5/97

Canada

ONTARIO

QUEBEC

D0792076

MAINE

NEW
LAND

Thunder Bay

Lake
Superior

Halifax

NOVA
SCOTIA

Sault Ste. Marie

Montreal

Ottawa

Augusta

Portland
Portsmouth
Hampton
Newburyport
Marblehead

WISCONSIN

Lake
Huron

Manotick

Montpelier

VT

York

St. Paul

Keswick

NH

neapolis

Green
Bay

Grand
Rapids

Scarborough

Chittenden

Concord

Waupaca

Toronto

L. Ontario

Albany

MA

Boston
North Adams

Madison

MICHIGAN

NEW YORK

Hartford

RI

Providence

WA

Milwaukee

Lake
Michigan

Detroit

Buffalo

Newark

CT

Franklin
Stratford

ibuque

Chicago

L. Erie

Lily Dale

New York City

Des Moines

South
Bend

Cleveland

PENNSYLVANIA

Merion

Trenton

Peoria

INDIANA

Mansfield

Pittsburgh

Philadelphia

Rancocas

Mary's

ILLINOIS

Williamsport

OHIO

Baltimore

NJ

Atlantic City

Indianapolis

Cincinnati

WEST
VIRGINIA

Harpers Ferry

MD

DE

Dover

sas City

Springfield

Washington DC

Annapolis

Webster
Groves

St. Louis

Covington

Charleston

Richmond

MISSOURI

Louisville

Frankfort

VIRGINIA

Norfolk

ngfield

KENTUCKY

Raleigh

Ozarks

Adams

NORTH CAROLINA

Outer
Banks

Nashville

Charlotte

RKANSAS

TENNESSEE

Little Rock

Memphis

Columbia

Wilmington

Atlantic Ocean

ckesburg

Yazoo
City

Decatur

Atlanta

SOUTH
CAROLINA

Birmingham

Oxford

Madison

Demopolis

GEORGIA

Charleston

Shreveport

Jackson

Montgomery

Savannah

Alexandria

MISSISSIPPI

ALABAMA

United States

LOUISIANA

Mobile

Jacksonville

Baton
Rouge

New
Orleans

Pascagoula

Orlando

LEGEND

Locations of hauntings

Major cities

St. Petersburg

Tampa

FLORIDA

Gulf of Mexico

Key West

Miami

Cuba

0   400 Miles

HISTORIC
HAUNTED AMERICA

Tor Books by Michael Norman and Beth Scott

Haunted America
Historic Haunted America

HISTORIC
HAUNTED
AMERICA

MICHAEL NORMAN
AND
BETH SCOTT

TOR®

A TOM DOHERTY ASSOCIATES BOOK

New York

This book is printed on acid-free paper.

A Tor Book
Published by Tom Doherty Associates, Inc.
175 Fifth Avenue
New York, N.Y. 10010

Tor Books on the World-Wide Web:
http://www.tor.com

Tor® is a registered trademark of Tom Doherty Associates, Inc.

Map by Mark Stein

Library of Congress Cataloging-in-Publication Data

Norman, Michael.
      Historic haunted America / Michael Norman and Beth Scott.—1st
ed.
          p. cm.
      "A Tom Doherty Associates Book."
      Companion to: Haunted America.
      Includes bibliographical references.
      ISBN 0-312-85752-7 (alk. paper)
      1. Haunted houses—United States. 2. Ghosts—United States.
3. Haunted houses—Canada. 4. Ghosts—Canada. I. Scott, Beth,
1922–94. II. Title.
BF1472.U6N68   1995
133.1'0973—dc20   95-23291
                                        CIP

First Edition: October 1995

Printed in the United States of America

0 9 8 7 6 5 4 3 2 1

Michael Norman wishes to dedicate this
book to his mother, Elizabeth J. (Bette)
Norman, and to the memories of his father,
James W. Norman, and his coauthor, Beth
Scott, who no doubt will find a typo somewhere on these pages. Thank you all for
helping me through life.

Contents

Foreword

This book is a companion of sorts to the collection of stories my late coauthor Beth Scott and I wrote under the title *Haunted America*, also published by Tor Books. What we endeavored to do in that book, as well as in this one, was to bring together in single volumes what we think are the most compelling *true* ghost stories from all across North America. Each state is represented, as well as the District of Columbia and many Canadian provinces.

Let me emphasize, however, that each work is original; there is no duplication of stories. The primary difference is that the stories in *Historic Haunted America*, are hauntings that may not continue on to the present day.

In some cases, however, as with "Yankee Jim" Robinson at the Whaley House in San Diego, or the dead gunslingers at Cimarron, New Mexico's St. James Hotel, a modern visitor might expect to encounter the phantoms you'll read about in these pages. At the General Wayne Inn in Merion, Pennsylvania, that will not be difficult. That hostelry has seventeen resident spirits that might materialize at any given moment!

Other stories are purely historical and the ghosts have probably left for parts unknown. But let me emphasize the word *probably*: ghosts are quite keen on capering about in the most unexpected places and at the most unanticipated times.

This is the fourth and final book on which Beth Scott and I collaborated. Our first volume of tales came from the state best known for beer, bratwurst, and the Green Bay Packers—we titled it *Haunted Wisconsin*. It demonstrated that there is far more that (doesn't) meet the eye than one might imagine in the land where "cheeseheads" reign supreme.

With the encouragement of our then-editor (now agent) Mark Lefebvre, we next looked for ghosts hanging around the Midwest. Surprisingly, no one had written a book about the subject. In *Haunted Heartland* we found no dearth of hauntings about which to write; indeed, there were far too many from which to choose, and so we included quite a few in this current volume and in the earlier *Haunted America*. Despite one critic's assessment of *Haunted Heartland*—that even the *ghosts* of the Midwest are boring, just like the region!—we believe these stories provide genuine, if gentle, chills in a section of the country not known for its Gothic mansions, fog-shrouded coasts, or abandoned ghost towns.

A twenty-year writing partnership was brought to an unexpected end with Beth's passing in February 1994. Beth was a wonderful colleague. I can honestly state that we never had a cross word or angry exchange. Our writing styles meshed so well that we didn't have to alter the way in which we put words, sentences, and paragraphs together. We shared the workload, each performing tasks as researcher, writer, and editor. I think that gave us an "ownership" in the work that is sometimes missing when one coauthor carries the greater part in writing or researching. We freely edited one another's work and didn't let our egos stand in the way of refining what we wrote. We trusted one another as professionals and as friends.

There are so many people who helped us along the way that to mention any is to risk forgetting innumerable others. But there are some individuals who deserve a special thanks. Beth's family—husband Larry and children Jonathan, Jeffery, and Rosemary—and my wife, Janell, and my son, James, put up with many late-night writing sessions, long phone conversations, and spouses or parents who spent far more hours than is healthy huddled in front of a typewriter or computer screen. The man who "discovered" us all those years ago, Mark Lefebvre, never left our side, and I am proud to say that he is still there. I am indebted to the faculty and administration at my school, the University of Wisconsin–River Falls, for allowing me time off to pursue this most peculiar of writing assignments.

More recently, I am indebted to my editor, Camille Cline, and the entire staff at Tor Books for their wonderful support and encouragement. I could not ask for a better group of people with whom to work.

To the hundreds of individuals who have contributed interviews, research materials, story leads, or moral support over the years, this book could not have been written without you. I am forever grateful.

But as with any product, one person must take final responsibility. Therefore, any sins of omission or commission are mine alone to bear.

Michael Norman
River Falls, Wisconsin
October 1995

THE UNITED STATES

ALABAMA

Family Remains

Mrs. Thomas Saunders had little doubt that the plantation her husband inherited two miles west of tiny Courtland harbored a ghost. A clanking of chains from the basement, persistent tapping in various rooms, and a pervasive sense of being watched bothered Mrs. Saunders so much that finally she confronted her fears.

"Either speak up, or go away and leave me alone," she shouted to an empty room. To her dismay a quiet voice answered, "Do not be doubting for I am truly here."

Later that same day, Mrs. Saunders, whose husband was a descendant of the plantation's original owner, saw a woman in the billowing petticoats of the antebellum South standing at the bottom of the majestic, spiral staircase. Assuming that the woman was involved with Courtland's centennial celebration and had gotten into the mansion without knocking, Mrs. Saunders reached out to shake hands with her unexpected guest. She vanished. The mistress of the house knew then it was the family ghost out to prove that she was "truly here."

Nothing remains today of Mrs. Saunders' home, Courtland's Rocky Hill Castle, on the road to Town Creek and the Tri Cities, save hard-packed earth where the house stood and the indistinct outline of the foundation. But for well over a century, the Castle was among the finest plantation homes in northwest Alabama.

Built in the late 1840s and early 1850s by James Edmonds Saunders, the plantation got its name from a six-story, medieval-style lookout tower Saunders had built adjacent to the house. From this vantage point, Saunders could keep watch over his cotton fields and the slaves who toiled in the broiling summer heat.

The house itself was a two-story brick affair with a plastered stucco facade. Identical porticoes built in Greek Revival style were attached to the front and rear, with four fluted Doric columns for added distinction. A cupola with arched windows sat atop the slate roof. Inside the front door, the vestibule was dominated by a handsome, sweeping staircase that widened as it reached the bottom floor. A polished mahogany banister ran the length of the staircase. The furnishings were as elegant as the house. As late as the 1920s, original furniture remaining in the house included two of Mr. Saunders's eighteen green velvet love seats, a marble-top table, a large dining room table, and several of the original oil paintings in exquisite gold-leaf frames. Nevertheless, it was the tower, with its cold, Gothic appearance, that gave the property its distinction.

Persistent rumors also circulated that the Castle was involved in illicit slave trading during the Civil War. A tunnel was said to lead from the nearby Tennessee River to the mansion's basement. Slaves were brought from ships and barges on the river and through the tunnel to the Saunderses' property, where they were then put to work in the fields.

Saunders was born in 1807 in Virginia and in 1828 moved to Courtland, where he established a law practice. He eventually acquired title to hundreds of acres of prime farmland.

The Courtland area stayed firmly in Confederate hands during most of the Civil War and Saunders became a colonel in the Confederate army. The Castle figured prominently in meetings of Southern military leaders. Among those entertained at the house was J. L. M. Curry, of Talladega, later the Confederate minister to Spain. Gen. Pierre Beauregard also spent time at the Castle.

Colonel Saunders survived the war, but his fortune was lost. He lived on at the plantation, however, trying several business enterprises, including vineyards. None was successful in restoring his prewar wealth.

His descendants continued to live in the Castle until 1926 when the property was sold to two Courtland businessmen. The house was lived in periodically until the late 1940s, when years of neglect caught up with James Saunders's glorious mansion. Vandals stripped the last of its interior furnishings, treasure hunters dug dozens of holes looking for buried valuables, and graffiti littered the once elegant walls. In a small cabin a short way from the old house, an aged black man kept watch over the old hulk. He reported that on several occasions he heard the ghostly sounds of a piano. He attributed them to mice running up and down the keyboard on that last piece of furniture in Saunders's crumbling mansion.

At about the same time, another phantom resident was heard from. She was the "lady in gray," a woman who reputedly lived in the mansion in the 1920s and had drowned with her two children when a bridge they were crossing collapsed into a rain-swollen creek.

The visages of the poor woman and her children were seen numerous times on the road leading from the creek to Rocky Hill Castle, even after the last remnants of the mansion had vanished from the earth.

A faint footpath through tangled underbrush, a few scattered weed-choked bricks, and the ghosts of a southern lady, a mother and her children are all that remain today of a once glorious estate.

The Musical Housekeeper

It is difficult to single out one Alabama mansion as the *most* beautiful in the state, but Gaineswood, a few miles north of Demopolis, has been termed a magnificent example of Greek Revival architecture in the state. It also is known for a musical ghost story.

Gen. Nathan Bryan Whitfield built the house between 1843 and 1860 for his wife and children. When his wife died before it was finished, General Whitfield hired a young woman from the East to care for the home and the children. She was an accomplished pianist, spending most evenings entertaining the family with her musical skills. In 1856, however, the woman fell ill and died. Her last wish was to be buried in her hometown.

Harsh winter weather delayed the shipment of her coffin to the East, and for some days or weeks (the records are not clear), the young woman's remains were kept under the cellar staircase.

She was finally buried according to her wishes, but not before visitors heard faint footfalls ascending the basement stairs and going into the drawing room. Delightful piano tunes favored by the deceased housekeeper would then be heard throughout the house.

Historians argue over the woman's name and even over whether or not a piano was ever in the original home. In 1976 a grand rosewood piano was given to the historic home by Mrs. Arthur Compton, a descendent of General Whitfield. There is some evidence that the piano may have been among Gaineswood's earliest furnishings.

The housekeeper apparently has not returned to play her beloved piano, but she may one day. Visitors should stay alert for unplanned recitals.

The Unfamiliar Guests

The historic Burleson/McEntire house in Decatur, on the south bank of the churning Tennessee River, shows the many scars of nearly 175 years of existence, including occupancy by both Union and Confederate forces during the Civil War. The stately white columns are pockmarked by bullet holes. But by far the most intriguing stories are those of the two ghosts who have been seen over the decades, scaring the home's residents and adding supernatural intrigue to the lore of the old plantation manor.

Built in 1824 by slave labor, probably by Tennessean Jesse Whorton, the house changed hands several times until the Civil War when it was owned by Mr. and Mrs. A. A. Burleson. They received it from her parents, the Alexander Pattersons. The war brought the house's most colorful period, when it was used as a hospital and command center by both the Blue and the Gray. It was around the home's dining room table that Gen. Albert Sidney Johnston planned the Battle of Shiloh on April 4, 1862. After the fall of Vicksburg, Union generals Grant, Sherman, and Blair held meetings there, and Gen. Grenville M. Dodge had his headquarters in the house in 1864.

A gruesome event during the war may be the cause of at least one of the hauntings.

Federal troops crossing the Tennessee River were frequently fired upon by Rebel soldiers hiding on the upper floors of the old First National Bank Building. One Union soldier was mortally wounded in an exchange of gunfire and taken by his comrades to the Burleson house, where he soon died. Confederate forces rapidly filling the city made it impossible for the Union soldiers to bury the man. Instead, they ripped up the floorboards in the front parlor and dug a hasty grave in the dirt below. Within a few days Union troops had recaptured the city, as well as the Burleson house, and were able to remove the soldier's corpse for a proper burial.

Shortly after the turn of the century, LeRoy McEntire Sr. told of his experience with a mysterious stranger. "I was walking home from grammar school," he told a newspaper reporter, "and when I got to the earth bridge, it's paved now, I looked up at the top of the house and saw Papa. At least I thought it was him."

He ran inside to ask his mother why his father was on the roof of the house. She said he wasn't home at all, but working several miles away. Young LeRoy bravely went up to the attic where he found all the doors and windows leading out onto the flat roof locked and bolted from the inside. The boy never did figure out who he had seen on the roof.

There are at least two other candidates for the male ghost in the house.

The Burleson house was one of only five buildings left standing in the wake of the fire and destruction that nearly destroyed Decatur during the war. Because of its central location and good condition, it became the headquarters for the hated carpetbaggers and the scene of most major political meetings and speeches.

The story of Judge Carlton, a Morgan County probate judge who occupied the Burleson house for a time, illustrates the extreme emotion rampant at the time—and could be another cause of the haunting. The judge was a carpetbagger and fervently anti-Klan. That was enough to engender nearly universal hatred for him in Decatur. There had been many threats against his life. Whether the danger grew too oppressive for him isn't known, but he made plans for a hasty trip to Mexico. He almost made it. He had gone to a Nashville bank to collect enough money for the excursion and was returning to Decatur to pack his belongings. Townspeople found his body midway between the railroad depot and the Burleson house, a distance of only a few blocks. The bank gold was gone. No one was ever convicted of his murder, although the Ku Klux Klan was assumed to have had a hand in it.

A third legend holds that an army paymaster, killed near the house's front gate, is the cause of the haunting. He was on his way to pay troops quartered in the house when he was slain and his bullion stolen.

There is also a second ghost, a woman in a flowing white gown whom no one has been able to positively identify.

In 1869, the Burlesons sold the house to Jerome J. Hinds. They had several children, including Grace, later Lady Curzon of London and Kedleston, the wife of the last Viceroy of India.

But it was another daughter, Jessie M., who was the first to disclose the presence of a female specter. According to her, an upstairs front bedroom that her parents occupied was haunted for many years. One night, her mother awakened with a start to find a dark-haired woman in what appeared to be a dressing gown staring at the couple from the foot of the bed. She held a lighted candle in one hand. A number of years later, Mrs. Frank Brown reported that when her family had rented the house when she was a child, the same specter returned. As children, Mrs. Brown and her sister shared that same upstairs bedroom. Both girls saw the ghost in a white robe carrying a candle. She looked sad, Mrs. Brown recalled. The ghost's flowing black hair cascaded down her back, the candle casting a soft glow on her delicate features. So terrified were the children that they turned the room over to their brothers, without telling them of the ghost. The boys didn't stay long for they saw the same apparition.

Later, a visitor sitting in the bedroom early one evening fled the room claiming she saw a lighted candle sway back and forth above the door to the hallway. She said it slowly moved toward her and then exploded a few feet from her face.

Although the upstairs bedroom is directly above the parlor under which the soldier was buried, there doesn't appear to be a connection between the two apparitions.

The stately Burleson/McEntire home bears its wounds and sorrows like badges of courage. Lovingly restored earlier in this century, the house is a reminder of an era long vanished from the American landscape. From its original iron fence to the hand-laid brick walk, eighteen-inch-thick inside walls, and wooden doors held together with wooden pegs, the house is sturdy enough to last for another century. And along with it, two infrequent spectral guests.

Miss Susian

The "Tinker Place" was built in 1835 for a Miss Susian Trumon Tinker, a strikingly beautiful belle and a leading cultural light in old Greensboro. Little is known of her life, or of the happy activities she must have engaged in at her home, but it seems that she was so attached to the house that she never left.

A Mrs. Turpin was the first to encounter the ghost of the home's first mistress. She startled her family one night many years ago with the news that a small woman in a gray dress had stood smiling at her from a doorway. She disappeared before she could be questioned.

In about 1934, Mrs. Charles E. Waller, Mrs. Turpin's daughter and the then-doyenne of the home, was entertaining several grandchildren when they asked about the curious woman standing a few feet from the dining room table at which they were seated. Since no one else could see anything, the children described the unseen visitor's actions. She was moving through the doorway now, the children said, and across the living room floor. The ghost, for that is what it surely must have been, faded away as it glided up the staircase.

A sick friend recuperating in the Wallers' home reported another strange incident. Unable to leave her bed, the woman called for Mrs. Waller to come up and turn on the light in the room. The words were barely spoken when the overhead chandelier light snapped on.

The lady at Tinker's place seems to prefer gray clothing. At times she is glimpsed warming her hands by the fire, or perhaps admiring the crystal and china displayed in a china cabinet. She always appears quite happy, but disappears as soon as anyone looks directly at her or tries to strike up an acquaintance.

However, she is not completely antisocial. Mrs. Waller recounted an incident that led her to believe the ghost was more of a guardian than a malevolent wraith.

It was the custom in Mrs. Waller's family for the first person up in the morning to make a pot of hot coffee. Early one day, just before the first rays of sun penetrated the old house, Mrs. Waller walked out of her bedroom toward the kitchen but was stopped in her tracks by the sight of the little lady in gray standing in a doorway through which she had to pass. A slight smile appeared on the ghost's sallow face and she turned and moved across the adjoining room. Mrs. Waller watched her disappear on the stairs.

"She was the image of Miss Susian," Mrs. Waller told a visitor sometime later.

The Blue Lamp

The Perry County mansion known as Carlisle Hall is an unusual structure, even by Alabama standards. It is an amalgam of Romanesque arches, Japanese temple–type hanging copper roof, and a balcony rail of Moorish derivation. All of this is wrapped in a generally Gothic design.

Built by Edwin Kenworthy Carlisle, a prosperous cotton merchant, in 1827 for the sum of $90,000, the house has had a variety of owners. For many decades it sat abandoned and decrepit. Shortly after Carlisle died, stories were first circulated about a blue lantern light that could be seen through the windows of his old bedroom. A young woman was said to sail down the staircase to greet her returning Yankee colonel sweetheart . . . long after the war and the lives of the lovers had ended. The lady may have been Carlisle's daughter.

During the 1930s, Carlisle Hall was restored and modernized by A. S. Hill, a retired naval officer and teacher at Marion Institute. World War II put a halt to his plans and his occupancy of the house.

W. E. Belcher owned the place after Hill, but he rarely occupied the home. Vandals ransacked Carlisle Hall, destroying all fifty-six windows, including several leaded Venetian glass masterpieces above the staircase. They ripped the banister apart, chopped to pieces a half dozen marble fireplace mantels, and shattered the exquisite imported plaster medallions in the ceilings of each room. As a final insult, the plunderers dug up trees and plantings in the yard.

A family was hired to act as live-in caretakers when Carlisle Hall was put up for sale. Not much was left of the grandeur that had once marked the mansion. And the caretakers left their own ghostly legacy. It was told that the family's baby fell to its death down the spiral staircase and left a bloody stain on the floor where it landed. Some people claimed the stain "cried out at night."

A Birmingham teacher, Kay Klassen, rescued the house from certain destruction. She "always felt sorry for old things," and Carlisle Hall seemed to be in need of gentle restoration. The young woman spent nearly seven years restoring the house. She and her parents searched all over the South for period furnishings, mantels, and chandeliers to replace those destroyed, to complement the extensive repairs they had to perform on the edifice itself.

Kay Klassen never reported seeing Edwin Kenworthy Carlisle or his daughter gliding about their old house, but one of the first things she noted when she moved into the house was that a section of flooring just below the staircase had been carefully removed. Just at the place where a dying baby's cries had been heard decades before.

ALASKA

The Crawling Woman

The tiny village of Wales, on the Seward Peninsula of northwest Alaska, faces the Chukchi Peninsula of Russia, fifty miles across the Bering Strait. Before the coming of the Europeans, Wales was known as Kingen. Strange events took place in this Eskimo settlement and at least some of the stories survive in oral tradition. The tale of the woman-who-crawled-on-all-fours goes like this:

In the days that have long since passed, boys fourteen or fifteen years of age left their homes to live with other boys in a large igloo called the *kazhgie*. The kazhgie functioned as a kind of boarding school. Tribal historians taught the culture and traditions of their tribe and during the evening hours hunters came to make or repair their equipment. While the elders worked, the boys watched and learned how to make and use the weapons that they themselves would soon be using. At the end of the evening the men went home, leaving the boys by themselves to play, sing, or dance until bedtime. They were not to leave the igloo. This honor system worked well until late one afternoon when a troublemaker spotted a young girl passing the kazhgie and set off after her.

Since the men of the village were on an extended walrus-hunting trip the remainder of the boys knew they wouldn't be caught at any mischief-making. They all rushed outdoors, caught the little girl and physically abused her. When she was able to wrench herself free she ran screaming to her grandmother, with whom she lived alone.

The grandmother, after listening to the sobbing child's story, determined to teach the rascals a lesson they'd never forget. She painted her face with ugly streaks and patterns, then turned around to her granddaughter. "They'll be scared of me now, won't they?"

The little girl shook her head and cried pitifully, "No! Oh no! That will make them laugh."

The old woman then smeared soot over her face and rubbed ashes into her hair. But the child wiped her tears and shook her head again. "There's no use, Grandmother. You can never scare those boys. You wouldn't even scare me."

The grandmother thought for one brief moment, then knew what she had to do.

Turning her back, she went into a dark corner and removed all her clothes.

With a sharp knife, she cut long, deep gashes in every part of her body. Then she got down on hands and knees and crawled toward the child, leaving a bloody trail behind her. The little girl cried and covered her face at the horrible sight. She knew that her grandmother would now terrify every boy in the kazhgie.

The sun had set and darkness shadowed the land as the old woman crawled toward the kazhgie. Her movements slowed as her strength ebbed and the blood drained from her body.

Standing just outside the igloo was a boy named Ahmezuk, the only fellow who had not abused the girl. He heard something coming toward him and grew frightened because he could not see what it was. He turned and ran inside to tell the other boys, but they called him a liar and made up a wicked song that poked fun at him.

With tear-filled eyes, Ahmezuk turned around and saw the terrible "thing" entering the igloo. The figure was smeared with blood and the eyes seemed to come from the top of its head. Ahmezuk ran into a dark corner, bit his fingers and pushed them into a crack in the wall. As his fingers swelled the crack held him fast, and he prayed that the "thing" could not pry him loose. Both of his hands ached and tears ran down his cheeks.

The "thing" pushed through the main door and the boys could not take their eyes off it, nor could they scream their fears. Only one boy yelled, "A ghost woman!" As the old lady crawled in a circle around the room the boys, mesmerized by the movement, crawled after her. Six times the torn and bloodied figure circled the room, all the while beckoning Ahmezuk to follow her. But of course he could not, even had he wanted to.

With a hideous grunt the ghost left the igloo, crossed the tundra, and started up the mountainside. The boys followed.

The next morning the men returned to the village. By this time Ahmezuk's knees trembled with fatigue and he felt faint. Hearing someone pass by the kazhgie, he called out. A man found him immediately and asked where the other boys were. "They were all taken away by a ghost," cried Ahmezuk.

All the villagers gathered at the igloo to free the poor boy. They had to cut away a portion of the wall before they got his fingers loose. Then they followed the tracks of the ghost and the boys. At the summit of the mountain they found the frozen bodies of all the boys. None was buried because each one had turned to stone. There was no sign of the old grandmother.

It is said that you can see them on the mountainside behind the village of Wales—grim reminders of boys who disobeyed their elders.

In Old, Haunted Tucson

The adobe house in Tucson's Old Pueblo has a history dating back to the 1850s, but its prominence derives mainly from its most famous owner, Carlos Ygnacio Velasco, and his wife, Beatriz, who lived there from 1878 until Carlos's death in 1914. He may still be there.

Located at what is now 471–477 South Stone Avenue, the Velasco house has three main rooms and an entry hall and dates from about 1850, about the same time the Spanish garrison settled in El Presidio. Other sections of the house, including those with fifteen-foot-high ceilings constructed of ponderosa pine and Douglas fir, were built sometime later, perhaps as late as 1880. A major renovation by Beatriz Velasco added a hip roof and new floors during the 1880s.

Carlos Velasco arrived in old Tucson during the 1860s, already famous as a Sonoran state senator and district judge. He was a native of Hermosillo. For thirteen years, until 1878, Carlos operated a general merchandise store but sold it to start a Spanish-language newspaper, El Fronterizo. A room on the south side of the Stone Avenue house accommodated the newspaper's office and a Washington hand press that had already served at least three newspapers. That original press is now housed in a Tubac, Arizona, museum.

Carlos Velasco ran the newspaper with a printer's devil, and eventually developed it into a respected publication with a circulation throughout southern Arizona and northern Mexico. Carlos continued as publisher until his death in 1914.

One of the earliest Hispanic insurance companies in the Southwest, the Alianza Hispano-Americana, also came about as a direct result of Carlos Velasco's efforts. Disturbed by what he saw as growing anti-Hispanic sentiment, Carlos formed the fraternal insurance society with himself as president in 1894. At its pinnacle in the 1940s, the insurance company had a membership of nearly twenty thousand and had paid out over $3 million in benefits.

But all of this is the known history of Carlos Velasco and his old home. That didn't prepare its new owners for what they believed was the reappearance of the former owner several years ago.

The house had undergone considerable remodeling following Carlos's death. Windows and doors had been boarded up when it was turned into apartments.

In later years, termites nearly destroyed the ancient timbers and the roof sagged from years of neglect.

The three new owners, Charles Brown, Bill Dillon, and William Cobb, took on the task of restoring the Velasco house to its original condition. Not long after the work began, Brown reported that he saw the head and shoulders of a shimmering figure hanging in the air in a bedroom behind the room used as the newspaper's pressroom. He said it seemed to be the upper torso of a Mexican man floating some eight feet off the floor. Although the room was dark and the walls charred from a fire sometime before, Brown was able to get a good look at the mustachioed image before fleeing. He later identified a photograph of Carlos Velasco taken in 1883 as being the nearly identical image of the man he had seen in the bedroom.

On at least three other occasions, witnesses have said they've seen a man standing in various parts of the house. Brown and a female companion were walking toward the back door when both of them stopped, stared at the doorway and then quickly went in the opposite direction. Both of them had seen the diaphanous form of an elderly Mexican man lounging in the doorway. He was looking directly toward them.

Two other visitors reported sighting a younger Hispanic man, once standing near a door and at another time bustling across the living room. On neither of these occasions did the witnesses say they were scared, merely startled by the mysterious figure's sudden appearance.

If it was the ghost of Carlos Velasco that inhabited his old house and office, he seemed not to be upset at the changes going on around him, although clocks seemed to be mysteriously reset and some furniture was strangely rearranged. Nothing wicked came from the old man's presence, only the understanding, perhaps, that new owners would have to contend with some unexpected company.

The Laughing Lady

Speedway Boulevard is one of Tucson's busiest thoroughfares. Restaurants, shopping centers, and a few homes share the long avenue with various other small businesses and incessant daily traffic. Until 1970 there was a house at 1017 East Speedway Boulevard that sheltered an ethereal young lady with a raucous laugh and a propensity for harmless pranks. No one knows who it might have been, or what became of her after the house was razed nearly three decades ago. Her story, however, is a reminder that even in the midst of urban development there can be places of deep puzzlement.

A former television news director and publicist for the Tucson Chamber of Commerce, Chris Helms, was the first to reveal the presence of the "Speedway Ghost." Helms was a University of Arizona student in 1963, living in the house with another university student, Dave Sonenschien, when the mysterious lady first came around. It had been a mild early summer in 1963 and the young men were accustomed to sleeping with the windows open. Early one morning, Helms later said, the clear, unmistakable laugh of a young woman drifted in through a window. It seemed to come from just outside, and below, a bedroom window. Helms, and later Sonenschien, both searched the yard but came up empty-handed. They said the voice was absolutely that of a woman, yet it had a hollow, almost unnatural quality about it. Another roommate, who had also heard the voice, later asked if someone had had his girlfriend over the night before.

The young men's pet German shepherd, Beaumont, had a difficult time sleeping through the night. He always slept in a front room, but would often sit up suddenly, alert to something in a distant room at the other end of a long hallway. His neck hair stood up and he growled, yet nothing discernible seemed to cause his anxiety.

Soon after Chris Helms married and moved out of the Speedway Avenue address in 1964, the lilting laughter took on a maniacal character. Whether "she" was upset at Helms's departure, or annoyed at the light-hearted way the young men treated her occasional appearances, the ghost soon changed her behavior.

Sonenschien was awakened one night by the plinking of what sounded like coins being dropped on the wood floor and then rolling around. He turned on the light to find his collection of military medals scattered about the floor, apparently having fallen somehow from atop his dresser. He told a newspaper reporter at the time that he couldn't figure out how *all* of the medals could have wound up on the floor. Sonenschien attributed the mischief to their distaff specter.

An especially disturbing incident led Sonenschien to think that the young ghost was becoming a bit too brazen. He lay in bed late at night with the sensation of being caressed by invisible human hands. He was so terror-stricken that he couldn't scream, although he very much wanted to. It was a "cold fear" that he had never experienced before, he said.

A University of Arizona professor of folklore, to whom Sonenschien had detailed the peculiar events, helped exorcise the spirit. The professor told Sonenschien that according to folklore, a ghost could be removed by placing a single candle in a darkened room. Sonenschien did so and waited. Nothing happened for about an hour, and then the candle flickered. A black, elbow-length woman's glove with pearl buttons suddenly appeared, skimming a few inches above the flame. It vanished, and with it the last trace of the ghost of Speedway Boulevard. Nothing more has been heard from her, although current residents and business owners on that street might be well advised to pay attention and listen for a woman's laughter, especially if it's late at night and no living being seems to be around.

Looking for a Body

A puzzled young woman, her dark hair pulled straight back and parted in the middle, stares fixedly through the small window of a Romance language laboratory in the University of Arizona's Modern Language Building. She has a delicate quality about her, heightened by the hand-knit shawl drawn tightly about her shoulders and a long skirt reminiscent of an earlier age. The students who may notice her curiosity and ask if they can be of assistance are startled when she scurries away, raising a thin hand to cover her face with a corner of the shawl.

According to those who have seen her, the bewildered lady was the victim of a ghastly murder at the turn of the century who has returned to claim her earthly remains. The origins of the haunting seem to be wrapped in the assertion that decades ago a young woman was killed and her body dumped in a well near what had been the women's athletic field. The Modern Language Building was built on that site in 1965. Construction workers are said to have found human skeletal remains as they dug the foundation, but didn't report their findings for fear a police investigation would have delayed the project. The recovery of those old bones is the object of the ghost's nightly sojourns.

An emeritus professor of English, Byrd Granger, was quoted in the university's student newspaper as saying the ghost was trying to recover the bones "so she can rest."

Descriptions of the ghost and her frequent appearances do not vary in detail. She is most often seen between eight P.M. and midnight, usually going through the south-wing entrances to the building. That portion of the structure apparently covers the old well. Sometimes she actually comes into a room, looks around in vague discomfort and then runs out the door, trying to hide her face from those who may have glimpsed her. At other times she has been spotted gliding down a third-floor hallway, a painfully emaciated shadow in white.

The nameless ghost never challenges those around her; she's intent only on somehow reuniting her body and soul.

Old Custodians Never Die. . . .

Across town at Catalina High School, a school ghost of another variety was reported in the early 1980s. This wasn't a lost young woman but a school custodian who had died a decade before, but nevertheless returned on occasion to help out with cleaning chores.

The man's name was Martin Valencia, a faithful worker who admonished less-than-honorable colleagues who might try to pilfer items from the home economics room or school kitchen, both his assigned responsibilities. Valencia was so conscientious that cooks would leave out cookies as a treat for him. He shared them with his coworkers but drew the line at allowing them to raid the kitchen's refrigerator or snoop through the drawers of the home ec classroom. Valencia suffered a heart attack and died while at his job.

Did Valencia remain, in spirit at least, at "his" high school? Some skeptics think it was somebody "playing tricks," noting particularly the eerie nature of dimly lit school hallways in the middle of the night.

Others are not so sure.

One custodian said he was positive he saw something while cleaning rest rooms before graduation ceremonies in June 1980. He was in a hallway at a few minutes past midnight when he heard the metal casters of a movable garbage container scudding down the hallway. He could just make out what looked like a man dressed in work clothes about twenty-five feet away, pushing the can along the floor. The custodian thought it was a fellow worker until a little later when he found everyone in the gymnasium setting up chairs for graduation.

Another janitor heard footsteps ascending a ramp close to him. He waited for whoever it was, but no one appeared. Exasperated, he went outside and found the rest of the night crew waiting for him so they could lock the building.

If it was Martin Valencia still cleaning the building, he seemed to have his own methods. Trash containers and custodial supplies would disappear or be found in different places from where they were left. Doors slammed shut. The late custodian wanted it to be known that he was still there, keeping an eye on Catalina High School.

ARKANSAS
The Hills Are Haunted

When the first frost nips the pumpkins and a chilling wind rattles the dry corn-stalks in the fields, Arkansans like to gather at their firesides to spin the legends of "haints" that once walked among them, and perhaps still do. In spite of the intrusion of television and other electronic marvels, these people retain a strong oral tradition. The ghostly stories are passed down from generation to generation.

Someone recalls a horseman who once galloped the back roads searching for his head; another remembers the weird moans and wails arising from bushes wrapped in fog; and yet another may have seen, only yesterday, the ghosts of a man and a woman, long dead, strolling hand-in-hand down a dusty lane.

In the backcountry, especially, it would be hard to find a person who hasn't heard about at least one ghost. Except for the African-American woman who complained that all her life she'd heard folks talk about haints, but she'd never seen one.

"The only strange thing I ever saw," she allowed, "was a little man without a head. And he turned into a dog."

The Killers

A hundred years ago Dr. Ferdinand Smith of Frankford, Missouri, moved his family to Lockesburg, Arkansas. This small settlement in the southwestern corner of the state had no physician and Dr. Smith, a man dedicated to curing the sick, wanted to go where his services were desperately needed. His wife, Isabella, and the children looked upon the move as a great adventure and talked of it for many years afterward. But not Genevieve. Genny, as she was called, was six years old at the time and the only one of the family to witness a murder.

The Smiths left Frankford early in the summer. Mrs. Smith drove the family wagon with the children, a few clothes, and camping gear (a wagon train would bring the family's household goods later), and Dr. Smith rode his horse on ahead as a scout. He looked the part, sitting tall and lean in the saddle. Although not a fearful man, he wore loaded pistols in his holsters to quell his wife's anxieties. They'd be traveling part of the way through unsettled territory and she was nervous about being held up by a gang of ruffians. There were also rifles in the wagon and Isabella Smith, like all pioneer women, knew how to use them.

The family had a pleasant trip over the hills and undulating prairies that were new to them. They cooked their evening meals over an open fire and slept under the stars. Whenever they met another wagon traveling north the two families waved greetings to each other and sometimes shared a meal. Although the Smith children enjoyed making new friends, the trip that had started out as fun grew long and tedious.

After they crossed the border into Arkansas, progress was slow as the horses plodded through the red clay soil made sticky by recent rains. But late on a July afternoon the weary family reached Lockesburg. Even with the delay, they had arrived sooner than they were expected, and the doctor knew their house might not be prepared. He'd have to find temporary shelter. Genevieve hadn't been feeling well for several days and now appeared to be seriously ill. They could not sleep outdoors another night.

Dr. Smith reined his horse at the general supply store and went in to introduce himself. R. A. Gilman, the proprietor, shook the doctor's hand, his fat face wreathed in smiles.

"I'm so glad you've come, Doc, but we didn't expect you quite so soon. Your house should be ready in a few days."

"Fine," said Dr. Smith. "Where can we put up temporarily?"

Gilman offered space in his own house but the physician declined. He did not want to impose, nor did he want to take a sick child into the home of strangers.

"I understand, Doctor." A curious expression crossed the storekeeper's face. "There is a double log house at the edge of the village. Since the owner died some of the women are keeping it clean and tidy. They jokingly call it our hotel. I think you would find it comfortable."

The house, in a grove of sycamore trees, appeared to be in fine repair, the logs tightly chinked, the door squarely hung, and the windows sparkling. The doctor dismounted at the yard gate, and after tethering his horse, removed saddle, blanket, and bridle which he carried into the house. His wife and children waited in the wagon.

In one corner of the front room, Dr. Smith noticed a large blood stain. He dropped the saddle over the spot and returned to his family. They unloaded only the items necessary for the night. While Isabella prepared beds in a rear room her husband made up a bed for Genny in a corner of the front parlor. He would sit up with her to provide medicine and to be certain that she was all right.

Toward midnight the little girl became delirious. She screamed that she saw four men were playing cards across the room from her. They were dark, ugly men. Suddenly, three of them jumped up, threw down their cards and pulled knives from their belts.

"Daddy! Daddy! They're killing him! They're killing that man in the chair!"

Dr. Smith, sitting at his daughter's bedside, held her hand tightly in his. Under his skillful and soothing questions the child described the men fully—red shirts open at the neck, brown shapeless pants tucked into dirt-caked boots, and hats pulled low on their foreheads.

There was more, she sobbed. With a terrifying scream, the victim fell to the floor and lay motionless. He'd been stabbed in the chest and then twice more in the back after he fell. His companions stomped out the door. Genny covered her ears and tears stood in her eyes.

"Daddy, the blood's all over the floor!" Genny cried, gripping her father's fingers with both of her hands.

Dr. Smith saw nothing. Isabella and the other children, awakened by Genny's screams, came running into the room.

"It's all right," he said quietly. "Genevieve had a terrible nightmare. I'm giving her a sedative. Go back to bed now and get your sleep."

The little girl fell into a deep and natural sleep. Her father lay on a pallet beside her, pondering the significance of the horrible scene that Genny had described. None of his children had ever had nightmares or suffered hallucinations, even when they ran high fevers. He was uneasy and did not sleep.

The next morning, Dr. Smith visited storekeeper Gilman. He asked about the child's health and was glad to hear she was better. "And what brings you to the store so early, Doctor?"

"What can you tell me about that house we're in? Has anybody stayed there recently?" Dr. Smith questioned.

Gilman, putting groceries on the shelves, hesitated.

"Not for several weeks," he replied, avoiding the doctor's steady gaze. "That was when four strangers showed up during a hellacious rainstorm and asked about shelter. I told them about the place myself and that's where they put up for the night. A little rough-looking but pleasant enough." His description of the men corresponded exactly to that given by Genny.

A cold chill swept over Dr. Smith.

"Tell me, Mr. Gilman, was there ever any trouble in that house?"

"Trouble?" asked Gilman.

"A murder perhaps?"

Gilman turned to face the doctor.

"Yes," he admitted. "There was a brawl the night those strangers bunked there. One of 'em was stabbed to death. Two women found the body on the floor when they went to tidy up the place the next day. Never did find out his name. We jus' had a little service and buried him out in the cemetery. How did you come to find out?"

"There's a large blood stain on the floor of the front room," Dr. Smith replied.

Gilman nodded. "The women scrubbed and scrubbed. Never could get rid of it. One of 'em claims the stain seems to grow larger each time she's out there. It's purely strange. Them murderers got clean away."

A small bell on the store's screen door tinkled as a customer came in. Gilman leaned over and whispered: "We don't like to talk 'bout it."

After Dr. Smith moved his family into their new home, he learned that the cabin was generally thought to be haunted. Several caretakers, at different times, had also witnessed the reenactment of the bloody brawl and all refused to go near the place again. Some swore they heard the shrieks of the dying man.

In time "progress" came to that part of Arkansas as it did to many other rural areas of the country, and the little cabin was abandoned to the elements.

Genevieve Smith grew up to become Mrs. James King of Marietta, Oklahoma. She never forgot her terrifying experience, and whenever the subject of ghosts was raised she remained silent—but mindful that there are those events which cannot be explained.

The Illusive Fiddler

The night Henry Albright saw ghosts he was so horrified that he never told anyone, and the sorrow of the experience stayed with him forever.

Henry moved to rural Arkansas as a baby, the only child of a middle-aged couple who tilled the land and kept a milk cow and a few pigs that they slaughtered from time to time to put meat on the table. Because there were no neighbors or relatives with small children living nearby, Henry played alone most of the time. He built castles with a set of crude blocks and played happily with the few store-bought toys that his parents could afford. Henry's father, a city man, had lost everything in the great stock market crash of 1929, and had moved to the hill country to try to eke out a living for his family. Henry's uncle, a bachelor, had come too, to help his brother build a new life.

When Henry started school he had already learned to read by choosing books from his family's small library and sounding out the letters. Reading came quickly and easily to him. He read books beyond his comprehension, but reread them again when he was older and understood what they meant. He was secretly fascinated by the metaphysical writers.

Henry's classmates, while friendly, didn't know what to make of him. They liked him, but knew instinctively that they couldn't call him "Hank." It was not a suitable nickname for a fellow who stood somewhat apart from the crowd. Henry never played ball, nor did he learn to hunt and fish. Mostly he hiked the hills, roamed the forests, and watched the changing of the seasons. His father once said to his wife that their son was growing up in the wrong place at the wrong time.

One day, in Henry's senior year of high school, his teacher announced that because of a statewide teachers' convention school would not be in session during the last week of October. The leaves were still golden and clinging to the trees and only the tingle of a light frost chilled the night air.

Since Henry's help was not needed at home at that time, he made plans of his own for the week. It wouldn't be exactly a vacation; it would be more like a retreat, during which time he'd camp alone in the woods and do some walking and reading, like a latter-day Thoreau. He was secretly pleased to share the same first name with the author-naturalist.

Packing his pup tent, lantern, some beef jerky and homemade sausages, along with a loaf of his mother's freshly baked bread and a few pots and pans, he set out over the hills. The air was clear, the sun bright and warm on his back, and only an occasional breeze teased his hair.

By late afternoon he had found a small, flat clearing beside a rushing stream a few miles from his home. It was one of his favorite spots and within sight of old Jeb Gibson's place. Gibson was a bachelor who was never called anything but "old Jeb." People said he'd lived in his little shack in the hollow since God created the Ozarks. Everyone loved him. In the morning Henry planned to hike down there and buy some milk and fresh eggs. He didn't know the old man well, but it would be nice to have a visit with him. Although old Jeb had little schooling, he had the wisdom of a homespun philosopher.

Darkness set in early, almost before Henry had finished his simple meal. Then, he lit his lantern and began to read. But the night was unquiet, disturbing. Suddenly, from out of the woods behind him came the sounds of a violin—sad, haunting notes played with a rich vibrato that trembled on the air. But of course he was imagining it. There was no house for miles around except old Jeb's down in the gap, and he didn't play the fiddle.

Henry put down his book and stepped out of the tent. No light shone anywhere, yet the music grew louder, insistent. What sort of crazy man was wandering the woods playing music at this time of night? And why? Henry was more curious than frightened and the hypnotic music impelled him to search out its source. He found a deer path and followed it on silent feet. At times the music seemed near him, at other times farther away.

Henry picked his way carefully around rock outcroppings and the black-haw bushes and, with his hands, parted low-hanging tree branches. Only a sliver of moon lit the path as he trudged on. The music grew harsher now as if it were a sentient being in pain.

Then Henry thought he saw in the distance a faint glow of light. It seemed to remain stationary, growing larger as he approached it. Coming to a small rise topped by a flat rock, Henry clambered onto it. Now he had a splendid view of the light. It was not a circle of light at all, but a rectangle glowing through what appeared to be an open door or unshaded window. Henry strained to make out the outline of the building, but he could see nothing—no walls, no roof, no sort of structure. Yet from somewhere near that light came the persistent notes of the fiddle.

Henry wondered if he had stumbled upon a moonshiner's still, the operator whiling away his time with his violin while the "brew" cooked. As he lay on the cold rock, his body tense, the music surrounded him. It seemed to come down from the night sky, from the trees, and even up from the ground itself. For a brief moment, Henry considered fleeing, but he knew he could not. He must walk to the light.

As he approached, the music softened, repeating the sad refrain he had first heard. Finally, he saw the outline of a small cabin, its open doorway filled with a steady light as from a lamp rather than a candle. At the same time he heard the stamping of a horse followed by a low whinny. Henry crept closer to the cabin. The music stopped abruptly and he saw two women framed in the doorway. One of the women was stooped, her hair gray. Her companion, a young woman with a beautiful, heart-shaped face, laid an arm protectively around the shoulders of the other. Both seemed to be smiling out into the darkness as if to greet an approaching visitor. Henry wondered if it was him they were looking at.

The women were oddly dressed, even for this isolated part of the Ozarks. Both wore long, full, calico skirts and tight bodices with lace insets.

As Henry stood speculating, a shot rang out, then another and another; the wild shrieks of the horse filled the night air. Then came another sharp report and flash of fire. Henry dropped to the ground and as he did so the young girl in the doorway fell face-downward across the sill. Another shot felled the older woman. A young man ran out of the woods, leaped over the crumpled, bloodied bodies and plunged into the cabin. Reappearing with a rifle, he shot again and again into the darkness. Henry heard the rush of feet hurrying away, snapping twigs underfoot as someone tried to escape. When the cracking of the rifles ceased, Henry saw the cabin's defender collapse beside the dead women in the doorway.

Henry never remembered returning to his camp. He knew nothing until long after the sun had risen above the eastern rim of the hollow. Old Jeb was standing over him, a smile on his wrinkled face.

Setting a jar of milk and sack of eggs beside the tent, he said, "Reckoned you'd be needing these." He turned away. Henry didn't stop him. Hill folk were loose of tongue only with their kin. Henry watched the old man trudge back to his little home until he was only a dot in the valley.

After Henry had eaten, he set forth to find the cabin. But tracks of man and animal crisscrossed among the trees and he didn't know which path to follow. He spent most of the day trying to find the place but without the music to guide him his search was futile. In the thickening dusk of evening he tramped wearily back to his camp.

The next day Henry got an early start, and by noon stumbled upon the cabin. At least what remained of it. It was a low log structure with one room and a lean-to kitchen. The ridge pole was broken and the roof caved in. The remnants of a door, its buckskin hinges shredded, leaned open against a wall, and the one window was broken. Henry stepped inside, picking his way carefully over rotted floorboards in which weeds grew up through the cracks. A once-handsome fireplace had collapsed, its sagging mantel covered with moss.

He went back outside to check the surroundings. To the left of the cabin stood a tumble-down stable surrounded by the remains of a stake and rider fence. Desolation and decay were everywhere.

There was no doubt in Henry's mind that this was the place that he had visited. Yet how could it be? Clearly no one had lived in the cabin for years, nor had a horse occupied the stable in recent times.

But Henry had come prepared to wait. He was sure he had heard the plaintive music from this place. Or was he going mad? He had often camped alone in the woods for weeks at a time, yet he had never had an experience that he couldn't explain.

He climbed up on the rock and waited, only a little fearful. As the last rays of sun dipped behind the western ridges, the plaintive whine of the violin permeated the silence of the forest. When it ended on a weird high note, Henry again heard the stamping and whinnying from the stable. Then the old woman and the young girl appeared in the doorway and finally the tragic face of the youth. But no din or tumult arose. The horse quieted and the figures faded away.

The day before Henry had to return home to prepare for school, old Jeb reappeared at his camp and asked the boy if he'd like to explore Simpson's Cave. Although Henry had heard about the cave several miles away, he had never been there.

Old Jeb led off. Henry was surprised by the brisk pace the old man set. It was a perfect fall day with just the slightest chill in the air.

Henry lost count of the number of ridges they crossed before coming to the cave. It lay beneath a rise, its entrance concealed by a thick tangle of vines. Old Jeb cleared a passage, lighted the small kerosene lamp he had carried on the hike, and the two descended a gentle slope. The cave had only one room. The old man strode around the cavern holding his lantern high and low and told of how the stalactites and stalagmites were formed and how this cave was a living one, constantly changing. Henry read the excitement in Jeb's face and guessed that his companion came here often.

After crawling up into the sunlight, old Jeb rearranged the vines to conceal the entrance. Then the two sat with their backs against the trunk of a tree and ate the sandwiches Jeb had stuffed in his pack. The old man lit his pipe and Henry joined him. Although Henry wasn't much of a smoker, he did carry a cob in his pocket and a sprinkle of tobacco. He especially enjoyed a smoke with his father and uncle by the fireplace after a hearty winter night's meal.

When the two explorers were ready to start for home, Jeb suggested a shortcut through the woods. With leaves crackling underfoot, Henry followed in the old man's footsteps. Suddenly he looked up and saw that they'd reached a cabin in a small clearing. As they approached it from the rear, Henry felt a chill sweep through his body. He said nothing, but as they passed by, he turned around to look at the front. It *was* the same dilapidated cabin that he'd already seen!

Henry touched the older man's arm. "Let's rest here a little and have another smoke," he said casually. If he spoke in a detached manner, perhaps old Jeb would tell him the story.

"Little further on," insisted old Jeb.

Henry estimated they had walked at least another half mile before his partner eased himself down upon a fallen log and clasped his gnarled hands about one drawn-up knee.

Presently, old Jeb lit his pipe and looked intently at his young friend. "You're wanting to hear the story of that cabin, ain't ya," he drawled, his remark more a statement than a question.

Henry nodded.

" 'Course you don't know it being as how you're not hill folk. My kin've been here for many a year. I'm the last of the old ones." Through heavy-lidded eyes, he scrutinized the face of his young companion. "I'll tell ya 'bout it."

"A hundred years ago," he began, "a boy was born in that cabin. It was a fine home then, sturdy and built just so. His name was Daniel. But he was a strange child; seemed like he never fit in nowhere." The old man shook his head.

"He hated farm chores and everything 'bout these hills. His kin worried 'bout him, but didn't rightly know what to do. Daniel always wandered 'round like he was dreamin', fidgety-like, looking for something, you know. It was said he never talked to nobody. But one day he spotted his pap's fiddle hanging over the mantel. He stood on a chair and got it down. Then he began to play, like it came real natural to him."

Old Jeb knocked out the cold ashes of his pipe and refilled it. "Anyways, the story went that he played such hauntin' melodies that the animals in the forest grew quiet. The whip-poor-will stopped calling, the wood dove quit cooing, and even the crickets no longer chirped. My pap said it was real strange how the boy had this power. Nobody could understand it.

"Then one day some city men came to the woods. I don't rightly remember why they was here. Anyways, Daniel talked to 'em a long time. He learned 'bout colleges and places to study music and things. Stuff nobody in this holla' knew about. Daniel got excited about leaving the gap and his father said the boy must go. But then a terrible sickness came through and Daniel's father died.

"Yet the boy never gave up hope to be set free of this place. He fiddled from mornin' to night like the music was telling the disappointment he couldn't say. His mam was driven to a frenzy by the wild music and hid in these woods when she couldn't stand it no longer.

"Then one morning he found a newborn colt in the barnyard. Its mother was standing over it to protect it. Well, that colt grew into a beautiful filly they say and Daniel loved it. Now he played a happy kind of music that made his mam real cheerful.

"As the young fella' grew older, he found another love—a girl named Hattie.

And a great change came over him. It was like he knew from the start he was marryin' her and I reckon she knew it too. Now he'd never leave the hill country but he paid it no mind. He figgered that after they married he'd play love songs through the cold, winter nights and when the babies come he'd put them to sleep with lullabies. People said it was just like God had planned it.

"'Cept another man already loved Hattie. He threatened a day of reckonin' if she turned him down. But Hattie was a real hill girl, Henry, and they have no fears. She tells him outright she's not marrying him. But she never tells Daniel about him."

All this time Henry had sat quietly on his end of the log, cradling his cob in his hands. He dared not light it for fear the old man would be distracted and not finish the story.

Old Jeb shuffled leaves into a pile at his feet. "The wedding day came along in October, same month as Daniel's mam was married years before. Well, that night Daniel and his wife went directly to his mam's cabin. She was wanting them to bide with her till they could settle into a place of their own. They laughed and sang and while Daniel played sweet songs his wife sang the words.

"Suddenly, a terrific noise shook the cabin near to pieces—shrieking and banging to drive a person stone deaf.

"'Oh, a shivaree!' cried Hattie. She and Daniel's 'mam rushed to the door to welcome the visitors. But you know, Henry, Daniel heard something else—a wild cry from his filly. He rushed to the barnyard and saw her dying, shivering on the ground and in a pool of her own blood.

"They said she was so terrified by the noises that she tried to jump the fence and a stake went right through her."

The old man's eyes filled. "I tell you, friend, Daniel knew this was no shivaree. This was a mad mob like them gangs of Baldknobbers or bushwhackers that used to gallop through the countryside, killin' and burnin'. Nobody knew who they were or where they'd strike next. Please to God there's none of that anymore.

"Anyways, Daniel was real skeered, a course, for his loved ones," old Jeb went on, "and he ran back toward the cabin. But jest as he came 'round the corner, he heard a shot and saw a flash of fire. Then he saw Hattie fall in the doorway."

Henry felt sick. He knew the rest of the story; he had seen it all before.

The old man knocked the tobacco out of his pipe.

"Before Daniel could reach Hattie there was another shot and another flash. His mam fell beside Hattie. Daniel jumped over the bodies and ran into the cabin. He grabbed a rifle and rushed outside. Then he jest opened fire into the woods in all directions—a raving maniac with a gun.

"In the morning my pap and two other men crept into the woods. They knew Daniel was crazy as a loon and they were a little skeered of what they'd find.

"But there was nothin' to fear. Daniel was laying dead by the cabin door beside his women folk, his rifle at his side. My pap found five more dead men laying on the ground at different spots. Daniel'd killed 'em all. One of 'em was the fella' that had made the threats, the one that Hattie threw over."

Old Jeb eased himself to his feet and rubbed the stiffness out of his legs. "We go on now, friend."

Henry felt old and tired as he trudged after his neighbor. He never even felt the sting of briar bushes through the legs of his pants.

Suddenly, old Jeb turned around in the trail. Looking Henry directly in the eye, he said, "That cabin back thar is full of haints."

"Yes, it is," Henry replied.

"Anyways, it is in October. That's when the ghosts of all them dead folks come back."

Henry nodded. It was a fact that he had witnessed a tragedy out of the distant past—a circumstance he had known nothing about. He had seen for himself that mysterious link between the living and the dead.

Eventually Henry moved away to the city to work and marry. But the wild music of the mountains never left him. His wife loved to attend music recitals. Henry didn't accompany her. Whenever she asked him to go, he said he couldn't. Eventually she quit asking. She never understood his reluctance.

Sarah's House

The pleasant young man sits with his hands clasped at a table typically occupied by visitors eating a quick lunch in the coffee shop adjoining San Jose's Winchester Mystery House, California's most incredible home. "The owners want the truth told about the house and its history," he emphasizes to a visitor.

A 160-room Victorian enchantment, the mansion was built over a period of nearly four decades by Sarah Winchester, an heiress to the company that manufactured the deadliest gun in American history. The house is now a tourist attraction, open year-round to the public.

The truth behind the incredible manse is as strange as any story in America. The wealthy Mrs. Winchester, at the age of 44 and recently widowed, traveled alone to California in 1884. After the death of her husband, the heiress had been told in a séance that to achieve any peace in her life she must appease the spirits of those killed by her husband's family's guns. She must find or build a house, and add to it—forever. That she did, for thirty-eight years, never allowing work to stop on the house, gardens, and surrounding farm fields. At its zenith Sarah's house rose almost seven stories and contained a dizzying maze of rooms, hallways, staircases, and doors unlike that of any other private home in the world.

But there are other, darker, questions about Sarah Winchester and her Llanda Villa, as she named it:

Was she a madwoman who added rooms and new wings truly at the behest of ghostly visitors?

Did she ever actually encounter any of the wraiths of the Indians, pioneers, and soldiers killed by Winchester rifles?

Was she hoping for eternal life if construction never stopped as, it is said, the "spirits" promised her?

And for what reason did she shun virtually all human companionship?

The most asked question, however, is a simple one: Is the Winchester Mansion haunted?

That question is not easily answered. "There are eerie things in this house," the young man, staff member at the house, continues. He notes that séances have been held in the bedroom where Mrs. Winchester died and in the eerie, isolated

Blue Room, with its thirteen hooks for ghosts to hang their wraps upon. It was there Sarah Winchester communicated with "good spirits" until the wee hours of the morning.

The man explains that several psychic investigators have been granted permission to spend a night in the house. Each has come away with the impression that there is considerable ghostly activity taking place within the literally miles of hallways and eightscore rooms.

"One psychic who has been through the house, Sylvia Brown, even said there was a room that has not yet been found," he adds. Within that room, according to Brown, are letters from Sarah Winchester. But there is little architectural proof that such a room exists.

Mrs. Brown and four other persons stayed overnight in the séance room in the early 1980s. She wanted to debunk the ghost legends unless she personally witnessed unexplained phenomena. She didn't because she did.

According to published accounts, Mrs. Brown saw a man and a woman dressed as servants hovering in a corner. She described their faces as filled with "fierce intensity." The psychic said she also heard organ music. During a late-night walking tour of the mansion, several members of Mrs. Brown's entourage felt intense cold spots and saw pulsating red lights coming from a source they could not detect.

At another séance, psychic Jeanne Borgen actually felt the presence of "one very gentle ghost," perhaps that of Mrs. Winchester herself.

The owners of the Winchester Mystery House are quite willing to accept the possibility that something of another world resides in their public attraction. It doesn't harm business. But even ghosts have a hard time competing with the real-life history of Sarah and her grand manor on South Winchester Boulevard.

Sarah L. Pardee Winchester was born into New Haven, Connecticut's high society in 1840, the daughter of Leonard and Sarah Burns Pardee. Her exact birthdate is not known. She was privately schooled in music, learned to speak four foreign languages, and quickly became one of the leading belles of the city. Sarah grew to only four feet ten inches tall, but her cultured speech and creamy complexion made her a favorite of New Haven's eligible bachelors.

New England in the decades before the Civil War was the home of men with names like Colt, Wesson, Sharps, and Smith who were forming companies to manufacture firearms. But another New Englander also had his eye on the armaments business. His name was Oliver Fisher Winchester.

Winchester was a remarkable man, self-made in the truest sense of the word. He and a twin brother had been born in 1810, the last of five children. Forced to go to work at the age of seven to help support his family, by age fourteen Oliver was apprenticed to a carpenter. In a few years he became an expert builder.

At the age of twenty, Oliver Winchester moved to Baltimore. He married Jane Ellen Hope in 1834 and to that union were born three children: Ann Rebecca, Hannah Jane, and William Wirt. Over the next fourteen years, Oliver Winchester became one of the greatest success stories in New England industrial history.

His interest in building waned for some reason and he went into the clothing business while his children were still quite young. One of the problems facing men of that era was ill-fitting shirts. The cloth hung from collar bands, causing the shirt to droop. Winchester determined that a shirt that hung from the shoulder would be a much more comfortable fit. He returned to New Haven and opened a factory to sew his new shirts. They were an immediate financial and sartorial success.

It's ironic, however, that a builder and shirtmaker is now best known for a rifle. And what's even more amazing is that Oliver Fisher Winchester didn't even invent the weapon that still bears his name. Entrepreneur that he was, Winchester became involved in the burgeoning arms business because of its potential for financial success.

With the earnings from his profitable shirt company, Winchester formed the New Haven Arms Company, later renamed the Winchester Repeating Arms Company, to manufacture a rifle that seemed to him the best design of any he had seen so far. Within a few years, he became the most successful of all the gunmakers in North America.

Sarah Pardee married Oliver Winchester's only son, William Wirt Winchester, on September 30, 1862. For the vivacious young debutante it seemed a perfect match—the son who would inherit his father's burgeoning manufacturing empire wedding the daughter of an old Connecticut family. Sadly, the happiness they sought eluded the prosperous young couple.

The first tragedy of their life together came in the fourth year of their marriage. A daughter, Annie Pardee Winchester, was born on June 15, 1866, but died a month and a half later of marasmus, a disease that is characterized by the gradual wasting away of the individual. In children it is sometimes attributed to improper feeding or nourishment. While it may appear that Sarah somehow contributed to the infant's death, historical accounts differ on her culpability. Sarah appeared genuinely inconsolable and was put under a doctor's care. She would have no more children.

By 1880, the seventy-year-old Oliver Winchester was making plans for the continuing operation of his family-owned company after his death. It was taken for granted by all that William Wirt would assume control of the company. The Winchester rifle was "winning the West" and the profits allowed Oliver's family a sumptuous lifestyle in the era before income taxes. Most of the stock was held by his wife, son William Wirt and Sarah, his two daughters, and a son-in-law.

On December 10, 1880, Oliver Winchester died. At about the same time, William Wirt Winchester contracted tuberculosis. By early 1881 it was clear that he was too ill to become president of the company. William W. Converse, Oliver's son-in-law, became chief executive officer.

William Wirt Winchester died on March 7, 1881, barely three months after his own father's passing. It was too much for the diminutive Sarah. Rather than see another physician, as she had done after her infant daughter's death, she started consulting Boston psychic readers and spiritualists. She wanted to find some reason behind the deaths of her daughter and husband. What she found was not solace but a kind of self-proclaimed avenging angel in the person of one unknown psychic she consulted.

The psychic told Sarah her loved ones died as retribution for the thousands of victims of her in-laws' deadly rifle. The spirits of all those killed were exacting a terrible, personal toll on poor Sarah. There was a curse on her, she was warned, that could only be lifted if she moved West, bought a house and added to it continuously, twenty-four hours per day, day after day after day.... The spirits would tell her what to build.

Sarah might also find eternal life in her building project, the psychic said the spirits promised. If she stopped, or failed to heed the spirits' directives, she would be haunted forever by the innocents who died with a Winchester rifle bullet in them.

Incredibly, Sarah evidently believed the psychic's every warning and directive. Three years after William's death, Sarah Winchester packed her belongings, a $20 million inheritance, and an estimated $1,000-per-day income from Winchester patents and moved to what would become San Jose, California. There she began to build her mansion, just as the spirits had directed her to do.

It is not clear why Sarah Winchester chose California as the site of her "spirit mansion." Nor is it recorded what attracted her to the then eight-room farmhouse owned by a Dr. Caldwell. Perhaps it was the opportunity to purchase a large amount of land—she eventually owned 161 acres—or maybe one of her spirits directed her to this particular location. But for whatever reason, for the next thirty-eight years, Sarah added room upon room to the doctor's original house, working her staff of carpenters, decorators, gardeners, and personal servants 365 days per year. Construction was never allowed to stop. She employed anywhere from forty-two to eighty persons at any given time. Barns and storage buildings went up, vast gardens and fields were planted, sweeping lawns were constructed, but foremost and always there was the mansion itself. A mansion built, Sarah said, because the spirits told her to.

Words such as "eclectic," "bizarre," the "ultimate rambler," and "Victorian monstrosity" have all been used to describe Mrs. Winchester's house. Starting with just eight rooms, she added to the structure so that it rose over seventy feet in the air and contained over 160 rooms in the years just prior to the devastating 1906 California earthquake.

Each night, Sarah would contact the spirits in the Blue Room. This particular room, buried deep within the structure, can only be reached after taking a winding path through various other rooms and halls. She built it this way so that any "bad spirits" following her would become confused and give up. A four-foot-high iron bar across the doorway was at just the right height for Sarah to slip under, but low enough so that any spirits that had managed to keep up with her would slam into it. When they cried out in pain, Sarah would simply slam the door in their ethereal faces! Only Sarah alone ever entered this sanctum sanctorum.

The tolling from the bell tower signaled the arrival of the spirits just after midnight and then their departure a few hours later. She would emerge from the room with architectural sketches on scrap paper and bits of tablecloth. There was never any formal blueprint for the construction and, in the end, only Mrs. Winchester knew the location of all the rooms, hallways, linen closets, and staircases.

With her vast wealth, Mrs. Winchester bought only the finest furnishings and construction materials from American and European sources. She had priceless Tiffany art glass windows made to order in Austria. One window alone cost $1,500 at the time and was made of German silver, bronze, and lead. It was designed so the sunlight coming through the crystal and rock quartz would cause colored light patterns to play across the room. But Sarah put it on the north side of the house— and then built walls outside so any view was completely blocked. Many of the house's two thousand doors are also inlaid with German silver and bronze.

The Grand Ballroom cost a then-staggering $9,000 when it was built in the early 1900s. Special carpenters from the East Coast were hired because Sarah didn't trust her own staff of builders. Not a nail was used on the seven different types of wood in the ballroom, an innovation at the time. Two art glass windows were commissioned, inscribed with two odd Shakespearean quotes: "Wide unclasp the tables of their thoughts" and "These same thoughts people this little world." Only Sarah knew what special meaning they held for her.

The vastness of the estate challenges the imagination. Consider that the house has: 40 bedrooms, 5 kitchens, 40 staircases with a total of 376 steps, 52 skylights, 47 fireplaces (gas and wood or coal burning), evidence of at least 17 chimneys, 2 ballrooms, and approximately 10,000 windows, some valued today at over $10,000 each!

Gold and silver chandeliers hung from the ceilings of many of the rooms, storerooms were filled with priceless furnishings bought but never installed, wash basins were hand-painted and imported from Venice, exquisite staircases were handcarved from flawless mahogany, as were several fireplaces. Wallpaper was imported from France.

Despite the immensity of her mansion and grounds, Sarah Winchester kept a close watch over construction details. One story is told that she instructed a repairman to fix a broken gate at the edge of the estate. A few days later she inspected the work, wearing as was her custom an ankle-length black dress and a veil covering her face, and asked where he had found the yellow-colored nails. He told her he had found them in a storeroom. "They're not copper," she said. "They are solid gold and I'm saving them for a special purpose." She ordered them replaced.

Sarah also installed numerous "modern" conveniences. Three Otis elevators carried her between floors, but one rose only a few feet to the next floor level. Two of them were powered by water pressure and the third by electricity. It is assumed that they were installed because severe arthritis in her later years made Sarah a virtual invalid.

A push button in each room allowed Mrs. Winchester to signal servants through an ingenious call box system. A bell signaled the servants on duty who could then talk to their mistress through a series of voice tubes. A light on the intercom also pinpointed her exact location.

The South Conservatory is called the "room of glass." Sunlight poured into the room all day long to nourish the plants and flowers she loved to raise. Sarah solved the problem of watering the plants by building a special floor that could be raised, exposing a zinc subfloor below. When servants watered the plants, excess water ran across the subfloor, through drains, and thence to the garden below.

It is not Sarah Winchester's extravagant spending, however, that is most notable about her mansion. Sarah's primary purpose in building the sprawling estate was to thwart the "bad spirits" that she feared would follow her all her days. Numerous visitors have said that the house seems to have been built by ghosts, for ghosts.

To that end, the Winchester mansion is filled with architectural anomalies, to fool even the most curious, albeit unwanted, visitors from this world . . . or the next.

Several staircases end abruptly at the ceiling. Perhaps they were built to reach an anticipated floor above, but their true purpose died with Sarah.

A switchback staircase has seven turns and forty-four steps, but goes up only nine feet. Each step is just a few inches high. The speculation is that the gradual incline made climbing easier for the arthritic mistress of the house. Or perhaps it was built to confuse pesky spirits. Another staircase descends to a landing without an apparent purpose. The only way out is up another staircase.

Many doors are only four feet high and several open onto solid walls. Other doors swing open over drops of several stories. One room has a cupboard one inch deep, but a pantry door a few feet away swings open to reveal a passage to the mansion's thirty back rooms.

Secret corridors led to isolated rooms, many of which remained unfinished at Sarah's death in 1922. And, of course, there is the "hidden room" that psychic Sylvia Brown said had not been discovered. Speculation is that this may be Sarah's "missing" wine cellar. The story is that one evening as she was dining with her secretary, the only person allowed to see her without a veil, Sarah excused herself to locate a particularly fine wine. She was the sole possessor of the key to the wine cellar. However, when she entered the room she found a black handprint on the wall, perhaps made by a thirsty servant. But fearing it was a "demon's hand," Mrs. Winchester had the room sealed off. According to legend, it has never been found.

As befitting a believer in the psychic world, Sarah Winchester was devoted to the number thirteen.

There are thirteen bathrooms in the mansion, but only a single shower with a shower head installed at the correct height for a person slightly under five feet in height. All the bathrooms have windows to the surrounding rooms. Sarah liked to keep an eye on her servants at all times!

There are thirteen windows and doors that open in the old sewing room, thirteen glass cupolas in the Greenhouse, thirteen ceiling panels in the Entrance Hallway and Guest Reception Room, thirteen stones in the Oriental Bedroom windows, thirteen panels in the wall by the thirteenth bathroom, thirteen windows in the thirteenth bathroom, and thirteen California Fan Palms lining the front driveway. There are at least a dozen more uses of the number thirteen in the mansion.

When the Ballroom chandelier arrived with only twelve gas jets, she added one more.

The 1906 northern California earthquake nearly destroyed Sarah's monument to the spirit world. Though the top three stories crumbled, amazingly only a few rooms on the first three floors were damaged because of the house's solid construction materials. Another of Sarah's peculiarities almost cost her her life in the quake. She had the habit of sleeping in a different bedroom each night . . . so the spirits wouldn't know where to find her. The servants were never sure where she could be found on any given morning. It took rescuers several hours to find her and dig her out.

Sarah feared the earthquake was a warning that the spirits were displeased with her efforts. Though construction on the house continued, she moved to an elegant houseboat she had built on a river nearby. She lived there for six years, convinced that the Pacific Ocean would rise to wash away all of California.

Much to her surprise, California survived and she moved back to her mansion. She had ordered the bedroom where she had been trapped boarded up and the front section of the house closed off. The elegant front hallway never received visitors and the Grand Ballroom never hosted a Christmas dance.

Sarah Winchester died on September 5, 1922, at the age of eighty-three. Nearly four decades of constant building didn't provide her with eternal life after all. She may have known all along that the spirits were not to be trusted. She wrote a will . . . with thirteen sections signed by thirteen people.

Was this a madwoman possessed by her own personal demons, or simply an eccentric, misunderstood and vilified by those who never knew her?

She seems to have been a mixture of both. Her architectural acumen improved over the decades. The stairways to ceilings, doors opening onto walls—or into space—and fireplaces without chimneys gave way to a kind of enchanting Victorianism that characterizes the house. Perhaps in the beginning Sarah was compelled by spirits, but toward the end of her life she seemed propelled more by a need to build an artistic monument never to be equaled.

That she was a recluse with a strong aversion to being recognized or photographed is well documented. On her infrequent trips into San Jose, she stayed in her heavily draped carriage while the proprietor of the general store brought out bolts of cloth for her to inspect. He handed them through the window curtains to her, and she passed back those that didn't suit her tastes. He never caught a glimpse of her.

The hedge around her estate was allowed to grow so that only the top floor of her estate was visible from the street. In this way, Sarah was shielded from prying eyes. She was never seen around the house without a heavy veil obscuring her face. Once when two workmen accidentally glimpsed her sans shroud, they were summarily dismissed, but with several months' severance pay.

So complete was her quest for privacy that she turned down all requests for interviews and audiences, including one by Theodore Roosevelt. As the tales of her eccentricity spread through the land, so did her retreat into her own private world.

At the end she died alone in her bedroom. She had spent all but $4 million of her inheritance, the balance going upon her death to a sanitarium in Connecticut, the William Wirt Winchester Annex for Tuberculosis in New Haven. The house and its furnishings were left to a niece, but with the stipulation in Sarah's will that it was hoped the house could be preserved. The niece took what she wanted and the rest of the furniture was auctioned off. Movers took six weeks to remove the household goods, primarily because they often became lost in the maze of dead-end hallways, secret doors, and endless rooms. Since 1973, the private corporation that now owns the house has restored it to its condition when Sarah Winchester died there nearly seventy-five years ago.

But what of the most important question: Is Sarah Winchester's rambling mansion haunted?

The answer is not simple. Certainly the current owners find it useful to perpetuate the "mysterious" nature of the house. They need very little help convincing visitors of that fact. It is the quintessential "haunted house." Knowing that Sarah built its catacomblike rooms at the direction of "spirits" only adds to its reputation.

Yet there have been incidents, minor perhaps, certainly not an inundation by the pale visages of deceased warriors and outlaws, but enough to warrant the tentative supposition that Sarah's house may contain more than architectural eccentricities.

While most of the ghostlore connected with the Winchester House is of relatively recent vintage—from the early 1970s to the present time—the first article detailing the builder's obsession with spirits appeared in the Sunday American Weekly on April 1, 1928, April Fool's Day. The headline read, "MRS. WINCHESTER'S EXTRAORDINARY 'SPOOK PALACE.'"

The anonymous writer limited himself to a description of the absurdities built into the mansion to please the good spirits and to thwart the nefarious missions of the bad ones. Among the former was the near total absence of mirrors. Ghosts, it is said, will instantly vanish upon seeing their reflections. There are just two mirrors, one in Sarah's bedroom and another in the adjoining bathroom. Even the mirror installed over the mantelpiece in the Grand Ballroom had its backside to the room in order not to offend a wandering specter.

Sarah's building plans also took into account a ghost's predilection for escaping up chimneys, thus accounting for the "fifty . . . popular spook escapes," according to the *American Weekly*, although current estimates are that no more than nineteen chimneys ever actually existed. Perhaps the writer counted fireplaces, of which there are at least four dozen. At any rate, when the bell tolled two A.M. and the spirits had to leave, they had a variety of exits at their disposal. Hopefully, they did not choose the one chimney that ascends through four floors, has three or four fireplaces attached to it, yet stops inches short of the fourth-floor ceiling!

Over a quarter-century passed, however, before the first account of an odd incident involving a visitor to the mansion. This and other mysterious events have been compiled by the staff of the Winchester Mansion.

A Fresno, California woman, Mrs. Arlene Bischel, wrote the staff of the Winchester House that during a 1955 visit she mysteriously "lost her eyesight" after touring several rooms. She had to be led around by her husband until a tour guide could take them out. Mrs. Bischel sat on a bench in the sun for several minutes and her vision came back. A subsequent visit by Mrs. Bischel in 1978 passed uneventfully.

Several prominent psychics claim to have had mysterious experiences while conducting séances in Mrs. Winchester's bedroom and in the Blue Room.

During the late 1970s, psychic Sylvia Brown, her husband, Dal, and four others, including writer Antoinette May, spent one night in the mansion, splitting their time among the Blue Room, the bedroom in which Mrs. Winchester died, and roaming the hallways. Mrs. Brown said she heard organ music in the séance room, although her companions could not. A recording made at the time allegedly contained sounds of an organ. When she was alive, Sarah Winchester sometimes played a pump organ in one bedroom until late into the night. Neighbors and passersby often spread tales of the haunting music that seemed to come from the sleeping mansion.

Sylvia Brown's group also felt "cold spots" and saw large "balls of red light that seemed to explode and then fade" in Mrs. Winchester's bedroom—which contains the original, hand-carved oak bed in which she died.

The psychic also described a phantom couple lingering in the corner of the bedroom clothed in servants' outfits appropriate to the early twentieth century. Several members of Mrs. Brown's group said they had the sense of being watched the entire night.

Psychic Jeanne Borgen and medium Joy Adams investigated the haunting of Winchester House on Halloween night, 1975. The pair conducted a séance in Mrs. Winchester's bedroom in the presence of several newspeople, according to later reports. During the séance, Mrs. Borgen, apparently in a trance, appeared to age suddenly. In the dim light, her hair seemed to turn gray and her face lined with deep creases. She looked to be in extreme discomfort. As she started to stumble, she awoke from her sleep.

The psychic said the spirit of Mrs. Winchester was "overpowering," but she described the late mistress of the house as a "gentle ghost." She had earlier reported the sight of a ghost with "a kind of white face and form" hanging about a hallway.

Sounds with no earthly source have been heard with some regularity in the mansion. A caretaker from 1973 to 1981 told a reporter that in one specific room there seemed to be someone breathing, though he was ostensibly alone in the entire house. He followed the sound of footsteps to the threshold of Mrs. Winchester's bedroom. Again no one but the man was about. At another time, he said he was awakened by the squeaking of a nail or large screw being pulled out of wood. It then seemed to drop to a wooden floor in the room in which he slept.

Mike Bray, a tour guide, told his supervisors that as he was closing the house on a night in July 1981, he heard his name whispered as he walked down a hallway near the bird aviary. He was quite alone.

Rich Cirivilleri and Jane Brusin, also tour guides, have reported hearing footsteps on different occasions. Cirivilleri said he had the feeling of being watched shortly before footsteps made a floor creak in a hallway. Brusin heard the same thing from rooms on the second floor that still show damage from the 1906 earthquake.

Two other tour guides had the singular experience of *smelling* phantom odors.

Amy Kinsch sniffed the distinct presence of chicken soup while sweeping the floor in the front kitchen. A few months later, during the summer months, Gina Aning was leading a tour group through the area when she and her entire entourage detected the same odor in the same kitchen. Aning also reported feeling the kind of steam heat given off by a boiling pot as she walked by the stove. A kitchen in the gift shop/restaurant was some distance away, but couldn't have been the source of the odor. They don't sell soup in the summer.

Another of the house's six kitchens figures in one of the few reported *appearances* by a ghost that may have been Sarah Winchester.

Sue Sale was an office manager at Winchester House. She saw a small, gray-haired woman sitting at a table in one of the kitchens. At first, she assumed one of the employees had been costumed to impersonate Mrs. Winchester for the amusement of tour groups. However, she found out later that no such promotion was occurring at the time she saw the woman in the kitchen.

Another ghostly image turned up in one visitor's photographs. Gary Parks, a friend of a former caretaker, had been invited to spend New Year's Eve at the mansion. He spent a good deal of time taking pictures with a camera he had received as a Christmas present. When he had the pictures developed a few days later, he found one negative with an image of "strange lights" that seemed to have moved when the picture was taken, and the image of a man dressed in overalls. Parks had seen nothing unusual in the room when the picture was taken.

Some of the phenomena seem to be the product of a poltergeist bent on disrupting the staff's routine through puckish behavior. Allen Weitzel, a director of food and merchandising at Winchester House, was puzzled by several episodes. One night he locked all the doors to the gift shop and headed into a storeroom to set the alarm system. When he came back out, a glass door leading to the courtyard had somehow been unlocked. No one else was around at the time.

About a year later, Weitzel was again by himself locking up for the night. He walked through the entire house turning off all the lights on the various tour routes. As he headed toward his car, he turned around to make sure he hadn't missed any. The house was dark. But when he reached his car and glanced back a final time, all the lights on the third floor were ablaze.

Weitzel also had one of two reported incidents at the house involving the strange appearance of water. In his case, Weitzel discovered his office soaked with water one morning. Everything from the paperwork on his desk to his chair and the floor was sopping wet. Even a pencil holder was filled with water. A light rain had fallen overnight, but not nearly enough to cause the extent of damage Weitzel found. And, most intriguing of all, the ceiling and walls were completely dry. There was no sign of water seepage anywhere.

A former director of operations, Roger LaFountain, reported finding that a light-bulb in the Blue Room had exploded overnight. He thought seeping water around the fixture might have caused the bulb to burst, although it hadn't rained in some time and water stains were not visible.

On Halloween 1979, four men, including LaFountain and psychic Warren Capling, spent the night in Mrs. Winchester's bedroom. Shortly after six o'clock, and as the quartet sat in the room with the lights off, Capling said he heard an organ playing and a dog's insistent barking. No one else heard anything. All of the men *did* see a beam of light with a blurred center moving across the room. It hovered near Sarah's deathbed and vanished.

The truth behind Sarah Winchester's fabulous mansion is far more bizarre than anything created by skilled publicists to lure tourists in search of supernatural thrills. A woman who kept dozens of carpenters building additions for thirty-eight years so that the "spirits" would not haunt her, and studiously avoided all contact with fellow humans, doesn't need any manufactured fame. There is enough on the record to puzzle even the most discerning skeptic. Yet in this house built "by ghosts, for ghosts," is it any wonder that the phantom architects, and the woman who carried out their plans, remain behind in their masterpiece?

Yankee Jim's Legacy

The diminutive director of San Diego's historic Whaley House Museum decided that the rainstorm would curtail the usual crush of visitors to the restored 1856 brick home. June Reading had shown only a handful of tourists through the exquisitely decorated nineteenth-century rooms that morning, proudly pointing out the 1853 Jenny Lind Piano, a unique collection of antique music boxes, Andrew Jackson's favorite sofa, and the dozens of other pieces of period furniture. So June left for an early lunch. A young woman who had worked as a guide at the house for only a short period of time was left in charge.

"When I got back she met me at the door," June recalled of that day several years ago. "She said that while I was gone she had heard the heavy tread of bootsteps not once but twice, at intervals, on the second floor."

June remembered that a young boy had toured the house just before lunch. He expressed a keen interest in the ghostly legends connected with the place. He even sat for a time on the stairs to see if he could "hear" anything. June hadn't paid much attention to him, but now she wondered if he could have somehow sneaked back into the house.

June and the young guide decided to look around. As they reached the top of the main staircase they were surprised to see a large hallway window standing open. Great rolling thunderheads rumbled in off the Pacific Ocean. Rain was blowing in the window, soaking the curtains and carpeting. June was sure the window had been closed earlier in the day. Had the young boy opened it and then climbed back in after he left through the front door? June wondered.

While June found towels to mop up the water, her companion quickly checked through the bedrooms. "She didn't think anyone had been up there," June said. "I then tried to close the window, but the white cedar frame was swollen. I could hardly get it closed. It was so hard to pull the bolt pin back that I said we'd have to get a hammer to pound it back. Finally, between the two of us we managed to get that bolt back and shut the window."

One thing was certain, however. The frame was so enlarged that a child the age of their young visitor couldn't possibly have opened the window in the first place. If not the young boy, who? June thinks the answer to that question is connected to the rest of her adventure that afternoon.

"We walked into the nursery and looked around," June said. She was still trying to find an explanation for the footsteps. One of the museum's proudest possessions is a collection of antique dolls in the nursery, arranged as if in waiting for the return of a favorite little girl. June's companion said she had been asked about the dolls while giving tours and wanted to know more about them.

"I started talking about them and ended up holding a doll so small that it's difficult to show unless you actually stand and look at it closely," June said. "I think they used to sell them for a penny apiece. It has a tiny hand-crocheted dress on and a little bonnet." The guide remarked that she had never seen anything so tiny as the doll June cradled in her palm.

In the next moment, from the dark hallway, came the baritone laugh of a man. Very pleasant it was, not malicious or evil, but clearly of human origin.

"Neither of us said anything at first. We didn't move. And then she said, 'Did you hear that?' I just kept looking at the doll and asked what she heard."

"A man's laughter," she said.

"I did too," June recalls with a shudder.

Both women fled down the stairs.

"It was the most profound thing that's ever happened to me," June emphasized. "Something happened upstairs in that nursery, something touched me. It was like an electric shock. That laughter hit me and went down my spine, my legs, my arms. I felt just like I had had contact with the unseen world."

For June Reading, that rain-swept afternoon was final proof that her beloved Whaley House is haunted. But to understand what spectral beings laugh and cry, and even occasionally are seen and smelled in the lovingly restored home, it is necessary to go back to the very origins of that dazzling southern California city on the bay.

San Diego was little more than a frontier outpost in 1849, the year Thomas Whaley first visited there. A well-educated member of an old eastern family that traced its lineage to early seventeenth-century Britain, Whaley couldn't have found a sharper contrast with his upbringing than life in the predominantly Spanish village, El Pueblo de San Diego.

The legendary Padre Junípero Serra founded his California mission, San Diego de Alcalá, nearby in 1769. It wasn't until the 1820s, however, that a small community grew at the base of Presidio Hill, the site of Padre Serra's church, and now the historic district known as Old Town.

What Thomas Whaley found was a rough-hewn collection of Mexican adobe and American wood-frame buildings clustered around a plaza. Only three years prior to Whaley's visit, in 1846, the American flag had been raised in the plaza of the old pueblo, effectively ending Mexico's dominance over the territory.

Thomas Whaley didn't stay long the first time he landed in San Diego. Sent by his company to start mercantile businesses in California, Whaley continued on to San Francisco. But he returned to San Diego in 1851 and started in business with a general store on the plaza. His partner was Philip Crosthwaite, who was later to become county clerk and sheriff.

By 1857, the year Thomas Whaley started building his red brick house, the eastern businessman was prospering. He returned to New York to marry Anna Eloise De Launay and brought her back to California. Whaley also started drawing up plans for a two-story, Greek Revival mansion, the likes of which had never been seen in old California.

But another, more sinister event would first take place, one that would forever shape the haunting legend that has come to envelop Thomas Whaley's home. That had to do with "Yankee Jim" Robinson, a tall, mysterious drifter with unruly blond hair.

No one really knows *who* Yankee Jim really was or where he came from. Historians think he may have been one Santiago Robinson, a Bermudan who came to California in 1842. Santiago is the Spanish name for James.

Or, Robinson may have been Nova Scotian, or even a so-called Sydney duck, one of the former Australian convicts who settled in early southern California.

He may have been the founder of a long-vanished settlement in Placer County, California, called "Yankee Jim's Diggings." According to state records, a man named James Robinson discovered gold in the vicinity in 1850.

Whatever his origins, it is known that one James W. Robinson, alias "Yankee Jim," was spotted rowing surreptitiously toward the schooner *Plutus*, a thirty-ton vessel sometimes called a pilot boat, anchored in San Diego harbor on August 13, 1852. Its owner, Capt. James Keating, was standing onshore and hailed the intruder. He thought someone might be trying to steal his ship, a hanging offense in early California. When Robinson did not reply, Keating fired several rounds of buckshot but missed the rowboat and Robinson.

Robinson made for shore and headed inland through the scrub oak. Keating waited until the next morning to make a report to the authorities in San Diego. Sheriff Reiner mounted a posse and soon brought in two men thought to be Robinson's accomplices, William Harris, alias William Harney, and James Grayson Loring. Both were charged with grand larceny. They supposedly admitted to being professional horse thieves.

Robinson, however, was not so easy prey. Sheriff Reiner warned residents near False Bay, where Robinson had put ashore, to be on the lookout for a tall man wearing a red shirt. Shortly after dark on Saturday, August 14, 1852, a man answering Robinson's description showed up at the door of a Mexican couple in a settlement known as Rose's Ranch. He asked for something to eat, but grew nervous when the couple acted suspiciously.

Robinson fled the house with the Mexican couple at his heels. The husband managed to throw a lasso around the suspect and then thwacked him on the head with a Spanish artillery sword. The couple lashed the unconscious and bleeding Robinson across the back of a horse and took him to the sheriff.

Three days later, Yankee Jim Robinson was tried and found guilty of grand larceny. On August 18, he was sentenced to be hanged exactly one month later. His accomplices were, for some reason, let off with lesser prison sentences.

The irony is that only Yankee Jim was sentenced to die for what seems now to be a minor crime. Later research established that it was the "intent" of Robinson and his confederates to steal the pilot boat *Plutus*, that resulted in the stiff sentence for Robinson, the mastermind of the attempted theft.

Robinson almost didn't make his thirty-day waiting period. There was no jail in San Diego. A number of citizens gathered on the afternoon of the verdict to hold a public meeting on the question of whether Yankee Jim should swing on that very same day. Cooler heads prevailed, however, and various local men took turns guarding the prisoner until the court-imposed hanging.

At two o'clock on the afternoon of September 18, 1852, Yankee Jim Robinson stood in the back of a buckboard, one end of a hemp noose knotted around his neck and the other attached to the gallows. Asked if he had any final words, Robinson launched upon a soliloquy that silenced the anxious spectators. Thirty minutes later, the desperado still hadn't slowed his patter. The crowd was nervous. By law, all executions had to be carried out by three o'clock in the afternoon and it looked like Robinson might talk until midnight.

Sheriff Reiner wasn't about to let that happen. With a brief nod of his head, Reiner signaled for the horses to pull the wagon away, silencing Yankee Jim in mid-sentence. But a ghastly error had been made. The scaffold had been built for shorter men. The toes of Robinson's boots scraped the ground. Yankee Jim Robinson slowly strangled to death.

Among the spectators at the hanging was Thomas Whaley. Four years later he would build his home on the precise spot where Robinson died an agonizing death.

Yankee Jim Robinson has never rested easily in his grave.

On September 25, 1855, Thomas Whaley paid the grand sum of $302 for a 150-by-217-foot parcel of land, eight and one-half acres, which included a freshwater spring—and the old execution grounds. Construction on his house began in May 1856 and was completed one year later.

The home Whaley designed was in the Greek Revival style, a popular motif in nineteenth-century America, but quite unlike anything else in early San Diego. Early Anglo settlers wanted everything they did, or built, to be American or, more precisely, eastern American. Amidst the Mexican adobe and wood-frame boxes there rose a Yankee mansion, the first truly "American" home in southern California.

Because of the expense in shipping materials to California from the East and the lack of building supplies on the frontier, Whaley had to supply his own. He established a brickyard three hundred yards from his future home to make bricks for the exterior siding. Tar for the roof came from the La Brea Tar Pits in Los Angeles. Plaster for the walls was mixed from horsehair, river sand, and crushed seashells, gathered by Indians.

The main house contained seven rooms: a kitchen, parlor, music room, and library downstairs, with four bedrooms on a second floor reached by a wide staircase in a spacious hallway. Whaley also built a dirt-floor granary next to his house that was eventually connected to the house. Behind her fine home, Anna Whaley planted a garden. She was particularly proud of her several varieties of roses.

The house cost $10,000 to build, a substantial sum in 1850s California.

Within a few years, the Whaley House became the social center of the community. Whenever citizens wanted to meet and discuss one issue or the other, Thomas Whaley generously offered the use of his airy rooms. Visiting dignitaries often stayed there, enjoying Anna's gracious hospitality and lavish parties. Presidents Ulysses S. Grant and Benjamin Harrison are known to have spent nights in the house. Union general Thomas Sedgwick was headquartered there during the Civil War. For a few years, a traveling theatrical company, "The Tanner Troupe," used the granary as a playhouse.

Except for a period of about six years, when Thomas Whaley traveled to Alaska and established the city of Sitka, members of the Whaley family lived in the home until 1953.

The most notable event connected with the Whaley House occurred during its use as the San Diego County Courthouse in the late 1860s. Thomas Whaley had offered the use of his old granary, bearing all the costs of remodeling it into a courtroom. He charged the county a nominal sixty-five dollars per year for rent.

Trouble was brewing, however. Tensions between the people of Old Town and a development in so-called New Town led to open conflicts. There was sentiment among some elected officials that the county should have a bigger courthouse in the newer section of town. Thomas Whaley obviously disagreed. He turned out to be on the wrong side of the argument. Despite the posting of guards and a declaration of martial law, on the night of March 31, 1871, a group of armed men led by county clerk and recorder Col. Chalmers Scott broke into Whaley's house and stole all the county records. Whaley was away on a business trip to San Francisco. His wife was forced back into her room at gunpoint when she got up to investigate noises in the county "offices."

Scott and his henchmen transported the records to the Wells Fargo building at Sixth and G Streets. That building was used as a courthouse until a new one was built in 1872. Whaley was left with an empty courtroom and six months' rent due. He never collected.

Thomas Whaley died in 1890, still bitter over what he considered the shoddy treatment afforded him by the city and county, particularly their refusal to pay for damages he claimed were caused by Colonel Scott and his night riders.

The colorful legacies provided by Yankee Jim Robinson, Thomas Whaley, and others, together with at least one alleged murder, provide the Whaley House with a history of hauntings that began at least fifty years ago.

The first to suggest the presence of ghosts was Corinne Lillian Whaley, Thomas and Anna's youngest daughter, who lived in the house until she died in 1953 at the age of eighty-nine. According to some accounts, she seldom ventured to the second floor. She wrote in her memoirs that a "force" of some sort didn't want her in the upstairs bedrooms. She said so many strange occurrences had taken place that she slept only fitfully and was always uncomfortable in her ancestral home.

Lillian remained a gracious hostess, however, right up until her death, often inviting old friends over for visits. Christmas was her favorite time of the year. She would have the descendants of other pioneer families stop in for refreshments on Christmas Day. Even when she became too frail to put up a Christmas tree, she took out her charming assortment of antique ornaments and placed them in the lighted windows and on the fireplace mantel.

What disturbed Lillian about the house also puzzled her visitors. Friends reported that as they sat chatting in the parlor, the distinct sounds of a man pacing in heavy boots were heard upstairs. Lillian tried to ignore the noises. Her friends often assumed another person was in the house. But as the afternoon or evening wore on no one else appeared.

Lillian Whaley said it was Yankee Jim who walked in her house.

In 1956, the Whaley House was scheduled for demolition when a group of San Diego citizens formed a Historic Shrine Foundation to buy the land and building. San Diego County eventually agreed to preserve the house as a museum and restore it to its original grandeur. The Foundation maintains it today as a reminder of the city's colorful early days.

June Reading spearheaded the efforts to save the house and served for over thirty years as the museum director. Even before the restoration was completed in 1960, she had her first experience with one of the four ghosts known to haunt Whaley House.

"We were moving all the furniture over here from storage," Mrs. Reading recalled. "Two men from the historical society were helping me move the big pieces of furniture in. I remember coming in, walking right straight through the house and opening the back door so the delivery men could bring in the furniture. They backed up the trucks as close as they could. We all heard the sound of someone walking the floor upstairs. Like a man's footsteps. The floors were bare at the time, so we heard his heels hitting the floorboards. It was a big man, from what I could tell, and it seemed like he was wearing boots. Both of the men helping me said there was someone upstairs. I thought it was probably one of the workmen, although it was funny that he didn't call out and identify himself.

"I started up the stairs and got about halfway up when I saw that the shutters were closed, and there were no signs of life. I did call out but I didn't get any response. Well, I turned around and came back down. I told them there was nobody up there. They looked kind of smug, then one of them said, 'Well, maybe old Thomas Whaley's come back to look the house over.' We all kind of laughed, but from that time on . . ." June's voice trails off as she shrugs her shoulders.

Thomas Whaley or Yankee Jim Robinson? Whaley was known to pace the upstairs hallway. He would also stand for hours on the balcony watching the distant harbor for incoming ships. Research has found that the old gallows stood where an archway leads from the entryway into the music room. June Reading thinks the man she and the workmen heard that day was Yankee Jim. She notes that he was a tall, heavyset man given to wearing tall boots.

Sometimes it's not just the pacing that upsets the staff. A tour guide was eating her noon lunch when she heard noises upstairs. She got up to investigate and saw a man wearing a frock coat standing at the top of the stairs. His face was turned away from her. Before she could call out, the figure faded away.

Mrs. Reading has also seen a ghostly figure of what she believes is Thomas Whaley near the stairs on the second floor.

"He appeared one Sunday afternoon when we were quite busy. A guide called out to come and look at something. I walked back to look up the stairs and sure enough there he was. There were people up there, but they were all looking in the doorways of the bedrooms. He had a black hat on with a wide brim and this long coat. He was solid, but only there for a moment. He was all by himself, right in the middle of the landing. I couldn't believe my eyes."

Whaley doesn't confine himself to the indoors. Several people have seen him strolling through the garden, near a fern bed at the rear of the house.

Sheila Furness has a delightful British accent, a decided belief in the supernatural, and an abiding interest in the Whaley House, where she works as a volunteer guide. She is often overwhelmed by the smell of cigar smoke. Whaley smoked a distinctive brand of Havana cigars. The odor is so strong that Mrs. Furness has to retreat to the front porch for a breath of fresh air.

Around Christmastime, other odors permeate the kitchen even though no one is cooking. Apple. Apple butter. Fresh baked bread. And coffee. Oddly enough, sometimes only one person in a group will detect the cigar smoke or baking odors, Mrs. Furness said.

A sickly sweet perfume is another smell that guides and visitors have noticed.

Jessie Keller, a longtime volunteer at the house, said it's so heavy it almost makes her sick. "I've smelled her [Anna Whaley's] perfume and have been the only one. The last time was right by the parlor door. Mrs. Reading was in the dining room. I asked her if she could smell that perfume. She came in here and only I could smell it. It's just so strange. It can be so heavy," Mrs. Keller said, shaking her head.

Anna Whaley has also put in a few appearances at the house Thomas built for her. Her most famous visit came in 1964 when TV star Regis Philbin spotted her early one morning while he was conducting an "investigation" of the house.

According to written accounts, Philbin and a friend were sitting on the Andrew Jackson sofa when an image identified as that of Anna Whaley materialized in the study, floated through the music room and into the parlor where Philbin was sitting. She evaporated when Philbin shined a flashlight in her direction.

Yet reports of Anna's ghost go back to even earlier times. June Reading recalls a visit by a man who said he delivered newspapers in the neighborhood when he was a boy. He said that he would stand opposite the house in the early morning hours waiting for the delivery truck to drop off his bundle of newspapers. He said he would glance across the street and see a lady dressed in blue standing behind an uncurtained window. There was no one living in the house at the time.

In more recent times, a rocking chair in Anna's old bedroom sometimes rocks back and forth, a bit upsetting for the tourists trying to listen to a guide's lecture about the house.

For several years, Mrs. Reading kept a log of the unusual phenomena observed by staff members and visitors. Several entries relate to the ghost of Anna Whaley:

• On January 5, 1963, a guide reported hearing music and laughter for about thirty seconds. He said it sounded like a woman singing "Home Again."
• The same guide, Lawrence Riveroll, saw the vague form of a woman in a hoop skirt in September 1964. He said the woman was very slight. She was standing in the hallway, but because of the dim light he couldn't see her face.
• A visitor told June Reading that two days after Christmas, 1964, he saw the ghost of a woman wearing a green plaid gingham dress. Her hair was long and dark, coiled up in a bun. She was sitting on a settee in Anna's old bedroom.

While Mrs. Reading and her staff held a meeting one afternoon to discuss an upcoming party at the house, one of her assistants took a photograph of the group sitting in the old courtroom. When the pictures were developed, there seemed to be the faintly outlined figure of a woman standing nearby. "She loved parties," June said. "Maybe our conversation drew Anna to listen in on the plans."

Anna Whaley is not the only female ghost to haunt Whaley House.

One of the strangest incidents involved what might have been the ghost of one of the Whaley daughters. In August 1976, an unusually high concentration of static electricity was plaguing the house, according to Mrs. Reading. One after-noon a visitor was touring the upstairs bedrooms when she reported a swarm of tiny, glowing objects darting about one of the rooms. She said they looked like fireflies. One of the strange "sparks" dropped to the floor and glowed.

June Reading called the California Parapsychology Foundation about the mys-terious, darting orbs of light. After an on-site investigation, an official told her the things were "ectoplasmic tubes" and that if several of them came together they would form a figure from the "spirit world." A few days later, a number of the so-called tubes melded and the life-sized figure of a young woman formed at the bottom of the bed. Mrs. Reading said it looked to her as if the figure was folding clothes or perhaps packing a suitcase. She thinks it was one of the daughters since the bizarre scene unfolded in their bedroom. The apparition lasted only a few seconds.

Sixteen years earlier, in October 1960, a Mrs. Kirbey of New Westminster, British Columbia, had an equally intriguing brush with a female resident of Whaley House's other world. While her husband, a prominent Canadian physician, stayed downstairs to discuss the early medical history of San Diego with June Reading, Mrs. Kirbey set off to explore the upstairs rooms.

A few minutes later, Mrs. Kirbey returned to her husband's side. She told Mrs. Reading that a soft breeze had blown across her head and a strong force pushed against her as she tried to climb the stairs. In each of the bedrooms, a strong sense of being followed, of being watched, caused her to turn around quickly several times to catch a glimpse of her silent companion. No one was ever there.

Dr. and Mrs. Kirbey and June Reading then walked into the courtroom, filled with display cases exhibiting documents and other memorabilia from pioneer San Diego. Mrs. Kirbey stopped. She said there was a dark-complexioned woman with dark hair and eyes standing in the corner. She wore a calico dress, had on gold hoop earrings and some type of cap on her head. Dr. Kirbey and Mrs. Reading saw no one.

Mrs. Kirbey seemed to sense that the woman lived in the courtroom and the trio was invading her "privacy." June was puzzled. No member of the Whaley family would have been described as having dusky skin.

The identity of this mysterious woman may have been discovered a few years later during a visit by Kay Sterner, founder and president of the California Parapsychology Foundation. Sterner wrote that she saw a ghost near the door of one of the Whaley daughters' bedrooms and then heard loud screams. A woman with black hair wearing a long, flowing skirt materialized. Sterner then saw the re-enactment of a violent quarrel in which a Mexican man seemed to be pointing accusingly at the woman. To Sterner's horror, the man plunged a knife into the woman's abdomen.

June Reading told Sterner that a Mexican couple *had* been tenants in Whaley House decades earlier. And the husband had, indeed, murdered his wife in nearly the same manner Kay Sterner described!

The other frequently noted spirit in Whaley House is that of a little ghost child known as the Washburn girl. She was a playmate of the Whaley children. One day while running to join her friends in the backyard she ran into a low-lying clothesline and fell, striking her head on a rock. She died in Mr. Whaley's arms as he carried her into the house.

Mrs. Reading remembered a particularly striking photograph that purportedly showed the littlest ghost.

"A lady came in during the holidays," Mrs. Reading said, "and took a picture in an upstairs bedroom. She got the figure of a little girl [in the photograph]. It was terribly impressive. She took it under very difficult circumstances because it was actually photographed through the glass." Panes of glass have been erected to prevent visitors from physically entering the second-floor bedrooms.

The little girl is confused, Mrs. Reading believes, because she died so very young. Her occasional return to the house occurs most often in the kitchen, where she amuses herself with the pots and pans and utensils, as she probably did in life.

"She plays around on the stairs and moves things in the kitchen," Mrs. Reading said. "One of the reasons we closed off the kitchen was that the meat cleaver on the rack in there would move. People were fascinated with that. We allowed visitors to walk through the kitchen, but we finally decided that wasn't a good practice. Everyone thought there was something mechanical that caused the meat cleaver to move."

The old courtroom, converted by Thomas Whaley from its original use as a granary, has been restored to appear precisely as it did when San Diego County first used it a century and more ago. The jury box, lawyers' tables, a judge's bench, and spectator benches all make it seem that a trial could be held there at any time. Display cases contain artifacts from early San Diego history. Historical photographs hanging from the plaster walls recount important events and personages from the city's past.

Whaley House ghosts sometimes clamor for the same attention tourists pay to the courtroom's physical fragments of history.

A group of seventy-five high school students from Chula Vista, California, witnessed one of the most bizarre events ever recorded at Whaley House. It happened in the courtroom.

The students were fairly typical. Along with several visiting teenagers from Mexico City, they had spent the day touring historic sites in and around San Diego. By the time they got to the Whaley House, late in the afternoon, a gentle early morning rain had become a severe storm.

"They hadn't made an appointment," June Reading said about the group that showed up on the front porch. "I had only one helper with me. I really didn't know how we were going to handle all seventy-five of them. We got them all seated in the courtroom after I got chairs from around the house. I found three chairs for the teachers. The bus driver just leaned against one of the showcases in the back."

Mrs. Reading took her place in front of the room, near the judge's bench. A low, wooden railing separated her from the students. Two chains stretched from either end of the railing to both walls, installed to prevent eager tourists from sitting in the judge's chair.

"I launched into the story of Thomas Whaley's trip around Cape Horn," Mrs. Reading recalled, an adventure that was a milestone in Whaley's life. It took him over a month to make the journey around South America, surviving exceptionally rough seas and a near-capsizing in a 106-foot schooner.

Mrs. Reading discovered that the students had just visited the Star of India, a majestic, nineteenth-century schooner berthed at the San Diego harbor. They buzzed with conversation about what it must have been like to have taken a long sea voyage a hundred years ago.

"I soon found, or thought I had found, that they were fascinated with the story because they were all very, very quiet," Mrs. Reading said. "I got to the part where Thomas was making the actual trip around Cape Horn. They were all looking at me very intently."

Mrs. Reading thought they were unusually quiet for a group of teenagers, but attributed it to a long day of walking and sight-seeing. But that wasn't the reason for the hushed audience, as she found out.

As June Reading described Whaley's hard trip around Cape Horn, the chains on either side of the railing were undulating in wavelike motions. The students, teachers, and bus driver all saw the phenomenon. Mrs. Reading was facing toward her audience. The chains to either side and behind her prevented her from seeing the unusual visual aid.

Once she discovered the reason for their rapt attention, Mrs. Reading had a difficult time getting the students back on the bus. They wanted to see that "trick" again.

"I thought to myself that it made sense. That trip around the Cape was a high point in his life," Mrs. Reading said. "The students had actually witnessed some kind of psychic phenomenon. I could have triggered it because I knew I was talking about something that was very important to him."

In mid-June 1988, volunteer guide Mrs. Jessie Keller said she returned from lunch to find three adults and a group of elementary school children gathered on the spacious porch. If it's a slow day, Whaley House is closed over the noon hour.

"One of the guides for the school had eyes like saucers," Mrs. Keller said. "She said she'd heard something. She was standing by the outside double-doors waiting for us to come back. All of a sudden the other door, on the left, started rattling. It was just like someone was in the house shaking it."

Two other adults witnessed the event, along with the children, who got very excited at the incident, too.

Odd events are reported almost weekly at Whaley House. A chance visit might include a meeting with Yankee Jim Robinson or Thomas Whaley himself. More likely, however, will be the soft rustle of a woman's bustle skirt, a man's heavy footfalls, giggling children by the music room door, a piano playing while no keys move, or perhaps it will be a child's footsteps pounding up the stairs.

If you're an animal lover, maybe Thomas Whaley's old dog, Dolly Varden, will race down the hallway in front of you, as she did a few years ago in front of several startled visitors.

Along with Winchester House, in San Jose, and the *Queen Mary*, berthed in Long Beach, San Diego's Whaley House occupies a prominent place in haunted California. But don't expect clanking chains or oozing slime dripping from the walls. You see, no one who works at Whaley House is ever really afraid.

"It's all very gentle," June Reading emphasized. With the possible exception of angry old Yankee Jim Robinson, and the murdered Hispanic woman, the ghosts are those of a family that dearly loved their home. And a little girl who found the house so nice to visit that she's never left. To their way of thinking they have every right to remain right where they are.

Home, sweet home.

COLORADO

The Pocahontas Mine Jumpers

A century ago Rosita, Colorado, was a peaceful hamlet. Except at night. When purple shadows darkened the green hills of Custer County, a ghost once walked. Dogs howled from the hilltops and residents stayed within the shelter of their homes.

No one knew for sure who the ghost was, but some said it was that of an old soldier named Colonel Graham who began his nightly prowls shortly after the discovery of gold and silver. His route never varied. With saber rattling at his side, he marched back and forth across a bridge that by day carried nothing spookier than a bouncing buckboard.

But the ghost didn't always march. A man returning home late one night claims he saw the specter swinging hand over hand from girder to girder on the underside of the bridge, while screaming unintelligible curses into the night air. By the light of a full moon he saw that the ghost wore a grim look with eyes like burning coals.

Was there ever a Colonel Graham? Yes. He was a mine jumper who, with two other villains, committed acts that led to the bloodiest skirmish in the history of Rosita.

A band of German prospectors discovered a mine rich with gold and silver deposits a short distance from Rosita and within sight of the village. They named the mine Pocahontas and set to work immediately to extract the ore. But before they could swing their picks, news of the mine spread far. Greedy fortune seekers came from all over the country, and the building of hotels, stores, and saloons scarcely kept up with the needs of the flood of immigrants arriving daily. Carnal needs were seen to by the prostitutes who followed the miners, setting up business in the upstairs rooms of each saloon whose owners welcomed a bit of extra income. There was even a newspaper, the *Rosita Index*, and a brewery in a three-story concrete building with an iron roof.

In less than three months from the discovery of the famed Pocahontas, Rosita had grown from a scattered handful of residents in rough cabins to a tough, bustling camp of more than a thousand persons. Few of the newcomers knew one another, or cared to make enduring acquaintances. It was every man for himself in the scramble to get rich quick and get out. The knife in the belt and the gun in the holster were worn only for protection, of course.

So it was that no one knew anything about a trio of bold and daring knaves among them: W.A. Stewart, a "Colonel" Boyd, and a "Colonel" Graham, whom a newsman reported to be "as mild a man as ever scuttled a ship or cut a throat." Neither of the "soldiers'" first names is known.

Stewart and Boyd, representing themselves as capitalists, opened a bank while their pal, Graham, ran a gin mill. Oddly, the villagers found them to be affable men and came to respect them.

Stewart had come from Denver, where he had passed as a rich gentleman, joined a church, and built a fine cottage on Capitol Hill. His hospitality attracted some of the most prominent citizens of the city and he was once nominated for mayor.

His name, however, was *not* Stewart. That was only one of many aliases he used while building a career as one of the boldest and most successful robbers in America. He had robbed at least thirty different banks in this country, and he and his confederates were the only thieves to have robbed the Bank of England. Stewart's share of the loot reached into the millions. But after members of his gang had been captured and hauled off to prison Stewart fled west to Denver. Yet he soon tired of playing the role of gentleman and longed for the association of thieves. When news of the opening of the Pocahontas mine reached him, he vanished from Denver and showed up at Rosita. There he met "Colonel" Boyd and "Colonel" Graham.

Boyd, whose army association was dubious, had once been mayor of Baxter Springs, Arkansas, a proprietor of faro banks and other dens of infamy. One night in a fit of rage, he killed two men. He disguised himself and escaped to the West. He had no money, but he had nerve. Stewart had both, so they made an ideal pair to operate a bank.

Graham actually *had* been an army officer and, after being discharged, squandered his mustering-out pay at the gambling table. At Hugo, on the Kansas Pacific railroad, he shot and robbed an army paymaster, then hightailed it to Denver where he lost his ill-gotten gains in a card game on his first day in town. Here he was arrested, tried for the crime of robbery, and sentenced to ten years in the penitentiary at Canon City.

But the wily colonel soon escaped and hid out in the mountains of Custer County. A sheriff and two deputies pursued him, found him unarmed and shot him. In his wounded condition, he was returned to prison and eventually recovered. He did not, however, serve his full sentence. Because of his physical suffering and his army service, the governor pardoned him.

Graham rushed to Rosita and opened a saloon to earn money. But saloonkeeping was not his intended occupation. Standing behind the bar, he used his uncanny ability to judge the men coming in to size up the right pair of thugs to help him "jump the mine," a frontier term for an armed takeover of a mining camp. The night Stewart and Boyd swaggered through the swinging doors, Graham knew he'd found his partners. They looked hard, they drank hard, and they didn't ask to go upstairs.

The three met later to plot the takeover, and on the next night they jumped the mine with the help of a gang of hired ruffians. All were well armed. Although besotted with whiskey, they marched back and forth, in shifts, day and night in front of the mine entrance, threatening to fire upon anyone who approached. The mine was worth half a million dollars and everyone knew it.

The sheriff was powerless to prevent the takeover and appealed to the governor for troops. But before the territorial militia arrived, Graham spied an enemy on the street and shot him. When two more passed, he killed them too in cold blood. Screaming, "My work is done!" he rushed into the mine where he hid for several days, protected by the drunken guard at the entrance.

Meanwhile, the men of Rosita, determined to end this reign of terror, formed an "army" of their own and started toward the mob in possession of the mine. They hadn't gone far when Graham emerged from hiding, brandishing a pistol in each hand. As the brigand started toward town the little group of citizens leaped behind a hill. At the moment that Graham started across the bridge, the townspeople opened fire and Graham fell, pierced by a score of bullets. Before the smoke cleared, the men at the mine had thrown down their guns and fled in all directions.

Boyd got as far as Canon City before he was captured and brought back to Rosita to be hanged. But at the last minute a reprieve was granted on the conditions that he turn over the keys to the bank safe and leave the county immediately. Boyd hastily complied. He reached Missouri and joined the infamous James boys, who shortly thereafter killed him for treachery.

But Boyd had the last laugh. The bank safe was empty. The late proprietors had taken the considerable sum of money deposited by trusting citizens.

Stewart safely reached New York, where years later a detective, who had been on the thug's trail for ten years, recognized him on the street. Stewart was tried for robberies, convicted and sentenced to life imprisonment at Sing Sing. There he made boots for the State of New York and presumably died in prison.

This might have been the end of the story, just another bloody tale of frontier justice long forgotten. But Graham never left the spot where he fell. His body was disposed of, but his pallid ghost remained at the bridge for decades, marching back and forth while screaming invectives against his murderers.

Rosita was officially abandoned years ago, its wooden buildings left to destruction by the elements, its dirt streets overgrown by weeds. But it did enjoy a flurry of excitement in 1957 when the Metro Goldwyn Mayer movie studio built new, if temporary, buildings for the filming of *Saddle the Wind*.

Today this beautiful Wet Mountain Valley is attracting residents once again. Forty people now live year-round in Rosita and another twenty make their permanent homes in the Rosita Hills subdivision. Many more families are building summer homes in the area.

Colonel Graham, presumably, won't bother the new residents . . . unless they accidentally disturb his fitful slumber.

The Blue Lights of Silver Cliff

May 1882. The miners' whoops and hollers echoed through Wet Mountain Valley as the buckboard lurched over the stony trail. It had been a good night of carousing—the drinks were hard and the women soft.

Now, the men were on their way home to Silver Cliff, one of the state's great silver mining camps. As the carriage rolled past the local cemetery, Jake Daniels, who'd been swigging from a bottle, dropped it and screamed, "Holy Mary of Jesus, look at them lights!"

A hush came over the revelers. Bright blue flames were dancing on top of the gravestones, chasing one another, disappearing, then reappearing. There were too many to count. Or were the men seeing the same ones over and over again? They couldn't tell.

Jake tumbled to the ground and his pals followed. Staggering over the ground, with arms outstretched, they tried to catch the elusive lights, but as soon as they got close to one it vanished. They stumbled, fell, got up again.

"The ghost got me!" screamed one man, falling facedown and narrowly escaping hitting his head on the corner of a granite stone. His besotted friends helped him into the buckboard and climbed in after him.

The next morning the miners told their story of the mysterious lights to the bemused townsfolk. Everyone laughed. A bunch of drunkards might just as well have seen the prancing devil himself. Yet a few persons were curious and decided to check out the report.

Several nights later, a small band walked the half mile to the old cemetery to conduct a "scientific" investigation. Jake Daniels led the expedition. Along for the night were: Harold Parsons, an assayer; attorney Hulbert Cowles; Ephraim Ballew, a photographer; saloon keeper Spike Norton; and sisters Anna and Emma Turner, milliners.

The two women took charge. They marched up and down between each row of tombstones, beaming their flashlights on every stone and calling out the names chiseled on each, as if to summon all the spirits of the dead. The men stood in a knot and scanned the dark sky, waiting for the lights to appear.

Although the day had been warm, the night was cold and the ground damp from a recent rain. Cowles felt the dampness seep through the soles of his shoes and stomped his feet to keep warm. He should have worn a sweater under his thin jacket.

"All right, Daniels," he said, "where are those damn lights?"

"I dunno," said the miner, shrugging his shoulders, "but they sure were here the other night."

Anna beamed her light in his face. "Jake Daniels, you have done nothing but lead us on a wild goose chase and we are leaving."

"Good night!" added her sister.

Arm in arm, the Turners started back to town. The men watched them go but said nothing. Then shortly after they'd left, each man, singly, drifted away from the cemetery, angry that he'd been duped by an ordinary miner.

Daniels stood alone now, hands in his pockets. Where were the lights? They *had* been there; of that he was, well, almost certain. He walked the perimeter of the cemetery and neither saw nor heard anything. Just as he turned to leave, he caught a bright flicker out of the corner of his eye. He swung around. A blue light danced atop a tombstone, then another and another. Trembling with excitement, he cupped his hands to his mouth and shouted, "The lights! The lights!"

The skeptics heard his cries, quickly retraced their steps and stood slack-jawed at the sight before them. Soon scores of blue lights swarmed like moths over the tombstones. Curiosity replaced fear as each man tried unsuccessfully to catch a tiny light as it floated past. The women, learning about the sighting the next morning, lived to regret their hasty departure. They never once saw the lights.

In the eleven decades since their first recorded appearance, those dancing lights have been the subject of endless speculation and numerous theories. Some said the lights were St. Elmo's fire, an electrical phenomenon that sometimes appears on ships' masts and other pointed objects before a storm. Yet the sightings often did not presage a storm.

Others thought the lights were will-o-'-the-wisps, a phosphorescent light caused by the spontaneous combustion of gases from rotting organic matter. Except that will-o-'-the-wisps occur in swamps and marshes. The Silver Cliff cemetery is on a rise of land grown up with yucca and cacti.

A reflection perhaps from lights in Silver Cliff? Hardly. There were no electric lights in those early days, and even as late as 1963, when all electric lights were turned off in several nearby communities the lights still appeared.

Longtime Silver Cliff resident Francis Wernette took a young man from Denver out to the cemetery. The visitor was convinced that the lights were nothing but reflections. He had a blanket with him and, seeing a light on the top of a stone, threw the blanket over it. Within seconds, the light popped up behind him!

Folklorist and anthropologist Dale Ferguson took a different approach to the puzzle of the lights. He says that the Cheyenne and other Plains people buried their dead on hilltops, and a number of Native American legends mention "dancing blue lights" on these sites. But unless there is a prehistoric burial site far below earth level, the Silver Cliff site was used mainly by German and English settlers.

After all these theories were discussed and dismissed the residents of Wet Mountain Valley concluded that the lights were on the helmets of long-dead miners, still seeking frantically for silver on the hillside. The ghost theory prevailed.

Wherever you find ghosts you find pranksters and charlatans.

One dark evening two young girls in black clothing prowled the cemetery, carrying small lanterns with blue-tinted globes. Their deception was soon discovered when a man who'd seen them headed for the cemetery got there first. He leaped out of a freshly dug grave, dressed as a cadaver. The girls ran for their lives.

A spiritualist from Pueblo hawked pieces of smoked glass that he said would enable the viewer to see a tiny human form in the center of each light. It isn't known how many gullible citizens, if any, bought the magic glass, but the man was quickly driven out of town.

Francis Wernette, in an interview taped in 1987, recalled stories his uncle told of going to dances by horse and buggy. As the rigs neared the cemetery the drivers beat the frightened animals to get past the place as quickly as possible.

Wernette added that the best time to see the lights was in the snow or rain, or on nights of heavy cloud cover. "There's no explanation for them," he said, "and as far as I know they've been out there with Geiger counters and I don't know what all, trying to find out what causes them."

Kathy Williams, after a 1982 visit to the place, said, ". . . the rocks beside the road glowed as well as [the] many, many lights."

The lights might have remained only curious local phenomena had they not been dignified by reports in *The New York Times* and the *National Geographic*.

After the 1967 publication of the *Times* account, written by W. T. Little, *Rocky Mountain News* special correspondent, tourists from all over the country flocked to the little burial ground to see for themselves what all the fuss was about. Some saw the lights and pondered their significance; others went away disappointed.

"I know they [the lights] are not all myth, for I, too, have seen them," Little concluded.

In 1969, Edward J. Linehan, assistant editor of the *Geographic*, toured the cemetery with Bill Kleine, a local campground manager who said he'd seen the lights many times.

"This is a good night for them—overcast, no moon," said Kleine. The two climbed out of the car and waited. Linehan strained to see something—anything—and, as his eyes grew accustomed to the darkness, he discerned the jagged rows of weathered tombstones.

Suddenly, the lights appeared.

"I saw them too," wrote Linehan. "Dim, round spots of blue-white light glowed ethereally among the graves. I found another, and stepped forward for a better look. They vanished. I aimed my flashlight at one eerie glow and switched it on. It revealed only a tombstone."

Today, only a handful of year-round residents live in Silver Cliff, and few speak of the cemetery lights. Outsiders, too, have been attracted to the beautiful and peaceful valley set in the Sangre de Cristo Mountains. Because of lights from new homes and ranch lights burning from dusk to dawn, the mystery flames are difficult to see. And when they're visible they seem to focus on six tombstones, all circa 1912.

Perhaps the concluding jingoistic words of editor Linehan bespeak the sentiments of many:

"No doubt someone, someday, will prove there's nothing at all supernatural in the luminous manifestations of Silver Cliff's cemetery. And I will feel a tinge of disappointment. I prefer to believe that they are the restless stirrings of the ghosts of Colorado, eager to get their Centennial State on with its pressing business: seeking out and working the bonanzas of a second glorious century."

CONNECTICUT

A Knocking They Did Come

Once upon a midnight dreary, while I pondered, weak and weary,
Over many a quaint and curious volume of forgotten lore—
While I nodded, nearly napping, suddenly there came a tapping,
As of some one gently rapping, rapping at my chamber door. . . .

Edgar Allan Poe, "The Raven" (1845)

The staff and elderly patients at Restmore Convalescent Home on Stratford's Elm Street didn't know what to make of it. Their peaceful lives were being disrupted by a rash of odd events—gurgling noises, tappings on the walls in the middle of the night, and other anomalies. Sometimes emergency alarms rang without apparent reason. A series of investigations showed no obvious causes for the disturbances. Even a psychic couldn't explain what was happening.

By the early 1970s, new owners of the nursing home, facing mounting financial problems that had nothing to do with the events, closed and boarded the home. A short time later the house at 1738 Elm Street—known for almost a century and a half as the Phelps mansion—was demolished.

Those elderly tenants were the final witnesses to the mysteries of one of the most notorious haunted houses ever recorded in the northeastern United States. It's a tale that begins with the saga of alleged poltergeist activity that beset the Reverend Eliakim Phelps family from March to October 1850. During that eight-month period, the Phelps family endured demolished furniture, broken windows, smashed china, and candlesticks prancing in the air. It was as if all the demons in Hell danced in their mansion.

A hundred years later, when the Phelps mansion was used as a rest home, the mysterious incidents seemed to suggest that the haunting on Elm Street had not ended.

There was little to foreshadow the future notoriety of the soaring three-story, Georgian-style frame house when it was completed in 1826. Prominent Stratfordian Gen. Mattas Nicoll gave it as a gift to his daughter and son-in-law, Capt. George R. Dowdell. He was the master of a clipper ship planning to retire from the sea when Nicoll financed the house.

Mrs. Dowdell considered carefully her husband's love of sailing ships in designing the home. For instance, the hallway was the exact dimension of a clipper ship's main deck, twelve feet wide by seventy feet long. At either end of the hallway, twin staircases rose to meet at a second-floor landing. Thus, Captain Dowdell could still stride across a ship's "deck," climb to the "hurricane deck," and descend again to the main deck.

Outside, four Doric columns stretched across the facade of the house, supporting a portico that gave it the appearance of an Athenian temple. Smaller Doric columns graced many interior archways. A half dozen chimneys soared above the rooftop. Acres of lawn and ancient trees stretched from Elm Street to the banks of the Housatonic River. The estate was as handsome a jewel as any found on an avenue known for its elegant homes.

From all accounts, the Dowdells spent a contented retirement in the mansion. Following their deaths, the house and grounds were sold in May 1849 to the Reverend Eliakim Phelps, a recently arrived minister originally from Massachusetts.

Reverend Phelps was nearing sixty years of age at the time, but had recently married a widow with four children, two girls and two boys. A graduate of Union and Andover seminaries, Reverend Phelps earlier served congregations in two New York cities and was secretary of the American Society of Philadelphia. He also had an abiding interest in the occult and clairvoyance, not unusual for ministers in the nineteenth century. The spiritualist movement later in that century counted many clerics among its converts.

Until March 10, 1850, few people outside Reverend Phelps's congregation had much knowledge of his or his family's personal life. Mrs. Phelps seemed a bit morose, but that was generally attributed to the difficulty of adjusting to life in a small town. She was used to bustling Philadelphia society.

The tenth of March was a Sunday. Reverend Phelps was accompanied to Sabbath services by his wife and children—the girls aged sixteen and six, the two boys, eleven and three.

When they left that morning, all was quiet in their Elm Street home. No one was in the house.

When they returned some hours later, however, their names and that of Stratford would be forever etched in the annals of strange psychic disturbances.

What the Reverend Phelps found was a house turned upside down. One of the front doors was draped in black crepe. Inside, furniture had been overturned or broken, personal effects were strewn about the rooms, and kitchenware had been pulled from shelves.

However, the most bizarre sight was found in the main parlor, where various pieces of female clothing had been shaped into human forms. The figures were on their knees "praying," or holding open Bibles in front of them. One was found with its "forehead" nearly touching the floor. A garishly misshapen figure was suspended from a rope in the middle of the room, rigged so that it appeared to be flying. In another room, the family found a shrouded dummy laid out as if for a funeral.

Within days all of Stratford and most of Connecticut had heard about the events on Elm Street. And that was only the beginning, for in the coming weeks and months not only were more dummies found in various rooms, but knockings, voices, apparitions, and spirit writing were all reported by various witnesses and family members. Crowds gathered on the street in the hopes of "seeing the spirits," reporters came from newspapers throughout New England, spiritualists and self-proclaimed psychics held séances. Civil authorities tried to make sense of the whole affair. The local livery was provided a handsome income from guided coach tours past the notorious house.

A newspaper reported a few of the more bizarre events:

• One of the boys was carried across the room by unseen hands and "deposited on the floor."

• That same boy's clothing was found cut to pieces.
• A fireplace shovel and tongs scooted to the middle of the floor and hopped about in a kind of dance.
• A dining table was tipped over when the room was empty.
• A brass candlestick flew from a mantelpiece and kept smashing against the floor.
• An oil lamp glided across a table, tipped and set fire to some papers.

In the April 22, 1850, issue of the Bridgeport *Standard*, a reporter turned in this amazing journalistic account:

"The carryings on . . . are becoming more and more dreadful. The furniture of the house becomes occasionally bewitched, and knocks itself to pieces and the deuce is to pay with the children's clothing. One of the enquiring visitants was sitting with the family the other evening, when an earthen pitcher got up from the table and flew at a young lady of the family, and just missing her went ker-smash against the side of the room."

The reporter obviously let his personal interest override his objectivity when, writing in the third person, he added: "The visitor thinking that the young lady was unusually attractive took her by the hand, when, he says, he received an electrical shock."

He concluded with this preposterous claim:

"A few days since, a scissors grinder stopped in front of the house, and in the view of several persons, he began to ascend into the air. He went up and up, turning his wheels steadily, all the while until he was lost to human view. The next day he came down in Waterbury. So they say."

The flying grinder story was later totally discredited.

Though fantastic accounts of the Phelps haunting were plentiful, it was the strange tableaus of lifelike dummies that aroused the most interest. A Dr. Webster told the *New Haven Journal*:

". . . the rooms were closely watched, and figures (dummies) appeared every few days when no human being could have entered the room. They were constructed and arranged, I am convinced, by no visible power. The clothing from which the figures were made was somehow gathered from all parts of the house, in spite of a strict watch. In all, about thirty figures were constructed during the haunt. Some were so life-like that a small child, being shown the room, thought his mother was kneeling in prayer with the rest."

Among the hundreds of visitors to the house was pioneer psychic Andrew Jackson Davis, the "seer of Poughkeepsie." Davis claimed the eleven-year-old boy was causing "vital radiations" that made objects fly toward him or his sister. However, at other times their "electricity" was stronger, and objects hurtled away from the children. Davis said at least five spirits were hovering about the house, guiding most of the psychic activity.

Reverend Phelps once took the advice of another visiting psychic who suggested that he might communicate with the spirits through a series of taps, each series of taps representing a letter of the alphabet. The good minister tried that route, but he was disappointed that most of the responses were nonsensical. He said the spirits sounded "like loafers on a spree."

Another witness, Mrs. Ellen Olney Kirk, went so far as to attribute the disturbances to a woman hanged for witchcraft nearly two centuries earlier. She wrote:

"One is tempted to believe that the spirit of Goody Bassett, hanged in 1651 for divers witch-like arts, was never fairly laid, and now, after an unquiet term . . . returned to walk the earth."

Mrs. Kirk provided one of the most colorful accounts of the Phelps haunting:

"There were rappings—not merely rappings, but thumpings, and thumpings too, as if a giant's strength were behind them; there were marvelous noises, with reverberations like thunder up and down the staircases and along the halls; there were apparitions, strange figures in strange places; there were messages from the unseen land of the spirits, not only spelled out in hard knocks and vibrations on the headboards of beds, on ceilings, doors and floors, but written out fairly on slips of paper, which floated down from the invisible like the leaves of the Cumaean Sybil."

Mrs. Kirk said that when vegetables from the cellar were peeled and sliced, they were found to contain "indelible characters" on their insides.

She said two "clear sighted and reasonable men," whom she did not further identify, heard unexplained knockings.

The men were "sitting alone in a room with two doors, one opening into a hall and the other into a clothes press, [when they] heard knockings on the inside of the closet door, which on opening they found to proceed from vacancy: as soon as the door was again closed the knockings proceeded, not only with a loud noise, but so vigorously that the very panels shook under their eyes. Sitting before the fire, they beheld the ornaments on the mantel piece spring from their places to alight unbroken on the floor; bricks started out of the air and were hurled across the room; pokers jumped up of their own accord and went crashing through the windows."

Dr. Phelps himself took great pains to carefully record each event, such as in this letter he wrote to a newspaper:

"For days and weeks together I have watched these strange movements with all the care and caution and close attention which I can bestow. I witnessed them hundreds and hundreds of times, and I know that in hundreds of instances they took place when there was no visible power by which the motion could have been produced. Scores of persons of standing in the community, whose education, general intelligence, candor, veracity and sound judgment were without question, were requested to witness the phenomena, and, if possible, help us to a solution of the mystery but as yet no such solution has been attained. The idea that the whole was a 'trick of the children'—an idea which some of the papers have endeavored with great zeal to promulgate as to everyone who is acquainted with the facts, is as false as it is injurious."

Was the supposition that the children were somehow involved in the "haunting" indeed erroneous?

A history of the city discusses the "Stratford knockings" and concludes that Mrs. Phelps, considerably younger than her husband, conspired with a "scheming" daughter and "precocious" son to stage the events. She was used to the "gaieties of the city and [was] dissatisfied with the solemn stillness of Stratford," the city history asserts.

Many of the activities *were* centered around Mrs. Phelps's teenage daughter and eleven-year-old son. In several cases, the children were the only eyewitnesses to the poltergeist activity. The "investigators" relied only upon their testimony, reason enough to suspect that they could have deceived the gullible.

A newspaper reporter and another observer spent a night in the Phelps house. He wrote of a chair being carried across a bedroom and thrown against a wall and the contents of a dresser drawer dumped on the floor. But these events transpired in the teenage girl's bedroom away from both witnesses. The visiting reporter saw only the smashed chair and disheveled clothing.

The suspect son was involved in an event described by a skeptical editor at the *New Haven Journal*:

". . . the boy went out of the room and soon one of the ladies of the house came running in, exclaiming that Henry was gone, and couldn't be found. A general scream followed by a general rush of men and women, young and old, clergymen, lawyers, loafers, etc., made a rush to the back of the house . . . till the boy was found under the hay against the side of the barn. When pulled out, he assumed a sleepy look. Eyes heavy shut, as though in a comatose state, together with the loss of consciousness and voluntary motion.

"We pitied the father, who seemed distressed by the apprehension of his son being strangled, as on a former occasion he had been found with a rope about his neck and perched upon a shelf in the closet. After nearly an hour of apparent stupidity the boy came out of his lethargic state, and when questioned, said he was flying his kite in the yard, and the next he knew he was in the barn."

The *Journal* thought the Reverend Phelps guiltless in the haunting, but wrote strongly that some sort of deception was taking place, without putting the blame on any single individual. The paper took this position, the editors said, because the events were at "variance with the known laws of nature and of Providence, and with the history of mankind."

There were *other* times, however, when the children seemed to be absent from the scene. On one such occasion, Dr. Phelps was walking alone across a room when a nail and key "flew" over his head and landed at his feet. Could it have been thrown by someone standing behind the minister? Perhaps. And again it was only his testimony given in this incident.

Still another time, the family had gathered at the dinner table when a turnip fell from the ceiling! That was the same evening that the silverware floated up and off the table. On another night, several spoons seemed to rise up and bend in half, and then were thrown by some force at the dinner guests. If this is an accurate rendering of what happened, it would seem that the deception was an extremely sophisticated contrivance.

The haunting continued unabated until October 1, 1850, when Mrs. Phelps and her children returned to Philadelphia. They spent the winter and early spring there and, when they came back to Stratford in mid-1851, nothing more was heard from the spirits on Elm Street.

Whatever had caused the "poltergeist" seemed to have resolved itself. The Phelps family lived quietly in the house until they sold it in 1859 to Moses Y. Beach, the founder of *The New York Sun*.

The house remained in the Beach family until the early twentieth century. Moses' son, Alfred E. Beach, lived with his family in the Phelps house for many decades. The longtime editor of the *Scientific American*, Alfred turned part of the mansion into the Stratford Institute, a private school for his children and the offspring of other wealthy city families. He remodeled and modernized the mansion in 1907.

Several other owners followed the Beach family until the early 1940s, when Mrs. Maude Thompson converted the Phelps house into a residence for senior citizens. In 1947, Carl Caserta and his wife, registered nurses both, bought the house from Mrs. Thompson and operated it as the Restmore Convalescent Home until the late 1960s.

It was during the Casertas' tenure in the house that rumors of supernatural activity were heard again on Elm Street.

The Casertas occupied a third-floor apartment. The elderly patients lived in rooms on the first two floors. Shortly after they moved in, Mrs. Caserta put her infant son, Gary, to bed in their apartment. Her husband was gone for the evening. As she left him sleeping in his crib, she draped a blanket over a wall light fixture so the glare wouldn't disturb his sleep. She wanted to keep the lights on so that she could find her way when she came up to bed.

Years earlier a series of electric buzzers had been installed on each of the three floors to summon household help. They were the last things on Mrs. Caserta's mind, however, when she left her apartment to join several staff members to finish some work they had begun in the basement. Barely a half hour later, the basement buzzer shattered the stillness. Mrs. Caserta and her two assistants raced upstairs to locate the source of the alarm. None of the patients on the first two floors were strong enough to reach the buzzers from their beds.

As she started up the stairs to the third floor, Mrs. Caserta smelled smoke. Her son began to scream as she charged into their small apartment. The blanket over the light was smoking; small holes already had burned through the material. She threw the blanket in the bathtub and carried Gary to safety.

The child wasn't big enough to reach the buzzer unit, and no one else would have been in a position to sound that alarm. But whatever set off the frantic buzzing also saved the young boy's life.

A few years later, another incident with the electric buzzers confirmed for the couple that if a ghost did reside in the Phelps mansion, it was a kind and benevolent soul.

Mrs. Caserta was on duty alone late at night, sitting at the nurse's station on the main floor. Her husband and young son were asleep in the apartment, all the patients were sleeping, and no other staff members were in the house. The sudden squeal of the buzzer on the main floor sent her scurrying from her chair. She could find none of the patients awake nor any sign of activity on the first two floors. On the third-floor landing, however, her gaze fell upon her son, by now a toddler, trying to climb over the railing. Before him was a straight drop of three stories.

The frantic mother charged up the stairs and grabbed young Gary just as he was about to fall. The child's unfocused gaze told his mother that he was sleepwalking. She shook him awake and led him back to his bed. He had no recollection of why or how he had wound up in the hallway. Nor did Mrs. Caserta ever discover why that buzzer sounded, only that for the second time its incessant blare had saved her son's life.

The rest of the story of the Phelps house is a sad one. The Casertas sold the rest home to the Alliance of Medical Inns, Inc., a New England company that operated nursing homes throughout the northeastern United States. Their plan was to build a large hospital adjacent to the Phelps house and use the house as office space.

However, financial problems prevented the company from carrying through with its plans and the Phelps house was boarded up. Within a short time vandals destroyed most of the interior, setting fires in its various rooms and punching holes in the walls. Someone even stole several of the Doric columns that graced the front of the mansion. In March 1972, the wrecking ball finally reduced Stratford's notorious haunted house to a pile of rubble.

In 1975, the town of Stratford opened the American Shakespeare Theater on a fourteen-acre parcel of land on the banks of the Housatonic River. A section of its parking lot was carved from what had been the backyard of the haunted Phelps mansion.

With a name change to the American Festival Theater, it was beset with financial problems in the 1980s and remains closed as of mid-1995. Its future depends upon whether millions of dollars in needed funding can be raised.

Should you happen to stroll the vacant theater's grounds, gaze off toward old, aristocratic Elm Street. You won't *see* Eliakim Phelps's mansion, but if there be ghosts, a few must linger still where they once enthralled all of Connecticut.

CONNECTICUT
Blood Orchard

Micah Rood was about as mean and dangerous an old rascal as ever walked the byways of Connecticut.

He kept his own counsel, glared at anyone daring to bid him a "Good Morning, Sir!", and generally behaved in ways to make even the most temperate citizen wish him ill.

The old man lived near what is now Franklin, then called Nine Mile Square. The first settlers had bought the land for seventy pounds from the Mohegan chief, Uncas. Rood scratched out a living on a miserable patch of rocky farmland in Peck Hollow, not far from the Susquetonscut River. The year was 1693.

No one knew much about Rood. A rumor at the time, for instance, held that he hated all Frenchmen; his father allegedly had been killed by the French in a Colonial conflict. Truth be told, Micah Rood harbored deep and sinister resentment against almost everyone, especially those who spoke with a foreign accent or dressed in "peculiar" ways. His mother lived with him for many years, a constant reminder of his father's tragic death, neighbors said.

Whatever the truth of his life, and it is nearly impossible to accurately portray this obscure man's personal peccadilloes three hundred years later, Micah Rood grew to legendary status in southeastern Connecticut because of a cursed apple: the "Mike Apple," as it became known.

The tale begins in the early spring of 1693, as farmers and villagers on the English colonial frontier emerged from another harsh New England winter. One of the few opportunities for excitement in the austere lives of pioneer homemakers came when peddlers arrived in the isolated settlements selling everything from brooms to fine gingham cloth. These wayfaring strangers were part salesmen and part entertainers, with a strong dose of malarkey in their spiel.

But the women in the villages and on the farms anxiously awaited their visits. On this particular day, an old peddler whose name may have been Horgan appeared on the Franklin Green. According to local legend, he visited the village twice yearly, spring and fall. Like many of his counterparts, his dress consisted of woolen castoffs and he spoke with a deep accent.

His display of trinkets, tinware, toys, and cloth was neatly arranged on the Green. Housewives, often with husbands and children in tow, began arriving on foot and by horseback shortly after the sun broke the horizon. All day long peddler Horgan explained how the various toys and trinkets worked, exhorting a reluctant shopper now and then to purchase a particular piece of merchandise—while filling his purse with his customers' hard-earned gold and silver coins.

By nightfall, his pack was nearly empty. It had been a particularly rewarding day as he had gotten his asking price for almost every item. There was little haggling over a few pennies with these Connecticut folks.

Horgan loaded the few remaining baubles in his pack. His bulging purse he tucked safely in the deep recesses of his heavy coat. From one of his last customers he inquired about where he might find lodging for the night.

Peddlers generally weren't welcome at respectable inns, and besides, the nearest commercial lodging was in Norwich, several hours away. He hoped that a family might spare him a room or, at worst, a hayloft in their barn.

The woman to whom Horgan directed his question paused only a moment before saying that he might find a room with Micah Rood, who lived only a short distance from town.

Horgan grabbed his pack and ambled off. The last anyone saw of him was as a receding figure in the twilight disappearing over the ridge above Rood's farmhouse.

As he approached the isolated homestead, Horgan gazed with immense pleasure at the apple trees in full blossom. Rood may have been a cussed bugbear, but he took pride in the beautiful orchard he had planted and carefully cultivated. So particular was Rood that his trees not be disturbed, he sometimes sat up at night with a blunderbuss across his knees to scare off local children who occasionally snatched some of the fruit. When his apples were the deepest red of any in the region, he donned a witch's mask and jumped out from behind trees to frighten interlopers.

But on this night, Rood pulled none of his tricks on Horgan. The peddler knocked and was admitted with some suspicion by the farmer. Horgan inquired about a room. He could pay. Rood was reluctant to give up even a square inch of his private domain to a stranger, but he brightened at the mention of cash and asked how much. The peddler turned his back, rummaged in his coat and pulled out a single gold sovereign. That was good enough for Rood. He pointed to a back room. There might even be some soup for an extra fee, Rood said, if the peddler didn't mind drinking from a rusty mug.

It did not escape Rood's piercing gaze that the peddler tried to hide his money bag.

All evening, Rood bustled around the tiny cabin trying to make the visitor feel "at home." He even lit a candle when he served the soup, something that surely grated his penny-pinching nature. His rare visitors had remarked that Rood went to bed precisely at nightfall. To save candlewax.

Rood prodded the peddler about his business that day.

Did he sell all his goods? What kind of prices did the assortment bring? Would people pay in gold? Silver? Perhaps a gem, a family heirloom, if the farmwife was short of cash?

Horgan was guarded in all of his answers. He was wary of this inquisitive farmer who was so interested in money and yet seemed to live in squalor.

Only the night before, the peddler had narrowly escaped robbers intent on relieving him of his day's receipts. He didn't think there was danger in this Rood fellow, but he hadn't traveled alone and safely all these years by being foolish. He would have to be careful here.

And so before turning in for the night, Horgan took his bulging money pouch from his coat, pushed it deep inside his pack, and covered it with odd bits of clothing and leftover goods. He lay down on a straw mat clutching the pack to his bosom.

If he had been with anyone but Micah Rood that might have been protection enough. As it was, so the tale is told, the peddler breathed his last sometime that night.

Early the next morning, passersby found Horgan's battered body beneath an apple tree. His sack had been ripped open, its contents scattered around the body. There was no sign of the peddler's money pouch.

Authorities launched an investigation that immediately centered on Micah Rood. Horgan's customers remembered that he had been directed to his farmhouse and he was last seen walking in that direction.

For his part, Rood heatedly denied any connection with the brutal murder, though he admitted that the peddler had spent the night at his home.

He said Horgan had mentioned being accosted by would-be thieves at the Blue Horse Tavern a day earlier, and suggested that when the peddler left that morning the villains had accosted him where the body had been discovered. But authorities pointed out that no other strangers had been seen in the neighborhood.

Rood reluctantly agreed to a search of his house and grounds, but not a single stray coin was found. Nor was there evidence of any recent digging to suggest Rood had buried anything.

The investigation ground to a halt. No proof and therefore no charges against Rood. If Rood did commit the murder, no one ever discovered what he did with the peddler's money. Horgan's body was buried in Potters Field, and slowly life returned to normal in Nine Mile Square.

Within a few weeks, the orchard at Micah Rood's farm was filled with sweet-smelling apple blossoms. But then folks around the region noticed a very strange thing—rather than the usual purely pink or white blossoms, each bud was streaked with scarlet. As one drew closer to where Horgan's body had been found, the apple blossoms grew more deeply crimson, so that the tree under which the peddler lay had buds the color of blood.

Villagers flocked to see the strange scene, remembering that the peddler's death had never been solved. They said it was a sign that Micah Rood had gotten away with murder. The peddler, with his dying breath, had placed a curse on the orchard so that his blood would forever flow in Micah Rood's precious fruit.

Rood withdrew even more from society, if that was possible. It is said that he lost his appetite, woke up screaming from horrible nightmares and let his fields, and apple orchard, fall into decay. A candle burned in his sparse living room until the wee hours of the morning. Rood's brooding figure paced back and forth before its flickering glow, peering anxiously into the shadowy corners because he thought he saw or heard the old peddler begging for his life. No one dared approach any closer than the edge of the road skirting the weed-choked yard.

All that late spring, curious neighbors watched the unnatural petals fall to the ground. Despite Rood's neglect, the fruit ripened on the trees and looked not unlike that of previous years. Perhaps this idea that the orchard was cursed, spread by the more superstitious of villagers, was nothing more than idle speculation.

When summer melted effortlessly into the first crisp days of autumn and the Rood apples were ready for tasting, a discovery even more astounding than the scarlet-tinged buds was made. It was because Micah Rood no longer stopped people from picking his apples. In fact when he found someone sneaking into the orchard he hollered for them to pick all they wanted.

"I don't want the accursed things," he screamed at one youthful trespasser.

Indeed there was clear reason for him to be so uncharacteristically generous. Not only were the blossoms stained, but so too was the inside of each apple mottled with bright red splotches. And apples on the very tree beneath which Horgan the peddler died had rich, white pulp marked with spots of red shaped precisely like drops of blood.

That was clear proof of the recluse's guilt, villagers and farm folks agreed. It was time to reopen the murder investigation and shake the truth from old Micah Rood!

But it was too late. A sheriff's posse found Rood slumped in a rocking chair next to his front window. He had been dead for several days.

Possibly the last thing Micah Rood ever saw was his cursed orchard.

The bloody orchard continued to produce the cursed apples for many decades. Even after those trees died, descendants of the murder tree, whose each and every apple had a stain the shape of a blood drop in its center, were found in Rood's old orchard well into the twentieth century.

It is said that even today a few of the apple trees in that region bear fruit with strange red blemishes on the pulp, reminders of Micah Rood, an old peddler, and a crime that was never fully solved. And a curse that cannot be lifted . . .

Mr. Justice Ghost

Samuel Chew was a large, imposing man with a resonant voice and a fine appearance. He would have made a grand preacher; instead he was an eloquent chief justice of the Supreme Court of Delaware. His social relations were warm, but discreet; a few close friends sufficed. A bachelor, he had long ago given up entertaining the idea of a wife and family.

Samuel Chew was fair and just both in and out of court, and the people of Dover, the state capital, generally liked and admired him. Yet his peculiar name brought out the punster in some. A few men couldn't resist a forced sneeze when meeting him on the street. "Ah Chew!" they would cry out. Others affected grinding motions of their jaws as if eating tough pieces of meat. The judge was not amused. He sternly rebuked the guilty ones, who then turned and covered their mouths so as not to show they were laughing behind his back.

Most of the justice's years in Dover were good ones. He enjoyed life and was one of those men who never seem to grow old. But at last on a night in 1744 he died in his sleep. He was in his eighties. The whole town turned out for the church funeral that followed a private service in Chew's large brick home.

Now that the good judge was dead the mockers would gather on street corners and sneeze and grind their jaws with abandon, laughing and punching one another as if they had all gone mad. People had a hard time understanding this silliness when the object of their derision was dead.

But the *spirit* of Samuel Chew was quite alive. He stood beside them, listening and watching. Finally, his anger was so aroused by this lack of respect that he determined to put a stop to it.

Farmer David Hendricks was the first to see the ghost of Justice Samuel Chew.

On a fall night with a nip of frost in the air, Hendricks was on his way to the Inn of King George III. He and neighboring farmers customarily met there after a long, hard day in the fields. Suddenly, in the moon-filled street a figure loomed up ahead. Its black robe flapped in the breeze like a crow lifting off a tree branch, and the big white wig on its head shone like silver in the moonlight.

Hendricks was so cold and so frightened that he started to sneeze. The ghost of Justice Chew, hearing the despised sound, gathered up its robes and gave chase.

Hendricks, who had never harmed a cricket, screamed with fright and raced home more swiftly than a hare fleeing from a pack of hounds.

Mrs. Hendricks heard the beating sounds of her husband's boots and threw open the door. Her husband slumped into an easy chair to catch his breath and it was several minutes before he could tell his wife and children what had happened. None of them slept that night.

In the morning Mrs. Hendricks told the story to her neighbor, Esther von Achtenburg, who told it to her husband, who told it to the blacksmith, who told it to . . . The reappearance of the old judge spread like a brushfire. Some persons allowed that such a thing was entirely possible, while others argued that farmer Hendricks had probably been at the tavern *before* seeing the "ghost."

The incident was forgotten . . . but not for long.

Late one blustery night a year later, Peter Droongoggle, the miller, was picking his way home from a tavern by lantern light. The wind was high, slamming the lantern against his thighs and threatening to tear it from his hands. Rain, laced with hailstones, pelted his head as he scrunched down into his turned-up coat collar. A blast of wind abruptly flung the lantern from his hand. Stooping to retrieve it beside a large poplar tree in the city square, he looked up directly into the face of Samuel Chew. The ghost towered above the quivering miller, leveling its malevolent red eyes and pointing a bony finger. Droongoggle recalled that he had mocked the judge once and now regretted it. His face turned white as flour. He dropped the lantern and fled.

Now everyone in Dover town was afraid to be out after dark. Children stayed indoors behind closed shutters and their elders spoke softly to one another, fearing that a loud remark of any kind might summon the angry judge. Each man searched his soul, trying to recall if, at some time in the distant past, he had intentionally or unintentionally insulted Justice Chew.

Shops closed before sunset and the streets were empty of people; a stranger arriving after dark might have thought that a plague had decimated the town. The public houses, of course, suffered most of all. Night after night not a single man stopped in for his usual drink and bit of gossip. And night after night the tavern owners sat with folded hands in front of their fireplaces, worrying about their mounting debts.

Finally, Mistress van Loon, herself a tavern owner, called her fellow citizens to a meeting beneath the poplar tree in the square. It was a warm, sunny afternoon and almost every resident showed up. Miss van Loon was a hardworking and respected spinster beloved by everyone. (If she had a first name no one recalled what it was.) If a man ran short of money she proffered him drinks anyway, and rarely did anyone "forget" to repay his debt.

Planting her fat hands on her ample hips, Miss van Loon looked over her audience—the miller, the dry goods merchant, the carriage dealer, the blacksmith, the harness maker, fellow taverners, the farmers, and wives with children and babies in arms.

"My friends," she began, "our town was once a cheerful place filled with happy, satisfied people. We have all worked together side by side, each to his own talents, to make our town a haven of prosperity and safety for all. But now the ghost of our late Justice Chew roams the streets, frightening all of us."

She paused, looking over her rapt audience.

"I have thought long and hard of how we might rid ourselves of this unwelcome spirit, and I think there may be a way. I have heard it said that in England a ghost who roams can be put to rest by giving it a nice burial."

The audience gasped. Bury a ghost? How?

Mistress van Loon anticipated the question, and explained that there must be another service for the deceased, followed by the burial of an empty casket under the poplar tree in the square. Justice Chew had always enjoyed pausing in the shade of that magnificent tree, and his ghost seemed equally attracted to the spot.

Miss van Loon waited for reactions. The notion of a funeral for a ghost seemed to strain credulity . . . yet, one after another the people silently nodded their assent. No one could offer a better solution.

The Reverend Charles Antwerp scheduled the service for the following Friday afternoon when the shops usually closed early. Every pew in the little church was filled and when the rites were over everyone agreed that it had been one of the finest funerals ever given.

The pallbearers carried the casket up the aisle while the black-robed choir followed, singing "Faith of Our Fathers." The solemn procession moved to the town square as the church bell tolled. There, the gravediggers lowered the casket into the ground. Preacher Antwerp said a blessing for the ghost of Samuel Chew, bidding it rest in peace until the day of resurrection. As the gravediggers started filling the hole, the families walked silently toward their homes.

That night the bravest men of Dover walked past the big poplar on the road that led to the Inn of King George III. There was no sign of a ghost—not then, nor forever after.

DISTRICT OF COLUMBIA
Pierre L'Enfant's Vigil

The United States Capitol is one of the most imposing public buildings in the nation. The central structure is of Virginia sandstone painted white, and the wings are of Massachusetts marble. Corinthian columns support the porticoes at the front and sides of the building, and the interior is adorned with tile and mosaic floors, sweeping staircases, and several hundred pieces of sculpture and paintings depicting historic events and personalities from America's history.

George Washington laid the Capitol's cornerstone on September 18, 1793. Congress moved here in 1800 from temporary headquarters in Philadelphia. The building would not be completed for another twenty-seven years.

From the beginning, the Capitol has been the object of numerous tales, not all of them political in nature. Legends involve no less than fifteen ghosts roaming the wide halls during the gaslight era.

The most notorious ghost and certainly the most persistent is that of French engineer Pierre Charles L'Enfant, the original architect for the city of Washington, D.C. His ghost paces the floor of the cavernous Capitol basement, awaiting payment of a bill—submitted two centuries ago!

L'Enfant had been commissioned by President Washington to plan the new nation's capital. He designed streets one hundred feet wide and one avenue four hundred feet wide and a mile long. Although Washington felt that such grandiosity was foolish for the fledgling capital, he endorsed the plan. But L'Enfant went too far. He ordered a wealthy landowner to remove his new manor house because it blocked a particularly beautiful view. When the owner refused, L'Enfant demolished the house. President Washington then dismissed L'Enfant and ordered others to complete the plan. Congress refused to pay the engineer for his work.

From time to time the ghost of this sad little man in archaic dress is seen hurrying along with a sheaf of papers stuffed under one arm, perhaps his designs for the city. And it's said that whenever a street change is proposed, the ghost moans and cries as he scurries along the corridors.

In Statuary Hall, filled with sculptures of prominent statesmen of the past, the luminous ghost of John Quincy Adams has been seen by Capitol staff. The hall was formerly the House of Representatives chamber and it was here that Adams, a representative from Massachusetts, used to orate at great length and with brilliant persuasion. He was a bit of a gadfly and often sided with the minority.

Adams was one of only a few former presidents to run for elective office after being the nation's chief executive. After serving as the sixth president from 1825 to 1829, he was elected to nine different terms in the House. On the morning of February 21, 1848, he entered the House chamber bright and in good spirits and took his seat. The Mexican War was over and to celebrate the country's victory President James K. Polk had suggested that Congress bestow honors on the generals who'd won the war. Adams had been opposed to the Mexican War from the start.

Now, as he rose to speak, he reeled suddenly and grasped his desk. Someone shouted, "Mr. Adams!" A nearby colleague caught the former president as he started to collapse. He was carried into the Speaker's chambers and as he was placed on a sofa, he whispered: "This is the last of earth; I am content."

Two days later, on February 23, 1848, John Quincy Adams died of a cerebral stroke. He was eighty-one. Adams had dedicated his life in service to his country. Does President Adams return to deliver the speech he never gave on that cold winter's morning? Those who believe they've seen him insist that he appears at the exact spot where his desk once stood.

President James Abram Garfield held office for only four months before he became the second American president to be assassinated. On July 2, 1881, he and Secretary of State James G. Blaine stood in the Baltimore railroad station waiting for a train to the New Jersey shore, where Garfield's invalid wife was staying. Suddenly a pistol fired. The president staggered and sank to the floor; he'd been shot in the back. Before the horrified spectators realized what had happened, Garfield and Blaine were quickly taken away in a carriage. The assailant, Charles Julius Guiteau, was seized and hurried off to jail to thwart the risk of a lynching.

Although President Garfield was expected to recover, he died in New Jersey on the night of September 19, 1881. His remains were taken to the Capitol Rotunda and viewed by thousands of mourners. Guiteau, a rejected office-seeker, had apparently shadowed the president for some time before having the courage and the opportunity to shoot. On January 25, 1882, a jury found Guiteau guilty of murder, and on June 30, 1882, he was hanged.

Several sources report that the assassinated president's ghost was seen in the halls of the Capitol while his body lay in state. Later, the ghost of assassin Guiteau was glimpsed in a Capitol stairway.

At least one American vice president haunts the halls of the Capitol.

Henry Wilson was vice president during Ulysses S. Grant's second presidential term. He died in 1875, halfway through his own term of office. But the Republican from Massachusetts, determined to complete his tenure in office, is sometimes seen in the Senate wing where he died.

Wilson's death was untimely. He caught a chill and died of pneumonia after bathing in the Capitol's basement. Italian marble bathtubs had been installed there for the convenience of senators wishing to relax after a long day of tedious committee meetings. As president of the Senate, Wilson was particularly fond of using these facilities during the late afternoon or evening hours. Long soaks in the hot water seemed to rejuvenate him and clear his mind for further hours of work.

Shortly after Wilson's death, Senate security guards said they heard mysterious sneezing and coughing outside the vice president's office—when no one was there. Sometimes, too, there is a damp chill in the doorway and the scent of old soap, like that once provided for the senators' ablutions in the long-vanished basement tubs.

With his busy mustache, dark piercing eyes, and long black hair, the ghost of Gen. John Alexander Logan is easily recognized. It appears at 12:30 A.M. at the door of the room once used by the Senate Committee on Military and Militia. As a U.S. senator, Logan, a veteran of the Mexican and Civil wars, had chaired that committee during the 1890s. The ghost listens to late-night hearings, and judging from the frequent frown on its face may be displeased with some of the decisions.

General Logan has also been seen poking around in a dark subbasement, searching perhaps for his horse. It's unclear whether his horse died in battle or of old age. However, the carcass was mounted to be put on display in the Capitol, but workmen mistakenly consigned it to a storage room.

The histories of many public buildings contain legends of workmen who died mysteriously on the job and whose ghosts remain. Their names and the exact circumstances of their deaths are seldom known. During the construction of the Capitol, a carpenter is said to have argued with a concrete mason and, in his fury, threw a brick at the mason's head, killing the poor man instantly. The carpenter sealed the body in a wall to prevent discovery of the crime. The mason's ghost is sometimes heard scrape . . . scrape . . . scraping the hardened mortar with a trowel in a vain attempt to call attention to his circumstances.

For years, the ghost of a custodian who died at work returned to help the flesh-and-blood crew with their nightly chores. He was especially fond of picking up a mop and swishing it across the marble floors. The trouble was only the mop was seen moving back and forth . . . causing those in attendance to flee for their lives.

The Library of Congress was originally housed in the Capitol. In 1814 part of the collection was lost when the British burned the city, and another conflagration in 1851 destroyed half of the Library's holdings. Nevertheless, the Library continued to expand and, in 1897, moved into larger quarters in a building across the street. Yet tales are still abundant about two employees who worked in the Congressional Library when it was housed in the Capitol.

A Mr. Twine was a conscientious employee even after he died. He visited his office regularly, stamping books with the standard mixture of alcohol and lamp-black in an office resembling a large iron cage. Guards heard the hard rubber stamp meeting flyleaf and knew that Twine was still at work in the place that had once been his office.

A coworker of Twine's died shortly after stashing $6,000 in government bonds between the pages of rarely used books. He was an elderly man with few friends and a deep-seated distrust of banks. Parsimonious by nature, he saved most of each paycheck, anticipating a comfortable, if lonely, old age. For years after his fatal stroke, guards said they heard the riffling of book pages as the old man's ghost sought the cache at the former library site. No one had told him that you can't take it with you. The money was never found.

* * *

The apparitions in the Capitol are startling, of course, to the percipient, but *one* in particular strikes terror in the hearts of all who meet it—and it isn't even that of a human being. For over a century late-night workers have feared encounters with the dreaded Demon Cat that lurks in subterranean corridors.

Several years ago, a guard, alone on patrol, came upon the creature. It padded toward him, purring softly, its black fur barely visible in the dimly lit hallway. Then, as it came closer, its body swelled—and swelled—until it was the size of a Bengal tiger. Eyes glowed and the purring changed to a savage snarl. With claws extended, the monstrous beast leaped upon the guard. He screamed and covered his face—but he never felt the attack! When he opened his eyes and peered down the long corridor, there was no sign of activity, feline or otherwise.

Other guards have allegedly fainted upon meeting the phantom cat, and in one case, a worker fled the building as the beast approached him.

Does the Demon Cat have any basis in fact? Perhaps. It is thought to be the last of a feline brigade recruited many years ago to control the Capitol's growing rat population. After the rats were exterminated, the cats' services were no longer needed. Most became house pets and others wandered off. Only the Demon Cat remained, seeking retribution perhaps for not having been adopted by humans.

Those who believe in the Demon Cat say it always appears before a national tragedy and at the time of the changing of administrations.

Miami Frights

The evidence for a haunting seemed persuasive:

- Cats were mysteriously strangled on several occasions when an iron gate slammed shut on them for no apparent reason.
- A chandelier on the front porch fell from its mooring and crashed to the floor.
- An owner heard odd noises from the kitchen. He found dishes and silverware littering the floor. No one was in the house with him.
- A path in the backyard echoed with the sound of phantom high heels.
- A timid, furtive woman darted silently down the hall, dressed in a frilly Spanish gown; her hair was pulled tightly into a bun. She vanished as quietly as she appeared.

During the 1970s and early 1980s, these incidents reported in the Miami news media gave North Miami Avenue's Villa Paula the reputation of being the most famous haunted house in the city. Was the notoriety deserved? Did this distinctive landmark actually harbor the ghost of the wife of the Cuban consul who lived there in the 1920s?

The answers, of course, depend upon one's proclivity to accept certain events as supernatural. But Villa Paula's owner during that era believed very much in his "lovable ghost."

Villa Paula was built in 1925 as the first Cuban consulate in Miami. The consul, Don Domingo Milord, named his residence after his wife, Paula. According to city legend, she died in 1931 under mysterious circumstances in one of the bedrooms from complications arising after she had a leg amputated.

The consulate was bought by a Muriel Reardon during the Depression. She lived there for over thirty years. The house saw a variety of owners during the 1960s and early 1970s until it became senior citizens' housing. By 1974, Villa Paula had become a haven for drifters. That's when Cliff Ensor bought the still-distinctive house from the Department of Housing and Urban Development for an undisclosed sum.

Ensor spent thousands of dollars remodeling the house to its original grandeur. He repainted the interior, scraped and refinished the flooring, installed glass chandeliers, and decorated the interior with his own nineteenth-century Empire-style cherry and oak furniture highlighted with whorls and intricately carved scrollwork.

Villa Paula is truly a grand dwelling. It has ten rooms, two baths, and ceilings eighteen feet high. Tuscan columns inside set off exquisite painted tiles installed seventy years ago by Dom Domingo himself. The exterior is yellow brick imported from Cuba with a white stucco covering. Ionic columns grace the front entrance.

Cliff Ensor put the house on the market in 1976, listed for $110,000. There weren't any takers. By 1985, the price had climbed to $185,000 and Ensor decided to auction off the property.

Part of the problem in selling the mansion may have been that Ensor was the man who spoke most freely about Paula, the resident ghost. She was "quite well-behaved, really," he told reporters. The house's location in the heart of Little Haiti might have discouraged other buyers. In fact, Ensor once said that residents in the neighborhood refused to walk on the sidewalk in front of the house. The auctioneer responsible for the 1985 auction said the house would be worth a million dollars if it were located in Coral Gables.

Cliff Ensor was quick to tell listeners that he couldn't testify for certain that he personally saw the mysterious, one-legged woman some took to be the consul's wife, Paula Milord. It was the psychics who visited the house at Ensor's invitation who reported the ghostly presence on five different occasions, usually in the front living room.

However, Ensor didn't have to see ghosts to know the house wasn't a typical city dwelling. Ensor reported plenty of other strange episodes during his tenure at Villa Paula.

The most disturbing was the freakish death of several cats.

Thick iron bars across the windows have protected the house for years, as has a front iron gate which, during Ensor's time, was always kept chained and pad-locked. However, another gate in back stayed unlocked. That was the one blamed for the feline finales. Somehow the gate would swing violently shut—on windless days—garroting cats caught in its murderous path. Ensor found three of his cats thus dispatched.

Muriel Reardon, the woman who bought the house from the Cuban government, allegedly hated cats, Ensor said. That may explain what happened to his pets, although there is no proof one way or the other. Ensor did determine that it was Reardon who once painted the house pink.

There were more peculiarities while he lived in the house, Ensor said. Many more.

Ensor said a steady rapping at his front door didn't necessarily mean guests. Often he would unbolt the latch, open the door and peer outside into . . . noth-ingness. One day his bedroom door slammed shut for no earthly reason. Later, an elderly neighbor who knew Paula Milord when she lived there said she played the piano in that room. She always closed the door beforehand to keep the draft away from her shoulders while she practiced.

Also in the bedroom, Ensor sometimes found his bedspread covers turned over.

And the smells. The strong aroma of Cuban coffee drifted out of the kitchen. A scent of roses in the dining room was not unusual, even though it occurred out of season.

Ensor told reporters that he caught reflections of "something" out of the corners of his eyes, almost as if a skittering shadow quickly dissolved before he could focus on it. He would rub his eyes not quite believing that anything was really there. In a hallway Ensor thought he glimpsed a swish of a gown as Paula, her jet-black hair pulled tightly back, seemed to vaporize at the hint of his presence.

Paula Milord may not have been alone in haunting her old villa. Other, more reticent ghosts at Villa Paula seemed most content to keep their identities secret. But there were those circumstances in which they showed themselves to phychics intent on exposing the spiritual nature of that architectural marvel.

At a séance in 1976, the Reverend Emma Tandarich, who called her home in Opa-Locka the Shrine of Spiritual Enlightenment, and later the Church of Psychical Science and Christianity, found a perplexing array of otherworldly beings announcing their habitation of Villa Paula.

During the séance, the Reverend Tandarich claimed to have played the Villa Paula piano better than she ever had before. "My body vibrated. I felt as if my head was expanding, my hair was coming out, and my ears were plugged up," she told a reporter. Wearing a white graduation robe, the Reverend Tandarich called upon her spirit guide, the Lady of the Roses, to help her navigate through the unseen world.

By the end of the session, the Reverend Tandarich and her dozen followers had identified four spirits visiting them that night.

There was a lanky, elderly man with a top hat; a fat lady wearing a red dress; another woman who cried that she had lost a medal in Villa Paula's garden; and a young Cuban woman desperately sad over having had an illegitimate child in the house decades ago. The baby had died at birth and had been buried near Villa Paula. She was seeking its grave.

Strangest of all, the Reverend Tandarich found another spirit who said she liked grinding Cuban coffee, placing roses in Villa Paula's various rooms, and playing music from *Carmen* on her beloved grand piano.

Could that have been Paula? Neither Cliff Ensor nor the Reverend Emma Tandarich could say for sure.

For some years, Villa Paula has been quiet. In a supernatural sense, that is. Cliff Ensor was able to sell the house. The neoclassical mansion is still beautiful, looking exactly like a typical Cuban home of the 1920s. In the early 1990s, it housed a physician's office.

Where once only spirits sought solitude, the ill and injured now seek the curative powers of medicine. But perhaps Paula is only waiting . . . waiting for her opportunity to show that there is more to heaven and earth than we imagine.

The Warehouse

A great untruth of ghostly activity is that it takes place only at night and only in ancient mansions. Some of the most startling events have unfolded in broad daylight in the most unlikely of locations, say a three-bedroom rambler in Middle America or a skyscraper in New York City.

Or a wholesale warehouse filled with trinkets and souvenirs in modern Miami.

Al Laubheim was a jovial, balding man who operated just such a Miami business, which he called Tropication Arts. He certainly didn't expect to find himself at the center of one of the most notorious cases of supposed poltergeist activity ever recorded.

From December 1966 until February 1967, over 224 separate incidents of flying boxes, crashing glasses, and tumbling containers mystified psychic researchers, journalists, a magician, and police officers who came to investigate. The public record of this haunting is extensive and detailed.

Just when the troubles began is not known. Observers believe the first disturbances could have occurred as early as the fall of 1966, when the owners began to notice a large amount of breakage in the thirty-by-fifty-foot warehouse. They attributed it to clumsy workers.

But it was over a period of just a few days during mid-January 1967 when all of Florida would know of Al Laubheim, Tropication Arts, and the supposed poltergeist.

The fast-moving set of events began with the first incident directly involving Laubheim on January 12, 1967. The next day, well-known ghost hunter Susy Smith, in town promoting a book, visited the warehouse at the invitation of a Laubheim employee. On Saturday, January 14, the police became involved. A day later, prominent psychic investigator William G. Roll was on the scene recording the events. Shortly thereafter, the warehouse poltergeist was headline news in the Miami popular press.

The large number of disturbances—sometimes fifty within just a few hours—caused many to suspect trickery, or that the owners were trying to publicize the business through some sort of elaborate hoax. Indeed, a nineteen-year-old Tropication Arts clerk eventually came under suspicion for instigating the mischief.

Was the case, then, one of genuine poltergeists? Or was it an elaborate fraud? An examination of the circumstances leads to many questions but few solid answers.

That first encounter Al Laubheim had with flying objects on January 12 occurred when he carefully placed a number of amber glass beer mugs on a shelf. As he walked away, one of the glasses fell to the floor. He told author William G. Roll that the mugs' placement well *away from the edge* seemed to make it impossible that a mug could fall of its own accord.

Between January 12 and the initial police investigation on January 14, Laubheim said boxes were constantly hurtling from the shelves. No sooner would he clean up one mess than another load of souvenirs flew from a shelf. A container of plastic back scratchers fell, scattering the contents over the floor.

As word of the events spread among the employees, many became terribly upset. Several female office staff broke down in tears, Laubheim claimed.

On Saturday, January 14, Laubheim decided that he couldn't solve the mystery himself. He called in the Miami police.

What they found was a situation not covered in police academy training manuals. There is no entry under *Poltergeist, Apprehension of.*

The first officer to arrive on the scene was Patrolman William Killin. He was met by Laubheim and Julio Vasquez, the young warehouse employee later suspected of triggering the mayhem. Killin searched the warehouse while Laubheim and Vasquez remained near the entrance. Killin heard at least one disturbance and subsequently found a highball glass on the floor, shattered. Later, Killin saw two boxes overturn, spilling their contents to the floor. Both Laubheim and Vasquez were within sight of Killin.

By early on the afternoon of January 14, Killin had been joined by a sergeant and two other patrolmen. A professional magician, Howard Brooks, had also been invited by Laubheim to join in the investigation.

The officers stood in front of the large room discussing the events. Laubheim, Vasquez, the magician Brooks and his female companion were in a separate group. Suddenly a box of address books fell off a shelf. Officer Killin said everyone was under observation when the box dumped its contents. He couldn't explain how it happened. The box was half a foot from the edge of the shelf. The officers tried and failed to dislodge a similar box by shaking the shelf on which it sat. Brooks searched for hidden wires or other devices. He couldn't find any evidence of deliberate trickery.

A German shepherd police dog summoned to sniff for clues unsuccessfully searched the building.

Although the warehouse disturbances grew in intensity toward the end of January, several witnesses claimed to have seen falling objects earlier in the month:

• Reporter Thomas Garcia checked out the warehouse story soon after he heard about it in mid-January. He stood with Laubheim and Vasquez at the front of the warehouse. Two boxes fell off a shelf. Garcia said nobody was near the shelf.
• As he checked the warehouse inventory on Friday, January 13, Laubheim's partner, Ben Lewis, said ashtrays, tumblers, and glasses fell from shelves shortly after he stacked them. That same day, William Drucker, the company's insurance agent, came by on a routine visit. He was told about the damage and saw debris on the floor from earlier episodes. As he was leaving the warehouse, he heard a crash from the rear of the room. After verifying that the three people inside at the time were far away from the aisle in which he heard the noise, he checked and found two boxes on the floor. An examination showed no evidence of tampering. Julio Vasquez was six yards away and in a different aisle. Drucker said it seemed impossible to him that Vasquez could have caused the accident.
• Also on January 13, warehouse clerk Curt Hagemeyer claimed to have seen a shot glass tumble to the floor. It didn't break. Later, he and co-owner Ben Lewis saw three small boxes fall off a shelf. In both instances, Hagemeyer said nobody was near the shelves.
• The following Monday, January 16, magician Howard Brooks again visited the warehouse. This time he was rewarded with a view of two cartons falling, seemingly of their own accord, from a high shelf to the floor. An off-duty police officer was at one end of the aisle, Brooks at the other, when the eight-by-ten-inch boxes fell. "Something did move those, and I couldn't figure out what," Brooks told investigator William Roll.
• Ruth May, an artist employed by Tropication Arts to paint Florida scenes on various novelty items, reported one of the more bizarre events on January 16. According to Mrs. May, a plastic tray flew from one shelf to another and then into a large cardboard carton. A few seconds later, a rubber alligator and some souvenir key chains dropped into the same carton from a box on the shelf above. Warehouseman Julio Vasquez and co-owner Lewis were at opposite ends of the room. Mrs. May said neither one was close enough to have triggered the events.

And on it went through most of January 1967. Based on eyewitness accounts, including his own, investigator Roll counted 224 separate incidents of flying, tumbling, or crashing objects from early January to February 1.

The single most "active" day seemed to be Monday, January 23, during which fifty two incidents were counted. Laubheim told Roll that in one instance a fifteen-pound box filled with large tumblers somehow scooted twenty four feet along a shelf before striking the floor. All the glasses shattered.

Co-owner Laubheim compiled a list of sixteen outside witnesses who had seen at least one falling or flying object, in addition to the observations of his own employees. Interestingly, few witnesses actually saw an object *start* its fall. Although he spent ten days examining the premises, Roll never saw an object begin its activity. However, he did witness objects in "mid-flight" and found the shattered remains of others after they had hit the floor.

There are two theories about what happened at Tropication Arts.

The first holds that elaborate trickery was involved, probably instigated by Julio Vasquez, the young clerk who was allegedly present during *all* of the disturbances. It was suggested that he used strong thread or rope to yank the objects off the shelves. Police even suspected Vasquez of burglarizing the warehouse in early February, but dropped their investigation when Laubheim refused to press charges.

Vasquez, a Cuban immigrant, heatedly denied that he was the warehouse "poltergeist." He said police had tricked him into confessing to the earlier warehouse damage after he was picked up on the burglary charge. His self-incrimination reportedly came after hours of questioning by police and threats to "send him back to Cuba."

Did Vasquez have the sophistication necessary to pull off such an elaborate hoax? Six police officers, a professional magician, several newsmen, two veteran investigators of the paranormal, and many others were all unable to find any hints of trickery, usually within seconds of seeing or hearing the falling objects. Yes, Vasquez *was* always present, but he was most often under partial or total observation by other persons. It would seem reasonable to assume that in at least a few of the 224 incidents, someone would have discovered Vasquez's methods of making the objects move.

A second, more controversial, theory concludes that Vasquez was responsible, but that he unwittingly caused the damage through psychokinesis, or PK, the ability to physically move an object through the use of one's mind.

In this scenario, Vasquez probably wasn't aware of his PK powers. In virtually all cases of supposed poltergeist activity, a troubled teenager is present. Vasquez seemed to fit that description. He was under constant suspicion, held a low-paying job that he believed was beneath his status, and resented his brusque treatment by other employees.

Could Vasquez have unconsciously *willed* objects to move in the warehouse? William Roll thought so. He brought Vasquez to his Phychical Research Laboratory in Durham, North Carolina. During various tests, Roll found that Vasquez scored above chance on certain tests for psychokinetic ability. Roll told author Susy Smith that Vasquez "could, to some extent, bring his PK powers under conscious control."

Vasquez grew agitated at times at the laboratory. He was tired from all the tests and anxious to return home. In one of those instances when he was particularly upset, a vase fell off a table in the hallway outside the testing room. Vasquez and the researchers were the only ones in the building.

Roll was careful, however, to couch his conclusions in cautionary terms. He told *Miami News* columnist Jack Roberts, "We're conducting scientific research. We want controlled laboratory evidence, not conjecture." Yet he also said, "We have certified to Mr. Laubheim . . . that no fraud or trickery was involved in the happenings at his place of business. I was able to observe with my own eyes numerous instances of movement of objects and check for the possibility of fraud or accident. Neither existed."

The truth behind the Miami warehouse poltergeist may never be fully known. Al Laubheim told reporters he was willing to believe that Vasquez had unusual mental powers which caused the damage. He noted that despite weeks of effort, nobody could prove fraud or trickery. Laubheim was content to let his business get back to normal. That it did. The warehouse poltergeist was gone, but it never, never, will be forgotten.

Tobe or Not Tobe?

*In the weird of night when the
lights are no more
And the clock on the mantel beats
slower than slow,
A man walks forth with a measured
tread.
He is not of this earth—the man's
from the dead.
He walks with assurance; his tread
is not light;
This man from the dead seems to
think he has right.*
                    "The Ghost of Orna Villa"
                    Mrs. Paul Campbell
                    circa. 1946

A comparison to Poe or Dickinson shows these rhyming couplets to be of dubious literary merit, despite the evocative images the lines project. Mrs. Campbell may not have been a poet for the ages, but she did have a knowledge of the subject that makes her verse all the more fascinating—she is a descendant of the men some say are the prime candidates as the phantom of Orna Villa, the oldest home in Oxford, Georgia.

The phantom could be her great-uncle Tobe Means, though Mrs. Campbell cast her vote for another of her uncles. But whichever one haunts Orna Villa, this ghost story has been an Oxford staple for over a century.

The origins of the classic plantation home situated on a small rise a few hundred feet off Highway 81 are obscure. A former owner contends that it was originally a one-room log cabin built in the early to mid-1700s. Heavy locks still on some of the doors are the work of English ironmongers and date to at least 1791.

Over the decades, the log house was expanded with the addition of numerous rooms and, eventually, a second story, so that the original log structure, if indeed it originated in that way, has been obliterated. It has been established that Orna Villa was weatherboarded and remodeled in 1822, because more recent owners tore down an ell and found a penny from that year in one of the upright studs installed during the remodeling. The heavy timbers used for the sills and corner posts were hand-hewn, while the wide floorboards, door-facings, and wainscoting show signs of having been hand-planed. Knife nicks can be seen in the carved mantels.

Today, the home is an excellent example of Greek Revival antebellum architecture. The two-story portico is framed by four columns, setting off a main entrance with side and transom windows. Decorative pilasters grace the corners of the main house and frame the doorway. Two single-story wings extend from the sides. A trio of limestone and stucco chimneys rise above the low-pitched roof. A small outbuilding used as slave quarters stands behind the main house.

Orna Villa is known locally as the Means House, after its most famous resident, Dr. Alexander Means, an educator, poet, inventor, minister, scientist, and fourth president of Oxford's old Emory College, now Atlanta's Emory University. During his remarkable life, Dr. Means enjoyed the company of the Prince of Wales in London, was a house guest of Sir Michael Faraday, entertained President Millard Fillmore at Orna Villa, and delivered the funeral oration for President Zachary Taylor in 1850.

Tobe and Olin Means were his sons. Mrs. Campbell was Dr. Alexander Means's granddaughter.

To say that Dr. Means was a man of extraordinary achievements is, at best, an understatement. This is especially true considering his humble origins. Born in 1801 near Statesville, North Carolina, Alexander Means acquired sporadic schooling before moving to Georgia around 1820. He taught at several schools, including one in Madison, Georgia. While there, he became an ordained Methodist minister and then studied medicine under the direction of Drs. Walker and Randolph. In 1825, he graduated from the school of medicine at Transylvania College, Kentucky.

Dr. Means formed a partnership with Dr. Henry Gaither in Covington, Georgia, and bought Orna Villa, then some distance from the city, in about 1828. When the Methodist/Episcopal Georgia Conference formed a manual labor school in 1834 at Covington, Dr. Means was elected its first rector. Two years later when Emory College opened nearby, Dr. Means was chosen as the first chair of its physics department. He spent 1837–1838 studying at Jefferson Medical College, Philadelphia, and returned to assume additional duties in chemistry. He remained a professor at Emory for four decades.

A fine scientist, Dr. Means also held deep religious principles throughout his life. He was described as "a preacher of rare eloquence" who was often called upon to give orations at the funerals of prominent persons, such as Dr. Wilbur Fisk, president of a Connecticut university, and the aforementioned President Zachary Taylor. His many published sermons, addresses, reviews, and scientific discussions were widely circulated.

Following a one-year presidency of Emory College, from 1854 to 1855, Dr. Means taught chemistry at both Emory and the Atlanta Medical College. But following a trip to Great Britain, he became intrigued with Sir Michael Faraday's experiments with electricity. That led to an amazing event at Atlanta's old city hall on June 2, 1857. Witnesses assert that on that day, Dr. Means exhibited the world's first incandescent light. Thomas Edison was ten years old.

Dr. Means had gathered a group of prominent Atlantans in the room and by turning a large disk on a machine he had invented, Means produced frictional electricity. It passed through wires attached to a chunk of black carbon, causing the material to burst into light. One witness said, "Never . . . have I seen a more brilliant light. Nothing in all the phenomena of our wonderful age has ever impressed me more than this exhibition and I can never forget it as long as my memory lasts."

Unfortunately, other memories didn't last. Edison is credited with inventing the electric light. Dr. Means didn't patent his electricity-producing machine, which is now housed at Emory University.

Much of the scientist's work was conducted at a laboratory he installed in a second-floor room at Orna Villa. He worked far into the night on his many interests, often rocking violently while trying to stay awake so that he could finish whatever project he was working on.

Part of Orna Villa's ghost lore centers on that old laboratory. Twentieth-century owners of the house have reported seeing bright, green-hued lights in the night and hearing the incessant squeaks of a rocker. They say it was Dr. Means, still trying to fight off sleep.

Orna Villa's ghost is believed by many to be Tobe Means, a rebellious iconoclast and the youngest of Dr. Means's nine children. However, the late Mrs. Campbell and others believe the haunting is by Dr. Olin Means, Tobe's older brother.

Tobe was, according to most accounts, a problem for his more conventional, success-oriented father. The younger man wanted nothing to do with being a minister or teacher or scientist. He ignored his family's proclivity to read extensively in the various arts and sciences. The final blow was the day Tobe told his father in no uncertain terms that college was not for him; he wanted to get his education by traveling the world. He proposed that the money Dr. Means would spend on college tuition be given to him to finance his journeys.

The "discussion" between Tobe and his father degenerated into a shouting match. The young man stormed from the room, slamming the door behind him as usual. Later that night, Tobe rode out of Oxford, never again to enter his family's home. In the months and years to come, family members sometimes heard pacing coming from the rear porch. They thought it was Tobe returned to hearth and home, but when they opened the door there never was anyone to welcome back.

If Tobe was the antithesis of his father, Olin Means was the old man's shadow. From his clear blue eyes to his small stature and erect bearing, Olin mirrored Alexander Means in every way except one. While his father was a man of eclectic interests, Olin knew from an early age that his career would be in medicine. He graduated from medical school and established a successful practice not far from his family's Oxford home.

His life's work seemed set until a completely unexpected call to the ministry interrupted his routine. Olin was nonplussed. He tried to ignore the nagging tug to follow his father's path into preaching. He stayed awake many nights weighing a decision to take up God's work, trying to convince himself that through his career as a medical doctor he was helping mankind. Although father and son talked often of this difficult decision, Alexander Means did not try to influence his offspring one way or the other.

As he tried to arrive at a decision, Olin paced the back porch, day after day, night after night. Sadly, the young man became gravely ill and died before making his decision. Mrs. Campbell and others believed it was logical to assume that it was Olin Means, not Tobe, pacing up and down, still trying to make up his mind.

Dr. Alexander Means continued to teach, speak, write, and conduct scientific experiments and was active in the turbulent affairs of his native state before and after the Civil War. He was a member of the 1861 Georgia Secession Convention, speaking strongly against leaving the Union, but later voting with the majority to secede. After the war, Dr. Means was appointed Georgia State Chemist, the first in the state's history, and held that position until 1877. He died on June 5, 1883.

Orna Villa was eventually transformed into a boarding house for Emory College students. Even the old slave quarters were used as a student bunkhouse. The small community of Oxford, which had grown up around the school, had a number of homes that functioned as student housing until a dormitory, Haygood Hall, was finished in 1915. When Emory moved to Atlanta the campus became Oxford College.

The first ghost stories connected with Orna Villa may have originated earlier in this century with "Uncle Billy" Mitchell, the grandson of Tobe Means's nurse. Mitchell was an Oxford handyman and longtime employee of Emory College.

He said that it was his grandmother who "divined" that the ghost was Tobe. Nurse and child remained close even as he and his father were growing apart. She claimed Tobe had died in Texas and would haunt Orna Villa if his body wasn't returned for burial in the local cemetery.

However, the legend of Tobe Means may be just that, a jumble of suppositions and rumors that have little to do with what is known of the man. This isn't to diminish the possibility that it *is* his ghost wandering Orna Villa, only that he was far from the peripatetic vagabond who vanished into the night.

Although the circumstances of his leaving are lost to memory, H. W. (Tobe) Means was certainly a successful man in his own right. He did, in fact, attend college, eventually receiving a Ph.D. from Emory University after it relocated to Atlanta. He was a principal in Pine Bluff, Arkansas, for two years and spent over fourteen years as principal of Peabody School in Little Rock. According to a newspaper article about Dr. Means, he was "widely known among educators for constructive execution of the training of the young, per civic usefulness and body building for nutrition and health work."

A man who owned Orna Villa in the 1960s and 1970s, James Watterson, said he once met Tobe's great-grandson when he decided to visit his ancestor's hometown. The man said Tobe lived to a "ripe old age" in Little Rock and was an educator like his father, Alexander. The great-grandson told Watterson that he knew nothing of the ghost legends at Orna Villa. Nor did he think it likely that Tobe had floated all the way back to Georgia to haunt his boyhood home.

If Tobe might be ruled out, there are several other candidates for the ghost of Orna Villa.

One legend even predates the building of the house. A small stream running through Oxford and nearby Covington is known as Dried Indian Creek. The strange name is derived from the story of an Indian chief vehemently disliked by white settlers. He was captured, murdered, and then staked out to "dry" near the site of Orna Villa. An early belief held that the periodic flooding of the creek was the chief's vengeance on future white settlers.

An old walnut grove on the Orna Villa property gave rise to another tale. Famed Confederate spy Zora Fair used the dark juice from the nuts to stain her face so that she could pass for a mulatto and slip through Yankee lines to give vital intelligence to Southern forces. But a Confederate general ignored her information. Zora is said to have died of a broken heart when her beloved South lost the war.

A fortune in Confederate gold may have been buried at Orna Villa, according to reports from the early 1940s. An old man who was familiar with local history told the *Atlanta Journal* he was "sure of it." A woman who once lived at Orna Villa said the base of a large chimney could have concealed the cache of riches. It isn't know if she ever searched for the lost treasure. There are no confirmed reports of any Confederate treasure being lost or buried in Oxford.

*   *   *

The first extensive accounts of a haunting at Orna Villa began in 1945 when E. H. "Buddy" Rheberg and his wife bought the house. The couple lived there for many years; it was Rheberg who tore down the ell at the rear of the house and found evidence of the 1822 remodeling. Ironically, the Rhebergs had another connection to the Means family. Mrs. Rheberg's father, James Boykin Robinson, was Tobe Means's closest childhood friend. Robinson said Tobe had spent his last night in Oxford with him at a local social gathering after the young man's falling out with his father.

Buddy Rheberg bought the house having heard all of the ghost stories connected with it but still skeptical that such things could happen. It did not take him long to discover that there may have been more truth in the tales than he thought.

Early one winter morning, Rheberg arose earlier than usual. He dressed and went to the kitchen to prepare a simple breakfast. A few minutes into his meal, he heard footsteps crunching on the gravel driveway. Expecting his handyman Walt to knock at the kitchen door, he waited expectantly. The footfalls climbed the porch steps, approached the door and stopped.

"Walt, come on in!" Rheberg shouted.

Rather than the door swinging open, Rheberg heard whoever it was cross to the other side of the open porch and then back again to the door.

"Walt, come in. Walt, don't you hear me!" Rheberg shouted.

He got up out of his chair disgusted that the man was ignoring his shouts. He could still hear the footsteps pacing the porch as he turned the doorknob.

Rheberg swung the door open; the footsteps stopped. The porch was empty. Walt didn't arrive until a half hour later.

The Rhebergs' daughter, Betty, used the upstairs north bedroom when she lived in Orna Villa. After returning from a date, she locked the main door, climbed the staircase and knocked on her parents' bedroom door directly across the hall from her room.

"Mom, I'm home," the girl whispered as she cracked open her parents' door.

"Your mom is asleep. Are you okay?" Buddy Rheberg asked.

"Yes, I'm fine," Betty replied and closed their door.

The young woman went to her own room, turned her dresser-top radio on low and slipped into bed. She was about to get up to turn off the radio when she heard somebody coming up the stairs from the bottom landing.

"Dad, is that you?" she asked. There was no reply. The door swung open. The girl let out a scream and her father came running out from his room across the hall.

"What's the matter?" he demanded.

"Didn't you see it?" she asked.

"No, I didn't see anything. What was it?" Rheberg asked.

The girl assumed that whatever opened her door would have to have been visible to her father. It wasn't. But the door had swung open, of that the frightened girl was certain.

Mrs. Rheberg told a reporter in 1946 that a couple of mysterious things had happened to her early in her family's tenancy at Orna Villa.

She tended to ignore the occasional sighs, creaks, and groans in various rooms, assigning them to the category of "old houses are like that," but when she found a man's footprint in the newly painted kitchen floor she got a "funny feeling." The doors had been locked from the inside, and no family members had been in the kitchen while the floor paint dried.

Mrs. Rheberg's southern-style biscuits had a tendency to disappear, causing the family to jokingly suggest, "There's Tobe again!" Milk and cake also vanished from the Rhebergs' kitchen.

Mrs. Paul Campbell, the granddaughter of Dr. Means and the author of "The Ghost of Orna Villa," was living in Atlanta at the time the Rhebergs occupied Orna Villa. She always thought the footsteps belonged to her uncle Dr. Olin Means rather than his brother Tobe. The only experience she had with the haunting was seeing a mysterious light emanating from the room where Alexander Means earlier conducted his experiments in electricity. It was also Tobe Means's bedroom when he lived at home.

Mrs. Campbell had a hard time believing that the ghosts of either of her uncles would steal the milk, cake, or biscuits. A rather "unspectral" thing to do, she sniffed to a reporter.

The ghosts of Orna Villa were relatively benign until 1967, when James and Glynora Watterson bought the house. "We just fell in love with its stateliness the very first time we saw it," James Watterson said, noting that he was the thirteenth owner. "No one really said it was a dangerous house. No one ever really came up with the term 'fear.' "

The couple had been aware of the ghost stories, but the house's spacious rooms and antebellum flavor won them over. James was also pleased that it would be the ideal house to display his extensive collection of Civil War artifacts, including uniforms, muskets, swords, and other priceless military paraphernalia.

The man from whom Watterson bought Orna Villa, John Rudesal, had remodeled the interior to accommodate his mother. However, she reportedly stayed only a short time because the house "hated her."

Rudesal told Watterson that a couple of peculiar things had taken place while he lived there. On one occasion a piano started playing all by itself. Windows and doors often rattled as if being shaken by someone.

Although Watterson never *saw* a ghost, he believed that Orna Villa was haunted.

"I can remember when we made a den out of that old back porch," he recalled. "It was very comfortable. We had a television set and rocker out there. It was a good place to sit. There were big long drapes on the windows and the view of the backyard and woods was just beautiful. I would sit there reading, either early in the morning or late at night. I like the quiet times of the day. But sometimes I would see little things, in the periphery of my vision. Something would move. I was constantly noticing that."

Once he was frightened by something well within his line of sight while he was relaxing on the porch. "There was a door into the hallway. To the left is a door to the kitchen, which was never kept closed, and then the door to the parlor. That was closed all the time. As I sat out there one night, I happened to look up and the door to the parlor swung open. Every hair on my neck stood up. The parlor lights were off and I must tell you I was real hesitant to go in there. I did though and then all through the downstairs. There wasn't anyone around."

Glynora Watterson had an odd, recurring dream that made the couple uneasy. It concerned a "lost" part of the house. In this dream, she would open a door and find a section of the house that was furnished with plush Victorian furniture. She explored the room but always woke up before finishing her tour. So vivid were these images, and so insistent the dream, that her husband searched for hidden panels.

"I carefully measured and drew the house plans but I could always account for all but a few inches," Watterson said. "So there was no such thing as a hidden room."

That didn't completely satisfy him. "Dreams probably are closer to the root of most experiences than anything else," Watterson noted. He was sure that his wife's dream had some relevance to the secrets of Orna Villa . . . even if he couldn't prove it.

Watterson had a separate room in which his military memorabilia was displayed, museumlike, in glass display cases and on wall-mounted brackets. An accident one afternoon in that room has always puzzled him.

"I had a rack of old Civil War artillery muskets, seven or eight of them, hanging on the wall with a long, glass showcase below it. My wife heard this terrible crash, and every one of those guns came off the wall. Fell right on that showcase."

Nothing broke even though the brackets were yanked out of the wall.

Neither were there any scratches on the antique glass showcase. Watterson increased the size of the bracket anchors and the guns never again fell.

A second incident in Watterson's Civil War room was equally mystifying. Six valuable lithographs hanging on another wall all fell off at the same time. But none of the glass over the pictures was broken, nor were the frames damaged in any way. The hooks had stayed in the wall, but the wire holding each lithograph came loose. *All at the same time.*

Watterson didn't calculate the odds of eight muskets or six lithographs falling at the same time, but they would be astronomical. Unless something supernatural had a hand in the affair.

A canary named Diana was a mysterious fatality while the Wattersons lived at Orna Villa. The couple had left on a short vacation, making certain to put a large bowl of water and plenty of seed in the canary's cage. The bird was quite a singer and Glynora was especially fond of her.

According to Watterson, they had only been out of the state for two days when his wife started having premonitions about the bird's fate.

"Something bad has happened to my canary," Glynora told her husband. He tried to placate her fears, even teasing her about it. Though they didn't cut their trip short, it was with great trepidation that they unlocked the back door upon their return.

Glynora's fears were well founded. The birdcage was lying broken on the floor. The hook that had held the cage to the wall had come loose, causing it to fall. After searching for a few minutes, Watterson found the yellow canary drowned in the aquarium.

"Now what drove that bird to such excitement, and what made that cage come off the wall I'll never know," Watterson avers. "Maybe the bird survived a day or two in the house without water and then drowned trying to get a drink from the fish tank. I just don't know. But that was the last straw for my wife. She knew there was something in the house that was against her."

In 1975, James and Glynora Watterson moved from Orna Villa to "High Point at Chestnut Grove," the name given to another beautiful antebellum home which the couple had moved to Oxford.

Despite the peculiar incidents at the old Alexander Means mansion, James has fond memories of the place.

"I never felt a presence, or cold spots or a breath down my back or chill in my spine. It was a good house. It was a comfortable house, and most forgiving of anything we did to it," he said.

A medical doctor bought Orna Villa in 1975 and moved in with his wife and six children, including two foster children. The family does not wish to have their identities revealed, but their experiences with unexplained phenomena during their first six months in the house nearly made them pack up and leave.

A twelve-year-old daughter had been assigned a bedroom off the enclosed back porch, the den James Watterson used as a reading room. No sooner had she moved in than she told her parents there were strange knockings on the walls and the knob on the door separating her room from the enclosed porch would turn of its own accord. The doctor's in-laws reported the same events when they stayed in the room during a visit.

On a calm day, a cleaning woman heard a door slam from somewhere within the house.

The couple's sixteen-year-old son and his mother saw a brilliant, white light near the room in which Alexander Means is said to have conducted his experiments with the electric light. The light they saw was brighter than any light in the house.

The four younger children all saw a man in their rooms at different times. Late at night, one of the five-year-olds awakened his parents with the question: "Daddy, who's that man in my room playing with my toys?" A couple of nights later, another of their children asked about the "man" in his room.

The doctor and his wife had at first considered the ghost of Orna Villa a colorful addition to the real historical significance of the house. But the accumulating stories from their own family members made them change their minds. By the time the couple had their *own* personal encounters with the supernatural side of Orna Villa they were willing to suspend their disbelief.

The doctor's wife saw a man she described as tall and thin walk past her open bedroom door. It disconcerted her. The children were asleep, her husband in another part of the house.

That same hallway was the setting for the doctor's introduction to the ghost of Tobe/Olin Means—in broad daylight. He saw a lanky man dressed in a long coat with a ruffled shirt and string tie lounging in the hall. For the few seconds it appeared, the doctor clearly made out the man's long, reddish hair and sideburns. Just as quickly as the ghost appeared, it was gone.

As a deeply religious man, the doctor tried to find answers in his faith. He believed that the ghost might actually be a "guardian angel" sent to watch over his family. Once when the rest of his family was away, he went through each room praying that if it was a guardian angel in his home it should keep itself invisible so as not to frighten his wife and children, and that if it wasn't a "protective" entity it should stay out of Orna Villa. Forevermore.

That seemed to work for about seven years, until a 1984 visit by two friends, both Methodist ministers, seemed to prove that the doctor's informal exorcism had worn off.

The men were overnight guests who had been given the bedroom next to the haunted enclosed porch/den. Although they had been asked to be awakened at eight the next morning, the doctor and his wife found the men dressed and sitting at the kitchen table drinking coffee when the couple came downstairs at the appointed hour. The ministers said that at precisely six o'clock, a loud pounding on their door had awakened them. That's when they learned about Tobe . . . or Olin . . . or whoever. . . .

The haunting of Orna Villa may be on the wane. After all, a hundred years *is* a long time for any ghost to hang around. Especially if some owners have tried to get rid of him. But if the ghost needs a new home, Glynora Watterson happily offers her solution.

"Tobe lived there all those years, had a nice roof over his head, and now they're throwing him out," she said. "Well, I'm inviting him here."

Memo: To Tobe Means
From: A Friend

If you find Orna Villa no longer satisfactory, you have an invitation to visit High Point at Chestnut Grove. It's on Wesley Street. You can stay there for as long as you like. And you can bring brother Olin along too. Mrs. Watterson said so.

Pele

If Pele get huhu [angry] with you, you
look out; she cover your land up with
fiery lava, she cover your house up, and
she cover you up, too.

—Hawaiian proverb

The native Hawaiians were certain that it would happen. *Kanakas* came from all
over the islands for the big celebration. At the edge of the great Halemaumau fire
pit, which glowed red with sulphurous fumes, the people were preparing a luau
of roast pig, *poi, okalehau,* and wonderful drinks. They waited in anticipation of
the moment the Kilauea craters on the big island of Hawaii would send towers
of flame and molten lava into the skies over the paradise of the Pacific.

On the other side of the island, Col. Donald S. Bowman, a longtime resident
of Hawaii, heard the rumors of the impending eruption. He set off for the old
Volcano House Hotel near the craters. The rough roads of 1904 made the going
slow and he didn't arrive until late in the evening.

The owner of the Volcano House at that time was a character named "Uncle
George" Lycurgus. His hotel was, and is, the closest accommodation to the Kilauea crater. For fifty years early in this century, Lycurgus presided over the famous hotel and acted as the unofficial historian of Hawaii's explosive volcanic
history.

On this night, Colonel Bowman persuaded Lycurgus to go with him to the
camp the native Hawaiians had established at the edge of the craters. With guide
Alec Lancaster, the men saddled horses and rode nearly four miles over steep trails
to a corral where the Hawaiians had tethered their horses. The final few hundred
yards to the fire pit itself had to be navigated on foot.

Bowman, Lycurgus, and Lancaster found many Hawaiians at the luau, sitting
or standing on the black lava, illuminated only by flickering lantern light, and
feasting on a variety of luscious tropical food. The visitors joined in the meal.

As the full moon finally made its appearance, climbing slowly over the lip of
Kilauea crater, a celebrant cried out in alarm and pointed to the edge of the pit.
A stooped, old woman, her long hair hanging in disheveled, gray strands about
her shoulders, hobbled slowly toward the craters, a twisted coffeewood cane
gripped tightly in one hand, seemingly oblivious to the activity only a few yards
away. At the shout, she turned to look back over her shoulder.

"Come and eat with us, old lady!" a man shouted. He didn't call her by name
for she was a stranger to him. Her dark features spoke of pure Hawaiian ancestry,
her deeply wrinkled face showing many decades of life under the Pacific sun.

"No thank you," she called. "I have work to do."

With those words, she disappeared into the crater. The Hawaiians and the *haole* observers were unbelieving. This old woman seemed to have walked directly into the fiery well of bubbling lava.

In the now brightly moonlit night, the men scrambled to the edge of the pit. She was nowhere to be seen. Had she taken the trail down to the horse corral and only seemed to have slipped into the pit? A dash down the trail brought them to the surprised wrangler at the horse corral. No one, he emphasized, had been on the trail since the arrival of Colonel Bowman and his companions. He would have seen them if they had; the trail was clearly visible in the moonlight.

The joyful luau had become somber at the horrible realization that this mysterious old lady had fallen, or walked, into the Kilauea crater. How could that be? they whispered to each other as they huddled at the edge of the rumbling volcanic crater.

And then the Hawaiian sheriff of Kau came up with the answer.

"It was Pele!" he shouted. "The old woman was Pele!"

As if in answer, a fountain of blazing lava soared a hundred yards into the air. The molten rock fell as sheets of steaming liquid, and out of Kilauea crater rolled the lava, covering the side of Mauna Loa with a "lake of fire." The men ran to their horses, escaping the deadly fumes and scorching lava with only minutes to spare.

Their experiences that night would stay with the men for the rest of their lives—as eyewitnesses to one of nature's most awesome spectacles and their personal encounter with Madame Pele, the legendary guardian goddess of Hawaii.

The story of Madame Pele is part traditional Hawaiian religion, for she is a deity associated with fire, and part ghost story, because believers in her powers have described numerous personal encounters over the decades with a mysterious woman who many believe is the goddess incarnate.

No true Hawaiian will deny that Pele exists. Too many people, like Colonel Bowman and his friends, have seen odd things happen before volcanos erupt or watched as a frail old woman, appearing for all the world to be corporeal, vanishes into thin air. There is a certainty in the life of Hawaiians that much of what happens on their beautiful islands cannot be explained by scientists, philosophers, or anthropologists.

To understand the deep belief Hawaiians have in Pele, it is necessary to walk back in time to the very beginnings of Hawaiian settlement by the ancient peoples of Polynesia.

Archaeologists have found the earliest traces of Polynesians on Oahu, but it is quite possible that other islands actually provided refuge to the first arrivals. With plentiful supplies of food and water on the lush islands, these seafaring settlers set about building villages—and giving proper acknowledgment to their gods.

The gods Kane, Kanaloa, Ku, Lono, and many other Polynesian deities were transplanted to Hawaii. Pele had been the Polynesian goddess associated with fire. She was from a family of gods, one of the seven Hiiake sisters. In most Polynesian settlements Pele played a minor role. Even in the Hawaiian islands, her importance was not that great except on the Big Island. There she achieved immense status and importance.

It is said that after first arriving on the island of Kauai, Pele searched the other islands for a home before discovering the Big Island, Hawaii. She dug in the ground until she found the warmth of the fire that burns beneath the earth. That place became her home, the Kilauea crater at Mauna Loa.

Hawaiians see no conflict between their acceptance of Madame Pele and a belief in the God brought centuries later by Christian missionaries. There is a similarity that many point to: salvation comes to those who accept Him and damnation to those who disavow His existence. With Madame Pele, those who meet her with kindness are rewarded by escaping the volcano's wrath, while meanness toward her or doubt about her reality will result in the destruction of all that one cherishes. Like the fire deity she is, Madame Pele disappears into the fiery volcanic pit as an old, decrepit woman only to ascend in flames, phoenixlike, as a young, extravagantly beautiful woman.

Beginning with Colonel Bowman's eyewitness account of Madame Pele's appearance in 1904, so many other stories have been told about her that it is worth wondering whether there is more here than Hawaiian superstition.

One of Pele's favorite gambits is to change her appearance to fit the occasion, as she did in this story from a small village on the Big Island reported many years ago by a *haole* librarian, Maude Jones.

Jones had been standing on a sea wall watching the strangely swirling clouds and turbulent seas when she saw an old man nearby, a stranger in the village.

"What do you think of this weather?" Jones asked.

"Why do you ask?" the stranger replied warily.

"Because this is volcano weather," she answered. "Do you know if anyone has seen Pele lately?"

"Why?" the old man demanded.

"Because this is the kind of weather when Pele is always seen."

"You know then!" The man seemed startled at a *haole*'s knowledge. "Yes, we saw Pele at Waipio."

"But Pele doesn't go to Waipio anymore!" the young librarian said in surprise.

"She hasn't for a long time." The old man nodded. "This time the lava will come down on that side of the mountain." With that he turned and walked away.

Cries of "Volcano is erupting! Volcano is erupting!" awoke the slumbering villagers in the predawn hours of the next day. A sharp earth tremor rattled their homes. Sure enough, lava flowed down the north slope of Mauna Loa, near Waipio, just as the old man had predicted. Maude Jones didn't know the man's name, if he even had one. He was never seen again. It was presumed that Pele changed gender for the occasion.

Gilacio Pascual was a truck driver for Anthony's Trucking Service, in Kapaa, in December 1945. His life was a simple, orderly one until the day he picked up a hitchhiker.

Pascual was on his way to Kapaa from Hanalei when he saw a young girl thumbing a ride near Koolau store. She was neatly dressed in a somber, black dress with white trim. She said she wanted to be let off at the Moloaa baseball park. As the truck rolled down the highway, they chatted, but she seemed extremely shy. Though Pascual told her his name and where he was from, she refused to reveal her identity. "The next time I see you, I'll tell you my name," she said demurely.

At a sharp highway turn near the ballpark, Pascual had to lean out his window to maneuver his rig around the bend. As he straightened his wheels, he glanced toward the passenger seat ready to resume his chat. The girl was gone, the door still locked. It seemed impossible, but somehow the girl must have jumped from the truck. He was worried about her welfare and stopped at Moloaa baseball park assuming that she would eventually arrive there. She never did.

Pascual told many people in Kapaa about his strange experience. They all nodded and gave the same reply: "It was Madame Pele."

Russ and Peg Apple coauthored the series "Tales of Old Hawaii" in the *Honolulu Star Bulletin*. In one installment, the couple shared a story of how Madame Pele reassured a young mother that an impending Kilauea eruption should not be feared.

The woman, her husband and children had a vacation home at Twenty-Nine Mile, a small community that got its name from the mileage between it and Hilo. Some in the community were retired persons, while others commuted to their jobs elsewhere on the Big Island. A few, like the young couple of the story, lived there only part of the year because of the village's refreshing climate in the cool rain forest four thousand feet above sea level. But there was fear in this Shangri-la, for the community experienced the earthquakes and eruptions common near the summit crater of Kilauea volcano.

Early one morning, as stars still filled the lightening sky, the mother awoke with a start. Her husband was working elsewhere on the Big Island. Her daughter stirred in the bed next to her, looked groggily at the clock on a bedside table, and then watched as her mother made her way to the window. A red glow covered the horizon as it seemed Kilauea was exploding. The fern forest appeared to be on fire.

She quickly made her way down the stairwell, a crimson-hued glow illuminating the house interior. Each window framed the shimmering rays given off by the approaching firestorm.

As she opened the door to her front porch, the red glow snapped off just as if a switch had been snapped off. The house was plunged once again into darkness. On the porch, the woman saw above her a clear sky. A gentle breeze stirred the verdant greenery in the distance.

It was then that she realized Madame Pele was responsible for this curious event. It was her way of warning the young mother that an eruption was soon to occur, and that it would not harm her family.

Two weeks later, on July 10, 1961, lava began filling the fire pit at Kilauea's summit. Scientists say more than seven million cubic yards of new lava was produced over a period of seven days.

The young family remained safe and enjoyed the spectacle—almost as much as Madame Pele.

When Pele get *huhu*—angry—with you, you'd better watch out. That's what the cast and crew of the television series "Hawaii Five-O" are said to have found out in 1974.

The popular police series had traveled to the Big Island to film an episode in Hilo and also near the Kilauea craters. While near the summit, crew members picked *lehua* blossoms and took away pieces of lava from a recent flow. Madame Pele considers it a sacrilege to take *lehua* and an affront to her beloved volcano to steal lava rocks.

Hilo was immediately hit with rain showers after three weeks of beautiful filming weather—clear skies and moderate temperatures. Even Waimea, a usually dry if not drought-stricken region, was rainy when the TV crew tried to film there.

Those who know say it is no coincidence that the rains came after the crew members showed such disregard for the sacred possessions of the fire goddess.

Al Pelayo, a more recent host/manager of Volcano House, the only hotel within Hawaii Volcanoes National Park, was another who also developed a fascination with the lore of Pele and the spectacular beauty of the craters of Kilauea. He would sit by the hotel's fireplace for hours on end, enchanting listeners with his knowledge of Pele's mysterious ways.

For instance, Pelayo carried on a tradition established by "Uncle George" Lycurgus of making an offering of alcohol to Pele. Pelayo maintained the schedule Lycurgus established of placing bottles of gin in Halemaumau Firepit, Pele's traditional home, on Christmas, New Year's, and Mother's Day. No one seems to know just why gin is Pele's drink of choice.

When he made the offering, Pelayo often took along chunks of lava sent back to him by tourists. Quite often the sender would include a note to the effect that they'd been plagued with bad luck and discovered that anyone who takes lava from the firepit faces misfortune.

To this day, park rangers regularly find lava "souvenirs" in the morning mail, being returned by visitors who want to take no chances.

In 1991, a news article quoted a typical letter sent to rangers at Hawaii Volcanoes National Park:

"Dear Madame Pele: Enclosed please find some lava that my husband and I took home as a souvenir in 1973 from a lava flow that closed the black sand beaches. We didn't realize that it was taboo to keep lava, and that it would make you angry. We certainly have had more than our share of bad luck, and we are terribly sorry to have angered you. Please accept these back, with our most humble apologies, and please release the curse."

The last words were in boldface, underlined with red.

Al Pelayo himself gave credence to the belief that regular sacrifices to Madame Pele brought good luck. He noted that soon after he started the sacrifices of gin, volcanic activity began after a long dormancy. It caused little damage . . . and it actually proved to be very good for the tourist business at the Volcano House.

A personal experience also made Pelayo wary of offending Madame Pele. For his first seven months at Volcano House, Pelayo lived in a small cabin. On many nights he was roused from a sound sleep when his outside door was pushed open. He initially suspected prowlers and slept with a shotgun at his side, but no one was ever apprehended. After several weeks, Pelayo took to calling out "Welcome!" whenever his door opened. It was Madame Pele, he thought, coming to check up on him.

Volcanologists had a more mundane explanation: the cabin was located on ground that "swelled" or rolled with the underground lava movement, causing the door to occasionally swing open.

Al Pelayo liked his theory better.

A series of unusual events near Hilo before the 1955 Kilauea eruption provided evidence that Madame Pele sometimes takes a form other than human.

Pedro Monzano was at the helm of his Hilo taxicab when it blew a tire on Saddle Road. As he knelt beside the flat tire, a large tire wrench floated up from his open trunk and dropped at his feet. He said it was like someone had picked it up to try to help him. Monzano got the tire changed in record time and roared off. Madame Pele was his unseen assistant, he believed, since Kilauea sent lava streams shooting from its craters a few days later.

"Spook lights," mysteriously illuminated orbs that have been reported in dozens of sites around the United States, also were seen on Saddle Road before the 1955 eruption. In Hawaii, these lights are attributed to Madame Pele's power.

Henry Macomber and his family were cruising down the road on January 31, 1955, when their truck shuddered as if it had been hit with strong wind gusts—except there was only a slight breeze at the time. A little later, they saw strangely shimmering lights near the highway. Several government officials traveling along the same section of highway some days later reported that they, too, had seen lights dancing along the road.

Geologists investigating earthquake and volcanic activity say these lights might be produced by vaporous gases escaping through fissures in the earth. It is not uncommon for strange lights to be seen in regions known to have earthquake fault lines or to be the site of slumbering volcanoes. But in the islands, people prefer to think it's the work of Madame Pele.

On the morning of March 26, 1926, fishermen on the wharf at Ho'opuloa were preparing their boats for a day at sea. Among them was a wealthy man named Ka'anana. He owned a large home in the village, several small shacks at the water's edge, and a vacation cottage on the south slope of Mauna Loa.

As he bent over his fishing equipment, an old woman whom he had never seen before hobbled up to him and asked if she might be given a particular kind of exotic fish. When Ka'anana insisted that he hadn't caught that fish for a long time, she said his luck would change this day and he should save some of his catch for her.

Ka'anana sailed away to his favorite fishing grounds and forgot about the woman. He had a particularly good day, including some of the fish the old woman had requested, and returned to the dock by mid-afternoon. A fish broker met him on the wharf and purchased his entire catch. However, as he was leaving the wharf, Ka'anana was accosted by the old woman. She asked for her share of the fish, but he said they had all been sold to the fish broker. Tomorrow, he said, there will be more. The old woman glared at him and replied that no fishing would take place the next day. With that she stalked off.

Now at about the same time that Ka'anana was out on his fishing boat, the woman who lived next door to his fine home in the village was preparing food to be cooked for supper. There was a knock at her front door. On the doorstep was the same old woman. What was the young mother doing, the grandmotherly woman wanted to know. Preparing dinner for my husband, my son . . . and Madame Pele, the homemaker said. Just why she added the name of Pele she was never able to say. Without uttering a word in reply, the elderly woman smiled and walked away.

Late on the night of March 26, Mauna Loa erupted with a slow flow of *a'a'*, or slag. Everyone in the region saw the red glow on the top of the mountain, including Ka'anana. At once Ka'anana thought of the old woman and of how he had neglected to save any fish for her. It must have been Madame Pele, he realized to his horror, and now she was showing her anger at his selfish ways.

Ka'anana discovered that the lava was flowing in two directions, one toward Ho'opuloa and the other in the direction of his mountain house. He knew from tradition that a sacrifice might appease Madame Pele. He quickly butchered his prize pig, roasted it in the traditional luau manner and took it to the south slope of Mauna Loa, as close to the lava flow as he dared approach. He placed the roasted pig directly in the path of the lava. Madame Pele was not appeased; the lava swiftly covered the pig and then destroyed Ka'anana's mountain retreat.

The second stream of slag was approaching Ho'opuloa. Ka'anana gathered together all the money he could find, about twelve dollars, and placed it on the fence behind his house and prayed that Madame Pele would accept this offering and spare his property. According to legend, the flow paused briefly at only one place in Ho'opuloa—directly at the fence behind Ka'anana's house—and then it thundered on, destroying his house, his fishing shacks, and his boat. Many buildings in the village were also smothered. The steaming slag flowed into the sea, creating a peninsula of lava. All the fish in the lagoon were killed. It was many years before fish returned to the area. Ka'anana lost his property and his livelihood.

The house next to Ka'anana's where the kind young woman said Madame Pele would find a place setting at her dinner table was spared.

Another story about fishermen and Madame Pele has the same unfortunate ending as befell Ka'anana. At Paaica on the island of Hawaii's Kona coast there was a pond three miles long that was abundant with fish. Several fishermen were hauling in large catches one day when a bent, old woman appeared asking for a few fish. They turned her away. Later that night, lava flowed from the 2,500-foot volcanic peak known as Hualalai. The fishermen knew then their visitor had been Madame Pele and her retribution would be awful. Indeed it was. The hot lava flow slid into the cool waters of the pond at Paaica and with a loud hiss all the water evaporated in great clouds of steam, never to return.

Also in the Hualalai region lived two families in a village on the western slope of that *puu*, perhaps Kalaoa. They lived at opposite ends of the same house. Each family had a daughter and the girls were the best of friends.

One day the girls were roasting breadfruit when Madame Pele, disguised again as an old woman, came by begging for food. One girl took pity and gave her part of her family's breadfruit. Her friend refused. Madame Pele smiled at the benevolent girl and told her to mark her family's door that night.

When they heard the story, the good girl's parents realized the goddess was abroad in the land and hung a tapa leaf on their door, the sign preferred by Madame Pele. In the wee hours of the following morning, while the village slumbered, a slender, meandering lava flow started down Hualalai. It became wider as it reached the girls' village. With little warning, the flow destroyed the section of the house the mean girl lived in, but it caused no harm to the home of the munificent child and her parents.

Some sacrifices have worked in appeasing Madame Pele's fiery appetite, as was once discovered by Princess Ruth, a sister of the great Hawaiian king Kamehameha (c. 1758–1819).

Hilo was threatened by a lava flow when Princess Ruth and eight of her suitors ventured to the erupting crater. With great ceremony, she plucked a chicken and threw it directly into the lava flow. Miraculously, Hilo was left undamaged when the lava flow veered around the beautiful town.

* * *

The historic Kapoho lighthouse on the eastern coast of the Big Island near Pahoa was saved from destruction in 1960 because, residents there say, they prayed frantically to Madame Pele for salvation from the searing lava streams.

And though the lighthouse was directly in the path of the lava, the lava divided for some reason shortly before it reached the lighthouse and poured into the sea. Nearly every other structure in the region was buried.

Does Madame Pele frequent one of Honolulu's most luxurious hotels?

Or was there something more sinister behind the appearance of a beautiful woman in a red dress at the Hilton Hawaiian Village, on Kalia Road?

The *Honolulu Daily Advertiser* reported in April 1959 that just such a woman requested help in finding a certain room number in Hawaii's largest resort complex. Whoever this "woman" was, she vanished while walking beside a hotel employee.

However, another story circulating at the time said the woman had been the victim of a hushed-up murder in the hotel some time before. It was her ghost the employees saw. There was even the rumor of the killing happening in a "secret room." No solid evidence so far unearthed supports this theory.

It *would* be just like Madame Pele to show up far from her native lava flows, looking for small kindnesses in the most opulent of surroundings.

There is little to be gained from cursing Madame Pele when her lava destroys your property. Wise Hawaiians accept such outbursts as part of the nature of things. Sadie Konanui Brown was just such a person.

In December 1986, lava poured over most of the fifty-two acres at Kapa'ahu that belonged to Mrs. Brown's family. To her it was not a malevolent act by Madame Pele, but the continuation of a relationship her family has had with the fire goddess since the late 1950s.

Sadie Brown sighted Madame Pele when Kapoho erupted and sent flows to the Puna's coast, according to an interview with Mrs. Brown in the *Honolulu Advertiser.*

"I actually saw her, in Kapoho. Her whole face, her very long hair. Her face and her neck and upper body, and her hands, but not her fingers. She was in the smoke," she said. "She's beautiful, with very long hair. Her face is really pretty, a pretty woman."

Mrs. Brown saw the figure for only a few fleeting seconds before it evaporated. The impression it made on her mind was still clear twenty-five years later.

The 1986 lava flow wiped out virtually all vegetation on her land and knocked down an old shed. The house in which she was raised was destroyed by fire years before, but other houses on the Kalapana Highway were swept away by the molten lava.

Mrs. Brown was angry with herself, however, when she surveyed the damage the flow had caused. Perhaps if she had brought a sacrifice Madame Pele would not have been so angry. They could have communicated.

"Too bad I didn't bring her gin," she said. "I forgot the gin. I should have brought it."

If there was a next time, Sadie Konanui Brown would remember. But on this day, Madame Pele quickly finished her work.

*   *   *

A very special relationship with Madame Pele was developed over three decades by Leatrice Ballesteros, a well-known *Kahuna* in Waipahu, on the island of Oahu. It all began with her infant son and continued through many personal encounters with Pele and miracles Mrs. Ballesteros attributed to the lady in red.

Mrs. Ballesteros told writer Alice Gilmore that Clifford Ballesteros was just six months old when his unusual behavior caused wise Hawaiian women to conclude that he was in touch with Pele. The young boy was the only one of Mrs. Ballesteros's six sons and one daughter to show these tendencies.

As he grew older, Clifford delivered messages from Madame Pele. He told his mother what kind of cloth and pattern should be used in making a *holoku*, or that he must be taken to Kilauea on the Big Island to pray to the fire goddess. The eruption of a volcano caused him to break out in a rash. And even though there were usually nine people crowded around the dining room table at the Ballesteros home, a special plate was always set for Madame Pele. In time, the young boy said she was with them many evenings while they ate their dinner; he would talk to her and then pass on what she had to say to his mother.

During his twelfth year, Clifford told his mother that he wanted to end his relationship with Pele. He passed on his powers to his mother and she built a long and lasting love and respect for the woman she calls "the lady in red."

Mrs. Ballesteros told Gilmore that Madame Pele was a presence very much with her. Often she saw an old woman and knew instinctively that it was Madame Pele.

The first time was on the Big Island, along a road leading to the volcano. Mrs. Ballesteros was riding in a car when it passed a silver-haired, wrinkled old woman in a white *mu'u mu'u* covered with lavender print flowers. A few yards down the road the car came to an inexplicable stop. Some force seemed to prevent Mrs. Ballesteros and her driver from turning their heads to look back down the road. When they finally did, the old woman was nowhere to be seen. "You can never see her leave. She just disappears," Mrs. Ballesteros said.

On two other occasions, she believed Madame Pele was testing her. Once Mrs. Ballesteros saw Pele as a beautiful young woman in a bright red dress in the lobby of a Waikiki hotel, and at another time the volcano goddess was disguised as an Asian girl who asked her for a match.

But Madame Pele's biggest task, Mrs. Ballesteros said, was in teaching her the old Hawaiian religious ways. Although she was a Christian, and remained so throughout her life, Mrs. Ballesteros saw no conflict between her belief in God and her devotion to the ancient volcano goddess. "I have served God for forty-five years and He has done a lot for me. I serve Him and Pele—He has done miracles," Mrs. Ballesteros said. She considered Pele an apostle of the Christian God.

Madame Pele was a good teacher. For instance, Mrs. Ballesteros learned the ancient Hawaiian chant that she would sing at the edge of the volcanic craters. Sometimes it was *Manu 'O'o*, or *Hale Ma'u Ma'u*. On other days, the Oahu woman might try a version of the more secular "Blue Hawaii" for Madame Pele's pleasure.

With the chant concluded, she followed tradition and threw in a bottle of gin, sake, or whiskey and thanked Madame Pele for receiving her prayers and offerings.

In her tidy Waipahu home, Mrs. Ballesteros began each day by placing a glass of water and the first cup of coffee on a small shrine dedicated to Madame Pele.

Nearby was a Christian altar with statues of the Virgin Mary, the baby Jesus, and St. Francis of Assisi.

The prayers Mrs. Ballesteros offered to Madame Pele at the *Hale Ma'u Ma'u* fire pit were often at the request of friends, relatives, and even strangers who knew of her special devotion to the volcano goddess and wanted her to intercede on their behalf. The petitioner himself might be ill, or someone in his family might need help. Perhaps it was something as simple as returning lava the unlucky person unknowingly stole from Madame Pele's "home."

On one day, it was a mainland woman who wanted relief from her constant pain. Would Mrs. Ballesteros pray to Pele on her behalf? The answer was yes, of course.

A Las Vegas entertainer was ill with cancer when his wife asked her to pray for his recovery. Mrs. Ballesteros said that after her prayers to Pele, the entertainer's doctor found his cancer in remission.

Park rangers eventually reserved a "special place" for Mrs. Ballesteros so near *Hale Ma'u Ma'u* that it was normally off-limits to visitors. Rangers allowed her to approach the fire pit with her prayers and offerings because she was such a recognized *Kahuna*. And, too, maybe they didn't want to take the chance of incurring the wrath of a goddess who could spew fire and lava across federal land.

Mrs. Ballesteros found out many things from Pele—that she is saddened by the despoiling of Hawaii by skyscrapers and freeways, that she would offer comfort to Mrs. Ballesteros in the night when she missed her late husband the most, and that Madame Pele responds most warmly to those people who come to her with love and trust and a "good heart."

In Hawaii, Madame Pele could not have had a better ambassador on earth than Leatrice Ballesteros.

The Bulgarian Monk

Every community has its eccentric character—an oddly dressed or reclusive man or woman, seeking no meaningful friendships, yet amiable enough when spoken to.

In Bayhorse, Idaho, the recluse was known by all as the "Bulgarian Monk of the Church of Jerusalem." Some said the monk had no ecclesiastical credentials because he never saved anyone from sin. But that scarcely mattered. He did *look* somewhat churchly, a young man, tall and lean with a long, black cloak flapping about his ankles and a red fez perched atop his head. He claimed to speak thirty-two languages and said he'd been a guide for Mark Twain in the Holy Land. All quite credible in nineteenth-century Idaho.

Two weary horses and a scrawny dog accompanied the monk as he wandered from one mining camp to another along the Salmon River. He never caused any trouble and if his strange appearance brought a comment from a newcomer to the area, the old-timers would say, "Oh, he's a harmless coot. Just part of the scenery." And they always said it with respect, for they both admired and sometimes feared this "missionary man" who lived among them. What proselytizing he did came in tolerable doses.

Rumor had it that the monk had a tiny cabin somewhere in the woods and that he was hospitable enough to the few lost travelers who stumbled to his door. He always left provisions for the taking.

The monk fished and hunted, his scarlet cap warning other hunters of his presence in the wilderness. Although generally he was uneasy with adults, children loved him. They came running from all directions when he stopped by the village store for supplies. It was as if they knew he was coming before they ever saw him. The smaller children thought he was so tall because he probably walked on stilts. At other times he would sprint down the road chasing after the children, the sides of his cloak flapping like giant wings, gales of laughter greeting startled passersby. Of course, he never caught them, for that would spoil the game. He would always fall flat on his face and cry and beat the ground, as if in great suffering.

In the harsh winter of 1890, shortly before Idaho became a state, the Bulgarian Monk vanished. A blizzard blew for endless days, the temperature dropped, and ice-crusted snow made it dangerous for search parties looking for stranded prospectors and families. Avalanches killed many miners, and trains between Shoshone and Ketchum were snowbound for days. Livestock and wild game starved.

And when the storm abated, people started reappearing, searching for family and friends. The old mining town of Galena had been hardest hit, but many had escaped in time.

And where was the monk? Some said he was in Bellevue, Idaho. He wasn't. Another said he'd seen him in Shoshone. He wasn't there either. Children sobbed, fearing their friend had died in an avalanche.

In fact, the Monk had been at Galena when the storm struck and he stayed on, camping on Titus Creek. But when the storm grew, he knew he'd have to get over Galena Summit to the safety of the mining camps on the Salmon River. He made snowshoes for his horses and for himself and, carrying the little dog through waist-high drifts, reached safety. He said in all the thirty-two languages he knew that he had "never traveled faster than 100 miles per hour."

In February 1891, the rains came. Roofs weakened by the weight of snow now collapsed under tons of water. Legend has it that in one section of Hailey Hot Springs people burned a whole block of shanties just trying to keep warm.

Meanwhile, a few miles outside Bayhorse, the Bulgarian Monk set about repairing his remarkably undamaged cabin. Some slabs of siding were gone and the roof had sprung a few leaks. He left for Bayhorse and the supplies he would need. At the village limits, he heard the running and the laughing of youngsters, and his heart quickened. He'd give them a good race this time. But, as he leaped over a boulder, he lost his balance and fell into the rain-swollen river. Pieces of his robe were found later tangled in some brush near the riverbank. The children wept and their parents mourned their lost apostle.

Yet two weeks later a visitor arrived in Bayhorse and was shocked by reports of the Monk's death. On the day of the supposed drowning, the stranger said, the monk was twenty-five miles away, playing with the children at Yankee Fork, Idaho.

Could the monk have been in two places at once? Not likely. But soon riders traveling the areas of Bayhorse, Bonanza, and Yankee Fork told of seeing a black-robed figure pacing the riverbanks. He held a lantern high in his hand, but always vanished at the approach of a rider.

Was it the Bulgarian Monk searching for his mortal remains, or maybe looking for new penitents? The questions still provide plenty of speculation around campfires in the Sawtooth National Forest.

Mr. Bookbinder and the Haunted Elm

The old man didn't know where he was going. He would never know. But he heard the rumbling of the wagon wheels beneath him and the voice of the kindly young driver who sat beside him on the seat. The horses stopped in front of a large gray building and the young man helped his passenger down.

Inside the building a uniformed guard, seated at a desk, glanced up. "What is your name, sir?"

The driver placed an arm gently around the old man's stooped shoulders, and said, "He doesn't speak. No one at the poorhouse ever learned his name. The only thing we know is that once he worked as a bookbinder. He has no relatives."

And that is how A. Bookbinder was admitted to the former Peoria State Hospital in Bartonville, where he would die in 1910. He was a mysterious and tragic figure, but perhaps no more so than many of the inmates of this new asylum for the insane.

The governor had appointed Dr. George Zeller as superintendent and his choice was a wise one. No longer were the mentally disturbed subjected to ice-water enemas, wrapped in rubber sheets, and kept in chains. Dr. Zeller recognized the dignity of each patient and insisted upon humane treatment by his staff.

The problems of the living were great, but the problems of the dying threatened to become overwhelming. Like Mr. Bookbinder, many of the two-thousand inmates were elderly and indigent, with no relatives to assume the responsibilities of burial. The hospital desperately needed its own cemetery and Dr. Zeller ordered a plot of ground set aside for that purpose. The graves would bear numbers, not names. Funeral services were simple, yet dignified, and often attended by persons from the community who had no personal attachment to the deceased.

Six strong men, supervised by a male attendant, dug the graves and then filled them in after the caskets had been lowered. Between burials the gravediggers kept busy placing markers, and weeding around the graves. Bookbinder watched the men for hours from the window of his tiny room, which gave a view of the cemetery. At night he dreamed that he was with them, setting the markers just right and clipping the soft green grass. Dr. Zeller himself noted the old man's interest and desire to work outdoors and assigned him to the gravediggers' crew.

At first the supervisor was hesitant to accept such an old man, but he would soon learn that "Old Book," as the inmates affectionately called him, was not as feeble as he appeared. His arms were lean and strong with taut muscles beneath the blue denim shirt, and his hands, blue-veined and gnarled, were equally strong. His agility was remarkable, the more so because he had spent a lifetime working indoors. He wore his visored cap tilted rakishly over one eye and whenever the supervisor asked him to do something, Old Book leaped to his feet, straightened his cap and saluted. Once shown how to do a task, he never forgot.

No one in the asylum ever forgot Old Book's emotional outburst at his first funeral. Ordinarily, when the casket was being lowered, the shovelers stood back, silently awaiting the end of the ceremonies. Then after the mourners had left they would complete the interment. But at the critical moment, Old Book removed his cap, wiped his eyes, and finally burst into loud weeping that startled everyone. He didn't even know the name of the deceased.

Old Book was possessed of a mania that robbed him of his reason and he found solace for his great sadness in tears. He wept long and copiously during each funeral, and many times tears stood in the eyes of the mourners.

Old Book developed an unwavering routine in his mourning. Standing with spade in hand, he would raise his left arm, then his right, to wipe away a tear. As the casket was lowered, he would walk over to the spreading elm tree that sheltered many of the graves. He embraced the ancient tree, burying his face in its rough bark while sobbing convulsed his body.

When Old Book finally became too feeble to work in the cemetery, his nurse kept him apprised of every funeral and usually accompanied him to the services. It was his only interest and his only exercise. No matter how severe the weather, Old Book assumed his place among the mourners. At the given moment, he would shuffle off to his elm tree.

And then it was his turn. Old Book died in his sleep. The news spread quickly and, because everyone had loved the strange old man, Dr. Zeller decided that all of the patients and the staff should attend the funeral. At high noon on a beautiful June day in 1910, patients, accompanied by their nurses, gathered at the grave site. Other nurses lined the hillside, looking like a great bank of lilies in their starched white uniforms. Townspeople came, too, some of them weeping unabashedly even before the service began.

The coffin rested upon two cross-beams over the grave with four men standing by to work the ropes by which it would be lowered. A small choir sang the traditional "Rock of Ages." During the last stanza, the men grasped the ropes and leaned forward to raise the coffin so that the supports could be removed and the coffin lowered into the grave.

At that moment the coffin bounded into the air, throwing the men to the ground. Mourners screamed and ran in all directions, some rushing to the grave for a closer look, others rushing out of the cemetery. A contingent of nurses panicked and ran inside the building. For some it would be the last funeral they ever attended.

Dr. Zeller, who was officiating at the service, helped the four men to their feet and called for silence. But before the commotion died, a wailing voice came from the direction of the old elm. Every man and woman stood transfixed. There stood Old Book hugging the tree and sobbing. There was no mistaking him, for he wore his old cap at a rakish angle as he'd done in life. The nurses who'd been at his bedside when he died, the undertaker, and the pallbearers all saw the old man clearly, standing in the dappled sunshine. So did the scores of spectators.

Dr. Zeller ordered the coffin lid pried open. The minute the lid was lifted the sobbing by the tree ceased. There lay the old man wrapped in his shroud with his hands crossed upon his breast.

"It was awful, but it was real," the superintendent wrote in *The Institute Quarterly* of 1916. "I saw it, 100 nurses saw it—300 spectators saw and heard it. I am not over credulous. Long residence among the primitive people of our Island possessions has schooled me against the acceptance of many popular beliefs, but this vision I can never dismiss from my mind."

Several weeks after Old Book's funeral the sexton appeared at the superintendent's office. "Doctor, I don't know quite how to say it, but our majestic elm is dying."

Dr. Zeller looked up from the papers before him on his desk.

The sexton's eyes filled. "It started at the top of the tree. The leaves all curled up and died. Then the lower ones went too. I had my men pour hundreds of buckets of water around the roots, but it did no good."

"Better call in a tree expert," suggested the superintendent. "He'll know what to do. It's probably some sort of disease." Experts came and went, but none could diagnose the problem.

By fall the tree was denuded, every leaf littering the ground beneath it and crackling underfoot. The gaunt branches reached skyward, resembling a human being in supplication. The tree struck fear and dread in all who saw it, and many of the inmates feared to approach it.

At last it was decided to cut down the old elm. One of the workmen sharpened his axe and struck the trunk—once. Then he dropped his axe and fled. When he was able to speak he said that as the axe struck the trunk an agonized cry of pain arose from the heart of the tree and it began swaying like a sapling in the wind.

Sometime later Dr. Zeller ordered the burning of the tree. It was a menace in its present condition. Firemen ignited a pile of dry brush at the base of the tree, but as the flames roared upward the men backed away. They said they heard the familiar sobbing. One fireman declared that he saw Old Book emerging from the clouds of smoke. Turning their hoses on the flames, they quickly doused the fire. The graveyard elm still stood.

The Curse of Old Lady Gray

On that final day, Mrs. Andrew Gray stomped into her back pasture, shook a bony fist skyward and shouted, "May this land turn into thorns and thistles and bring ill luck, sickness, and death to its every owner." Then she and her husband vanished from the village that was Peoria in 1847.

Had Mrs. Gray lived in different circumstances, in a different century, she might not have been a shrew. But she hated frontier life and all the hardships it brought. Her vegetable garden was ravaged by rabbits, field mice, chicken hawks, and other critters. Fighting back with broom, hoe, and arsenic, she managed to save only a portion of the produce. Year after year her garden grew and year after year the scavengers ate their fill.

Yet there was a tenderness and a yearning for beauty in the old lady's heart. She loved the wildflowers that grew along the riverbank and the violets that lined the narrow wooden sidewalks of the village. Dandelions were the kiss of the sun upon the earth.

But suddenly, Mrs. Gray's small measure of happiness faded. Her ne'er-do-well brother died, leaving her to raise his wayward teenage son. The boy slept through the summer days in the shade of his aunt's cherry tree and dozed through the winter nights by the warm fireside. He bestirred himself only to shuffle down to the riverbank taverns, returning home each night so drunk that he couldn't recall who he'd been with or what he'd done.

Soon he was in trouble with the law. Mrs. Gray was frightened and had no idea how to handle her nephew or where to get help. Mr. Gray wanted to throw him out of the house, but his wife wouldn't hear of it. Kin take care of kin, she reminded him.

About this time a young attorney named David Davis arrived in Peoria. He was a quiet, unassuming young man whom everyone liked immediately. He wanted the experience of practicing law in a rural area before testing his skills in the wider world. Eventually, he became one of the most noted jurists and politicians in the country, a U.S. senator and Supreme Court justice. But for now, those were distant dreams. Davis rented a little pine shanty on the banks of the Illinois River and tacked up a neatly painted sign:

DAVID DAVIS
ATTORNEY AT LAW

Inside the shack, an upended box served to hold his modest law library, while other boxes served as stools for his clients. By a quirk of fate, Mrs. Grays' drunken nephew was the lawyer's first case. But there was a problem. Neither the young man nor his aunt had cash enough to pay him. It occurred to Davis that a mortgage upon the old woman's lot in the village's original plat would be good security for the fees that he suspected he'd never collect. On November 10, 1847, the Grays made a trust deed to Davis on lot 7, block 27, as security for his fee. When payment was due and the nephew was unable to pay the fee, Davis foreclosed on the mortgage.

Mrs. Gray insisted that she had never signed any papers, but when shown the notary's seal she knew she was beaten. She drove the nephew from her home. Fearing his return, sympathetic villagers offered the Grays assistance in finding a new home; Mrs. Gray slammed the door in their faces. Three days later the nephew's body was found floating in the Illinois River.

Mrs. Gray, now lost in melancholia, screamed her curse into the night air. Its effect would last for seventy-seven years.

After the Grays left the area, ex-Governor Thomas Ford and his wife rented the house, but tragedy would strike. After the Civil War ended in 1865, their two sons were killed. The elder son was murdered in Kansas. His younger brother was presumably murdered while seeking his brother's killer. Legend has it that their parents died of grief.

Meanwhile, lawyer Davis had neither the time nor the interest in keeping up the property. The house was a cheap, flimsy structure and no one wanted to live there. The land was soon overtaken by thorns and thistles, just as the old lady had predicted. Finally, wind and rain and an army of rats rendered the house untenable.

In a short time the ghost of the nephew returned to the house to beg his aunt's forgiveness. No one dared go near the place. Late one night, in the midst of a blizzard, the empty house burned to the ground, and the story circulated that old Mrs. Gray herself was gleefully dancing in the flames.

The villagers, aware of the role Davis had played in driving the elderly couple from their home, turned against him. They took their legal problems elsewhere, and Davis soon moved to Bloomington, Illinois.

Shortly after the Civil War, a wholesale grocer bought the land for taxes due and gave it to Tom Lindsey, one of his father's former slaves. Like most ex-slaves Lindsey had no money and no means of securing a living. But he was a hard worker, able to feed himself by growing crops and by fishing and hunting. He found a shanty in liveable condition and moved it to the exact spot where the Grays' house had stood. Three months later the shanty was struck by lightning and burned.

Someone then told Lindsey about the terrible curse and he packed his few belongings to move on. But he never did. One of the village men offered him a petrified rabbit's foot found in the graveyard. With this lucky charm in his possession, Tom Lindsey built a modest home on the cursed land and lived in it peacefully until his death twenty-five years later. He had buried the rabbit's foot under the stone doorsill and decorated the walls of every room with horseshoes.

After Lindsey's death a banker bought the property and built a large, imposing house befitting a man of his position in the community. He married a beautiful young woman who, in due time, had a child. Less than eighteen months later, mother and baby were dead.

A year after the baby's death the bereaved husband remarried and his new wife bore a child. But a strange phenomenon took hold of the baby. Whenever he was taken near the fire burning on the hearth he would scream until his little face turned purple. His parents finally moved his cradle into a chilly hallway and covered him with only a thin blanket because whenever they tried to keep him suitably warm he cried endlessly. The child became critically ill. After his death, his mother's health broke and she was permanently hospitalized in Minneapolis.

The grief-stricken banker moved out of the house and it was then turned into a boardinghouse. The keeper's daughter drowned in the lake and her son fell from a balloon and was killed.

A group of milliners rented the house, but didn't stay long because of a strange odor. They had the house searched several times, but nothing was ever found to account for the smell.

In 1894 the ground was acquired by the Peoria Public Library and the new building begun in 1895. The old lady's curse seems to have marked each successive librarian.

E. S. Willcox, appointed the first librarian, in 1896, was killed when a streetcar ran over him.

His successor, S. Patterson Prouse, died from a heart attack during a heated argument at a board meeting in the library on December 14, 1921.

Dr. Edwin Wiley, the next librarian elected by the board, died unexpectedly from poisoning on October 20, 1924. He was fifty-two years old.

The curse then seemed to have been fulfilled. Dr. Wiley's successor, Earl Browning, lived to be ninety-four years old, and those who followed him have lived out their normal life spans.

Today, the librarians in the Peoria Public Library rarely speak of the curse of old lady Gray, even those familiar with it. Although some portions of the story are in dispute, it has passed into the folklore of the city, to be recalled each Halloween.

Tippecanoe and Tecumseh, Too

William Henry Harrison, the ninth president of the United States, and the great Shawnee chief Tecumseh were of two different worlds. Yet their lives were intertwined. Each was a great leader of his people, each was a bitter enemy of the other, each would die an untimely death—and each has become the center of strange legends. Ghost soldiers from the army Harrison commanded in the Battle of Tippecanoe still walk the Indiana soil, and the most devastating earthquake in American history occurred shortly after Tecumseh promised to "make the earth tremble" as retribution against faltering Indian allies.

Although he was born of wealthy parents near Richmond, Virginia, William Henry Harrison shunned the comfortable life of a gentleman for the vicissitudes of the military. After dropping out of medical school, Harrison joined the army in 1791, where he served with distinction in the early Indian wars in the wilderness that became Ohio and Indiana. He rose quickly to the rank of lieutenant.

President John Adams appointed him governor of the Indiana Territory in 1800 when he was still commandant of Fort Washington, Ohio. In later years, Harrison would serve as congressman, U.S. senator, ambassador to Colombia, and, of course, for only thirty-one days as the ninth American president. On the rain-chilled day of his inauguration the old soldier contracted pneumonia, and died a month later. He became the first president to die in office.

Harrison is also remembered for the famous political slogan of his 1840 campaign, "Tippecanoe and Tyler too." John Tyler was his running mate, and the man who finished Harrison's abbreviated presidency.

The Tippecanoe phrase came about from Harrison's popular victory over the Shawnee at the 1811 battle on the Tippecanoe River, a few miles northeast of present-day Lafayette, Indiana.

Ironically, Harrison as governor of the Indiana Territory had banned the sale of liquor to the Indians and ordered that they be inoculated against smallpox.

But his largesse did not extend to treating the Native Americans as equals. In 1809, he negotiated a treaty with Shawnee leaders whereby nearly three million acres of forest on the Wabash and White rivers were forfeited to white settlers.

Several Shawnee leaders, however, disagreed vehemently with the new treaty, including the proud chief of the Shawnee, Tecumseh, and his brother, Tenskwa-tawa, also known as the Prophet. Both declared their intentions to regain their ancestral lands.

Early in 1811, Chief Tecumseh set out on a long journey that took him to tribal villages throughout the Middle West and southern United States. To the Sioux and Apache warriors in the West, and the Alabama people along the southern Mississippi River, Tecumseh talked of a war to drive the white settlers back into the sea. He met with only partial success. Although many joined his band of warriors, others doubted Tecumseh's promise of eventual victory over the whites.

One tribe of Alabama people who made their camp on the banks of the Mississippi was especially contemptuous of Tecumseh. "Promises are like the wind. The wind is free. Talk is nothing," their chief told the Shawnee leader.

As the snow of an early winter swirled through the Alabama camp, Tecumseh made a promise to his hosts. When he returned to his people near Detroit, Tecumseh said, "I will stamp the ground, the earth will tremble and shake down all your wigwams. You will remember Tecumseh!" The Alabama Indians shook their heads derisively.

Tecumseh's curse seemed to come true only a few weeks later!

On December 16, 1811, the most violent earthquake in the history of the United States roared through the lower Middle West. The New Madrid Earthquake, named after the epicenter located near that small Missouri town, shook homes—and wigwams—from Cincinnati to Kansas City. The Mississippi River actually reversed its southerly flow, throwing riverboats against the shore.

Forty thousand square miles of undulating earth swallowed farms and villages. The exact number of human casualties is unknown, but estimates range from several hundred to many thousands.

The Alabama Indians said it was Tecumseh's prophecy coming true. "He has stamped his feet at Detroit," the terrified Indians said.

A silly coincidence? Perhaps. But Tecumseh *did* say he would make the earth tremble.

The nations that joined with Tecumseh terrorized white settlers up and down the length of the Wabash River Valley in late 1811. Westward immigration had steadily increased the number of settlers in Indiana and eastern Illinois. The land was being stripped of its virgin wilderness, replaced by farms and pioneer settlements. Tecumseh, his brother the Prophet, Tenskwatawa, and their followers refused to accept the prospect of being driven from their homes to new land in the West.

Thus it was that William Henry Harrison, as governor, took control of the Indiana Territory militia and marched northward from the capital of Vincennes to Terre Haute, where he built a fort to defend the Wabash Valley.

General Harrison left Terre Haute with his troops in the first week of November, 1811, to forcibly remove the remaining native people from the new "federal" land.

As the armed force approached the mouth of the Tippecanoe River, near Americus, Indiana, they were met by a delegation of Shawnee from the village of Tecumseh's brother Tenskwatawa, the Prophet. They wanted to talk. Although he was suspicious, Harrison agreed to meet with them the next day, November 7, 1811.

In a freezing drizzle just before dawn, however, Harrison's troops were swarmed upon by the Shawnee warriors. The soldiers had slept in full battle attire, and kept the Indians at bay until daylight, when the soldiers mounted a counterattack.

In the bloody hand-to-hand combat, sixty soldiers were killed and more than one hundred were wounded. Scores of Shawnee fighters were also killed and wounded. The Prophet's men fled shortly after dawn. Harrison then marched on the Indian encampment and burned it to the ground. The Prophet and most of his followers escaped. Harrison returned to Vincennes a hero.

Tecumseh was in southern Indiana when his brother attacked Harrison's soldiers. He had not approved the foray, and criticized Tenskwatawa for upsetting his careful plans to wrest control of the territory from the Americans.

Tecumseh and most of his followers fled to Canada, where they joined the British in their fight against the United States in the War of 1812. But the Indian wars in the Middle West ceased for all practical purposes when Tecumseh was killed in the Battle of Thames, in Ontario. The British had virtually abandoned their posts in the Middle West by 1813.

The Indian wars may not be over for General Harrison's militia: their ghostly remains still march across western Indiana on the way to a *phantom* Battle of Tippecanoe.

For many decades, a two-story frame house, twelve miles north of Williamsport, in Warren County, has been noted as the scene of peculiar activities. It is on the precise route that General Harrison and his militiamen took on their way to the Battle of Tippecanoe.

On certain nights in early November, the unmistakable cadence of hundreds of marching feet approaches from a southerly direction. With drums rolling and steps reverberating against the empty, cold fall air, the spectral sounds grow louder as they approach the house and then gradually recede as the parade passes to the northeast. There are never any apparitions, only the echoes of a vanished army on the march.

IOWA

Desperado

Each year, on the second weekend of October, the little town of Winterset, southeast of Des Moines, attracts some thirty thousand visitors to Madison County's Covered Bridge Festival. They come from every state to photograph or paint century-old covered bridges, listen to a fiddlers' contest, clap to the country music—to savor the sights and sounds of a vanishing American landscape. The popularity of Robert James Waller's best-seller, *The Bridges of Madison County*, and the subsequent movie with Clint Eastwood and Meryl Streep, has made this idyllic corner of Iowa a national mecca.

Movie star John Wayne's restored birthplace in Winterset is another popular tourist attraction. The small frame house is open year-round and features memorabilia from the actor's childhood and movie days.

The six remaining covered bridges in Madison County, all listed on the National Register of Historic Structures, are unique in that they were built by carpenters and farmers, using none of today's tools—and they were built to last. Even now, at least one of these barn-red wooden spans—the old Holliwell Bridge—bears heavy traffic.

But before there were literary characters like the photographer Robert Kincaid and the lonely farm wife Francesca Johnson there was the one, special covered bridge that captivates everyone, including fictional lovers, who sees it—the Roseman Bridge, five miles west of Pammel State Park. Its fame predates Waller's novel, however, for it has been known for decades as the "haunted bridge."

Folks in the region say the legend began on a moonless night a hundred and more years ago when a convict escaped from the Madison County jail in Winterset. When the alarm was sounded, two posses formed. The men strapped on their pistols and rode after the brigand. The posses agreed to rendezvous at Roseman Bridge. As they approached from either end the lawmen saw the escapee dash onto the bridge.

Hearing the shouts of the hunters and the snorts of their steeds, the desperado knew he was trapped. Or was he?

In a frantic attempt to escape, he climbed the heavy wooden support timbers and broke through a weak spot in the roof. What happened to him next isn't known for certain. He either made his way across the roof and hid in the wooded countryside or tumbled into the Middle River and was swept away. At any rate, the posses never found their man or his remains.

Yet *something* of his presence remains.

Fishermen report hearing laughter coming from the top of the bridge and foot-steps running across the roof on misty summer evenings. The "escape hole" was mended long ago, but visitors still notice the repaired section through which the convict allegedly slipped.

The Roseman Bridge has another legend connected with it to account for its haunted reputation.

A young man is said to have been hanged on the bridge after being accused of theft—falsely as it turned out—by a father who didn't want him marrying his beautiful daughter. The unfortunate suitor's body was left hanging overnight, but mysteriously disappeared the next day.

Some people feel a cold spot in the center of the bridge where the man was hanged, and dogs, with hackles raised, sometimes howl and refuse to go across.

During festival weekends buses with guides make a two-hour tour of all the Madison County bridges, with a stop at two of them. The ghosts of dead high-waymen, thwarted suitors, and fictional lovers are not on the public itinerary.

The Beacon

When darkness blankets the Iowa prairie, the tapestry of fields is stitched together by lights burning in barns and farmhouses. But a half mile south of St. Mary's in Warren County, a different sort of light illuminated the landscape for many years.

Beginning in 1874, a glowing light was seen floating like a globe along the perimeter of a 160-acre tract of the Storz farm. The light was said to be fifteen or twenty inches in diameter, bright red in the center, and shading to orange at the edge. It would flash bright, intermittent "signals," then dim. Although it usually traveled in the same horizontal plane close to the ground, some observers said they saw it shoot straight up into the sky. Several young people tried to catch the light at various times, but none was successful.

For seventy years people tried to explain the light's origin. Realists said it was swamp gas, ball lightning, or reflections from the moon. Others said it was the spirit of a young girl who had died a violent death in the area. Or was it, as some thought, the spirit of a certain Mrs. Wallace who had supposedly burned to death in a house that once stood on the Storz land? Neither story has been adequately documented.

In the 1930s the light was especially active. C. A. McNair, proprietor of the general store and café at St. Mary's, was driving home one night when he glanced out the window of his Model T Ford. Seeing the light hanging in the sky at the south end of the Storz farm, McNair floorboarded the gas pedal. He told friends later, "That old car never traveled so fast!" In the opposite direction from the light, it might be added.

Orval Berning, a local farmer, saw the light a number of times and, on one occasion, wished he hadn't. At one-thirty on a wintry morning, Berning was walking home from a card game with his cronies. As he passed the Storz place, he noticed a light floating along slowly, just inside the fence line. Berning covered the rest of his way home in record time.

In the morning, Berning told everyone who would listen, "That light was no more than twenty-five feet from me. There was no moon and there was no one in the field with a lantern."

Berning also said he'd seen the light many times from a window of his house, which was three-quarters of a mile east of the Storz place. He said it would flit about until one or two o'clock in the morning, going along the ground, then soaring away above the treetops.

Witnesses to the light who talked to news reporters in the 1930s said the fiery orb never left the Storz place, but it apparently did, at least once. Nobel Nixon was riding past the Storz farm of an evening when his horse suddenly bolted. Nixon pulled on the reins and swung around in the saddle. The light was bobbing down the middle of the road after him! It increased its speed . . . and so did Nixon's nag. The farmer sat hunched in the saddle holding on for dear life. He never remembered reaching his home and he never forgot the wild ride. Neither did the horse; it refused to leave the corral for a week.

In the 1940s Bill Brentano was farming the Storz land. He claimed he'd never seen the light, knew no one who had, and was a firm disbeliever. However, by this time tales of the mysterious light had spread far beyond Warren County and, at the conclusion of World War II when gas rationing was lifted, amateur ghost hunters came from near and far to see the spirit light for themselves. Carloads of visitors descended upon Brentano's farm and made his life miserable, trampling his shrubbery, uprooting trees, and stealing his chickens. On several occasions he called the sheriff to disperse the crowds.

Some visitors claimed to have seen the light and didn't know what to make of it. But sixty-year-old Roy Whitehead, of Indianola, Iowa, did. In 1947, he made a startling observation. While standing at the edge of a field watching the light bob and blink along its accustomed route, Whitehead said he'd heard the "cry of a lost earthbound soul" coming from inside the mysterious object.

Today, there is little talk about the mystery light. Either it has ceased its prowling or the people of tiny St. Mary's have been too busy to notice. But in the dark of the moon when autumn winds crack the dry stubble of cornstalks in the fields, a few of the old-timers may sit by their windows, watching and waiting. . . .

KANSAS

Nine Ghosts Nine

Everybody knows that ghosts inhabit antebellum homes of the South, vintage clapboard houses of New England, and an occasional windswept lighthouse on the lonely Oregon coast. But who'd believe specters in the orderly, rational world of a modern army post?

At Fort Leavenworth, the nation's oldest continuously active military post west of the Mississippi, nine ghosts are thought to be permanent residents, with scores more passing through. No one knows for sure why this historic post has drawn so many creatures from the netherworld, but experts say that any place in which a number of traumatic events have occurred will attract spirits.

Here then are some of the fort's favorite legends:

The Woman in the Attic

The woman lives in the garret at 18 Sumner Place and spends much of her time peering out the high, round window, smiling at passersby far below.

Not an unusual activity . . . except this woman isn't real. She first materialized in the 1970s and is said to be Fort Leavenworth's most celebrated ghost.

The occupants at the house on Sumner Place discovered her one night in the kitchen, quietly washing the family's dinner dishes. They didn't know if she came with the house, but they'd never seen her before. She reappeared on many occasions—a matronly figure dressed in a heavy, black woolen skirt. Sometimes the adults felt a presence brush past them on the staircase and their arms would grow cold from the contact.

It soon became apparent that the ghost loved children and resented grandparents and baby-sitters. At least one grandmother said she'd been pushed out of the nursery by unseen hands. And sitters complained that as soon as they'd turned down the children's beds they would suddenly be remade. One small boy, after learning that his parents had canceled their evening plans because the sitter couldn't come, told them, "You go out. The nice lady will take care of me."

Another child said that an old lady read him stories until he fell asleep. In the morning a book was found in the youngster's bedroom. The family said it did not belong to them.

Maj. John Reichley of Fort Leavenworth's Historical Society doesn't believe in ghosts, but he told Allen Seifert, a reporter from the *St. Joseph News-Press/Gazette*, that he visited the house at one time.

"I did see a middle-aged woman in black, and when she appeared it suddenly became very, very cold in that area. There were some strange goings-on in that house which can't be explained," he conceded.

Sometimes items that were put down in one place would reappear in another. Most families who occupied the house regarded these antics as amusing, but the family living there in 1975 was unnerved by the phenomenon, and prevailed upon an army chaplain to perform an exorcism. Twelve laymen accompanied the chaplain. The rite was performed in secrecy; not even the closest neighbors knew of it.

Apparently it was a success because the specter in black was never seen again in *that* house. However, strange incidents soon began occurring next door at 20 Sumner Place. On one occasion three persons watched the attic doorknob turn ever so slowly. After they learned about the lady in black they knew that she'd moved into their house. They never saw her, but they'd hear soft footsteps on the attic floor and an occasional rattle of the doorknob.

Animals were uneasy in the house. Cats sleeping on the landing near the attic door would awaken suddenly and stare at the door. Then, with fur bristling, they'd leap down the stairs as if something were chasing them. Dogs would bark and stand with hackles raised, gazing up the stairway from the main floor. Few would go to the second floor unless accompanied by a family member.

And so far as anyone knows the ghost is still "living" in the attic at 20 Sumner Place and watching the passersby in the street below.

The Phantom in the Fire

In the early 1970s a new family moved into the large home at 605 McClellan. One evening while her husband was out, the wife was entertaining a neighbor. Suddenly, the back door opened and banged shut and heavy footfalls raced up the stairs. Not expecting her husband home so early, she went to the foot of the staircase and called up to him. There was no answer. Fearful that a burglar had gotten inside, she phoned her husband to come home immediately. He did, and after searching the house thoroughly, found nothing that could account for the footsteps his wife and her friend had heard.

On a chilly autumn evening the family sat watching the changing pattern of flames in the fireplace. Suddenly, one of the children pointed at the fire and screamed. The profile of a man wearing a mustache and goatee appeared in the center of the blaze. Horrified, yet transfixed, the family stared into the fire. When it had burned down to coals the phantom's face appeared on the back wall of the fireplace.

A short time later perplexing events began to occur in the house. Loud crashing sounds awakened the family in the middle of the night, and icy blasts chilled them. Feet stomped up and down the staircase nightly. Then, as quickly as the phenomena had begun they vanished, and an eerie stillness descended upon the house.

Weeks later the noises began again and family members shivered as the temperature dropped outdoors. Thumping, banging, and scratching noises were heard throughout the house at all hours of the day and night. Some of the racket seemed to come from the third floor, which the family did not use. To keep their dogs from going up there they had blocked the stairs with a folding baby gate. One night the gate rattled and footsteps scurried up the stairway. The husband got up to check and found the gate in place and no one on the third floor. The dogs were sound asleep. The minute he crawled back into bed the sounds were heard again—and again—keeping the family awake for the rest of the night.

But these manifestations did not last. One week the house became enveloped by a silence that calmed the family. Without speaking of it they knew that they'd finally been liberated from a force they couldn't understand.

No further activity was reported until the 1980s, when a different family occupied the quarters at 605 McClellan. One morning the father got up to shower and shave. As he entered the bathroom he nearly collided with a tall, thin, dark-haired man who stood in front of the mirror with shaving cream on his face and a razor in his hand. The father, still blinking awake, said, "Goodness, son, you're up pretty early." The father went back to bed. He learned later that his teenage son had not been in the bathroom at that time of the morning.

At dawn on another day the daughter of the family was awakened by the presence of the same thin man standing in her bedroom doorway. He wore an army uniform and a cap tilted at such an angle that she could not see his face. Sitting bolt upright with the bedclothes pulled up under her chin, she screamed, "What in heaven's name do you want?"

He paid no attention to her as he crossed the room and walked into a closet. The family learned that this closet had once been a hallway connecting the girl's bedroom to the master bedroom.

Fort Leavenworth appears to be home to an eclectic assortment of other ghosts. Some hold tea parties, one plays a harmonica, soldiers on horseback ride through the old infantry barracks, and Civil War soldiers stride through the nearby woods.

But of them all perhaps Catherine Suttler is the most beloved.

On a cold morning in 1880, her children, Ethan and Mary, went out to collect firewood. They did not return.

A search party found nothing, and that winter Catherine died of pneumonia—and grief. Her bereaved husband returned to his Indiana home, and later learned that his children had been found alive and would be returned to him safe and sound. But Catherine still wanders, searching for her beloved children.

Trick-or-treaters at Halloween are always asked to watch for her. If they see her they are told to call out, "Catherine, your children are safe!"

What's in Albert Taylor Hall?

Theaters are notoriously haunted. The ghosts of countless actors and actresses tread the boards, craving applause they hope will never end.

In Albert Taylor Hall at Emporia State University some say the ghost of Albert Taylor himself steals the footlights, upstaging the actors. But Taylor's legend does not coincide with the known facts. Taylor was a faculty member, and, in 1882, was named president of the school. The assertion that he was also a student there is not true.

The *legend* goes that sometime late in life, after the turn of the century, Taylor took a leading role in a theater production. One evening, fearing he'd be late to go onstage, he dressed in his stage wardrobe at home—a glittering white costume with a cape and a colored neckerchief. He jumped into his flivver, one of the first in the city, and sped toward town. He crashed head-on with another car. Both drivers were killed instantly. At curtain time the ghost of Albert Taylor appeared onstage, wearing the glittering costume . . . stained with blood. The performance was canceled.

Is there any truth to this story? Probably not. In 1983 Deborah Anne Heffley, a student at the university, researched Albert Taylor. She learned that he had resigned from his position at Emporia at the close of the 1900–1901 school year in order to accept the presidency of James Milliken University in Decatur, Illinois. Here he presumably died. Further, Albert Taylor had been a student at Lincoln University in Decatur, and *not* at Emporia.

Then what is it that haunts the theater? The ghost's identity may never be known, but he is probably the liveliest and best-known ghost in Emporia. Legend has it that he wanders throughout the theater, from basement to stage, frightening untold numbers of persons.

From interviews with students, Heffley collected the following accounts:

The basement contains a number of small rooms, dank and dark. One day a woman employee was sent to the basement on an errand. When she had finished, she snapped off the lights and turned to go up the stairs. Something cold brushed against her shoulder.

"It sure is dark in here!" a voice said to her.

She raced up the stairway, vowing never to return to the basement alone.

In 1966, the scene shop foreman had a similar experience. After turning off the basement lights he pulled a cigarette from his pocket. He heard a match strike and a voice said, "Do you need a light?" The foreman dropped his cigarette and ran. Although this incident occurred during a run of *Dracula*, when pranks were common, the fellow didn't think this encounter was a gag.

Many disturbances occur on the catwalk, two levels above the stage. In 1978 an employee was working up there when he screamed. Students, rehearsing below, looked up to see the man leaning over the railing with his shirt pulled out in front of him. As the students rushed to his aid, the invisible force tugging at the man's shirt let go.

During that same year the students were working on an operatic production in which one character dies onstage. During a rehearsal, the "dying" actor lay on the stage floor gazing up at the catwalk. An elderly couple dressed in black were standing up there. The woman wore a veil and had been seen previously in other parts of the theater. No one knows who she is.

The production of *My Fair Lady* in 1981 drew unexplained activity. During the first performance of the musical an actress was applying makeup in a dressing room. Feeling someone watching her, she swung around on her stool. In the doorway stood a man in a black cape. He vanished when several other actresses entered the room. They said they'd passed no one. However, the stranger may have ducked through a small door that provides access to the theater's organ pipes.

But the stranger in the cape was not to be dismissed. During another performance of *My Fair Lady* he stood in the middle of the catwalk watching the play. One character in the play wore a cape, but he was elsewhere at the time.

Perhaps the most frightening incident occurred during a rehearsal of the Lerner and Loewe musical. Since the backstage plumbing is loud and can be heard out front, the cast often uses facilities in an outer hall. There is no light switch in the room because the lights are on a main panel. Two girls went into the restroom with a third girl holding the door open to give light from the hallway. One actress opened a stall door and found a man in a black cape standing on the toilet! She screamed and other women rushed into the room. No one was there.

A custodian working alone in the building one night heard a fourth-floor toilet flush. All the lights were off up there and no one came down.

One of the strangest incidents involved a St. Christopher medal left on top of a pile of street clothes in an upstairs room. Mike, the medal's owner, asked a friend to go get his clothes and the holy medal burned the fellow's fingers! He carried the clothes down, taking care not to touch the medal again. When Mike touched the medal it was cold.

So long as the prankish ghost "lives" in Albert Taylor Hall many more tales will be told. Today's students think the spirit may be that of Franklin L. Gilson, organizer of the "Gilson Players," and the grand old man of theater at Emporia State University. The Players, founded in 1916, performed in fifteen different states and hundreds of small towns throughout Kansas. Dr. Gilson himself took the lead role in many productions, and members of his family held supporting roles in a number of casts.

Legend says that Gilson died onstage while directing a production, but according to the *Emporia Gazette* he died in St. Mary's Hospital in January 1946. He was seventy years old and had been ill with a heart ailment for about two weeks.

The *Gazette* of January 29, 1946, also reported, "Funeral services for Mr. Gilson will be held in Albert Taylor Hall at Emporia State College at 4 o'clock Tuesday afternoon."

For over a generation Franklin Gilson was identified with the campus and particularly with its theater. Is it possible that he has never left?

Virginia's Place

Virginia was hanging by her neck from the chandelier in the ballroom. That's where Walter Stubbs, governor of Kansas, found his maid. He'd been called back to the state house in Topeka on that warm April evening in 1911. Arriving at his home in Lawrence after a tiring thirty-mile drive, he rang the doorbell. Virginia didn't answer. Perhaps she was resting.

No matter. Virginia was a conscientious servant and Governor Stubbs felt fortunate to have her. He unlocked the door with his key. Lights were burning and everything was in order, even the mahogany tables glistened with a fresh coat of polish.

On the way to his bedroom, the governor had to pass Virginia's room. Her door was wide open and the bed made. He called, but got no answer. After searching the first two floors of the house, he mounted the stairs to the third-floor ballroom. There swung the ghastly corpse of the maid, her eyes bulging. Rope burns on her neck glowed purple in the dim light.

Murder? Or suicide? The house showed no signs of having been broken into, and, so far as the governor knew, Virginia had no enemies. The maid's sunny disposition seemed to rule out the taking of her own life.

The tragedy was never resolved. And the legend of Virginia's haunting began.

In 1922 the governor's family sold the house to the Sigma Nu fraternity at the University of Kansas. The men had heard the story of Virginia and believed she was entombed in the massive stone fireplace, above which hangs a cryptic plaque: "The world of strife shut out, the world of love shut in." It has a blank recessed area at the bottom where birth and death dates are usually engraved. Funeral directors have said that such a plaque is rarely used in a home.

The hearth is neither cheerful nor inviting, but a dark and brooding place. Originally used for cooking, it opened into both an entryway and the former dining room. The dining room side of the fireplace was walled up before the Sigma Nus bought the house, and a swinging iron hook that once held pots now swings only into the entry.

For more than sixty years the fraternity brothers have reported strange goings-on in the house—two sets of footsteps running down the stairs, and glimpses of a ghostly form. Stories told by the men from earlier years are remarkably similar to those heard today. Most of the ghostly activity takes place in April, near the anniversary of Virginia's death.

Some of the students, of course, ignore the noises and scoff at the story. The huge old house is just naturally spooky, they contend, with its dark nooks and crannies and its creaking floors and stairways.

But Dave Randall, a former resident of the Sigma Nu house, knows that something not of this world is in that house. He too laughed at the story until a weekend night in April 1978. He and a friend were studying past midnight when suddenly the silence was ruptured by the sounds of two sets of footsteps racing up and down the front and back stairways—up to the former ballroom (since converted to bedrooms), then down to the fireplace, making a circle through the house.

Few men were there that weekend, but Randall and his friend figured that the guys were just having fun running through the house. Annoyed by the disturbance, they waited at the foot of a stairway to catch the culprits. The footsteps stopped directly in front of them.

The pair checked the rooms of the men who were in the house and found them all asleep.

The last bedroom they entered was in the area of the old ballroom where the maid's body had been found. It was vacant. Suddenly, the room door began to rattle. It was not a windy night and the windows were all shut and locked.

Randall told a reporter from the *Lawrence Journal World* that as they left the room and walked down the hall, the bedroom light went out and the noise ceased. Going back to check the light, they heard the door rattling again.

"The closer we got to the door," Randall said, "the more violently it would shake. I have to admit, we were really terrified at that point."

The friend, still thinking it was a joke and that some of the brothers were hiding behind the door, kicked it wide open.

The men returned to their studies, but could not concentrate. Something impelled them to go back up to the old ballroom. This time they opened the door, but did not turn on the light. A vague figure materialized, a misty form moving rhythmically, and clearly visible against the surrounding darkness. The men heard a slight noise, as if tree branches were brushing against a window—except there were no trees nearby.

Randall told the newspaper reporter, "I was overpowered by a sense of extreme dread and terror that seemed to come from the *outside.*"

The men finally went to bed but did not sleep well.

In that same year, while Randall and others were frightened witless by what they thought were supernatural activities, Keith Sevidge took on the story of Virginia as a journalism class project. His extensive research seemed to indicate that the story had no basis in fact. Someone had died in the house in 1911, but Sevidge could not learn the person's identity. Virginia supposedly died in April 1911, but death certificates were not required in Kansas until later in that year. Only relatives of the deceased with an interest in the estate can obtain a copy of the death certificate. Sevidge concluded that Virginia is a legendary figure created by earlier fraternity men to add a measure of notoriety to the old house.

Yet he has some reservations. "One summer," he told the *Journal World* reporter, "when there were only two of us in the house, we would both just get the creeps."

Then there's that mysterious plaque above the fireplace. It casts long shadows. "It's a major heebie-jeebie," Sevidge said, shaking his head.

Beware the Gray Ladies

It is not unusual for female apparitions to be known by the color of their attire. Whether one considers Chicago's infamous Resurrection Mary hitchhiking rides in a shimmering white prom dress, or the grieving, ghostly widow in black stalking her old Mississippi mansion, the distaff side of the spirit world presents the conclusion that attention to fashion need not end with physical death.

The gentle ghosts of Kentucky are no different. Two of the most celebrated Kentucky hauntings are by ladies in gray. Mrs. Margaret Varick is the historic ghost at elegant Liberty Hall, in Frankfort; and a young woman spurned by no less than the Marquis de Lafayette bemoaned her fate even after she died at Covington's oldest residence, Carneal House.

An act of kindness killed Margaret Varick. At the age of sixty-five, Mrs. Varick agreed to undertake an arduous trip from New York State to frontier Kentucky in 1817 to comfort a favorite niece, Mrs. Margaretta Mason Brown, the mistress of Liberty Hall, who, according to some accounts, had lost a child to one of the many diseases so common to pioneer Americans. Mrs. Varick had raised Margaretta after her mother died.

Mrs. Varick's month-long journey by coach and horseback was too much for the old woman. By the time she arrived, the already-frail Mrs. Varick was exhausted. She died of a probable heart attack in an upstairs bedroom of the brick mansion. Some records indicate she was buried in a small family cemetery near the garden. Later, her remains along with those of other family members were removed to the newer Frankfort Cemetery. However, there is some uncertainty about the exact location of her grave.

The solicitous "Aunt Margaret" hasn't left the home she barely knew in life. For generations, this "lady in gray" has haunted Liberty Hall, perhaps to remind the living that she rests in dismal anonymity.

Though Mrs. Varick is the most famous ghost at Liberty Hall, she is not the only one. An opera singer who vanished during an evening stroll in the mansion's gardens even before Mrs. Varick's visit is glimpsed periodically running across the lawn.

* * *

Built in 1796 by Kentucky's first U.S. senator, John Brown, Liberty Hall is an exquisite example of eighteenth-century Georgian architecture. The city of Frankfort was only a decade old (and Kentucky a state for just four years) when Brown completed the house from plans drawn by Thomas Jefferson, in whose law office Brown had studied law. The place was deemed one of the finest homes in all of Kentucky, if not anywhere west of the Allegheny Mountains.

Senator John and Mrs. Margaretta Mason Brown spent lavishly on furnishings. Bricks were fired on-site for the exterior walls, while fine hardwood was dried for over two years before it was used for the flooring, rafters, and framing. Brass door locks, window glass, mirrors, and fine furniture were transported by flatboat and horseback from the East. Among the matchless items acquired by the Browns were Parisian furnishings brought back to the United States by the senator's brother, James Brown, the ambassador to France during President James Monroe's term in office. (Another member of this august family was Dr. Sam Brown, who introduced vaccinations to this country.)

Mrs. Brown in particular was most anxious to soften the austere life she found on the frontier. She ordered fine silk fabrics, a grandfather clock, and other touches of the refined life she had left behind in eastern society. Her father, Rev. John Mason, had been George Washington's chaplain at West Point.

Over the ensuing years, the Browns entertained the elite of early American society. During the year of 1819 alone, Liberty Hall played host to a sitting president and two future chief executives—President James Monroe, Col. Zachary Taylor, and Col. Andrew Jackson. General Lafayette stopped by, as did Aaron Burr and, in later years, William Henry Harrison and Theodore Roosevelt.

The home remained in the Brown family until 1956, when the Colonial Dames of America assumed its administration as a living museum of Kentucky history. The Dames restore and preserve historic American homes. The last private owners of Liberty Hall were Mary Mason Scott and her brother John M. Scott. When the Scotts announced in 1922 their plans to donate their home to the Dames upon their death, one newspaper termed the mansion a "genuine treasure," while another asserted that it contained "more genuine antiques and actual heirlooms than probably any other home in Kentucky."

Tales of the Gray Lady of Liberty Hall began circulating in about 1820, just a few years after Mrs. Varick died. She is the "inside" ghost, nearly always described as a small, neatly groomed woman in a gray housedress, quite intent on performing some sort of useful household chore. She is not at all upsetting or frightening to those she encounters. Indeed, she is a calming presence, a munificent, albeit indiscernible, "auntie" trying to help out around the house. It's only when she's up at night opening and slamming doors that her solicitous behavior is not so appreciated.

The first person to see the Gray Lady was the young bride of Benjamin Gratz Brown, the grandson of Sen. John Brown. She had been assigned the room in which Mrs. Varick had died. On this occasion, the ghost simply walked silently across the floor, much to the bride's astonishment.

Benjamin Gratz Brown's sister, Margaretta Brown, saw the ghost, as did one Rebecca Averill of Frankfort. Rebecca was a guest in the home and claimed Mrs. Varick showed up standing next to the fireplace in her bedroom. Not a word was exchanged between the two, nor did Mrs. Varick make any movement. Rebecca quickly pulled the sheet over her head and prayed that Mrs. Varick would soon be on her way. When next the young woman peered from beneath the covers the chamber was quite devoid of otherworldly intruders.

There isn't a room in the house in which someone hasn't reported Mrs. Varick's sudden arrival, but that one upstairs bedroom and the staircase are her favorite haunts.

Mary Mason Scott, a niece of Benjamin Gratz Brown, saw her ancestor on several occasions. The two women were said to have physically resembled one another. According to one account, Miss Scott was unaware of Mrs. Varick's ghost until her return home from college. She was given Mrs. Varick's old bedroom. On her first night back, Miss Scott awoke to the matronly ghost standing next to the bed.

A story from the 1920s, when Miss Scott still lived in the house, claimed that Mrs. Varick was using Miss Scott as a "medium" to try and convey the location of her unmarked grave.

Contemporary stories of the Gray Lady emphasize the nonthreatening aspect of this particular sprite, although the unexpected nature of any haunting can be quite upsetting for the accidental witness.

That was the case with a Colonial Dames employee who portrayed "The Gray Lady" at Halloween during the early 1980s. In period dress, she walked back and forth in front of a Liberty Hall window holding a candle in her hand.

She never actually *saw* the "real" Gray Lady, but she didn't have to in order to believe the stories that she had heard. The woman had lived for a time in a small apartment above Liberty Hall's kitchen. Late one evening she left the bathroom door open as she was taking a bath. She told *Louisville Times* reporter Laurice Niemtus what happened next: "I was just thinking 'I wish I'd closed that door' when I decided to wash my hair quickly and hurry up and finish my bath. While I was washing my hair, the door closed by itself. And it's a big, heavy door; it didn't normally open or close by itself."

A library door sometimes opened and closed when the woman lived there. Once a music box that she'd owned for decades (and that hadn't been played for about that long) began to play—with the lid closed and without being wound! She'd been thinking wistfully about the boyfriend who had given it to her many years before.

Accounts of the Liberty Hall haunting were kept by the Brown family and later by the Colonial Dames. They document incidents both casual and confounding:

- Overnight guests sometimes awoke to find themselves being tucked in by a smiling woman; in the morning they may have found blankets folded or some mending finished.
- A former curator discovered three gold bracelets on a nightstand in the upstairs "ghost" bedroom. They weren't listed in the house inventory, but a jeweler said they were probably created about the time Mrs. Varick visited her niece. No one admitted knowing how the bracelets got on the table.
- Mrs. Varick is sometimes noticed standing at an upstairs window by passersby. A college professor who wanted to see if moonlight caused those appearances stayed in the house for six weeks, during an entire moon phase. He found the moonlight did not cause any unusual reflections in the windowpane. But on one

of his last nights in Liberty Hall, the man was startled awake by a touch. Standing beside him was the faintly smiling Gray Lady.

• The same curator who discovered the gold bracelets claimed to have taken a photograph of the ghost. During the home's restoration, she took pictures of the various stages of reconstruction. In one photograph is the faint image of a woman coming down the staircase . . . even though there had been no one on the stairs at the time the curator snapped the picture.

Some of the strongest evidence for a haunting at Liberty Hall came when two men stayed there for several nights following a 1965 fire.

The mansion would have been destroyed if the fire had not been quickly reported and extinguished. As it was, a hallway was gutted and several pieces of irreplaceable furniture were burned.

A Frankfort fireman, Butch Barber, and Bob Watson, an employee of the local newspaper, volunteered to stay in the house at night to guard against vandalism. They told their story to newspaperman Sy Ramsey.

"Since there was no electricity we decided to put candles in the rooms and on the stairs," Watson said. The men roamed through the house on the first night. They ended at the attic door, which is flush with the floor and must be pulled up to go into the attic. The men went inside the attic, but as they looked around "someone or something slammed the (attic) door."

The pair clawed at the door, got it open, and ran all the way downstairs.

Later that night, "we found the (attic) door open again. We had closed it behind us the last time."

Problems with that door reoccurred on their second and third nights in the house. The men would close it—and find it open a few hours later. That third, and final, night also brought strange cries, moans, and groans, Watson recalled, and a new rash of incidents in which candles would suddenly be sniffed out.

"You bet your sweet life I was convinced," Watson told newsman Ramsey. "I don't know the answers, and none of us are scaredy-cats. But there's something weird going on in that house."

Is there also something "weird" going on *outside* Liberty Hall?

A second, less well-known, legend surrounding Liberty Hall is that of a beautiful Spanish opera star who ostensibly vanished while visiting the estate in 1805. No one is certain what the woman's name might have been, but the young soprano had been asked to present a concert in Frankfort. John and Margaretta Brown invited her to stay with them during her visit, and even threw a gala party after the concert.

During the party in her honor, the señorita slipped outside for a walk across the spacious grounds. Even though the night was especially humid, she seemed glad for the opportunity to have a few moments to herself. At least that's what those who caught a glimpse—a final glimpse as it turned out—of the ill-fated star thought at the time.

Liberty Hall's gardens swept down to the Kentucky River. The last anyone saw of her was as she strolled toward the water.

And was gone forever.

Extensive searches found not a trace of her. The river was dragged but with equally disappointing results. It was theorized that she was abducted by a roving band of Indians or bandits attracted by the lights and party sounds, and the sight of a woman walking alone. The wilderness came literally to the edge of Frankfort in 1805, and it would not have been difficult for ruffians to have quickly slipped away from the frontier settlement.

In subsequent years, a dark-haired apparition was seen running through the Liberty Hall gardens on hot, humid nights, her mouth frozen open in a soundless cry of terror. The anonymous diva was last seen more than two decades ago. She is due for an encore.

At Carneal House in Covington, the "lady in gray" walks the hallways of that ancient house because of a broken heart.

The year was 1824 and the Marquis de Lafayette was touring the new Republic at the invitation of Congress, which had earlier voted to give him $200,000 and a township. A grateful nation wanted to show its appreciation for his military prowess in the American Revolution by honoring him at festivities all across the new land.

At that time, Carneal House was known as the Southgate Home. The marquis was an overnight guest during his stop in Covington. A dance was held in his honor where, according to the story handed down from generation to generation, a young woman in gray chiffon asked the marquis for a dance. The dashing Frenchman declined for some reason. Later that night the woman hanged herself.

Subsequent residents of Carneal House claim the despondent lady will not leave the site of her unkind dismissal. Specifics are vague, but it seems that this lady in gray makes her presence known by sound and action, not by sudden and awkward appearances.

A young couple had a close encounter with the murky specter when they lived in an apartment at Carneal House in 1973. The story they told was of "something" hiking around their rooms several times a week and of early-morning door slammings followed by footfalls on the staircase.

"There were uninterrupted sounds of someone walking up the stairs through the apartment door. Without the door opening," the husband recounted. His wife also heard the footsteps.

An intense cold descended on the rooms whenever the lady in gray was pacing around.

A quiet evening of piano music ended in an especially frightening episode with a rocking chair. It rocked. All by itself.

"The drapes weren't moving so we knew the rocking wasn't caused by the wind," the husband told a reporter, adding that a friend of his was playing the piano at the time. "My friend stopped playing . . . and we both froze into a cat-atonic state. The rocking continued for three to five minutes, then stopped. . . ."

More recent occupants have said nothing unusual happens in the house, aside from the usual problems inherent in old homes. There are the occasional creaks and groans associated with age. But they're quite certain that it is all perfectly . . . natural.

Ladies with a preference for gray apparel aren't the only ghosts to call old Kentucky home. Indeed, the state is among the richest in the nation when it comes to tales of spectral beings. Here are a few other celebrated Kentucky haunts:

White Hall. Two ghosts have been known to bump into tour guides at the historic Richmond estate of Kentuckian Cassius Clay, the noted abolitionist, ambassador to Russia, and a founder of the Republican party. Neither ghost is Clay, although a child ghost may be one of Clay's two children who died at White Hall. One boy died of typhoid fever and the other was poisoned by a slave. A supervisory tour guide saw the second ghost—an old man in dark clothing. He lurks in the basement on stormy days.

Hunt-Morgan House. The Creole nurse Bouvette lived in this Lexington home during the nineteenth century; her ghost is of a more recent vintage. Those who saw her will never forget the red shoes sported by this benign wraith. The ghost *and* her shoes are no longer seen—but Bouvette signals her continued presence by helpfully opening a door or closing a window.

Norma Arnold House. Time has not improved the organ-playing ability of Molly Kylie, the ghost in this Versailles home. An ardent but mediocre musician, Miss Molly's discordant tunes are still heard here a century after her death . . . if all the stories are to be believed.

My Old Kentucky Home. This historic home at Federal Hill, Bardstown, was built by Judge John Rowan. There were stories in the 1940s about headless horsemen on headless horses pounding by the old mansion, and chains dragged across its floors, but most of those accounts were dismissed at the time by curator Mrs. James Arnold. However, peculiar incidents involving a monument to Judge Rowan at his gravesite have been attributed to his disgruntled spirit. The judge was quite adamant about *not* having a tombstone mark his resting place. His will included the following proviso:

"There is to be no monument nor to be placed over my grave any tombstone. In this sentiment I am emphatic and it must not be violated. When my venerated and beloved father and mother died, they, like the multitude in that day, were interred without tombstones. My children have been buried in the same way—neither of them has a tombstone, nor shall I have one. It would be cruel to their memory. . . . Besides there is no pride among the dead; pride is an unfit associate of death and the grave. I therefore again forbid a monumental stone of any kind."

Judge Rowan's wishes were not followed when some years later a column was erected to mark his grave. One morning, the marker was discovered toppled over. It was reerected but soon thereafter dumped over again. Judge Rowan's admonition was recalled. He would never rest in peace as long as his grave was memorialized against his wishes.

Mr. Holt's Kith 'n' Kin

New Orleans and southern Louisiana are rife with tales of screaming skulls, bloody apparitions, evil voodoo priestesses who would as soon slit your throat as speak to you, and countless other tortured souls impossible to confine to their spectral environs.

Cajun country, however, is somewhat different. There one can find kinder, gentler ghosts who would rather gaze idly through wispy drapes at the occasional passerby than wrap their bony hands around the nearest warm neck.

Just why this should be the case is a mystery. Perhaps these courteous old plantation wraiths were taught in life to respect the privacy of others. Why shouldn't the well-born retain their dignity even if they have been dead for over a century?

Take kindly Mr. Holt, for example.

For most of his life, he was secretary to Frederick Conrad, the popular owner of The Cottage, a lush plantation that once graced the Great River Road landscape south of Baton Rouge. In the decades before the Civil War, Conrad entertained the likes of Zachary Taylor, the Marquis de Lafayette, Jefferson Davis, and Henry Clay. Francis Parkinson Keyes wrote *The River Road* while living there. Even before the plantation burned to the ground nearly four decades ago, various ghostly tableaus were played out in its stately rooms. To this day, the grounds on which The Cottage stood are not immune to eerie events.

The most well-known tales concerned Mr. Holt himself. He was born in 1802 and died in 1880, but that's not the least of it. As far as is known, he is the only Louisiana ghost to have had his photograph taken . . . a half-century after his death!

But first the story of Mr. Holt himself.

He was so devoted to his employer, Frederick Conrad, that when Federal troops occupied The Cottage in the waning days of the Civil War it wasn't surprising that both men were tossed in prison. Conrad died there, but Mr. Holt was at last released and returned to The Cottage to live out his remaining years.

Prison apparently warped the faithful retainer's mind. In the dozen years or so that he lived at The Cottage, he developed a pathological fear of poverty. As the lone tenant of the old mansion, he saw to it that each shred of cloth was carefully stored away, unused pieces of twine wrapped on a spindle, and even spare biscuits tucked away for some future repast. Long after his death in 1880, Mr. Holt's insurance against indigence was being unearthed by The Cottage's subsequent owners.

Added to his odd behavior was the physical appearance of Mr. Holt himself. The occasional visitor would report that the old man was an insomniac who wandered through the plantation's hallways all night long in a tattered white nightshirt, his scraggly beard splayed across his narrow chest. All the while he took great pains not to alarm guests or call undue attention to himself. A true gentleman's gentleman.

Beginning late in 1880, shortly after Mr. Holt's demise, his ghost was seen on many occasions, reenacting his nocturnal wanderings. Right up to The Cottage's conflagration in 1960, the old man's countenance peered mournfully from the mansion's ancient windows. It was at one of those windows that a photographer caught what was said to have been the ghost of shy Mr. Holt staring through the glass. The picture was reputedly published many years ago in *The Elks Magazine*, although officials at that publication have not been able to verify its existence.

Mr. Holt may not have been the only Cottage spirit.

Vague dancing forms and faint fiddle tunes and banjo music occasionally graced the generous front verandah on quiet, humid evenings. But these were musicales performed by ghostly slaves at some ethereal soirée. Long after The Cottage was nothing more than charred ruins, passersby noted the occasional laugh or patter of tapping feet coming from what was once a grand and glorious estate.

The Case of the Promiscuous Jurist

Just how many ghosts *are* there at the Myrtles Plantation?

There's old William Winter, who makes it only as far as the staircase's seventeenth step . . . the green-turbaned Chloe, hanged for her bad manners . . . a couple of blond vixens . . . a ballet dancer in a black tutu . . . a rambunctious girl who bounces on freshly made beds . . . a Confederate soldier or two . . . a voluptuous, naked Indian girl who lounges around the gazebo waiting for . . . well, one gets the idea.

Fabled throughout the South as the region's most haunted plantation, the Myrtles resides serenely within a grove of moss-draped oaks and pink-blossomed crepe myrtle trees thirty miles north of Baton Rouge, just outside St. Francisville. During the daylight hours it seems impossible that this gaily painted lady could harbor anything nastier than an occasional attic bat or swamp rat. Lacy wrought-iron outlines wide verandahs sporting porch rockers to while away the afternoon. A small pond in the backyard includes an island upon which a gazebo has been built. Cozy seats seem ideal for an intimate after-dinner assignation. Perhaps with the Indian maiden.

Do not be deceived.

This mien of benign gentility masks a history more frighteningly real than a Poe short story, for within the walls of the Myrtles, or very close by, at least ten people have been murdered over the past two centuries. And wandering the staircases, bed chambers, dining rooms, and grounds are no fewer than a dozen spirits; the ones above join company with two others—a wailing voodoo priestess and a strange little man in khaki who tells curious visitors at the gate that the Myrtles is no longer open for business.

The story of this Plantation begins in 1796, when a leader of the infamous Whiskey Rebellion, Gen. David Bradford, fled Pennsylvania for the Louisiana frontier. It seems that President George Washington had placed a price on his head, and General Bradford found the bayous of Louisiana more conducive to a long life than the hills of his native state.

Not much is known about General Bradford other than that he once owned over 650 acres planted in cotton and indigo, and he built the Myrtles, one of the finest examples of southern antebellum architecture to be found anywhere. Each of the mansion's twenty-two rooms is furnished in exquisite nineteenth-century antiques, most of them once owned by the Ruffin Gray Stirling family, which bought the plantation and fields in 1834. Exquisite plaster friezework and faux bois complement the Gothic decor.

Recent owners have undertaken a loving restoration, planned so as not to interfere with the Myrtles' status as a popular bed and breakfast inn.

The plantation's bloody past seems to begin after its sale in 1817 to General Bradford's son-in-law, Judge Clark Woodruffe. The promiscuous jurist engaged in indiscriminate affairs with countless women, including the French mulatto governess for his children. Her name was Chloe. Woodruffe tired of the illicit liaison and told her to stay away from the family. However, he discovered her a few days later eavesdropping on a business discussion. In his rage, Woodruffe sliced off her ear.

Chloe plotted to avenge the judge's ghastly punishment. She asked the family for permission to bake a cake for the birthday of the judge's oldest daughter, a kind of peace offering as it were. That she did—but mixed in with the sugar and cocoa were poisonous oleander flowers. Chloe was successful in her retribution. The deadly treat killed two of the Woodruffe children and the judge's wife.

But the Woodruffe slaves were outraged at Chloe's deed. They dragged her to a tall tree near the Mississippi River and hanged her. Her corpse was thrown in the river.

The ghost at the Myrtles with the green turban is Chloe, usually espied wandering around the mansion in the middle of the night. Sometimes a baby's cry accompanies her nocturnal strolls. An otherwise sound sleep can be interrupted by Chloe lifting the mosquito netting over the bed and peering intently at the faces therein. She always seems disappointed at who she finds.

Is Chloe the same specter as the old lady in a tattered green bonnet? Perhaps, or perhaps the story of the ghost's origin has changed with time. This ghost, too, wanders from room to room searching for something or someone. She also seems sad to not find who or what she's after.

A former owner of the Myrtles, Frances Kermeen, told the Los Angeles Times in 1987 that it was definitely Chloe she saw just after she bought the house.

"I . . . was asleep in a downstairs bedroom. Suddenly I woke up. Hovering nearby was a black woman in a dark, flowing gown wearing a green turban. She held an old tin candlestick. I hid my face and screamed and screamed. Finally, I forced myself to look again. I reached out to touch the gown but—there was nothing there but air, and she faded away."

Despite that experience, Miss Frances, as she was called by her staff, enjoyed the ghosts. "They're really quite friendly and civil," she said.

* * *

From 1860 to 1871, the Myrtles was owned by William Winter, a lawyer, and his wife Sarah Mathilda. Winter's ghost haunts the plantation because of the bizarre way in which he died.

Winter was called out to the front porch by a stranger on horseback. The attorney was shot in the chest as he came out the front door. He managed to stagger back in the house and started up the stairs before collapsing and dying in his wife's arms. He expired on the seventeenth step.

Winter is heard but not seen, thumping across the floor and up seventeen of the twenty steps to the second floor.

His widow, Sarah Mathilda Winter, was a member of another family cursed during their tenancy of the Myrtles. Her father was Ruffin Gray Stirling, who bought the plantation in 1834. He and his wife expanded their holdings to five thousand acres and five hundred slaves, one of the largest, if not the largest, prewar holdings in Louisiana. It's their furnishings that still decorate the home, including eighteenth-century furniture and a Baccarat crystal chandelier.

Although they added indiscriminately to their material gains, the Stirlings' personal lives played out like a Shakespearean tragedy.

There were nine children in the family—eight boys and one girl, Sarah Mathilda. Six of the boys died in the Civil War, one was murdered while gambling in Scotland, and the eighth, Steven, who took over after his brother-in-law William Winter was murdered, lost the entire estate over a gambling debt in 1888.

There's little evidence that any of the Stirlings haunt the Myrtles—although it's said that a substance that looked like blood once oozed from a spot near the front door; it was supposed to have come from one of the Stirling men, shot and wounded on the porch shortly before the Civil War began. With so many ghosts to choose from, however, a Stirling in the bunch wouldn't be improbable.

The origins of the other ghosts are as murky as their countenances.

One writer swore that he awoke to find two blond-haired little girls standing at the foot of his bed. Are they the same children who peer through the windows at night?

There's another child who is said to delight in jumping up and down on freshly made beds. She is trailed from room to room by a young woman attired in a maid's uniform smoothing the wrinkled bed linen.

The Confederate soldier marches across the porch. The man clad in khaki waits at the gate to warn away customers, when no one is supposed to be stationed there.

A ghostly tableau plays out from time to time. A black woman holds something in her hand while chanting mysterious words over the still form of a young girl. One claim is that she's a voodoo priestess who was unable to use her magic to cure the child of a fatal disease.

Old-timers in the parish say the Myrtles was built over Indian graves. That might account for the backyard gazebo's frequent visitor, the nude Indian girl. She looks lonely.

The most recent owners of Myrtles Plantation have taken advantage of the house's notorious reputation by holding Mystery Weekends and giving tours. Overnight guests can also be accommodated. Ghosts are not included in the price.

Current information can be obtained by writing The Myrtles, St. Francisville, Louisiana 70775.

Topless Wraiths

At least four headless apparitions haunt three different Louisiana plantations.

Lacy Branch Plantation, near Natchitoches in northwest Louisiana, can be thankful the ghost who haunts the nearby road hasn't yet made an appearance near the mansion grounds. Those who have seen him, or it, can't forget the experience—a headless body appearing suddenly from the ditch to scare the wits out of motorists and late-night pedestrians. Sometimes the thing is on horseback. No one seems to know under what circumstances the ghost lost its head, or even *who* the hapless victim was.

An aimless, headless man shuffles about Skolfield House, near Baton Rouge, harmlessly scratching about for the rest of himself. His identity, too, is unknown. An earlier Skolfield specter wasn't so nice. She was the wife of a former owner who resented her husband's new bride. Around the kitchen this woman-ghost scorned would rattle, knocking pots and pans to the floor and slamming doors. She vanished when death claimed her former husband. Their battles on "the other side" are probably dreadful affairs.

Kenilworth Plantation, below New Orleans, is a poignant reminder that true love knows not even earthly bounds.

A man and a woman stroll hand in hand through the rooms and hallways. Sometimes his arm is about her corseted waist. Both are dressed in elegant antebellum garb. Neither speaks a word, nor can they. Each is absent its head!

Sixteen Ghosts on a Dead Man's Chest . . .

Some Louisiana plantations have intriguing stories of legendary buried treasure connected with them. Guarded by the undead.

A bevy of specters haunts ancient St. Maurice Plantation, outside the town that gave it its name, between Shreveport and Alexandria. An intriguing fellow hovers a few yards from the house, supposedly over the location of secret treasure. However, a number of years ago the plantation's owner tried digging there. His metal detector indicated the presence of metal. A few feet further down he found . . . a pickax.

The visitor may have more success in spotting one of St. Maurice's other ghosts—a lady in the attic, several playful children, and a former caretaker. The plantation has been open for occasional tours in recent years.

St. Bernard Parish is on a desolate peninsula southeast of New Orleans. The Mississippi River Gulf Outlet Canal slices through the tract, while the Biloxi Wildlife Area stretches across the parish's thumb, near Lake Borgne. There are no settlements east of tiny Yscloskey.

One of Louisiana's most gruesome lost treasure tales arises from this dismal region, at the old Mercier Plantation, and dates back over a hundred years.

One humid summer night, an old black woman who worked as a Mercier Plantation cook nearly collided with the ghost of her former owner, old Mr. Mercier himself, when she stepped out onto the porch. He called her by name—"Sarah"—

and told her to meet him behind the milkhouse that night. He would show her where a fortune in gold was buried.

Not only did she *not* want to meet him anywhere, but she screamed her head off at the sight of the dead man, summoning nearly the entire household to her side. As she stammered out her story, everyone else's eyes blazed with the thought of hidden riches.

News of the episode soon reached the ears of a black minister who volunteered to lead a delegation to the milkhouse treasure. The group met at eleven o'clock at night—the ghostly Mr. Mercier's stated time—and the preacher began to dig. Suddenly, he dropped his shovel and screamed in pain. He said the devil had grabbed him; witnesses said they could hear the sound of a whip snapping at the preacher. Awful welts rose on his back; blood oozed through the fresh rips in the man's shirt.

Sarah pushed through the throng. She could "see" Mr. Mercier, she cried out; it was he who wielded the whip. He was angry that Sarah had disobeyed him and allowed others to hunt for the treasure.

According to the legend, the minister died of the terrible injuries a few days later. No one knows what became of the gold supposedly buried at Mercier Plantation.

Roadghosts

Not all of Louisiana's ghosts live in antebellum homes and ancient plantations. Some mysterious things have been seen in the desolate countryside of the Pelican State.

The old Roddy Road in Ascension Parish, about twenty miles south of Baton Rouge, was once called the Lighted Lane of Gonzales. Fascinating, dancing lights were often seen there late at night. Witnesses said they saw what looked like a match being struck, with the light then moving alongside the roadway. One legend maintained that a young woman was buried along this road and a light placed over her grave to keep the night away.

Sheriff Hickley Waguespack reportedly saw the strange light in April 1951. He said it had a "yellowish cast" but didn't create a distinct beam. The light wouldn't let anyone approach it.

Swamp gas, or phosphorous fire, is said to be prevalent in this part of Louisiana. Caused by rotting vegetation, the swamp gas is sometimes seen as a shimmering light in rural areas.

Ponchatoula is a small town in southern Tangipahoa Parish, thirty miles north of Lake Pontchartrain. There is a haunted gum tree there that weeps with the pearllike tears of a young woman who committed suicide under its branches.

The ghosts of soldiers buried in unmarked graves haunt the woods near Marksville, on the Red River in east central Louisiana. An old legend holds that a Civil War battle was fought on the road near the woods and the dead buried in a trench. At night the decapitated men still march among the trees.

An avenue of oak trees leading to Parlange Plantation in Pointe Coupee Parish is the setting for a particularly poignant ghost story.

Parlange was built by the Marquis Vincent de Ternant of Dans-ville-sur-Meuse, France. He obtained the land from the French crown.

The marquis' son, Claude Vincent de Ternant, had four children with his second wife, Virginia Trahan. One of their daughters, a beautiful girl named Julie, went mad on her wedding night. As hundreds of guests looked on, she started screaming and ran hysterically down the oak alley pursued by her distraught husband. She collapsed and died several hundred feet from the house. Her sobbing specter arrives on moonlit nights running down that very same path at Parlange.

A shadowy man haunts Destrahan Manor House, St. Charles Parish. A former employee swears she saw the furtive figure on five different occasions, including once in the old nursery and again as a flickering image in a downstairs mirror. At other times old-fashioned mysteries emerge, such as the front door slamming shut, a feeling that someone is watching from the front porch, and plodding feet (bodyless, of course) on the floor above.

Is it any wonder that a man who built his own coffin and regularly slept in it at night haunted his old home?

That was precisely the case at Oakland Plantation, near Haughton, in Bossier Parish. Ex–Confederate Colonel Sutton believed firmly in the importance of providing for one's own future. He placed the burnished wood casket in his own bedroom and regularly passed the nights in peaceful slumber within its cozy interior.

Impossible to believe such a thing could happen? Neither did the two handymen employed at Oakland years ago. That changed when they swore old Colonel Sutton's regular stroll across the squeaky floorboards of his bedroom ended when he climbed in the spectral coffin. From that night on, the men slept behind locked doors with an ax and a pick as their only companions.

Colonel Sutton doesn't seem to have any connection with the other legendary ghosts at Oakland Plantation, a quartet of horsemen who charge their mounts around the grounds. An amazing sight it must have been one evening after nightfall when the horsemen clambered onto the verandah, still mounted, pounded through the doorway, down the long hall and out the back door. The veracity of the story may be questioned owing to the fact that the horses have never left behind any pungent reminders of their unpredictable visits.

The Pearl River is haunted by Indian spirits or the ghosts of early Spanish settlers, depending upon whom you believe.

The captivating music people have heard issuing from its depths comes from Indians who drowned there. Then, too, a group of Spanish settlers may have marched stolidly into the swirling currents to avoid capture and torture, fifes and drums and flutes a-playing. The Pearl River is wide enough to hide the dead of many nationalities.

Dead Ships and Old Curses

If we are to see ourselves as reasonable and rational human beings, such peculiar occurrences as might be described, let us say, in a ghost story, are impossible to comprehend. The very existence of the human *organism* argues against any plane of reality beyond that of our senses. The physical world—a sphere of sight, sound, touch, and smell—encompassess all that we are confident is indisputably reliable. To say that anything beyond this is possible, however improbable, is to court ridicule from our more pragmatic brethren.

Yet is there not *something* in each of us that says we cannot know all there is to understand? That we cannot proclaim with irrefutable certitude that within the observable universe there is all understanding?

The mere existence of ghost stories, of true tales of the supernatural, is evidence of belief by some individuals that a level of being other than our own may occupy some fragment of space or time. And that on rare occasions those who live and work and play in the physical world may brush up against *this other universe*, if only for a moment. When the two worlds collide, when matter beholds nonmatter, we see beyond ourselves and into the void.

Dead Ships

By all accounts Homer Grimm was a cautious man. His affair with the passionate Mrs. Googie Bragdon of Wolfe's Neck on Casco Bay, off Portland, Maine, was a perfect example of his deliberate avoidance of trouble.

Homer lived on Staple's Point, a short distance across the water from Wolfe's Neck. That would seem to be the ideal situation for illicit passion; Homer could reclaim his lady love anytime he desired. But he always stayed well clear of Wolfe's Neck—except on those days when the fog lay so thick along the coast that a man could extend his arm and not see the tip of his fingers. On those days, Homer jumped in his rowboat and made his way to a point on Wolfe's Neck where the earthy Mrs. Bragdon waited. Together they went over to Punkin Nubb, at the mouth of Freeport's harbor, and . . . well, the couple were the happiest on foggy days.

This was one of those days, an August afternoon early in World War II. The entire vicinity of Casco Bay had been taken over by the U.S. Navy and its allies, most notably His Majesty's Navy at the back cove of Cumberland Foreside. All manner of floating war vessels moved in and out of the bay, from Portland on up to Yarmouth and Harpswell and clear across to Westpoint and Popham Beach. The locals knew that when destroyers gathered, there was surely a convoy headed out the next morning. Patrol boats swept back and forth across the waters. The newly installed radar machines watched where no man's eyes could reach.

On this August day, the fog descended like an impenetrable wall of dusky cotton. Mrs. Bragdon and her paramour had just settled down to business on Punkin Nubb when the sirens wailed with the warning that an intruder had penetrated the defense perimeters. Immediately, all the ships in the bay sprang to life. Guns were unsheathed, gongs brought soldiers and sailors scrambling to battle stations. The HMS *Moidore* swept out of Cumberland Cove while the American navy closed in from all other sides.

The *Moidore* fired its cannon as it came. One shell landed on Punkin Nubb and knocked off a chunk of rock a few yards from where Homer and Mrs. Bragdon were enjoying each other's company. Gawdamighty, thought Homer, Mr. Bragdon knows what his wife is up to and aims to blow us to pieces!

The couple peered around the corner of the shattered rock ledge. It took a while for their eyes to grow accustomed to the fog, but, when they did, Homer saw that heavy artillery was not going to be the main problem.

Sweeping past Punkin Nubb, directly under the gaze of the startled pair, was a tall ship, her sails full of wind as she tore through the waves. Homer saw sailors on deck straining to see through the mist. In the distance but closing in quickly were the HMS *Moidore*, the U.S. Navy, and the Coast Guard, all with guns rattling and sirens wailing

Homer couldn't believe his eyes. But it wasn't the excitement of watching the Allies chase a dangerous, or naive, interloper. No, Homer caught the name on the stern of this sailing ship as she swept by his trysting place.

The *Dash*. And Homer knew her story.

She was a pirate ship that had vanished—130 years before!

As it turned out, Homer Grimm and the Allied forces were merely the latest witnesses to the arrival of Maine's most famous phantom, a vessel known to generations as the "Dead Ship of Harpswell."

Thought by some to be simply a floating derelict occasionally sighted during the nineteenth century, the *Dash* was a privateer launched in 1812 to look for British ships. She was built at Porter's Landing, Freeport, for Seward and Samuel Porter of Portland.

There is some confusion about which ship is actually the one being referred to in the Harpswell-Freeport region. The ship was never actually *from* Harpswell, and another ship, the *Sarah*, is sometimes considered "the ghost ship of Harpswell-Freeport."

Much of the quandary arose from John Greenleaf Whittier's poem "The Dead Ship of Harpswell." It is his paean to "the Flying Dutchman" legend:

> *What weary doom of baffled guest,*
> *Thou sad sea-ghost, is thine?*
> *What makes thee in the haunts of home*

A wonder and a sign?
No foot is on thy silent deck,
Upon the helm no hand;
No ripple hath the soundless wind
That smites thee from the land!

Whittier's dead ship was the *Dash*, but he added many forlorn details to the known legend. His ship never quite reached port, but was always stopped just short and then drifted helplessly back out to sea stern-first, only to arrive again with the next fog and repeat its hopeless quest to find safe haven.

The writer Robert P. Tristram Coffin used a ghost ship in his *John Dawn* since, as a Harpswell native, he had heard the legend of the *Dash* from his earliest childhood. He actually knew men who had seen the ghost ship in some of its unearthly passages off the Lookout at Harpswell Center and near Bailey and Orr's Island.

As for the *Dash*, only a little is known about her disappearance. She was successful at chasing down British ships—a patriotic quest for the new Republic, a lucrative haul for the Porters. During fifteen sorties, nothing untoward befell her, so out she went on number sixteen.

That was the end of the *Dash*.

The ship and her crew of Freeport lads were lost forever. Some thought a squall hit while her "chasing sails" were up and she went over; another theory was that she struck uncharted shoals and ripped apart.

The *legend* of the *Dash* began a few months after that final mission when a fisherman named Simon Bibber was working off Punkin Nubb (the same island on which Homer Grimm and Mrs. Bragdon carried on their assignation). A fog thicker than cream abruptly descended, but the fishing was good so Simon worked on. Suddenly, a full-rigged sailing ship hove into view no more than thirty feet away. So close was she that Simon could make out the figures of men on deck and hear the creak of her lines.

And though she was laid over with sails billowing, there was no wind! There never is in a thick, coastal fog.

As Simon watched unbelieving, the ship's stern slid by and he saw this phantom's name: "DASH—FREEPORT." Finally, the ship that was thought to be lost had come home to port.

The fisherman quickly raised anchor and rowed to the Freeport landing. There was no sailing ship in the harbor. Simon questioned some of his dockside cronies, but was met with derision.

"Where the hell you been!" demanded Mort Collins. "The *Dash* was lost long ago!"

For a very long time, Simon Bibber thought he was losing his mind. But then one day Roscoe Moulton took him aside and allowed as how he'd seen the *Dash* over by Crab Island. "She flew past me like a whirlwind, and they warn't a breath of air stirring, thick o'fog and flat-arse calm. I seen her!"

Then over the months and years many others saw that dreadful sight—including all seventeen members of the Banks schooner *Betty Macomber*. She was heading into port with a load of cod when the *Dash* zipped right past her.

Each time it was the same, whether she was off Crab Island or Pound o' Tea or Eagle Island. The air was calm and the fog was thick as the old schooner slipped past, her lines creaking and the water slapping at her hull, and gathered all along the railing were her Freeport boys trying to see home through the impenetrable haze.

But is it the *Dash* spotted along the coast of southern Maine? She may not be the only ghost ship navigating those waters.

There is the *Sarah*, which old-timers will tell you has as strange a history as any sailing ship in nineteenth-century America. She was built in 1812 by two young Portland men, George Leverett and Charles Jose. Charles's uncle and George's father gave them the necessary financial backing. The men had plans to use the ship in the lucrative West Indies trade, hauling wood products and fresh fish to the Caribbean and bringing back cane sugar, rum, and coffee. George would be captain and Charles the first mate. The Soule yard in South Freeport laid the keel, and it was there the troubles began.

Sarah Soule was the daughter of the yard's owner. A beautiful young woman in her late teens, Sarah charmed both men. Charles was the most persistent in his attentions, but it was George with whom Sarah fell in love.

The men argued all the way back to Portland. It is said that Charles tried to push George and his horse off the Yarmouth bridge and into the Royal River. Charles eventually backed out of the partnership and left the city. He was rumored to have ended up in the West Indies, there to make his own fortune.

George Leverett proposed to Sarah and they planned to marry a few days after the ship was to be launched, in September 1812. He had decided to name the vessel after his bride-to-be.

The launching went smoothly, but not so the wedding: the church was too small for all the invited guests and the wedding had to be moved to a large workroom at the shipyard; the bride's minister turned out to be unavailable and a substitute was brought in from Yarmouth; and the time of the vows was changed to early evening. The old spinsters said three black marks against the young couple so early in a marriage meant nothing but ill fortune. Their words were more prophetic than anyone realized!

As he prepared to enter the shipping business, the now-Captain Leverett had to contend with the rumors of bad luck swirling around, centering on his argument with Charles Jose over Sarah Soule and then the problems with their wedding. Sailors refused to sign aboard the newly christened *Sarah*. Men from all the way over in Portland eventually came aboard as officers, and crewmen were rounded up from various small communities around Casco Bay.

Captain Leverett finally sailed from Freeport and into Portland to pick up his load of cargo bound for the West Indies—but ran straight into his next problem. A mysterious three-masted bark, painted black and flying no flag, had been seen lurking about just offshore for several days. When Captain Leverett arrived in Portland harbor, the bark trailed him in.

The mystery ship's crew was a rag-tag band of Cubans . . . led by none other than Charles Jose, now captain of the *Don Pedro Salazar*, as the bark was named. He said he had found the ship abandoned on a reef near Cuba, bought it for salvage, made repairs, and set off for Maine to register it at his "home port," Portland.

Now Captain and Mrs. Leverett, along with her mother, all had made the short voyage from Freeport to Portland. The women were to return to Freeport by packet boat when the *Sarah* sailed for the West Indies. Plans changed and they took a stagecoach back.

A strange incident befell the packet near Clapboard Island when she was stopped by a rough band of swarthy sailors aboard a whaleboat. Their leader demanded that Mrs. Leverett be turned over to them. For what reasons he did not say, nor would he identify himself or the others. When the packet's officers persuaded him she was not on board—and indeed she was not—the strangers jumped back aboard the whaleboat and rowed off. No explanation of why they were seeking Mrs. Leverett was given and no investigation was undertaken. It was later assumed the men were part of Charles Jose's crew.

Meanwhile, Capt. George Leverett set sail for the Caribbean and the West Indies. But within hours of his clearing Portland harbor, his lookout spotted a trailing ship—the *Don Pedro Salazar*. During the *Sarah's* entire run down the Eastern Seaboard, the dark ship was always just on the horizon. Leverett's men grew increasingly nervous. Near the Bahamian island of Abaco, the captain made the decision to alter course and head straightaway to Nassau, where he would report the *Don Pedro's* aggressive behavior.

Captain Leverett never made it. His nemesis aboard the *Don Pedro* must have realized what the change of course meant, for he hoisted the "skull 'n' crossbones" of the Jolly Roger, rolled out heavy cannon and overtook the slower *Sarah*. The fight was brief and bloody. Everyone but Captain Leverett was slaughtered by Jose's skilled cutthroats, who then looted the merchant ship. Jose's men lashed George Leverett to the mainmast. The helm was tied down, the *Don Pedro's* men jumped back aboard their ship, and the *Sarah* was left to drift on the high seas.

Here is the beginning of the *legend* of the doomed ship *Sarah*. As the *Don Pedro* fell away in the distance, the bloodied and nearly unconscious George Leverett sensed a change of direction for his ship. As he looked around, he saw his dead crew come back to life, run up the sails and head for home, his first mate standing at the helm. Not a word was passed among the men; Leverett lost consciousness.

Weeks later, fishermen near Harpswell, Maine, saw a square-rigger loom into view, navigate the precarious channel between Haskell's Island and Potts Point, and finally drop anchor in Potts Harbor. A single, silent man stood at the helm. The few people who saw the strange vision claimed the ship's name was obliterated by cannon shot, her superstructure destroyed and the shredded sails flapping limply in a stiff breeze. Some men who saw her, though, said she had the unmistakable lines of the *Sarah*.

Sailors seemed to materialize as if from nowhere, lowered the single remaining lifeboat and made for land. Once ashore, they placed the limp form of Capt. George Leverett on a grassy bank, his log next to him, and rowed back to the ship.

Suddenly, a fog bank swept in from the sea, obliterating the harbor. When it lifted, there was no sign of the strange, battered ship, although Captain Leverett was found barely alive on the shore. The last entry in the log recorded a course change to Nassau. George Leverett said he remembered absolutely nothing after that . . . and he never again set foot aboard a sailing ship.

So we have the privateer *Dash* and the ill-fated merchantman *Sarah* vying for attention as the "ghost ship of Maine's coast." There is ample evidence, at least in waterfront folklore, to suggest that each vessel commands substantial support among the various partisans who claim it is *their* old sailing ship that reappears with notable infrequency.

The *Dash* surely disturbed the American and British navies on that August afternoon—not to mention the serene lovemaking of Homer Grimm and Mrs. Bragdon. Once the couple figured out that their nest had been discovered, they hastily departed for Wolfe's Neck, where Homer would deposit the lady back onshore. It wasn't quite that easy. Navy ships prowled the harbor looking for their quarry but only came upon Homer rowing for his life. His answers to their inquiries about a sailing ship were disturbing to the sensibilities that prevail in the armed forces. He allowed as how it was most certainly the *Dash* he'd seen and that it was no more.

The U.S. Navy was forced to accept Homer's account when other inhabitants around the bay told investigators it must have been the *Dash* trying again to make port. What other possible explanation could there be? they asked incredulous MPs.

The chronicle of the incident in Casco Bay was swiftly buried in government archives. Officially, the *Dash* remained just another piece of Maine folklore. Homer Grimm knew better. But he wasn't about to say anything different. The navy didn't want anything to do with him. And he most assuredly wanted to forget all about that dreadful afternoon.

Old Curses

The Old Gaol (jail) in York, Maine, stands guard over the village center as it has done since 1719. It is the oldest remaining public building of the former English colonies. Saved by local residents from destruction in the late nineteenth century, the Gaol has served as a museum of local history since 1900.

Jail cells and even the jailer's quarters have been restored to their eighteenth-century appearance. Archivists have collected dozens of historic items—from a first edition of a novel by Sarah Sayward Barrell Keating Wood, Maine's first female novelist, to a 1610 Breeches Bible.

Then there is on display the Old Trickey Bible, sometimes called The Pirate's Bible. And there is its curse.

The book is old and stiff, and some will tell you that it will not stay open because its former owner, a man called Old Trickey, didn't use it enough. It is a haunted volume.

Francis Trickey was a fisherman who lived in a cabin at the mouth of the York River. He was listed on the tax roles as residing in Kittery in the 1650s. A more ill-tempered, disreputable, prickly man would have been hard to find. His meanness, however, went beyond mere unpleasantness; his was a wickedness and malevolence that singled him out as a character to be avoided at all costs. His tongue was sharp. In surely what must have been one of the first such cases in the early colonies, a man named Dennis Downings sued him and his wife for slander in 1656 following an argument between Mrs. Trickey and Mrs. Downings. No one knows over what.

Old Trickey, as he was known in the region, was so wicked that when he died and went straight to Hell, Lucifer himself decided upon his punishment, to haunt Bra'boat Harbor until the end of time, hauling loads of sand with a rope until his Master was satisfied. Trickey's foul curses only made the Devil laugh harder.

On those nights when the rain and wind swept across Cape Neddock from the North Atlantic, Trickey's wraith was at work, galloping over the landscape screaming "More rope! More sand! More rope! More sand!" until those frightened residents who heard him had to press their pillows against their ears to shut out the horrible voice.

Even today, at the hint of an approaching nor'easter, when the sea roils against the jagged rocks and the gales send all but the foolhardy into their sturdy homesteads—on days like these folks still say, "Old Trickey is binding and hauling sand tonight! God save the fishing-smacks from harm!"

The more prosaic habitués of this section of the Maine coast calmly assert that Old Trickey's ghost was laid long ago and that his curse was lifted. The only remaining vestige of his existence is his grave outside York.

Yet there is that ancient Bible . . . and the few who swear the covers have slammed shut in their hands. A curse is a dangerous thing with which to tamper.

This tale of the haunted sea could rightly be called "the curse of the open door." It takes place at the lighthouse on Matinicus Rock, a stony outcropping best known as a birdwatcher's paradise.

The old light was once located in a tower at one end of the lightkeeper's dwelling. The tower has not been used in decades and was always kept locked. Coast Guard crews said it was because the place was beset with a ghost.

A long time ago a lightkeeper, perhaps driven crazy by the loneliness and desolation of this speck in the Atlantic, went up into the tower, tied a rope to a rafter and hanged himself. People on Matinicus Island discovered the death when they noticed the light hadn't been lit for several evenings.

Guardsmen swore the old man still clumped around the tower, causing trouble wherever and whenever he was heard. Dishes were broken, furniture tipped over, and supplies thrown into disarray. The men stationed there thought they'd figured out how to stop the haunting when they locked and barred the door going into the tower. Maybe he'd stay put, they reasoned.

He did. For a while. But then some crewmen had to fetch material from the tower and he'd open the door and new problems tormented the station. The light did not work, machinery malfunctioned, or the foghorn developed laryngitis.

Only so long as the door stayed locked did the lighthouse remain curse-free.

Mrs. Ridgely and Associates

The Hampton House, north of Baltimore, is filled with grief and sadness and the phantoms of those who lived and died there more than a century ago.

This grand Georgian house was built by Charles Ridgely, a member of the Maryland House of Burgesses from 1773 to 1789, and also a member of the committee appointed to frame a constitution for the state. On two thousand acres of land willed to him in 1772, Ridgely built his legacy. It is one of the largest and most magnificent houses of the post–Revolutionary War era. Its two-and-a-half-story main section is capped with a cupola and flanked by one-story wings. Ridgely died just months after its completion in 1790.

The estate passed to his nephew, Charles Ridgely Carnan. To conform with an odd provision of the will, Carnan changed his name to Charles Carnan Ridgely. *This* Charles Ridgely served as governor of Maryland from 1815 to 1818, and it was he who brought national attention to Hampton House through several grand additions. Formal gardens enhanced the grounds, stables were filled with the swiftest horses, and elaborate dinner parties were held for the state's aristocracy.

But Hampton House brought no happiness to the governor's wife, Priscilla. Although she bore eleven children, she seemed to take little interest in them, or in anything else for that matter. Indeed, she felt imprisoned within the great stone walls of a benign fortress. While her husband entertained important guests, Mrs. Ridgely remained in seclusion upstairs, reading her Bible for hours on end. Sadly, even her religion brought no comfort. Thirty-two years after entering Hampton House, Priscilla Dorsey Ridgely died a lonely, mentally unbalanced recluse.

But now she may be traipsing through the passages and rooms she avoided in life, always dressed in a gray gown.

On a winter's day years after Priscilla died, a new bride in the Ridgely family heard a faint tapping at the front door. She opened it to find a thin, frail woman shivering on the doorstep. She wore no coat, only a plain cap on her head and a plain dress.

"Won't you come in and warm yourself by the fire?" asked this Mrs. Ridgely.

The stranger hesitated, peered through the open doorway, then turned abruptly and vanished into the crisp night air. A servant told the young bride that it was the spirit of Priscilla, still searching for the happiness that eluded her in life.

* * *

Over the years, the deaths of Hampton's first ladies have been foretold by a haunted chandelier. Everyone in the house at the time hears the crash of the ceiling fixture as it falls to the floor. Trouble is, all the beautiful crystal chandeliers are always hanging in place.

The fifth mistress of Hampton House was enjoying the company of her family one springlike Easter Sunday when they heard the dreaded crash. The children and housekeeper scattered in all directions. They searched every room, but found nothing amiss. However, the mistress of the house was dead within twenty-four hours, perhaps giving rise to the legend of the chandelier.

It is not only the women of Hampton whose deaths have been foretold by psychic phenomena. Legend has it that whenever a master of the house dies away from home, his soul returns in a spectral coach.

Charles Ridgely IV had taken his young sons to England to enroll them in a boarding school, after which he proceeded to the Continent to vacation in Italy. One wintry night during his absence, the caretaker's wife was awakened by tinkling sleigh bells and the thud of horses' hooves on the packed snow. She arose and peered out the window. The landscape was an unbroken and glistening white in the moonlight. There was no sleigh. There were no horses. The next day word reached Hampton House that "Mr. Charles" had died in Rome. His family was already in mourning.

Of all the tales of haunting associated with Hampton House, the most poignant swirls around Governor Swann's beautiful daughter who died at the mansion in the nineteenth century. Miss Swann had fully recovered from a serious illness and Hampton's first lady, Eliza Ridgely, invited her to the house. Eliza was very fond of the girl and always called her Cygnet, or "little swan." She thought the fresh country air might help to restore her strength.

Sadly, that was not to be the case.

One morning the girl appeared at the breakfast table looking quite pale. Dark circles rimmed little Cygnet's blue eyes and her long golden hair lay in tangles about her face. Eliza feared she'd taken a turn for the worse, but the child assured her hostess that she felt well. It was just that she'd had a nightmare, she said, a terrible dream of death:

An old man with a scythe had chased her through endless fields of wheat, she said. After she narrowly escaped his desperate clutches, he shouted, "I'll get you yet, my golden-haired beauty!"

In the suddenly silent dining room, Eliza finally spoke as she reached out to pat Cygnet's cold hand: "It's nonsense, child. Everyone has bad dreams once in a while. They mean nothing. Come now, we'll sit outside on the terrace and rest."

That evening, Eliza staged a ball to cheer the sickly child. But when she failed to appear, a servant was sent up to her room. Poor little Cygnet was slumped over the dressing table, one hand still clutching her hairbrush. A doctor called her death "mysterious," but no investigation ever looked into the circumstances.

Throughout the years visitors to Hampton House claim to have seen Cygnet in her old northwest bedroom. She sits in her satin ball gown, combing her golden locks.

The ghosts of Priscilla and Cygnet may not be the only ones in the house. One raw January afternoon about seventy years ago, a young woman interested in historic houses visited at Hampton. She'd been invited by the Ridgelys to "stop anytime."

A formally dressed butler answered her knock and said that, although the family was not in residence that day, he'd be pleased to show her around. As he escorted the guest from room to room, she became amazed at his knowledge of the Ridgely family history. He identified portraits hanging on the walls and spun stories of bygone days. Finally, when the woman started to leave, she tried to offer him a few dollars for his helpfulness.

"Thank you, ma'am," he said, shaking his head, "but I need for nothing. Nothing . . ." His voice trailed off.

Several days later the woman telephoned Mrs. Ridgely.

"I'm sorry you weren't home the day I stopped at Hampton," she apologized. "But I want you to know how much I appreciated the wonderful tour of your home with your butler. He seemed so devoted and so knowledgeable about the family."

"My butler?" exclaimed Mrs. Ridgely, completely mystified. "But I have no butler. As you must know, it's very hard to find help these days."

The unexpected caller described the butler down to his formal clothing and kindly manner. Mrs. Ridgely was silent for several moments before speaking again. "That must have been old Tom. He was born on the place and served us well for many years."

She paused again.

"But Tom died thirty years ago."

The Ridgely family occupied Hampton House for more than 150 years, but no one ever determined the specific identity of another ghost, one who roams the mansion at midnight opening doors.

People say they have heard latches lifted, bolts withdrawn, and doors opened. A check of the premises finds no disturbances. In any old house, floorboards may squeak under human weight, a certain window may rattle in a high wind, but at Hampton House it's the metallic clank of the bar over the south portico door that brings alarm. This door opens into the Great Hall and was never used after dark. Anyone arriving home late used another door.

One night when young John and Stewart Ridgely were sleeping in a room on the south side of the house, they were awakened by the scrape of an iron bar.

Burglars, they whispered.

Shivering with excitement tinged with fear, the boys climbed out of their beds, grabbed a flashlight and tiptoed through the quiet hallway. At the top of the staircase, the boys hesitated, then descended one step at a time, each clutching the other's arm.

Inside the Great Hall, John snapped off the flashlight and threw on the light switch. In the sudden blaze of light, the huge room appeared in order. The ponderous hasp on the outside door had not been disturbed.

In 1948, the Avalon Foundation, a philanthropic organization, acquired Hampton House and donated it to the federal government. The Society for the Preservation of Maryland Antiquities acts as custodian. Hampton House is now a National Historic Site operated by the National Park Service. The house is open to the public.

The hauntings continue.

Park Service employees staying in the house have heard harpsichord music coming from the bedroom where sad Cygnet died, but, according to all available records, no harpsichord has ever been in the house.

On one occasion, the Great Hall was used for an exhibition. In the middle of the night the ranger on duty was awakened by a terrifying crash. Rushing into the Hall, he found all the display racks thrown to the floor.

But the old tack room may be the busiest and certainly the noisiest of all the "empty" rooms. Rangers have heard chains beating against the walls, and when they look in they see saddles and harnesses swinging back and forth from pegs in the walls. The windows and doors are kept tightly closed.

Some speculate that Jehu Howell, Hampton House's original carpenter, has returned to take one more ride. Howell had received more than $6,000 and sixty-eight quarts of rum for his labors, but he didn't live to enjoy his financial and liquid windfall. One night in November 1787, Howell rode his horse into a rain-swollen creek. He may have misjudged the water's depth or, more likely perhaps, been blinding drunk after emptying off part of his payment. No one will ever know.

In the morning, Jehu Howell and his horse were found dead on the streambank.

MARYLAND

Death in the Library

Annapolis, the capital of Maryland, is known for its spit-and-polish naval cadets, picturesque wharves, and handsome colonial mansions. Less well-known may be its other landmarks—revenants who refuse to believe they're dead.

At the Brice House, 42 East Street, ghosts have shadowed the rooms for the past two centuries. They show no signs of leaving.

This two-story brick mansion dates to 1761. John Brice began its construction, but he didn't live to see its completion. When he died in 1766, he left the unfinished house to his second son, twenty-year-old James. For seven more years, bricklayers, masons, and carpenters toiled to complete the thirty-three-room edifice. Walls supporting the steeply pitched roof are three feet thick and the chimneys at each end of the home rise ninety feet above East Street.

Colonial Annapolis was in awe at what was in its time the most beautiful home in the city. Those who saw it certainly agreed that it was a fine wedding gift to Juliana Jennings, whom James Brice married in 1781. In 1776, Brice had been commissioned a colonel in the Maryland militia, and now, with Juliana at his side, he began to entertain lavishly and frequently. Dinner guests might include General Washington, the Marquis de Lafayette, James Madison, or Gen. Nathaniel Greene.

Colonel Brice's political career and his position in Maryland aristocracy were well assured. In 1782 and again in 1788 he was elected mayor of Annapolis and also served on the governor's advisory council. For two years, from 1791 to 1793, he was acting governor of Maryland after the sudden death of George Plater.

The vivacious Juliana never tired of opening her home to vast numbers of relatives, friends, and a variety of other visitors. There were certainly enough rooms to house a veritable congregation of guests.

Perhaps the warmth of Juliana's hospitality encouraged some to overstay their visits—James Brice himself lingered for years after his death in 1801. Through the years, James has been observed hurrying along the corridors of his still-exquisite house, perhaps checking on last-minute preparations for one of Juliana's parties. On at least one occasion, he wore a plum-colored suit with lace fichu, knee breeches, and a powdered wig.

Following the colonel's death, the house was occupied by his eldest son, Thomas Jennings Brice, a bachelor. A well-liked, friendly gentleman, Thomas treated everyone with equanimity. His generosity was well known, even among his servants, to whom he made a large provision in his will. The fact that he planned to provide an inheritance to his servants may have played a role in his death, according to legend.

Thomas Brice was found dead one morning on the floor of the library. He'd suffered a fatal head wound. Just what caused the injury is the subject of some conjecture. He may have had a stroke and, in falling out of his chair, hit his head on the floor. Or, he may have been murdered. The popular theory was that Thomas had been bludgeoned to death by blows from a hammer, possibly wielded by one of his servants. But that was never proven. However, Thomas's valet disappeared at once and was never located. At least not in the flesh. Some say that the ghosts of Thomas Brice and his valet periodically reenact a murder scene in the library.

But such violence is an anomaly in the Brice House, for the majority of ghosts who "live" there are gentle souls who threaten no one. They do not groan, glare, or bang on doors and windows at midnight. Indeed, they seem to go about their business (whatever that might be) with quiet dignity.

A wispy figure of a young woman used to hover near the wine cellar. She would move upstairs just before the candles were lighted at dusk. She had the unnerving habit of staring directly at those she met. In the parlor, she'd stand by the mantel and hold her face in her hands, as if weeping. When the candles were lit, she vanished with the light. Her visits were thought to have something to do with "treasure" hidden in the walls.

That's what Thomas Murdock thought.

One day he was whitewashing walls in the cellar and discovered a loose stone. He removed it and found a large, dark recess behind it. However, before he could peer into the cavity, he claimed that a spider of epic proportions attacked him. Its head, he said, was as large as a child's and it was armed with ferocious fangs. That's what he said.

Murdock struck the creature with the handle of his paintbrush, which the spider bit off and swallowed. He shoved the stone back into place and fled. He said that if there'd been money hidden in that wall, it wasn't meant for him. He never returned to finish the job. And, if the weeping woman found her "fortune" no one knows about it.

Upstairs an unknown nursemaid cares for infants once in residence, feeding them and quietly rocking them to sleep.

In the 1930s the Brice House was converted into faculty apartments by St. John's College. A professor at the Naval Academy resided on the ground floor. One day he had the strangest experience of his life and told his story to his friend and former colleague, William O. Stevens.

"I was leaving my room after a sound sleep," began the professor, "with a bundle of papers under my arm, starting off for my eight o'clock class. It was bright daylight. As I stepped outside my door, I saw to my astonishment, diagonally across the hall, an old gentleman standing at the door of what was once the library. His white hair was worn rather long and his black clothes were of an old-fashioned cut. As he was someone I had never seen before, I stood still and looked at him in surprise. As I stared, the old man gradually faded into the door behind him and disappeared."

The professor was a reputable, sober-minded academic who had gone to bed early the night before.

Sometime later, a naval officer's wife and her daughter also claimed to have seen the same elderly white-haired man dressed in black, but both were reluctant to speak of the encounter with Stevens. Was Thomas Brice awaiting his assailant?

Although William Stevens acknowledged that he'd never seen the ghost, he wrote that he chose "to believe that the Brice House ghosts are as real as its chimneys."

Another professor who lived in the house for a time saw two spirits whose identities have never been established.

After a particularly trying day of examinations and student conferences, Prof. Allen Blow Cook was unable to relax. He went to bed early, but didn't fall asleep. At about three-thirty in the morning, he got up and prepared to make a cup of tea. Glancing idly out of his kitchen window, he noticed a man and a woman standing in the backyard. The woman's light-colored hoop skirt reflected the moonlight; Professor Cook knew that she was not of this age.

Apparently, the couple had had an altercation of some sort, because when the man offered his arm to her she abruptly turned away. He stomped into the house and spent the rest of the morning pacing the floor upstairs. The good professor never slept that night.

In 1953 the Brice House was purchased by the Wohl family. They knocked out partitions and restored the place to its former grandeur, including the addition of antique period pieces.

The Wohls were evidently happy in their "new" home; they never saw a ghost. After the death of Stanley Wohl in 1979, the Brice House was again placed on the market. It was sold at public auction in 1982 to the International Union of Bricklayers and Allied Craftsmen.

The Brice House is now technically the Union's headquarters, but it is not always occupied—by living persons. By 1992, only the central section of the house had been renovated for Union use, with plans for a "masonry museum" in the basement. Meanwhile, the Brice House is rented out for various functions, including the annual Historic Annapolis Tours. Those touring the mansion are cautioned to count the number in their group at the beginning *and* end of their ramble through the mansion. One never knows who, or what, might tag along.

MASSACHUSETTS

Curse of the Bloody Pit

In the rugged and beautiful Berkshire Hills of western Massachusetts, where mists draw patterns on the peaks, ghostly legends have prevailed since the earliest days of settlement. Around campfires and by the warmth of wood-burning stoves, old-timers tell of persons who vanished, never to be seen again; of weird night sounds echoing down the valleys; and of grown men, sound of mind, filled with undefinable fears.

One of the most popular legends is that of the haunting of the Hoosac Tunnel at North Adams.

The digging of this railroad tunnel is a saga of blood, sweat and tears. Begun in 1851, it wasn't finished until 1875. During those twenty-four years, hundreds of miners, using mostly crude black powder and pick and shovel, chipped away at the unyielding rock of Hoosac Mountain. By the time the tunnel was finished, two hundred men had lost their lives in what came to be known as "the bloody pit." Most died in explosions, fires, and drownings, but one death may not have been accidental.

In 1865, the explosive nitroglycerin was introduced to America and used for the first time in the construction of the Hoosac Tunnel. On the afternoon of March 20, 1865, explosive experts Ned Brinkman, Billy Nash, and Ringo Kelley planted a charge of nitro and ran toward a safety bunker. Brinkman and Nash never made it. Kelley had prematurely set off the charge, burying his coworkers alive under tons of rock.

Soon after the accident, Kelley disappeared. He was not seen again until March 30, 1866. His body was found two miles inside the tunnel in the exact spot where Brinkman and Nash had died. Kelley had been strangled to death.

Deputy Sheriff Charles F. Gibson estimated the time of death at between midnight and 3:30 A.M. An investigation was carried out, but with no suspects, the murder was never solved.

Some of the workmen, however, came to their own conclusion. They *knew* that Kelley had been killed by the vengeful spirits of Brinkman and Nash. Fearing the tunnel was cursed, they balked at entering it. Even visitors became uneasy inside the dark, dank cavern with water dripping continuously from the ceiling and streaming down the walls.

Paul Travers, a mechanical engineer employed on the Hoosac project, toured the tunnel with a Mr. Dunn. Travers had been a highly respected cavalry officer in the Union army. In a letter to his sister in Connecticut, dated September 8, 1868, the engineer wrote," ... the men constantly complain of hearing a man's voice cry out in agony and refuse to enter the great shaft after nightfall. Mr. Dunn has reassured them time and time again that the strange sound is nothing more than the wild winds sweeping down off the mountainside. Our work has slowed to the point where Mr. Dunn asked me to help him conduct an investigation into the matter.

"Last night Mr. Dunn and I entered the great tunnel at exactly 9:00 P.M. We traveled about two miles into the shaft and then stopped to listen. As we stood there in the cold silence, we both heard what truly sounded like a man groaning out in pain. As you know, I have heard this same sound many times during the war. Yet, when we turned up the wicks on our lamps, there were no other human beings in the shaft except Mr. Dunn and myself. I'll admit I haven't been this frightened since Shiloh. Mr. Dunn agreed that it wasn't the wind we heard. Perhaps Nash or Brinkman—I wonder?"

A month later, on October 17, 1868, the worst disaster in the tunnel's history occurred. Thirteen miners died in a gas explosion that blew apart a surface pumping station. Debris filled the central shaft where the miners were working.

Glenn Drohan, a correspondent for *The North Adams Transcript*, reported that a miner named Mallery was lowered by bucket and rope to search for survivors. Brought back to the surface, and almost unconscious from fumes, he gasped, "No hope."

Without an operating pumping station, the 538-foot shaft soon filled with water. Bodies of some of the dead miners surfaced. More than a year later the remaining bodies were found on a raft the men had built to float on the rising water. They had suffocated from the vapors of deadly naphtha gas.

Drohan wrote, "During the time the miners were missing, villagers told strange tales of vague shapes and muffled wails near the water-filled pit. Workmen claimed to see the lost miners carrying picks and shovels through a shroud of mist and snow at [the] mountaintop.

"The ghostly apparitions would appear briefly, then vanish, leaving no footprints in the snow, giving no answers to the miners' calls.

"But, as soon as the raft-bound miners were found, and given a 'decent' burial, the visitations ceased."

Yet deep inside the tunnel, the eerie moanings persisted, and workers were terrified.

Four years after the gas explosion, a Dr. Clifford J. Owens visited the tunnel, accompanied by James R. McKinstrey, a drilling operations superintendent. Dr. Owens wrote the following account, which was thought to have appeared first in a Michigan newspaper:

"On the night of June 25, 1872, James McKinstrey and I entered the great excavation at precisely 11:30 P.M. We had traveled about two full miles into the shaft when we finally halted to rest. Except for the dim smoky light cast by our lamps, the place was as cold and dark as a tomb.

"James and I stood there talking for a minute or two and were just about to turn back when suddenly I heard a strange mournful sound. It was just as if someone or something was suffering great pain. The next thing I saw was a dim light coming along the tunnel from a westerly direction. At first, I believed it was probably a workman with a lantern. Yet, as the light grew closer, it took on a strange blue color and appeared to change shape almost into the form of a human being without a head. The light seemed to be floating along about a foot or two above the tunnel floor. In the next instant, it felt as if the temperature had suddenly dropped and a cold, icy chill ran up and down my spine. The headless form came so close that I could have reached out and touched it but I was too terrified to move.

"For what seemed like an eternity, McKinstrey and I just stood there gaping at the headless thing like two wooden Indians. The blue light remained motionless for a few seconds as if it were actually looking us over, then floated off toward the east end of the shaft and vanished into thin air.

". . . I am above all a realist," he continued, "nor am I prone to repeating gossip and wild tales that defy a reasonable explanation. However, in all truth, I can not deny what James McKinstrey and I witnessed with our own eyes."

On October 16, 1874, Frank Webster, a local hunter, vanished. Three days later, a search party found him stumbling along the banks of the Deerfield River in a state of shock. Webster said that strange voices had ordered him into the Hoosac Tunnel, and once inside he saw ghostly figures wandering about. Suddenly, something seized his rifle from his hands and beat him over the head with it. When the searchers found the hunter he had no weapon with him and he couldn't recall leaving the tunnel.

During that same year, with tunnel headings completed, workmen removed rubble, completed the grading, and laid track. On February 9, 1875, the first train went through the tunnel. It pulled 125 people on three flatcars and a boxcar. North Adams had become "the Western Gateway" to much of New England.

But even with the completion of the tunnel, frightening tales still circulated.

In the fall of 1875, Harlan Mulvaney, a fire tender, was driving a wagonload of firewood into the tunnel late one night. Suddenly Mulvaney turned his team around, whipped the horses across their flanks, and careened out of the tunnel.

A couple of days later, workmen found the team and wagon in woods three miles from the tunnel. Mulvaney was never seen or heard from again.

Joseph Impoco, a former employee of the Boston and Maine Railroad, believes there may be some truth to this legend. He went to work for the railroad at the age of eighteen and claimed the tunnel ghosts saved his life. Twice! In an interview that appeared in *The Berkshire Sampler* of October 30, 1977, Impoco told reporter Eileen Kuperschmid that he was chipping ice from the tracks one day when he heard a voice say, "Run, Joe, run!"

"I turned and sure enough there was No. 60 coming at me. Boy, did I jump back fast. When I looked there was no one there," he recalled.

Impoco said he heard the voice before he heard the train. He added that he'd seen a guy with a torch pass by and wave, but he paid no attention to him. The voice that had come from somewhere saved his life.

Six weeks later, Impoco was using an iron crowbar to free freight cars stuck on icy tracks. Someone shouted, "Joe! Joe! Drop it, Joe!" He dropped the bar and it was instantly struck and smashed against the tunnel wall by eleven thousand volts of electricity from a short-circuited overhead power line.

Later, while removing trees from the tunnel entrance, Impoco was nearly crushed when an enormous oak fell in his direction. He outran the falling tree, all the while hearing a strange, unearthly laugh. He was certain it hadn't come from one of his crew members.

Joseph Impoco quit his job and moved away. But every year he returned to visit the tunnel and to pay homage to the ghost who had saved his life. He was certain that if he didn't go tragedy would befall him. In 1977 he stayed home. His wife was ill and she wanted him with her. In October of that year she died.

In 1976 a parapsychologist from Agawam, Massachusetts, visited the tunnel and claimed to see the figure of a man wearing old-fashioned work clothes. The man appeared within a glowing white light. Could it have been the apparition that Owens and McKinstrey had seen 104 years earlier?

Ali Allmaker, a philosophy professor at North Adams State College and part-time ghost hunter, wrote in the *Berkshires Week*, issue of July 6–12, 1984: "I have been in the tunnel only once, accompanied by a railroad official, and can attest to the claim that it *is* an eerie place. I had the uncomfortable feeling that someone was walking closely behind me in the darkness and would tap me on my shoulder or, worse, pull me into some unknown and unspeakable horror at any moment."

Allmaker also reported that, on one occasion, college students took a tape recorder into the tunnel, turned it on and left. When they retrieved the machine, sounds like muffled human voices were heard on the tape.

Although today's visitor to the area may be tempted to enter the tunnel, he risks his life in doing so because the Boston and Maine Railroad runs a dozen or more freight trains through the tunnel every day. But he can gain an appreciation of this enormous engineering feat by visiting the Hoosac Tunnel Museum in the Western Gateway Heritage State Park that opened in North Adams in 1985.

And if the visitor talks to certain old-timers, he'll learn that reports of chilling winds, shrieking noises, and floating apparitions still occur. Perhaps the Mohawk Indians had correctly named Hoosac Mountain. In their language it means "the Forbidden Mountain." And did they also, as some believe, put a curse upon this place to keep it safe from white invaders?

The Eternal Wanderers

Storm clouds roiled and lightning slashed the western sky. The man in the rickety carriage glanced over his shoulder, then whipped his bay horse into a faster gallop. Beside him, a little girl, eyes wide with fear, clutched his sleeve with both hands.

Since that day in 1770, Peter Rugg and his daughter, Jenny, have been trying to get home to Boston. For years after the American Revolution, many persons claimed to have seen the pair in all parts of New England.

"Which way to Boston, my good man?" Rugg called out to the fellow travelers he might encounter. And each time the road was pointed out to him, Rugg sped off in the opposite direction.

Storms always followed the travelers, drenching them with rain, pelting them with hail. The child shivered in her thin cloak and pressed closer to her father. As they passed through nameless villages, townsfolk called out to offer food and lodging. Rugg always shook his head. "For the sake of the child," they pleaded. "Must get to Boston tonight!" shouted her father. The pair usually vanished before anyone saw them go.

Adonariah Adams, the veteran driver of the Portland mail, claimed to have met Rugg and his daughter near Newburyport, the great bay horse overtaking Adams with such speed that his own horses leaped from the road and wrecked the coach against a rock outcropping.

"I saw Peter and his daughter glowin' with fire like a horse-shoe as it's taken from the blacksmith's hearth," Adams told his friends. "At the very same time, there was flames and sparks comin' from the mouth and ears of that huge bay horse and I was almost choked by the smell of brimstone . . . I know that what I saw was the devil's shade of Peter Rugg!"

Who was Peter Rugg? He was a horse and cattle dealer with a lovely, hardworking wife and a beautiful young daughter. The family lived on Middle Street in Boston, and was well respected by their neighbors. Although Rugg was said to have a violent temper when crossed, he was generally good-humored, fair in his business dealings, and generous in providing for his family. They never lacked for necessities and Mrs. Rugg was always the first to comfort a troubled neighbor woman.

One fall day Rugg hitched his horse to the chaise to make a business trip to

Concord. Because it was a warm, sunny morning, he took ten-year-old Jenny with him for company. She loved riding in the open carriage and especially liked taking the reins from her father to guide the horse over safe, open stretches of road. Her father's trust in her made her feel grown-up and confident.

But as the two started home, a violent storm overtook them. Rain, driven by a rising wind, seemed to come from all directions at once. Rugg slowed the horse as he squinted to see what lay ahead. Only the steady hum of the carriage wheels assured him that he was on the roadway. On either side, trees bent and groaned and spilled the last of their colored leaves.

By the time the pair reached West Cambridge, they were cold, drenched, and hungry. Rugg stopped at Tom Cutter's place for a quick dram of rum, but when Cutter suggested that the two spend the night there, Rugg's temper flared. "Damn the storm!" he bellowed. "I'll see home tonight, or may I never see home!"

He leaped into the carriage beside Jenny, whose thin clothes were pasted to her wet body, and raised the whip to his horse. He did not reach home. Searches were made, but Peter Rugg and his daughter were never found.

Late one night the following May, Sven Parson, another resident of Middle Street, got out of bed to take some medicine. Suddenly, he heard a carriage clattering over the cobblestones. No, he thought, it must be his imagination. No one would be out driving at this unseemly hour and on a rainy night. He went back to bed, but did not sleep.

Thomas Felt, the gunsmith, was awakened by the same noise and leaned out of his window. Through the mist he saw a carriage approaching. He could discern the forms of Peter Rugg and his daughter seated in a weatherbeaten rig, but they seemed enveloped in a phosphorescent glow. Felt shuddered, closed his window and drew the shade.

In the morning the gunsmith learned that other neighbors had seen the strange spectacle, but all agreed not to tell Mrs. Rugg. Another search was begun, to no avail.

Newspapermen, fascinated by the tale of the missing couple, vied with one another in reporting new sightings. The tolltaker at the Charles River Bridge said that the pair crossed his bridge many times at midnight, never slowing to pay the fare. On one occasion, the angry tollman threw a stool at the horse, but it passed right through the animal. The stool ended up leaning against the guardrail on the other side of the bridge.

In the summer of 1820 Jonathan Dunwell, a New York businessman, traveled to Boston. He sailed by packet to Providence, then went by stage to Boston. Because all the seats were filled in the stagecoach, he was obliged to sit up with the driver, a pleasant, agreeable man. They had not traveled far when the driver asked, "Do you see the horses' ears?"

Dunwell noticed that the animals' ears were flat against their heads. At that moment a man and a child in a rickety carriage raced around the stage at an incredible speed. After they were gone the horses' ears went up. How peculiar, thought the traveler, and asked about the people in the carriage that had overtaken them.

"I've met them at least a hundred times," said the driver, "and the man stops only long enough to ask the way to Boston, even when he has come from that direction."

Dunwell studied the driver's face. "But who is he?"

"They say his name is Peter Rugg and the tavernkeepers claim that he and his daughter have been traveling these parts for fifty years. I'm told they never stop to eat or rest."

Dunwell thought it an unlikely story, but said nothing. The driver looked up at the darkening sky. "A storm always follows the wanderers, but we'll make Polleys tonight."

The stage reached Polleys Inn just as the storm burst. The driver and the innkeeper helped the passengers alight, unloaded their trunks, and then stabled the team and coach. After the horses had rested the driver fed them.

A short time later, a peddler with a cart of tin merchandise arrived at the inn. The man was drenched. After he had dried himself before the fire, he recounted a remarkable story. He said he'd met the man and the girl in the carriage in four different states within the previous two weeks. Each time after the man asked the peddler the way to Boston, a thunderstorm followed, soaking the peddler and his merchandise. He smiled and said, "It's enough to make me want to get marine insurance on my wares." Then his face became grave. "That rig doesn't belong to this world."

Three years later Jonathan Dunwell was in Hartford on a business trip. While standing on the doorstep of Bennett's Hotel he heard a man exclaim, "Why look! There goes Peter Rugg and his child! And farther from Boston than ever."

As the rig clattered past them Dunwell knew that was the man he had seen years before. The speaker then told Dunwell what he knew about the wanderers. When he finished he said, "I have heard it asserted that Heaven sometimes sets a mark on a man either for judgment or a trial. Under which Peter Rugg now labors, I cannot say; therefore I am rather inclined to pity than to judge."

On Dunwell's next trip to Boston he went to the address on Middle Street where he had been told Peter Rugg once lived. A Mrs. Betsey Croft, an elderly widow, answered the door. No, it was not Rugg's house; it was hers. Nevertheless she, too, had a tale to tell.

"One night last summer, just at twilight, a stranger knocked at my door. He looked frail and tired in his tattered clothes and he had a sickly looking child by his side. At the curb stood an ancient carriage drawn by the biggest black horse I've ever seen."

Mrs. Croft wiped her hands on her apron and looked up at Dunwell. "Oh, do forgive me. Won't you please come in."

After they were seated in a small, modestly furnished parlor, Mrs. Croft continued:

"Well, this stranger asked for Mrs. Rugg. I told him the woman had died more than twenty years ago at an advanced age, and this was my house now. Of course, I gave him my name. But he said no, it was his house and the child said she used to sit on the stone doorstep. 'Didn't I, Daddy?' she pleaded.

"Her father nodded, then shook his head slowly. 'So Catherine Rugg has deserted her husband and child. But pray tell me, madam, has John Foy come home from sea? He's a relation and could maybe give me an account of my wife. He lives just above here on Orange Tree Lane.'

"Now, Mr. Dunwell," the widow continued, "there is no such place in this neighborhood. I told the gentleman that the streets were all changed or gone and the people were all dead. He mentioned other streets that I never heard of and remarked that he must have made a mistake. He wanted to get to Boston, but when I told him he *was* in Boston he said no because his horse would have taken him directly to his home. All this time, the child twisted her hair in her fingers and stared at the pictures on my walls. A very odd girl indeed. I thought she seemed somehow unreal."

When Dunwell pressed for more details, Mrs. Croft offered to send for James Felt, an elderly neighbor who knew more than anyone else about the Rugg family.

Mrs. Croft excused herself to make a pot of tea. When her neighbor arrived she introduced the two men and all three sat in the parlor.

Mr. Felt took a philosophical view toward the story of Peter Rugg. "I knew him in his youth," he began, "and of course his disappearance was a great shock. The rumormongers set to work spreading all kinds of tales that weren't true. The man owed no one any money so he wasn't escaping creditors. And he certainly wasn't committing any crime. He took his daughter and his own horse and chaise."

Felt set down his cup and looked at Dunwell. "Who knows why Peter Rugg vanished? He had his reasons, of that I'm certain. It's been about fifty years now and he's forgotten, at least in this neighborhood. We've all heard stranger tales."

Dunwell studied the old man's face with its wrinkles so placed that it gave his mouth a constant smile. He was the kind of man you liked instinctively without knowing exactly why.

"Mr. Felt," Dunwell said, leaning forward in his chair, "Peter Rugg is alive. I've seen him and his little daughter in the chaise drawn by the big black horse. Please tell me more about him."

Felt shifted in his chair. "Yes, Mr. Dunwell, Peter Rugg *could* be alive. I was eighty last March and he was only ten years older than myself. But the girl Jenny was ten years old when she and her father vanished. If she were now living she'd be more than sixty."

So the old peddler had spoken the truth: *That rig doesn't belong in this world.* Dunwell thanked his hostess and her neighbor and returned to his hotel.

A short time later the Reverend Samuel Nickles, a circuit preacher, left Wickford for Providence astride his old near-sighted nag, Romeo. That evening they were caught in a severe thunderstorm. The preacher hunched down in his upturned coat collar, relaxed his hold on the reins and let the horse lead the way.

As they entered a narrow trail between two hills, Nickles heard a fast-approaching carriage headed straight for him. He looked up to see the driver pulling frantically on the reins while a child beside him clutched his sleeve. The horse drawing the rig was huge, and its eyes shone like live coals.

Romeo, frightened and frothing at the mouth, reared up and somersaulted his rider onto the back of the great bay horse pulling the carriage. The terrified minister screamed, and at a clap of thunder the horse dashed up the side of a boulder.

In the morning sunlight, Reverend Nickles regained consciousness. He was lying at the base of a huge stone. Stiff and bruised, he staggered to his feet and then saw, with horror, cloven hoof prints in the solid rock. Romeo was nibbling on grass nearby—but not for long. Nickles eased himself onto the back of his horse and the two sped away as fast as the old nag could go.

Now Reverend Nickles had something more interesting than moral admonitions to give his congregations. For years afterward, people flocked to view the strange hoof prints in the rock. And for all anybody knows, Peter Rugg and Jenny are still trying to get to Boston.

MASSACHUSETTS

Mercy Denied

A thin sickle moon hung over the little coastal settlement of Marblehead, Massachusetts, on the night of September 21, 1690, barely lighting the unpainted clapboard houses that pockmarked the shore. The settlers, numbering less than one thousand, were proud, resourceful folks who built sturdy homes with their own hands and took care of their own needs.

What food they didn't grow came mostly from the sea. Several times each year all the men who were physically able sailed off to the Grand Banks, hoping to return with a good haul of haddock and cod. Retired seamen and women, many with babies and small children, were left alone for weeks at a time. It was a harsh, lonely existence. On warm, sunny days, women, with chores finished, would sometimes gather at the beach. While the adults visited, shy children hid in the folds of their mothers' long skirts and older ones played tag on the sand.

But there were fearful moments, too, and they always seemed to occur when all the able-bodied men were away. The seventeenth century was the era of piracy, and Marblehead had its share of mysterious ships that anchored at Oakum Bay (later Little Harbor) after dark and slipped away before dawn. The bay was a harbor of refuge for *any* ship needing to wait out rough seas.

During the long evenings people sought entertainment at the local tavern. There, by the fireside, they'd tell tales of Ned Low, the infamous Boston pirate, and Peter Quelch, who terrorized scores of coastal villages from Canada to the Caribbean. But young wives whose husbands were gone were made uneasy by such talk and seldom left their homes after dark. They hurried their children indoors at dusk and closed both windows and shutters, "against the damp night air," they told one another.

On that September night in 1690, the young men were gone to sea. The air seemed still and heavy. An inlander might have predicted a tornado. There was a sense that the waters lay motionless, that the ocean had somehow ceased rolling. Seafaring people have their superstitions, and the people of Marblehead knew that something sinister was upon them. It was written on the faces of the four old women and the five old men who had gathered at the tavern.

Without a word, ancient Lucas Manley grabbed a lantern and stepped out of the tavern. With the light in one hand and his cane in the other, he hobbled partway down a thin strip of rocky beach. He returned to report "there aren't nuthin' to be feared of." A few careful observers thought his eyes said otherwise.

Lucas's words broke the tension. Men and women, now reassured of their safety, glanced at one another and smiled. Lucas was the patriarch of the town whose advice was sought by everyone. He'd signed on as a deckhand on a schooner when he was sixteen, spent over six decades at sea, and was now eighty-two years old. People said there was nothing about the natural world that Lucas didn't know, that he even talked to the stars and they answered him.

As the villagers began strolling back to their homes, Tim Locksley, the tavern-keeper, closed up and retired to his bachelor quarters at the rear of the building.

Just before midnight it happened. A woman cried out, "Lord Jesus, save me! Dear Christ, have mercy on me!"

Amanda Cartwright heard the shrieks.

Hortense Potter heard the shrieks.

Emily Langham heard the shrieks.

Amanda was molding candles and spilled hot wax on the floor. Hortense was spinning wool yarn and the wheel stopped suddenly as if struck by some hidden force. Emily was weaving and would never remember leaving her loom. All three women were alone in their houses with small children. They extinguished their lanterns immediately.

The screams came again . . . and again, each time growing fainter. "Help me! Please help me! Oh God, have mercy!"

Then a rough male voice shouted, "You'll be shuttin' up, you slut! Do you want to waken the dead?"

Amanda put her trembling hands to her face. The unfamiliar voices came from Lovis Cove just below her house. The pirates had landed! Their ship would be anchored out in the bay.

Amanda's children were awakened by the screams and their mother herded them into her own bed and warned them to be quiet. "Stay still and we won't be hurt." The baby sniffled while the older ones, both boys, said they wished they could meet real live pirates.

Amanda fell to her knees and crawled to the sill of the one narrow window that overlooked the water. She had forgotten to fasten the shutters and now she dared not go outside to do it. Between boulders and clumps of sea grass she saw a lantern shining over the sand, and by its light she detected the form of a young woman kneeling at the water's edge. A ruffian was bending over her. Would he rape her? Torture her? Kill her? Amanda felt the tears slide down her cheeks. Her heart ached for the suffering stranger. But what could she do? Nothing. Nor could any of the handful of women and the feeble old men left in the settlement.

Amanda's knees hurt and her head throbbed, yet she dare not stand. If the pirate's lantern was swung upward she might be caught in its beam. She could not risk her own life nor the lives of her children.

"Oh God, have mercy!"

The words drifting upward were so faint now that Amanda barely heard them.

Then came silence and with it the awesome fear of not knowing what had happened and what could yet happen. Amanda crawled to the door to be certain it was bolted, then, wrapping herself in a heavy blanket, lay down on the bare wood floor beside the bed that held her children.

*　　*　　*

The buccaneers had captured a Spanish galleon loaded with wines, laces, silks, and satins and all manner of expensive goods. Immediately after boarding the vessel they had murdered the crew and begun to divide the loot. With heavy seas running, the pirates knew they'd have to take shelter. They had put in at Marblehead after dark and would leave before dawn. Having heard that all the able-bodied men of the community were on the Banks fishing, they expected no trouble. A single lantern faintly illuminated the ship's deck.

Suddenly, the door leading into the after-cabin opened and a heavyset man with red hair and a scarred face advanced onto the deck. From out of the shadows by the railing emerged a younger, handsome man wearing velvet breeches and a shirt of fine linen open at the throat. Caressing the hilt of his sword he said, "I see that you are prompt, Crotch."

The other nodded. "Ben Crotch's word is always good." He grinned and his eyes flashed cold in the lantern's light. "You know the cargo don't interest me," he went on, "and it don't interest you either, De Longe. We both know that. Let the gang fight over it." He stepped forward. "It's the wench I want and you want her too. There's only one of her and two of us."

Capt. Temple De Longe leveled his eyes on his rival and fingered his black mustache. "Why not let the lady decide?"

"You bastard!" Crotch screamed. "What kind of a chance do you think I'd have against the likes of you?"

"Remember, Crotch," said De Longe in a controlled, even voice, "I'm captain here. Go fetch the girl."

A few minutes later Crotch emerged from a cabin, dragging the reluctant and frightened young woman. She was a beautiful English girl whose husband had been killed along with the ship's crew. Squeezing the girl's forearm in his rough hand, Crotch gestured toward De Longe. "The captain there says you must choose between us. What d'you say?"

The girl trembled and glanced from one man to the other, her eyes wild with fright. "No, no, not that! Please," she begged, "please let me go!"

"See!" Crotch exclaimed triumphantly. "For all your finery you're not better than me." He glared at his rival. "There's only one way, De Longe. I'll fight you for the wench."

De Longe agreed and ordered more lanterns to be brought to the deck.

Crotch shook his head. "Not here. One of your men could sneak up and run me through. We'll go ashore, you, me, and the girl."

A skiff was lowered and the trio climbed in. Crotch rowed with strong, even strokes while De Longe never took his eyes off the girl. When the boat swung into Lovis Cove, De Longe helped the girl wade ashore. Crotch shouldered the stern of the boat and heaved it onto the beach.

No words passed between the men. Each understood that this duel would be fought with no formalities. Crotch unsheathed his heavy cutlass; De Longe bared his slender Spanish rapier. With only the radiance of the stars and the faint reflection of the water to guide them, each man advanced. Steel clashed against steel, and the young woman, mesmerized by each thrust and parry, clenched her hands until they ached.

Suddenly, De Longe screamed, "Oh, my God!" He leaped back, his sword snapped in half. Crotch sneered. He cut the captain down with one lunge and then stood over him, watching the sand turn crimson.

He turned toward the girl, who seemed only a dim shape in the darkness. "I won! D'ya hear? I won! Now you're all mine!" he screamed.

She stooped to pick up something from the sand. Crotch saw the glitter of steel, a piece of the captain's rapier. She lunged at him, but the sword only grazed his shoulder. Crotch seized her by the throat, laughing as her screams trembled on the air. When they had died away, Crotch hurriedly covered her body with sand, sheathed his cutlass and bore the corpse of Captain De Longe to the skiff. Only the dip of oars broke the stillness of the night.

At daybreak, Hortense and Emily appeared at Amanda's door. They had left all the children in Emily's house with fourteen-year-old Sarah Potter in charge. Beneath their bonnets, the faces of both women were pale and drawn. Hortense said she had slept fitfully, and Emily said she hadn't slept at all.

Amanda, leaving her boys to tend the baby, accompanied her friends down the winding path that led from her house into the cove. Lucas, a couple of the old men, and the one old woman were already there. Lucas was the first to spot the slight mound of sand partially hidden by rushes. He began digging with his strong, gnarled hands. He did not have far to go. The woman's battered and bruised body was only a few inches beneath the surface. The fourth finger of her right hand had been severed. The women thought she might have been wearing a jeweled ring that the pirates couldn't remove.

The little knot of mourners stood in a circle, heads bowed, each praying silently for the repose of the poor woman's soul. Only Lucas saw the pirate ship, now a dot on the horizon. Only he had heard the splash when the ship dropped anchor the night before.

For many years the people of Marblehead avoided Lovis Cove. Each year on the anniversary of this gentle woman's death, the rushes heave slightly over her grave. Again and again her screams—"Help me! Save me! Lord, have mercy!"—shatter the night air.

MICHIGAN
Nights of Horror

Marge and Ted Brower were thrilled with their new home in southwest Grand Rapids. They moved in during Christmas of 1964, after searching for a long time for just the right house to restore. For months they scraped layers of paint from the woodwork, steamed off stained wallpaper and hung new, and waxed the hardwood floors to a mirror finish. They bought handsome colonial furniture and braided rugs. This was the couple's first home and they wanted everything to be just right.

But it wasn't. From the beginning the house seemed strange. There was a certain coldness in it. Ted worked nights on the railroad, and one morning he got home to find a large upstairs closet door open and the light on. The rear of the closet opened into an attic where the couple stored out-of-season clothes and items needed only occasionally.

Now, Ted saw the contents of large boxes scattered all over the floor. He called Marge. She said she hadn't been in there. Together they searched both closet and attic for an opening through which a squirrel might have entered, but the house was tight. There was no way in which an animal could have gotten through.

Ted locked the closet door, but for the next five mornings he and Marge found the door unlocked, the light on, and the closet and the attic ransacked.

On the sixth morning they discovered a woman's expensive watch lying on a pile of clothes on the attic floor. Marge saw it first, the diamond-encrusted watch band glittering in the sunlight pouring through a small window.

"Gee, it's expensive!" said Ted, fingering the watch. He and Marge debated what to do with it, and finally decided to leave it there. The antics in the attic abruptly ceased. Several days later the couple packed the watch away.

Marge was uneasy. She wondered if she had met the owner of the watch. She'd never said anything to her husband about the mysterious caller who had come to the house one spring afternoon. The woman wore a calf-length silk dress, a wide-brimmed straw hat blooming with artificial flowers, and white lace gloves on her tiny hands. Marge wondered why she was dressed in such dated clothes.

The woman asked to see the house, but never went beyond the living room. Or needed to. Smiling faintly, she said, "I lived here once. I remember it well."

Marge felt a chill sweep over her as she looked into the stranger's pale face and watery eyes. The poor woman must be sick.

"But . . . but are you happy here, my dear?" The woman's voice seemed faint.

Marge nodded.

"Well, that's nice," said the visitor, glancing around the room once more. "Well, thank you. I must go now."

The woman seemed to float down the walkway. After she'd gone Marge went to the kitchen to make a cup of tea, but her hands shook as she held the cup to her lips. She was overly tired, she decided; she and Ted had done too much work in too short a time. The visitor was probably a nice, if eccentric, old neighbor lady who'd come calling, and Marge regretted that she hadn't invited her to stay for tea.

But in the next few days Marge would learn that no one in the neighborhood had ever seen the woman she described.

At any rate, the house was peaceful and Marge was beginning to relax and enjoy it. She and Ted invited friends to dinner and were pleased to receive compliments on their lovely home. Neighbor women dropped in and Marge soon felt a part of her new community.

Then it happened. One night at midnight something scratched at the first-floor bedroom window where Marge was sleeping. She awoke screaming, as from a nightmare. Ted was at work. She got up, turned on all the lights and went back to bed. She never closed her eyes, nor did she dare to open the curtains.

When Ted returned from work, Marge told him what had happened.

"It's nothing, Marge," he said, "probably just the branches of that bush outside the window. The wind must have been blowing them against the glass."

Marge was not comforted. It had not been windy outside. The next night she heard the scratching again and stayed up all night with the lights burning.

When Ted got home and heard the same story he put an arm around his wife. "Gee, hon, you've never been so jumpy. I can't understand you."

"No," she snapped, "and I can't understand what's going on outside that window."

They fought, and finally Ted said, "Okay, I'll cut the damn bush down!" With saw in hand, he stomped out of the house.

The next night he understood his wife's fear. He awakened as something clawed at the window, something that sounded like fingernails dragging over a blackboard. There was no bush outside that window. He broke into a cold sweat and briefly considered going outdoors to check, but thought better of it. He and Marge sat in the kitchen drinking coffee until dawn.

The following night the couple did not go to bed at all. They sat up waiting for the noises that never came.

For a week after those hectic, sleepless nights the house was quiet. Marge was no longer afraid to go to bed alone while Ted worked. Some nights she was so exhausted that she never remembered getting into bed, nor did she wake up until her husband got home and kissed her good night.

Then something *entered* the house! Marge was awakened by heavy footsteps pacing upstairs. The sound was loud and clear, and the young woman was more fearful than ever. She sat up again, waiting for her husband to come home.

When Ted heard about the footsteps he was alarmed. He immediately quit his railroad job and took one in a gas station near home. If his wife were in danger he could get home more quickly.

There was a door at the foot of the stairway in the couple's house that closed off the main floor from the second floor. The door had no lock, but Ted figured a way to keep it from being opened. He wedged three table knives into the door-jamb. Now Marge would have peace of mind, knowing that whatever was up there could not get downstairs.

That same night Marge heard the familiar footsteps overhead. Then something came down the stairway. Suddenly, there was silence. The "thing," whatever it was, stood on the other side of the door. Marge opened her mouth to scream, but no sound came out.

She heard the plunk of a knife on the bare floor. Another plunk—and then the third! Burying herself in her bedclothes, she fought back tears. Something moved across the dining room floor, through the kitchen, and out the back door. After the door slammed shut, Marge lay still, listening. A neighbor's dog barked and, in the distance, an ambulance shrieked.

When Ted came in the front door, he stood aghast at the sight of the knives lying on the floor. Marge stood, trembling. Ted knew then that something wanted him and Marge out of the house. But they had poured much love and money into it. It was their home, damn it. They would *not* be driven out!

When strange noises arose from the basement one day, Ted thought it was a prowler and boarded up all the basement windows. But when sawing and rasping noises arose, Ted knew that someone had gotten in down there. As he started down the basement stairs, a step collapsed beneath him; he staggered, but did not fall. With his flashlight, he discovered that the step had been sawed through from the underside! Ted's tools lay untouched. No one was in the basement—at least no one he could see.

The locked closet, the barricade of knives, the boarded-up basement windows—could nothing keep the "thing" out?

Ted bought his wife a German shepherd. The dog would protect her and frighten away any prowler. He wished he had thought of it earlier. As an extra precaution he locked the kitchen door that led to the basement and wedged a solid oak table leaf under the doorknob. It was impossible for anyone to get past *this* barricade.

The days were once more peaceful. Marge loved the dog and together they took long walks every afternoon. One evening a week later, the dog stood over the floor register in the living room, howling, then pacing around it. Marge heard faint noises coming from the basement, but could not identify them.

The next night terrible wailings came from the basement, as if someone were in great pain. The dog was frantic. It barked, howled, clawed at the register. Heavy footsteps started up the basement stairs—slowly, purposefully. Marge phoned her husband at work. He told her to stay on the telephone, that nothing could come through that door.

An ear-splitting noise like a shotgun blast shook the house. Marge screamed and dropped the phone. Flinging a coat over her shoulders, she ran all the way to the gas station. She was hysterical and determined to stay in the station office all night. Ted raced home.

In the kitchen he found the table leaf split right down the middle and lying in two pieces on the floor. The door to the basement was still locked! The dog stared at the door, growling and baring its teeth.

Ted and Marge Brower never returned to live in the house. They moved to another city and do not like to talk about the demons that drove them out of their dream home.

The mystery was never solved.

Buried Bones

Mrs. Hattie Sebastian, a widow with five children, needed a place to live. In the summer of 1910 she found it, a second-floor apartment of a ramshackle frame house at 486 Pleasant Avenue in St. Paul. The rooms were clean and the rent affordable. Mr. Sebastian had died six years earlier in an industrial accident, and the insurance settlement was barely enough to cover the necessities of daily living. But Hattie Sebastian had her pride. She told her friends that the house was a perfect place to raise her family.

But it was far from perfect. From the day they moved in, the family was disturbed by odd noises that shook the walls and windows of the entire house. (The first-floor apartment was vacant at the time.) Hattie searched the rooms, but found nothing to explain the noises. When the youngest children became too frightened to sleep, their mother moved the family to the slightly more expensive first-floor apartment. The noises continued, but Hattie dared not complain to the owner of the building for fear of being ridiculed or maybe even evicted.

One night between Christmas and New Year's, eight-year-old Hazel and eleven-year-old Rosie started down the cellar stairs with a blanket to make a bed for their dog in the small upper cellar. As they bent over a box to arrange the blanket, they heard soft footsteps padding below. Then an ugly, stocky man started climbing the rickety wooden stairway that led up from the deep, lower cellar. He wore a hairy overcoat and moccasins. In the dim light of their lantern, the girls saw his shining black hair, his black mustache and dark eyes. They screamed, snatched up the dog, and stumbled up the stairs.

In the kitchen, mother and daughters slammed shut the door to the cellar and threw their weight against it. Hazel thought the doorknob turned, but the others didn't notice, nor did they feel anyone pushing against the door from the other side. The dog slept in the kitchen.

Sometime later, Hattie lit a lantern, cracked open the door and peered down the stairway. It was empty. She tiptoed halfway down and shone her light in all directions. It revealed the coal pile in its wooden crib, the furnace ducts that snaked in all directions, and the cobwebs that were strung from rafter to rafter. There was no sign of any intruder.

Hattie didn't know what to make of the episode. She wanted to believe her girls, yet there was no solid proof of what they said they had seen. She said nothing more to her children. With the recent move, she was still busy trying to get everyone settled into their rooms and arranging her furniture and unpacking her kitchen utensils.

But one day in the middle of January she went into the cellar to split wood for the cookstove. Just as she lifted the axe, a shaft of white light passed before her eyes. There was no way to account for it. She threw down the axe and dashed upstairs. The noises the family had heard when they first moved in were now increasing in intensity, and soft footsteps shuffled through the rooms. Hattie was becoming uneasy.

One evening, a Mrs. J. Pryor, of 31 Douglas Street, and Mrs. E. A. Hempel, her next-door neighbor, visited Hattie. The three women had been close friends for years and Hattie was delighted to see them. They discussed the day's news over their teacups and Hattie refrained from saying anything about the house. They passed a pleasant evening.

When the visitors were ready to leave, Emma Sebastian, twenty-two years old, and Minnie, her sister, went into the bedroom to get the ladies' coats.

"It was a terrible experience," Emma told a reporter from the *St. Paul Pioneer Press*. "A curtain separates the bed from the rest of the room and this I tried to draw back. But I couldn't. Ordinarily a child could throw it along the pole, but the combined efforts of myself and my sister were useless. Suddenly it moved slowly back of itself and then, in the glare of the lamp I held in my hands, I saw the figure of a man. He wore a hairy overcoat and a pair of moccasins. A black mustache hid his upper lip and I distinctly remember that he had brown eyes.

"I stood perfectly still for a few moments, fascinated," she continued. "Then, as I began to draw back, a feeling that I shall never forget came over me. He seemed to move toward me until, just as I felt his arms were about to clasp me about the neck, the lower part of his body faded away. Slowly, while I stood terror-stricken, the other part disappeared. I screamed and I don't remember what happened until I awakened to find myself in the living room."

"She fainted," Hattie pronounced.

The family later learned that a young man who had once slept in that room awakened, gasping for breath, in the middle of the night. The heaviness on his chest was so great that he couldn't sit up. Something was pressing him down by the shoulders. When he was able to free himself and sit up, the covers were jerked off him. He fled at dawn.

The night that Emma fainted her mother moved the family into the homes of friends and neighbors to sleep. By this time the youngest children were so frightened that Hattie kept them out of school. Although the family continued to rent the apartment and lived in it by day, they never again slept there.

One morning Hattie opened a closet door to remove some clothing and stared into the eyes of a black-haired man. She felt her head spin and she grabbed the doorjamb. The stranger vanished through the wall.

Hattie knew now that she must call the police. Something was most definitely in the house. Four officers arrived and, with drawn revolvers, searched the house from the attic to the lower cellar. They found no one, nor did they find evidence that a prowler had gained entry to the house.

The owner of the house, Chief J. J. Strapp of the St. Paul Fire Department, was contacted, and he said he'd take care of it. Whatever "it" was no one learned, because the chief never came around. At least Hattie never talked to him.

Meanwhile, news of the haunted house had leaked out and newsmen jumped on the story. Everyone in St. Paul talked about it. Neighbor men patrolled the grounds in shifts each night, harassed at least part of the time by motorists who shouted that they'd come to see the ghost. During daytime hours mothers pushed baby carriages slowly past the house and held the hands of toddlers who dragged behind. The streetcar company did a thriving business with special excursions, as did the taxi drivers.

One day in mid-winter a cold spell froze the water pipes. Hattie dug a hole in the dirt floor of the subcellar to pour warm water over the pipes. She had almost dumped the first bucket when her eye caught the glint of an object in the hole. Pulling her lantern closer, and getting down on her knees, Hattie gazed upon a pile of bones intermixed with crucifixes and rosaries which she feared to touch. To one side lay a folded sheet of paper, its edges crumbled. She lifted it out and spread it open. It appeared to be a letter written in French, which she could not read. Hattie hurried upstairs, inexplicably burned the letter in the kitchen stove, then called the police again.

The officers tramped down to the cellar, dug out the artifacts and turned the bones over to the coroner. He asked anatomy professors from the University of Minnesota to study the bone fragments, but they could come to no conclusion. The largest bone, the humerus, exists in both man and animal, and the sample that was found was too far deteriorated to make a determination of its origin.

F. J. McCarthy, a dealer in ecclesiastical goods, examined the rosaries and expressed amazement. He found them to be very old. He was especially attracted to the bone rosary and the crucifix. With a finger he traced each hand-carved bead of the rosary. "I should say this belonged to an old French settler. The work was done in France, I am sure . . . Catholics who settled in this vicinity years ago possessed such rosaries."

McCarthy said the mother-of-pearl rosary was extremely rare because the beads were joined with silver chains. The figure of Christ was also raised rather than being stamped on the cross. And the beads that were split by the shovel during the digging showed them to be made of wood and brass wire. Such rosaries were worn only by nuns. The letters J and M were engraved on two of the rosaries.

The crucifix too was of great antiquity, being made of bisque instead of modern metal.

Who had buried these ancient artifacts? And why? A clue came from Chief Strapp. He said his father had built the house in about 1880, and the Strapp family occupied it until 1900. In 1905 the house was rented to a Frenchman.

"I do not recall his name nor know what has become of him," Strapp said. "He was a man of medium height and weight and with a heavy black mustache and dark eyes."

This description matched that of the man the Sebastians claimed to have seen. Had he buried the rosaries and the crucifix? The letter Hattie had unfortunately destroyed might have provided this information.

Meanwhile, the crowds that had been wandering past the house day and night were no longer content to wander. Many persons, wanting to inspect the inside of the house, knocked at the front and back doors. Hattie was always on hand to greet them, and gave tours of the house, pointing out the places where the figure had been seen. But the continuous stream of visitors soon exhausted her, and dark circles rimmed her eyes. The children too were fretful.

Hattie knew that she and the children could not stay in the house any longer, and kindly neighbors and sympathetic friends packed the family's furniture into one room, ready to be moved when a suitable place could be found.

But before the family located other quarters, George Van Cook asked for permission to spend a night in the old house. Van Cook was a soldier who had built a reputation for "de-spooking" haunted houses. He was certain he could catch the man in the hairy overcoat. At twilight Van Cook, pistol at his side, settled down for a long night's vigil in the bedroom where Emma had fainted. Van Cook pushed back the curtain on the pole and sat with his back against the wall. But the silence was enervating and he found himself nodding off from time to time, then jerking awake. Twice, to keep himself awake, he got up and walked through the apartment. In the morning Van Cook reported that he had seen and heard nothing.

Several days later a séance was held at the house and again the ghost failed to materialize. A neighbor's child whispered loudly, "I bet there's some pigeons and rats in the attic." The spiritualists concluded that the Frenchman preferred a quiet, homey atmosphere and would not reveal himself in the interest of "science."

When a suitable apartment became available on Goodhue Street, the Sebastians moved away. The old house remained vacant for some time, and then two families moved into it. Neither one had heard the story of the ghost, nor did they report any supernatural activities.

Today the 400 block of Pleasant Avenue is gone, replaced by a section of Interstate Highway 35E. The story of the man in the hairy overcoat has passed into obscurity.

The Warriors' Return

Lake Mille Lacs, one of the largest and most beautiful bodies of water in Minnesota, is a sportsman's paradise. Walleye, northern pike, and bass abound in its clear waters, and deer, pheasant, and grouse frequent the nearby wooded areas. A visitor, standing on a pebbled beach on a cloudless, calm day, can see blue outlines of the opposite shore twenty miles away.

But such serenity did not always prevail. Three centuries ago the Sioux tribe that occupied this area was driven away and nearly annihilated by the Ojibwa who lived on the shores of Lake Superior. Out of the bloody battle came the legend of the haunting of the lake. For many years, settlers near Vineland reported seeing vague, white forms moving through the immense groves of sugar maple, and hearing chilling moans rising on the night air. The ghosts were believed to be the souls of the dead Sioux warriors.

In the closing years of the seventeenth century, a battle erupted, even though old antagonisms between these two great nations had been set aside. A Sioux maiden, who was being courted by two young braves, one Sioux, the other Ojibwa, chose the Ojibwa suitor. The jealous Sioux brave killed his rival. The act did not result in immediate hostilities, but it did remind the warriors of both tribes that their people had once been enemies. Any further aggravation would close the trails between the villages of the two tribes and sever the fragile bond of friendship that had been forged.

That aggravation was not long in coming. An elderly Ojibwa, father of four sons, lived at Fond du Lac, an important Ojibwa village at the head of Lake Superior near present-day Jay Cooke State Park. Although not a chief, the man was a great hunter highly respected by his people. He belonged to the Marten Totem family. His sons, full-grown and handsome men, made frequent visits to the villages of the Sioux. And the Sioux women, highly attracted to these visiting braves, usually gave them presents to take home.

Shortly after the quarrel over the Sioux maiden and the death of her Ojibwa suitor had occurred, the four brothers set forth to pay a friendly visit to the main village of the Sioux at Mille Lacs.

They made the trip easily in two days. But evidently their intentions were suspect, and their words misunderstood, for one of the brothers was treacherously murdered. The other three escaped safely to their father's home.

The old man listened with disbelief to the sad news. "Probably they have taken the life of my son through mistake," he reasoned.

Shortly afterward, when the surviving sons asked their father's permission to visit the Sioux lodges again, he told them to go. The brothers reached the village on the shore of Mille Lacs, and this time two of them were killed.

When the remaining son returned home, the father blackened his face in mourning, and his head hung low in sorrow.

Again the surviving son asked permission to travel to Mille Lacs Lake in order to visit the graves of his deceased brothers. The father said again, "Go, my son, for probably they have struck your brothers through mistake."

The son did not return. After a month had passed, the sorrowing father knew that the Sioux had murdered his last child. There was no mistake. Now, for the first time he began to weep. And as the tears flowed he planned his revenge.

First, he used the fruits of his hunt to obtain ammunition and other materials for a war party. Then he sent his tobacco and war club to the most remote villages of the Ojibwa,·detailing the evil that had been done to him, and inviting the warriors to assemble at Fond du Lac.

When preparations were completed, almost all of the men from the shores of Lake Superior gathered at Fond du Lac with muskets and scalping knives ready. Invoking the Great Spirit to aid them, the large war party set off on the trail toward the Sioux stronghold at Lake Mille Lacs.

The Sioux had established large villages at Cormorant Point and at Kathio, both on the west shore of the lake. Another village lay a few miles south of Kathio on First Lake, which was connected to the large lake by a portion of the Rum River. These villages consisted mostly of earthen lodges.

The vanguard of the Ojibwa attacked the Sioux at Cormorant Point early in the morning and nearly annihilated them. So swift was the action that the main battle was almost finished before the rear guard of the Ojibwa arrived. But the warring nations were unevenly matched. The Ojibwa, who had had long contact with white people, had acquired firearms from the French traders and training in modern warfare from French officers. The Sioux, who had no knowledge of gunpowder, relied on their traditional, unsophisticated weapons—bows and arrows, spears and clubs—all useless against the muskets of the enemy.

Nevertheless, a small remnant of Sioux managed to flee Cormorant Point in their canoes and reach Kathio. Here the Ojibwa struck with all their forces and the Sioux took refuge in their lodges. The enemy pursued them, dropping bags of powder into the smoke hole of each roof. The bags, ignited by the fire burning beneath the smoke hole, spread death quickly to all the unfortunate beings crowded within.

A few Sioux warriors survived, however, and escaped in the middle of the night to the village on First Lake. Here they made their last stand. The Ojibwa pursued and vanquished their enemy in three days.

The old man from Fond du Lac was satisfied. The deaths of his sons had been avenged; the Sioux were swept away from their favorite dwelling place forever.

The Luminescent Attic

That October day in Eveleth had been harsh and ragged, with wind-borne rain tearing leaves from the trees and pasting them to the ground. Darkness came early and now, in the shadowed gloom, Tim Mack pulled his car up in front of the old house.

"You wait here," he said to his wife and two young daughters, "while I take up the luggage." He tried to sound cheerful, all the while thinking that there was something oppressive about the place. It had seemed cheerful enough when the landlord showed the second-floor apartment to him days earlier. But now no lights welcomed him. The house seemed desolate.

Mack grabbed two suitcases and climbed the stairs to the front porch. Setting down one suitcase, he pulled the key from his pocket and unlocked the front door. Mack felt his way up the narrow inside stairway, the suitcases banging against the walls. Near the top of the stairs a light popped on. Mack was astonished. He recalled that the switch for the stair light was inside their new apartment . . . behind the still-locked door.

After depositing the suitcases inside the apartment, Mack turned on other lights and went back down to their landlord's apartment. A note on the door read, "Gone fishing for a week. Please make yourselves at home." Then who turned on the light?

The Macks settled into their new home. Tim tried to forget about the light's mysterious "greeting" and concentrated on his job as advertising manager of the *Mesabi Daily News*.

But his new apartment produced other mysteries.

Three weeks later, in November 1980, the Mack family was watching television in the living room when a loud explosion came from the kitchen. They rushed en masse to the room to find a drinking glass shattered on the counter.

"It was just powder," Mack said, shaking his head. "It wasn't a cheap glass, either. It was from a set of wedding present glasses that had survived a number of moves."

Mack's wife, Jan, was not uneasy, but she never knew what to expect next.

"One night we came home and saw all the lights burning in our apartment," she recalled. "I knew I hadn't left them on. I wouldn't go up those stairs alone."

There were other perplexing episodes with the frisky lights. Tim asked the landlord about the problem, but the man offered no help. The broken glass incident wasn't mentioned. "That was just too strange," Tim offered.

Then there was the attic.

The attic of legend is filled with bats, groans, and chains that clank in the night, but not *this* attic. It was a quiet, pleasant place.

"If I went up there during the daytime or nighttime hours," Jan Mack remembered, "there was a translucent light, a warm, friendly glow. I never felt afraid. It made me feel at peace."

Tim added that the attic ceiling was extremely high. "You could walk around up there without touching the roof. You almost didn't need lights."

There was a skylight at one end, but at night, of course, no light filtered through. The street lights were not bright enough to seep through several wall vents. The couple simply could not account for the attic's faint luminescence at all hours.

The couple found curious similarities between their new Eveleth home and their old house in Webster City, Iowa, including attics where oddities occurred.

In Iowa, the Macks had discovered "witches' shoes" in the attic, old narrow black leather shoes with pointed toes. They were so tiny that their young children couldn't get them on. Newspapers from the 1890s had been stuffed inside them to keep their shape.

Their Eveleth attic didn't conceal old shoes, but one day Tim Mack did find one of his guns lying on the attic floor. It was the top one from his gun rack, which was kept in the attic. Neither Jan nor the girls ever touched the guns, and there was no way it could have fallen to where Tim found it.

Their houses may have also shared hauntings.

The Macks believed their Iowa home had held a friendly spirit. On that first day in Eveleth when the light quickly came on above the stairway, they wondered if the ghost had perhaps traveled with them.

"Who knows?" Jan asks. "There are experiences we can't always explain."

In February 1981 the family moved into a trailer outside Eveleth. They wanted more space around them. Jan said they were all much happier after they'd moved from the apartment. And nothing *else* left with them.

Of his short stay in that Eveleth apartment, Mack said, "There wasn't any outstanding incident, but there was definitely something in there. I've always felt that there is another world, some other plane. There are things that I don't think anyone could ever explain."

The Mack family later moved to Plainview in southern Minnesota, where Tim and Jan published the *Plainview News*, the *St. Charles Press*, and the *Lewiston Journal*.

Publishing three newspapers kept the family busy. Glancing around her husband's cluttered office, Jan sighed. "Sometimes I wish we had a friendly spirit around here to help with things."

But the friendly spirit evidently stayed up north.

"Fishing for walleyes, no doubt," said Tim. He grinned.

Mysteries of the Gulf Coast

A skeletal pirate captain guarding his buried treasure . . . strange songs drifting across the Pascagoula River . . . a robed woman walking the beach in Mississippi City.

From Bay St. Louis close by Louisiana, to Pascagoula in the east, the Gulf Coast of Mississippi is fertile territory for ghost legends of all manner. Dastardly pirates roamed its swampy coasts and sandy beaches for a century, while wealthy planters built grand mansions among magnificent oaks. The haunted places along the coast are among the most fascinating in the American South.

The Singing River

The humming reminds one vaguely of a swarm of bees in flight, melodic but distant, growing louder the more intently a person listens. It seems to issue from deep within the dark waters. Especially on a warm summer night, an eavesdropper can believe in all the legends of the Pascagoula River. The singing river, it is called.

Scientists have tried to explain what it is one hears ever since the humming was first noticed as long ago as the eighteenth century. It may be the grating of sand on the slate floor, natural gas escaping from the sand, a current rushing past a hidden cave, or maybe it's a peculiar school of fish producing their own sounds. No one theory has ever been proven.

Judge Charles E. Chidsey described what it sounded like to him in an 1890 issue of *Popular Science Monthly*. He lived in Scranton, at the mouth of the Pascagoula River:

"An old fisherman called me from the house where I then was, to come down to the river bank and 'hear the spirits singing under the water.' . . . If what I heard cannot be properly called music, it was certainly mysterious. From out of the waters of the river, apparently some forty feet from its shelving bank, rose a roaring, murmuring sound, which gradually increased in strength and volume, until it had reached its height, when it as slowly descended."

The most widely told origin of the singing river is a Romeo and Juliet story of love and honor.

The Pascagoula Indians were a gentle, handsome people of small stature and delicate features living on the river's banks. Nearby lived the warlike Biloxi tribe, jealously guarding their self-described status as the "first people."

A Biloxi princess, Miona, had been promised to the warrior Otanga, but she had fallen in love with a young Pascagoula, Clustee. Her family demanded that she end her romance, but she stubbornly refused. Instead she sought refuge with her lover's tribe.

Otanga was outraged. He gathered his warriors and declared war against the Pascagoula. The fierce Biloxi badly outnumbered the Pascagoula. Clustee begged his tribe to turn him over to Otanga so that his people might be spared horrible deaths. The tribe refused. They would either protect Clustee and Miona or die in the attempt.

It soon became apparent that the Pascagoula could not survive the attacks by Otanga's forces. The tribe gathered to decide what their fate should be, defeat and subjugation by the Biloxi—or suicide. They chose the latter. With Miona and Clustee walking hand in hand to lead the way, all the men, women, and children of the tribe walked into the river, singing their songs of death "until the last voice was hushed by the engulfing dark waters."

It is the Pascagoula death song one hears from the singing river.

Interestingly enough there is some truth in the Indian legend. The Pascagoula had been allies of the French in the Seven Years' War, known in the Americas as the French and Indian War (1756–1763). By the terms of the Treaty of Paris, signed in 1763, the English received all of the territory on the Gulf Coast. Rather than live under their former enemies, the Pascagoula Indians followed some of their French allies into Louisiana territory. The tribe probably did march into the river in 1764, but then out again to settle in Louisiana to the west.

The Sentry

More than two centuries ago when buccaneers still operated along the Gulf Coast, a certain pirate ship anchored off Deer Island. The captain had a chest of gold which he wanted to bury.

He came ashore with several trusted men and dug a hole in the sand in which to bury the treasure. He asked for a volunteer to remain behind as a guard. A novice pirate anxious to please his captain quickly offered his services. He didn't realize the ramifications of his generosity. The captain drew his cutlass and sliced off the man's head. His remains were buried with the treasure chest—a sort of eternal sentry, as it were.

Many decades later, three fishermen were camped on Deer Island. As they finished their supper, the nearby palmettos softly rustled. They couldn't see anyone past the light of their campfire and figured it was just the wind or one of the island's wild hogs rooting around.

The rustling continued, drawing ever closer. Suddenly at the edge of the fire's glow a headless skeleton staggered toward them. They threw down their utensils and fled back to their boat, where they spent the rest of the night. At daylight, the trio bravely returned to fetch their tent and gear. No trace could be found of their horrible visitor.

Whenever a visitor to Deer Island camps too close to the pirate captain's buried treasure, the headless skeleton appears to show his displeasure.

Waveland's Pirate House

Hurricane Camille rid the Gulf Coast of the infamous Pirate House, on North Beach Boulevard in Waveland. Eight ghosts once inhabited the former lair of a New Orleans man who moonlighted as a privateer.

Among the ghosts was the one Mrs. James W. Faulkner claimed to have seen in the 1930s. She was halfway up the staircase when she screamed. At the top of the stairs stood a man with a hypnotic stare.

Another of the ghosts was an alcoholic who committed suicide. He was seen many years ago by a Mrs. Lister. He would stand at the cocktail bar looking longingly at the liquor bottles. When Mrs. Lister tried to engage him in conversation, he would fade away. She said he wore a fedora and a black coat with tails over a stiffly starched white shirt, and seemed to have gray hair and a faint mustache.

There was also a busybody old lady specter who followed a maid around in her daily chores.

But the pirate ghost at the Pirate House presented the ugliest sight. A party guest saw him once on the front lawn wearing wide, black boots, a flapping coat, a ruffled shirt, but no head. Blood streamed from his neck!

Built around 1802, the house belonged to a New Orleans businessman/pirate who was supposed to have been the agent for the infamous Jean Laffite and his band of Barataria pirates. In this "safe house," the New Orleans man installed all manner of conveniences for his nefarious business. A secret tunnel led from a subbasement to the Gulf. Pirates could transfer their booty from ship to shore with nary a chance for discovery. A dungeon was for anyone who crossed the buccaneers, and may also have held illegally smuggled slaves. A well in the backyard may have been used as a convenient grave for the bodies of at least three men. A specter in shirtsleeves was seen for decades around the well.

Despite the house's horrific history, most of the residents said the ghosts were not at all disruptive. They were usually well mannered, although they sometimes broke plates or overturned vases.

Nothing of substance was left of the Pirate House after Camille's two-hundred-mile-per-hour winds. A pile of bricks, some broken doors and twisted pieces of decorative grillwork were all that remained. The last owners collected the usable rubble and built a smaller cottage nearby.

Old Leathers' Place

The house that used to sit at 1460 Beach Boulevard in Mississippi City is unusual in the annals of Gulf Coast hauntings. Though the ghost seen nearby was always a robed woman walking on the beach, often accompanied by ethereal piano music, there are at least four candidates for just *who* she might have been in life.

Some facts about the house are known. New Orleans physician William Balfour built it in 1845 as a wedding present for his daughter when she married Dr. Horace Blackman. That was about the last nice thing that happened to Mrs. Horace Blackman.

Her life was suffused with tragedy. Both her father and her husband died when she was still quite young, leaving her with two children to raise. In later years, her son was convicted of murder and sentenced to life in prison. Mrs. Blackman used nearly her entire fortune on lawyers in unsuccessful attempts to defend him against the charges. Within a short time her newlywed daughter died unexpectedly.

In her final years, Mrs. Blackman lived alone and penniless in the once grand mansion. A friend found her seriously ill one day in 1888. She died a short time later.

The first reports of a mysterious robed figure walking the beach near the house came not long after Mrs. Blackman passed away. Piano music could be heard during the sightings. Mrs. Blackman was an accomplished amateur pianist.

In the 1890s, a ship captain bought the Blackman house for his wife. He often docked at nearby Pitcher's Point. In this way, his wife could watch for his schooner as he returned from long voyages.

Late one night, when the captain was long overdue from a particularly hazardous voyage, she suddenly ran from the house crying.

"I hear him calling me!" she wailed, plunging into the storm-tossed waves. Her body washed ashore the next morning.

The captain had been lost in the storm.

The robed woman in the water might be the captain's wife.

Or perhaps it's one of two other former occupants.

There is the sweet young woman who was shot by her former lover as she sat playing the piano in the front room. The man had crept under the open window and shot her through the heart. No names are attached to either person.

Maybe it's the young mother who, along with her child, contracted leprosy while they lived in the old house. She played the piano to pass the long, lonely days. No one was to know they had the dreaded disease. An elderly servant looked after them, and buried them in the backyard when they finally died.

It's possible that a yellow fever epidemic that swept the Gulf Coast in 1897 is connected with the house's bad reputation. A story made the rounds that a family with yellow fever lived at the East Beach address. It's understandable that the place was to be avoided.

Strangely enough, the name by which the house came to be known—Leathers' Place—had nothing to do with the ghost legends. The name came from James Leathers, a prominent Gulfport attorney who bought the house in 1906.

Through all the decades, despite rumors of ghostly music and pale, strolling women, Leathers' Place survived until 1968. A fire destroyed the storied house . . . and, presumably, its ghosts.

Chapel of the Cross

The young Belhaven College student had mapped out several routes between his Yazoo City home and the campus in Jackson. His favorite took him down Highway 16 and past the historic Chapel of the cross, between Madison and Flora.

He often traveled with three other young Belhaven students. Occasionally they stopped at the chapel, a Gothic edifice that looked for all the world like some remnant from ancient times. With its graveyard of crumbling stones huddled close by, the little brick church at twilight caused even the boldest visitor to draw a sharp breath at the slightest sound.

The four college friends usually stopped at the chapel for only a few minutes to stretch their legs. But on one moonlit evening they found themselves actors in an otherworldly drama.

On this night, the young men had separated to do a bit of informal sleuthing. One walked around behind the church, another peered in a side entrance, a third was near the chapel's front entrance. The driver, who recalled the events in a newspaper interview years later, was trying to read the old tombstones in the graveyard by flashlight.

Each then heard or saw something entirely disquieting. One looked up quickly as he heard the tower bell ring, another caught a fleeting glimpse of a face in one of the windows. The other two men, each on different sides of the church, heard organ chords.

One of them also saw the heavy front door open and a figure appear. It then passed directly through the locked iron gate that protects the old wood door and vanished down a path.

Each of the students described what he had seen, but none was absolutely ready to believe the others. After all, only two of the students had shared in one of the weird events—organ music coming from inside the chapel.

There would be other nights when they would be far more certain that something haunts the Chapel of the Cross.

The chapel was built by Mrs. Margaret L. Johnstone as a memorial to her husband. John T. Johnstone was a wealthy planter in antebellum Madison County. The

Gothic design was by Frank Wills, an English architect who later worked for the Episcopal Diocese of New York.

Consecrated as an Episcopal church in 1852, the chapel has been called "one of the best examples of Gothic architecture in the state" by historian Mary Wallace Crocker. Architect Wills gave the church a striking "pointed look" with sharply tipped windows and a pointed-arch front doorway protected by an iron gate. Dramatic buttresses form a steep bell cote. The interior woodwork and plaster labels carry through the apex design. The Gothic effect is heightened by unusual iron fences around the adjacent cemetery.

The human story of the chapel's founding family is dramatic—and tragic.

John T. Johnstone was the younger brother of Scotland's Earl of Annandale. He made his way to Madison County in 1820 from North Carolina, where he had first settled after emigrating to the United States. Johnstone left his wife Margaret behind in North Carolina while he made the journey alone. She joined him later when he completed a two-room log cabin on the large acreage he purchased.

The house grew along with his family; the Johnstones raised fifteen children over the ensuing years. The oldest was Fannie, for whom her father built Ingleside House in 1846. The youngest was Helen, who played a central role in the most famous legend of the Chapel of the Cross.

Johnstone became one of the wealthiest planters in Mississippi, and made plans to build a magnificent mansion he would call Annandale, after his Scottish ancestral home. He died in 1848 before his dream could be fulfilled.

His widow vowed to complete her husband's vision. The lack of a satisfactory church in which to hold her husband's funeral, however, induced her to put off Annandale's completion until a proper church could be built. Sunday services had often been held in the Johnstone house or in a local schoolhouse.

Mrs. Johnstone donated ten acres of land to the Episcopal Diocese of Mississippi. Artisan slaves baked bricks for the building of the little church, while Mrs. Johnstone made sure its furnishings would be of the finest quality. The baptismal font, made from a single stone, and the original stained glass windows were made in France. A furnace, highly unusual for that era, was included. The pews, altar, chancel rail, and pipe organ were imported from England.

By Christmas 1855, the chapel was complete and John Johnstone's legacy, Annandale, was now under construction by his widow. The great mansion would eventually rise to become a three-story Italianate villa with forty rooms.

During that same Christmas season, Mrs. Johnstone and her sixteen-year-old daughter, Helen, were visiting daughter Fannie and her family at Ingleside.

One afternoon during the holidays, the dashing young Henry Grey Vick, son of the founder of Vicksburg, was traveling on the nearby road when his carriage became mired in the mud. Servants at Ingleside freed the carriage, but it was determined that several days would be needed for repairs. Vick was invited to stay at Ingleside. During those few days, the beautiful Helen Johnstone and Henry Vick fell in love.

Mrs. Johnstone was not displeased at the match, but she insisted that the couple wait until Helen reached her twentieth birthday. Their love persevered and a wedding date was set for May 21, 1859.

A few days before the wedding, Henry Vick traveled to New Orleans looking for furnishings for their new home and a wedding suit for himself. By ill fortune, he came across one James Stith, a man who claimed that Vick had harmed him in an earlier business deal. The men argued and Stith challenged Vick to a duel.

Vick tried to retreat from the challenge, perhaps worried over Stith's reputed excellence as a marksman. But the thought of being called a coward was too much, even with the prospect of losing his life. He agreed to defend his honor, which in the South of the 1850s was to be expected from all gentlemen. While duels were officially banned, they were privately condoned.

The two men met at Holly's Gardens in Mobile; Vick, as the challenged, had decided upon long rifles as the chosen weapons. With their backs to one another, Vick and Stith marched off thirty paces, turned and fired. Vick aimed into the air. Stith did not. The groom-to-be fell to the earth mortally wounded.

Mrs. Johnstone broke the tragic news to her daughter as she prayed in the Chapel of the Cross. Helen insisted that Henry Vick's body be brought back so that he could be buried in the new church cemetery. Shortly before the planned wedding day, Vick's remains, packed in a piano box with ice and charcoal used as preservatives, arrived at Annandale.

Some say that Helen insisted the wedding go forward. Henry's wedding band was placed on her finger before he was laid to rest in the chapel's graveyard. The inscription on his tombstone, shaped as a cross, reads: HENRY GREY VICK, ENTERED INTO REST MAY 17, 1859. Carved into the stone are the replicas of a dog and a gun.

Helen was inconsolable. She sat by her lover's grave for hours upon end, speaking in a quiet voice of what their life together would have held. Mrs. Johnstone was naturally worried that the tragedy might permanently destroy her daughter's mind. She decided to close Annandale and take Helen on an extended tour of Europe. They were gone for several months. When they returned Helen seemed to have overcome her grief, at least by all outward signs.

Helen later married the kindly Reverend George Harris, but she never truly overcame her love for Henry Vick. She died in 1916. Her body rests at Rolling Fork plantation, which became her home after her marriage to the Reverend Harris.

The four Belhaven College students were never certain that they saw Helen's ghost at the Chapel of the Cross. But other visitors have reported seeing an attractive young woman sobbing near Henry Vick's grave. Grief is apparent in her face, and she fades away when a visitor dares to approach.

On a subsequent visit to the chapel, the students decided to stay together. Three of them were watching the front door—the one protected by the iron gate—when it opened and two figures came out. The door closed behind them as they passed *through* the bars of the iron gate. Then the most peculiar event ever reported at the chapel took place. The figures walked over to a nearby tree, climbed up its trunk and out onto a stout limb. They sat there for about half a minute before finally fading away.

All three young men saw the events at the same time. The men did not attempt to talk to the mysterious figures at any time. Whatever, or whoever, they saw seemed to want to avoid contact with human interlopers.

Although Helen Johnstone's ghost is most often seen at the chapel, there is another, far bloodier legend associated with it.

The chapel had a caretaker many years ago. He cleaned the church, opened the doors for Sunday services, and kept the grounds well groomed. He was married to a most obnoxious woman, a shrew who giggled incessantly.

The caretaker's duties took him to the chapel late one night. A few minutes after he arrived, his wife came in the door, giggling uncontrollably as usual. Something snapped inside him. He yelled at her to stop. When she giggled even louder, he picked up an axe and with one swift stroke severed her head.

He dragged her body to a bench outside the front door, retrieved her head and propped it atop her bloody neck. Because he was a fastidious, conscientious employee, he mopped up the blood and put away the axe. Then he hanged himself from a rafter.

The woman's giggle has not gone away, some people say, and the bloodstains from that murderous night reappear from time to time on the stone floor.

A duel may also have produced other ghosts at the chapel, although its factual basis is much in doubt.

Two men were in love with the same woman. They agreed to a duel in the graveyard. The winner married the woman. All three are supposed to be buried side by side, although there aren't any three graves close to one another with dates that would coincide with this legend.

The Annandale mansion itself burned to the ground many years ago. But a ghost story prevailed there for quite some time.

During Mrs. Johnstone's tour of Europe with Helen after Henry Vick's death, the women met a young, hunchbacked former governess named Annie Devlin. The women took a liking to the little woman and invited her to return with them to Annandale for a visit.

Annie agreed and her stay extended for several months, not unusual in that era. The Johnstones enjoyed Annie's quiet ways, and, in turn, she assumed that her life at Annandale could go on indefinitely. But Mrs. Johnstone and Helen decided to take another extended trip and close Annandale. They told Annie she would have to leave. She was surprised and hurt by the news. This was the first real home she had ever known.

Annie's health soon began to fail. Mrs. Johnstone instructed the servants to watch her carefully, but on a morning in June 1860 a maid found Annie's door blocked by something inside. Through the keyhole they saw her lying on the bed, her arm dangling over the side. When they forced their way into the room, Mrs. Johnstone found a bottle of laudanum, a form of opium. Annie Devlin had taken her own life. She was buried at the Chapel of the Cross. On her tombstone was the Latin IMPLORA PACE.

Some years later, after Mrs. Johnstone died, a guest at Annandale asked Helen Johnstone if her mother had been a short, slightly stooped, red-haired woman given to wearing a shawl.

"You're describing Miss Devlin," Helen cried. "But where did you see her?"

"I just met her on the staircase," the guest replied. "I spoke and went toward her, but she vanished."

Servants and guests found Miss Devlin visiting different rooms in the mansion right up to Annandale's demise. She was always said to be a "friendly little ghost" who especially liked to pluck the covers from visitors staying in her old bedroom.

Meanwhile, the hauntings at the Chapel of the Cross continue. A posted notice forbids entrance to the grounds after six o'clock at night. The regulation is probably designed to prevent vandalism, and that is good. It may also give the graveyard ghosts all the privacy they ever expected.

The Witch's Curse

Every city has its secrets. Long buried or passed along in whispered conversations, the mysteries of the past give each community stories not often shared with casual visitors.

Take Yazoo City, for example. It is a fairly typical southern community of middling size. The mysteries of its past are no more unusual than those of any other similar locale. Take the question of the derivation of the name Yazoo, for example. There were Yazoo Indians in the region in the old days, but the precise meaning of the word itself is unknown. Is it the sound of the wind blowing through enemy scalps that hung from tall poles in the village? That's one story. A most unusual variation is that Yazoo means death, in the forgotten Yazoo language. So, it might then be Death City on the banks of Death River. That's a secret city tourism officials may want to keep to themselves.

Somewhere beneath the gentle waves of the Yazoo River is another secret, the precise location of two Civil War–era gunboats—the USS *Baron DeKalb* and the USS *Petrel*—sunk during battle. At the old river landing on Water Street, the ghosts of dead Union soldiers, perhaps those lost on the gunboats, wail in despair on a moonless summer's night.

And there are other secrets—of how Mound Street was built on an ancient Indian burial mound. The array of bones and artifacts dislodged during construction of the road may have been all that was left of a race of giant people from whom the Yazoo Indians wrested the territory. It is said that the giants will return some day.

The most fascinating secret from Yazoo City's past may be just who is buried in the "witch's grave" at the city's old Glenwood Cemetery. And did the grave's "occupant," an accused witch, also accurately predict a devastating city fire in 1904?

As with any good story, the facts have gotten lost in the telling and retelling of the tale. Some things about the mysterious legend are known. There was an unmarked grave in Glenwood Cemetery. A slab of marble was the only sign that a body lay in the ground. Around the plot was a length of chain with one link missing. It is also certain that no one alive today knows for certain who is buried in that plot.

Yazoo City was most certainly nearly destroyed by a fire on May 25, 1904. A woman who lived on Mound Street was preparing to show off her wedding trousseau when she discovered her parlor in flames. Someone, a servant perhaps, had accidentally knocked over an oil lamp. The fire quickly spread to adjoining buildings. Before the flames were extinguished by firemen from as far away as Jackson and Greenwood, Yazoo City was in ruins. Not a business was left standing in the downtown area, and many beautiful old homes were charred ruins.

The next day, several persons visited the supposed witch's grave. A link was missing from the chain. The story of the witch and how that chain came to be there now becomes the legend and the subject of some dispute.

Skeptics say that famed author Willie Morris made the whole thing up for his book, *Good Old Boy*, a remembrance of his youth in Yazoo City. The story of the witch is contained in its pages. Other longtime residents of the city are not so sure. One oldster said the story of the mysterious grave was known in the very early 1900s, but instead of a witch buried there it was a man so mean in life that folks put up a chain to make sure he didn't try to escape from his grave.

This is the story of the witch:

During the 1880s, a mean, ugly old woman lived an isolated life on the banks of the Yazoo River. No one knew her by name, although her cunning cruelty was whispered among all the people of the town. She would lure fishermen to her squalid home, they said, and murder them in most barbaric ways. She buried them on a wooded hillside and danced on their graves.

Joe Bob Duggett knew the stories. He found himself thinking about them as he guided his raft past the witch's shack on an autumn night in 1884. He heard moaning coming from inside and steered toward shore so he could investigate. Peering through a window, Joe Bob saw a terrible sight. Two dead men were stretched out on the floor. The witch woman, dressed in a filthy black dress, was dancing around the corpses, waving her hands in the air in a horrible incantation.

Joe Bob ran back to his raft and paddled furiously to town. He told the sheriff what he had seen and, together with several deputies, rode horseback out to the witch's house.

No one answered the sheriff's pounding on the door. The men broke it down and went inside. The bodies were gone and the house looked empty. Upstairs, though, the men made a hideous discovery. In the attic a dozen emaciated cats prowled dazedly beneath two skeletons hanging from a rafter.

The witch had fled, or so it seemed. Just then they heard the crunching of footsteps on fallen leaves. The sheriff looked out a second-floor window and saw the old woman scurrying away toward the swamps. He yelled at her to stop. She started to run.

The sheriff's men and Joe Bob Duggett took off in pursuit. She apparently didn't know the swampy ground as well as she thought. By the time the pursuers came upon her, the witch was caught in quicksand up to her neck. Only her frightfully scarred face was visible above the muck. With her last breath she uttered a curse that stayed with Joe Bob for the rest of his days: "I shall return," she cried. "Everybody always hated me here. I will break out of my grave and burn down the whole town on the morning of May 25, 1904!" With that she disappeared beneath the quicksand.

Her body was eventually retrieved and buried in the center of Glenwood Cemetery. Around her grave, the sheriff strung the toughest chain link he could find. "If she can break through THAT and burn down Yazoo," he said, "she deserves to burn it down."

The witch's curse was practically forgotten until May 25, 1904, the day of the great fire in Yazoo City. When those who remembered the witch's curse found a link missing from the chain around her grave the next day, they said her prophecy had come true. Through some supernatural effort, she had broken free of her dank prison and instigated the fire. The link remains missing to this day.

Is the story of the witch's curse from a storyteller's imagination, or could it be true?

The records of who was buried in Glenwood Cemetery prior to 1904 were destroyed in the fire. No formal monument was ever known to be on the grave, although a simple stone with the initials T.W. (The Witch?) was on the neatly tended square plot for many years. A sexton at the cemetery said he got more questions about the witch's grave than any other. And it's not unusual to find bouquets of fresh flowers lying on it.

The truth behind this mystery may never be known. It's probably better that way . . . the real story might not be nearly so interesting.

More Phantasms

On drizzly, foggy nights when the countryside turns to cotton candy, a headless man glides along an Ozark highway as if on roller skates.

Since pioneer days, travelers on the old Wilderness Road (State Highway 13) in Stone County, near Kimberling City, have reported close encounters with the specter. On at least one occasion, the ghost was seen rolling along with its head cradled in its arms.

On one particularly rainy night, it lay down to rest in the wet brush, and its horrible moaning so terrified a team of mules that they ran over the nearest hill.

Once it settled astride a horse, behind a young man riding home from his sweetheart's house. The fellow, daydreaming about his girl, didn't see the ghost approach. But he felt the thump. An icy draft frosted the hairs on the back of his neck. Breath from a headless ghost?

At the next bend in the road, the hitchhiking ghost vanished.

Tomp Turner, who lived near Kimberling Bridge on the White River, scoffed at tales of the headless ghost . . . until one night in 1915. As Tomp was galloping south on the highway, his horse turned skittish. Tomp peered between the horse's ears and saw the ghastly figure approaching.

The horse bolted into the brush, snapping twigs and twanging tree limbs in its frenzy to escape. When Tomp regained control of the beast, the ghost was nowhere in sight.

From that night on Tomp listened, with rapt attention, when talk turned to the headless ghost.

Ghosts sometimes hang out at the scene of violent crime, but no one recalls a murder on the old Wilderness Road that might explain the haunting.

"Old Raw Head"

In the restive years following the Civil War, highwaymen and bushwhackers terrorized many communities throughout Missouri, destroying property and murdering in cold blood.

For some reason, residents of Morgan County seemed especially vulnerable to these depredations and murders. The sound of approaching hoofbeats late at night chilled the hearts of the bravest men, for no one knew where a roving band would strike next.

After that bloody era of Missouri history ended, the ghost of one victim, familiarly called "Old Raw Head," was seen in various parts of Morgan County.

John A. Hannay spotted the specter one night in a field near Versailles. It straddled a strawstack, its translucent torso and limbs shimmering in the moonlight. As Hannay drew near, he saw the bloody stump where its head had been. The ghost slid down the opposite side of the stack and vanished.

Hannay's grandparents had seen the same specter many years before. The couple were riding in their wagon on a backcountry road when the headless ghost materialized. It arrowed between the horses, then disappeared, leaving Hannay's grandfather perplexed and his grandmother in hysterics.

The Dance Hall Ghost

Years ago, Johnny Griffin and his family lived in a rambling old house on Back Creek, near U.S. Highway 67, south of Farmington. Griffin trusted everyone and loved good times. On Saturday nights the Griffins threw open their doors to friends and neighbors who came to "party." With furniture pushed against the parlor walls, a spacious "ballroom" was created. Fiddlers sawed and twanged, while couples danced the night away.

Word of Johnny Griffin's hospitality spread, and strangers began arriving at his door. That's when the trouble started. The Griffins didn't know many of the people who thronged their house. Boisterous men they'd never seen before swaggered through the doors; some, seeking "entertainment" of a different sort, caused nervous neighbor men to keep close watch over their wives and daughters.

For the most part, there were no unpleasant incidents. But one night a fiddler spotted Griffin talking to his sweetheart. He threw down his fiddle and rushed his host. In the next instant, he beheaded Johnny Griffin with a Bowie knife. Two women fainted and the rest of the crowd fled, screaming.

For years afterward, farmers reported seeing the headless ghost of the victim in the upstairs windows of the old house. Although the ghost appeared to be very tall and Griffin had been short, people who saw the specter were certain it was Johnny's ghost. And some heard the rattle of chains that the ghost shook whenever curious tourists approached the house. The man who, in life, had loved people, was condemned in death to frighten them off. It was almost as if he feared a second death, one even more macabre than the first.

The Legend of Mint Spring

Many years ago, Oliver Busbee and his wife, Margaret, acquired a vast Ozark acreage with choice woodlands and steep fertile valleys. Oliver bought the land because it had been well cared for, and Margaret never tired of the ever-changing view from the farmhouse windows—the butternut and sugar maples that flamed golden-red each autumn on the northern slopes, and the gnarled junipers that clung to rocks on the southwest hillsides.

One November afternoon, when the sun was warm, Margaret walked down the path to Mint Spring, named for the many varieties of mint that grew along its banks. She often gathered mint for tea and cress for salads.

Now, as she kneeled beside the mint bed, she saw the body of a young girl floating facedown in the water! Margaret leaped to her feet and ran to get Oliver. When they returned to the spring the body had vanished. Oliver thought his wife had seen some sort of reflection. She hadn't.

For years afterward, in November, the girl's lifeless form appeared in the cold waters of Mint Spring.

When Oliver questioned some of the older farmers in the neighborhood about the apparition, he learned this story:

Twenty years earlier the Busbee property had been owned by Jerry Hutchison, a wealthy farmer whose love of the land was exceeded only by his love for his beautiful daughter, Rachel, whom he delighted in spoiling.

When Rachel turned eighteen she asked for a horse of her own. She loved to ride, and with her own horse she could ride whenever and wherever she pleased.

Three weeks later, Jerry Hutchison came home leading a handsome and spirited chestnut-colored horse, and carrying a sidesaddle. Rachel was ecstatic and begged to ride immediately. Her father saddled up the horse and helped her to mount. Then away she galloped, up into the wooded hills as fast as the young horse could go.

Day after day Rachel rode through the woods and the valleys, never seeming to tire. Returning home each evening, she would ride to Mint Spring to let her horse drink. Then she'd gallop back to the barn, remove the saddle and turn the beast out to pasture for the night.

One November evening, the young woman rode home and through the gate down to Mint Spring. Her father had opened the gate for her and now leaned against it, watching his lovely daughter ride past. He would wait there for her. But she didn't return. The riderless horse galloped up toward the barn.

Hutchison called for his daughter but there was no response. He ran to the spring. There, floating facedown on the surface of the water, was his beloved Rachel. For some reason she had been thrown from the horse and had drowned or hit her head on one of the jagged rocks jutting from the spring.

Jerry Hutchison never recovered from his grief. Two years later, he and his wife sold their land and moved away. None of their friends ever heard of them again.

The Haunted Hog Wallow

Many communities across the country claim legendary haunted houses or grave-yards, but maybe none can boast of a haunted hog wallow except Reeds Spring, Missouri. Three miles west of this tiny Ozark village, by a hog wallow known as Dead Man's Pond, strange, unexplained incidents occurred for many years.

Mrs. May Kennedy McCord, who was raised near Dead Man's Pond, admitted, even in her adult years, that she'd never go near the place alone after dark. As a child she had heard many of the eerie, and sometimes chilling, tales, but one was especially baffling.

A fellow named Willie Webber saw a woman dressed all in black late one afternoon while he was by the pond. The woman wore a red apron over her dress and her hands were wrapped in the apron's flounce. As Webber watched her coming along a path, he tried to recall who she was. He'd never before seen anyone in the area dressed like that. Suddenly, she vanished. The day was clear and the sun still bright and Webber could see several hundred yards in all directions, yet the mysterious woman had disappeared before his eyes.

Another baffling experience happened to Palmer E. Sharp as he was returning home from a party late one night. According to his brother, Will, Palmer and his girlfriend had each ridden a horse to the party and Palmer, having seen the girl safely home, was returning to his own house and leading the girl's horse. It had been a splendid evening and Palmer sat relaxed in the saddle, his face tilted to the sky flung with stars.

As he passed the pond, Palmer noticed that the horse he was leading had slowed down. He turned and saw a man in the saddle. In the next instant, the figure vanished. Will said later, "My brother was not afraid of ghosts, but what did he see?"

Perhaps Palmer was not afraid of ghosts, but he never passed Dead Man's Pond again after dark.

Places associated with dark deeds and violent deaths are said to harbor the ghosts of the victims, usually because the corpses haven't been given proper burial. That may explain, in part, the hauntings of the hog wallow. Shortly after the Civil War two bank robbers were killed at Dead Man's Pond.

A skull and other human bones were found in the mud. Whether the remains were those of the robbers or of some innocent travelers gunned down by outlaws would never be known.

Dead Man's Hill

The spectral horseman is a frequent traveler throughout the Midwest, galloping down dark and lonely roads and frightening all who see him. He may be a cavalryman killed in some distant battle, a highwayman gunned down while plundering a wayside inn, or perhaps an early settler mortally wounded in an Indian attack. In any case, he's compelled to travel the route he rode in life, presumably searching for his slayer.

Near Bolivar, the ghostly rider was a horse thief who was shot to death and buried on the top of Dead Man's Hill, about a hundred yards east of State Highway 13. When the farmer whose horse was stolen reported his loss, a posse of citizens from Greene and Polk counties was formed and gave chase. The culprit fled and as the posse gained on him, he leaped from his horse and dashed to the top of the high knoll. There, shielded by the rocks, he kept his pursuers at bay for some time.

Whenever the attackers seemed ready to storm his fort, the thief fired a round and the posse would fall back. All during the night scattered shots came from the hilltop.

At dawn, the posse determined to take the thief dead or alive. The men charged the hilltop, dodging from rock to rock and keeping up their fire. Soon no response came from the summit. The men found the horse thief dead behind a pile of stones. No one knew him.

That afternoon the women of the neighborhood dug a shallow grave at the hilltop and buried the victim. A brief burial service was offered with a song and a prayer. A headstone, without inscription, was later erected at the spot.

For many years, wildflowers occasionally appeared on the grave, leading some people to speculate that someone in the community knew the thief's identity. Or perhaps a kindly soul was moved to compassion. At any rate, the trail from the highway to the grave was used often enough to keep it free of underbrush.

But the grave could not contain the restless stranger. People passing near the hill at night often saw a ghostly figure sitting astride the stone that marked the grave. If they attempted to draw closer, the figure would leap from the stone and dash from rock to rock.

There were reports too that the horse thief's ghost stayed, at least part of the time, in an old house opposite the hill. A succession of tenants moved in and out of the place.

The old thief was not content to stay indoors, or sit on his tombstone. Many a swain returning home from an evening of courting would hear the clatter of horse's hooves on the highway behind him. Turning in the saddle, he'd see the spectral rider coming after him at full gallop, his brown homespun coat flapping in the wind and his two big Colt revolvers swinging at his sides.

The young man, hair bristling at the back of his neck, palms sweaty on the reins, would ride his mount at breakneck speed to escape the apparition.

But one man didn't escape. Overtaken by the ghostly rider, he fell from his horse. In the morning, passersby found him barely conscious in the underbrush by the side of the road. His horse was gone. The man said he'd been struck in the shoulder by a bullet fired by the passing horseman. The back of his coat had a freshly burned hole in it, but his body bore no mark!

The natives were so frightened by this inexplicable incident that for many years afterward they avoided riding or walking past Dead Man's Hill, especially after dark.

The Screaming Ghosts of Breadtray Mountain

To the people of Stone County, Breadtray Mountain is a place of haunting mystery. Tales of buried treasure have been associated with this bald-topped mountain soaring over Table Rock Lake at the junction of the James and the White rivers for as long as anyone can remember. And, in the more recent past, unexplained screams and moanings in the night have terrified travelers in the vicinity of the mountain.

One of the earliest legends tells of a band of Chickasaw Indians who mined silver near Breadtray. They were eventually conquered by an enemy tribe, but not before hiding their vast silver horde in a cave of the mountain. No one knows if the Indians ever returned to claim their treasure, but many people believe it is still there, sealed for eternity.

Another story tells of a band of Indians who lived on the top of Breadtray. For many seasons hunting was poor, and when the people were close to starvation a lovely maiden from another tribe appeared with the message that if she married the chief's son prosperity would be restored to his people. The wedding took place and her promise was manifested; fish and game became plentiful once again and the people thrived. But the medicine man who had profited by the tribe's misfortunes resented the marriage and cursed the young wife. In sorrow she left the village with a vow that the people would be driven from the earth. The hill folk say that is why, even today, nothing grows on the mountaintop.

But the legend that most keenly stirs the imagination concerns a band of Spanish conquistadors who, like the Chickasaw, mined silver near Breadtray and hid it in a fort near the mountaintop. They forced the Indians to work their mines and after amassing a large quantity of the precious metal they decided to leave the area. They secretly planned to take a group of Indian maidens with them. But the canny tribe learned of the abduction and attacked the soldiers, killing all but three of them. The survivors fled into the hills and, after hiding out for a time, returned for the treasure. The indomitable Indians, however, were waiting, and the three hapless Spaniards lost their lives.

In the 1880s the notorious Bald Knobber gang pillaged throughout Stone and Taney counties and were thought to have cached their loot in a cave near the base of Breadtray. In 1889 the entire gang was captured and executed. But one outlaw escaped from the prison at Ozark, and some say he returned to the cave to recover the loot.

For many years treasure hunters have combed the mountain, searching for the various silver caches and the outlaws' loot. Breadtray has never yielded its treasures, if in fact they exist, but it has sounded terrifying alarms of its ancient history. Local residents and passersby tell of hearing hideous groans and sobs and stifled screams issuing from somewhere deep within the mountain late at night.

Are they the death cries of those unfortunate Spanish soldiers condemned to reenact their violent deaths at the hands of the Indians? Many people think so.

Or do the bone-chilling screams arise from the ghosts of a Chickasaw band who were slain by an enemy when they returned for their silver cache?

And are the eerie sobs those of the lone Bald Knobber who returned to seize his loot, only to meet death in some brutal, unknown fashion? Or something else?

Leonard Hall's Dream

The swift-flowing Current River winds through Ozark country past villages named Akers, Jacks Fork, and Owls Bend. The cold, clear water rushes through gorges between bluffs two hundred fifty feet high, bisects meadows and forests of hickory, oak, and pine. Wild turkeys live in these ancient hills, and so do bands of deer that come to drink at night at the water's edge.

But it wasn't the stealth of an animal that awakened Leonard Hall on that August night in 1941. Camped on the upper Current River, Hall thought he heard the sound of voices close by. He rubbed the sleep from his eyes and reached for the tent flap. Peering out, he saw a ring of campfires in the clearing scarcely a hundred yards away. Tall, bronzed Indians, naked except for breechcloths, tended the fires, moving quietly and talking in hushed tones. Hall was astonished. Then he noticed figures seated around one fire; they wore the heavy armor and the visored helmets of the Spanish conquistadors. One soldier rotated a sword in his hands, the long blade reflecting the firelight. From somewhere in the distance came the gentle neigh of a horse.

Hall, convinced that he was dreaming, turned over in his bedroll and went back to sleep. He never bothered to awaken his companions.

In the morning, Hall found no trace of the Spanish encampment, no sign of a single recent fire. He never told anyone about his eerie experience, but many years later he read that the Spanish explorer Hernando de Soto had been in the Ozark area of the Current River in August 1541.

De Soto and his men did travel as far west as the eastern slopes of the Rocky Mountains in their futile search for gold. Although the explorer's exact route is not known, it seems possible that the party, with its Indian guides, could have camped on the meadow where Hall had seen them—exactly four hundred years later!

The Peddler's Revenge

In 1853 a peddler was crossing Missouri with a light pack and a full purse. Approaching the house of Daniel Baker, near Lebanon, he asked to spend the night. "Of course," said Baker, receiving the stranger warmly.

And that was the last anyone saw of Samuel Moritz. Some of the neighbors remarked on Baker's sudden prosperity, but others figured the stranger had probably left town early in the morning before anyone was up and about. Anyway, the peddler's disappearance was of no importance. Nobody knew the man.

On a moonlit night in 1860, Reverend Cummings, an area clergyman, was riding home in his buggy. Nearing a bridge on a dirt road by Baker's farm, he saw a man standing there. The man had a pack over his shoulder and a stick in his hand, and was peering down intently at something beneath the bridge. Cummings called out a greeting and offered the stranger a ride. The man looked directly at him, then pointed to the edge of the bridge with his stick.

The clergyman glanced down, but saw nothing except strands of mist that laced the gully. When he looked up the man with the pack was gone. Just then the horse snorted and plunged ahead and it took Cummings several minutes to bring the animal under control. When he looked back, the man had reappeared on the bridge and was looking over the edge of it.

The minister told his neighbors about his experience and in the morning two of them accompanied him to the bridge. There, swinging from a bridge support, was the body of old man Baker. It was exactly beneath the spot where the stranger had stood. And there were no footprints in the damp earthen surface of the bridge. Cummings knew then that he had seen a ghost.

In cutting down the body, the three men accidentally dislodged dirt and gravel from a reinforcing bank. A skeleton lay half concealed in the weeds and rubble. Fragments of clothing on it were identified as belonging to Samuel Moritz.

Was it conscience or craziness that drove Daniel Baker to kill himself above the grave of his victim? No one knew. Perhaps it didn't matter. The peddler, in revealing his murderer, had his revenge.

The Invisible Family

In 1956 Mr. and Mrs. S. L. Furry bought the former Henry Gehm house on Plant Avenue in Webster Groves. The two-story structure of wood and brick was set well back on its wide lot and surrounded by a garden that ensured privacy. The Furrys were not unsociable people, but they preferred to spend most of their time with their own family. The couple had been married for twenty years and had two young daughters.

The events that enveloped the Furrys and a later family in that house on Plant Avenue constitute one of St. Louis's most widely reported ghost tales.

Mrs. Furry was the first to realize that something was wrong with the house. She woke up at two o'clock each morning with the chilling sensation that someone had shaken her awake. (Mr. Furry slept in an adjoining bedroom.) On one occasion she was roused from sleep by the sounds of a hammer striking the headboard of her bed. She threw off the covers, leaped out of bed, and snapped on a light. No one was in the room.

She slept poorly the rest of the night and in the morning decided against telling her husband. He was a practical man who believed that everything could be logically explained.

During the daytime hours, Mrs. Furry began to hear footsteps racing up and down the stairs when her children were not in the house. They were the steps of someone in a hurry, someone familiar with the house. But the footfalls always stopped on the upstairs landing.

Early one morning Mrs. Furry went downstairs to make breakfast and found a heavy wall ornament lying on the living room floor. How could it have fallen? Its mate was firmly attached to the wall. Mr. Furry did not notice.

After several weeks of strange goings-on, Mrs. Furry became so nervous in the house that she told her husband she thought the house was haunted. He replied that he too had heard strange noises in the night, but they were probably caused by the settling of the house. All old houses did that. Mrs. Furry knew otherwise.

One night shortly after this discussion, Mr. Furry awoke from a deep sleep to see a translucent shape in his bedroom. It glided past him, out the door and into the hallway. He jumped out of bed and followed the misty form into his younger daughter's bedroom. The child lay curled in bed, sleeping soundly, one arm hugging her teddy bear. The form vanished. When Mr. Furry returned to his room he decided that he either had been dreaming or had seen lights reflected from passing cars.

The couple never discussed the strangeness of the house in front of the children, nor even between the two of them to any great extent. Mrs. Furry wanted some painting and wallpapering done, and soon she and her husband were involved in so many decorating decisions that they ignored the unexplained noises.

Then one morning their three-year-old daughter asked who the lady in black was who came into her room at night. No house guests were staying in the house, and neither parent could recall any visit by a woman dressed in black.

But the lady reappeared and the child said, "She spanks me with a broom, but it doesn't hurt."

Mrs. Furry felt faint. She asked no questions because she knew she could provide no answers. She pushed the episode from her mind, but fears nagged her and she came to resent the real estate agent who had sold them the house.

After nine years of living with shadowy shapes that drifted in and out of rooms and unceasing footfalls on the staircase, the family had had enough. When they moved, they told the neighbors the house was no longer suited to their needs.

In the fall of 1965, another family rented the house. The Whitcombs knew nothing of its history, but they liked the quiet neighborhood. Two of their children lived with them: ten-year-old Tricia and twenty-year-old Sarah.

Mrs. Whitcomb, a biochemist, was somewhat psychic and felt that the house was "peculiar" when she first toured it. In fact, she was rather delighted to have her suspicions confirmed when she saw her first ghost—a white mist the size and shape of a human being floating through her kitchen one evening as she prepared dinner. In the coming days blasts of cold air enveloped Mrs. Whitcomb in the kitchen and in her bedroom. There were never any windows or doors open that could have created drafts. And from time to time she heard the crying of a tiny child, which upset her considerably.

Like Mrs. Furry, Mrs. Whitcomb was awakened in the middle of the night. The house seemed to come alive at four o'clock, with footsteps hurrying up and down the staircase and presences hovering in dark corners. Mrs. Whitcomb, unlike her predecessor, determined to learn something of the history of the place. She found out from the man across the street that the builder and original owner, Henry Gehm, had lived in the house until his death. He worked in some capacity for a circus, but no one knew exactly what he did. The neighbor said that Mr. Gehm was supposed to have hidden valuables all over the house and had come back to look for them—or so the rumor went.

Mrs. Whitcomb was fascinated. That night she was awakened at midnight by a musty odor that permeated the room. She thought it smelled like death. Her husband, a chemist, thought little of it—until the next night, when the odor filled his bedroom. He could not identify it.

One day while cleaning upstairs Mrs. Whitcomb found the door to the attic standing open. She thought her husband or one of the girls had taken something up or brought something down. But after finding the door open morning after morning she questioned her family. They had all heard the footsteps on the stairs and thought some other family member was in the attic!

Mrs. Whitcomb wondered if Mr. Gehm had left any valuables up there. Feeling a little foolish, she decided to investigate. One morning, on hands and knees, she

climbed the attic stairs, examining each tread as she went. Then she discovered
a tread that had been hinged. She lifted it up to find a box—empty and laced
with cobwebs.

Mrs. Whitcomb started then to keep a journal of her discoveries and also a
record of the various manifestations in the house and the dates of their occurrences. It might be useful in determining whether a pattern was developing. Besides, it was an interesting game and the record-keeping forced her to become
unusually observant.

On March 1, 1966, she was working in the kitchen when a strange sensation
came over her. Someone, or something, was urging her to go up to the attic. She
had heard no noises, but now, as in a trance, she started up the stairs. Her steps
led her into a small room where she had stored packing boxes. She had noted, at
the time, the neatly stored pieces of old furniture and wondered who had left
them and why. There were large desks, marble-topped bureaus, and walnut chairs.

But now the furniture had been moved around and the room was in disarray.
A drawer in a heavy, ornate chest had been pulled wide open; it was stuffed with
papers. Mrs. Whitcomb picked up one. It was a blueprint, and the bottom of the
sheet bore the name HENRY GEHM. A chill ran down her spine and she hurried
back down to the kitchen.

Early the next morning Mrs. Whitcomb heard footsteps pacing in the hallway
outside her bedroom door. She looked out, but saw no one. She went back to
bed, but couldn't sleep. Suddenly, she seemed to receive a message: she must
open the bottom drawer of her bureau and take out the music box. It was an old
one that had belonged to her mother and had been broken for years. She lifted
out the box and when she opened the lid it began to play. Who had fixed it? No
one in her family; of that she was certain.

Her journal recorded that on March 6 she was awakened at four A.M. to find
the drawers of her bureau open and clothes strewn across the floor. Then she
knew. She was occupying Mr. Gehm's bedroom and he had come for his valuables.

Two days later Mrs. Whitcomb was working in the basement when she heard
running feet in the dining room, the light footfalls of a child. Perhaps Tricia had
brought a friend in to play. But when she called out to her daughter, there was
no answer. She went upstairs to investigate. The house was empty. Tricia was
outside playing in the garden. Were there two ghosts in the house?

Several days later Mrs. Whitcomb was doing the laundry in the basement and
had hung a clean sweater on a hanger to dry and looped the hanger over a rafter.
All of a sudden the sweater and hanger arced through the air and landed at her
feet.

"Mary Gehm, why did you do that?" she asked.

After she'd uttered the words she was astonished. Why did that name come to
mind? And why was she talking to a ghost?

In the morning she had the irresistible urge to return to the storage room in
the attic. A trunk was open in the middle of the room and a doll house had been
moved. In the dust of a chest was the handprint of a small child!

Now, Mrs. Whitcomb knew without a doubt that a family was living up there—
a family caught in a time warp, remaining in the house they had once occupied
and loved.

In the morning sounds of voices drifted down through the open attic door.
None of the Whitcombs were up there. But from that moment on, activities
occurred almost daily. Tricia found her typewriter had been used during the night

and a doll had been moved from its usual place. The living room lights went on and off by themselves, and wrapped candies vanished from a dish and were never found.

The Whitcombs got the message: they were not wanted in the house any longer. Tricia became so upset that she dared not go into the attic, and her parents had become increasingly uneasy in the house. Finally, one day Mrs. Whitcomb said, "Let the ghosts have it."

The Whitcombs built a new home and on moving day the voices of the invisible family drifted down from the attic, along with footsteps scurrying up the stairs.

Old Judges Never Die. . . .

Bob and Dorothy Card and their three children moved into the house on Holter Street in Helena, Montana, in March 1969. The imposing nineteenth-century mansion had been built in 1887 by Theodore Brantly, a justice of the Montana Supreme Court. It commands a sweeping view of the city from high atop a hill on what was known a century ago as Spruce Street.

The mansion had been converted into four apartments sometime before the Cards bought it. Bob planned to restore it to the beautiful family residence that it had once been. Oak had been used extensively throughout and the original dining room held a magnificent built-in breakfront fitted with leaded glass doors. Judge Brantly spent freely to create a home that befitted his social and political aspirations. Even the family name—BRANTLY—was carved in the sidewalk in front of the house.

When the Cards moved in they took the second-floor apartment with its three bedrooms. It would be spacious enough for the family until they could afford to make the changes they wanted. The first-floor and basement apartments were still being rented out at that time.

In 1973 Bob Card was financially able to begin the remodeling. He gutted the vacant third-floor apartment, turning it into two rooms: a combination living room/TV room, and a playroom for the youngsters. He also removed the staircase between the second and third floors and substituted a spiral one.

That's when the trouble began.

"You could almost feel the unrest in the house," Dorothy Card said. "Now maybe there had been funny goings-on that we had passed over without even thinking about them. When we started remodeling that's when things started to get worse."

Dorothy was alone in the third-floor family room watching television when she heard the big outside door of the house swing open and then slam shut.

"I thought somebody had come home," she said, and then called out a litany of her family's names. "Debbie! Bert! Jim! Bob! No response. I went downstairs, down the main staircase, and I actually heard somebody coming up the stairs, but there wasn't a soul there."

The pattern continued on many occasions. She wasn't alone in discovering the mysterious presence.

"The kids would say the same thing if my husband and I were out for an evening. They would hear the front door close and then the footsteps. My older son was scared to death to stay in that house by himself."

It was always the same. Footsteps ascended the main staircase all the way to the third floor, occasionally interrupted by various doors being opened. It was, Dorothy thought, as if somebody had come home and was now checking to see that everything was all right.

Sounds produced from inside the sealed-off attic space above the Cards' bedroom disturbed Dorothy's sleep. "They were definite footsteps. Somebody pacing back and forth. My husband heard them too, but he said they were probably mice." They would have been mice wearing cowboy boots, however, according to Dorothy's recollection of the heavy steps.

The Cards never figured out how to get to that particular concealed attic area. Bob did locate a false wall inside a downstairs closet and thought possibly that a stairway might have once been there. Dorothy, reluctant to disturb any further whatever was still in the house, persuaded her husband not to remove the wall. An attempt to locate pictures of the original interior also proved futile.

Dorothy did learn something about Judge Theodore Brantly himself. He habitually returned home late at night long after the rest of his family had gone to sleep. He climbed the stairs to his third-floor office where he would mull over cases before the court until the wee hours of the morning, weighing each with a deliberation and acumen that he thought was lacking in his colleagues.

When not engaged in legal matters, he was engrossed in genealogy. With the help of historians, he finally learned that his family had roots in the American Revolution, and he was delighted.

Justice Brantly was a frontier version of today's "workaholic." Although friends begged him not to work so long and so hard, he paid them no heed. For Theodore Brantly, hard work was his salvation. He came out of Tennessee in 1877, determined to succeed in the wild American West, not by brawn, but by brains. He was twenty-five years old and well educated. He was the first faculty member of the College of Montana in Deer Lodge, and later opened a law partnership. When the law firm failed, he berated himself for not having worked harder. Then, in 1887, only ten years after his arrival in Montana, the people of his adopted state elected Brantly to their highest court. The young barrister from Tennessee had become a much-admired self-made man of the frontier.

But Justice Brantly learned that his prominence had come at great personal cost. In his grueling schedule, he rarely made time for his wife and children. His two sons grew up without an attentive father in their house. A daughter left home to attend school in the East.

Judge Brantly's health began to fail in 1919. He lived for another three years before death claimed him at the age of seventy. His descendants owned the house until 1963. Six years later the Cards bought it.

Dorothy said that just as they were getting used to the footsteps, other oddities began to happen. One warm evening the family went out for a car ride, as was their habit during the summer. Before leaving the house, she told the boys to turn off a TV in their second-floor room.

"When we got home the TV was blaring and the lights were on in the boys' room. This happened several more times, but the boys always insisted they had nothing to do with it," Dorothy said. The house had been rewired so defective wiring was an unlikely cause.

A tenant in the basement apartment, a young woman named Barb, also had her problems.

"Have you been eating my candy?" Barb asked Dorothy Card one afternoon. "I had a whole bowl of M&Ms and I haven't eaten any. Now they're all gone."

"Oh, those dirty little poltergeists are after us again." Dorothy laughed uneasily.

Barb knew nothing of poltergeists or the Cards' problems, but after Dorothy briefed her, she admitted that this wasn't the first time candy had vanished. The women reluctantly dismissed the episode as a "funny little thing."

The Cards sold their dream mansion in November 1977. Ghosts and poltergeists, or at least footsteps and missing candy, didn't drive them out. Their daughter had gotten married, and an older son turned eighteen and wanted to be out on his own. Only Dorothy and Bob and their younger son remained.

"We just had too much room," Dorothy remembered. "I told Bob it had gotten to the point where all I was doing was cleaning. It was way too much house for us. The remodeling of our apartment had been finished, but the rest of the house wasn't. And besides, my husband wasn't feeling well."

A physician bought the house as an investment. She traveled extensively and rented the apartments, with a resident manager and his wife in charge.

One morning the manager called Dorothy at her new home to say that a package for her had been delivered to their old address. Could she please come to pick it up? Dorothy detected an uneasy edge to his voice and asked if there was a problem. After some hesitation, he asked her if she'd noticed any "funny happenings" in the house when she lived there.

Dorothy talked about the footsteps on the staircase, doors opening and closing, and the television incident. The man said he and his wife had experienced all those things—and more!

"He said they were going to move out because his wife was a nervous wreck," Dorothy said. "One day he came home from work and was talking to his wife in the middle of the living room. All of a sudden the large rhododendron plant that I'd left there rose three feet off the floor and just hung suspended in the air. Then it [the plant] started to shake, fell over and died. The pot was smashed. While they stood there, the vacuum cleaner in the kitchen turned itself on and started to move across the floor."

The resident manager and his wife moved. He told the new landlady about the ghosts, and she purportedly replied, "Yes, and they're my ghosts and I'm going to hang on to them."

Bob Card died not long after the couple sold the house. Dorothy moved to another part of Helena. When friends asked her why she lived for eight years in a haunted house, she had a ready reply.

"The poltergeists, or whatever they were, really weren't that disturbing. We kind of laughed it off and as long as they weren't destroying things and making life completely miserable for us, we knew we could live alongside them."

The Card family had two sons and a daughter. So did the Brantly family. Had the old justice returned to his home to find the family life he'd never had? Or was he still working on a legal case that he never finished? Was the inaccessible attic his old office? Or . . . ?

For her part, Dorothy dismisses all questions about the sealed attic. "I don't ever . . . *ever* . . . want to know what's up there!"

Ghostnabbers

Nebraskans have a lively history of storytelling, due perhaps to the lonely existence of so many early pioneers. Before the era of electronic communications, frontier folks had to amuse themselves with stories taken from events around them. Sometimes the stories those early yarn-spinners told were invented to amuse listeners; at other times a kernel of truth resided in the tales. The stories that follow are in the latter category; each one is said to be absolutely true!

Maud DeVault, Schoolmarm

Redington was once the liveliest outpost of civilization in Nebraska's western border country. Its reputation was acquired, in part, by tales of a ghost that frequented the scene of a gruesome murder.

On the night of September 30, 1883, Charles Adams was brutally killed. His head was chopped off. There were no clues to the identity of the assailant, but the motive was apparently robbery. A large sum of money was missing from Adams's cabin, along with a diamond shirt stud and other valuables. The search for the murderer was futile and, after the initial excitement had worn off, interest waned.

The community, located about ten miles southwest of Bridgeport on today's State Highway 88, was growing. By 1886 a post office was established and stores and sod houses were being built by the new settlers. The Adams murder took on a new twist, however, when locals said they saw a ghost visiting the little cabin where Adams had lived and died. On the anniversary of his murder, Adams was spied riding a white horse, carrying his head in his hands like the immortal Ichabod Crane. For years the headless horseman returned, frightening everyone who saw him.

The legend grew throughout the region until 1913, when the Redington School's new teacher, an adventuresome young beauty named Maud DeVault, said she'd surely like to meet this phantom horseman. Pranksters heard about Miss DeVault's wish and saw the opportunity for a practical joke. They decided that teacher and ghost should meet.

One young man consented to pose as the ghost, and draped himself and his horse with sheets. He was to conceal himself directly behind the dilapidated Adams cabin, a mile south of Redington, and at the given signal he was to ride out into the road and gallop away.

At precisely nine o'clock on the night of September 30, 1913, the thirtieth anniversary of Adams's death, the village ghost hunters arrived in front of the cabin to wait and watch. Their patience was soon rewarded; the ghost galloped boldly toward them. The citizens panicked, nearly trampling one another as they tried to flee. That is, everyone but Miss DeVault. She stepped forward, seized the horse by the reins, and demanded an explanation of the rider's periodic visits, punctuating her request with a couple of shots from her trusty revolver.

The frightened horse bolted, crashed into a wire fence and lost its trappings. Spectators peered into the gloom and saw several white sheets float to the ground. The "ghost" had been killed! Women shrieked and fainted and men groaned.

The "ghost's" sister, a formidable figure of nearly 280 pounds, was so stricken with fear that she sprinted toward Redington to spread the news. An automobile sent in pursuit overtook her only with difficulty. Brought back to the scene, the sister discovered it was her brother and not a ghost who rode horseback that night. And her brother was alive and unhurt. She collapsed, and a physician had to be called.

When the episode was finally explained to everyone later that night, Miss DeVault said she had expected plotters to arrange a joke on the schoolmarm and had loaded her revolver with blank cartridges. She earned the respect of everyone.

The Redington post office was abandoned in 1962 and the "haunted Adams cabin" itself burned in 1974. A church, a rural school, and a cluster of families are all that remain. Yet Redington's distinctions have probably never been matched. This little pioneer community had a legendary ghost, a real live spook, a ghost buster, and a 280-pound lady sprinter—all at the same time. It was probably enough to make the spirit of Charles Adams flee to Omaha.

Nick Foley's Bridge

No one now living knew Nick Foley. And few people living a century ago ever knew the exact spot where he was buried. But in the 1880s, Nick's name was on the lips of everyone living in northern Nebraska. Because of a brutal murder he committed, Nick was hanged from a bridge by an incensed mob. His body was then cut down and thrown in a shallow grave. That crossing was known thereafter as Foley's Bridge.

Simon Knox had heard the gruesome stories of the murder and the lynching, each teller adding new and more lurid details. But now, as Knox and his team lumbered across the rolling prairie, he tried to forget all about that. He'd have to cross Foley's Bridge after dark and the thought made him weak. He wasn't necessarily superstitious, he told himself, only a little . . . wary . . . of places tainted by evil.

Darkness closed in and stars pin-pricked the sky. Knox huddled low on the wagon seat listening to the creaking wagon wheels. He smiled to himself as a plan took shape.

At the next town, he hitched the horses in front of a saloon and went in for a drink. Then another. And another. Then he bought a bottle of "red eye" for the road. Back in the wagon, he held the reins in one hand and the open bottle in the other, swigging himself into a blissful stupor. In such a state, he'd be across the bridge without even knowing it. Well, that was the idea, anyway.

It didn't work out quite that well. As he crossed the bridge, Knox realized he was cold sober. Worse, the horses stopped, cried in terror, and refused to move. The dank night air pierced his woolen coat; he saw the stars dim. He managed to climb down from his seat and look out over the bridge. Standing on the rail several feet away was a man wrapped in mist. A phosphorescent light illuminated the body, then the face—of Nick Foley!

Knox, quaking like an aspen, leaned against the shoulder of the closest horse. Both horses fought their bits, twisting their heads away from the bridge as if to escape the thing on the railing. The south wind quit blowing and roosting birds screamed in the treetops and took flight.

Knox assessed his limited options: going ahead or going back. Deciding to proceed, he screamed at the ghostly figure, "Nick, I command you in the name of the Redeemer to fly to your eternal home, and haunt this region no more!"

As if on cue, the light went out and the misty shape floated down the river gorge. Knox climbed into the wagon and his team took off across the bridge, and didn't stop until they reached the saloon in the next town. Knox told his tale to the skeptical crowd, who accused him of being too drunk to know what he'd seen. He swore it was all true.

For a long time afterward, no one crossed Foley's Bridge after sunset. A few people would not cross it at all.

Blazing Chickens

In the western part of Madison County was the old settlement of Emerick. With its upland and valleys rich in the native grasses that ensured excellent pasturage, and its exceptionally fertile soil, the region was most attractive to settlers. Perhaps no one was more attracted to it than Carl Preuss. A hardworking farmer, he knew he could make a fine living from cereal crops and possibly an orchard.

By 1900, Preuss was one of the most prosperous farmers of Emerick. Then the trouble began.

On a cold, moonlit night in February, the Preuss family was awakened by thousands of nails rattling down the slopes of their house's tin roof. At least that's what it sounded like. Preuss and his wife leaped from their bed. What kind of jokester would be up on the peak of the roof dumping kegs of nails over the shingles? Preuss buttoned his mackinaw over his nightshirt, lit a lantern and rushed outside. The frozen ground crunched under his feet, the air was still. He circled the house, swinging the lantern upward toward the roof. Only a thread of smoke arose from the chimney. Preuss found no nails, nor anything else for that matter to account for the frightening noise.

He went back inside as puzzled as before. No sooner had he shut the door than one of his children, nose pressed to a windowpane, shouted, "Look at the chickens!" They weren't exactly chickens, but fiery fowls of a kind seen only in children's picture books. The shimmering creatures, on legs like golden wires, strutted about the yard, pecking bare batches of dirt and fluttering and cackling in an unearthly manner.

As Mrs. Preuss passed a window at the back of the house that overlooked the barn, she screamed and the family came running. In the doorway of the barn stood a black dog of massive proportions, its eyes as large as the gas lamps on the streets of Lincoln.

Preuss grabbed a buggy whip and raced out of the house. He raised the whip over his head, but before he could bring it down on the canine, it vanished through the side of the barn, leaving no trace of its presence. The family went back to bed, but sleep did not come that night.

Night after night the Preusses were awakened by the resounding clatter of nails, by the cackling of fiery fowls in the yard. And each evening, the ferocious dog appeared at the barn door shortly after dark and remained until dawn. He never left the barn dooryard. Every time Mr. Preuss attempted to reach him with a whip, the animal faded away.

Preuss finally summoned Rev. Ed Hoffman to exorcise the ghosts, but, in his presence, the oddities never appeared.

The last time Preuss talked to a news reporter, he swore all the events had happened just as he described. The ghosts were still at large.

Today the only vestige of old Emerick is the pioneer cemetery still used for burials. The turn-of-the-century buildings—the Methodist church, the blacksmith and wagon shop, the creamery, the general store, and the post office—are gone, replaced by modern farm buildings and livestock feedlots spread over the rolling hills.

If the phantoms of Emerick are still on the loose, their present whereabouts— and antics—are unknown.

Angel of Death

Why do humans fear death?

In the thousands of years that men and women have inhabited this planet, perhaps we have never escaped a primitive fear of the unknown. The void that comes after life is the greatest unknown of all. Out of these dark fears, superstitions developed. It was said that a black angel—the angel of death—would appear in a community and select its followers by giving a sign. The knock at the door of a house in which an ill person lived portended imminent death. So did the clock that stopped running, or rappings on the walls.

When the black angel came a-calling, there was no escape.

But the people of Long Pine, Nebraska, were unprepared for the angel of death that came to their village in the guise of a child—a fair-haired, innocent-looking tyke. The child made several forays into the village, and his coming always brought disaster to the person seeing it.

One day a resident met the child for the first time. The man was deeply touched. Surely the little fellow was lost and must be returned to his parents. When the man reached out for the child, his fingers closed upon empty air. The tiny figure jumped into the river and vanished beneath the waters. Minutes later, the man's son was kicked by a horse and died.

On another occasion, a rider on horseback saw the diminutive ghost and he, too, assumed it was a child who had wandered from home. He reached down to grab the boy, but was thrown from his horse and suffered a broken neck.

An Act of God?

One young choir member had to finish geometry problems. Another's car wouldn't start. Two members were so caught up in a radio program they had to hear the end. A mother had to call her daughter twice from a nap and both were late. The minister, his wife and daughter were all late because Mom hadn't finished ironing the girl's dress.

Of the fifteen members of a church choir in Beatrice, there were ten different excuses that kept *all* of them from being on time at their 7:20 P.M. choir practice on March 1, 1950.

It was an incredible coincidence, or an unconscious premonition, because at precisely 7:25 P.M. the church building was destroyed by an explosion caused by a faulty furnace. All of the choir members arrived minutes after the conflagration thinking they were late for practice. Instead, they offered prayers in thanks that each and every life had been spared.

Mathematician Warren Weaver calculated the odds of a church exploding at a time when choir practice was scheduled, and when all members were simultaneously late as a billion to one.

Parapsychologists might say that unconscious premonition played a role in the event. Did someone in the choir have a premonition that this was going to happen, and did the other members of the choir unconsciously pick up the "vibrations"?

Life magazine, in its account of the incident, called it one of the strangest events they had ever reported.

Back Berry's Race

Although there are no statistics to prove it, there may have been at one time more ghosts in Boyd and Holt counties than in all the rest of Nebraska put together.

In the early days of this century, people living in those sparsely settled sandhill counties saw numerous strange sights: balls of fire that leaped from one hill to another, causing dogs to bark and armed men to quaver and turn pale; ghosts floating along the willowed banks of the Elkhorn and Niobrara rivers, sending armed vigilantes running for cover.

Mavelius Libe, Hugh O'Neill, and John Hunt of Atkinson, and William Coleman of Spencer knew the stories; they had experienced the fireballs and the river ghosts. So had scores of others. But, out of all the supernatural excitement of the period, one folk hero emerged—Back Berry. He had a close encounter of the spectral kind.

It seems that once when Back and his buddies were "ghosthunting," an apparition emerged from a clump of bushes and took off after 'ol Back. He ran like a fugitive, fleet-footed on level ground, slugging through the scattered woodlots. Finally, near exhaustion, he dropped onto a log to rest. The ghost ran up and sat down beside him.

"We've had a great race, ain't we?" asked the ghost.

"Yup," Back allowed. "And by gawd, we're goin' to have anothern."

With that he took off once again.

Back Berry never said who won the contest.

Cochran's Brain

In the summer of 1880, John Cochran passed away. He had been visiting the C. H. Lane family of Pawnee City and died in their home. Since the cause of death could not be readily established, an autopsy was performed by four physicians. Cochran's brain and heart were removed and taken by one of the doctors for further study.

The night after Cochran's burial, the Lanes were awakened by loud knocks at the front door. They looked out the window and saw the dead man standing on the doorstep, vacant eyes fixed in his pallid face. Again, his gaunt fist struck the door, demanding that he be admitted.

A moment later, the family heard footsteps downstairs. No sooner had Mr. Lane started down the hallway to investigate than the translucent form of John Cochran shuffled toward him. In sepulchral tones, he demanded the return of all his body parts.

Every night thereafter the Lanes were visited by the ghost of the disassembled Mr. Cochran. Finally, Lane demanded that the physician return Cochran's organs for burial. This was done in the presence of witnesses. The corpse was appeased and kept to its grave.

The Ghosts of Dead Men's Island

Long stretches of undulating prairie highlands bank the Platte River where it flows through Dodge and Colfax counties in eastern Nebraska. In territorial days, settlers built their homes in a line, east to west, along the old military road that hugged the river. They formed close bonds, united for mutual protection against the dangers of the frontier. Indian depredations were unpredictable, thieves and desperados roamed the land, and justice by gun prevailed.

Late one afternoon, a settler galloped from homestead to homestead with the news of horse thieves in the area. A band from the Southwest had struck the Platte valley, raiding several corrals in western Dodge and eastern Colfax counties. Now they were headed back with their stolen horses. There was no time to lose. Each settler, in turn, grabbed his gun and swung onto his horse; within minutes a heavily armed posse was on its way, charging after the desperados.

With darkness coming on and the posse at their heels, the six thieves hatched a desperate, but ill-fated, plan. Pounding along the north shore of the Platte, west of where the hamlet of Rogers now stands in Colfax County, they noticed a small island. Like other islands in the river, it was little more than a sandbar fringed by scrub willows and grasses. To the gang's leader, however, it looked like a haven. At his signal, the men forced their horses into the water and made them swim to the island. The thieves would camp there for the night, then at dawn they could make it to the south bank and be well on their way before the settlers' posse could cross farther down and head them off.

Their scheme misfired. The "island" was actually a bar of quicksand. The weight of the horses set in motion the soft, shifting mass; men and horses were trapped. Across the dark roiling waters, the posse heard the cries of the terrified animals and the despairing shrieks of the men.

At dawn there was no sign of life; the deadly sand had buried men and horses. Retribution had been made, but the price was great.

For years afterward, on every storm-choked night when rain lashed the country-side, the thieves were forced to reenact their suffocating deaths. Ghastly shrieks and groans rose from the island, terrifying all who heard them. The settlers chris-tened the place "Dead Men's Island," and pointed it out to travelers.

Finally the island was washed away in a flood, and with it the memories of that accursed night.

Dead Miners, Old Bars, and a *Bucca*

Restless spirits are almost as difficult to find in Nevada as are towns in Eureka County—the total population of that forsaken patch of earth is less than two thousand people. Nevada ghosts probably number many hundreds fewer! A state that is best known for gambling and naked chorines, and whose official song is the unforgettable "Home Means Nevada" by one Bertha Raffetto, may stake most of its reputation on pleasures of the flesh rather than tales of the fleshless.

This is probably to be expected.

After all, in this most geologically inhospitable state of all, early settlers spent most of their time merely trying to survive. Nevada has less rainfall than any other state, and vast stretches of land are laden with alkali. Farming and ranching depend almost entirely on irrigation. Although the state's rugged natural beauty is among the most spectacular in the lower forty-eight states, it is tourism and high-stakes gambling that keep Nevada from being as impoverished as any Third World nation.

Archaeological research near Las Vegas has dated human habitation there to twenty thousand years ago, but the first accurate information about the region was provided when Capt. John C. Frémont mapped the Sierra Nevada and Great Basin regions from 1843 to 1845. A few years later, Mormon pioneer Brigham Young included most of present-day Nevada with Utah in his State of Deseret. Young petitioned Congress to admit his "state" into the Union, but the federal government instead created the Utah Territory in 1850. The Nevada Territory was constituted in 1861 and admitted as the thirty-sixth state in 1864.

The single most extraordinary event in pioneer Nevada, however, and the one that has given rise to sundry ghost stories, was the 1859 silver ore strike near present-day Virginia City. Several miners reportedly discovered the rich vein nearly simultaneously, but Henry T. P. Comstock took public credit and gave his name to what became the Comstock Lode. Within weeks, Carson County and Virginia City saw their meager populations swollen with an influx of hundreds of wealth-seeking prospectors from all over North America. By 1860, the county population had reached nearly seven thousand persons, many of them rowdy, lawless miners who thought nothing of murdering a rival if it meant a few more ounces of silver in their packs.

It's little wonder, then, that so many mines and abandoned mining camps are said to be haunted by the implacable seekers of El Dorado.

Ghost Tailings

The men and women whose professions place them in dangerous circumstances nearly each and every day are a superstitious lot. There are few more so than those who work deep underground in dank, dismal, claustrophobic tunnels, chipping away at the earth's mineral resources.

The miners of the Comstock Lode were no different. Many were ill-educated European immigrants who brought their beliefs in various demons and spirits to their new lives on the American frontier.

Irishmen called the ghosts *puca*; the Welsh name was *pwca*; an Englishman might consider them a form of *Puck*; but to a Comstock miner recently arrived from Cornwall, England, the spirits who inhabited mines were the *bucca* (or *bucca-boo*), and, to avoid disaster, they had to be appeased. Originally a Celtic sea god, the *bucca* took on the nature of a spirit among the fishermen of Cornwall. They placated the *bucca* by leaving a fish from their catch at the shoreline. Soon, the *bucca* found their way into the mines of southwestern England and discovered the surroundings were much to their liking. The dark, moist atmosphere actually made them prosper and multiply!

The Cornish who migrated to Nevada to work in the newly discovered silver mines brought the *bucca* with them, and, too, their belief in the necessity of leaving gifts for their unseen companions.

One of these Cornishmen was known as "Cousin Jack." He unknowingly had a *bucca* stow away in his rucksack on the lengthy journey from England to Nevada. The critter escaped and took up residence at the mine in which Jack found employment. Now Jack knew that unless he left a pastie (a kind of Cornish meat pie) from his dinner bucket for the *bucca*, misfortune would plague him. His kerosene lamp might not stay lit, his tools could vanish, or one of the support timbers might loosen and rock and gravel fall dangerously close. Jack was careful always to please his impish companion, for as long as the *bucca* was happy, a miner would not be harmed. Should a cave-in be imminent, for instance, the *bucca* would issue a warning by tapping urgently against the tunnel walls.

Which silver mine "Cousin Jack" worked in isn't recorded, but it could well have been the Baltimore Mine. A strange incident was reported there by the Virginia City *Chronicle* in late 1884.

While Cornishmen and the Irish believed spirits such as the *bucca* caused any tapping heard in mines, Englishmen thought the chilling sounds more likely caused by the ghosts of dead miners. Such was the case of the two prospectors the newspaper said heard the clicking of hammers as they climbed down the Baltimore Mine stope, a kind of excavation that took the form of steps when the silver vein was steeply inclined or vertical.

Soon the men saw the source of the noise: two hammers floating in midair striking alternately at the head of an old drill. Though no human was in sight, the hammers banged away at the drill—which turned as if under its own power!

Even more bizarre, the men claimed to have heard an animated conversation from whatever entities held the hammers.

When they told their story to men at the mine entrance, they were laughed at.

Until, that is, they dragged several doubters to the location and they, too, saw the hammers flailing away, the drill turning—and even heard snatches of conversation floating toward them. From thin air!

The ghost of old Henry Comstock himself put in an occasional appearance at Virginia City's Ophir Mine, located on the site of his original strike.

Miners at first believed that one of their own was playing pranks. Candle lanterns on the walls would suddenly be extinguished, casting the gloomy tunnels into darkness. On some occasions, the shift foremen actually saw the lanterns going out. But when peals of laughter roared from areas of the tunnel where no man was working, every miner knew the ghost of old Henry was on the premises.

A most puzzling and frightening episode unfolded late one winter's night in the year 1874. The story is that a brilliant, flaming light erupted from a shaft at the Ophir Mine. Citizens rushed to the mine afraid that the fire—for that is what it appeared to be—would destroy the timbers supporting the tunnel. However, when the crowd reached the entrance to the old tunnel, there was no fire at all. What appeared to be a beam of light shone up through the hole, far brighter than any light source known at that time.

Strangest of all, witnesses later claimed, the *chink-chink-chink* of a miner's pickax striking stone drifted up from about the seven-hundred-foot level of the mine shaft. Yet that area hadn't been mined in years!

No one volunteered to enter the mine shaft that night, and everyone went home puzzled about the curious episode. Early the next morning, the foreman on the first shift claimed to have heard the bell signaling for the elevator, a kind of "cage" in which the miners rode up and down the mine shafts, to be lowered to the seven-hundred-foot level. He obliged and down it went. Minutes later, the signal came to raise it. As it came into view, everyone saw that the cage was empty. And since the foreman knew no workers had been at that level for a very long time, the mystery of who or what was playing pranks in the mine only intensified.

Enter Frank Kennedy, a nervy young miner who boasted to anyone within earshot that he feared neither man nor beast. Why even the Devil himself, he thundered, would come out second best in a rasslin' match with Frank Kennedy!

The shift foreman grinned and allowed that it *just might be* Old Scratch himself down there. Would the brave Irishman care to go take a look-see? Kennedy jumped in the elevator cage and told the operator to lower away.

At the dreaded seven-hundred-foot level, Kennedy climbed out of the basket and, with his lantern held out in an unsteady hand, started walking down the tunnel. Blackness stretched away before him down the abandoned mine shaft. The young miner was about ready to give up and return to the surface (though he was reluctant to admit defeat and was even now dreaming up his account of "the Devil versus Frank Kennedy") when he thought he heard the faint, rhythmic sound of a pickax. It seemed to be coming from the far end of the tunnel, just around what Kennedy figured must be the final bend.

The lantern penetrated only a few feet ahead as Kennedy peered around the corner. A man that Kennedy recognized immediately as Henry Comstock crouched near a rock outcropping, his pick resting against the wall. As Kennedy's lantern light penetrated the darkness, Comstock quickly rose and turned toward the intruder. Kennedy nearly fainted at the ghastly sight—pieces of flesh hung from Comstock's face; vacant eyesockets seemed to emit a kind of blue light. A faint glow as if from some unseen lamp surrounded the figure.

This ghoul, this . . . thing . . . in the abandoned mine shaft was not pleased with having his work disturbed. He roared at Kennedy, shook his fist and sprang forward.

Quite forgetting his earlier boasts, the young miner nearly slammed into an ancient timber support in his haste to terminate this unexpected meeting. All the way back to the elevator, Kennedy felt Henry Comstock's looming presence a few steps behind. Or was that his imagination?

Frank Kennedy never ventured into that mine again, nor any other. He decided there must be a safer line of work somewhere on the surface. Where the sun shines. And where reanimated miners don't lurk at the ends of dark passages.

Perhaps because their work was so dangerous, Nevada silver and gold miners saw harbingers of disaster in all manner of unexplained sights and sounds.

A candle sputtering when a man walked by meant he would soon die unless he gave up the underground life. Strange noises were said to be the shrieks and cries of comrades killed when tunnels collapsed. The screams were meant as a warning that danger was looming. No man ventured below ground on that day.

Ghost Town, Nevada

If there is one town in all of Nevada with the most colorful history—and the most ghosts per square block—Virginia City must surely be it. Once the largest of the old western mining towns, Virginia City boasted a population estimated at thirty thousand and amenities that belied its location 6,220 feet up in the Virginia Range, twenty-three miles southeast of Reno. Founded in 1859, just two years after gold and silver were found in the nearby mountains, Virginia City became a center of civilization in an untamed land: world-famous entertainers played Piper's Opera House; women dressed in the finest European fashions; and swiftly built mansions outfitted with European furniture bought sight-unseen by miners turned into instant millionaires when they struck a rich vein. Nothing was beyond the reach of the unimaginable wealth that flowed in and out of Virginia City.

The rough-and-tumble life of the mining camp turned metropolis became known worldwide when Mark Twain wrote about this frontier outpost in *Roughing It*.

But Dame Fortune did not smile for long. Less than twenty years after its founding, Virginia City's population started dropping as the rich ore deposits became too costly to mine or simply gave out. By the mid-twentieth century, Virginia City had become a popular tourist center as one of the authentic "ghost towns" in the American West.

Not everyone who once lived in Virginia City has left. If one is to believe the stories, some of the best "conserved" vestiges of the community's heyday are its ghosts. Visitors say a few show their vaporous forms in the most unexpected places.

Father Patrick Manogue was a miner-priest who built a four-story brick domicile that became St. Mary Louise Hospital, and the abode of Virginia City's most famous specter—the White Nun.

What her name was in life isn't known, but she is said to have been in charge of the hospital operating room and to have died under "mysterious circumstances" sometime in the 1880s. But her earthly history is mostly conjecture. In more recent years, the White Nun still roamed the former infirmary's corridors and peered out of a second-floor window, as if waiting and looking for the next wagonload of injured miners or feverish children. She is sometimes observed in the company of a small boy, stricken with polio. His legs are encased in metal braces. The ghostly pair are on the front staircase of the old hospital; he is at the top of the stairs crying, obviously afraid that his awkward gait will cause him to fall down the steps. The White Nun scurries back up the staircase to comfort the tyke. To those who have watched this scenario played out late at night, the emotional impact is jarring. One observer said there was "a pleading about her gaze that seems to ask for help, but how does one help a ghost?"

The other macabre haunting at the former St. Mary Louise Hospital was the rare appearance of a "dead wagon," which would pull up near an out-of-the-way entrance to haul away the most recent corpses. No sound would issue from the swaying coach or snorting horses as the driver claimed his ghastly cargo.

Mysteriously replayed scenes such as those above—as if a videotape were being shown over and over again—are common in ghost lore. The phantom horse-drawn hearse arriving at St. Mary Louise Hospital is not the only strange manifestation tourists might see in Virginia City.

On an old dirt road from the Washoe Valley to Gold Hill, several miles outside Virginia City, a buckboard filled with mining camp supplies goes out of control and careens over an embankment. Horses, cargo, and driver crash down the sheer mountainside . . . and vanish in an instant!

The actual accident is reported to have happened decades before the "Geiger Grade" paved road was built. Several young women out for a trail ride once saw the ghostly reenactment. They claimed their horses reared up in panic. The horsewomen galloped for home.

The Woman in Red may greet passersby should they venture past a certain old house on F Street at twilight. She spends most of her time in the attic's rocking chair, but on occasion will post herself on a second-floor veranda and wave to people on the street. A former saloon keeper, the Woman in Red sometimes is seen in the company of hazy miners who seem to appear from nowhere.

Meanwhile, the red brick Mackay Mansion on D Street is the home to at least three ghosts: a mysterious female who makes incessant trips up and down the staircase trying to finish some long-forgotten job; another woman who spends most of her time lingering on the third floor; and the Colonel, a former owner, who spent his final days on earth sitting in the kitchen. That's where he remains.

A local cemetery contains the grave of one Julia Bullette, the most famous of all Virginia City's numerous prostitutes. Or does it?

A story circulated some years ago that the apparition of a slender young woman would rise up from Julia's alleged resting place. Dressed in a brown, bustled dress with a collar and cuffs of dark velvet, the woman looked nothing like Julia. The ghost of a small child played at her feet, providing further doubt that Julia was really buried at that place.

Katie Hillyer was a Virginia City writer who died in 1968. For several years after her death, various people claimed to have seen her scurrying down the street dressed in a heavy, old jacket and baseball-type cap. She was on her way to visit the bookmobile during one of its frequent Virginia City stops, an activity she much enjoyed during life.

At a local saloon she sometimes frequented, Katie's filmy silhouette lounged at the bar railing. She smiled and nodded in what one observer said was a "detached" sort of way.

Camels were introduced in Nevada in the mid-nineteenth century. The theory was that their ability to thrive for days and weeks without water would make them useful to the cavalry, prospectors, and settlers. The beasts didn't work out as planned, and most were removed to Arizona by the end of the century. The last herd of camels was supposedly seen in 1936 near Penelas.

But Virginia City has its own camel legend. High above the town on Sun Mountain a red camel appears on moonlit nights, scampering up and down the steep slopes.

In the nearby state capital of Carson City, the most famous Sierra Nevada stage driver made appearances at the Ormsby House, or so it was told.

Hank Monk was the driver's name, and he spent his final days slumped in a chair near a stove in the bar. Monk died in 1883, but for a long time after that the barkeep found Monk's old chair pulled up to the stove each morning—even when the puzzled bartender had pushed it to the other side of the room the night before!

The Black Rock Boogie Man

Two separate but possibly related incidents in the foothills of the Black Rock Mountains of northwest Nevada have given rise to the legend of a horrifying, pickax-wielding madman who attacks unsuspecting travelers.

In April 1875, prospector James N. Sharp was battered to death by his partner, Joseph W. Rover, in those mountains. Rover was tried and convicted of the murder. He was hanged in Reno on February 10, 1878.

But Sharp's ghost is not at peace.

As recently as 1965, a California prospector was allegedly attacked in the Black Rock foothills by a stranger wielding a pickax. The prospector, Richard E. York, had set up camp near an abandoned mine. The white-bearded, oddly dressed intruder, looking not "from this century," York recalled, showed up during York's second night in the desert. He wore a frock coat and beaver skin hat, and carried the pickax menacingly in front of him. The old man said not a word as he swung the lethal weapon at York.

The California prospector barely reached his Jeep in time to make his escape. The attacker threw the pickax at York's truck, but it glanced off.

Old-timers said the "Black Rock Boogie Man" had struck again, after a silence of nearly three decades. Some thought the attacker was the ghost of James N. Sharp looking for justice.

Ironically, the man hanged for Sharp's murder haunted his own Reno execution site. Several people claimed to have seen the ghost of Joseph W. Rover. He maintained until his dying moments that another partner had actually committed Sharp's murder.

Express Car No. 5

Tales of railroad ghosts are as common in Nevada as in most other states. Incorporeal conductors and anomalous railcars seem to be a permanent fixture in American folklore.

Wells Fargo men aboard the Southern Pacific's Express Car No. 5 in Nevada complained that when the railroad lost a body being shipped back East in 1881, the incident unleashed a most insistent ghost. He would suddenly show up demanding to know "What was done with the corpse?" No one was ever able to give him a satisfactory answer!

The deaths of two trainmen led to hauntings in Carlin and at Monument Point, near the Nevada-Utah border.

At Carlin, a conductor was accidentally killed, but his ghost was often seen in the railyards, while train crews on the Southern Pacific line at Monument Point had a different problem on their hands. A fireman had been killed there in a horrifying derailment. For years afterward, train crews said they often saw a swinging red lantern, the danger signal, alongside the tracks. After bringing the train to a standstill, they'd look for the person swinging the warning light, but never found a trace of anyone.

A Chinese cook murdered aboard a Nevada, California, and Oregon Railroad dining car in 1889 wouldn't stay dead. His ghost plagued his successors so regularly that the NC&O finally abandoned the haunted dining car.

In the northern Nevada region near the Kings River and Oregon Canyon are mysterious lights sometimes associated with railroads (or automobiles), although the Nevada ghost lights appear to be unconnected to either source.

Cowboys and sheepherders near McDermitt have seen lights in that high desert region, nearly 4,500 feet above sea level, for many years. The red or yellow lights seem to float a few feet above the ground and are about the size of automobile headlights. The lights appear almost "intelligent" by dodging and weaving whenever someone gets too close. Although ranchers claim they've chased the lights for several miles, no one has ever reported getting closer to one of the shimmering orbs than twenty or thirty feet.

The most persistent Nevada ghost light is probably that at the Kings' River Ranch, west of Oregon Canyon. Reports are that several hundred people have seen lights there similar to those found outside McDermitt.

The causes of both sets of lights have never been adequately explained.

The Cursed Isles of Shoals

A gale ripped the Spanish brig's two headsails and the spanker. The helmsman tried desperately to keep his ship on course, but knew his efforts were futile. The sky was the color of pewter. As the clouds lowered, a blizzard lashed the ship. On that January day in 1813, every sailor aboard the ship some believe was the *Sagunto* knew he was doomed.

The ship was blown toward Smutty Nose, a treeless, rocky island ten miles off Portsmouth, yet no hysteria erupted on shipboard. In the tradition of those who lived by the sea, each crewman performed his accustomed duties with silent resignation to his fate.

After the brig broke apart on the rock-strewn shore it was every man for himself. Those who were uninjured scrambled over the boulders and headed toward a light ahead of them. It would be a lantern in the window of a settler's cabin. They'd be safe. But as the men struggled against the biting wind and the blinding snow, they seemed to be no closer to the beacon.

In the morning, Samuel Haley, the island's permanent resident, found the bodies of fourteen sailors who had succumbed while crawling toward his lighted cabin. The bodies of two more seamen were found hung over the stone wall fronting Haley's home. Their ebbing strength had not allowed them to climb over the barricade. Their mouths were frozen in a final, frenzied cry for help.

Planks of cedar and mahogany stuck up haphazardly from crevices in the rocks, wedged there by the force of the collision. Crates of foodstuffs were scattered along the shore.

Haley and his family had slept through the storm. Now they stood stricken by the horrible scene before them. They buried the unknown sailors side by side on the island, and placed unadorned stones at the head of each grave.

But the Spanish seafarers did not rest in peace. For years afterward their ghosts walked the shores of Smutty Nose, signaling passing vessels to beg passage back to Spain.

Although some historians believe that the *Sagunto*, after a stormy voyage, put safely into a port, there is general agreement that a craft of uncertain identity did founder on Smutty Nose Island on January 14, 1813, and that all hands were lost.

* * *

Smutty Nose is not an isolated outcropping in the Atlantic Ocean. It's one of seven small islands collectively called the Isles of Shoals. Although they were once permanently inhabited by fishermen, the American Revolution hastened the decline of the fishing industry and these harsh, remote specks of land soon became places of mystery and violence—of fire and pestilence, of horrifying deaths, and of buried pirate treasure. Even today it is said that the ghosts of two pirates pummel each other in a church attic, fighting over the division of gold they'd left behind, or perhaps loot abandoned by some earlier buccaneers who once controlled the islands.

One of the most gruesome murders occurred on Star Island. Years ago "guinea boats" used to put in at various harbors of the Shoals. These long, narrow, rather nondescript vessels were berthed in Boston and manned by Italian and Portuguese crews. After a long, hard day of fishing, the men would relax around a cask of wine and swap yarns. It was always a contest as to who could come up with the most improbable tale.

Then, early one evening a member of one of the crews got drunk and staggered ashore. In the yard of a cabin he accosted a fisherman's wife. When she spurned his advances, he threw her to the ground. She screamed and fought him until he plunged a knife into her breast. As she lay dying, he returned to his boat. His mates, suspecting what had happened, said nothing. In the morning they set sail for Boston.

Now the islanders, upon discovering the woman's crumpled body, were certain that her husband had killed her. The couple had never gotten along well. The husband was accused of murder and police officers arrived from Portsmouth. But a storm came up before they could return to the mainland with their prisoner, and they all remained in the house.

At midnight, at the height of the storm's fury, the accused man leaped through a window, ran to the beach and launched a dory. Neither he nor the boat was ever heard from again.

Months later, the same crew of guineamen returned to the fishing banks off the island. They knew of the murder, of course, but did not speak of it among themselves. Late one foggy night as their boat lay anchored in the harbor, terrifying screams arose from the bowels of the craft. The men rushed below to find one of their mates waving the bloody stump of his arm; it had been severed at the wrist. A sailor who had remained on deck said he'd heard the dip of oars and, through a break in the fog, had seen an indistinct figure in oilskins quickly rowing away in a dory.

From that time on no guinea boat was ever safe in a harbor of the Shoals. On every stormy night a crewman would be found mutilated in a hideous way. One had an ear lopped off; another an eye torn from its socket; and still another a foot chopped off at the ankle. And always on board the cursed vessel someone claimed to have seen a ghostly figure in a dory.

The nefarious Captain Teach—Blackbeard to his victims—was a frequent visitor to the lonely Shoals. He supposedly buried immense treasures here. Legend has it that his many wives were ordered to stand guard over the caches until his return. Some performed their tasks until their dying day, and now their ghosts walk the sands searching the endless horizon for their mate's return.

Many persons claim to have seen the beautiful wraith of White Island, where a number of Blackbeard's victims may have been buried. The ghost is tall and shapely, wrapped in a long cloak. A mane of golden hair tumbles about her shoulders. Her round face is as pale and cold as marble. She stands motionless on a point of land; no breeze ever ruffles her cloak.

Another comely specter haunts Appledore Island. In the fall of 1826 a man who had gone to the islands thinking the fresh sea air would cure his failing health caught sight of a young woman looking out to sea. Thinking she was awaiting the arrival of a husband or a lover on a fishing boat, he said, "Well, my pretty maiden, do you see anything of him?"

She turned sad blue eyes upon him. "He *will* come again."

She then disappeared behind a boulder. The man followed, but found no sign of her. He asked the islanders, but no one knew of any woman who matched the description he gave.

In sunshine and storm the ghost stood at the water's edge, sometimes wailing like a banshee when the sea grew rough. And whenever the stranger stood beside her, he always heard the same words: "He *will* come again." Whether he heard them in his mind or upon his ear he couldn't say. Shells never shattered beneath her light footsteps.

Later the man learned that one of Blackbeard's comrades, a Captain Scot, had brought this lovely lady to the island where she lived and died, guarding his considerable treasure.

Yet another female ghost appeared to party-goers on Duck Island. The young people, seated on the beach, had finished their picnic supper and begun to harmonize to the accompaniment of a guitar. It had been one of those perfect, lazy summer days, warm and pleasant with only a gentle breeze to stir the water.

Finally, two of the men who had never been to the island before decided to go exploring. Setting forth on foot, they promised to return before sunset. Recent rains had turned the hollows into bogs, but the adventurous men slogged on.

Soon they reached a weatherbeaten shanty that had evidently served once as a fisherman's cabin. The windows, now gaping holes, were tenanted by sea birds, and the tilt of the building itself indicated that it hadn't been used for many years.

The men entered the shack and found nothing but two empty rooms that reeked of mustiness. Outside again, one of the men turned around to look back. The face of a beautiful young woman filled a window opening! Where had she come from? There was only the one door by which the men had entered.

They stood spellbound. And as they watched, the woman's face changed into that of a hag, a frightening creature who appeared old enough to have been guarding the place since the beginning of time.

Was the vision a trick of the light? The men shifted their position, but the ugly face remained. The sky paled and the hideous creature seemed to grow even uglier. Yet there could not be anyone inside the shack. The men reentered the gloomy place. As before, both rooms were empty. Only the crying of the gulls and the whisper of a rising wind broke the silence. The visitors hurried back to their friends and cast off immediately from the island. So far as is known, none of the young people ever again returned to Duck Island.

But today, hundreds of people come to the Isles of Shoals during the summer months and many return year after year. Some attend religious conferences on Star Island, others come to study at the Shoals Marine Laboratory on Appledore. Ships from Portsmouth carry day-trippers who want to experience, if only for a short time, the harsh beauty of these lonely islands—and listen to the mysterious tales of those who lived and died and may remain forevermore on the rocky shores.

To Dance with the Devil

Jonathan Moulton died in the fall of 1787 and was buried in his home town of Hampton. Because of a series of unexplained incidents, superstitious neighbors demanded that his grave be dug up and the casket opened. It was empty!

Little is known about Jonathan Moulton except that he was a real person born in Hampton on July 21, 1726. Records show that he became a hero during the French and Indian wars, slaying incredible numbers of the Abenaki tribe, and rising to the rank of general. At the age of twenty-three he married Abigail Smith.

The general and his wife lived in a handsome home acquired, in part, with Moulton's army pension. They were happy and comfortable, lacking none of the accoutrements of fine living. But Jonathan Moulton was a restless man; he missed the tension and excitement of battle. Surely there was more to life than the tedium of daily living.

So much for facts. Here the fantasy takes over, tales spun from half-truths, gossip, and speculation.

One morning, at breakfast, Moulton pounded a fist on the table and cried, "Abigail, we need more money—lots more! More wealth! More riches!"

Abigail, frightened by her husband's outburst, tried to calm him. "Jonathan, what has come over you? We have plenty of money—money to burn, in fact!"

"That's it, Abby! Money to burn! That's exactly what I want!" He leaped from his chair and began pacing the room. "I'd sell my soul to the Devil to gain all the gold on the face of the earth!"

Abigail covered her face with her hands and fled from the room.

Moulton stood by the fireplace, hands clasped behind him. Suddenly a shower of sparks flew from the chimney. He wheeled around to face a stranger. The visitor was dressed head to toe in black velvet. Not a speck of soot soiled his ruffled jabot or lace cuffs that protruded from the sleeves of his jacket.

"You called me, sir?" The stranger smiled.

Speak of the devil, muttered the general to himself as he backed away.

"Your servant," Satan began, "but please do hurry."

He picked up a glowing coal and checked his watch. "I'm expected at the governor's mansion in fifteen minutes."

Moulton felt beads of sweat stand on his forehead. It was not possible for anyone to reach Portsmouth in that short a time.

"Let us understand each other," said Satan, "is it a bargain or not?"

Moulton had often bragged that no one, not even the devil himself, could beat him in a deal. He casually took out his jackknife and began to whittle. The devil took out his and pared his nails.

"How do I know you'll do what you promise?" asked the general, averting his gaze from the evil face grinning at him.

The devil shook his cape and a shower of golden guineas cascaded to the floor. Moulton dropped to his hands and knees and chased the coins to the farthest corners of the room.

Old Nick smiled even more broadly.

"Now are you convinced?"

Moulton nodded but was unable to speak. Thereupon the devil drew up a contract promising to make Moulton the richest man in the county in return for his soul. Then he read the document aloud to be certain that there was no misunderstanding:

"In consideration of your agreement, duly signed and sealed, to deliver your soul, I engage, on my part, on the first day of every month, to fill your boots with golden guineas like those before you."

Satan paused and shook a diamond-studded forefinger at his host. "If you try to play me any trick, you will regret it! I know you, Jonathan Moulton, and shall keep my eye upon you, so beware!"

Moulton signed.

The demon pocketed his copy and Moulton hid his copy in the false bottom of a desk drawer.

As the legend goes, General Moulton scoured the town to find the largest boots possible to hang from the fireplace mantel. He finally settled for trooper's jackboots that reached nearly to his waist. Just as the Devil had promised, the boots were filled on the first of every month and soon the general was the richest man in the county.

To the general's credit, he did not squander his "inheritance." Seeking acclamation from townspeople, he spent some of his money to benefit his hometown. Neighbors began to admire him, and even those who had never before liked him smiled and nodded to him on the streets. He had become the hero of Hampton.

But over the years the general's greed became boundless. The more he had, the more he wanted. One day he cut the soles out of the boots. The devil poured the guineas from his sacks until the room below was filled and the chimney clogged. That night Moulton's house burned to the ground. Jonathan and Abigail escaped in their night clothes. But the general was not upset over the loss; the guineas probably had melted into a mass which he would later retrieve from the ruins. He found not a single nugget of gold.

But Moulton had stashed away enough money to build another fine house in Hampton. Soon after he and Abigail moved in, she died under mysterious circumstances, and Moulton married again immediately. The thirty-six-year-old bride was Abigail's best friend, Sarah Emery, a physician's daughter. She inherited all of the first Mrs. Moulton's fine jewels, including even the wedding ring that Abigail had worn for more than twenty-five years.

In the middle of one night Sarah awoke shrieking and writhing in pain. She screamed to her waking husband that the ghostly form of a woman had come to the bedside, seized her hand and torn the rings from it. Moulton stared at his wife's hand. There were no rings, only red, bloody ridges around her finger.

The general lit lanterns and rushed from room to room, but found nothing. Besides, all the doors and windows were still locked from the inside. Nevertheless, he slipped a cloak over his nightshirt and ran outdoors to search the grounds. There were no footprints anywhere in the damp earth. A cold chill swept through him; was it possible that Abigail had come back to retrieve the jewels that were rightly hers?

Sarah thought so. Every day she heard the swish of a woman's skirts and caught glimpses of a shadowy figure floating silently from room to room. Abigail had come home to stay.

At the age of sixty-one, Gen. Jonathan Moulton died, leaving Sarah to live alone in the house with only the ghost of Abigail for company.

After Sarah's death, Hampton House, as it was known, was lived in by many families. Sometimes the thunder of boots on the stairs was heard and the screams of a woman in an upstairs bedroom filled the night air. Residents often reported seeing the ghosts of women rushing through the house.

It is not known exactly who learned of Moulton's hellish contract, but the story spread that Moulton had indeed sold his soul to Satan. When the general's grave was opened, the empty casket proved to everyone that the devil had come to collect his debt.

Hampton House was moved at least once in the early part of the twentieth century and the ghosts exorcised. Today it is a private home.

Are the Van Wickles Home?

Everybody knows the old Evert Van Wickle house is haunted. Edward Murawski and his wife Kathleen know it so well they'll never forget it. In the summer of 1975 the couple moved into the beautiful eighteenth-century house in Franklin Township. Hidden in a grove of trees, the house is accessible only by a narrow, winding road. There is a Revolutionary War–era cemetery on the property. The Murawskis anticipated peace and privacy, and got neither. During their three-year stay they were bedeviled by invisible mischief-makers.

On her first day in the house Kathleen was sitting in the living room in a chair that had been left by the previous occupants, a family named Bogan. They had lived in the house from the 1950s until the early 1970s. Kathleen Murawski got up to go to the kitchen and when she returned found a puddle of water on the chair seat. There was no leakage from the living room ceiling and it hadn't rained. There was simply no accounting for the puddle's appearance.

One evening a short time later Kathleen was again in the living room, this time walking across the floor. Something flew past her head. It sounded like a bat, yet she and her husband found no evidence of one.

The next day Kathleen found a doily on the floor at the opposite end of the living room from the chair on which it had been placed. She thought maybe it had "flown" across the room. But a doily flying? Preposterous, she reasoned. And why hadn't she and Edward discovered it during their search the night before?

Soon the family's pets were acting in strange ways. The dog sat in the living room, wagging his tail while staring up at the ceiling. The cat sat beside him and hissed.

Soon there were unexplained noises. Doors slammed. A radio came on at all hours of the night, but that wasn't always an annoyance. On several occasions Edward overslept and would have been late for work had not the blast of the radio awakened him.

Most frightening to Kathleen was the night she heard a woman's soft voice:

"Edward . . . Edward . . ." it called.

Kathleen told her husband about the incident the next morning. He said he, too, had heard the voice. But he also said that whatever was in the house probably wouldn't bother them anymore.

"I told 'them' that if they didn't stop I'd burn the house down and they'd have nowhere to live," Edward reportedly told his wife.

It didn't work.

Early in the morning a few days later Edward awoke to encounter what he claimed were five apparitions hovering about him. They seemed like a family. Two of them stood while others sat on the edge of the bed.

Edward said the figures seemed to be covered by a blanket of mist. It was impossible to see any facial features or how they were dressed. As if on cue, the group floated into the bathroom. Edward, who had grabbed a gun from his nightstand, ran after them in hot pursuit. The bathroom was empty.

Kathleen Murawski told Robin Hope Axelrod, associate editor of the *Somerset* (N.J.) *Spectator*, who gathered the information about the Van Wickle haunting, that her husband does not dream, or at least had never remembered a dream before he encountered the ghostly quintet. Edward said the house was definitely haunted.

The day the couple moved out the people who lived upstairs were away on vacation. Edward made a last trip inside to get the dog. He heard footsteps on the staircase, then what seemed to be furniture scraping across the attic floor. Were the spirits, now that they were to be alone in the empty house, rearranging things to suit themselves? The Murawskis thought so.

In 1976 Franklin Township officials bought the house, planning to restore it as a historic site. Matthew and Leslie Curran moved into the place two years later, in June 1978. Matthew was the caretaker and Leslie was hired as the curator. The second-floor living quarters had been renovated for the couple, and Matthew was starting repairs and restoration on the main floor.

During their first night in the house the couple heard the front door knocker. Matthew answered the door but found no one there. A search of the grounds proved fruitless. Matthew had been particularly nervous over the previous few days because an anonymous arsonist had threatened to destroy a historic home in the county.

The couple's sleep was disturbed several more nights by the errant knocker until Matthew decided to spend as much time as necessary sitting hunched on the floor right inside the door.

Waiting.

The moment the knocker sounded he threw open the door. The knocker was moving all by itself!

Matthew and Leslie had stepped into a world quite removed from anything they had previously known.

Household items left in one place would magically reappear in another location or vanish completely. They heard sounds coming from the attic. Leslie thought it was rats. Matthew knew better. He had learned every inch of their new home and found no openings large enough for rodents.

There was the touch Matthew felt on his shoulder when he was installing a conduit in the crawl space under the house. His fingers froze as he glanced fruitlessly behind him.

Lights seemed to have a will of their own; wall switches were found to have moved to the "off" position when the Currans were elsewhere.

One early evening as Matthew and Leslie ate dinner, a woman's voice called "Matt!"

Twice Leslie awoke to see a middle-aged woman standing at the foot of the bed. Her clothing had a decidedly antique cast to it. Yet the Currans somehow learned not to fear her; in fact they came to believe that for some reason she was there to protect them—but from *what* they did not know.

In April 1979, the Currans left and Franklin Township Manager Harry Gerken moved into the upstairs apartment that Matthew Curran had renovated. By this time the place had come to be known as "The Meadows," and Sunday concerts were a regular feature.

When Gerken moved in, "The Meadows" foundation president, Mary Jane Post, handed him a slim leather book with the following inscription on the fly leaf:

This logbook is an ongoing record of events and work at The Meadows.
Please enter the following information by date: visitors, including ghosts. . . .

Gerken was amused.

But not for long. On the morning of May 29, 1979, Gerken heard the yowling that augured a cat fight. It wasn't. As he listened from his bed, he heard a blood-curdling scream. Distinctly human, he thought, and seemingly coming from somewhere beneath the kitchen window. He cautiously got up, tiptoed to his bedroom window and looked out. Nothing was stirring, and all was quiet for the rest of the shortened night.

In the morning, however, Gerken found a potted plant smashed in the middle of the floor. It had been on the kitchen windowsill. The window was closed. He was more puzzled than frightened.

Even a few days later when he shouted, "You'll have to live with me because I'm not leaving," Gerken thought many of the mysterious events were pranks, if unexplainable ones. Certainly not . . . ghosts.

In June, Gerken's daughters came to visit. Seven-year-old Jill slept in the single bedroom, ten-year-old Gwenn occupied the couch, and their father curled up in a sleeping bag on the living room floor. Not quite asleep, Gerken felt "something" brush past him. Gwenn was fast asleep a few feet away.

In the morning Jill asked her father if he'd washed dishes in the middle of the night. She complained that she heard pots and pans banging and the clatter of dishes. Gerken then explained the curious history of the Van Wickle House.

Once more, in November 1980, Gerken heard that anguished cry from beneath the kitchen window. This time he didn't get up. He just lay awake until dawn.

Harry Gerken does not live there anymore. Another caretaker occupies the house, which is still undergoing restoration. Only the ghosts remain behind.

Is there an explanation for what happened there? Perhaps. Ghostlore suggests that a house can act as a "reservoir" of emotions from previous occupants. These emotions may be manifested at certain times under certain conditions. To die young is to not be at peace. A person's spirit may return to try to finish out a normal life span. On the other hand, if a person died a violent death he, or she, may come back to wreak vengeance upon the living, or reenact his death scene to the understandable bewilderment of the living.

Papers found in the attic of the Van Wickle house indicate that Evert and Cornelia Van Wickle lived in the house between 1752 and 1757, and that it had been built for Evert at the time of his marriage. Both died young on March 3, 1757, although the cause of their deaths is not known. The couple lies buried in a grove of trees on the property.

Two facts seem significant. First, since both Evert and Cornelia died on the same day, the possibility of illness seems unlikely.

Second, the graves contain not the *bones* of Mr. and Mrs. Van Wickle, but their *ashes*. Since cremation was considered a pagan rite at that time, and was censured by the church, it seems possible that the couple burned to death in a fire. Indeed, one of the walls of the attic is badly charred. The terrifying screams that shattered Harry Gerken's sleep could be the reenactment of the Van Wickles' horrible death cries.

Yet, there are also ghosts *inside* the house. Leslie Curran was visited by a middle-aged female specter and Ed Murawski saw a group of five apparitions. They may have been later occupants of the house. Their identities may never be known.

John Dobson, Soldier

John Dobson was a quiet, pleasant young man, if a bit eccentric. Rumor allowed that he wore a tricornered, Revolutionary War–era hat to the dinner table, but since no one had seen John for two hundred years the statement was hearsay. What may not be speculation is that in 1972 Dobson's ghost went to live with the Frank Graisberry family in their new home in Rancocas Woods, south of the Delaware River, near Philadelphia.

There, he fiddled with electric lights and poked around in the closets, no doubt amazed to see strange newfangled gadgets and clothing.

The Graisberrys did not have to be told their house wasn't . . . typical. Every time they sat down to dinner a cold chill swept through the room. When Mrs. Graisberry set an extra place at the table, the coolness vanished. From that moment on an extra plate was always set for dinner. The room stayed warm and cozy.

Although the Graisberrys—Mary; her husband, Frank; and children, Tom and Polly—were never frightened, they were not entirely comfortable either.

The family contacted the Mental Horizons Society, a group that studies psychic phenomena, to try to identify "their" ghost. Mediums held a series of séances, and the Graisberrys learned an amazing story. Their resident ghost was one John Dobson, a Revolutionary War soldier. He said, through the mediums, that he was a well-to-do Virginian, raised at Oldfields Plantation, his father's estate near Roanoke. In life he had been a courier for Gen. George Washington.

Dobson, only nineteen years old, was carrying a message to Washington in November 1777 when he became lost in Rancocas Woods and died of exposure. During that bitter winter, sometimes referred to as "a little ice age," General Washington's ragtag and starving troops billeted in Valley Forge while the British and Hessians enjoyed the relative comforts of Philadelphia.

Dobson made it clear that his spirit could never be at peace because the Graisberrys had built part of their home over his grave.

The family was fascinated by these historical tidbits and wanted to learn more about Dobson. They contacted David C. Munn, then an editor at the New Jersey State Library's Archives and History Bureau. The Graisberrys wanted him to run a genealogical check on soldier Dobson.

Munn found that not one but four John Dobsons from Virginia and North Carolina had served in the War of Independence. The final records of two Dobsons were available; two could not be found. Neither of the traceable Dobsons seemed a likely candidate for the Graisberrys' John Dobson. However, David Munn did learn that a courier service was in place between troops in South Jersey and Washington's headquarters at Valley Forge during November 1777.

Meanwhile, the ghost of young John Dobson (whichever one he was) became much at ease, almost playful. He hid freshly laundered pillowcases, causing Mary Graisberry to chase through the house to try to find them. In another séance, he also changed the story of his death, saying he'd been executed after being caught as a deserter; he said he was carrying quinine to his sick mother.

One morning four-year-old Polly Graisberry startled her mother by humming a strange new song.

"It's called 'The World Turned Upside Down,' " Polly told her inquiring mother. "John taught it to me."

The song was later identified by Gordon Myers, a professor of music at Trenton State College, as the one played by General Cornwallis's fife-and-drum corps and sung by his troops as they marched to surrender to General Washington. It was first published in *Gentleman's Magazine* in London, in 1767. The tune is that of "Down Derry Down." It goes like this:

> *If buttercups buzzed after the bee,*
> *If boats were on land, churches on sea,*
> *If ponies rode men,*
> *And if grass ate the cows,*
> *If cats should be chased into holes by the mouse,*
> *If the mamas sold their babies to gypsies for half a crown,*
> *If summer were spring, and the other way 'round,*
> *Then all the world would be upside down.*

When it seemed certain that John Dobson had become a permanent resident in the Graisberry home, the possibility of an exorcism was raised. The Graisberrys refused. They really liked their ghost.

But they did move away from New Jersey.

The old, cold bones of John Dobson are still buried under that house in Rancocas Woods.

Adobe Wails

From the moment in 1993 when Greg Champion laid eyes on the historic St. James Hotel in Cimarron, New Mexico, he knew there was something special about the place. After more than a decade of working in various capacities for a major hotel chain, most recently in California, Champion was ready for a change and was looking for his own business to purchase.

"[I wanted] an opportunity to do something for myself," the Seattle native said. "You learn so much in a structured environment like that [at a major hotel], it's logical to want to do your own thing after doing it for somebody else. If you can live without a guaranteed paycheck."

When he learned that the 1880s-era hotel on the historic Santa Fe Trail in northeast New Mexico was for sale, Champion decided to look it over. What he found was a genuine piece of western Americana.

Begun as a saloon in 1873, the hotel, with its two-foot-thick adobe walls, tin ceilings, and antique furnishings, has been in continuous operation since it was added in 1880. Some of the most famous characters in frontier history stayed there: Annie Oakley, Buffalo Bill Cody, Clay Allison, Bat Masterson, Wyatt and Morgan Earp (who stopped on their way to Tombstone and the gunfight at the O.K. Corral), and Doc Holliday. Zane Grey finished portions of his Western novel *Fighting Caravans* in Room 22.

The infamous Bob Ford was a guest. He was the "dirty little coward who shot Mr. Howard and laid poor Jesse in his grave." Mr. Howard was of course Jesse James—who actually used the name R. H. Howard when he, too, signed the St. James guest register.

Davy Crockett II and two accomplices murdered three black cavalrymen from nearby Fort Union in the St. James Saloon and took off on a six-month crime spree. He ended up in Cimarron's boot hill, shot and killed by the lawmen who tracked him down.

There have been twenty-six documented killings at the St. James Hotel, most of them the result of saloon gunfights, brawls, or knifings.

But Greg Champion found that he was looking at more than a historic artifact; the St. James Hotel has the reputation of being one of the most haunted places in the American West. The ghosts of at least three guests still walk its worn floorboards.

"There were some jokes from the Realtor about it being a haunted hotel, but I laughed," he remembered. "We have a videotape at the hotel about an 'Unsolved Mysteries' [NBC-TV series] episode [about the hotel]. To be honest with you I never, ever looked at it until we purchased the hotel and got here. I was just so in love with the hotel."

Champion first saw the hotel in February 1993. It was love at first sight, but he was savvy enough to know that buying a property as aged and as off-the-beaten-path as the St. James was first and foremost a business decision.

"I knew I really liked the hotel, but I wanted to hear someone else's perspective," Champion said. He asked a friend with a background in marketing to come along as a kind of "devil's advocate" to help him decide if the hotel could attract customers and become a paying proposition.

The hotel's owner at the time was Ed Sitzberger, a Cimarron native who had grown up across the alley from the St. James. He had bought the hotel in 1985 with his then-wife, Pat Loree, and refurbished it throughout after retiring as a mechanical engineer at Los Alamos National Laboratory. At the age of sixty-two, however, Sitzberger decided it was time to retire from the seven-day-per-week schedule.

Upon his arrival, Champion eagerly took in the Victorian western ambiance of the crystal chandeliers, velvet curtains, brocade wallpaper, and heavy furnishings. On the walls he saw photographs and newspaper clippings about the famous guests who had stayed at the St. James, once described as the most modern hotel between the Mississippi River and San Francisco.

As he went through the hotel, Champion heard all about its haunted nature. "Hearing the ghost stories, and everything else that had happened here, I didn't really pay much attention to it. In my own mind, I never really believed," Champion said.

He did think it was curious that one area remained off limits to him . . . until just before he left.

"The only room I hadn't looked at was Room 18, which is always kept locked," Champion said. On the floor outside the door of that room was a vase of dead flowers. Sitzberger said the room had been left unrenovated and was never rented to guests.

But that was only partially correct.

Room 18 is occupied by the ghost of one T. James Wright, a man who died a violent death in the hotel after supposedly winning it in a poker game. His ghost refuses to leave his old room and doesn't take kindly to intrusions by the living.

"Just before I left, Ed let me go in and look," Champion said. "On the credenza was a half-full bottle of Jack Daniel's and an empty shot glass next to it. There were some playing cards, poker chips, and cigarettes. And some notes to T. J. Wright. I thought it was pretty neat. What a good way to keep the 'spooks' at bay."

Champion concluded without too much hesitation that purchasing the old hotel was a good business decision—and that the stories of ghostly apparitions and mysterious events reported over the years were perhaps not mere imaginings.

"The first night we had dinner with the [Sitzbergers] and then went up to bed. It was about nine or ten o'clock. I sat up in bed and was talking to the ghost like some idiot!" Champion laughed. "I didn't see anything, but I said out loud, 'I really love this hotel and I'd love to buy it. If you guys have any problem with that give me a sign.' And obviously nothing happened."

At least not right away.

Champion flew back to California. Except for his wife, no one knew about his trip to Cimarron. But if he was looking for a "sign" about his decision to buy the St. James, Champion thinks he found it in an uncanny conversation the next day with one of the employees at the hotel where he worked.

"I was making the rounds through the hotel. We had maybe two hundred employees. I walked into the reservations office and one of the girls said, 'Greg, I had a dream about you last night.' She really had to tell me about this dream. She proceeded to tell me about the St. James in great detail!" Champion was astonished.

The young woman recounted the features of the dining room and correctly identified it as a saloon back in the 1880s and 1890s. In her dream, she and Champion were in the room but only he knew the people present.

"Finally someone invited us to go upstairs and have a drink," Champion said she told him. "She explained in great detail going up a steep staircase from the first floor, going around a corner and then down a hallway into a room on the right. And that is exactly where Room 18 is. She and I went into the room. I talked to a gentleman who was in there but whom she didn't know. We ended up having shots of Jack Daniel's. I'm not a Jack Daniel's drinker and she certainly isn't."

Champion was "in shock" after hearing her story. Later, he showed the woman pictures he had taken of the St. James. "She turned white as a ghost," he said, only half in jest. Champion was dumbfounded that the woman had the dream on the same night he stayed at the St. James. He took it as the "sign" from the ghosts for which he had asked.

With its turbulent and colorful history, the St. James is the near-perfect repository for restless spirits not satisfied with their brief time on earth.

The hotel was built by Henri Lambert, a cook for Gen. Ulysses S. Grant and President Lincoln's personal chef. Lambert came to New Mexico in 1866 to search for silver and gold but found he could make more money running a saloon. He opened one in Cimarron in 1873 and added the St. James as a hotel seven years later.

Lambert's wife, Mary, liked the hotel so much her ghost haunts one of the rooms and periodically strolls the hallways. Her presence is detected by the sudden, strong fragrance of old-fashioned toilet water.

The great attraction New Mexico held for gunslingers and desperados was the virtually nonexistent law and order in the region. The first statewide law enforcement agency, the New Mexico Mounted Patrol, wasn't formed until 1906. And so into the territory rode a parade of badmen who, it seemed, gravitated sooner or later to the St. James Hotel, a social center then (and now) in northeast New Mexico. Not a few of them ended up leaving the establishment feet first.

One story concerns the notorious, and probably psychotic, Robert Clay Allison, who once led a mob to nearby Elizabethtown where they broke into the jail and hanged an accused killer named Charles Kennedy. Allison decapitated the corpse and stuck the head on a pole, which he placed prominently in the St. James

Saloon. He is also said to have danced on the bar, but it isn't known if he did that to "celebrate" the beheading. He killed at least one other man in a gunfight in the saloon and left his body behind a chair, where it was discovered by owner Lambert the next morning. Allison got off on a plea of self-defense.

Some twenty-two bullet holes still pockmark the *new* (1903) tin ceiling of the old saloon, now the dining room. The original ceiling had to be replaced because hundreds of bullets had shredded it. Fortunately, Henri Lambert had put two layers of heavy wood above the tin so stray shots wouldn't kill guests sleeping in the rooms above.

The violence at the hotel was a near daily occurrence in the old days. A history of the hotel written by former co-owner Pat Loree notes that "on a typical Saturday evening, it wasn't uncommon for the bartender, as the result of gunplay, to drag out several dead bodies and replace many shattered chimneys from the kerosene lanterns that hung overhead."

But with the outlaws came other, more easygoing, visitors. Gov. Lew Wallace, author of *Ben Hur*, stayed at the St. James, as did artist Frederic Remington, who occupied Room 24 during his stay in Cimarron to sketch the nearby Sangre de Cristo foothills. Buffalo Bill Cody and Annie Oakley planned their Wild West Show in the dining room while Gen. Philip Sheridan was a guest in Room 9 in 1882. He was touring army forts, including Fort Union, southwest of Cimarron.

Despite the owners' attempt to emphasize the hotel's elegance, hospitality, fine food and service, the ghosts of the St. James demand considerable attention from visitors and employees.

At least three specific ghosts have been identified by psychics and former owners: Mary, the wife of builder Henri Lambert; the Imp, a puckish entity who appears as a small, wizened old man who plays tricks on people; and T. J. Wright, the malevolent spirit in Room 18.

Mary's piquant perfume gives away her presence in the hotel's hallways. One young couple stayed in Mary's old room. When the husband found the room too stuffy for comfortable sleeping, he tried to open the window. He couldn't get it to budge. He said it was like someone was pushing down on it from the top. After several tries, however, he managed to get it partway open.

Sometime in the night he awoke to a tapping on the window pane. He got up and looked out, thinking a tree branch might be rubbing against it, but none was anywhere near. He shut the window halfway and went back to bed. A few minutes later there was more beating on the window. In exasperation, he closed it completely. The couple weren't disturbed the rest of the night. When the young husband told his story to the hotel staff the next morning, their response was that Mary probably didn't want the window open after dark.

The second ghost is something of a prankster. No one knows who he was—in life. Now he's called "the Imp" because of his penchant for causing minor annoyances. Glasses in the kitchen may crack for no reason, lamp shades suddenly tilt, or a pen or calculator may vanish from one location to show up in another soon after.

The Imp may also have been responsible for a bizarre episode in the hotel's kitchen in early January 1995.

Perry Champion, Greg's brother and co-owner of the hotel, was having a discussion near a service counter with one of the cooks. A plastic bucket about six inches tall and packed with steak knives stood on a shelf above the counter a few feet away from where the men stood. Suddenly one of the steak knives sailed out of the bucket and across the counter, and stuck in the floor between the men.

"My brother is not one to get very excited," Greg Champion said, "but he was like 'I'm not crazy. I saw this. There's no way that someone threw that knife. I watched it come out of the bucket and stick in the floor between the two of us.' "

It is rare for any of the ghosts to show themselves, but it happened once with the Imp.

Former co-owners Loree and Sitzberger hired a young lad to come in early mornings to sweep and clean the lobby and bar. Early on the boy's first scheduled day of work, the couple were surprised to find his mother sitting close by.

The teen sheepishly explained that she was there for "protection."

From what?

Well, he allowed, when he got to work that morning, he had seen a gnomelike man sitting on a barstool laughing at him! The boy had run home to fetch his mother so she could stay with him while he finished his first—and last—day of work at the hotel.

The entity residing in Room 18 is more problematic. The spirit is said to be that of T. James Wright, a man who signed the guest register three times in 1881 but of whom little else is known. On his third, and last, stay at the St. James, Wright is supposed to have won the hotel in a poker game, but he died in a gunfight before he could stake his claim.

No one can rent Wright's former room, Number 18. It is kept permanently locked, the vase of dead flowers placed conspicuously in front of the door. There is an evil associated with this spirit that is not evident in the other hauntings at the St. James.

T. James Wright does *not like* intruders. And he makes that sentiment known.

A visiting California physician and investigator of the paranormal said she was knocked over by "something" as she entered the room.

A hotel chef saw a hazy figure standing outside the room's door.

Former co-owner Pat Loree had a startling episode in Wright's old room.

Loree wrote of her experience: "In the upper left hand corner of the room there was a spiral, swirling, milk-white something. I couldn't see the corner of the room. I stopped speaking [to a guest], and just as suddenly, this mass came sweeping down across the room at me, passed on my right side, sending me to my knees."

Ed Sitzberger has been quoted as saying about Room 18: "I know he's there, and that's his room."

Greg Champion doesn't have to be convinced. He had his own encounter with the strangeness of Room 18.

It happened late in 1994. As Champion explained it, a woman from Clayton, New Mexico, about two hours east of Cimarron, had been making frequent business trips between her home and Angel Fire, a ski resort near Taos.

"She had to drive through Cimarron a couple of times a week," Champion said. "She never knew the St. James was here because you can't see it from the highway. But every time she drove through, she was drawn to the town for some reason. She even had dreams about an old hotel and a particular room in it."

The woman finally stopped in Cimarron and located the hotel.

"She didn't know what she was looking for, she didn't know why she was here, only that she'd been drawn here by something," Champion said. "My brother and I were in the lobby [when she came in] and we thought it was another kook showing up at the door. But we didn't have much to do so we took her on a tour of the hotel. We got up in the hallway where Room 18 is and walked right past it. She stopped dead in her tracks. She wanted to go in, but we said sorry, it's not renovated and we don't let anyone occupy it. We usually *don't* tell people that's where the ghost lives!"

Champion said the woman acted strangely from the moment she saw the room, rubbing her hands across the door while "talking to herself." He thought at one point they might have to call the police to escort her out.

But then the transom above the door popped open. "I thought she was pushing real hard on the door and somehow pushed it out," Champion recalled. His brother whispered that they would have to go in later and get it closed.

"She did this [rubbing the door and talking] for three or four minutes," Champion said. "There's a chandelier in the middle of the room and you can see it through the transom. It started to slowly spin in a clockwise manner like somebody had put their hands on it and spun it around. The intensity never slowed."

Greg and his brother were stunned. No one was in the room, the windows were tightly shut, and no amount of vibration could have caused such a distinct movement. The entire hanging light fixture was moving in about a six-inch circular arc.

"The lady decided it was time for her to go," Champion said. "We took her downstairs and she gave us her phone number. Perry and I walked back upstairs to look at the chandelier. It continued to spin. It went on for about forty-five minutes from start to finish before it stopped. There's nothing that would explain it. I would say that's as dramatic as it gets [here]."

Champion said Room 18 may be remodeled eventually and rented to guests. Perhaps it will be known as the T. J. Wright Room, to go along with the other rooms that bear the names of famous guests. But for now they're leaving Mr. Wright to his privacy.

Sometimes the ghosts in the St. James turn up just out of reach and, of course, not always at night.

"My wife will sometimes be the first one here at the hotel in the morning," Champion noted. "In our dining room is a big, antique bar with the front of it all mirrors. As you walk into the room you can look into the mirror and see what's behind you. On two occasions now she's gone in [early in the morning] and seen someone's reflection standing behind her. She'll turn around thinking it was a hotel guest who came down to check out, but they'll be gone."

The last time it happened, the reflection was that of a big man in western clothing wearing a cowboy hat. When Mrs. Champion turned to speak to him there was no one in sight.

"I have waitresses who will hear someone behind them ask a question, but when they turn around there'll be nobody back there," Champion said.

With the extraordinary number of killings documented at the St. James Hotel, along with the less bloody mayhem committed over the years, few observers are truly surprised that the place is haunted. Several psychics have said the hotel is filled with far more ghosts than have declared themselves. A psychic from Amarillo, Texas, told Champion the spirits are there reliving enjoyable experiences from their life on earth in what is now their afterlife.

"I think that's a pretty neat way to put it," Champion agreed.

For his part, the thirty-six-year-old innkeeper has come to terms with running a hostelry for the living and formerly living. He seems more bemused than frightened.

"When it comes right down to it, I need to be convinced of things in a logical, rational manner. I still do that to this day. I think about what might have caused this or that, what physical things can I attribute it to. I used to always do that. Now I don't do that as much. Things just seem to happen for whatever reason. There are people who are freaked out every single day of their lives here. I don't know why all these things happen, but I'm not afraid. . . ."

The St. James Hotel is open year-round. Guests may stay in one of the thirteen rooms in the historic section, ranging from the Waite Phillips Suite, featuring a separate bedroom, sitting room, and private bath, to the Remington Room with a double bed and shared hall bathroom. A modern motel annex has twelve rooms. Reservations are recommended during the summer season.

Lost in Santa Fe

New Mexico's three-hundred-year-old capital of Santa Fe has no scarcity of haunted places. Perhaps it is the dazzling mixture of Hispanic, Native American, and Anglo cultures that has produced so many ghostly legends, or perhaps it is this way in any city that has witnessed centuries of often violent history unfold on its dusty avenues. Or behind adobe walls.

Abraham Staab found his fortune supplying general merchandise to U.S. Army posts in the New Mexico of the 1880s.

Staab was well on his way to becoming Santa Fe's richest man when he returned to his native Germany to marry Julie Schuster. She eagerly took up her new life in Santa Fe as a wealthy merchant's wife.

Abraham and Julie's elegant 1882 brick home today forms the core of La Posada de Santa Fe, 330 East Palace Avenue, one of the city's most refined hotels and itself the centerpiece of a manicured six-acre complex which also includes separate adobe cottages and lovely gardens.

The exterior of the original two-story Staab house is no longer discernible, but some inside areas remain. A visitor will be shown the house's staircase leading up to the old bedrooms. The second floor of the old Staab house has changed only marginally. Some of the rooms are used for meetings and private dining.

There is also Room 256, Julie Staab's old bedchamber. It is a guest room—with a difference. Mrs. Staab may still be there.

Julie Staab was, by most accounts, a gracious and popular hostess. Her home was a center of Santa Fe society and culture. Her personal life was not nearly so perfect. Although seven of her children survived childhood, she may have had several miscarriages. One child died while still a toddler.

Julie Staab died at the age of fifty-two, but nothing was said in the obituaries about Julie's personal travails. It was rumored that she had been mentally ill for several years before her death.

Her old bedroom on the second floor retains much of its original southwestern Victorian elegance. A large chamber of some six hundred square feet, it is outfitted with a king-size brass bed, antique furniture, and exquisite area rugs over the original hardwood floors. Even the modern color television set is hidden in a beautiful armoire.

Julie Staab is not a *frequent* visitor to her room, but only a fleeting glimpse of a figure wearing a long, flowing robe with a hood covering her head. Since her room was renovated in the early 1980s, however, she hasn't been there nearly as much as she has visited other parts of the hotel.

A dining room on the second floor is a favorite haunt of hers. Waitresses say a gust of wind blows through the room when there should be none, often as they set up or clear dishes for private parties. If candles remain lit after dinner guests depart, somehow they are extinguished, thin wisps of smoke curling toward the ceiling.

An employee said he had a run-in with Julie as he cleaned the floors. He straightened up to rinse his mop when he caught her looking at him. She was translucent, but her dark brown eyes seemed to bore right through him.

A reporter staying in Room 256 several years ago didn't see the ghost of Mrs. Staab, although he stayed up all night waiting for her to appear. At about four o'clock in the morning, however, the bathroom door slammed shut for no apparent reason. The window drapes were drawn, no air was moving. The journalist couldn't explain what caused the door to close so suddenly but he *wasn't* ready to think it was Julie Staab come a-calling.

Mrs. Staab may also like to browse through the hotel gift store, no doubt impressed with twentieth-century amenities. Employees have reported hearing the sounds of books falling off shelves after the store is closed for the night. Though some attribute the noise to one of the hotel's occasional stray cats, others are not quite so sure.

In another instance, an employee heard the same sound—books being dropped—but this time it came from the lobby. When he investigated he found no one around, nor any disturbance that could have accounted for the distinctive noise.

The main floor bar, which is near the Staab house's original staircase, was the scene of another odd experience. A security guard was passing it late one night when he heard the voice of a man coming from inside the closed lounge. The four or five sentences he heard were not intelligible. And a quick look inside showed him what he expected to find. Nothing. Yet he was absolutely certain of the deep, male voice he had heard.

The possibility of a male ghost also inhabiting La Posada is supported by the stories of a guest and an employee. A girl visiting from Denver awoke in the night to see a man dressed in a waistcoat standing at the foot of her bed. When she asked him what he was doing there, he vanished.

An employee working in an office off the lobby late at night glanced through the open office door. She saw a man lounging near the front door. She turned back to her work, but realized no one should have been out there so late. Another look told her he was gone. She said he had been wearing a long, old-fashioned coat.

There have been other incidents over the years—pots and pans rattling in the empty kitchen, a cut-glass chandelier in one of the dining rooms swinging violently back and forth. And, once in a while, awful sobs come from everywhere, and nowhere, in the halls of La Posada. Julie Staab is on the move.

* * *

Another Santa Fe hotel was, at the turn of the century, the Exchange Building, a notorious center of dancing, gambling, and drinking. Today it is the sedate La Fonda Hotel, 100 East San Francisco, which advertises itself as "the inn at the end of the Santa Fe Trail."

The famous hotel's centerpiece is La Plazuela Dining Room. Diners might find more than an attentive waitstaff hovering about them.

The story is told that the dining room was once a patio with a deep well in the center. One particular gentleman lost his wealth and all his possessions at the gambling tables. In a drunken, suicidal rage over his bad luck, he dove headfirst into the well and drowned.

On occasion, visitors have told staff members that in the middle of an otherwise fine meal they have seen the hazy image of a man seem to vanish into the floor. At the same time, the surroundings blur and the guests see furnishings as there might have been a century ago.

The Sisters White

The Hopi woman, a weaver at the School for American Research, on the west side of Santa Fe, was decidedly uneasy. A late-night round of solo billiards in the school's game room had become an exercise in barely restrained fear. On the wall, an oil painting of one of the school's founders, Martha White, stared down at her. The face was smiling and pleasant, but the toga in which she was attired bespoke an eccentric personality.

The young weaver was not especially disturbed by the fantastic painting, but it added to the gloomy scene. What *really* bothered her the most was nothing *inside* the room. It was the faint laughter she heard, a murmur that seemed to come from somewhere outside. Yet she was quite certain no one was about on such a cold winter night.

One of the corners of the room was only faintly lighted. While she didn't actually "see" anything there, her attitude was akin to thinking that something awful might jump out from a darkened closet or grab an arm if one probed too deeply under the bed at night. The young artist quickly turned off the lights and left. The "presence" she sensed was so malevolent that she never again returned to that room.

Spinster sisters Martha and Amelia White donated the buildings and land upon which the school was built. The women were extremely wealthy; Amelia employed a butler to look after the house. She died in a room used by visiting scholars. The remains of both sisters are buried under a gazebo on the property. About twenty rare Afghan and Irish wolfhounds raised by the sisters were buried in marked graves.

The sisters' eccentricity may account for some of the tales associated with the property, but there may be other reasons. A story not easily substantiated holds that a student committed suicide there in the 1940s. It's also thought that an ancient Indian pueblo stood on the school site.

On the same night the Hopi weaver was in the billiard room, another woman stayed late to work on several written reports. Suddenly, the bell on the front door clamored. Someone had come in. Footsteps crossed the hallway but no one appeared. She waited. A few moments later the footsteps came back down the hallway, the bell jangled and the door slammed shut. She was quite positive she would have seen any visitor. The event would be repeated on several subsequent nights.

A teacher at the school often felt someone watching her near the gazebo that holds the sisters' remains. But the feeling was a contented one, as if the Whites were pleased at their legacy.

An anthropology professor, however, had a distinctly different impression in the office she used while working at the school. She had the perception of being followed around, like someone was always "reading over my shoulder."

Sometimes her office door was open in the morning, when she was quite sure she had closed it the night before. Her dog growled and bristled whenever she brought him over at night. Some items in her office seemed to have been rearranged, although nothing was ever missing. She suspected the butler did it— Amelia White's old servant hanging about to make sure the house was always tidied up.

The butler may also look after Amelia White's old room, the one in which she died. A person staying there returned from vacation to find the door open. It had been locked when the person left several days before. Again, nothing had been taken.

An arroyo near the school holds additional mysteries. Laughter like that heard by the Hopi weaver comes from there. It sounds like a late-night assembly . . . but with no visible guests.

Sister George

Many years ago, a religious order known as the Sisters of Loretto operated a school in the area now occupied by the Inn at Loretto. The lovely shops in the 200 block of the Old Santa Fe Trail were actually once used as the school's chicken coops!

Former shop owners say several unusual events have led them to believe that block may be haunted. And not by chickens.

A woman's light laughter and footsteps were heard in a printing shop several years ago, but that wasn't nearly as odd as what occurred to the two owners of a nearby clothing store. On their first night in business, they closed the shop and counted their receipts. Regardless of how they compared their sales slips with the money in the cash register, an extra ten dollars was always there. For the next week, they found an extra ten dollars each night. They never figured out the discrepancy.

Local folks suspect the ghostly culprit may be Sister George, a lively, caring nun known for her enormous generosity. Many years ago, she taught free special education classes for poor children and gave away homemade Spanish-style suppers each night. The good nun may still give to those who toil in her old neighborhood.

The Original Love Potion Number Nine?

A residence known appropriately enough as the Oldest House, at 215 East de Vargas Street, was once the home of two witches, termed *brujas* in Spanish. They sold charms and spells and brewed a mysterious potion eagerly sought by all the love-starved young *caballeros.*

One such young man came by of an evening seeking a potion that would help him win the hand of one of Santa Fe's loveliest señoritas. The *brujas* complied. He departed with their assurances that the woman would be forever his—once she drank of the elixir.

Although the young woman drank the potion, she married another man.

The spurned young *caballero* stormed into the Oldest House demanding the return of his money. One of the *brujas* grabbed a long butcher knife and with a single swing separated the young man's head from his torso.

A persistent legend insists that on the anniversary of the rejected lover's gruesome demise, his head rolls slowly down the Old Santa Fe Trail on its way to El Palacio Real looking for his refund. And the rest of him.

The Villagra Building

Few employees at this building in the Santa Fe capital complex will discuss "their" ghost openly.

What some (un)lucky witnesses see is an old woman, in a gown from the late 1700s, bustling down a hallway with a small dog incongruously perched on her shoulder. She waggles her finger at those who see her, inviting them to follow. She vanishes before they can take her up on the offer.

One story is that the woman was hanged as a witch in old Santa Fe, at the same place where the Villagra Building now stands. Or, others say, there may be a cemetery somewhere beneath the structure and the spirit of one of the deceased was disturbed. Either way, it's best to look up and down the hallway when you leave one of the government offices.

A Grieving Mother

The Public Employees Retirement Association Building, known as PERA, faces the Old Santa Fe Trail, across from the capitol on Paseo de Peralta. A large parking lot separates the building from the busy street. A small lady in a long black dress, a *mantilla* pulled tightly about her head, scurries across the parking lot. Should you see her, speak kindly. She won't acknowledge your greeting—ghosts rarely do—but she deserves sympathy.

Her son was a student at the old St. Michael's College, actually a boarding school with many youngsters from distant and isolated villages.

The child contracted smallpox, an always fatal disease in the old days. He was buried quickly. Even his gravesite was obliterated so that Santa Feans would not panic at the thought of an epidemic sweeping their city.

Because her village was many miles from the nearest trail, the lady who haunts the PERA parking lot was not able to be with her son in his final hours. School officials refused to tell her where he was buried and she died of a broken heart. Her spirit still searches for her little boy's earthly remains.

The Old Haunts

Any collection of American ghost stories is incomplete without the inclusion of at least a few of the more intriguing spirits who linger just beyond our ken in New York City. Perhaps no other metropolis has such a rich history of hauntings, due no doubt to its centuries-old legacy of colorful characters, vibrant commerce, and, shall we say, exotic nightlife. It is a daunting task to exclude certain revenants in favor of others, but what follows is a trio of intriguing ghost stories from "little old New York."

Peg-Leg Peter

The church sexton hurried down the cobblestone sidewalk toward St. Mark's in-the-Bouwerie. The late-night hour was an unusual time for him, or anyone else for that matter, to be visiting the church, but he had to retrieve some important papers for the rector. It couldn't wait until morning.

The night was especially clear for New York City in the mid-1860s; industrial smog was becoming a real problem. On this night, however, a half moon illuminated the empty streets. The only sound was the scraping of the sexton's boots on the stones until... he detected the crunch of other footsteps a few yards away. Only these steps were quite different: a single footfall was accompanied by a thump... thump... thump. Like a piece of wood hitting the ground.

The sexton squeezed his eyes as he peered into the dimness. Coming toward him was the old Dutchman himself, Peter Stuyvesant, with his walking stick raised menacingly in the air. As the churchman staggered backward, he knew that what he was seeing could not possibly be, for Stuyvesant had been dead these two hundred years! He was buried in the churchyard. At least that's where he was *supposed* to be.

The sexton took off running, screaming for help as he fled down the path.

Neighbors were roused from their sleep by the sexton's screams and ran to the church. He stammered out his incredible tale. Then the bell atop St. Mark's began to ring out wildly. Someone was now inside. With the shaking sexton in tow, the small band of onlookers hurried to the large front door. It was locked. Someone retrieved a key.

With lanterns lit they stood hesitantly in the narthex while the bell continued to peal. Just as suddenly as it had started the ringing stopped. The men moved cautiously forward. As they shone their lanterns upward, they saw to their astonishment that the bell rope had been broken off several feet above their heads. It was as if some superhuman agent had torn it apart. The puzzled assembly backed out of the church and locked the door.

With the first light of morning, the sexton was back at the church, his bravery restored by the sun's warming rays. He was absolutely certain that he had seen Peter Stuyvesant the night before and, of course, he and the others *had* heard and seen the mystery of the bells. He would investigate for himself whether the outside of the crypt was undisturbed. He found that wasn't the case when he opened the protective gate. On the floor lay the torn length of rope. The sexton had not been dreaming. He *had* seen old Peter . . . just before his ghost evidently began yanking wildly at the bell.

It was said old Peter might have been particularly upset on this night because the city had begun to extend Second Avenue through the church's graveyard— passing too near his own mortal remains!

The tales of Peter Stuyvesant's ghost began almost from the day in 1672 when he was laid to rest in the vault of a chapel he had built in 1660. That chapel was later incorporated into St. Mark's in-the-Bouwerie, at the corner of Second Avenue and Tenth Street.

Stuyvesant was the last governor of New Amsterdam, from 1646 to 1664, when the Dutch still ruled Manhattan Island. His nicknames of "Peg-Leg" and "Silver Nails" came about because he had a wooden leg with a band of silver around it. He had lost his right leg in battle when he was director of the Dutch West India Company in Curaçao.

The English fleet captured his beloved New Amsterdam in 1664 and renamed it New York. Stuyvesant decided to stay on even though he chafed under British rule. He lived quietly on his farm, in what is now the Bowery.

The Dutchman was famous, or infamous as it were, for many personal traits, including his hot temper and harsh leadership. He was known to raise his hickory cane against almost anyone who incurred his wrath. Not a few persons sighed with relief when he died at the age of eighty in 1672.

Stuyvesant's ill temper may not have ended with his death, if stories of his ghostly appearances are to be believed.

The sexton's encounter with the Dutchman's ghost sometime in the mid-1860s is just one of many Stuyvesant sightings recorded over the years. In 1774, for instance, his old farmhouse burned down. Within hours of the blaze, stories of an old man stomping around angrily in the ruins were spreading through the growing metropolis. Those who saw the ghost identified it as Stuyvesant—the wooden leg and waistcoat gave him away. They said he looked to be cursing the bad luck that had taken his beautiful home from him.

The ghost was particularly active as houses, businesses, and streets invaded his once pastoral acreage. He didn't like the intrusion of so many people. Grumblings and rappings were heard coming from the vicinity of the Stuyvesant family vault, with an occasional appearance of old Peter himself to scare away an unwary intruder. His attire was always the same—immaculate white lace ruffles and knickerbockers with a polished black boot on his single good leg. In the century after he died, he seemed to particularly enjoy scaring Englishmen, whom he loathed in life . . . and death.

The last direct descendant of Peter Stuyvesant died in 1953, and the vault was permanently sealed. Will that be enough to satisfy the ghost of the man known as "Silver Nails"? Only time will tell.

Ghosts Center Stage

A walk backstage at the Palace Theatre in the minutes before the audience comes in could produce some surprises. Walk downstage and peer through a small peephole in the curtain. If the auditorium doors are still closed and the house is empty of people, there is the possibility of seeing the reenactment of a tragic death.

Stagehands and actors have seen the ghost of a tightrope walker balancing dangerously on a thin wire high above the orchestra pit. He wobbles dangerously, looses his balance, and then plummets horribly to the floor.

It is a ghost scene played in this theater, an event that reportedly happened in the 1950s. The performer was Louis Borsalino, part of a high-wire act called "The Four Casting Pearls."

Borsalino fell and was rushed to the hospital. He died before regaining consciousness.

Think twice about looking for this ghost. Bad luck may come to those who see his death plunge.

David Belasco was one of the most eccentric playwrights and producers in the history of New York theater. Consider his dress and his office: he usually wore a monk's robe with a cowl covering his nearly bald head, and he decorated his office like a monastery. Belasco died in 1931.

His prominent place in theatrical history is assured through innovative stagings of such plays as *Madame Butterfly* and *Laugh, Clown, Laugh*. His ingenious stage and lighting designs were well ahead of their times.

The ghost of David Belasco appearing in the theater named for him is not as well known.

Stagehands working on the 1995 Broadway production of *Hamlet*, starring Ralph Fiennes, told a stage doorman they had heard "strange sounds." Other crew members thought there were unauthorized people in the house when they saw draperies move. However, there were no reported sightings of the flamboyant Belasco.

Actors rehearsing scenes in the theater named for him have seen him sitting in his favorite seat. When the last patron has left for home and the lights have dimmed, the stage curtain doesn't always stay down. Some say it rises halfway, pauses and then lowers. As if Belasco is taking his own special bow.

An old elevator whirs to life on some occasions, rising to Belasco's former offices on a top floor. The trouble is the elevator hasn't worked for years.

The new Metropolitan Opera stage at Lincoln Center is too new to have a ghost. The same cannot be said for the old Metropolitan Opera house. It was haunted by a plump old dowager who insisted upon making her opinions about the productions known—long after she was dead.

In life she had been Madame Frances Alda, the wife of director Giulio Gatti-Casazza. One particular story about her intrusive behavior is supposed to have happened in about 1955.

Early in the opera season, a woman who usually attended the performances with a friend had to take in a matinee performance by herself. She turned in the extra ticket to the box office. As she took her seat, she found her friend's seat already occupied by a large woman wearing a silk dress. During the first act, the stranger squirmed in her seat, rustled her program, and mumbled aloud about what she considered poor performances. Most annoying of all, she often jabbed at the arm of the increasingly annoyed woman next to her. "Flat, flat, flat!" she stage-whispered whenever a particular aria displeased her.

Finally, in exasperation, the woman had had enough of the obnoxious patron. She marched up the aisle at intermission and told the manager of her problems with her seat-mate. She showed off a black-and-blue mark on her arm where the portly critic had squeezed it. The manager sent an usher down to the seat to warn the woman to stop her behavior.

The puzzled young man returned to say there was no one in the seat. Nor had there been all during the first act, according to other people seated nearby. The ghost of Madame Alda had struck again.

Roxy Rothafel, the designer of Radio City Music Hall, left that theater as his premier architectural legacy. Whether *he* left is in some dispute.

The classic, art deco design of Radio City is unique in the world. The story is told that Rothafel traveled throughout Europe in search of inspiration from the opera houses and music halls of the Old World. He found none. They all lacked "style," he told friends. On his return voyage to New York he found what he wanted. As he sat in a deck chair, Rothafel watched the sun set in the western ocean. That magnificent scene was what he tried to re-create in Radio City Music Hall. And, most critics agree, he succeeded admirably.

Later, Roxy Rothafel had his favorite seat for Music Hall performances. It was down aisle D, front row center on the third mezzanine. Knowledgeable tour guides sometimes tell visitors of his infrequent visits to the theater. Decked out in top hat and tails, Rothafel strolls down the steps but vanishes before he takes his seat.

A Mythical Ghost?

The most famous "haunted house" in all of New York City may not be. Haunted, that is.

The sprawling Morris-Jumel Mansion, which sits on the highest land in Manhattan, at West 160th and Edgcombe, has long been the reputed site of appearances by the notorious Eliza Jumel, widow of former owner Stephen Jumel and, later, briefly the wife of the notorious Aaron Burr.

The 230-year-old mansion is certainly replete with enough intriguing history to invite visitors from the spirit world. But the accuracy of the stories has been questioned by many people associated with the historic home. Nevertheless, the rumors of ghostly visions persist.

The Morris portion of the mansion's name comes from its builder, Lt. Col. Roger Morris. He bought an old farmhouse and some land in 1765 and erected the mansion, his summer home, a short time later. Modesty was not one of his stronger qualities. He named his new home Mount Morris.

Morris was a devoted Tory on the eve of the American Revolution. Though his family spent only their summers in the mansion, which was far removed from New York City in those days, the outbreak of the Revolutionary War meant the near-certain dissolution of his estate. He fled to England in 1776. He managed to return in 1777 to become the inspector of the claims of refugees, though he never again set foot inside Mount Morris. With the signing of the peace treaty in 1783, Morris and his family returned permanently to England.

Mount Morris was already under the control of American troops by 1776, and served as Gen. George Washington's military headquarters for a month after the Battle of Long Island. He was later forced to abandon the property to the British. British administrator Sir Henry Clinton occupied it until the end of the war.

From 1783 until about 1810, the mansion changed hands numerous times. It was an inn, a tavern, and a farmhouse over the years. President George Washington once joined several members of his cabinet for a brief visit to his old headquarters.

The woman who was to become Madame Eliza Jumel was actually born Betsey Bowen in 1775 at Providence, Rhode Island. Her mother was apparently a prostitute who bore several illegitimate children. Betsey was her first child. She was sent to live in a workhouse as a child because her mother could not care for her. During her teens, Betsey herself had an illegitimate child she named George Washington Bowen, and whom she promptly abandoned. There is some speculation that she tried to pass the child off as the product of a liaison between herself and the president, though there is little evidence to support such a claim.

Young Betsey was a bright, vivacious woman who used her guile to work her way out of poverty. Her move to New York while still in her late teens was planned to help her achieve financial and social success. She found the former after a fashion, but never the latter. Throughout her life, she tried to create for herself the image of a woman born to wealth and good social standing. Only in old age did she seek out her blood relatives, and only then to provide companionship in her desolate final years.

Betsey's first conquest was a Frenchman, Captain de la Croix, to whom she may have been married. He took her to live in France where she embraced all things Gallic, preferences that would reappear in her later life. After a time, Betsey wearied of her French lover and returned to New York. If she had indeed married the captain, the records do not indicate that there was a divorce. Nevertheless, she was soon back on the social scene—but curiously this time with a new name, Betsey Brown.

Her relationship with wealthy wine merchant Stephen Jumel did not begin under the most auspicious of circumstances. He was in his mid-forties when Eliza came into his life; a native Frenchman, Jumel lost a fortune when his Santo Domingo sugar plantation was destroyed by insurrectionists. He arrived in New York penniless but soon built a thriving business selling wines and liquors.

Eliza became Jumel's mistress and for four years he gave her all the material possessions she could desire, but even those could not give her the respectability of "proper" society that she so desperately sought. Only marriage, she reasoned, would do that. Jumel resisted the idea, but Eliza had her own plan. She feigned a serious illness and begged Jumel to grant her "one last wish." That, of course, was to be married. Believing her to be on her deathbed, Jumel acceded.

According to legend, no sooner had the priest married the couple and left the house than Eliza sat up in bed and began brushing her long red hair. Her detractors snorted that the "recovery" was nothing short of miraculous.

Despite the obvious subterfuge, Stephen Jumel accepted his marriage bonds and set about to help his new wife enter New York society. They found the Roger Morris house and bought it in 1810 as their "country home" (they lived on Whitehall Street at the time of their marriage). Stephen spent thousands of dollars rebuilding and furnishing the house. He could just as well have saved his money, for they were still shunned by the society Eliza so ardently desired to join.

A large estate can be a lonely place for just two people. Madame Jumel's solution was to invite several of her nieces to come live in the mansion. From her mother's many illegitimate children, there were quite a few of them. Within a few years, however, even a houseful of relatives was not enough to assuage the couple's bitterness over their exclusion from genteel society.

The Jumels moved to Paris. They were accepted by the French nobility, making up in a way for the snub by New York's grand dames. However, for all her social success in Paris, Madame Jumel returned to New York within a year, some say because she espoused the Bonapartist cause when it was not popular to do so. Others maintain she had a violent quarrel with her husband.

Whatever the cause of her retreat to New York, all seems to have been forgiven because Madame Jumel soon sailed back to France and stayed for five years. But she again returned alone to the United States, this time to stay by herself in the mansion. She had Jumel's power of attorney and proceeded to take over his business and real estate holdings. Without his apparent knowledge, she also put everything in her name. She had a keen sense for business and actually accumulated holdings worth over three million dollars, a considerable sum in those pre–income tax days.

Mrs. Jumel raised several nieces in the house. The most prominent was Mary Eliza, whom Madame Jumel adopted, and who later married Nelson Chase. They stayed with her throughout her life. In return for providing them with a grand lifestyle, Madame Jumel insisted that they remain under her roof. She used her ample wealth to provide all of life's necessities. Her relatives' spouses were discouraged from working. The social acceptance she was never able to receive, Eliza Jumel bought with her wealth from the grateful Mary Eliza and her other kin.

Stephen Jumel was elderly when he finally returned from France. He and his wife lived in isolated splendor until his accidental death on May 22, 1832.

Madame Jumel wasted little time in casting her net for an eligible bachelor. In the fall of that year, she became reacquainted with the elderly Aaron Burr, the disgraced former vice president, and a social pariah like herself. There is some evidence that Burr had been one of the few prominent New Yorkers to have become friendly over the years with the Jumels.

In 1833 the couple were married—she was fifty-eight, he twenty years her senior. The marriage didn't last long. Ironically, since Madame Jumel had less than a sterling reputation herself, Burr had a taste for women that marriage didn't end. She divorced a year after their marriage; he died in 1836.

Madame Jumel lived on for nearly thirty years, dying as a virtual recluse, and very possibly insane, at the age of ninety-three in 1865. She is buried in a corner of Trinity Cemetery, 155th Street at Broadway.

* * *

Rumors of a haunting at the Morris-Jumel Mansion began a few years after Madame Jumel's passing. A governess for a child of one of Madame's nieces said dreadful rappings would occur in the floors and walls of the old woman's former bedroom. One relative said her ghost, clad all in white, actually stood by his bed.

Nothing more seems to have been reported until several incidents made the news in the 1960s. One witness swore he saw a Hessian soldier marching up a staircase; a group of schoolchildren visiting the mansion claimed a red-haired woman came out on a balcony with a finger pressed to her lips. She rebuked them for their noisy behavior. Her husband was ill and not to be disturbed, she chided. Later, the children saw a picture of Madame Jumel and said she had been the woman on the balcony.

There are many reasons to visit this beautifully restored historic mansion. From its columned facade and imposing entryway to the arched central hallway and Georgian dining room, the Morris-Jumel Mansion is a jewel from America's colonial past. Rooms with exquisite antique treasures fill a visitor with awe. By closing one's eyes, a person can almost hear the voices of Roger Morris and General Washington . . . and Eliza and Stephen and Aaron. *Real* ghosts they may not be, but their *presence* in their old home cannot be avoided.

Aaron Burr is associated with a number of haunted places in the United States, including the famous Octagon House in Washington, D.C. Although he has never been sighted at the Morris-Jumel Mansion, his ghost is supposed to roam his old neighborhood in lower Manhattan.

The ghost of a man often associated with Burr, Alexander Hamilton, has been heard in Greenwich Village.

Burr shot Hamilton in a duel on July 11, 1804, when both men were running for governor of New York. Their feud extended back to 1800, when Hamilton backed Thomas Jefferson for the presidency over Aaron Burr.

In the duel, Hamilton fired first but missed. Burr was more accurate. Hamilton was taken to his doctor's house at 27 Jane Street, in today's Greenwich Village. He died a few days later after being returned to his own home. No one has reported *seeing* Hamilton's ghost on Jane Street, but there have been periodic reports of strange noises and heavy footfalls in the night. The home in which Hamilton actually died was razed years ago.

Remains To Be Seen

The village of Lily Dale in far western New York state has a unique and intriguing history. It's a 114-year-old community founded by spiritualists and still governed according to their principles.

The central tenet of spiritualism is a belief in the ability to contact the dead through the intercession of mediums or psychics. At Lily Dale, however, the community itself has taken its beliefs one step further and incorporated them into the city structure. Only spiritualists can buy or rent houses, for instance, and alcohol is banned. Each summer for decades thousands of spiritualists from around the world have descended on Lily Dale to give psychic readings, hold séances, and demonstrate other disputatious spiritualistic activities.

The spiritualist movement has always been outside mainstream American religion, even though believers attend their own churches. Until quite recently, spiritualist mediums employed such devices as ear trumpets for spirits to speak through and blackboard slates upon which spirit "messages" were written. Today most mediums employ "mental mediumship" and disavow the showy props of past decades.

Spiritualism had its beginnings in 1848 when the controversial Fox sisters—Catherine and Margaretta—claimed the ghost of a murdered peddler was communicating with them through a series of knocks. Although the girls later said they produced the noises themselves (by snapping their toe joints!), a grisly discovery long after their deaths added credence to their original claims of the supernatural.

Were the Fox sisters communicating with the spirits of a dead man? Or did they perpetrate a hoax and, in the process, give birth to a spurious religious movement? An examination of the facts, culled from various narratives of the time, provides few definitive answers.

The Fox girls were born two years apart in the late 1830s to Margaret and John David Fox, pious Methodists who led unremarkable lives until history first records their presence in 1848 at the tiny settlement of Hydesville, New York. At that time Margaretta was thirteen and Catherine about eleven. Four older siblings were grown and lived away from home.

John Fox was a farmer who moved his family into a small, simple house in the tiny cluster of homes known as Hydesville. There had been rumors that the house was "haunted" by mysterious noises even before they moved in. Within a few months it seemed the local gossip might be true. Sporadic, nearly inaudible rappings perturbed the family. At other times it seemed as if furniture was being moved. What eventually enveloped the Fox family is remarkably similar to the Canadian haunting known as the Amherst Demon.

Margaretta and Catherine were at the center of the disturbances, especially at night as they slept in their shared bedroom. They became so frightened they moved their beds into their parents' room. The rappings grew in intensity so that the beds physically shook and rattled. Sheets and blankets were "pulled" off the girls' beds. Catherine claimed to have felt a "cold hand" on her face.

Despite their best efforts, the family apparently could not locate the source of the problem. They grew increasingly frantic because the nights had become a series of jarring episodes that kept everyone awake practically from dawn to dusk. John Fox would search the darkness of the small house with candle in hand, but the noises actually seemed to follow him around.

The last two days of March 1848 would prove to be the apex of the mysterious rappings.

On March 30 the knocks came with a special urgency. Constant pounding, thumping, and bumping drove the family nearly to despair. The several doors in the house were the main target. Mr. Fox would throw one open when it seemed to be possessed only to find nothing on the other side. At other times, he stationed his wife on one side of a door and himself on the other. The rappings issued from *within* the door itself!

The family got virtually no sleep that night, so that by the morning of the next day, Friday, March 31, 1848, their nerves were nearly frayed. Mrs. Fox even confided to her adult son, David, who lived on a farm outside town, that she, for one, was now absolutely convinced her house was haunted.

In the evening, mother, father, and two daughters retired early after nearly two days of sleeplessness. But there would be no respite this night from the puzzling phenomena. The Foxes learned there was an apparent intelligence behind the rappings.

After so many days and weeks of the almost rhythmic raps, Margaretta and Catherine had become impertinent. As the knockings barraged the family with nary a pause, Catherine abruptly called out, "Hey you, Mr. Splitfoot! Do as I do."

She rapidly clapped her hands, the echo of which was then quickly repeated by the mysterious rappings. Was it a reply to Catherine's command?

Margaretta took up the challenge. "Now do just as I do," she cried. "Count one, two, three, four."

Rap, rap, rap, rap came the response.

Catherine was delighted. She slowly made circles in the air with her hand. The rappings counted off the number of times she made the motion.

"Oh, Mother, it can see as well as hear," Catherine exclaimed to her baffled parents. "But, wait. April Fool's Day is tomorrow. Someone is trying to trick us!"

Her mother decided to trip up the trickster.

"Count to ten," she demanded. The rappings counted off the precise number. "Now, how many children do I have?"

Seven raps came in rapid succession.

Ah-ha! Mrs. Fox thought. It *was* a trick being played on the family. She had just six children. After a moment she paled. Of course, she realized, she did have six *living* children—but a seventh had died as an infant.

Mrs. Fox excitedly continued her interrogation of the entity.

Give me the children's ages, she asked.

With a pause between each series of raps, the correct answers were supplied.

A rather complicated communication system emerged as the family "talked" to . . . whom? If this was a ghost, its identity was still a mystery.

Within hours, the family determined that no raps to a question was meant as a negative answer. Two raps signified a "yes." When Mrs. Fox asked if a human being was behind the communication there was silence. "Is this a spirit?" she then queried. Two sharp raps followed.

Though the task was arduous, the family discovered that their "guest" was a thirty-one-year-old peddler who had been murdered in the house. His body was buried in the basement. Further, the spirit predicted the perpetrator would never be apprehended.

John Fox realized that these fantastic discoveries would probably be laughed at by the townsfolk. He needed witnesses to verify the story. The Redfields were the closest neighbors. When they arrived, their questions were answered correctly.

Next a William Duesler joined the burgeoning circle of witnesses. That was a propitious circumstance. He had lived in the Fox house many years earlier. He asked if either his father or himself had been the person to harm the spirit. No answer. Duesler then asked the spirit to rap if he heard the name of the man who had killed him.

Duesler called out several names without any response.

"John C. Bell?" Duesler asked.

Everyone's eyes widened as two rapid taps resounded. The neighbors recalled that Bell had lived in the Fox house with his wife and a hired girl about five years earlier. They had suddenly moved away from Hydesville with little explanation.

Duesler pulled further details from the murdered man's spirit. The story that emerged was a grisly one:

The peddler had shown up at the Bells' door with a knapsack bulging with merchandise, a wooden trunk . . . and five hundred dollars in gold coins. He had been offered overnight lodging and took it. In the middle of the night, he awoke to find John Bell looming over him. Bell grabbed him by the throat and stabbed him repeatedly with a butcher knife. Bell dragged the peddler's body to the basement, sliced off the man's head and buried the remains beneath the packed earthen floor.

The name of the spirit was also established through painstaking questioning. The family and neighbors didn't quite know how to find out *who* this man was until David Fox, who had been called in from his farm to help control the growing number of spectators, came upon the idea of asking the spirit to rap twice when a letter of the alphabet matched a letter of his name. Fox started with the first letter of the victim's first name and worked through the alphabet thirteen times.

Slowly the letters came:

C . . . H . . . A . . . R . . . L . . . E . . . S . . . B . . . R . . . O . . . S . . . M . . . A.

Charles B. Rosma.

Curiously, considering later events that seemed to discredit the presence of the spirit and placed the blame for the rappings with Margaretta and Catherine, the two girls were apparently absent during some of the questioning. They had been taken to a neighbor's house to get away from the curious onlookers.

That final day in March was by far the busiest day for the spirit. As word spread of the curiosity, contemporary reports indicate that as many as five hundred persons gathered in and outside the small Fox house over the weekend. But by Sunday night, April 2, the rappings had largely diminished.

On Monday morning, David Fox led his father and several neighbors downstairs to the basement in an attempt to verify the information they had gleaned from Rosma's spirit. Earlier, David Fox had asked the spirit to signal the exact spot in the floor where his remains were located. That it had done and Fox marked the section.

With shovels and spades the men dug up the dirt floor. They gave up after only a couple of feet because water seeped into the hole. Recent rains had made the low-lying ground around the house sodden, and some of the water had inundated the Foxes' basement. They would have to wait until the ground dried enough to allow them to continue.

Several weeks later the excavations resumed, this time with much greater success. Their shovels brought up bits of cloth, traces of quicklime, and pieces of what looked like hair and bone. A medical doctor inspected the remains. He pronounced the hair and bone as having come from a human skull.

William Duesler was able to locate the hired girl who had worked for the Bells in 1843. Her name was Lucretia Pulver and she told Duesler that she clearly remembered the morning Rosma the peddler came to call.

She thought the visit began oddly, because although the man was a stranger to her, Mrs. Bell seemed to know him. They held whispered conversations. Lucretia thought she overheard them exchanging "personal" information.

A few hours after the peddler arrived, Mrs. Bell suddenly announced that Lucretia would be terminated. The family could no longer afford her services, Mrs. Bell volunteered. As she was going to be visiting a neighboring village that night, Mrs. Bell offered to take Lucretia home. Before she left, however, Lucretia asked the peddler to stop by her own home in the next day or so. She had seen several utensils in his case she thought her mother might be interested in.

John Bell was alone with the peddler when the women left before nightfall. Charles B. Rosma never made it to Lucretia's house, nor was he ever again seen alive.

Within days Lucretia was suddenly summoned back by the Bells. No explanation was given for the "reversal" in their financial situation. One morning Lucretia discovered Mrs. Bell restitching two heavy wool coats. They were too big for her husband, she said, and had to be extensively altered. Reaching into her sewing basket, Mrs. Bell brought out a new thimble. "Here, Lucretia. This is for you. I bought it from the peddler."

In fact there were several items from the peddler's knapsack in the house, the servant girl noticed. The Bells seemed to have bought quite a bit from him. Strange, she thought, that he never showed up at her own house.

A few days later Mrs. Bell sent Lucretia to the root cellar in the basement for some preserves she had put up the previous fall. As she walked across the dirt floor, Lucretia stumbled in some soft earth. Her shouts brought Mrs. Bell running.

"Must be the work of rats," she said at once. "I'll have Mr. Bell fill those up right quickly." A few days later the hollow was filled in and smoothed over. Nothing more was said.

Mr. and Mrs. Bell grew increasingly edgy, Lucretia remembered. They had good reason to. First Lucretia, then the Bells were accosted by strange noises and foot-steps. The basement door swung open. Mrs. Pulver, Lucretia's mother and a friend of Mrs. Bell's, accused the family of trying to terrorize her daughter into quitting her job. The Bells vehemently denied her accusations.

In less than a month the Bells vacated the house for good and moved to Lyons, New York. Between the time the Bells left and the Fox family moved in, at least two other families lived there. One woman saw a man dressed in a black frock coat in the bedroom next to the kitchen.

Duesler led a delegation from Hydesville to Lyons, where they confronted John Bell with Lucretia's story. He denied killing the peddler—and produced an affi-davit signed by dozens of Lyons citizens attesting to his integrity. Evidently the case against John Bell was dropped at that point.

The story of cold-blooded murder and dismemberment offered by the spirit, and Lucretia Pulver's corroborating testimony, made for compelling circumstantial ev-idence that Margaretta and Catherine Fox had contacted the spirit world. With-out a complete, identifiable body or eyewitnesses, however, it was impossible to declare the knockings genuine efforts by the dead to reach the living.

The lives of John and Margaret Fox, their two daughters, and their other chil-dren would continue in turmoil for the rest of their days. The knockings never went away. They would diminish for several days or weeks, but then return in full force. Mrs. Fox's hair is said to have turned white within weeks of the first oc-currences. The girls were sent to live with siblings—the theory being that if they were absent the knockings would go away. It's not clear if the house was ever quiet in their absence, but the "spirits" traveled with the girls. Catherine lived for a time with her married sister, Mrs. Leah Fish, in Rochester, New York. Mrs. Fish gave private music lessons. She had to give that up when the knockings continually interrupted her students' recitals. Margaretta also lived with Mrs. Fish and on her brother's farm outside Hydesville. The knocking persisted in both locales.

Over time Margaretta and Catherine began getting more detailed messages from "the other side," such as:

"You have been chosen to convince the world."

And:

"You have a mission to perform. Make ready for the work."

Eventually the girls rented an auditorium in Rochester where they could lecture about the spirit world. This they did to a large audience, including many skeptics.

Disbelievers challenged the pair to submit themselves and their home to an examination by impartial observers. They agreed. First one committee, then an-other and another questioned the girls, searched their Hydesville home, and probed the content of the messages the girls received. All of the "investigators" pronounced the girls genuine. This public vote of confidence seemed to spur even more interest in spirit communication. Margaretta and Catherine began traveling and lecturing widely, including a New York City appearance backed by newspaper publisher Horace Greeley. Meanwhile, Catherine achieved notable success in Great Britain holding séances with Sir William Crookes.

For the remainder of their lives, Margaretta and Catherine Fox devoted them-selves to spirit communication, but it was far from a happy experience for either of them. Both women married men who died soon after their marriages, both were often physically exhausted from the demanding schedules of séances and lectures, and both, in the end, became alcoholics. Catherine died at age fifty-five in 1892. She never fully recovered from the unexpected death of her husband, Englishman Samuel Jackson, shortly after the birth of their only child. Margaretta passed away nine months later.

Margaretta seemed most unable to cope with the fame brought about by the strange events in her little Hydesville home. On her deathbed, she renounced her belief in spiritualism and confessed that she and her sister had produced the mysterious sounds by cracking their toe joints. However, her most loyal supporters said she had been coerced into the denial by detractors. Sources disagree on whether Catherine, too, disavowed belief in spirit communication. Her unhappy adulthood did make her cynical toward life . . . and life after death.

However, the spiritualism movement had grown beyond the point where controversy surrounding the last days of its founders would have a marked impact on its many adherents. Though Margaretta's disclosure caused many to abandon their belief in spirit communication, spiritualism itself continued in popularity and does so to this day in the spiritualist communities of Lily Dale and Cassadega, Florida.

There is a bizarre footnote to the Fox sisters' claims. On November 22, 1904, a ghastly discovery in the cellar of the old Fox house cast a new light on Margaretta and Catherine's early claims.

The house was vacant—indeed it had been given the sobriquet "spook house" by residents of the community. Children often went inside on "dares" by their playmates. On this occasion, youngsters playing in the basement somehow caused a wall to partially collapse, exposing a cavity between it and the foundation. Human remains were discovered in the rubble.

The *Boston Journal* of November 23 wrote that the home's owner, William H. Hyde, investigated and found an almost complete skeleton between the wall and the foundation. The newspaper said it was "undoubtedly" the bones of the Charles B. Rosma, the peddler, murdered sixty years earlier.

The theory forwarded was that John Bell had indeed murdered and then decapitated the peddler before burying him in quicklime in the basement's floor. When Lucretia Pulver stumbled in the loose earth, Bell removed the remains and secreted them behind a false wall. That would account for the fact that the excavations made by David Fox and others in 1848 had found only a few bones and bits of cloth.

John Bell also made a mistake in assuming that quicklime, also known as lime or calcium oxide, would obliterate the body. The substance is strongly basic (alkaline) and will dissolve soft tissue such as skin, muscle, fat and internal organs. However, quicklime will not break down hard tissue like bones and teeth.

By the time the peddler's skeleton was found, the apparent murderer, John Bell, was long dead and thus beyond prosecution—*just as Rosma's spirit had predicted.*

Did the finding of human remains in the old Fox house vindicate the girls and place spiritualism in a new light?

If the facts of the discovery are to be believed, it seems Margaretta and Catherine did, somehow, divine the peddler's murder and, perhaps, his ghostly presence. It's possible of course, if somewhat improbable, that the girls had been told about the murder by some unidentified third party who had knowledge of John Bell's awful secret.

Spiritualism has never taken root in the American mainstream. Perhaps it was the gimmickry associated with its early days—ear trumpets, Ouija boards, crystal balls, automatic writing, and such—that kept it on the fringe. Or maybe it was the inability of its practitioners to prove beyond a reasonable doubt that they were in direct contact with the spirit world.

Sadly, Margaretta and Catherine Fox were themselves spirits when some proof of their own incredible story was unearthed in their old home's basement. Then again, maybe they *were* watching as those children stumbled upon John Bell's grisly legacy. . . .

NORTH CAROLINA

The Mysterious Outer Banks

The barrier reefs off the coast of North Carolina are a series of thread-thin islands arranged like a giant necklace upon the waters. Collectively, they are called the Outer Banks. Stitched together by bridges or car ferries, with some of the more remote islands accessible by private boat only, the Banks divide Pamlico Sound on the west from the Atlantic Ocean on the east.

Although a few villages are scattered throughout the islands, most of the territory comprises the Cape Hatteras National Seashore—a wilderness of sand, surf, and solitude where commercial enterprise is prohibited. Dunes anchored by giant sea oats shelter vast beaches; gray surf runs high with white-foam breakers as a storm explodes; and blowing sand may uncover the rotted ribs of a sailing vessel that went down two or three hundred years ago. You may walk a beach for miles with only the gulls for company.

But the Outer Banks were not always so tranquil. An odd series of events has bequeathed a legacy of mystery, dread, and bloodshed upon them. It was here on Roanoke Island in 1585 that Sir Walter Raleigh's first English colonists landed. Within two years they had vanished, their fate still unknown.

Nearby, at Kill Devil Hills, in 1903, Ohio bicycle mechanics Wilbur and Orville Wright proved that man was capable of controlled powered flight.

It is the endless sea, however, that has given the Outer Banks its unique heritage—and two of its most spine-tingling tales.

On the tiny island of Ocracoke the pirate Edward Teach—Blackbeard—was finally cut down.

And on the frigid morning of February 1, 1921, a splendid five-masted schooner appeared on the shining waters off Cape Hatteras, a gray cat its sole occupant.

The Return of Blackbeard

Blackbeard was born to be a pirate. Standing nearly seven feet tall with dark, menacing eyes, a black beard that reached to his waist, and a swaggering gait, he was feared by both friend and foe. His savagery was known to every seaman of the early eighteenth century. Once, during a drinking bout, he grabbed two pistols and shot his loyal first mate, Israel Hands. One weapon misfired, but the ball of the other shattered Hands's kneecap, crippling him for life. The merciless brigand explained that if he didn't shoot one of his men from time to time they'd forget who he was.

On another occasion, spoiling for excitement on a becalmed sea, Blackbeard invited his crew to come below where they'd raise a little Hell of their own. A few men accepted the invitation and joined their captain in the hold. Casks of sulphur were lowered and lighted and the hatches shut tight. The men, choking on the fumes, screamed for air. After the hatches were opened and the men staggered to the deck, Blackbeard roared with delight that he'd held out the longest.

Two facts are known about the pirate leader's background: he was born in Bristol, England, in the late seventeenth century, and he was christened Edward Drummond. At that time Bristol was the roughest port in England, turning out uncounted numbers of buccaneers.

It was perhaps natural then that Drummond went to sea. Starting as a cabin boy, he soon worked his way up to merchant seaman. It was an honest way of life and the young sailor loved it. But soon England was caught up in Queen Anne's War with France. Anne had come to the throne in 1702 when she was thirty-seven years old. Both ignorant and indolent, she let her ministers make decisions for her and the war, begun in 1701, dragged on until 1713. But England was victorious, and now formidable throughout Europe.

During the war, many British ships were licensed as privateers. Under this arrangement, such a ship could attack any ship flying the French flag, imprison the crew, and divide the captured ship's cargo. Such actions saved the crown enormous sums in crew's wages, supplies, and general upkeep of vessels. The government called it "patriotism." The captain of a privateer was on his own; he took orders from no one and if, by error or design, he seized the ship of a friendly nation, it made little difference to the British crown.

But after the war ended and a peace treaty was signed with France, Queen Anne offered amnesty to privateers who would end their high jinks at sea and surrender all captured ships to Her Majesty's navy. It seemed an odd resolution to what had actually been government-sanctioned thievery.

Drummond had served under a privateer by the name of Benjamin Hornigold. After the captain decided to take up residence again in England, he turned over his ship to Drummond—or Edward Teach, as he had begun to call himself.

Teach renamed the ship *Queen Anne's Revenge*, assembled the toughest crew he could gather and sailed for America. After his first victory over a British man-of-war, the captain and his motley crew celebrated by smashing open casks of rum and drinking until they fell. Finally, only Teach was left standing on deck. "Call me Blackbeard!" he bellowed to those conscious enough to hear him, and from that moment on no one called him by any other name.

Before every battle, Blackbeard twisted his beard into corkscrew curls and tied them with bright red ribbons. A bandolier, tightened across his chest, bristled with several braces of loaded pistols, and from a wide belt at his waist swung his heavy cutlass and an assortment of daggers. He lined the brim of his hat with a slow-burning band of punk, and as the smoke wreathed his face, he looked like the Devil incarnate.

Now he had only one ambition: to become the bloodthirstiest pirate of them all. He installed forty cannon on *Queen Anne's Revenge*, enough firepower to blast the largest merchant ship to hell and beyond. Yet that still wasn't enough—he set about to acquire an armada of vessels, all flying the skull and crossbones.

In the Bay of Honduras he met Stede Bonnet, a pirate who had already captured prizes off the coasts of Pennsylvania, Virginia, and the Carolinas. Bonnet's ship was also named the *Revenge*. He readily agreed to join up with Blackbeard. As both ships headed north to Turniffe Island to refill their water casks, a sloop named *Adventure* was spotted heading for the same landfall. It was promptly seized and every crewman, trembling in his boots at the sight of a blackbearded giant, signed on with Teach.

This scum of humanity, as many called Blackbeard, soon added several more ships to his fleet and began ranging the sea lanes farther out into the ocean, plundering any unwary ship he could find and frequently unloading the booty in Havana. But he needed more hideouts. He began staking out several upriver refuges along the Virginia and Carolina coasts where terrified plantation owners offered both shelter and provisions. On one occasion, short of medical supplies, he blockaded the harbor of Charleston, South Carolina, and threatened to torch the city if drugs were not delivered and a sizeable ransom paid. The demands were promptly carried out.

Ocracoke Inlet of North Carolina's Outer Banks became Blackbeard's favorite haunt. The waters were treacherous enough to present a challenge to him in picking off cargo ships, and he could hide out in a cove on the north side of the inlet, shielded by yaupon and live oak trees. He could also peddle goods to Ocracoke Island's merchants at a reasonable price and without any British tariff. It was rumored that Charles Eden, the colonial governor of North Carolina, was protecting all pirate ships along his shores in exchange for a share of the plunder.

Possibly Blackbeard and others were so protected, but the day came when this most wicked of all sea brigands summarily announced that he was quitting the sea. He said he was tired of climbing the scuppers of strange ships, of engaging in hand-to-hand combat, and of training honest sailors in the ways of piracy. Now all he wanted was to settle into a calm and peaceful life. He and twenty of his men traveled to Bath, North Carolina's colonial capital, surrendered themselves and received the king's pardon.

Before long Blackbeard bought a house in Bath and turned it into a showplace befitting a successful "mariner."

He gave lavish parties to which he invited all of the leading citizens. The finest of furniture, table linens, and silverware were in evidence. Rum flowed freely, bolts of silks and satins and splendid jewels were proffered to female guests.

But soon such dissipation began to pall. Blackbeard was not to the manor born. The endless talk of cotton crops and politics by the rich southern planters and the sophisticated gossip of their wives bored him. He longed to feel a deck beneath his feet, the thrill of the chase in a choppy sea, the flash of dagger and cutlass. He would return to Ocracoke. But before he slipped away, a young lady, smitten by the rough charms of the bandit, hastily married him. She could not know that her husband had already acquired thirteen wives in other ports of call!

Back on Ocracoke, Blackbeard devised a masterful plan. It would prove to be his undoing. In his scheme, Ocracoke was to become a sanctuary for all pirates, a kind of "club" to which members would pay dues. In return for his protection of "members," Blackbeard would take 10 percent of the money.

It might have worked had not merchants and ship owners learned of the plan and appealed to Governor Spotswood of the Virginia colony for help. Spotswood dispatched two sloops of the Royal Navy with orders to take Blackbeard dead or alive.

On a clear, cold November morning in 1718, these ships slipped into Ocracoke Inlet, where Blackbeard and his men were aboard the ship *Adventure*.

The British sailors were unfamiliar with the treacherous channel, and one sloop ran aground. Blackbeard yelled orders to open the gun-ports of both sides of the *Adventure* and run out the cannon. Then he made straight for the *Ranger*, under the command of British lieutenant Robert Maynard. He'd take the grounded ship later.

As the pirate ship bore down on him, Maynard feared a collision. But at the last second Blackbeard deftly swung his ship around to starboard and ordered all cannon fired. The *Ranger*, hit bow-to-stern, shuddered in the water. Maynard saw a few of his men fall and yelled to the others to get below. In came the *Adventure* for another raking of the sloop. After the smoke cleared, the pirate saw no one on the deck of the *Ranger*. He'd taken yet another prize, he thought. But at the moment the grappling irons were thrown from the *Adventure* to the *Ranger*, Maynard hollered for his men to attack. They thundered topside, armed with pistols, daggers, and swords.

Blackbeard leaped over the gunwales of the sloop and faced the commander. With eyes flashing and the punk burning under his hat brim, Teach was quick to charge. Maynard was quicker. The ball from his pistol grazed the pirate's hand and threw him off balance. Blackbeard seized his cutlass, but before he could run it through the commander, one of Maynard's men plunged a sword into the pirate's neck. Crazed with pain and nearly blinded by blood pouring from his wounds, Blackbeard closed in for the kill. Maynard was ready and parried the thrust.

Finally, Teach fired his pistol, then fell facedown on the deck. He heard the clash of steel on steel and the ring of pistol shots as his men fought the Britishers, but the sounds grew fainter. The giant who had murdered countless innocent seamen was dead. When Maynard's men examined the body, they discovered twenty-five major wounds. Blackbeard's head was chopped off and hung from the bowsprit of the *Ranger*. His corpse was dropped unceremoniously overboard.

Meanwhile, Blackbeard's men, panicked by the death of their leader, jumped from the ship and swam ashore. All were rounded up, convicted of treason and hanged. Israel Hands, who had turned state's evidence, was allowed to return to England.

A cove on the Pamlico Sound side of Ocracoke Island is known as "Teach's Hole," the place where the pirate made his final stand against the British navy. And some say that the ghost of the infamous buccaneer still prowls the waters. Local fishermen have reported seeing the headless figure swimming around just beneath the surface of the water on a moonless night. It seems to emit a phosphorescent glow. When a strong wind blows inland, the tramping of heavy boots may be heard, and a distant, mournful cry: "Where is my head?" Sometimes the ghost is seen carrying a lantern. From time to time a ghost ship is sighted.

And what of Blackbeard's treasure? Did he hide it up and down the East Coast as legend says? For over 270 years, adventurers have sought to locate the pirate's bounty. Is there a fortune in old coins buried in some obscure sand dune or beneath the trees of Ocracoke Island? Probably not. Blackbeard lived well and he lived for the moment. What he looted from innocent ships he probably spent on a lavish lifestyle. It's unlikely that he buried any treasure anywhere. Tomorrow would always come, and with it another ship to plunder.

Port of Doom

In the days of sailing vessels, long before today's sophisticated navigational aids, every captain of bark, sloop, and schooner feared the Diamond Shoals off Cape Hatteras. When the Gulf Stream current and a strong southwest wind collided, ships were frequently driven onto these sand spits, where they floundered sometimes for days while waiting for a shift of wind. But too often that wind shift slammed in from the northeast, piling up surf that pounded the stranded vessel to pieces. It was not unusual to find timbers, name plates, bolts, and rivets scattered for miles along the coast of this treacherous sweep of ocean that is still known as "the graveyard of the Atlantic."

The night of February 1, 1921, was a quiet one at Cape Hatteras Coast Guard Station. Only a light breeze blew. Some of the crewmen had gone on to bed while others sat up for a time playing cards and swapping stories. They were well acquainted with one another; together they'd launched boats into heaving seas in attempts to rescue seamen from vessels in distress. Sometimes they succeeded; sometimes not. But every guardsman knew his duty: "You have to go out, but you don't have to come back."

The lookout that night never took his eyes off the black sea. He saw no lights anywhere—no passing ships or signals of distress. He could not know that in a few hours he would be involved in one of the most baffling mysteries of the Carolina coast, a mystery that to this day has never been solved.

As gray dawn lightened the eastern sky, the lookout turned to pour himself a mug of coffee. When he looked back to the water, he saw a splendid five-masted schooner out by Outer Diamond. Was he dreaming? He rubbed his eyes and swigged another mug of coffee. But the schooner remained, canvas sails unfurled, like a picture pasted on a paper sea.

However, when the lookout reached for the telescope, the picture turned grim. The ship had run aground on Outer Diamond, and each onrushing wave drove it harder into the sand. The guardsman sounded the alarm and his buddies leaped from their bunks, throwing on whatever clothes were at hand and slipping into warm jackets as they ran.

The lookout started the motor of the surfboat and the guardsmen, heading out to sea, speculated on the sight before their eyes. What was this ship and why had she not called for help? She must have reached Cape Hatteras during the night, yet no lights had been observed and no distress calls received.

As the boat drew near the schooner, the men saw no one on deck. They circled the ship twice, calling out but receiving no answer. They did notice the name CARROLL M. DEERING painted on the stern in large, bright letters that showed no signs of wear. The sails too were snow white and without patches; the schooner surely must have been on her maiden voyage when she floundered. Oddly, no anchors were in sight, nor were there any lifeboats.

* * *

The stern man hollered one final "halloo," but only his own voice echoed across the water. No one appeared on deck. The guardsmen, although curious about the vessel, could only return to their station. A law of the sea prohibits anyone from boarding another man's ship without his invitation. And the schooner was in no immediate danger.

Back at the Coast Guard Station, the station master studied his naval register to learn the owner of the ship and its home port. He soon discovered that the ship had been built the previous year and launched from the Bath, Maine ship-yard. The owners were contacted and permission granted to board the schooner.

The surfboat set out once more through an increasingly choppy sea. While two of the guardsmen remained on the launch, the others climbed the ship's ladder and leaped over the portside rail.

Although the day had turned unseasonably warm and sunny, the men boarding the schooner were shivering. Was it from imagined cold—the apprehension of what they might discover? A few felt that someone was creeping up behind them. They jerked their heads around and then, finding no one, tried to laugh at their fears. Two by two they began their exploration of the mystery ship. At first every-thing seemed in order, the captain's quarters and the first mate's quarters in perfect condition, without even any liquor missing from the storage compartment. But then, with a shudder, the men realized that no navigational aids were in sight—no sextant, no quadrant, no telescope, and not a single map of the Middle Atlantic coast! The log book also was missing.

Then, one man pointed to the steering apparatus. It had been smashed by a sledgehammer that was propped against the wheel. No wonder the ship had run aground. With rudder swinging free, the helmsman had had no way to steer his vessel.

Meanwhile, men searching other parts of the vessel called for their mates. In the beautiful dining salon with its splendid teakwood furnishings, the tables were set with linen cloths upon which rested full plates of a meal served but never consumed. Serving dishes filled with food had also been placed in the center of the tables.

In the galley, kettles of food had grown cold on the stove. The captain and his crew had abandoned the ship in a hurry. Why? Suddenly a scratching sound came from somewhere behind the stove; something was moving. The men stepped back, keeping a cautious eye ahead. A large gray cat appeared, the only living thing on board. It seemed to have been well fed. The men named it Carroll and took it with them.

Meanwhile, an intensive investigation had begun back at the Cape Hatteras Coast Guard Station. Events were slowly and painstakingly pieced together. The *Carroll M. Deering*, under the command of Capt. William Merritt, had left Port-land, Maine, in the summer of 1920 bound for Rio de Janeiro with a cargo of coal. At the port of Lewes, Delaware, Merritt complained of illness and left the ship. His son accompanied him.

At Lewes, a new captain by the name of William B. Wormell was summoned from New York to take command of the ship. Wormell was a well-liked and highly respected seaman with years of experience on most of the oceans of the world. He brought his longtime first mate with him. Other crewmen included six Danes, a Finn, and an African-American steward.

The ship sailed out of the Delaware Breakwater at Lewes and reached Rio de Janeiro on December 3. On the return trip, Captain Wormell stopped off at

Barbados, where he received orders to proceed directly to Norfolk, Virginia, with no cargo. But evidently the captain had some trepidation about bringing the ship back. He confided to the ship's agents at Bridgetown, Barbados, that the crew had been most uncooperative and that he himself did not feel well.

Later, a few Bridgetown natives would testify that they'd overheard some sailors from the *Carroll M. Deering* swearing, on a street corner, that they'd "get the old man." Did they mean Captain Wormell? He had always been popular with every crew he had commanded.

With his original crew, Captain Wormell left Barbados. The date was January 9, 1921. On January 23, the ship cleared the Cape Fear, North Carolina, light. Six days later she passed the Cape Lookout lightship—a distance of only eighty miles. Why had she taken so long?

At the Cape Lookout lightship, a man on the deck of the *Carroll M. Deering* yelled through a megaphone that the ship had lost her anchors in a storm and asked for help in notifying other ships to keep clear of her. The lightship captain was perplexed because the man on deck did not appear to be dressed like a ship's officer nor did he act like one. The crew wandered aimlessly around the deck. Furthermore, there had been no storms.

After the Hatteras Coast Guardsmen investigated the empty vessel on the morning of February 2, Coast Guard stations all up and down the coast were alerted. Every inlet, bay, and cove was searched for survivors or bodies, but no human being, dead or alive, was ever found.

The most exhaustive investigation in maritime history was conducted, involving the navy and the Justice, State, Treasury, Navigation, and Commerce departments. On a single chart salvaged from the ship, Captain Wormell's daughter identified her father's handwriting up until January 23. After that date the records were written in a different hand. She feared that pirates had seized the ship. A ship without cargo? Not likely.

A more commonly held theory was that of mass suicide. Had the crew contracted an incurable tropical disease and drowned themselves? If so, why were the lifeboats missing?

What of the conversation overheard in Barbados that indicated the crew of the *Carroll M. Deering* planned to "get the old man"? Had they murdered their captain, cast off in the lifeboats and later burned them on some secluded beach? Some charred remains of the boats would surely have been found.

All the governmental departments involved in the investigation finally admitted defeat. The sails and some of the furnishings of the mysterious vessel were salvaged and sold at auction. Then she was left to the vagaries of the weather. She went to pieces off Hatteras in a howling winter gale.

Yet, there are those who claim that the captain and the crew of that ill-fated ship live on, their shrieks and moans carried clearly to shore during February storms. They seem to be calling, "Save us! Please save us!"

Sky Lights

It had rained hard all day and now, in the darkness of the night, only a fine drizzle fell like a beaded curtain. The freight train rattled along between scrub pines and deep underbrush, headed for the village of Wilmington, near the southeastern North Carolina coast.

To conductor Joe Baldwin the chugging of the old wood-burning engine made a comforting sound, especially as the train neared the end of its long day's journey. Joe liked his job on the Wilmington–Florence–Augusta line and felt fortunate to have secured such a fine position. Some of his friends who had returned with him after the Civil War ended two years earlier were still looking for work.

Although tonight there were no scheduled pickups or drop-offs of freight before Wilmington, Joe called out each station in turn. That was his job. Now as the train neared Maco Station, he slid open the rear door of the next-to-the-last car and expertly leaped across the network of pins and couplers. But as soon as he jumped to the last car he knew something was wrong. It had lost momentum. Beads of sweat stood out on his forehead. With sickening dread he realized what had happened. The last car had become uncoupled and was rolling to a stop. An express train filled with passengers was only minutes behind his fast freight.

Joe seized his lantern firmly in one hand and jerked open the rear door of the car. Then, stepping out onto the platform, he peered down the tracks. The head-lamp from the oncoming passenger train grew, first as a pinprick in the far distance and soon, all too soon, as an enveloping bath of blinding light. Joe Baldwin frantically swung his light in great arcs to signal the oncoming engineer. His screams were cut off as the screech of metal striking metal punctured the night air; soot and sparks showered the brush on either side of the glistening rails.

Joe Baldwin was decapitated. His mangled body was found sprawled across the tracks, but his head was never recovered. He was the only one killed.

Not long after that tragic accident in 1867, a mysterious light appeared by the tracks near Maco Station, a scattered handful of farmhouses a dozen miles west of Wilmington. It was unlike anything that had ever been seen in the area. Soon throngs of people gathered each evening to watch for the eerie glow. And after newspapers picked up the story, curiosity seekers from all over the country descended upon the little outpost. Many hundreds of people claimed to have seen the light.

Some witnesses believed the light to be Joe Baldwin's lantern still swinging its futile warning to the approaching train. Others think the light is the conductor himself searching for his head. One observer reported seeing the lantern burning in a swamp near the place where it had been found on that fatal night.

John Harden, veteran newsman and collector of Carolina legends, described the light in his book *Tar Heel Ghosts*: "... the light is first seen at some distance down the track, maybe a mile away. It starts with a flicker over the left rail, very much as if someone had struck a match. Then it grows a little brighter, and begins creeping up the track toward you. As it becomes brighter it increases in momentum. Then it dashes forward with a rather incredible velocity, at the same time swinging faster from side to side.

"Finally, it comes to a sudden halt some seventy-five yards away, glows there like a fiery eye, and then speeds backward down the track, as if retreating from some unseen danger. It stops where it made its first appearance, hangs there ominously for a moment, like a moon in miniature, and then vanishes into nothingness."

The Maco Light's appearance is unpredictable at best. It may show itself night after night, especially if a fine mist is falling, or again it may disappear for weeks at a time.

In 1873, a second light appeared. This one traveled west rather than east, and the two sometimes met. More than one frightened engineer, believing another train was coming toward him on the track, yelled at his brakeman, squeezed his eyes tightly shut and prayed. At the dreaded moment of impact, the light vanished. Finally, signalmen began carrying both red and green lanterns. Given a green light, an engineer could push his behemoth fearlessly down the tracks past Maco Station.

In 1886 an earthquake jolted southeastern North Carolina and the strange light disappeared. But three years later, it returned.

One day during that year, President Grover Cleveland was riding a train toward Wilmington when it stopped at Maco Station to take on fuel and water. While waiting, the president decided to take a stroll down the tracks. Seeing a signalman swinging a green lantern in one hand and a red one in the other, he asked about this curiosity. When told the story of the light, he didn't know what to make of it.

Numerous attempts have been made to explain the phenomenon. A machine gun detachment from the United States Army's installation at Fort Bragg was once sent to investigate. The men fired repeatedly at the light, but were unable to hit it as it hopscotched down the tracks.

Reflections from automobile headlights coming from nearby roads have always been a popular explanation for anomalous lights. On one occasion at midnight all roads near Maco were cordoned off for an hour with guards posted to turn back motorists. The light appeared, hovering about three feet above the tracks and traveling east.

Old-timers always smile at any "scientific" explanation for the light; they know it appeared long before automobiles were built and roads carved into the area. They're certain it was Joe Baldwin's ghost.

In 1977 the tracks were torn up, and the light has once again gone away. But no one can say for certain if this time the Maco Light has been extinguished for all time.

The Brown Mountain Lights

In the mountains of western North Carolina, peaks bear fanciful, and often unforgettable names: Blowing Rock, Grandfather Mountain, Clingmans Dome, Rattlesnake Knob, and Chimney Rock, from which the Cherokee Indians once sent smoke signals.

But the most famous mountain of all goes by the prosaic name of Brown Mountain. Hardly qualifying as a mountain, it spreads across the Blue Ridge foothills at an elevation of only 2,600 feet and straddles Burke and Caldwell counties. Brown Mountain, located fourteen miles northwest of Morganton, is long and flat as a tabletop. It lacks any distinguishing characteristic . . . except at night. Then lights of various colors rise above its treetops, shimmering and dancing, disappearing, then reappearing.

Descriptions vary from one observer to another. One person reported seeing a bright red light that vanished in less than a minute. Another said he watched a pale white light whirl inside a halo, disappear for twenty minutes and then reappear. A minister described the light as cone-shaped and larger than a star. When two more arose, he, and his sons who were with him, watched through field glasses. The lights rose high in the sky and terminated. Other persons said they saw yellow lights that moved upward, downward, or horizontally. Sometimes clusters of lights appear and rise so fast that it's impossible to count them. When viewed through a telescope, the lights resemble balls of fire.

No one knows when the mysterious lights first appeared, but legend says they were visible before the Civil War, possibly as early as 1850. In that year a woman of the area disappeared. Neighbors suspected that her abusive husband murdered her. Shortly afterward, while search parties were scouring Brown Mountain in search of the woman's body, strange lights began bobbing above them in the night sky. Some suspected the spirit of the victim had returned to haunt her murderer; others thought the light had been sent as a warning to end the search. The woman's remains were eventually found under a cliff.

If the woman's spirit intended to haunt the murderer, it has outlived its mission. For nearly 140 years the lights have appeared with some regularity. They are well known to Tarheels and to increasing numbers of out-of-state visitors.

Many theories have been advanced to explain the weird anomaly. At first the lights were thought to be a will-o'-the-wisp, a phosphorescent light that hovers or flits over swampy ground at night, possibly caused by combustion of gas emitted by rotting organic matter. However, there is no marshy ground near Brown Mountain.

Could it be foxfire, a phosphorescent glow produced by certain fungi found on rotting wood? Hardly. Foxfire is a weak, pale light that would not appear as colored globes floating in the sky.

An amateur explorer once reported that he'd found at one end of the mountain a piece of pitchblende, a radium ore. But the rays from radium are invisible. And geologists have since confirmed that Brown Mountain is composed of ordinary cranberry granite.

Moonshiners once operated in the vicinity of Brown Mountain, screening their stills to conceal the fires. Whenever the covers were removed and the fires raked out, clouds of rising steam reflected the firelight from below. But uncounted numbers of stills would have been required to create lights in the sky on a regular basis. Besides, the era of moonshining has long since passed and the lights still appear.

St. Elmo's fire was yet another theory set forth. This is an electrical discharge from sharp-pointed objects during a thunderstorm. Sailors are well acquainted with it because it often appears at the tip of a mast during a storm. But the phenomenon requires a solid conductor and never occurs in midair. Also, the Brown Mountain lights appear on clear nights with no storms brewing anywhere in the area.

For a time the Andes Lights were given as an explanation. This is a phenomenon observed in the high mountains of Chile in which silent discharges of electricity pass through clouds to the mountain peaks. These discharges often produce round, shimmering lights that can be seen sometimes for more than three hundred miles. However, they occur only at elevations over fifteen thousand feet, not at the much lower level of the Blue Ridge foothills.

At least two studies have been made of Brown Mountain by the U.S. Geological Survey. In 1913, the first geologist arrived and determined that the lights were caused by headlights of locomotives and automobiles in the Catawba Valley, south of Brown Mountain. But three years later, in 1916, a massive flood washed out railroad tracks and bridges and turned the primitive roads into quagmires. No traffic of any kind moved, yet the lights appeared as usual. They do not appear, however, after a long drought.

In 1922, a second geologist came to Burke County. He carried with him a fifteen-inch plane table, a telescopic alidade, field glasses, topographic maps, a barometer, compasses, camera, flashlights, and other research aids. Each time the lights were sighted, their appearance was checked with the train schedules. After two weeks of diligent work, the investigator completed his study. He determined that 47 percent of the lights originated from automobile headlights; 33 percent from locomotive headlights; 10 percent from fixed lights; and 10 percent from brushfires. The geologist believed that the lights originated in a deep valley several miles away and that atmospheric conditions caused the lights to appear to rise over Brown Mountain. Mist and dust particles rendered the lights colorful.

Although residents respected the geologist for his hard work and sincere efforts, they agreed among themselves that he too had failed to reach any final conclusion about the nature of the lights.

At least some of the mountain folk believe the lights are of divine origin. John Harden, in his book The Devil's Tramping Ground, quotes from an account written by J. L. Hartley, a state fire warden. Hartley said: "If God could make Brown Mountain, could he not also make the lights?"

Hartley had lived in the area for sixty years, thirty of them spent as a fire warden. He continued, "I have fought forest fires on every mountain from Linville Falls to Blowing Rock at all times of the night and have seen these lights a great many times from Grandfather Mountain above any human habitation. It is true there were hunters with lanterns, but please tell me whoever saw a lantern ascend up into the elements where no game exists. . . ."

There may never be an explanation for the Brown Mountain lights, but many people don't care; they are fascinated by the unexplained.

If you'd like to look for these mystery lights, summer evenings after eight o'clock are best. There are three popular vantage points: Beacon Heights, just off the Blue Ridge Parkway near Grandfather Mountain; Wiseman's View, on North Carolina Route 105 near Morganton; and on the scenic North Carolina Route 181, also near Morganton. At the latter location the U.S. Forest Service has erected a sign telling about the lights.

NORTH DAKOTA

More Legends of the Plains

The contemporary visitor to Fort Abraham Lincoln State Park will see an exquisitely restored cavalry post on the Missouri River, six miles south of Mandan, across from Bismarck. It is North Dakota's most visited state park. A reconstruction completed in 1989 includes the blockhouses of the earlier Fort McKeen, earth lodges from an ancient Mandan village, and a museum with displays from the eras of Native American habitation, the Lewis and Clark explorations, and George Armstrong Custer.

The fort is famous in American history as the site from which General Custer and the troopers of the Seventh Cavalry rode off to annihilation by Sioux and Cheyenne warriors at the Battle of the Little Big horn.

General Custer and his wife Libby were at the center of Fort Lincoln's frontier social life in the mid-1870s. Their home, now restored for public viewing, was considered an "open house," which meant that other officers and their wives gathered there for dances, amateur theatricals, and card parties. Their parlor was frequently used for Sunday morning religious services.

The summer of 1876 began like most others. With the coming of warm weather, the hunting of fresh game was suspended because of the fear of Indian attacks. Only government-issue beef was available. Eggs had to be shipped in from St. Paul. Fresh fruit was even harder to come by. Mrs. Custer later said she had strawberries only once during her years at Fort Lincoln. Each military family did have a small garden plot near the river, so some variety in homegrown produce was possible.

Despite the obvious privations of the frontier, the fort boasted weekly concerts by a military band and even a baseball team that played against soldiers from Fort Rice and town teams from Mandan and Bismarck, across the river.

It was the custom for officers' wives to help with July 4th celebrations, but 1876 was different. General Custer and the Seventh Cavalry, along with Major Marcus Reno and his men, had ridden west a short time before. Libby Custer and a number of others said they were not in a mood to celebrate and so they declined.

The circumstances of that ill-fated expedition are known to nearly every educated American. General Custer and all of his men were killed. Some soldiers under Major Reno's command, involved in a battle nearby, survived.

What is not so well known is that Libby Custer may have psychically sensed that her beloved husband would never return.

She had joined her husband on Sunday, June 25, for the first day of his march westward into Indian country. She returned to Fort Lincoln the next day. Later, she spoke of her dark foreboding:

"With my husband's departure, my last happy days in garrison were ended as a premonition of disaster that I had never known before weighed me down. I could not shake off the baleful influence of depressing thoughts. A presentiment and suspense such as I had never known made me selfish and I shut into my heart the most uncontrollable anxiety and could lighten no one else's burden."

The officers' wives at Fort Lincoln often gathered to sing hymns in order to keep their spirits up. On the day her husband died at the Little Bighorn, Libby Custer was with other wives for this nearly daily ritual. She fainted at about the time it is estimated George Armstrong Custer breathed his last!

The wounded were brought back to Bismarck aboard the steamship the *Far West*, under the direction of Capt. Grant Marsh. Included among the wounded was the horse Comanche, ridden by Captain Keogh of Major Reno's regiment. A soldier named Jim Carnehan sent out the first word of the battle from the telegraph office in Bismarck when the steamboat docked there.

A Dr. Porter was the physician attending the wounded. It was his sad duty to break the news to the military at Fort Lincoln. The officers' wives were brought to the commandant's office. When Mrs. Custer entered the room, however, she held up her hand to stop Dr. Porter even before he began. "You don't need to tell me, I know," she said.

Libby Custer eerily predicted her own widowhood. She died in 1933, two days before her ninety-second birthday.

Phantoms of Devils Lake

In northeastern North Dakota, Devils Lake spreads like a great inland sea across nearly thirty miles, although its irregular shape makes the distance from corner to corner, by water, closer to sixty miles.

Called Minnewaukan ("spirit water") by Native Americans, Devils Lake is unusual for a freshwater lake. Its water tastes salty for one thing, giving rise to its sobriquet of "miniature ocean." Its shoreline is nearly three hundred miles in length, with greatly varying geological formations. At some points, meadows stretch for miles away from the lake, while elsewhere, bluffs several hundred feet high rise from the shore. Other shoreline areas are steep and rocky.

According to geologists, Devils Lake was formed by the projecting point of a vast, prehistoric glacier. The lake has no visible outlet, but it's thought the water flows through subterranean fissures to the Sheyenne, James, and Red river basins. Although the water has distinct elements of sulphite and carbonates, it is crystal clear.

What gives rise to numerous legends about Devils Lake, however, is the extraordinary twisting shoreline, with its numerous arms and bays ranging in length from several feet to a dozen miles. It is entirely possible to take several days to go by boat around the lake's perimeter.

One of the earliest tales connected with Devils Lake comes down from the Sioux and the Ojibwa, enemies in earlier centuries but in later years abiding by an agreement that made the lake neutral ground. The reason for the truce was a tribal legend common to both peoples. Two large war parties, one Ojibwa and the other Sioux, were engaged in a fierce battle on Devils Lake when an immense storm blew up and all the warriors were drowned. Although the Devils Lake Sioux Indian Reservation abuts the southern shore, the legend of the lost war parties kept all but the bravest men off the lake for decades.

There are no true islands in Devils Lake, but fog and mist can give the illusion that there are. And it may have been the odd formations of rocks jutting into the lake, seen in bad weather, that have given rise to the most persistent ghost stories connected with Devils Lake: tales of phantom ships.

At other times, however, perfect weather has been the norm for such sightings, such as the time J. Morley Wyard said he saw two ghost ships on July 17, 1893. He was crossing Devils Lake aboard the steamship *Minnie H.* from the old Chautauqua grounds to Fort Totten on the south shore. He described the water as calm and the sky as cloudless. "Along the shore the trees in summer beauty reproduced upon the crystal surface," he wrote in the *Park River Gazette Witness*.

When the *Minnie H.* was in the center of the lake, Wyard said there appeared near the southern shore, west of Fort Totten, what looked like the hull of a large vessel, without mast or spar or sail, the color of new timber. The ghost ship was motionless, about a dozen miles away from Wyard's vantage point. An outcropping of shore called the Point of Rocks eventually cut off Wyard's view.

Wyard's return trip across the lake a few hours later provided an even more amazing sight.

"Far down the strait," he wrote in the *Gazette Witness*, ". . . there appeared the glint of a sail, that, emerging from the distant outlet came more clearly into sight. Though the air was breathless, the fairy craft swept along with wonderful rapidity until it might have covered ten miles in about as many minutes. Its rapid flight could be definitely measured. Upon the shore the taller trees were outlined against the sky, and the mystic yacht sped past them close under the land, until it, too, like the sail-less and motionless hull of the earlier trip, disappeared at the boulder point near Fort Totten."

An 1893 sailboat moving at sixty miles per hour? It hardly seems possible, yet Wyard was quite definite in his account. He didn't speculate that the ships could have been mirages or imaginative renderings of shoreline formations, as seems likely. Wyard was a romantic, as is obvious from his poetic final words about the adventure. "All melted into air, like the baseless fabric of a vision."

The Morrison House

Every city in the United States has its own "haunted house." Perhaps it's the old home of an elderly man or woman who glares at children walking across the lawn, or the abandoned dwelling of a family that left most of its possessions behind for some unknown reason. But in North Dakota, towns of any size are few and far between. It often happens that houses with the reputation of being "haunted" are in the country.

That's the case with the old John Morrison home, about three miles northwest of Englevale in Ransom County. The house was one of the first to be built in the county, but Morrison didn't live there very long. His two children died at birth, and his wife died soon after the second childbirth. Mother and children were buried in a copse of trees near the farmhouse. Morrison left soon thereafter.

A series of individuals and families lived in the house after Morrison moved west, but none for very long. One man said his dishes rattled in the cupboard at night. Another family recounted how a rocking chair in the front parlor began to rock even after they shone an oil lamp on it. They kept at least one lamp lit each night after that.

Two other families who lived in the house some years later said a tall, slender figure in black sometimes roamed through the grove of trees where Mrs. Morrison and her babies were buried. The mysterious intruder moaned as he walked about.

A bachelor who bought the house and land said he wouldn't spend the night there. He felt hot breath on his cheek as he tried to sleep at night.

The Morrison home disappeared years ago, but not the legends surrounding this haunted house of the plains.

The Bewitched Schoolhouse

On a spring day in 1944, eight pupils at the Wild Plum School near Richardton, in southwest North Dakota, were jolted out of their ennui by a series of odd events.

As teacher Pauline Rebel explained a lesson, lignite coal in a bucket beside the stove began to stir. Seconds later, lumps of coal flew out of the scuttle, struck the walls of the room and bounced back. Little Jack Steiner was hit on the head and bruised. The bucket tipped over and the lignite ignited.

Window shades began smoldering. A bookcase burst into flames. Finally, as a dictionary slid unassisted across the table and the children screamed, Mrs. Rebel telephoned for help.

By the time school officials arrived, the commotion had subsided. But the coal was still agitated by some unknown force; pieces trembled in the men's hands. The school was temporarily closed and the children sent home.

State Fire Marshal Charles Schwartz said later the combustions were "simply beyond belief."

Chemistry professors at South Dakota State College analyzed samples of the coal, but found nothing unusual. The FBI tested pieces, along with the scuttle and the dictionary. They, too, came up empty-handed.

Mrs. Rebel and her pupils took lie-detector tests. On the basis of the tests all were said to have been telling the truth.

The story of the "bewitched" schoolhouse received national attention because it coincided with the publication of a book, *Mr. Tompkins Explores the Atom*, in which author George Gamow, a physics professor at George Washington University, set forth the idea that such spontaneous phenomena are possible. The theory was first developed by the late physicist James Clark Maxwell, and was known as "Maxwell's Demon."

To see how it might work, it's necessary to understand that a fundamental law of thermodynamics is the principle of increasing disorder, or entropy. In the normal state of matter, molecules move erratically, bumping against other molecules to create increasing disorder that results in a more or less even distribution of energy, or heat, throughout an object.

But, said physicist Gamow, a group of molecules might, once in several billion years, accidentally arrange themselves in an orderly movement that would upset this normal condition. For example, all the air molecules in a room could, theoretically, collect under a table and levitate it. Or, as in the North Dakota case, a group of molecules might fall into a pattern of collisions that would concentrate energy at a particular point, thus igniting lumps of coal.

Did "Maxwell's Demon" invade a little prairie schoolhouse in 1944? Or was there another explanation for the bizarre events?

To this day, the mystery remains unsolved.

The Regan Light

In 1977, a most unusual news dispatch from Wilton, North Dakota, captured the attention of readers across the nation. Writer Frances Wold had published a story in the Wilton *News-Washburn Leader*, later distributed nationwide by the Associated Press, of strange lights sighted near Regan, about fifteen miles east of Wilton.

The story began on a Saturday night in early February 1977 as Mrs. Barney Strand Jr. drove with her daughter Sindy from Regan to their ranch home in Canfield Township. Sindy was at the wheel of the family's pickup truck.

A few miles outside Regan, the mother and daughter noticed a bright glow about the size and intensity of a farmyard light close to their truck. It hovered behind and above them, slightly higher than the power lines along the country road.

Somewhat frightened, Sindy pushed down on the accelerator until she reached some fifty miles per hour. The light kept the pace. Mrs. Strand, though as anxious as her daughter to escape the speeding light, cautioned her daughter to be careful on the dark road. Both women thought that the light would disappear once they turned onto the road leading to their farm. It did not, following them right into their yard.

"I told Sindy that when we got home she was to get out of the car and into the house as fast as she could," Mrs. Strand told reporter Wold. "We both ran in, but we didn't turn any lights on."

Mrs. Strand grabbed a pair of binoculars and watched the bouncing orb as it pulsated near a grove of trees at the west side of the house. It made no sound. Through the glasses, Mrs. Strand said the light had a shimmering orange hue about it, although to the naked eye it seemed to be clear yellow in color. The light stayed in the yard for a short time before it moved away, growing smaller and smaller as it faded in the distance.

"It seemed to be twirling slowly as I looked, but maybe it was the changing colors that made it look that way," she said. "For awhile I could see it through the glasses after Sindy couldn't see it any more, but then I lost it, too."

Mrs. Strand and her daughter were not the first to see the Regan light. For at least two years, other area residents had been followed in their vehicles by the light. Sometimes it dipped so low that it seemed to be traveling parallel with a car's windows. All the witnesses said that no matter how fast or how slowly they were driving, the light stayed with them.

Her experience made a believer out of Mrs. Strand, too. "It kept right up with us," she said. "I don't know what it was, but I can tell you it was really frightening."

There were a number of theories offered at the time as to the light's origin. Some said it was someone's idea of a practical joke. The culprit was aiming a light at innocent motorists from another car or a fixed location. That seems far-fetched and very difficult to achieve.

Others believed it was caused by electromagnetic or atmospheric disturbances that caused reflections or lights to occur. Scientists have found that earthquake activity deep within the earth can produce lightlike effects through barely discernible fissures.

UFO proponents said the light was just another case of earthlings being visited by intelligent life from another world.

Whatever the cause, reporter Frances Wold concluded, the light did produce one concrete result. Those who saw it were scared half to death.

Ceely Rose

A hundred years ago Celia Rose murdered for love, and even today her ghost returns, watching for the boy who spurned her.

"Ceely," as she was known, was a large, raw-boned farm girl who could strangle a chicken with a flick of the wrist. Although ungainly and unattractive, even as a young child, she was treated kindly by most of the neighbors in the close-knit community of Pleasant Valley, outside Mansfield.

Ceely's father, David, operated the small farm and a grist mill with the help of his son, Walter, who was much older than Ceely. Her mother, Rebecca, tried to teach her daughter embroidery, tatting, crocheting, and other skills common to women of the late nineteenth century. Ceely seemed either uninterested or unable to learn. Since her parents had been middle-aged when Ceely was born, her mother often wondered if that had made her daughter "peculiar."

School was a heartbreaking series of defeats for the unfortunate child. By the age of thirteen she could barely read and was always in classes with children much younger than herself. Many youngsters teased her for her poor grades and her pronounced stammer whenever she was called upon to recite. With the cruelty that children often inflict upon one another, they would scream, "Dumbbell Ceely! Ugly old Ceely!" Yet a few of the more mature and compassionate girls befriended Ceely and walked her home from school.

Ceely came to know sisters Cora and Tracy Davis in this way and she sometimes invited them into the house. As the Davis girls talked about boys at school, comparing one with another as to looks and personality, Ceely listened with both awe and envy. She had seen both girls with boys, heard their laughter and sweet talk, and she longed to have a boyfriend of her own.

Meanwhile, Cora and Tracy grew increasingly uncomfortable in the Rose house. Mrs. Rose always hovered nearby and the girls hesitated to exchange confidences. Eventually, Ceely's friends stopped coming to the house. Nevertheless, Ceely was able to build a close friendship with the girls.

Ceely struggled on in school and attended high school for a while. By the time she was twenty-three, she had developed into a full-busted young woman more in control of her unwieldy body. New feelings arose within her, strong feelings that frightened her. She knew they had something to do with boys and she was determined to make them notice her. On long, lazy summer days she strolled down the dusty lane and watched young men working in the fields.

Eighteen-year-old Guy Berry especially attracted her. As he turned the soil or pitched hay in his family's field, sweat glistened on his brown body, naked above the waist; the muscles rippled in his arms. Once in a while he'd stop to wipe his face with a bandana tucked into the waist of his pants, and then he'd come to the fence to talk to Ceely, usually about crops and the weather. He always looked directly into her face, his eyes lit with kindness. No boy had ever talked to Ceely Rose before—not in a good-hearted way, at any rate.

Now Ceely, whenever she could escape her mother's attentive eye, hurried over to the Berry farm, which adjoined her father's small two-acre spread.

Guy's father, George, noticed that Ceely was hanging around his son and he didn't like it. He called on Mr. Rose and stated firmly, but politely, that Ceely was distracting Guy from his chores. To his surprise, David Rose sympathized with him, explaining that his daughter had become unmanageable. She refused to help around the house and wandered about as if in a daze. Her mother worried constantly about her. George Berry might have said, "What can you expect from an imbecile?" but he was not a brutish man.

One day, toward the end of June, Ceely and Guy went out for a walk at dusk. She told him that her family would be out of town for a few days visiting relatives and invited him to come see her whenever he could get away. He did not go.

On June 30, 1896, David Rose was found dead in bed in his home; he was sixty-seven. His wife, Rebecca, past sixty, was ill and died soon afterward, as did her son, Walter, thirty-nine. Autopsies revealed that all had died of arsenic poisoning.

The triple murders stunned the community, and neighbors demanded that justice be done.

The father of Ceely's girlhood friend Cora Davis suspected all along that Ceely was the murderer and he set out to prove it. Even though he learned that he would receive no reward for information leading to the conviction of the girl, he was certain that his daughter, Cora, could trick Ceely into a confession.

Cora was working in Bellville at the time of the murders, but returned home at her father's request. He outlined to her his plan to trap Ceely, who now lived alone in the family's home. On the afternoon of a sweltering day, Cora set out to visit Ceely. Because of the heat, Cora suggested that they go out to the barn and lie in the cool hay.

Cora spoke of many things, especially her job and the fun she'd had with her cousins near Bellville. Suddenly, she propped herself up on an elbow and looked intently at the girl lying beside her.

"You know," Cora began, "I loved a fella' once. It was when we lived in Tennessee. I never told you about him, never told anyone here about him. He had hair the color of wheat and his eyes were as blue as a summer sky. He had freckles, too, so I guess you couldn't say he was exactly handsome. But he was a real hard worker—good husband material, people said."

Cora's eyes filled and she crumpled a handful of hay between her fingers. "We wanted to get married eventually, but . . . he wasn't good enough for me and I wasn't good enough for him. That's what our parents said."

She paused and the tears spilled down her cheeks. "Ceely, I still love him and

I know he still loves me. I want to be his wife. But what can I do? His parents threaten to throw him off the family farm if we marry."

Ceely turned eyes of steel upon her friend. "Kill 'em, Cora! Kill 'em all! That's what I did." Then she told the story of how she had put two tablespoons of arsenic into a pepper box and then mixed the poison into the family's bowl of cottage cheese that they ate each morning.

Now they couldn't stop her from seeing Guy Berry. Ceely told her friend that as her father lay dying she went outdoors and dumped the remaining cheese into the barnyard, then threw the pepper box into the weeds. The chickens died within minutes and she buried all of them.

She was free at last, she went on, to marry Guy Berry. She knew he had always loved her. Why else had he stopped his farm chores to come to the fence to greet her? Now they could live together in her family's home. But Guy still had not come around, she told Cora, and she was puzzled by that.

Mr. Davis was hidden behind a buggy on the barn floor beneath the hay loft. He'd heard everything.

Ceely lived on alone in her parents' home for several days. No one came. Out of fear and loneliness, she turned to her parents' good friends, the John Ohlers, who lived two miles away. She told Mrs. Ohler about the poisonings and was quickly arrested. The people of Pleasant Valley were shocked. They were also divided as to the guilt or innocence of Ceely Rose, despite the testimony of Mr. Davis and Mrs. Ohler; rancor split the community.

Constable Pluck, prosecuting attorney Augustus A. Douglass, and Cora Davis visited Ceely in jail. The purpose of the visit apparently was to hear what she would say in the presence of her friend. But the prosecutor warned Ceely that anything she said could be used against her in court. Nevertheless, she confessed to poisoning the cheese with the intent of killing her family.

Later, at the request of the prosecutor, several physicians who had treated the family in their fatal illnesses visited Ceely in her cell, and again she talked freely about the poisonings.

The trial of Celia Rose for the murder of David Rose opened on Monday afternoon, October 12, 1896. The courtroom was packed, many of the spectators coming from long distances.

Both the prosecution and the defense agreed that the main issue to be determined was the responsibility of the defendant for the crime. Was she mentally unstable? Did she understand what she had confessed to having done? Establishment of guilt was the secondary issue. The jury must resolve both issues.

The prosecution called coroner George W. Baughman, who testified as follows:

"I was telephoned on June 30 by Dr. Rudd of Perrysville to come to the Rose homestead immediately. By the time I reached the house David was already dead. I talked to Celia about her family, but avoided any mention of sickness. When I called again, however, upon the death of Walter Rose, I talked with Celia about the cause of sickness. She said she couldn't account for it at all, but didn't think the deaths had been caused by anything the family had eaten.

"When I went back to the house after the death of Mrs. Rose, I strongly suspected that Celia had murdered her family by putting poison in the coffee. At the inquest of July 7, Celia denied it.

"But at the cemetery, following her mother's burial, Celia took me aside and confessed the crimes in detail."

The question then arose as to admitting the coroner's testimony into evidence.

With the jury removed from the courtroom, both prosecution and defense argued at length, and the court finally held that Dr. Baughman's testimony should go before the jury. The trial proceeded.

Ceely's friend Tracy Davis was called to the stand.

"I live about a mile from the Rose house," she began, "and have known Ceely for about fifteen years. During that time Ceely and I became good friends. We often attended parties and literary society meetings together. When I asked about her father's death, Ceely said she didn't want to talk about it. She talked mostly about Guy Berry and the wonderful life together that they would now have. I told Ceely she had better tell the truth about the deaths and she said she would tell me a week later. This was before she went to stay with the Ohlers. Then, Cora, Ceely and I went to the Roses' barnyard and found the pepper box under the weeds, just where Ceely said she'd thrown it. She picked it up and exclaimed, 'Oh, there's some of it right now. I thought I'd washed it all out.'"

When Guy Berry's father, George, was called, he said he lived next door to the Roses and he had complained to Mr. Rose about Celia going out to the fields to interrupt Guy and his brother, Clyde, at their work. Mr. Rose said there was little he could do. Mr. Berry said he was at the Rose house again when the family was sick, and that on his way home he had noticed several dead chickens in the Roses' yard.

Physicians who had participated in the examination of the victims testified that each had died of arsenic poisoning.

On Wednesday afternoon, October 14, witnesses for the defense were sworn in. Ceely Rose took the stand and admitted that she had murdered her family, then told the court how she had done it. She had killed them, she said, because of their refusal to let her see Guy Berry and also because of other family troubles.

Had Guy induced her to murder her family? No, she said, the devil had instructed her to do it.

The judge reminded the jury that a question sometimes arises as to the degree of credit to be given to admissions of guilt by a defendant. He told them that much depends upon the situation of the accused and of the witnesses, and the attendant circumstances. "The evidence of verbal confessions of guilt," he explained, "is to be received with great caution."

Rev. E. H. Dolbeer, of Lucas, Ohio, was called to testify as to Ceely's sanity. While he admitted that he was not an expert in mental matters, he said he had testified before in murder cases and had more than a rudimentary understanding of insanity.

"Celia will not do a thing if told not to do it," be began. "If Celia had been taught for years that murder was wrong she would have known it was wrong. But she was not of sound mind when I first saw her. She is not a raving maniac but she is definitely insane."

Lavina Andrews, who lived one-half mile north of the Roses, testified that she'd known Ceely for sixteen or seventeen years and had been in school with her. She said that Ceely did poorly in her schoolwork and seemed mostly interested in watching the boys play ball. Lavina said she didn't think Ceely capable of murder.

Emma Halderman, a teacher in the Valley Hall district where the Rose family lived, stated that Ceely was weak-minded. And Mrs. John Ohler made a similar statement, saying that Ceely could never earn a living, that her mind was not well balanced.

Eva Tucker, who taught Celia Rose during the winter of 1893–94, testified that she considered the accused silly and of unsound mind. She believed that Ceely had never been taught right from wrong and that she did not realize the enormity of her crime. "She could not get along in the world without being directed and taken care of," Mrs. Tucker concluded.

Mrs. Willard Darling of Perrysville had also taught Ceely, and her testimony reflected that of Eva Tucker. Mrs. Darling said that she considered the defendant an imbecile with a very limited idea of right and wrong. Said Mrs. Darling, "She wouldn't know it was wrong to commit murder."

The judge gave further instruction to the jury and they retired for deliberation. Ninety minutes later the verdict was handed down: not guilty by reason of insanity.

Celia Rose was returned to jail, as there were two more indictments against her for murder: one for poisoning her mother, and a second for poisoning her brother.

She was finally adjudged irresponsible because of psychosis and was committed to the Toledo State Hospital until the Lima institution for the criminally insane was completed. She died there at the age of eighty-three.

Sometime later, Louis Bromfield, the Pulitzer Prize–winning author and conservationist, bought a large tract of land in Pleasant Valley, including the old Rose place, and created Malabar Farm. He built a thirty-two-room country home for his family, and welcomed friends who sought relaxation in the beautiful rolling countryside.

Today Malabar is a state park open to the public. It is still a working farm with dairy cows, beef cattle, horses, ducks, goats, and chickens. All of the original buildings, including the "Big House," remain, and a number of them have been renovated.

The farm manager and his family live in the old David Rose house. They know the story of Celia Rose, but have never seen the ghost of the insane little girl who grew up there believing that the boy next door would marry her.

Some of the more romantic, however, say that on certain nights Ceely's face can be seen pressed against a window, watching for the strong young man who pitched hay in the summer fields.

Aunt Jane Among Others

Oklahoma is a land of such wide-open spaces that ghosts have a hard time finding places to hide. This may account for the dearth of hauntings the state can call its own. Those which have been reported are often connected with the old days of the tumultuous Oklahoma frontier.

Who Killed Aunt Jane?

A rustic grave at old Fort Washita holds the earthly remains of one Aunt Jane. She died sometime between 1842, when the fort was built, and 1861, the year Confederate forces overran it. Exactly who she was remains a mystery. Two facts *are* known—she was murdered, and her ghost makes infrequent appearances at the fort's ruins.

The legend of Aunt Jane has numerous twists and turns. For example, there is the question of how she died.

That she met a premature death is unarguable. But who committed the homicide? Either thieves or rogue soldiers killed her, it is posited, and she may have been beheaded in the process. Once, Aunt Jane's ghost, dressed in a snowy white gown, was seen by a young woman near the fort. The apparition was headless. The eyewitness didn't say how she knew it was Aunt Jane.

However, even the vacancy above her shoulders is in dispute. Another witness swore that Aunt Jane's ghost occasionally rode full-tilt through Fort Washita, her long black hair billowing out behind her.

The *why* of Aunt Jane's murder is clearer than the *who* behind her demise. She was rumored to have secreted a cache of money somewhere at the fort and was killed by blackguards trying to wangle its location from her—without success. Despite many attempts to locate this alleged buried treasure, it has never been found.

One man said that treasure-seekers faced Aunt Jane's presence even if they couldn't see her. When they tried to dig into the ground, "some force would hold the pick and not let it touch the ground."

Dr. Stalcup was a physician in the vicinity of Fort Washita around the turn of the century. He claimed that Aunt Jane's ghost bothered him for years. When his daughter Molly was born, he said the unrelenting revenant occasionally "possessed" her. One night the ghost threatened to cut off all the little girl's hair. Only when the child's mother fell to her knees in prayer did Aunt Jane end her threats!

Another Oklahoma army post has a ghostly component to it. The century-old officers' quarters on the Old Post Quadrangle at Fort Sill Military Reservation was the subject of a spate of ghost stories in the base newspaper during the mid-1970s.

Workmen making repairs in one of the houses frequently heard running footsteps coming from an upstairs room. They knew no one was supposed to be up there. And no one was—they checked twice. According to one account, the men completed the job in record time and left.

A Case of Mistaken Identity

Proctor is a speck on the Oklahoma map, lying in western Adair County a handful of miles from the Arkansas border. Its lack of centrality to the social fabric of the state, however, has no bearing on its suitability as the hometown of a ghost.

A house in the village had been built well before statehood by a man who later died under what is usually characterized as "unknown circumstances." By and by, it was relatively well known in the community that the man's ghost "lived" in the attic of his old residence.

An older couple later owned the house. They knew the stories, as did their grown children. As it happened, one of their daughters, whom we shall call Barbara, came visiting with her small children. A few days with Grandpa and Grandma. And a ghost.

Barbara and her mother stayed up late one night talking. When they finally turned in for the night, Barbara settled into the carpeted front bedroom, sharing it with one of her children. Her mother and father slept in a back bedroom, separated from her daughter's room by a shared bathroom. Doors into the bathroom were left open.

Barbara crawled into bed and turned out her light, casting the house into darkness. Moments later, Barbara heard the springs of her mother's bed squeak. Footfalls across the linoleum floors of the back bedroom and bathroom approached Barbara's room. They scuffed across her carpet. She thought her mother had come to tell her something.

Barbara was puzzled when her mother didn't speak up.

"Mother, what do you want?" she whispered, trying not to awaken her sleeping child.

No reply was forthcoming. The presence remained.

Again she repeated her question, this time at full voice.

"MOTHER, WHAT DO YOU WANT!"

From the distant bedroom came her mother's answering query, "What did you say?"

The Pesky Window

There was something wrong with the Kight House, neighbors said, especially up on that second floor. That's where an east bedroom window had the peculiar tendency not to hold its panes of glass. They'd break or fall out just as fast as they were replaced. For no apparent reason. Well, perhaps one. A ghost in the room may have had something to do with the difficulties.

The house was built in the late 1800s by Dr. A. J. Lane, a well-known general practitioner in northeast Oklahoma. He was the attending physician at the birth of humorist Will Rogers. His home in the Oowala region west of Foyil was a showplace, a solid frame home snuggled amongst a verdant cedar grove. He built it to house a large family. That was not to be.

Doctors still made house calls in that bygone era, and one night during a driving rainstorm Dr. Lane set out to visit several patients. He developed pneumonia after riding around for hours in wet clothing. He died not long after, in his forty-fifth year.

During Dr. Lane's final days, the story is told, he occupied the bedroom with the annoying window.

The house eventually passed into the hands of H. Tom "Big Tom" Kight, a congressman and lawyer. About 1938 he rented the place to a family that seemed to have the most trouble with the bedroom window. Its glass broke or tumbled out for no real reason. Even the rags they stuffed in the opening wouldn't stay put. The family always believed it was the ghost of Dr. Lane still hanging around.

A visiting relative was warned about the bedroom, but he decided to stay there anyway. In the middle of the night he came sprinting down the staircase carrying his blankets. A face had appeared in the cracked window, he sputtered.

After the family moved out in 1947, the house stayed empty for many years until it was eventually razed by the government. Oologah Reservoir now covers the land on which the house stood.

Head Hunter

The fields around Dalton Hill, near Owasso, northeast of Tulsa, have yielded several burial sites of ancient people. One grave hasn't been found—that of an Indian woman beheaded by a Spanish traveler sometime in the nineteenth century. Until it is, her ghost will continue its wandering ways.

The Spaniard was one of the many explorers who passed through the region. Why he killed the woman isn't known, only that he met her and left only her bloody torso beside the trail. He took her head.

Native American belief holds that a body must be whole to have eternal peace. Until then, the soul is condemned to walk the earth.

Should you see a headless woman dressed in Indian garb in that region of Oklahoma, be gentle with her. Perhaps even help her look for what she's lost. It would be a very good deed.

Old Cowboys and Moonlit Nights . . .

There are scores of abandoned ranches strewn across the Oklahoma landscape. Where once cowboys and cattle roamed, only memories and crumbling foundations remain. Gone are the days when distant neighbors gathered to swap stories and songs as they helped to raise a new barn, to brand cattle, or to celebrate Independence Day.

A few miles south of Ponca City was just such a ruin: the remains of the famous 101 Ranch and its three-story stucco villa known throughout the territory as the Whitehouse.

The 101 Ranch was a sort of headquarters for the cowboys and cowgirls who made up an Oklahoma "show biz" contingent for the western shows so popular at the turn of the century. Well into the 1920s, it was not unusual at all on a spring night for the likes of Pawnee Bill and his wife, May Lillie, the Miller Brothers—Zack, Joe, and George—Ike Club, Col. Zack Mulhall, and Will Rogers himself to gather around a campfire at the 101 Ranch exchanging stories and singing range ballads.

The Whitehouse has been gone for decades, but the songs and stories still linger. Legends of mysterious voices and snatches of melancholy piano music coming from the old 101 Ranch site are spread among those who believe that sturdy old singing cowboys can ride the range forever.

Pawnee Bill was the leader of the "Oklahoma Boomers," a singing group based in Rock Falls in the early 1880s. He later formed his own wild west show before Buffalo Bill Cody persuaded him to come along with his. To have heard Pawnee Bill criticize Cody, however, it's a wonder the union lasted. "He was the vainest man I ever knew," Pawnee Bill said of Cody. "Spent hours before a gold-framed mirror in his private car on the show."

The old Pawnee Bill ranch is now a landmark, just outside the town of Pawnee, off U.S. Highway 64.

The Miller brothers, also raised on an Oklahoma ranch, owned the largest wild west show in the nation by the mid-1920s. Their outfit traveled in a train one hundred cars long!

Col. Zack Mulhall formed his own show and gave Will Rogers his start as a trick roper. The homespun cowboy-philosopher is regarded as one of the greatest ropers of all time.

Rogers was always a guest at his old compatriots' ranches whenever he appeared in northeast Oklahoma, which was all too infrequently. He had become world-famous by the Roaring Twenties through his appearances in the Ziegfeld Follies and Hollywood movies. He was also a writer whose column of humorous comments on the news was syndicated to 350 daily newspapers.

On one night around 1925, Rogers had played an engagement in Ponca City. After the show, he joined his old compatriots at the shimmering, white stucco 101 ranchhouse. Pawnee Bill and his May were there, as were the Miller brothers, Colonel Mulhall, and many others. It may have been one of the greatest gatherings of western show business veterans ever assembled.

Rogers roamed through the crowd, joining in the romantic songs, although his nasal twang wasn't suited for even the most artless range ballad. Witnesses say he gnawed on pickled pigs' feet as he spoke to one and all of his great new love—flying.

"Some day we will be flying around the world," he told anyone who would listen. "And I intend to do it as soon as possible."

Rogers was killed along with pilot Wiley Post ten years later in a plane crash at Point Barrow, Alaska.

Pawnee Bill's wife, May Lillie, who had stayed at home on her ranch after her husband joined Buffalo Bill's show, played endless cowboy ballads on the old piano. The wind soughing through the elms and unkempt cedars carried her music and the untrained cowboy voices through the nighttime. In the distance a coyote howled.

Hour after hour the gifted Mrs. Lillie played for her cowboy troubadours. It didn't matter that most of them were no more on key than the irritated coyote, for their songs came from their hearts and their sentimental remembrances of range campfires from long ago.

A steady wind and a moonlit night can produce some odd sounds and shadows where the old 101 Ranch Whitehouse once stood. If you listen especially carefully, even snatches of Will Rogers's guileless twang might reach your ears.

OREGON
Rue and Muriel

Heceta Head Lighthouse has been a welcoming beacon for maritime travelers for a century. Situated thirteen miles north of Florence, Oregon, the lighthouse is by all accounts one of the most photographed West Coast landmarks. Its automated light, the most powerful in Oregon, is visible for twenty-one miles at sea.

The light itself is operated by the United States Coast Guard. Visitors to the lighthouse grounds, however, will see much more than a conical brick tower housing the five-hundred-watt lamp. Below the lighthouse is Heceta House, a lovingly restored Queen Anne–style structure built a century ago and used as a residence by the early Lighthouse Service and later Coast Guard lightkeepers and their families. So picturesque is the house that it's been used as a backdrop for several motion pictures, including service as actor Patrick Duffy's rented house in the CBS Television film *Cry for the Strangers.*

Heceta House was named to the National Register of Historic Places in 1978 and is all that is left of a once-thriving, small nineteenth-century community forced by its isolation to be completely self-sufficient. The three families normally stationed at the lighthouse and a few nearby pioneer settlers even had their own schoolhouse. The thirteen-mile trip to Florence took an entire day by horseback or buggy. Heceta House was actually a duplex designed to accommodate two families. Another house used for the chief lighthouse keeper has been demolished.

A unique arrangement among five state and federal agencies is responsible for operating Heceta Head and the adjacent grounds. The light itself is maintained and monitored by the Coast Guard from its base in Florence. Devil's Elbow State Park, which surrounds the lighthouse grounds, is administered by the State of Oregon. Two small, offshore islands are wildlife preserves managed by the U.S. Fish and Wildlife Service. The spit of land known as Heceta Head and several acres around the lighthouse are owned by the U.S. Forest Service. And Heceta House is operated by Lane Community College under a lease from the federal government. The college provides a caretaker, maintenance, and repairs, and has used the house as a classroom building for coastal extension classes.

Perched as it is several hundred feet above the pounding surf and surrounded by undulating coastal mountains blanketed with pine trees, Heceta Head causes most visitors to gasp at the breathtakingly dramatic vista. But there are other reasons visitors might draw a sharp breath. It would happen should they see Rue, the ghost that some say walks upon Heceta Head.

Unlike the ghosts that might be found in other old, isolated places, Rue's appearances are of relatively recent vintage. Accounts of her infrequent visits go back only twenty years.

In the early 1970s, Lane Community College hired a young man and his wife to act as caretakers at Heceta House. At about the same time, the Forest Service contracted with a local carpenter to perform some remodeling at the old house. All three people were the first to experience the haunting at Heceta House, as they detailed in numerous interviews over the years. However, the caretakers did not wish to be interviewed for this book. The details of what happened to them are based upon various interviews they gave to the media.

Shortly after the caretakers moved in, they noticed certain things that they could not attribute to the normal creaks and groans of an old house, even one buffeted by the winds and storms of the Oregon coast. A clicking like that of a light switch being flipped on and off, or footfalls coming up from a cellar, for instance. The house was always warm in the middle of the night—highly unusual given that most haunted houses seem colder than normal—so that the couple woke up literally sweating from the heat. Cupboard doors tightly latched stood open hours later.

One evening, the caretaker, his wife, and some guests blanched during a card party when a high-pitched scream seemed to come from the middle of the room in which they sat. The couple's two cats jumped at the sudden cry. In another anomalous episode, rat poison placed in the attic was gone the next day. In its place was . . . a silk stocking.

Living an isolated life on the seacoast might cause all sorts of imaginings, especially during the frequent storms that pummel the Oregon coast, but the caretakers have said this is definitely not the case at Heceta House.

If the husband had any doubts, he told one reporter, they really started to disappear the night he ran up the staircase to get his car keys from the bedroom. As he rounded the last landing before the top floor, he caught Rue "off guard." What the caretaker saw was a portion of a long skirt quickly crossing the hallway. With a distinctive swish, the figure melted through a locked door and into an unused bedroom.

Several college students taking a class at Heceta House reported seeing a "gray puff of smoke," long and flowing, moving up the same staircase.

The caretaker's wife also saw Rue. The young wife was bringing dishes into the kitchen from a dinner party when she glimpsed a "full person" going through a doorway. The ghost was holding something in her hand.

On another night, three dozen dishes stored in kitchen cupboards started rattling "just as though there was an earthquake." When the husband reached the kitchen, the noise suddenly stopped.

The most dramatic experience with Rue occurred when carpenter James Anderson was hired to make some repairs to Heceta House. The Forest Service developed a long-range plan in the 1970s to restore the grounds and exterior of the house to its 1893 appearance. That has been beautifully accomplished. Plans also called for restoration of Heceta House's interior so that occasional tours and open houses could be held, especially during the city of Florence's Rhododendron Festival each May.

What happened to James Anderson, however, gave Heceta House its first regional notoriety as the home of a ghost, according to Stephanie Finucane, author of a historical study of Heceta Head.

Anderson was working in one room of the attic. He had been puzzled by a couple of minor annoyances. Tools vanished only to turn up in another room, sandpaper didn't stay where he placed it. The room Anderson was in can only be reached through a trap door in the upstairs hallway. The high ceilings, however, made it necessary for him to pull himself up through the trap door after standing near the top of a stepladder.

On this day he was polishing the inside of an attic window. As he wiped his cleaning rag over the glass, he caught sight of the reflection of someone behind him. He turned around and gasped. Coming toward him was a very old woman, dressed in a floor-length skirt. She wasn't walking, but rather seemed to float a few inches off the floor.

Anderson edged back against the wall but the ghost kept coming. The open trap door was only a few feet away but to get to it he would have to brush past the woman. As she drew closer she seemed to be growing less distinct. Summoning all the courage he could, Anderson rushed toward the trap door—passing directly through the fading apparition.

The carpenter literally leaped through the trap door and to the hallway floor below. He ran from the house, shouted for his helpers, and all three jumped in his truck and roared off.

He told few people of his experience, but did describe the events to the caretaker when at last he did return several days later to finish the job. The caretakers thought Anderson's experience fit with the earlier ghostly activities in the house.

Anderson decided to stay out of the house for a while. He figured it would be "safer" to finish what exterior scraping and painting and repairs had to be done before regaining his nerve to go back in. He was wrong. Rue was not through with James Anderson.

Earlier, the workmen had broken another attic window when a ladder fell against it. The glass shards were still scattered on the attic floor. Anderson was standing on the scaffolding finishing repairs to the window when he glanced inside. Rue was hovering on the other side of the glass. He took a long, hard look to convince himself his mind wasn't playing tricks, maybe even blinking a time or two. It was her, all right.

The carpenter backed down the scaffolding, packed up his tools and left Heceta House. Enough was enough.

Rue apparently decided to finish the repair work herself. That night as the caretaker and his wife lay in bed, they heard what sounded like the swoosh-swoosh-swoosh of a broom sweeping across hardwood floors. It was coming from the attic. The next morning they found all the broken window glass swept into a neat pile near the new window. There was no broom in the locked attic, although there were distinct broom marks on the dusty floor.

But who is Rue? And why does she haunt Heceta House?

The most frequently told legend relating to the ghost's identity concerns a young baby who died while her family lived at Heceta House decades ago. She was said to have been buried near the house. There is a claim that old photographs of the house appear to show a tombstone in the yard. A daughter of lighthouse keeper Olaf L. Hansen, who worked at Heceta Head from 1904 to 1920, claimed that a cement slab on a point of land between the house and the lighthouse marked the child's grave. The marker, if it was indeed a tombstone, is now overgrown with weeds.

It is surmised that Rue could be the child's mother, come back to claim her baby. Or perhaps she's looking for the abandoned grave. A few say it's the child herself haunting the house, but that seems unlikely. Unless there are two ghosts, of course.

One man who took a keen interest in Heceta Head and its protection is Loyd Collett, a research assistant with Siuslaw National Forest, the agency responsible for Heceta House.

"We don't know where the grave is," Collett said of reports that a child had been buried on the Head. "We don't even know for sure if the story is true. If there was a child buried out there, we don't know if it's been moved or what."

Collett has two theories about the identity of the woman who haunts Heceta Head. The first holds that it might be Mrs. Frank DeRoy, the strong-willed, domineering wife of an early lighthouse assistant. Collett describes her as a fastidious housekeeper remembered for being the first person to repaint the drab, government-gray walls of Heceta House. It's entirely possible, he thinks, that she's still hanging around looking after "her" house. However, nothing in the official record indicates that Mrs. DeRoy lost a child.

Collett has a second idea about the ghost's identity. It might be the wife of another long-ago lighthouse keeper, a "mother who lost a child and is still not able to cross over to the other life. She can't separate from the child who had this premature, perhaps tragic, death. It must have been a very emotional time for the family," Collett said. The lighthouse's isolation from even the most basic medical facilities made the simplest childhood diseases potentially fatal.

"I believe there was a child that died, but I don't believe it's buried there," he said. If that's the case, the baby's rambling mother may never rest in peace, unless someone gently tells her to be on her way.

Collett has had no direct experience with the ghost at Heceta House, but he is willing to suspend his disbelief.

"I think he [the caretaker] is sincere. My own sensitivity to those things probably doesn't permit me to see a ghost. But I believe there can be such things. I've talked to people . . . there are things going on out there that can be explained in no other way."

The Girl from the Sea

If the identity of the ghost at Heceta Head remains a mystery, there is no question about who probably haunts the former lighthouse at Yaquina Bay State Park in Newport, Oregon. The ghost is one Muriel Trevenard, and her unsolved death 125 years ago has resulted in one of the most persistent legends of the Oregon coast.

Even without its ghost, the Yaquina Bay beacon is unique among historical Oregon coastal lighthouses for several reasons.

The lighthouse was in use for just three years, from its construction in 1871 until 1874, when a new lighthouse went up just three miles north at Yaquina Head. The federal government decided the Head was in a better position to protect shipping along the rugged coast. Light tender Charles H. Pierce, his wife Sarah, and their ten children were the only full-time occupants of the building. They left when the Yaquina Head light was turned on.

The lighthouse is a single structure. Rather than building a separate light tower, the whale-oil light was placed in a tower above the lightkeeper's living quarters. The clapboard structure is the second-oldest lighthouse in Oregon, and the oldest structure of its kind in the state.

From 1874 to 1896, the house was deserted. Later, the Coast Guard used it to house guardsmen, and the Life Saving Service moved in about 1906. Yaquina Bay State Park directors lived in the lighthouse during the 1930s. But the lighthouse has been vacant for most of its history.

The Lincoln County Historical Society succeeded in saving the rapidly crumbling structure by having it declared a historical landmark in 1956. Extensive renovation by the State of Oregon was begun in 1974. The old lighthouse is now a popular museum of coastal history.

The story of Muriel Trevenard and her ghost is passed along to all who ask about her when visiting the Yaquina Bay Lighthouse. Much of what is known about the tragic young woman derives from an account compiled by Lischen M. Miller, the sister of noted poet Joaquin Miller.

Shortly after the government abandoned Yaquina Bay, the frontier settlement of Newport was startled by the appearance of a sloop sailing into the bay. It docked at the wooden wharf. Most of the crewmen were described as "ruffians" commanded by a dark-browed sailor with an ugly scar stretching from the edge of his lip to his ear.

But the crewmen treated one man on board with unusual deference. He was dressed as a "gentleman" and spoke both cultured English and the unintelligible dialect of sailors. With him was his beautiful daughter, a girl in her late teens.

The stranger introduced himself as Mr. Trevenard. His daughter's name was Muriel. He said nothing of their travels, although he did mention that they were on their way to Coos Bay, farther down the coast. He requested fresh water, their primary purpose in landing at Newport, and sent the crew off to fill the water barrels.

While they were gone, he asked the villagers if his daughter could stay in Newport until his return from Coos Bay. She was not taking well to the sea voyage, and he wanted to spare her any further discomfort.

As was the custom in isolated pioneer settlements, townspeople agreed to provide shelter for the girl. They assured Trevenard that his daughter could stay at the Yaquina Bay Hotel, an establishment far less grand than its name would imply. The landlady promised that she would be responsible for young Muriel's well-being.

With that Trevenard hopped aboard the skiff and rowed back to the sloop with the rest of the crew. Within minutes the ship had weighed anchor and set sail into the Pacific.

The weeks passed, and Muriel settled comfortably into the community. She made friends easily and showed an artistic flair, spending countless hours at the oceanside sketching the dramatic scenery spread before her. And perhaps wondering where her father had gone.

The girl was especially friendly with a group of young people who had come down from the Willamette Valley to vacation along the coast. The mild weather was ideal for picnics and bonfires at the beach, hikes in the forests, and star-gazing at night. Late one afternoon, the group decided to visit the recently abandoned lighthouse. The hotel landlady had been left in charge of the only key and she readily loaned it to the young people.

The youngsters explored the lighthouse, going through the various rooms on the first and second floors, and then climbed to a small room that made up the entire third floor. An iron ladder gave access to the light tower itself, but the way was blocked off. However, the teens noticed a closet off the third-floor room. Shelves covered three of the walls, but a fourth wall was bare.

A young man named Harold Welch, who was particularly smitten with the charming Muriel, noticed that a piece of the wainscoting was loose. When he tugged at it, the boards fell away to disclose an iron door. He was able to remove it, revealing a tunnel about seven or eight feet long. At its end, it appeared to dip downward. Some said the tunnel looked as if it led directly down to the sea. Several of the group laughed nervously about smugglers or pirates using the hidden tunnel for their nefarious purposes.

Darkness and a quickly descending fog convinced the group to leave the house. Harold Welch had the key in hand and stayed behind to close a stubborn front door lock. Muriel stayed with him while the others started down the trail toward town.

At this point, the story takes a most peculiar turn. For some reason never made clear, Muriel asked Harold to let her back into the house. She had left her scarf on the second floor, she explained, and wanted to retrieve it. She told Harold not to trouble himself by going with her. She would be just a few seconds and would let herself out through the kitchen door.

Harold relocked the front door and walked around to the kitchen. When Muriel didn't appear after several minutes, he rejoined his friends who had, by now, gotten about halfway down the trail. He thought she must have gone on without him. Muriel wasn't there. They were deciding what to do about the missing girl when a woman's scream came from the lighthouse.

Harold led the group at a run up the trail. Once inside the house they looked quickly around the first floor. They found bloodstains that appeared to lead up the main staircase.

In the third-floor closet the youngsters found Muriel's bloodstained handkerchief near the iron panel. Oddly, the wainscoting had been replaced and the iron door could not be jimmied open. Earlier, they had left the entrance to the secret tunnel open.

Newport was alerted and searches were made of the lighthouse, the ocean beach, and the surrounding grounds. Muriel Trevenard was never seen again. Nor did her father and his rough crew ever return from the sea.

Stains that look very much like blood still dot the stairs, but it's doubtful that they are Muriel's since the house has undergone extensive remodeling.

A very odd and recent incident at the lighthouse, detailed by author Mike Helm, adds a contemporary twist to the legend of Muriel Trevenard.

A hitchhiker heading north on Highway 101 decided to spend the night near the lighthouse. He climbed the high fence and made his camp adjacent to the house. After cooking his supper over a small fire, he settled into his bedroll. Sometime later he was awakened by the front door opening. Silhouetted in the door frame was a young woman standing in front of a much older man. The room behind them was filled with flickering light, as if coming from wick lamps.

The strange young woman came down the steps. "Harold," she called out as she got closer. The hitchhiker couldn't make out her features in the dim light. When he didn't answer, her tone changed and she spoke directly to him. He would find a job in Newport, she said. With the money he made he could continue on his journey. With that she turned on her heel and disappeared through the front door. The older man followed her inside and shut the door. And just as the mysterious visitor predicted, the traveler soon found work in town.

Author Helm also maintained that a coastal tugboat and a private aircraft reported seeing lights in the lighthouse on the same night the hitchhiker saw the ghostly couple. That is not at all an unusual phenomenon at Yaquina Bay Lighthouse. The Coast Guard and police authorities routinely receive and file such reports under the heading of "Ghosts, Lighthouse."

Inn of the Seventeen Ghosts

On Monday nights in 1972, the 284-year-old General Wayne Inn in Merion, Pennsylvania, was usually closed. But this was a special occasion at the well-known restaurant near Philadelphia. Jean and Bill Quinn and four other psychics were seated at the polished mahogany table in a private dining room on the second floor. Joining the circle were owner Barton Johnson, his wife, and two of his sons. Flickering candles provided the only illumination. Tape recorders with sensitive microphones whirred quietly in the center of the table.

Jean Quinn anticipated a long session. She asked each person to put on a jacket against the anticipated cold, loosen their shoelaces and belts and visit the washroom.

Barton Johnson rose to close the doors. A penetrating chill descended upon the room as if the windows had been thrown open. No sooner had Johnson seated himself once again than both doors flew open. No one entered the room or stood in the dimly lighted hallway. At least no one they could see.

Johnson was impressed.

Jean lowered her head and immediately went into a trance. Within a very few moments, the small group was astonished as the "voices" of a procession of entities introduced themselves. Using Jean and the other mediums to vocalize, each took a turn speaking. First came Wilhelm, one of the Hessian soldiers hired by the British to fight in the American Revolutionary War. He seemed to be the leader. Others followed. Two maids, Sara and Sadie . . . a sad little boy . . . a Native American . . . an African-American . . . *and eight more Hessians.* By the time the séance concluded that night, seventeen ghosts had made their presence known!

Even without its ghosts, the General Wayne Inn has a colorful history. Built on land purchased from William Penn, the stone and timbered inn is reputedly this nation's oldest hostelry in continuous operation. Robert Jones, a Quaker, opened what he called the Wayside Inn in 1704 to provide accommodations for travelers on the nearby Old Lancaster Road from Philadelphia to Radnor. It became the General Wayne Inn in 1795 to honor local resident and celebrated war hero Gen. "Mad Anthony" Wayne.

The handsome three-story building was designed to resemble an English coaching inn. Large, open fireplaces grace each end of the first floor. Small sleeping rooms were provided upstairs near an overhanging porch on which weary guests could visit in comfortable rocking chairs.

Although some alterations have been made, and it no longer provides for overnight guests, the inn looks as it must have in the decades before the founding of the nation. Its unique characteristics have made it a registered National Historic Landmark.

Barton Johnson, a history buff and officer of the Lower Merion Historical Society, bought the General Wayne in 1970. As a child in Merion, he grew up listening to tales of the old haunted inn.

He was, however, far more interested in the mortal record of the inn. That was well documented. There were, for instance, its many uses over the centuries— first as an inn and restaurant, of course, but also later as a post office (Ben Franklin sorted the mail there), a general store, and a social center for newly arrived Welsh immigrants.

Johnson knew that many Revolutionary War battles had been waged around Merion. Indeed the inn had been occupied variously by American patriots, British Redcoats, and the Hessian hirelings.

Johnson had been told that Gen. George Washington and the Marquis de Lafayette had dined on the inn's famous squirrel ragout and pigeon stew.

During the 1800s, wealthy Philadelphians vacationed in the area. Many took meals at the inn, including Edgar Allan Poe. He is said to have written several stanzas of "The Raven" while seated at his favorite table. Until the 1930s a windowpane inscribed with the initials *EAP* etched by the poet himself could be found there.

All of the inn's past Johnson knew as well as his own life, but it in no way prepared him for what was to come. Ironically, he had mixed feelings about his immortal tenants. "I don't believe in ghosts," he said, "but I know they're here. Figure that one out."

Johnson's curiosity was permanently aroused in 1971 when he met Jean and Bill Quinn. The famous New Jersey psychics contacted him to seek permission to study the inn. The couple had heard that the hostel was haunted and wanted to make their own investigation. Johnson said they were welcome at any time.

The Quinns took him at his word and arrived unexpectedly a few weeks later on an extremely busy Friday night. Remembering his promise, Johnson asked what they would like to see. The basement, the Quinns stated.

Johnson escorted the couple down the worn wooden staircase to the cellar and watched in vague interest as Jean ran her hands along the ancient stone walls looking for cold spots. Johnson shrugged his shoulders and left to attend to his customers.

Two hours later, the Quinns reported back. The restaurant was haunted by many entities, Jean told her bemused host. Indeed, she had "spoken" to one spirit, a "very nice guy" named Wilhelm, she said. Although he took an immediate liking to the Quinns, Johnson didn't think much of her discovery.

Another year passed before the Quinns returned in 1972 for the séance at which all the ghosts were identified.

Wilhelm, the spokesghost, told Johnson, the Quinns, and the others at that séance that he had been killed during battle. He was unhappy because his commander saw that he wore a fine uniform and a new pair of boots that could be used by another soldier. They stripped his body and buried him in his skivvies. Wilhelm said he was still searching for his clothes so that be might be buried in proper attire.

His ghostly companions were generally satisfied with their afterlife at the inn, but a few things didn't sit well with them, Wilhelm said through Jean. Weird things.

They loved the dinner music, but couldn't abide the crash of the drummer's cymbals. And the gin and beer didn't taste quite right; nor did the wine. The only thing they really liked was the tea—which, he said, they drank constantly!

All of the spirits seemed to have problems important enough to keep them from resting in peace.

The little boy ghost had lost his mother. He couldn't stop crying long enough for the psychics to learn his name or anything more about him.

Sara and Sadie were saucy revenants from the mid-nineteenth century. They had both worked at the inn and died with a most distressing problem on their minds. A peddler had arrived with a wagonload of Persian rugs. To own such fine carpets at that time was considered the epitome of luxury. He told the women that he was expecting a buyer to meet him at the inn. Several days passed and the prospect still hadn't showed. The peddler asked Sara and Sadie to look after the rugs while he searched for the missing buyer. The girls agreed.

Days lengthened into weeks and weeks into months and the peddler never returned. The women feared that they would be accused of having stolen the rugs. At the séance, both women said they were still afraid of being accused of theft— even after a century and a half! It was difficult to get their story because, as Johnson recalled, "they were reluctant talkers and treated us [at the séance] as intruders." They didn't say how or why they died so young.

Johnson was certain the African-American was a twentieth-century ghost, a man called Chase, a longtime employee who had been working at the inn when Johnson bought it. Chase's job was to open the clams and oysters and help with the salads and desserts.

Two weeks after Johnson took over the inn, Chase confided in his boss that he had talked to Mr. McClain on the previous night. Johnson remembered the conversation clearly.

"No, Chase," Johnson replied. "You couldn't have spoken to him. Mr. McClain is dead." Richard McClain had been the previous owner of the inn.

"I know that," Chase insisted. "And I spoke to him."

"Well," Johnson said, not wishing to offend the man, "if you ever see Mr. McClain again, tell him I said hello."

A few weeks passed and Chase again pulled Johnson aside. "I saw Mr. McClain again last night and gave him your regards. He said to say hello to you."

"Thanks," was all Johnson could manage to say.

Several days later Chase was dead.

There was one ghost Jean Quinn and her group did not meet that night in the early seventies. He would appear several years later and is, or rather was, another Hessian soldier named Ludwig. He may have been one of Wilhelm's comrades. His story is the strangest of all.

It begins in 1976 when Johnson was away on vacation. A part-time contractor and psychic named Mike Benio from Olyphant, Pennsylvania arrived at the General Wayne with a peculiar request. Every morning at two o'clock, Benio was accosted at his house by a ghost that came into his bedroom and sat on the bed. The apparition explained that he had been killed in a Revolutionary War battle and was buried in the basement of "an old inn" near Philadelphia . . . in a place called Merion! The ghost wanted Benio to dig up his body and bury it in a cemetery.

When Johnson returned and heard the story from employees, he telephoned Benio. Johnson gave his permission to dig on the condition that he didn't endanger the foundation and that he would repair any damage.

Benio spent two days in the basement. He discovered a small room extending under the parking lot at the front of the building. Some broken pottery and what appeared to be bones were scattered on the earthen floor. Were they human remains? Neither Johnson nor Benio was able to find out.

Ludwig must have appreciated Benio's efforts, however, as he never again made an appearance.

All the Hessians left quite an impression on the inn. There are several other accounts of encounters with old soldiers who never die.

A picture of one of the German soldiers hangs on a wall of the gracious main dining room. His severe posture seems quite out of place in the elegant warmth and gentility of this room, with its aged ceiling beams and plank walls. Gleaming brass chandeliers throw gentle light on tables set with snow-white linen.

Several employees say they have seen someone who matches the man in the painting. A maître d' had so many run-ins with the ghost in the basement that he finally refused to go downstairs. A luncheon hostess met several soldiers in various places at the inn—striding through the dining room, sitting in the bar after hours, and upstairs in the private dining rooms.

But most uneasy of all may have been Nathan, an elderly porter who cleaned the floors at closing time.

The inn opens for dinner at four o'clock on Sundays, but Barton Johnson usually goes in earlier to inspect the place. One Sunday he found an irregular line of trash strewn across the middle of the dining room floor. He called out for Nathan, but there was no answer. On a hunch, he telephoned the porter's home. Nathan answered.

Why hadn't he finished his work? Johnson asked.

"Well, Mr. Johnson . . ." Nathan hesitated. "I was sweeping that dining room when a fellow just like that picture you have [on the wall] came over and walked right through me. I left."

If the ghosts at the General Wayne Inn are sometimes frightening, they are also playful. It is not uncommon, for instance, for young women sitting on the barstools to feel someone blowing on their necks. Johnson blamed his ghosts and said that "game" was played for over a year.

Despite Wilhelm's assertions that his spectral friends didn't like modern alcohol, the ghosts do frequent the bar late at night. When Johnson told Jean Quinn of the after-hours tippling, she loaned him a tape recorder. She directed him to load it with a fresh tape, place it on the fireplace mantel near the bar counter and turn it on when he left for the night. He followed her advice.

Johnson played the tape the following morning. He heard nothing for a long time, but then came the familiar noise of swiveling barstools, a noise unmistakable to the veteran tavernkeeper.

Then someone, or something, in the perfectly empty building turned on the water faucet and held a glass under it.

The revelry had begun about a half-hour after Johnson closed for the evening.

A ghost may also have been in the bar on another occasion. An elderly woman and frequent customer had been out to dinner and a movie with her nephew. She asked him to stop by the General Wayne for a nightcap. Johnson recalls that she loved to sit on the barstool, listen to the musical combo playing in the lounge, and sip nothing stronger than ginger ale.

On this night, her nephew reminded her that it was Monday and the inn was always closed on that day, but to placate her, he drove past. There were no cars but she insisted that someone appeared to be inside. Her nephew pulled into the parking lot and waited while she looked through a window. In the dim light filtering from inside, she saw a man sitting on a barstool, slumped over the counter. He wore a peculiar-looking soldier's uniform. As he turned toward her, she fled back to the car.

Only once have the ghosts become malicious.

Johnson opened the inn one morning to find the cash register drawer partly open and each compartment filled with water. He glanced toward the ceiling expecting to see stains where the roof had leaked. He saw none. Instead his gaze settled on a row of carafes sitting on a shelf. They were used to serve wine. But on this day each was filled with water.

He emptied the glasses, dumped the water out of the cash register and tried to work it; the machine shorted out.

An insurance adjuster inspected the roof for leaks and found none. He asked Johnson what had happened. "I don't really know," Johnson replied cautiously. Although he has no absolute proof of how the water mysteriously appeared, he believes the inn's ghosts were somehow responsible. To him, it is the only "reasonable" explanation.

As word spread of the haunting of the General Wayne Inn, area media ran a number of feature stories, usually around Halloween. A television station got wind of the ghosts and sent a crew to interview Johnson and perhaps capture one of the unbidden visitors on film. They stayed all day, but nothing out of the ordinary happened until . . .

The story was scheduled for several days later at 11:20 P.M. during a regular newscast.

The bar was full of patrons when Johnson turned on the television set above the bar. He told the customers about the feature. The first half of the news program went fine. But then the ghosts got into the act.

Johnson described what happened next.

"When our segment came on the whole picture started going around—a perfect picture with no flopover and no snow, but it just kept going around the whole time until our segment was over. It's never done that before and it's never done that since. All of my customers were watching in disbelief," he remembered, shaking his head.

He checked with neighbors to see if they had had trouble with their sets that night. None of them had.

The ghosts seem to be particularly active in the winter months. Johnson recalled one incident that, once again, left him puzzled.

A late-winter blizzard struck early one afternoon. A few hours later snowdrifts lay high against the front door and Johnson decided to close early. He had served only two lunches and knew there would be little if any dinner business.

Johnson locked the doors and went into the kitchen to tell the chef, who had been cleaning the refrigerators and washing a huge mixer with many attachments.

"Let's go right now," Johnson told his chef. "It's getting worse by the minute."

He waited for the man to put away the mixer's attachments and noticed for the first time a pile of clean hand towels folded into neat squares on the butcher block table. He decided to leave them there until the next morning. The men left together.

By morning the storm had abated and the inn opened for business as usual. A few minutes after the staff arrived, the chef stopped Johnson.

"Who was in here last night?" he asked.

"No one," Johnson replied.

The chef waved him into the kitchen, where the mixer attachments were scattered across the floor and the clean towels thrown into disarray.

Johnson wasn't particularly surprised; peculiar things like that were happening all the time. On several occasions, the housekeeper found both front doors unlocked when Johnson or one of his sons had securely bolted them the night before.

The ghosts also harassed Barton Johnson's wife.

The business office is on the third floor. After a busy day, Mrs. Johnson helps the bookkeeper with the paperwork. Charge cards, in particular, require several forms to be filled out.

In the beginning, Mrs. Johnson would add a column of figures on the small adding machine and decide the total didn't look right. It might be fifty or a hundred dollars off. Then she would "test" the machine. Two plus two equals . . . five? It gave the wrong answer. She would add columns of simple numbers and get erroneous results every time.

Then she had an idea. Was it possible the ghosts hovered nearby and tinkered with the adding machine? On an impulse she ordered the "guys" out of the room. She had work to do, she scolded. The adding machine worked perfectly from then on.

The coauthor of this book had a firsthand look at one of the ghosts in 1986.

Barton Johnson and Mrs. Scott sat at a table conversing near the bar when a distinct figure of a woman in a long, billowing white skirt and long-sleeved blouse hurried past the dark paneled wall. Her hands and feet were invisible. As the ghost turned, it appeared to be wearing a Dutch-style cap with upswept points at either side. Could the figure have been Sara or Sadie awaiting the return of their peddler, the Dutch cap mistaken for a bonnet? It seems quite possible.

Johnson is remarkably calm about the ghosts wandering the premises of his inn. He seems to understand that the place belongs to them as much as it does to him. He has never capitalized on their antics and has no idea whether they have helped or hurt business.

He also realizes that "his" ghosts are not the horrifying specters of fiction.

"They are certainly not earth-shattering stories," he explains. "But they are what has happened. And they *are* unexplainable."

The Palatine Light

The story of the sloop *Princess Augusta* is one of the most enduring and romantic legends of Block Island, which lies in the Atlantic Ocean some ten miles off the coast of Rhode Island. It is also the most controversial. Although undeniably based on fact, the details of what happened to that fair ship vary considerably. The information that follows is based, in part, upon accounts published in the newspapers at the time.

In August 1738, the three-hundred-ton *Princess Augusta* sailed from Rotterdam bound for Philadelphia, carrying 340 religious and political refugees from the Palatinate, a district on the lower Rhine River of Germany. Although she never reached her destination, the ship has been "seen" on and off for 250 years.

The passengers were a happy throng as they boarded the ship. No couple was happier than Emil Schultz and his wife, Erna. They had saved for years to pay for the passage to America, where relatives had already preceded them and built cottages and even a small country church. Emil wore his best suit and Erna her only silk dress to celebrate the sailing. Sometimes she had to pinch herself to be sure she wasn't dreaming about her new home in a new land. When she thought these thoughts her round face was wreathed in smiles.

But the voyage of the beautiful ship was doomed from the start. Capt. Andrew Long, a popular and able seaman with many years of experience, could not have foreseen the tragedy that lay ahead. The water supply for the *Princess Augusta* was loaded in Rotterdam in casks that previously had contained red and white wines. Mold had formed in the barrels and contaminated the water. By mid-Atlantic, 250 passengers and several crewmen had died and were thrown overboard. Captain Long was one of them. Erna and Emil lived.

A new master, Andrew Brooks, was put in charge of the ninety survivors and the stricken ship continued on its way to America. No one knew much about Captain Brooks. He had tight little eyes that seemed to see everything at once without a turn of the head. His taciturn manner and unsmiling face created uneasiness among the passengers and the crew. Some of the wealthy passengers who had brought their servants with them feared that Brooks might plunder the ship, robbing them of their clothing and their jewels stored in the hold.

But it was not to be looting—not at first. It was extortion. Brooks and several of his crewmen confiscated the food supply and hatched a plan to sell the hard, moldy biscuits for fifty-six dollars each. Those poor souls who couldn't pay starved to death and were dumped into the sea. Erna read the worry lines in her husband's face, but dared not speak her fears. They each ate one biscuit a day, slowly, to ease their hunger. Some days Emil said he wasn't hungry and insisted that Erna eat the two biscuits.

Then, on a raw December morning, Captain Brooks summoned his first mate. "We're going to get a little sea," he said, squinting toward the horizon. The mate nodded. Several hours later, the gale struck. Water rose in great mountains whipped into froth by a merciless wind. Waves roared over the gunwales, silencing the screams of the passengers.

Suddenly, the lookout yelled that land was in sight and Brooks thought that he could make Delaware. But the *Princess Augusta* was blown off course hour after hour, time after time, until she was so badly battered that the captain ordered the mizzen mast cut away. At the same time a leak developed near the "square of the stern," making the ship now nearly impossible to steer.

The weather grew colder and the first flakes of snow heralded a blizzard. The stricken passengers, hungry and freezing to death, huddled close to one another for warmth and comfort. But the heaviest coats and warmest sweaters could not still their shivers. Emil held Erna tightly in his arms and began the hymn, "O God, our help in ages past . . ." and soon every person's voice was raised in song.

Snow piled in drifts in the corners of the deck. The horizon had long since vanished. Visibility was barely three times the length of the ship. The captain finally hoisted a distress flag up the main topmast, but no ship came to the rescue. He calculated that he must be somewhere in the vicinity of Block Island, a rocky speck of land off the coast of Rhode Island.

Then it happened. The vessel struck ground with a tremendous impact, tearing a nine-foot plank out of her bottom and sending the passengers screaming and clutching at one another. Some, in their panic, leaped over the rails and, with broken limbs, dragged themselves to shore.

Here the story of the *Princess Augusta* becomes an inseparable mix of fact and fantasy, of speculation so embellished over the years that no one will ever know exactly what happened. The ship struck the shoals near Block Island either on the night of December 26 or in mid-afternoon of the following day.

According to the one version, the ship was lured to its death by a group of island fishermen known as "wreckers" or "mooncursers." They tied a lantern to the neck of a scrawny nag and sent it grazing on Clay Head, a dangerous rocky place of little turf. The "beacon" would lure any unsuspecting ship to its destruction, after which the greedy perpetrators would take to their longboats to ravage it. Any deaths that might occur on the vessel would be attributed to the mysterious forces of Providence.

On this day, however, the passengers were not killed, but taken to shore. All except one half-crazed woman, Mary Vanderline, who cried that she was waiting for relatives to come aboard to help her protect her gold and silver.

The wreckers then set fire to the sloop and she drifted out to sea on an ebbing tide. The woman's screams were heard until the flaming hulk sank beneath the waves. Some thought that another woman stayed with Mary Vanderline.

* * *

Is there any truth to this report? The eminent folklorist Edward Rowe Snow believed the *Princess Augusta* ran aground on the afternoon of December 27 because Captain Brooks and his crew intended to plunder the ship.

Snow said this is what happened:

Brooks and his men reached shore in a small boat bearing their own belongings and probably those of the wealthiest passengers. When the passengers tried to leave the ship the captain ordered them back. But when its broken bow was carried far up onshore with high tide, the *Princess Augusta* wasn't sailing anywhere. Yet on the next tide she could float away, carrying the passengers to certain death. It was every man, woman, and child for themselves as they fought one another to climb to safety.

Some, too weak and exhausted to walk, fell motionless upon the sand. Others made their way above the rise of the tide where cold, raw winds beat them mercilessly, freezing hands and feet.

It may have been minutes or it may have been hours before help came. But the men of Block Island distinguished themselves that day as they never had before, and their brave, unselfish acts were never forgotten. They plodded through snowdrifts four to five feet deep, bearing armloads of woolen blankets. Then each man hoisted a survivor onto his back and carried him or her to a warm cottage. The two nearest cottages were a mile south of the wreck, and when those were filled the men took the remaining immigrants several miles farther to food and shelter.

Erna Schultz made it to shore and to the safety of a family's cottage. She drifted in and out of consciousness, and cried out for Emil. There was never an answer.

Where were Captain Brooks and his crew? The captain was required to file a report with Simon Ray, chief warden of Block Island, so he and his men presumably spent the night on the warden's farm.

After the rescue, fishermen were able to retrieve twenty chests from the *Princess Augusta* which they stored and later returned to their rightful owners. They finished the unloading only minutes before Captain Brooks appeared and ordered his crew to loosen the ship's cable. At high tide she floated away, and on December 29 supposedly went to pieces on the western shore of the island. The two women on board were never found.

Some of the Palatinate refugees eventually reached Philadelphia; the remaining handful lived out their lives on Block Island. The kind, elderly couple who had taken in Erna continued to care for her. They often found her sitting on a cliff, her ragged silk dress blowing about her knees as she gazed across the water. When she died she was buried in one of the two unmarked plots known as "the Palatine Graves." Eventually the land was plowed and the graves obliterated.

That might have been the end of the story, but the year after the tragedy, scores of reputable seamen began reporting that a mysterious vessel appeared offshore. Her description was always the same: a sloop under full sail, riding low on the water and ablaze from bow to stern. Some even maintained that they'd seen figures in the flaming rigging. Every fishing boat who saw the image hastened to the rescue, but the burning ship sank beneath the waves as quickly as she had appeared, leaving only an angry sea. Southeast gales usually followed the sightings.

Joseph P. Hazard of Narragansett Pier promoted the belief in a connection between the *Princess Augusta* and the apparition of the burning ship, which would come to be known as the "Palatine Light."

Observing it in the summer of 1880, Hazard wrote:

When I first saw the light it was two miles off the coast. I suspected nothing but ordinary sails, however, until I noticed that the light, upon reappearing, was apparently stationary for a few moments, when it suddenly started towards the coast, and, immediately expanding, became much less bright, assuming somewhat the form of a long, narrow jib, sometimes two of them, as if each was on a different mast. I saw neither spar nor hull, but noticed that the speed was very great, certainly not less than fifteen knots, and they surged and pitched as though madly rushing upon raging billows.

Hazard believed that the ill-fated ship had been lured to her death by wreckers, plundered, and then set on fire. It was this version that John Greenleaf Whittier immortalized in his poem "The Palatine," which earned him the wrath of most Block Islanders.

Here is Whittier's account:

> Old wives spinning their webs of tow,
> Or rocking weirdly to and fro
> In and out of the peat's dull glow,
>
> And old men mending their nets of twine,
> Talk together of dream and sign,
> Talk of the lost ship "Palatine,"—
>
> The ship that, a hundred years before,
> Freighted deep with its goodly store,
> In the gales of the equinox went ashore.
>
> Down swooped the wreckers, like birds of prey
> Tearing the heart of the ship away,
> And the dead had never a word to say.
>
> And then, with ghastly shimmer and shine
> Over the rocks and the seething brine,
> They burned the wreck of the "Palatine."
>
> In their cruel hearts, as they homeward sped,
> "The sea and the rocks are dumb," they said:
> "There'll be no reckoning with the dead."
>
> But the year went round, and when once more
> Along their foam-white curves of shore
> They heard the line-storm rave and roar,
>
> Behold! again, with shimmer and shine,
> Over the rocks and the seething brine,
> The flaming wreck of the "Palatine!"

> So, haply in fitter words than these,
> Mending their nets on their patient knees,
> They tell the legend of Manisees.

Whether the ship was actually burned is a matter of conjecture, but over the years further evidence seemed to indicate that she had been torched. A century after the incident hundreds of persons reported sighting a blazing ship off the north coast of Block Island. All were not superstitious folk whose imaginations might have supplied the details of a burning hull, spars, and sails of a specter ship.

Dr. Aaron C. Willey, a resident physician of the island, saw the light twice. In a December 1811 letter he wrote to a friend in New York, Dr. Willey described it as follows:

This curious irradiation rises from the ocean near the northern part of the island. Its appearance is nothing different from a blaze of fire; whether it actually touches the water, or merely hovers over it, is uncertain, for I am informed that no person has been near enough to decide accurately. Sometimes it is small, resembling the light through a distant window; at others expanding to the highness of a ship with all her canvas spread. When large it displays either a pyramidal form, or three constant streams. This light often seems to be in a constant state of mutation; decreasing by degrees it becomes invisible, or resembles a lucid point; then shining anew, sometimes with a sudden flare, at others by a gradual increase to its former size. Often the mutability regards the luster only, becoming less and less bright until it disappears, or nothing but a pale outline can be discerned to its full size, then resuming its full splendor in the manner before related. The duration of its greatest and least state of illumination is not commonly more than three minutes. . . . It is seen at all seasons of the year, and for the most part in the calm weather which precedes an easterly or southerly storm. . . . It has been known to appear several nights in succession.

On another occasion a freighter spotted a ship burning not far distant. As the crewmen watched, the mizzen mast flared and dropped into the sea. The ship was instantly engulfed in flames. The freighter's captain ordered full steam ahead and lifeboats lowered. But as the freighter closed the gap between itself and the sloop, the ship vanished. Only a flat sea shimmered in the twilight.

"Aye," said the captain, drawing on his pipe, " 'twas the ghost of the *Princess Augusta*, the Flying Dutchman of these waters."

A gentleman whose cottage was close to the sea once told his neighbors that the light shone through his windows and illuminated the walls of his room. He judged it to be half a mile offshore.

Mr. R. T. Gardiner, a longtime island resident, said he'd seen the ship three times. And in the summer of 1880 Mrs. George S. Rathbone saw the light and thought it came from a steamer.

Noel Powell, writing in the July 1956 issue of *Yankee*, stated that he talked to the only living islander who had seen the Palatine Light. In a modest home tucked beneath the Mohegan Bluffs, the wife of a sea captain told Powell that, as a child, she had lived on the north shore. One night her parents woke her up and for several moments she watched in awe a flaming ship riding the waves and then suddenly vanishing beneath the water.

Today Block Island is a popular destination for bird enthusiasts. Large tracts of land have been preserved for the thousands of waterfowl and other birds that use the island as a sanctuary on their annual migratory flights up and down the East Coast. Many residents help track flight patterns through bird banding. Islanders also possess a strong sense of preservation for historic structures. Efforts were under way in 1994 to raise nearly two million dollars to move a picturesque lighthouse away from a nearby cliff being eroded by the pounding seas.

Is the weird and fantastic tradition of the fiery phantom ship no longer a part of preservation efforts and now passed into history? Hardly. Although the phenomenon is sporadic, reports of sightings have occurred in modern times. In 1969 a number of islanders witnessed the appearance of "a great red fireball on the ocean," although they could not identify it as a ship. The incident was never explained.

Could there be a scientific explanation for this story? An official of the United States Geological Bureau has suggested that the light might be caused by gas escaping from vast ore deposits below the ocean floor. The gas, upon reaching the surface, would ignite.

Folklorist Snow speculates that menhaden, an inedible fish living in American Atlantic waters, could be responsible for the light. These fish are oily and phosphorescent and are used as a source of fish oil, fish meal, fertilizer, and bait. They travel in large schools and, under certain conditions, give off a considerable amount of light. If gas were to rise and unite with the phosphorescence, could this union not create a gigantic and towering will-o'-the-wisp? It seems plausible until one remembers that fishermen are accustomed to reading the seas year-round in all kinds of weather. They claimed to have never seen the apparition of a burning ship until after the wreck of the *Princess Augusta*.

Perhaps there is no satisfactory explanation for the Palatine Light, but the legend will live on so long as there are islanders to tell it: a ship with never a home port, condemned to sail forever.

Old Boney, of Charles Towne

Charleston is South Carolina's jewel by the sea—a colonial port city that still retains its charms of 150 years ago. It is a living museum of antebellum homes with formal gardens, narrow cobblestone streets, and grand old churches, all surprising perhaps in a city that has been ravaged by two major wars and a number of natural catastrophes.

During the American Revolution, British troops led by Sir Henry Clinton laid siege to the city. The colonists, outnumbered in men and firepower, captured only a few transports and supply vessels before surrendering on May 12, 1780. With the fall of Charleston the entire South was effectively conquered. Although Sir Henry offered pardons to all those who would swear allegiance to the Crown, most remained true to the cause of freedom. In 1788 South Carolina would enter the Union, the eighth of the thirteen original colonies.

The War Between the States began on April 12, 1861, when the Confederate army bombed Fort Sumter, in Charleston harbor. The subsequent fifteen-month shelling of Charleston by the Union navy destroyed much of the city and killed 25 percent of its male population. Years of suffering and poverty lay ahead until, in 1902, the U.S. Navy established a base here that provided thousands of jobs. Today the naval facility is home to submarines and ships.

Charleston has also been wracked by devastating natural calamities. In 1886 one of the greatest earthquakes in American history rocked the city. Hundreds of buildings crumbled and aftershocks continued for nearly two weeks. In the 1920s two great fires swept through the city. And, on September 21, 1989, Hurricane Hugo roared up the mouth of Charleston harbor, packing winds of 139 miles per hour. It was the most destructive storm ever to hit the continental United States.

But the people of Charleston are survivors.

By the spring of 1990, houses were repainted, roofs repaired, and the last of the fallen trees hauled away. Visitors say the city is more beautiful than ever before. Tourists come to visit the homes and gardens; to enjoy the music and drama of the world-famous Spoleto Festival held each spring; and, of course, to look for the ghosts, for which Charleston is famous.

Charles Towne Tours provides ghost hunters with a detailed map, a prerecorded tape, and a printed guide outlining the routes past the abodes of some of the city's prominent wraiths, many of them located on colorful Legare Street. These amorphous residents, however, are not the frightful kind that drag rusty chains up the cellar stairs. For the most part they're courtly and friendly and are either treated like members of the family or left alone to their contentments.

Boney

Boney was a slave. With his wife and children, he lived in a small house on King Street in the late 1790's, behind the Charles Towne mansion of their owner, a Colonel Andrews. The colonel also owned a large Waccamaw River rice plantation from which he shipped grain to the port of Charles Towne. Rice was one of the major products of eighteenth-century South Carolina. It was exported, along with indigo, to England and other nations around the world.

Boney worked days on the wharves of Charles Towne, unloading Colonel Andrews's ships. He was lean and wiry, befitting his name, and he was unusually strong. He rarely complained about heaving sacks of rice from schooner to dock, and he always had an eye out for a less able worker who needed a hand with the back-breaking work.

Boney had another talent too. His vision was nothing short of phenomenal. He could see what others could not. As vessels approached the port of entry, even from the distant ocean side, Boney discerned the figures on deck, describing the men's clothing long before the ships docked. His sight never faltered, even on overcast days. It was as if he were seeing the world through binoculars. Fellow slaves said Boney had "crazy eyes." They said he lived under a curse and some feared him. Their attitudes made Boney uneasy, and once he asked his wife what she thought. She didn't give him a straight answer.

Now Boney took to hanging around the docks of Charles Towne at night. He liked the peace and quiet. Mr. Peters, the agent for several planters, was usually there, working in his tiny waterfront office, emerging occasionally for what he called a "breather." Peters was a large, affable man with a perpetual squint brought on by too many hours in the sun and too many hours at his books. His job was to sell the rice, invest the planters' money wisely, then take his commission on the sales. Peters especially welcomed the arrival of Colonel Andrews's ships because the colonel's rice did not require processing at the McLaren mill in the harbor. The husks had already been removed at Colonel Andrews's plantation mill. Rice that was ready for immediate shipment meant higher profits for both seller and agent. Colonel Andrews was widely known as one of the wealthiest planters in South Carolina.

It seemed natural then for the friendly white agent and the colonel's slave to engage in conversation during the evening hours. Boney knew the size of his master's incoming rice shipments, the number of vessels, and the dates of arrival at the port. Peters, of course, had this information, but somehow Boney always had it first. Peters liked the young African American, in fact grew genuinely fond of him and wished from the bottom of his heart that the man could be set free. One night in 1796 he broached the subject.

Sitting at the water's edge, he said, "Boney, haven't you ever wished that you could be a free man?"

Boney nodded his head. "Yes, of course," he began, "but Colonel Andrews would never let me go." He paused. "I serve him well."

Peters thought a moment. "You know, Boney, if you could do something that would bring you fame you could earn your freedom." He told Boney the story of a slave named Caesar who had developed an antidote for rattlesnake bite. Caesar had taken plantain, horehound, and goldenrod roots, soaked them in rum and lye, then wrapped the bundle in rum-soaked tobacco leaves. This concoction was believed to draw the poison out of the body. Peters said that in 1750 the South Carolina legislature ordered Caesar's prescription published for the benefit of the public. Upon its publication, the slave was set free.

The agent studied the young man beside him. Silence hung heavy between them. "No," said Boney, finally. "There is nothing I know how to do."

Just at that moment, something prompted Boney to swing around. He saw St. Philip's Church in the distance. The old brick church, built in 1710, was called "the most elegant religious edifice in America." Its cupola, housing two bells and a clock, soared fifty feet into the air. Boney, of course, had never been inside the building, but he had heard Colonel Andrews speak of the beautiful heart-of-pine box pews and altar rails and the exquisite stained glass windows. The colonel was an Episcopalian, as were most of his fellow planters, and he was a member of St. Philip's. In fact, he had been married in the church.

Boney squinted into the dark night. "I must go," he said. "The church steeple is on fire." If there was urgency in his voice, Peters missed it. Before he could respond, Boney had leaped to his feet and raced toward the church. Peters, staring after him, saw nothing save a sliver of moon in the night sky.

Boney, heart pounding, reached the church and looked up. A thread of flame was burning in the wooden steeple, high above the clock, high above the bells. He started to climb a wall, slipped back, tried again. His agile hands sought fingerholds in the wall, found them in the rough cement between the bricks and in an occasional outcropping of mortar.

Slowly, painfully, Boney climbed. His legs ached and the wind roared in his head. Although accustomed to hard labor, he had never climbed a nearly vertical wall. But there was no turning back. Once past the clock and the bells, Boney was dismayed to see how much farther he had to go. At the top of the spire one cedar shingle burned. It was the flame that the slave had seen from the waterfront; he could not understand why the fire had not already roared through the other shingles and engulfed the historic church.

At the top, Boney extended one hand toward the burning shingle and, with great effort, wrenched it free from the pegs that held it in place. He threw it as far from the building as possible, then tore off his shirt to smother the flames that were now licking the other shingles. When Boney was certain that the fire was out, he backed down the wall. His hands were burned and he couldn't stop shivering.

Peters and several dock workers were waiting with blankets and hot tea. The agent treated Boney's hands and gave him lodging for the night. Boney said he had done only what he had to do. He had seen the pinprick of light in the tower in the same way that he saw deckhands on ships before they entered Charles Towne harbor. Now folks said his talent was a blessing, not a curse.

The next morning, Boney had just started to unload sacks of rice from Colonel Andrews's vessels when he was summoned to Peters's office. The colonel was there too. Peters looked at Boney and said, "I've already told him what happened last night."

Boney looked from one man to the other.

"If any deed deserves the gift of freedom, this one does," said the planter.

When the colonel held out his hand to Boney, the slave's cheeks grew hot and he stared at the floor. Had he heard correctly? "Yes, sir," he muttered, taking the hand that was proffered.

Free! Boney left the office, turned his back on the wharf and went home to tell his wife and children.

Boney spent his days and most of his nights sitting in the cemetery that adjoined St. Philip's Church. He sat motionless for hours at a time, gazing upward at the steeple, and, amazingly, regretting the deed that had earned him his freedom. He longed to be back on the docks, hoisting the sacks of rice, enjoying the camaraderie of his fellow workers. That was all he knew.

Soon, Boney stopped eating. Death soon followed.

Boney was buried in the cemetery at Colonel Andrews's Waccamaw River plantation. But his spirit did not rest. For decades afterward, visitors to the graveyard reported seeing a man sitting with his back against a tombstone, gazing into the distance, as if watching for something. Those who saw him said his skin and hair were dark, but his eyes were pure white, as if he'd been frightened to death. They knew he was not real and they hurried on their way.

Ruth's Marriage

The year was 1783. The Revolutionary War was over and the society matrons of Charleston once again unpacked their ball gowns in readiness for the glittering social season ahead. This promised to be the most memorable one in many years with the upcoming marriage of Ruth Lowndes and Francis Simmons. The bridegroom-to-be was a charming and wealthy planter who would have been the "catch" of any season. Ruth's friends were envious, but at the same time glad of her good fortune.

The couple was married in one of Charleston's largest churches and the pews were filled with friends and relatives. Ruth looked radiant in her ecru satin gown with sweeping train, but Simmons appeared not to notice. At the altar he mumbled his vows and stared at the floor. He didn't kiss the bride, nor did he take her arm as they walked back up the aisle. Ruth's cheeks reddened with embarrassment. Her mother said her daughter was just flushed with excitement.

At the door of the church the couple stepped into the gilt carriage that was waiting, and rode off to their new home at 131 Tradd Street. While watching them go, a few people lingered beneath the trees and spoke in low tones about the strange actions of the groom.

No one knew what to make of Francis Simmons.

They would soon find out.

Well before his marriage, the folks of Charleston knew Simmons as a vain man who liked to have his name embroidered on his silk shirts and linen handkerchiefs by his sister, Anne. She was older than Francis and delighted in performing handwork for the brother whom she adored.

At a fashionable ball one night, Francis Simmons met Ruth Lowndes. The two danced together, and just before the traditional midnight buffet was served they stepped outside on the balcony. A servant brought two glasses of champagne. In taking hers, Ruth accidentally bumped the servant's hand and a few drops of her drink spilled on the front of her dress. Simmons offered her his handkerchief, and when Ruth saw the beautiful embroidery she exclaimed, "Francis Simmons, what a lovely name!"

"Well, since you like it so much, will you accept it?" Simmons asked. He meant the handkerchief. She thought he had proposed.

Ruth beamed. Just at that moment her father passed by. She told him that Francis Simmons had asked her to become his wife. Within minutes Mr. Lowndes had announced the betrothal to the assembled guests, and the well-wishers celebrated far into the night.

Francis was stunned. He could not shame the older man; in those days honor was more important even than life. And so Francis Simmons and Ruth Lowndes, casual acquaintances at best, were married.

At least, they went through the ceremony. The marriage was never consummated. On her wedding night, Ruth Lowndes Simmons slept alone in the Tradd Street mansion. Her husband returned to his plantation on Johns Island.

The years rolled by. Simmons built a fine brick home at 14 Legare Street and moved in. He lived there alone with his servants while Ruth spent her time on Tradd Street. But once each year he and his wife held a magnificent reception at Legare Street. Arm in arm and smiling, they appeared to be the happily married couple. At the end of the evening Ruth returned, alone, to 131 Tradd Street.

Twenty years after his most peculiar marriage, Simmons's servants found him dead, slumped over in a chair in the drawing room.

Ruth Simmons died some time later. Her face was often seen at the window of her bedroom, waiting and watching for the husband who never came. There is no longer a house at 131 Tradd Street, but Charlestonians say that Ruth's carriage, bearing her restive spirit, still travels between the two locations, clattering across the cobblestones in the old port city.

The Hunter's Return

James Heyward's two loves were books and hunting. He spent long hours in the library of his mother's city home, then rode out into the country to go bird hunting in favorable weather. Mrs. Heyward was accepting of her son's routine even though in one way she was disappointed. Her husband, William, had been killed in the American Revolution, and she hoped that James, her favorite child, would assume responsibility for the family's rice plantation. James, however, had no interest in planting.

At the end of the war, the widow Heyward built herself a comfortable two-story house at 31 Legare Street. She had many friends in Charleston and she loved entertaining and being entertained. Although her social calendar was always filled, she welcomed visits from her children and, of course, saw James regularly.

On the morning of January 14, 1805, Mrs. Heyward went into the library as usual. She saw her son seated at his desk in the alcove. He held his head in his hands. She wondered why he was still there since he'd told her that he and a friend were going out to the plantation early to hunt quail.

"James," she said, walking over to him. "I thought you'd gone to the plantation. Are you ill?"

Young James did not answer.

Furthermore, when his mother reached out to him he vanished. The chair was empty!

Mrs. Heyward screamed, then fainted. The servants called a doctor, but by the time he arrived the woman was sitting up in a chair. Yet Mrs. Heyward knew that something had happened to James. The vision she had of him in the library was a warning of danger. She begged the doctor to ride out to the plantation to check on the boy's well-being.

At that moment, footsteps pounded across the front porch. The door swung open and the body of James Heyward was borne into the front parlor by plantation workers. The young man's grieving friend trailed behind.

As the men had galloped across a field that morning, he told Mrs. Heyward, James's horse had shied at a cow that appeared suddenly in front of the riders. James was thrown from the horse and killed instantly.

Mrs. Heyward found that she had "seen" and spoken to her son that morning at the precise time of the accident.

Now, two hundred years later, James Heyward still returns to his beloved books. His ghost in the library of the house at 31 Legare Street appears comfortably situated while he reads, or sometimes gazes absently in the distance toward the plantation and hunting trails that vanished long ago.

The Headmistress

Madame Talvande was a French-Haitian emigré who operated a fashionable boarding school for girls at 32 Legare Street. In the years before the Civil War it was customary for wealthy cotton and rice planters to send their daughters away to school, and Madame Talvande's academy was considered one of the finest in the antebellum South. It offered a not-too-rigorous scholastic program, firm discipline, and thorough training in the social skills requisite to Charleston society.

And that is why Marie Whaley became a student at the school. She was raised on the barrier island of Edisto, and her father wanted her to have an education befitting his social status. When Mr. Whaley went into Charleston on business trips, he often took little Marie with him. He showed her the lovely mansion that housed the school and explained to her that one day this would become *her* school. The child was excited by the idea. Life on the island was dreary and lonely for her; few children lived on Edisto, and she had no playmates her age.

Then, on a fall day in 1829, Marie Whaley unpacked her steamer trunks at Madame Talvande's school. She had just turned fifteen. Shy at first, she soon made close friends among her classmates and began to flourish in the exciting, new environment. Whenever the headmistress planned parties for her students, Marie was the first to volunteer to help. On rare occasions, Madame Talvande invited "proper" young men of Charleston to the school's social functions.

As it happened, during a bed check following one of these parties, Marie Whaley turned up missing!

Madame Talvande felt sick. No student had ever before left the school without written permission from her parents. "Mon Dieu!" the good headmistress cried, and wept into her hands. She could not sleep that night, and in the morning sent word to Mr. Whaley to come immediately to the school.

Marie was found, eventually. Marie *and* her new husband!

The story was that she had sneaked out of the party and rendezvoused with a New Yorker named George F. Morris. He was known to Marie's father and despised. One version of the legend claims the couple eloped; another says Marie and her lover were wed in St. Michael's Episcopal Church. At any rate, Madame Talvande was embarrassed; her reputation as a guardian of flowering young womanhood had been shattered, and she took immediate steps to ensure that none of her charges would ever again escape her watchful eyes. Within the week masons erected a high brick wall and studded the top with broken glass bottles, making Madame Talvande's school more like a fortress prison than a finishing school for the dainty belles of South Carolina society. No further "escapes" were ever reported.

The school has been a private residence for many years, yet even now, more than a century later, Madame Talvande's spirit is said to keep a watchful eye on her girls. She walks the halls, checks the bedrooms, then vanishes.

Sometimes a gentleman ghost comes calling late in the night. One family heard the front door swing open and heavy footsteps clump through the entry to the north hall. The family's cook claimed she saw a spectral cavalier walk through the large old dining room on his way to the game room.

Could it have been Marie Whaley's husband?

The Spectral Rider of Bobo's Mills

Wind rattled the skeletons of trees and a hunter's moon rode high. In a small clearing surrounded by dense woods, a thread of smoke rose from the chimney of a log cabin, while through an uncurtained window a lantern cast a square of light upon the frozen ground.

Inside the snug cottage, well chinked against the wintry blasts, an elderly Quaker gentleman rocked by the fire, reading his Bible and puffing on his pipe. In earlier years, David Miles and his wife, Esther, had cleared the land, planted the gardens, and raised a few pigs for butchering. Sometimes it seemed like only yesterday that she had worked beside him, but eighteen years had passed since Esther's death and he was left alone with his children, who were now young adults.

Nineteen-year-old Charity bent close to the lantern to check the stitches of her knitting. Occasionally she glanced at her brother, who was seated on the floor cleaning a gun, and once in the reflection of firelight she saw a tear glisten on her father's cheek. She knew he was fearful, not for himself, but for his children. The Revolutionary War was raging and the Redcoats, under General Tarleton, were sweeping across South Carolina. Sometimes distant gunfire seemed to shake the cabin's walls, and the old man stirred uneasily in his sleep. It was always on these nights that young Henry Galbreath, a Continental Army scout, came calling.

Charity had warned him many times not to come, but he laughed and said, "Why not? I've escaped the Tories many times. Besides, no one knows this countryside as well as I."

It was true, of course. Henry knew every rock, tree, and stream, and where to cross the Bush River, which ran close by.

Suddenly, out of the night sounds came the hard pounding of a horse's hooves. It stopped near the rear of the cabin. Silence. Charity put down her handwork. Her father closed his Bible and her brother loaded his gun.

An urgent rap shook the door. Charity cracked it open. Henry's uniform was rumpled and sweat beaded his face. Charity reached for his hands and pulled him inside.

"Henry," she began, "you must not come here. You promised me."

The tall young horseman flung off his cape, took Charity into his arms and tilted her chin to kiss her full on the mouth.

"But I love you, Charity, and I shall come as often as I wish."

Charity hid her hands in the pockets of her calico apron.

"I love you too, dear, but you must not risk your life. Hide out with friends until this bloody war is over. I couldn't bear knowing that something had happened to you." Tears stood in her luminous brown eyes, but Henry paid her no heed.

He strode to the fireplace to shake hands with David Miles and his son, both of whom had risen to greet him.

Charity made fresh chicory coffee and the four sat at the rough-hewn table beneath a wall festooned with strings of dried apples and peaches. For several moments no one spoke. Then Henry, warmed and relaxed by the coffee, said: "Charity, hear my words. One year from now I shall return to you, whether or not the war is over."

Charity fought back the tears. Surely the fighting could not last so long.

"I shall wait," she murmured.

Only the old man heard the beginnings of the blizzard. He always bragged he could hear the snowflakes fall long before the wind howled. Suddenly, out of the rising storm came the thundering of many horses, and then rough voices shouting at the cabin door.

"Come on out, you scoundrel, and don't try no tricks!"

Charity ran to douse the fire with a bucket of water kept for such emergencies while her brother pushed Henry through the opening of a removable plank in the cabin's wall that opened onto the backyard.

Rifle butts smashed the front door and two Tories, coats ragged and soiled, plunged into the room.

David Miles never moved from his chair. "You was wantin' something?" he asked.

One soldier swaggered up to the old man. "Where is he?"

David reamed his pipe. "Haven't the foggiest notion who you'd be talking about. Ain't nobody here but me and my family."

The Tories, after a brief look around, ran out through the battered front door. "Surround the house!" they yelled.

Too late. Henry had already mounted his black charger and stuck the spurs to its flanks. The band of Tories followed in hot pursuit, firing shots wildly into the night, but Henry escaped on wings of wind. He turned only once in the saddle to fire a single shot and the British troops, knowing they couldn't find their way in the storm, retreated.

Days lengthened into weeks and weeks into months and there was no word of Henry Galbreath. Sometimes, when a regiment of the Continental Army passed through Bobo's Mills, Charity asked about Henry's fate. No one knew.

Charity performed her household chores and often sat for hours staring out the window. Then one night after her father and her brother had gone to bed, a strange spell came upon her. She kept hearing Henry's words: *One year from now I shall return to you.* The year was not yet up, but she was certain that something or someone was outside. She pulled open the door. Drawing a shawl around her shoulders, she stepped out into the moonlight.

Suddenly, from out of the woods came a strange light and out of its brightness galloped a horseman, tall and erect in the saddle. He was dressed in black, his long hair streaming out behind him. He had ridden hard, for his black charger bore heavy foam on its sides. Racing past the cabin, the rider looked neither to left nor to right, intent upon a mission known only to himself.

Charity knew then that Henry Galbreath was dead, but she said nothing. The specter returned night after night through sleet and snow, darkness and moonlight. His appearance never changed and he rode with the fury of one pursued.

But the rumor spread, as rumors always do, that Galbreath's ghost returned, riding a phantom horse.

Then, on a December night during the last year of the Revolution, the Mileses sat close to the blazing fire on the hearth, each rejoicing silently that the battles had ceased. The only sound was the furious whip of wind lashing the sides of the little house with icy sleet.

Because it was the anniversary of Henry's leavetaking, Charity put on a new dress she had made and bound her hair into long shining braids. Perhaps she had been mistaken about the identity of the spectral rider. Perhaps even now Henry was hurrying to her.

Suddenly, the storm abated and the door flew open. A blinding light filled the cabin and out of the light stepped Henry Galbreath wearing a tattered army uniform. His eyes were vacant sockets in a haggard face and his long hair hung in frozen strands that fell to his shoulders. When he looked upon Charity, she cowered. But as quickly as Henry had appeared, he was gone—just as he had left five years earlier. The wind rose, but the wild tramping of the charger tamed the wind's roar.

Charity never married. Nothing was ever discovered about Henry Galbreath's death; it was assumed that he had been killed in battle.

The snug little cabin of David Miles rotted to dust many years ago, but even today some say that on a certain December night when a storm is raging, a fiery charger bearing a tall rider dashes out of the woods near Bobo's Mills. No one knows where he goes, and no one would dare to ask.

SOUTH DAKOTA

Larry

The actor decided to stay late at the theater. Rehearsals for a mystery/comedy, *The Girls in 509*, had been over for hours but Ray Loftesness wanted to study some particularly difficult stage business and lines that he, and other amateur actors, would be performing in public within a few days.

Now well past midnight, Loftesness was alone, speaking aloud his part as he strode about the set, illuminated only by work lights above the stage. At one place in his role, he had been instructed to look out toward the balcony.

On this very late night, however, as he shot a glance toward the darkened gallery . . .

"As I looked up into the balcony there became apparent this very steady glow, which was what I would call an aura, rather of a blue color. I assumed someone was playing with the lights.

"I thought for a moment that it was just a blue bulb that someone had turned on, but it began expanding. There was no sound to it. The aura gradually expanded to several feet in diameter and [was] very high.

"In the center was a man. I could not tell his mode of dress, but he was either pointing or beckoning to me. He seemed to be trying to tell me something."

At about the same moment Loftesness glimpsed the pulsating orb, a stream of cold air enveloped him. It seemed to come from the empty auditorium.

Loftesness said the icy blast felt as if a freezer door had been suddenly opened, and then slammed shut. There were no auditorium doors open on that cold October night.

The thirty-seven-year-old actor may have encountered the legendary "Larry," a ghost whose origins have been lost in the annals of the old vaudeville theater that houses the Sioux Falls Community Playhouse.

Some accounts say Larry was a construction worker killed when the building went up around the turn of the century. Or, he might have been a stagehand killed in an accident when the place was a vaudeville house.

But the fact that Ray Loftesness saw a ghostly figure in the balcony may lend credence to the speculation that Larry fell in love with a married woman and was murdered by a jealous husband—in the balcony of the old theater.

Attempts to trace the ghost's identity have been fruitless. Many newspaper records from earlier in this century were lost in a fire at the newspaper offices decades ago.

Built as a vaudeville house shortly after the turn of the century, the old theater's written history is meager, too. The Community Playhouse organization has owned the building since 1954, when the group bought it from Minnesota Amusement Company. The auditorium had been used as a movie theater since the 1920s.

Sightings of Larry are extremely rare. Ray Loftesness may be the only man who has actually seen what he believes was a ghost.

"That feeling of fright began settling into me and I knew I had to leave," Loftesness said of that night in 1959. "I left the theater as hurriedly as possible. I remember going out and locking the door behind me, getting in the car and coming home. I spent a sleepless night."

Loftesness returned to the theater the next morning to see, in his words, "if perhaps someone had been in the theater after I left." No one had, but the young actor had another surprise waiting for him.

"What did you do down here last night?" the theater's technical director, Gay Spielman, asked him. Loftesness said he didn't know what the man was talking about.

"Well, when I came in here this morning, every fuse in the theater had been blown," Spielman said to him.

"I couldn't explain that," Loftesness remembered.

An electrical malfunction was extremely unlikely, as the theater had been recently rewired.

Another incident during dress rehearsals for this same play made Loftesness wonder if, indeed, he wasn't the target of some hostile entity.

"This happened to be a 'whodunit' show and I was playing the villain," Loftesness said. "One of the actions was that a net was to be dropped down over me, trapping me beneath it.

"We went into dress rehearsals and the scene came and the technicians dropped the net over me. But apparently they hadn't correctly tied a sandbag which was necessary weight to bring it down correctly over me. The sandbag hit me on the head and knocked me out."

Theater accidents are not infrequent, and Loftesness, though shaken from the incident, was assured by the crew it would never happen again. Technicians readjusted the net and weighted sandbag, hoisted it to a higher level and conducted several more rehearsals to make sure it worked correctly. They had taken "every precaution," Loftesness was told.

But on opening night when the net fell over "villain" Loftesness, the sandbag again went awry and hit him on the head. He collapsed unconscious. The show was stopped for several minutes while the actor was revived. No one on the production staff could explain how the sandbag could have strayed off course. Loftesness admits it took him a long time to again feel comfortable on the Community Playhouse's stage.

The actor was also involved in a single, unusual episode of precognition, the ability to "see" future events, a decade after he saw a ghost in the Sioux Falls theater balcony.

Loftesness has had a long and distinguished career in show business, broadcasting, and public service. From 1969 to 1975, he was a manager with Fred

Waring and the Pennsylvanians, a popular musical group for nearly fifty years. The late Mr. Waring is known, too, as the inventor of the popular Waring blender.

He was also psychic, according to Loftesness.

"Waring was a remarkable person, of course, with tremendous ability. He led a very interesting life. But very often when I was working closely with him he would make a reference to dreams he had. He would say something 'good' was going to happen today, or something 'bad' will happen. Invariably something of that nature would happen.

"He was a very deep thinker and he just seemed to have an ability, or some method, to know [future events]."

Some of Waring's precognitive abilities may have rubbed off on Loftesness. He maintains that once he foresaw tragedy—near the beginning of a tour by the Pennsylvanians in 1970.

"I happened to be out on the road ahead of the show. As manager I would contact the theaters in which we were to appear, basically a series of one-nighters. One morning I suddenly saw the image of the tour bus, which Mr. Waring always insisted upon riding in with his 'kids,' literally crawling under a huge semi-trailer truck," Loftesness said.

So clear was the vision that Loftesness thought about calling back to Pennsylvania to see if anything bad had taken place. He decided against it because the phone call might have appeared "foolish."

He thought the incident a "personal nightmare" until a phone call from Waring three hours later.

"He said their bus driver had fallen asleep and the bus had slid under a semi-trailer truck. Two people were killed and many members of the cast were injured," Loftesness said. The bus was just leaving Pennsylvania to begin its tour of two hundred cities. Waring himself escaped serious injury because he was riding in a rear compartment of the bus.

Although the bus accident occurred a quarter-century ago, Loftesness still can't get it out of his mind.

Two very inexplicable brushes with the supernatural left Loftesness with no explanations of why or how the events occurred, only very certain of their reality.

"I don't understand it, but I do know that something very unusual happened that night [in the theater]. Some people have told me, whenever I bring the subject up, that surely I'm joking. What I say is that I don't understand the experience, but it was as real as any human experience that I've had since. It will always remain with me."

Jack Mortenson is a vice president of a telemarketing firm in Sioux Falls and was a technical director at the Sioux Falls Community Playhouse. In 1972, he too confronted the unexplained on the theater's historic stage.

One stage set had been taken down, "struck" in theatrical parlance, in preparation for a Young People's Theater production. Mortenson was going to be that show's technical director. As a final check before starting the new set, Mortenson, like Loftesness before him, found himself alone on the stage late one night.

"I was sweeping the stage before the next day when we brought in the kids to start working together [on the set]. I had started sweeping from the front of the stage, from left to right. I overlapped the broom about a half-stroke each time to be sure it was clean.

"Coming back from stage left to stage right on about my fourth or fifth pass, I guess, I sensed a sound behind me, if that sounds reasonable."

Mortenson didn't hear a clatter of any sort; rather he seemed to "perceive" that something had happened behind him. He turned around to look and didn't immediately see anything. He glanced down. About three steps behind him was a small, square object on the floor.

"I had just swept that area and it wasn't there before," he remembered.

Mortenson walked over and picked up an old tintype photograph of a bearded man who appeared to be in his mid-thirties. His cheeks were tinted rosy, as was the custom in the late nineteenth century. It was slightly larger than postage stamp size.

"I wondered where it had come from because it certainly wasn't in the broom. I had just swept back and forth across the stage and knocked the broom against the floor several times as I went along."

Mortenson turned on additional work lights which would illuminate the grid above the stage. He thought perhaps someone was hiding up there and had thrown the photograph down as a practical joke. There was no one up there and seemingly little chance that the tintype could have fallen of its own accord.

"I stood there holding this picture, looking at it for what seemed like a long time. Well, the thought of Larry had been there for a time and it suddenly got real cold where I was standing. I just turned and put the tintype on top of the light board, didn't turn off any of the lights, and I walked out very quickly, locked the door and went home."

Mortenson told his wife about the tintype. She was amazed, and not a little amused, at her husband's story. The next day, Mortenson returned to the theater. He found the tintype where he had placed it on the lighting panel. Several of his colleagues asked about it and laughed when Mortenson revealed its mysterious origins. But they always worked with all the lights turned on from that day forward. The tintype remained on the light board for many years until a new electrical system was installed. It disappeared after that, but Mortenson thinks it still may lurk somewhere in the theater.

Jack Mortenson still doesn't know where the tintype came from. As the theater's technical director, he had climbed all over the grid above the stage and never seen it. The stage was bare as he pushed the broom across the floor. And, if someone had dropped it earlier, why didn't he see it the first time he cleaned that section of the floor? Mortenson had on only the work lights, but it was bright enough to work by. He saw the picture several steps away when he turned at the faint sound he thought he had heard. Why couldn't he have seen it a few feet in front of him?

"There's more doubt in my mind about things that we can't explain," Mortenson said. "I'm like the Cowardly Lion. All of a sudden, I do believe!"

Reports of allegedly supernatural events at the Sioux Falls Community Playhouse are very rare and difficult to verify. All good theaters, it is said, should have at least one spectral patron. Jack Mortenson and Ray Loftesness can say that at least in this case, the supernatural may not be a product of dramatic imaginations.

TENNESSEE

Family Troubles

Nearly two centuries ago, the most famous apparition in southern history, and probably the most thoroughly examined haunting in all of America, made its first appearance in Robertson County, Tennessee. The Bell Witch, as it was and is to this day called, plagued the family of John Bell from about 1817 to 1821.

The name "witch" is a misnomer. Whatever caused the haunting was most definitely not a witch in the traditional sense. The events began with mysterious poltergeist-type noises, such as scratchings from within the walls of John Bell's home, progressed to disembodied voices, and culminated in the appearance of a female specter who called itself "Kate Batts, witch."

An ancient ghost may be dismissed as the fantasies of lonely homesteaders, but this phantasm cannot be so easily banished to the murky past.

Ask Carney Bell. He is a direct descendant of John Bell and a prominent businessman in Springfield, Tennessee, only a few miles from the site of his ancestors' troubles. He has had enough peculiar incidents in his life to make him wonder if the Bell Witch is not still active.

"Several years ago when my mother was still living she called me real early one morning," Bell said. "It was springtime and she wanted me to come right down. I asked if there was a problem and she said yes. I went running down the street and she met me at the door."

"I need you to help me," Mrs. Bell insisted.

"What happened, Mom?" Bell asked.

"Somebody's been in this house, I think, and he may still be in here."

"Well, we can find out right quickly."

Bell kept a gun at his mother's house. He took it out of a cabinet, loaded it and began a search.

"I checked all the doors and the windows—there are seven outside doors in the house, all of which lock from the inside. I started checking windows, but they were all locked. So whoever was in there had to still be in the house. But I went through every closet, the attic, the basement, under the beds, everywhere, and could not find anyone."

Carney Bell's mother insisted someone *had* been inside. As proof she pointed him toward a pantry between the dining room and the kitchen. Floor-to-ceiling cabinets with glass doors lined both sides of the small room. Bell drew a sharp breath.

"Both sets of doors were open and all the china Mom had stored in there was out on the floor, everything. Even the little salt shakers, cups and saucers, vases, everything was on the floor. The crash of them hitting the floor had awakened her upstairs."

But *nothing was broken!*

"Oh, some of it was cracked, but those were the old pieces [already chipped]," he said, shaking his head at the memory. "I'll say 150 pieces [were on the floor]. Those cabinets are all the way to the ceiling and they have four or five shelves in each one. Whoever did it must have stuck his hand in and pulled everything out. But [my mother] didn't hear multiple crashes, she just heard one."

Try as he might, Carney Bell couldn't figure out how all that china ended up on the floor without one piece being broken. Nothing else in the house had been disturbed.

Bell was not ready to blame it on his family's old ghost trouble, but, after this and two earlier incidents, he was certainly left with many questions. One of the previous incidents again involved his mother.

"She had become ill and had gone to the hospital and I was staying in her house," Bell recalled. "The telephone rang and it was the neighbor. He asked if I was watching television. He told me Channel Five was having a special about the Bell Witch. So I punched in the channel and it was all 'zebras.' I could hear it but I couldn't see it. It was the same on all three television sets in the house. Every time there was a station break, [the signal] would come in perfectly, but when it switched to the Bell Witch story it'd go out. The neighbors all around me said later they had seen it. It was working everywhere except there. One of the TVs had rabbit ears and the others were on an antenna."

Coincidence? Carney Bell truly isn't prepared to give a definitive answer, even though a third incident makes it seem that some kind of guiding, invisible presence still surrounds the Bell family.

Bell is a funeral director in Springfield and, quite naturally, spends a good deal of his time in cemeteries. But he has more than a professional interest in such places. For most of his life, he searched in vain for the grave of his great-great-grandfather, Joel Egbert Bell, John Bell's son. That is until one day when he was out with his four sons:

"I was hunting on a farm out near Highway 41 north of Springfield towards Adams. . . . We had jumped a rabbit and shot at him and he ran into a thicket. We were stomping around trying to kick him up so we could get another shot and my feet became entangled in some honeysuckle. It was real thick in that area. I had a loaded gun with me and I began to fall. I put the gun down and reached over to put my hand on what I thought was a stump of a tree covered with honeysuckle.

"I regained my footing and then I noticed it wasn't a stump at all. I peeled the honeysuckle off and it was a cemetery monument."

And not just any monument, but the headstone for Joel Egbert Bell. On each side was buried a wife (he married twice). With his first wife was the grave of an infant. She had apparently died in childbirth.

"It was so weathered we couldn't tell what it said [at first] so we got a clump of dirt and rubbed it across [the inscription] and we finally figured out that it said 'Joel Egbert Bell.' Now that's coincidental."

Carney Bell was still amazed at the oddity of these personal anomalies even though several years had passed since they had occurred. He knows well the history of his family, as do a great many people in Tennessee and throughout the South.

John William Bell Sr. was born in Halifax County, North Carolina in 1750, into a prosperous farming family of English descent. He didn't marry until he was thirty-two years old, quite late in that era. His bride was Lucy Williams, the daughter of another well-to-do farmer in nearby Edgecombe County.

Bell Senior was a thrifty, hardworking man who accumulated a good deal of wealth in the early decades of post-Revolutionary America. By the early 1800s, he and Lucy had six children; Chloe, a slave owned by Lucy Bell, had eight children. Seventeen people to feed and clothe stretched the resources of even this affluent farmer, and in 1804 he decided to emigrate to Robertson County, Tennessee, where he knew several families who had earlier left North Carolina for what was then the western frontier.

According to some sources, however, Bell Senior was not entirely the upstanding citizen portrayed in so many accounts of the Bell Witch. He may have killed an overseer on his North Carolina plantation, a man named John Black. The reasons behind the murder are obscure. He may have mistreated slaves owned by the Bells, but there is some evidence that Black may have been attracted to Lucy Bell (or vice versa).

Bell Senior purchased a thousand acres of rich farmland on the banks of the Red River, a few miles from the Kentucky border near what is today Adams, Tennessee. He moved his family into the house already on the property, a seven-room, story-and-a-half, double-log dwelling covered with weatherboarding; an ell added several additional rooms and a passage. A wide front porch ran the length of the home. It was considered one of the finest homes in northern Tennessee.

The house had been built by the grandfather of Richard Powell, a schoolteacher in the area at the time of the Bell Witch activities. Powell was a close friend of the Bell family, perhaps was even living in the house when the first strange occurrences were reported, and may have had a hand in creating at least some of the mischief. There were said to have been secret passages built in the house as a precaution against Indian attacks. Powell was probably aware of them.

The precise date the "troubles" began isn't known. The first public disclosures came in 1818; earlier incidents had been kept within the family. Richard Williams Bell, one of John Bell's seven sons, wrote a memoir of his remembrances of the Witch. Although he was only six years old at the time of the events, his book is one of the few accounts written by one of the observers.

In it he wrote:

". . . strange appearances and uncommon sounds had been seen and heard by different members of the family at times, some year or two before I knew anything about it, because they indicated nothing of a serious character, gave no one any concern, and would have passed unnoticed but for [later] developments. Even the knocking on the door, and the outer walls of the house, had been going on for some time before I knew of it, generally being asleep, and father, believing that it was some mischievous person trying to frighten the family, never discussed the matter in the presence of the younger children, hoping to catch the prankster."

John Bell Sr. in particular, didn't want anyone outside the family, or even his youngest children, to know what was happening. He pledged his family to secrecy and forbade anyone to keep a diary of the incidents. The scratchings at the walls were first attributed to the branches of the large pear trees in the front yard rubbing against the house. Even the appearances of "strange animals" in the woods which looked like dogs or wolves but leaped into the air and sometimes "walked like a man" were kept a secret.

The quiet world of the Bells changed forever in May 1818. The weird noises moved inside. Richard recalled it was on a Sunday night when he and three of his brothers were awakened by what sounded like "a rat gnawing vigorously on the bed post." He and his brothers—John Junior, Drewry, and Joel—lit candles and looked all around. They found nothing unusual. They had just dampened the candle and climbed back into bed when the noise started up again. Another fruitless search ensued. Richard estimated that he and his brothers were up and down a half-dozen times that night, all the while trying to find the nonexistent "rat."

The noises continued almost nightly for weeks, often traveling from room to room during the night so that the entire family was roused from their beds. Nothing was found or accomplished, Richard wrote, ". . . beyond the increase of our confusion and evil forebodings."

Soon there were even more puzzling oddities. Richard noted that it seemed as if every evening something would be added to the mix. Late one night he felt his hair being twisted, and then he was pulled up so hard from his bed that "it felt like the top of my head had been taken off." Covers and sheets were wrenched from the beds "as fast as we could replace" them. Some family members heard lip-smacking and choking. No one ever saw anything, nor was there ever any indication of the source.

The two family members most affected by the haunting were the father and his daughter, Elizabeth (Betsy) Bell, twelve years old in 1818 and the only girl among the seven children still at home. Her only sister, Ester, had married Alexander Bennett Porter in 1817 and moved to Mississippi.

Betsy has been described as a young woman of "unusual good looks" who was "popular among her neighbors, a devout Christian and perfect character." She was a "roguish beauty" even at such a tender age.

Meanwhile, John Bell Sr. was the target of hateful attacks all during the three to four years the Witch was most active and, tragically, paid the highest price of any member of his family for the turmoil they endured.

Sometime in late summer 1818, which is only an estimate of the date since it is based upon Richard's memory, John Senior decided to tell his neighbor and close friend James Johnson about what was happening. Bell thought Johnson might be able to help solve the mystery. Instead matters got worse both in the house and, later, when word eventually leaked to the entire community that the Bell home was plagued by supernatural events.

Johnson and his wife agreed to spend a night in the house. He led everyone in prayer, read a chapter from the Bible, and asked for divine intervention in freeing the Bells "from the frightful disturbances, or that its origin, cause and purpose might be revealed," Richard Bell remembered.

It didn't work.

As soon as darkness settled, the racket began anew—scratching, gnawing, pounding on the walls, chairs overturned—as if whatever was present wanted Johnson to know that it wasn't about to be intimidated by religious fervor.

Johnson said the entity was beyond his comprehension. He thought it was an "intelligent" being of supernatural origin. His advice was to ask others in the area to come in and investigate.

Meanwhile, the entity had turned its attention to Betsy. Her cheeks sometimes turned crimson after she had been slapped by hands that no one could see, her hair pulled so roughly that she screamed in pain.

As word spread through Robertson County, visitors appeared on the Bells' front porch, intent upon solving the mystery. Groups of neighbors took turns staying awake all night in the house trying to discover whatever or whoever was responsible.

Meanwhile the entity was causing mischief outside the house.

Mysterious lights darted through the yard and among the trees, while bricks and small pieces of wood were hurled about. No one ever claimed to have seen the agent responsible for this particular rascality, and the incidents were increasing in frequency and viciousness.

For some time it had been thought that if communication could be established with this unseen force, there would be a better chance of understanding its motivations and, everyone hoped, encouraging it to leave. Everyone visiting the Bells began urging the being to talk. At first, the questions posed were simple: How far is it to a certain destination? How many persons are present? How many horses are in the barn?

Suddenly, answers came in a series of taps on the wall, much like a man rapping his knuckles against wood. The number of raps invariably coincided with the correct numerical answer to the question.

And then the demon spoke.

Richard Williams Bell remembered the first sounds as a sort of "whistling voice," but which soon progressed to a "faltering whisper" clearly articulating syllables and words. To the question of "who are you," the voice said it was "a witch . . . once very happy but [I] have been disturbed." Later, it claimed at various times to be a demon from hell, a person whose grave had been disturbed, an Indian ghost, a witch millions of years old, the ghost of a child buried in North Carolina . . . and once it claimed to be looking for a lost tooth!

The most intriguing explanation the phantasm ever gave of who it was came when it claimed to be "Kate Batts, witch." That's the derivation of the names that have been attached to this Tennessee phenomenon ever since: "Old Kate," and "The Bell Witch."

Kate Batts was a real person. She was an eccentric neighbor of John Bell's who died at the beginning of the troubles, and in the midst of an argument with Bell over property boundaries, a fairly common type of dispute in frontier America. Her husband, Frederick Batts, had an affliction that made his wife responsible for the family. She was probably what would today be termed a "character." For instance, she had the habit of begging pins from any woman she met. The superstitious believed that giving someone a pin gave that person supernatural control over you. In 1818 Tennessee, people were quite willing to believe that Kate Batts had returned as a ghostly "witch" to torment John Bell and his family.

The Witch seemed truly confused about who or what it was. Despite many questions, it never gave out any more information, nor did it ever seem pleased to talk about itself. But that didn't stop the chats. Once the Witch found its voice, nothing could shut it up.

A unique aspect of the Bell haunting was the Witch's penchant for engaging in witty and caustic debate. On topics ranging from religion to politics, the Witch displayed a voracious knowledge of the Bible, classical literature, and political topics of the day. It even brought news from distant places to these isolated pioneers. That could be done, the Witch said, because as a ghost it could range freely over the landscape!

The Witch managed to "attend" Methodist and Baptist church services each Sunday—thirteen miles apart—and then proceeded to mimic both preachers in a recitation of the sermons.

Unfortunately, the Witch turned into a "backslider" and took to raiding a neighborhood still, later turning up drunk at the Bells', cursing and singing drunken ditties until the wee hours of the morning.

Another time, it claimed to be the spirit of an early emigrant who buried a large sum of money and died without divulging the secret of where it was hidden.

Despite very specific instructions by the Witch, nothing was found during a day-long hunt along the Red River where it said the treasure was hidden. That night the Witch laughed at the easy gullibility of those it induced into conducting the search.

Betsy Bell was usually the target of the Witch's attempt to exhibit its power. She was poked, prodded, and slapped, her hair pulled relentlessly, combs yanked from her hair, shoelaces on her boots untied, and the boots themselves thrown across the room by unseen hands. So afraid for Betsy's welfare was her family that two girlfriends alternated spending the nights with her; even when Betsy stayed over-night with these or other friends, the Witch traveled along and tormented her and her friends wherever they ventured.

Young Betsy had other afflictions which at the time were attributed to the Witch but now seem to indicate a type of epilepsy or a muscular disease.

Richard Williams Bell wrote in his memoirs of the problems Betsy had: "Sister was subjected to fainting spells followed by prostration, characterized by shortness of breath and smothering sensations, panting as it were for life, and becoming entirely exhausted and lifeless, losing her breath for nearly a minute between gasps, and was rendered unconscious. . . ."

Little was known about epilepsy or similar disabilities in the early nineteenth century. It's quite easy to imagine that such drastic physical behavior change in a young woman of "robust health" might have been ascribed to supernatural agents.

John Bell Sr. and his wife, Lucy, were also marked for special treatment by the Witch but in quite different ways.

The Witch's abiding hatred for John Senior was never fully understood. He began to suffer from sudden illnesses, attributed to the Witch, which were de-scribed as a curious feeling in his mouth, a stiffness of the tongue, and "something like a stick crosswise, punching each side of his jaws," his son Richard wrote. As the Witch increased her appearances, John's predicament worsened. His tongue became so swollen that he couldn't talk or eat for hours at a time. Modern science might think his illness symptomatic of strep throat or a muscular disorder.

Whatever the cause, the Witch took great glee in his misfortune. It cursed and screamed at "old Jack Bell" and swore to torment him to death.

Lucy Williams Bell was quite another story. The Witch loved Mrs. Bell and often sang songs to her, gave her gifts, and showered her with altogether more affection than anyone else in the household. "Old Luce [sic] is a good woman," the Witch said.

In September 1820, Lucy was stricken with pleurisy. The Witch was so upset that it kept up a steady stream of chatter, asking what it could do to make Lucy better, how she was feeling each morning, wondering if it could sing a new song and so forth. Nearly everyone was driven to distraction, but Lucy seemed to tolerate the smothering attention quite well.

On a day when several neighbor women visited Lucy, hazelnuts mysteriously materialized and dropped into the sick woman's cupped hands. She put them on the bedspread but said she didn't have anything with which to crack them. Within minutes all the nuts were broken open. Several days later, grapes suddenly appeared in the same way. The Witch took credit.

The Witch also predicted events and passed along information from great distances away. When twenty-seven-year-old John Junior made plans to travel to North Carolina to settle an estate in which his father had an interest, the Witch warned against the long journey.

"Bad luck if you go on the trip," the Witch's voice intoned. "The legal proceedings will not be finished and you will return with nothing."

"I don't take orders from an invisible imp!" John Junior shot back.

The Witch tried a different ploy. There was "an elegant young lady from Virginia . . . on her way to visit friends in Robertson County." She is "wealthy," the Witch whispered, but if he left he would never have an opportunity to meet her, perhaps even to ask her to be his bride.

John Junior ignored the warning. He was gone six months and, true to the Witch's prediction, returned penniless. The legal work on the estate had not concluded before he had to return. Further, a rich, raven-haired enchantress had shown up in the county during John Junior's absence, but left after several weeks without ever having met the young bachelor.

The Witch also kept Lucy informed about events back in North Carolina, events which were confirmed in letters she later received from family and friends.

Strangers were also confronted with information about themselves, such as the time the Witch told one man who stopped by, and who was unknown to the Bell family, that "he is the grand rascal who stole his wife. He pulled her out of her father's house through a window, and hurt her arm, making her cry; then he whispered to her, 'Hush honey don't cry, it will soon get well.' " The man confirmed the accuracy of the account.

Gen. Andrew Jackson is said to have personally visited the Bell farm to investigate the Witch, although there is some dispute as to whether or not the event actually took place. Richard Williams Bell does not include any reference in his memoir to a visit by the great military hero. The only version of the visit is contained in M. V. Ingram's 1894 history of the Bell Witch, and there the report is attributed to a prominent Clarksville, Tennessee lawyer, Thomas L. Yancey, who was told about the visit by his grandfather.

It is highly probable that General Jackson had heard about the Witch. He was living in Nashville at the time, some thirty-five miles distant, both Jackson and the Bells were from North Carolina, and John Bell Sr. and his son Jesse had served in the Tennessee militia during the War of 1812.

General Jackson's diary of that period doesn't mention a trip to see the Bell Witch in action, although he may not have wanted such an event to be permanently recorded, especially if he had his eye on Washington. Nevertheless his supposed visit is an essential part of the legend.

The story begins with General Jackson coming out from Nashville with several other men, including a "witch-layer" who claimed he could face down any form of sorcery, in a wagon loaded with a tent and provisions for several days. The men rode on horseback behind the wagon. While crossing a dry, level piece of ground near the Bell home, the wagon wheels became stuck. No matter how hard the driver whipped the team, the wheels would not turn.

General Jackson thought awhile, and then exclaimed: "By the eternal, boys, it is the witch!"

Suddenly from the bushes along the road came a sharp retort: "All right General, let the wagon move on. I will see you again tonight."

With that the horses jumped ahead and the wagon rolled along smoothly. A search of the area produced no explanation as to the origin of the mysterious voice.

John Bell Sr. welcomed the prominent party into his home and insisted they accept his hospitality to stay inside rather than camp out. To that offer the travelers readily agreed.

During the evening, the brawny witch-layer bragged endlessly about his exploits of "undaunted courage and success in overcoming witches." Across his lap he held a big flintlock army pistol—with a silver bullet in its chamber.

As the hour grew late, General Jackson became annoyed at the witch-layer's swaggering assurance of his invincibility.

He leaned over and whispered to a friend: "Sam, I'll bet that fellow is an arrant coward. By the eternals, I do wish the thing would come, I want to see him run."

The general didn't have long to wait.

From a corner of the room came the same voice the men had heard alongside the road.

"All right, General, I am on hand ready for business."

The witch-layer leveled his gun in the direction of the voice and pulled the trigger. It didn't fire.

"Try again," cried the Witch. He did, with the same result.

"Now it's my turn; look out you old coward, hypocrite and fraud. I'll teach you a lesson."

Over tumbled the witch-layer as the sound of something slapping him on the face filled the room. Whack . . . whack . . . whack.

"Oh, my nose! My nose! The devil has got me. Oh Lordy, he's got me by the nose!" he screamed as he was dragged around the room by something no one could see.

The door flew open as if by magic and the chastened witch-layer ran out, crying and jumping at every step, as if being shoved and pummeled. The last anyone saw of him was his backside as he sprinted down the road toward Nashville.

"By god, boys, I never saw so much fun in all my life. This beats fighting the British." General Jackson laughed. He and his witch-hunting buddies were convulsed with mirth. So too was the Witch.

"How the old devil did run and beg," the Witch chuckled. "I'll bet he won't come here again with his old horse pistol to shoot me. I guess that's fun enough for tonight, General, and you can go to bed now. I will come tomorrow night and show you another rascal in this crowd."

Despite Mr. Bell's request that they stay several days, General Jackson and his party left the next morning for Nashville. They'd had enough of witch-chasing to last a good long while.

The Witch sometimes used different voices to address its audience. Once it said it was actually a "witch family" with four members: Blackdog, Mathematics, Cypocryphy, and Jerusalem. Cypocryphy and Mathematics had soft, feminine voices; Jerusalem spoke like a young boy; Blackdog was a foul-mouthed disciplinarian who often "beat" the other spirits for disobeying his orders. All four appeared drunk one day, infusing the house with the pungency of whiskey.

While the Witch usually confined its activities to speaking and mischief, there were many times when it took on tangible form, as something that could be either seen or felt. It claimed to be able to appear as various animals, for instance a large dog or rabbit, especially true early on; of course, there were the many times it slapped Betsy Bell and different visitors.

Calvin Johnson once shook the Witch's hand.

He was a neighbor of the Bells during the height of the Witch's antics. He and his brother, John, are said to have carried on many conversations with it. Calvin conceived of the idea of asking to shake the Witch's hand. Only after he promised not to "grasp or hold the hand that would be laid in his" did the Witch agree. He held out his hand and felt a touch that was "soft and delicate like the hand of a lady." Another man, however, also shook hands with the witch, but he described it as being touched with a hirsute substance.

William Porter was another neighbor fond of engaging the Witch in extended conversations, the only way anyone had found to keep it from engaging in further naughtiness. Porter was a bachelor, and a good thing, too. Kate tried to sleep with him one night.

"It was a cold night and I made a big log fire before retiring," Porter told friends several days later. "As soon as I got in bed I heard scratching and thumping about the bed, just like Kate's tricks. . . . I felt the cover drawing to the back side, and immediately the Witch spoke.

" 'Billy, I have come to sleep with you and keep you warm,' the familiar voice said.

" 'Well, Kate,' I said, 'if you are going to sleep with me, you must behave yourself.'

"I clung to the cover, feeling that it was drawing from me, as it appeared to be raised from the bed on the other side, and something snakelike crawling under. The cover continued to slip in spite of my tenacious grasp, and was twisted into a roll on the back side of the bed, just like a boy would roll himself in a quilt, and not a strip on me."

Porter jumped out of bed, noticed that the Witch was all rolled up in the covers, and decided to end its reign once and for all. He grabbed the bundle and intended to throw the blanket, Witch and all, into the fire. Halfway across the room the load suddenly became quite heavy, and an overwhelming stench rose from the parcel. Porter dropped the blankets on the floor and ran out the door for a breath of fresh air. He returned a few minutes later and picked up the blankets, but any sign of the Witch had vanished. Even the horrid smell had gone.

The Witch's attacks on John Bell Sr. grew in viciousness so that by mid-1820, nearly three years after the first inkling that something was preying on his family, the mysterious ailments had made him a near invalid. Richard Williams wrote that the "spells" were occasioned by "the jerking and twitching of his face, and the swelling of his tongue, fearfully distorting his whole physiognomy."

The episodes lasted for days on end, but would then go away and he would return to normalcy. As 1820 progressed, however, he had fewer days of good health. One of his children accompanied him on those rare occasions when he went outdoors, should he experience one of the spells.

The Witch, who had promised to see "Old Jack" dead, was delighted at the man's declining health. It grew angrier and more violent toward him, cursing his every breath; toward Mrs. Bell it continued to be kind and loving.

The end came in December 1820. On the morning of the nineteenth, the family found their father and husband in a deep slumber from which he could not be roused. John Junior ran to the cupboard where his father's medicine was kept. The bottle was missing, in its place a vial about one-third full of a mysterious dark liquid. No one could account for the missing medication, nor did anyone know what the new vial contained.

The family doctor was sent for. He examined the substance and declared he had no idea what it was. The Witch was smug: "It's useless for you to try to relieve Old Jack," its voice sang out through his bedroom. "I have got him this time; he will never get up from that bed again. I put it [the vial] there, and gave Old Jack a big dose out of it last night while he was asleep, which fixed him."

A cat was given a small bit of the brown liquid found in the vial and promptly dropped over dead.

John Bell Sr. died on the morning of December 20, 1820, without ever having regained consciousness. He was buried in the small family cemetery. At the funeral, mourners heard the Witch drunkenly singing and laughing in the distance.

After John Bell Sr.'s death, the Witch seemed to lose interest in persecuting the household. Strangely, as Bell slipped toward death, the Witch relented in its attacks on Betsy and she recovered completely from her illnesses. Now days would pass without any sign of the Witch's presence. Neighbors continued to visit, giving comfort and condolences to the family, but rarely was the Witch heard from, although it continued to object to a relationship that was blossoming between Joshua Gardner and young Betsy Bell.

Gardner was her schoolmate, came from a prominent family, and was considered a "good catch" in the region. He was full of promise and hope for a future that, he implored, included marriage to Betsy.

All during the Witch's appearances, and particularly its attacks on Betsy and her father, Joshua Gardner had stood by her side, his love and devotion never wavering. The Witch had on many occasions cursed the young woman and begged her not to marry the young man.

As the Witch's visits waned during the spring of 1821, Betsy, who was only fifteen years old, decided that Joshua would make a good husband and became engaged to him. Their happy future was not to be.

On Easter Monday, 1821, the couple had gone fishing on the Red River with several other young people. Joshua had just thrown his line into the river when it was seized by a fish witnesses described as two to three feet long, and of a variety they'd never seen. The giant fish yanked the pole from Joshua's hands and swam away upstream, dragging the pole and tackle with it. A few minutes later, it came back downstream holding the pole in its giant mouth.

And then as if issuing from the sky above came the familiar but now melancholy voice of the Witch: "Please Betsy Bell, don't have Joshua Gardner!"

The young woman tore the engagement ring off her finger and gave it back to her lover. He tried to plead his case, but Betsy said the Witch's constant presence—"the thorn that now pierces my heart," she called it—would not allow her to live in peace if she married him.

Joshua Gardner reluctantly accepted Betsy Bell's decision and a few days later moved to west Tennessee, where he married and became a magistrate; he died in 1884 at the age of eighty-four. Joshua and Betsy never saw one another again.

With Joshua out of the picture, the local bachelor schoolmaster, Richard Powell, started courting Betsy. He had been her teacher for several years who "relished every opportunity for praising her virtues to her mother, telling Mrs. Bell what a bright, sweet girl she was . . . ," according to one history of the events. Powell's birthdate and background are not known, but he was many years Betsy's senior.

Powell is an interesting actor in the Bell Witch drama, one who may have played a greater role in the "troubles" than perhaps anyone at the time realized.

Described as tall, elegant, and well spoken, Powell was a politically ambitious man who later became a state legislator, sheriff, justice of the peace, and a captain in the state militia. He also read widely in the "occult sciences" and was said to have mastered the techniques of ventriloquism and possibly hypnotism.

But despite the disparity in age, Powell's courtship of Betsy was looked upon with favor by her family. He didn't force himself on her in any way and, indeed, bided his time for four years until she agreed to marry him.

The Witch apparently "approved" of Richard Powell, for in late spring 1821, it announced that it would leave, but promised to come back seven years hence.

By 1828, only Lucy Bell, and her sons Richard and Joel, lived on the farm. All the others had married and moved away. True to its word, the Witch returned, exhibiting the same pattern of scratching on outside walls, gnawing of the bedposts, and pulling off of bedclothes. This time no one in the family told outsiders of the disturbances, hoping that if they kept it a secret the problem would go away. And it did, after about two weeks, never to return in the original family's lifetime.

Lucy Bell died in late 1828, the farm divided among the children. The old house remained vacant and was eventually torn down.

We are left then with a conundrum: whether to believe that an unseen (for the most part) entity brought unimaginable anguish to this early Tennessee family, or that some human agent was responsible for the deprivations suffered by the Bells. Perhaps the truth lay somewhere in between.

Modern research into the causes of the Bell Witch hauntings has focused on the schoolmaster, Richard Powell, as a man who had far more than a passing interest in the Bell family and, most especially, the marriage prospects of young Betsy. Powell was the best-educated man in the community, an intellectual for his day, but an individual who was disappointed that he could not dissuade the frontier community from their religious fundamentalism, which often equated supernatural events with the doctrines of Christianity.

Powell had ready access to the family. He may have lived with the Bells for at least part of the time the Witch was most active, and there is substantial evidence that his grandfather built the house with several secret chambers. Powell knew their location and could have used them to prowl about the house undetected.

He had ability, perhaps, as a ventriloquist and a hypnotist. Accounts of the Witch's activities claimed that its voice sometimes came from a household object such as a chair or vase, and that it often mimicked members of the community, including the Methodist and Baptist ministers. Hypnotism, called "mesmerism" in those days, may have been a factor in convincing people they had grappled with an "invisible force," or that the Witch was dragging the person along by the nose, another oft-told occurrence.

The word "heretic" was often used to describe the Witch's activities because it engaged in tempestuous debate on subjects ranging from the belief in God to politicians of the day.

Richard Williams Bell wrote: ". . . the propensity for religious discussion was strongly manifested, and in quoting the Scripture the text was invariably correctly cited, and if any one misquoted a verse, they would be promptly corrected. . . . It delighted in taking issue on religious subjects, with those well versed in Scripture, and was sure to get the best of the argument. . . ."

Unless one accepts the possibility that a supernatural entity was at work, it seems reasonable to assume that the cultivated, well-educated Powell, by throwing his voice or secreting himself in an unknown passage, could have easily argued biblical passages with the unlearned frontier settlers.

Powell also had contacts throughout the community and could freely have gained information that he, in the guise of the Witch, then passed along during its visits. As the schoolmaster, Powell had access to virtually every household and family secret in Robertson County. He was known to have been especially friendly with the few other educated citizens in the community, including the ministers.

It has also been alleged that Powell had informants in North Carolina who passed along information about the Bells' family history, and also kept him apprised of news from the old north state. One source claims that Powell murdered the two informants when they threatened to blackmail him by exposing his ploy.

But what would have been his motivation?

Richard Powell was, of course, politically, economically, and socially ambitious. Some might even say ruthless. John Bell was very wealthy for his time, and one of the most prominent men in Tennessee. Powell may have seen marriage to Betsy Bell, even though she was in her teens at the time, as a way to exploit the family fortune. With John Bell out of the way, Powell might have assumed he would become de facto head of the family. The Witch did claim that it had gotten rid of "old Jack Bell." Although it cannot be proven at such a late date, Bell's death was suspicious, to say the least, and quite possibly deliberate murder.

According to some accounts, Powell was also present at the fishing party at which the "giant fish" stole Joshua Gardner's pole and Betsy gave him back her engagement ring. Powell may have seen Joshua losing his fishing pole as a perfect opportunity to again impersonate the Witch. Adding to the evidence of a plot by Powell is that after Gardner left the county, his land supposedly came into the possession of . . . Schoolmaster Powell.

The superstitious folks of Robertson County were easy prey for a man with the sophisticated wit and intelligence of Powell. And they didn't necessarily want the Witch to go away. The citizenry "concluded that a good spirit had been sent to the community to work wonders and prepare the good heart for the second advent." Investigations of the Witch's appearances were not thorough, and when the "witch-layers" and doubters were driven away by the entity's caustic tongue, people in the community were secretly delighted.

Powell may have been a philanderer as well. He was purportedly attracted to Mrs. Lucy Bell and her daughter-in-law, Martha, who had married the Bells' oldest son Jesse in 1817, interestingly enough the same year in which the Witch first made its appearance with the mysterious rappings. He may also have been involved with a minister's wife, who aided him in his Witch impersonation.

It is easy enough to presume that once Martha decided to marry, and Lucy Bell showed no interest in him or rebuffed his adulterous overtures, Powell turned his attention to young Betsy, albeit wrapped in the guise of a teacher devoted to the success of his bright, and attractive, pupil.

She probably didn't comprehend his motivations, or chose to ignore them, preferring the attentiveness of boys her own age. She was, after all, only eleven years old in 1817 and barely fifteen a few years later when she spurned Joshua Gardner's engagement. It was shortly after that when Richard Powell became her "persistent suitor," although their marriage didn't come until several years later; the exact date isn't known, but the couple were married for just seventeen years. Powell's date and cause of death are not known. After her husband died, Betsy moved to Water Valley, Mississippi, where her daughter lived, and died there on July 10, 1888. She always maintained that her marriage to Richard had been a happy one.

One writer has suggested other explanations, such as Betsy having a deep-seated hatred for her father, perhaps as a result of a childhood sexual assault, with the Witch being the physical manifestation of her unconscious self, perhaps culminating in the actual death of her father. This author, Dr. Nandor Fodor, asserted that John Bell's illness was "psychosomatic. The inhibition of the power of speech suggests that Bell had a guilty secret, perhaps the hypothecated assault on the infant Betsy."

There may be some truth in Fodor's theories, but any precise analysis nearly two centuries later is, of course, impossible. Perhaps there were psychological problems with father and daughter that resulted in physical disturbances usually associated with poltergeists, perhaps Richard Powell did prey upon the naïveté of the community in impersonating the Witch . . . but perhaps there was something more to the haunting, something that cannot be explained by rational means, especially when one learns that the Bell Witch has never really left Robertson County.

The Witch's last documented visit occurred in 1828 to Lucy Bell and her two sons. Joel Bell and his son had run-ins with what they thought was the Witch in 1852 and 1861, and two other odd events were reported in 1872, but the Witch's promise in 1828 to return in "one hundred years and seven" went unfulfilled. The mid-1930s passed Witch-less, despite a reunion by the Bell family in 1937 at which the spirit was an invited but nonattending participant.

Carney Bell's curious experiences in his mother's house and with his serendipitous discovery of Joel Bell's grave are only two of the many contemporary hauntings attributed to the Bell Witch.

One of the most mysterious places associated with the story is the Bell Witch Cave, on the banks of the Red River. It was used by John Bell as a storage place, and it is in this dank cavern that many people have encountered strange phenomena.

Situated on a bluff on the south side of the river, the cave has two large rooms, and can be traveled through safely for about one hundred yards. A small stream flows along its gravel floor. There is little if any animal life. Collapsing rocks and large limestone formations block access to many portions of what is likely an extensive network of caverns. The cave has been open to the public, but visitors should check with the owners of the property.

A young woman wrote to the authors about her visit there in 1987. Kelly Barnett and a friend decided to go exploring:

"As we were in the back chamber, we suddenly heard the sound of a woman singing and playing a guitar. Though the words were muffled, the voice was very feminine, pretty and melodic, somewhere between a low soprano and high alto range. It lasted for about fifteen seconds, and when we turned to go, it stopped.

"Back in the front chamber, I saw this blue shadow being thrown on the rocks behind this light, and it intrigued me so much, I took a picture of it."

The photograph Kelly Barnett took has an eerie, cloudlike formation in the upper right corner. She said the mist was not in the cave when she took the picture. Earlier, she had jokingly asked the daughter-in-law of the cave's owner if she thought "Kate" would mind her taking some pictures.

"Kate won't mind," the young woman told Kelly, "but there's no guarantee they will turn out."

Just to be on the safe side, Kelly asked Kate for permission, too. Evidently Kate tried to make her nearness known.

Other visitors have seen a raven-haired woman floating through the cave, or report being touched by someone. Rattling chains and footsteps trouble others. A young boy had his cap snatched off his head and dropped on a ledge thirty feet up the side of one chamber.

Even tough soldiers are no match for what haunts the cave. Several army enlistees from nearby Fort Campbell, Kentucky, visited the cave in 1977. One young man was boasting of his bravery and allowed as how he didn't believe in ghosts when something none of the men could see grabbed hold of him and pinned him to the ground. He said it was as if a large person was sitting on his chest, squeezing the breath out of him.

A Nashville author, H. C. "Buddy" Brehm, has collected many of the stories associated with the Bell Witch in the twentieth century.

He said sometimes things are seen, swirling, vaporous forms that dematerialize in an instant. The longtime owner of the farm on which the cave is located, Bims Eden, was guiding a group of young people through when several shouted, "Look there!" Near the front entrance was a figure that looked like a white, "bulky snowman," but with its back to the group. They could see its head, shoulders, arms, and torso, but nothing below the knees. It gradually faded away.

A woman touring the cave with her husband and son began screaming when she saw the figure of a woman floating near the cave's ceiling. But only she could see it. She was so overcome at the sight that her knees buckled and she collapsed on the floor. As her husband helped her out of the cave, the group heard labored breathing coming from behind a limestone wall, followed by what seemed like a person's death gasps. The woman was nearly hysterical by the time the group made its way out the entrance. She thought perhaps Kate had died a terrible death and this was her way of showing it.

The Bell Witch has become such an integral part of life in Robertson County that it is blamed for all sorts of odd events and nefarious deeds. As long ago as

1875, two men were acquitted of a murder they told the court had really been committed by the Bell Witch.

Author Brehm said the strangest incident blamed on the Witch took place late at night in the year 1968. A soldier from Fort Campbell was driving his girlfriend to her home in Cedar Hill and had to pass through Adams on Highway 76. As he approached the outskirts of town, a child darted into the path of his car. He tried to stop or swerve to miss the tyke, but it was too late and both he and his girlfriend felt the impact of a body hitting the car.

The soldier brought the car to a stop, jumped out and ran back up the highway. There was no body on the road. He thought maybe the child had crawled off the highway, but a quick search of the roadside brush proved fruitless. Since it was quite late, he decided to take his girlfriend home and call the sheriff in Springfield, Tennessee, to report what had happened.

He met lawmen and rescue workers in Adams and showed them on Highway 76 where his car had struck the child. They searched along the highway and adjoining fields for several hundred yards, and even brought in searchlights so they could continue until dawn.

No body was ever found, nor did anyone in Adams or the surrounding area report a missing child. The soldier was certain he had struck something; his girlfriend confirmed that both had felt the impact. He also said that a check of his car shortly after the accident turned up what he said was a small handprint in the dust on the front bumper. A rescue worker claimed that what looked like blood drops were found in the roadway.

The soldier later said of the incident:

"I saw her and felt the impact when she was hit. I know I hit her. The road was clear, the headlights were bright, and I was not drinking. Yes sir, I know I hit her, and I haven't gotten over it yet, and I don't think I ever will. I know I hit the child, but we never could find her. I don't know what happened, but it's driving me crazy."

Visitors to Adams, Tennessee, know right away they are in Bell Witch country. A state historical marker on Highway 41 tells a highly condensed version of the story, an old schoolhouse is now the home of country music's Bell Witch Opry, and the cave of the Bell Witch can be toured. East of Adams, on Highway 41, is the Bellwood Cemetery with a tall marble memorial to John Bell Sr. and his descendants. Bell, his wife, Lucy, and three of their children are buried in the family cemetery on the old farmstead, which is on private property. Tangled undergrowth makes it nearly impossible to find the gravestones, although John Senior's is the only one with names and dates on it. The original Bell home and outbuildings have long since vanished.

The story of the Bell Witch is still very much alive, however, particularly among southern storytellers. Even in Adams, as writer Don Wick noted, "Kate is still an almost tangible presence, and whenever something out of the ordinary happens, the residents around here are likely to shrug their shoulders and simply say, 'Kate probably did it.'"

And most folks think it's doubtless true.

The Prairie Poltergeist

The small town of Cisco is a center for oil and gas production, diversified agriculture, and manufacturing. But in the last century it was a tiny settlement on the vast frontier of north central Texas.

In 1877, a farmer named B. G. Woodson moved his family by covered wagon to a quarter section of land he'd purchased six miles south of Cisco, along the Leon River. Corn and cotton grew successfully in the fertile soil and wild pecans, growing along the riverbanks, could be harvested and sold in town. In time, pecans became the family's chief cash crop.

The existing house on the property, however, was poorly built and much too small for a large family. Woodson and his sons replaced it with a large log cabin of three rooms: a main room and the kitchen downstairs with fireplace and chimney and a sleeping room upstairs for the four sons who were still living at home. The seventeen-year-old daughter presumably shared the main room with her parents. The cabin also had a covered front porch and wooden floors within rather than the usual dirt floors. It was considered a splendid home in this small German settlement. And the Woodson family was well regarded; they were hardworking, devout people who eschewed the use of tobacco and read the family Bible regularly. In fact, the Good Book was their most prized possession.

But Mrs. Woodson felt uncomfortable in the house and didn't know why. She said nothing. Then, on a windy night in March 1881, there came a knock on the porch wall. A neighbor come to call, B. G. Woodson thought as he opened the door. No one was anywhere around. A harness hanging on the side of the porch must have banged in the wind. He took it down.

The next night the knocking occurred again, and the next night, and the one after. Even stranger, they were always preceded by three mewings of a cat. Woodson ruthlessly destroyed the family's six cats. The mewings continued. Oddly, the family's outdoor dogs never barked or whined or acted upset in any way. The rappings usually ended at midnight with a sound similar to that of a large bird flapping its wings.

The Woodson boys, ages ten, twelve, thirteen, and twenty-eight, told their parents that when the knockings started each night, an animal of some kind ran up the stairway to their room, hid behind a trunk and ground its teeth. Their father suspected they were telling tall tales, but they insisted that it was the truth. Once, they claimed to have seen beady eyes peering out from behind the trunk, but not one of the boys would leave his straw mattress to investigate.

Sometime later, Mrs. Woodson discovered a man's shirt lying on the stairway. A glove had been placed on either side of the shirt and a hat in the center. If there was a meaning in the arrangement, it was lost on the Woodsons. The items belonged to Mrs. Woodson's eldest son, Sylvester, who had stored them in the trunk before he left for a neighbor's ranch to work for several weeks. She put them back in the trunk.

Stories soon spread about Woodson's "spook" house, and before long visitors were coming from a hundred miles away to find out for themselves what was going on.

Although no one could offer an explanation, one person suggested that the phenomenon might have something to do with buried treasure. Tales of lost wagonloads of gold from Spanish days were common in the neighborhood, and supposedly a farmer living north of Woodson had lost a buried treasure trove to three strangers. He'd given them permission to dig on his land, provided that he receive a share of the loot. Later, the trusting farmer discovered a deep, rectangular hole in the river bottom on his acreage. He was certain that the strangers had dug up a chest filled with gold, but, of course, he couldn't prove a thing. He never found the men.

Soon, however, theories of buried treasure were abandoned. A new phenomenon descended, literally, upon the Woodson household. Rocks of all shapes and sizes fell down the ladder from the upstairs room of the cabin, two or three falling every minute and continuing for several hours. They would stop, then start up again. Poor Mrs. Woodson, alone in the house, trembled with fright as the rocks landed close to the doorway of the kitchen where she worked. Sometimes, when the "rain of rocks" began, she hurried to a neighbor's house for a cup of tea and comforting words. At night, the family gathered up the stones. Each one bore a letter, but no matter how they were arranged, no message was spelled out.

At first, Woodson suspected deviltry on the part of his three youngest sons. One day, on a hunch, he climbed a ladder to the roof and found several stones lying there. He threw them off. Obviously, the boys had been throwing stones *over* the house. But who had thrown stones down an *inside* stairway and for what purpose? Woodson knew beyond a shadow of a doubt that his boys would never do such a thing. Not one of them would wish to risk injury to his mother. Besides, the boys were seldom in the house when the rocks fell.

Sometimes, rocks fell outdoors when the family was in the barn, milking. They would hear them crashing through the trees, breaking the branches and tearing the leaves.

Inside the house, the hail of rocks was soon replaced by a bombardment of butcher knives, dishes, silverware, and miscellaneous kitchen equipment, all hurtling down the stairs. All of the objects belonged to the family.

The front door was secured by a wooden pin inserted at an angle into a hole bored in the doorjamb. One evening, after the family had just cleaned up a pile of shattered kitchenware, the door flew open. The pin was found on the floor.

Woodson replaced the pin, then ordered his wife and children to join hands with him in a circle in the center of the room. The pin was again somehow removed from the door, not once or twice, but five times! No matter how watchful the Woodsons were, they never saw the pin flying through the air; they saw it only after it had landed.

And then there was the problem of the disappearance of eggs from beneath a sitting hen. On a frigid night with the hint of snow in the air, Woodson feared the hen might not survive in the drafty coop, so he brought her and her nest indoors. The hen clucked and settled herself into a corner of the main room.

Suddenly, the family felt and saw the yolks and the whites of eggs trickling down upon them from cracks in the ceiling. No one was upstairs. For whatever reason, the hen was not disturbed by her now-empty nest. Woodson swore the family to secrecy. This incident, more than any other, was too improbable to discuss, even among themselves.

But as improbable as that incident seems, another even stranger one came shortly after the hen was removed from the house. Mrs. Woodson suffered from occasional bouts of indigestion. Neighbors suggested that she chew a little tobacco when she felt an attack coming on. One night, in discomfort, the woman sat by the fireplace wishing for tobacco and regretting that none of her men used it. In the next instant, a plug of tobacco dropped into her lap. She chewed it, she went back to bed, and she slept soundly.

And she *never* told her husband.

Soon, the most startling manifestation of all occurred. Late one night Columbus Woodson, the older middle brother, and Charlie Rucks, a family friend who had built the family's stone fireplace, sat talking by the fire. They spoke in hushed tones so as not to disturb the other members of the sleeping family. Then, as if from nowhere, a dusky child appeared before them. He spoke not a word and vanished as quickly as he had come. Columbus would have thought he'd been dreaming had not Rucks also seen the apparition.

Folklorists say that in earlier centuries the Devil was commonly known as the Dark Man, and death befell those who saw him.

It seems far-fetched to suggest that the child was the Devil's emissary, but Columbus did die the following winter. No one suggested that the appearance of the child was a death warning.

Exactly four weeks and one day after the first knocking had roused the family, a single rock was thrown down the stairway just before breakfast. That was the end of the inexplicable sights and sounds.

Surely the Woodsons were relieved, but did they also feel a sense of loss? They had been the center of attention in Cisco and had been visited by strangers from near and far. The following months and years saw the family settle into the quiet routine of life on the prairie of north central Texas. They were never again visited by their mysterious poltergeist.

Succeeding generations of the family kept the story to themselves for fear of being ridiculed. As the years passed, the Woodson cabin, ravaged by time and the elements, vanished from the earth. For several years the chimney stood as a lone sentinel, until it, too, collapsed.

Is there an explanation for this prairie poltergeist? Parapsychologists who study the movement of objects by nonhuman means believe that a teenager in the house may *unconsciously* create a phenomenon of moving objects, called psychokinesis. Unresolved tensions, often of a sexual nature, may create within the youngster a "vibration" that leaves the body like a radio impulse and plays havoc wherever it hits. The Woodson family had one prepubescent and two pubescent sons. They could have been the antagonists.

While these strange incidents from over a century ago were frightening, they were far from unusual. Similar cases have been reported for centuries from all over the world. Thankfully, the Woodsons were relieved of their poltergeist after only a short time.

The Nearly Departed

The Great Salt Lake encompasses nearly 2,350 square miles of northern Utah and is, next to the Dead Sea, the saltiest body of water in the world. Conversely, it is quite shallow, with a maximum depth of just twenty-seven feet. Although its shoreline varies yearly, the lake is on average seventy-two miles long and thirty miles across at its widest point.

All of this is by way of saying that the *known* facts about this briny American inland sea are readily available to the inquisitive person. What may be less known is the story of a Salt Lake City gravedigger who was exiled to an island in the lake for his ghoulish crimes against the dead. He disappeared without a trace. But some claim his ghost is still around.

His name was John Baptiste (or John the Baptist in some accounts) and he was one of the first gravediggers (or sextons) in Salt Lake City. All most people knew about him was that he lived at K Street and South Temple in a house consisting of two rooms and a lean-to. It was well furnished for that era, according to those who knew him.

John was a hard worker, always punctual in carrying out his appointed duties at the city cemetery. The graves he dug were straight and deep. He went about his dismal task with few citizens bothering to notice his comings and goings. Until . . .

About three years into John Baptiste's city employ, a man died in Salt Lake City and, of course, was given over to the gravedigger for final interment. Now it happened that the dead man's brother lived in the East. Not being familiar with the Mormon religion, he journeyed to Salt Lake City to see how his brother had been buried. The grave was uncovered. As the casket was pried open, gasps went up from the brother and the few others gathered with him.

The corpse was nude. And the body itself was lying facedown—as if it had been unceremoniously dumped in the coffin.

The man's brother was justifiably outraged. He threatened to sue the city, the Mormon church, the state—anyone and everyone who might have had some responsibility for this indignity.

Police immediately launched an investigation which quickly focused on the sexton, John Baptiste. Several men were assigned to maintain surveillance of the cemetery. Soon after another burial, Baptiste was spied pushing a wheelbarrow from the direction of the fresh grave to a storage shed. Authorities stopped him and found a pile of clothing hidden under a layer of brush. The fresh grave was unearthed. This corpse, too, had been stripped of clothing, which was identified as that found in the wheelbarrow.

Baptiste was arrested and his home searched. His two rooms were filled with piles of clothing. He used some of it as curtains for his windows, or drapes around his four-poster bed. In a cellar below the back room Baptiste had placed a large vat filled with water in which he soaked the clothing removed from the human remains. After it had dried, he would have it laundered by a family across the street. Apparently they never asked where Baptiste had acquired so much apparel.

The news of the gravedigger's outrages spread quickly around Salt Lake City. Bereaved, and now sickened, families swooped down on the city cemetery to see if their loved ones had been victimized. When the examination was at last concluded, authorities said he had stolen clothing from corpses in at least 350 graves!

All of the clothing still in Baptiste's home was gathered up and taken to City Hall for identification by relatives. A check of city pawnshops found that Baptiste had also sold items of jewelry taken from the graves for cash. That, too, was collected and returned to families. All the articles that he had stolen, and that could be located, were returned to the appropriate casket.

And what became of John Baptiste, the graveyard ghoul?

He was tried and convicted of robbing from the dead, branded and sentenced to exile on an island in the Great Salt Lake, northwest of Salt Lake City. Two islands vie as the site of his exile—the small, barren Fremont Island, or the larger Antelope Island.

Baptiste was cast ashore and told never to set foot in Salt Lake City again.

But that was not to be the end of the story.

A few weeks after the exile was carried out, lawmen returned to the island to check on their prisoner. He was gone. A search revealed remnants of a fire and a rudimentary shelter, but the man himself was nowhere to be found.

Speculation at the time centered on his having escaped on a raft built from logs and pieces of lumber, or that he may have swum to shore or to another island.

In any case, John Baptiste was never seen again. Not in the flesh, anyway, because for decades to come his ghost was sometimes seen on the beaches of the Great Salt Lake, wandering forlornly toward the water's edge, a heap of dirty, musty old clothing clutched to his chest.

Lost in Space

THE TIME: Late on a warm night in September 1979.
THE PLACE: An abandoned Central Pacific Railroad bed at Sinks of Dove Creek, Utah.
THE EVENT: A park ranger engaging in a historic reenactment pulls late-night guard duty. He is as alert and as cognizant of his surroundings as any man could be—yet he is wrenched back in time and hears and sees events that unfolded a century before.

The spectral repetition of scenes from the past is not an unusual phenomenon. At the turn of the century, two English schoolteachers visiting the Versailles Palace's Petit Trianon, outside Paris, claim they were somehow conveyed back in time to the late eighteenth century. As recently as 1955, mysterious people in the dress of the 1700s have been seen strolling in those same Versailles gardens.

Outside the village of Puys, France, near Dieppe, witnesses saw a phantom army reenacting a rehearsal for D-Day—in 1951!

All over the world, historical events are said to be repeated over and over again, even though their participants long ago turned to dust.

Even if he knew the commonness of these small, spectral dramas, that Utah ranger was in no way prepared for what he chanced upon that night, or what he learned in a later investigation.

The Sinks of Dove Creek, near Kelton in northwest Utah, was the site of one of many labor camps built by the Central Pacific for the Chinese laborers who helped complete the transcontinental railroad. The Golden Spike National Historic Site is southeast of Dove Creek. It was there, at Promontory Point, that the Central Pacific and Union Pacific tracks were joined on May 10, 1869, to form the first direct rail link from the Pacific Ocean to the Atlantic coast. Within days of driving the final, golden spike, the worker camps that had supported the heroic effort were abandoned. Many of the Chinese migrated back to the West Coast after they found hostility and suspicion, and only menial employment, in the raucous western towns that sprang up along the railroad.

The Central Pacific line at the Sinks of Dove Creek was deserted long ago. The county built a road in the right-of-way, yet few but hunters, hikers, and campers dared navigate its treacherous length. It was along this railbed that the park ranger and several friends made their camp as they reenacted a march by the Twenty-first Infantry, the army unit assigned to protect the railroad workers, right down to authentic military uniforms of the post–Civil War era.

The reenactors put up their tents and built their campfires at what they discovered to be an abandoned labor camp for Chinese workers. They even found weed-filled dugouts that had served as the foundations for the workers' huts.

With nightfall came the decision of who would pull guard duty—a necessary requirement even if you're "playing" soldier, and nothing more sinister than a stray bobcat might disturb the night. Or so they thought.

The park ranger drew the late-night shift, from two A.M. to five A.M. Stars shone bright in the clear sky as they seem to do only in the American West. No moon was out. The heat of a high desert day lingered as the ranger shouldered his .45-70 Springfield rifle and paced the old railroad grade.

Suddenly, and almost without notice, the atmosphere changed. Everything seemed out of kilter—as if it were 1869 all over again.

The ranger heard the locomotive as a distant rumble. He couldn't believe his ears. Surely he must be dreaming. Yet it wasn't the wind, for the night was still. He peered into the distance and noticed a pinprick of light like that of a kerosene lamp swinging back and forth. It was moving inexorably toward him at a high rate of speed. By now he recognized the far-off roar as that of a steam locomotive pounding along the vanished rail!

Suddenly, it was on him. He could hear the thunderous chugging of the engine, saw the bobbing light—but that was all there was. He saw nothing else and felt nothing as the iron horse passed directly overhead in a great clatter of iron wheels against iron rails and hissing steam.

He staggered back to camp and slumped in front of his tent. Was he going mad? Having a nervous breakdown? The most unnerving part of all was the absolute *reality* of what he had just experienced. Yet, it could not possibly be . . . or could it?

The ranger gathered up his rifle and marched back to the old rail line. Despite his misgivings, he didn't want to wake the next guard and certainly couldn't abandon his post.

If hearing a phantom locomotive race by was bewildering, the ranger was next to step even further into this enigmatic time bend.

Faint voices and soft footsteps now surrounded him. He couldn't quite detect what was being said, although it seemed the word "A-melican . . . A-melican" was repeated several times. That had a familiar ring. When he lived in San Francisco, the ranger's Chinese landlady had referred to Caucasians in that manner. The ranger was hearing Chinese laborers talk about him, the "A-melican." Somehow these were snatches of conversation from 110 years before! Only now they were talking about him, the "A-melican" walking among them.

The voices were soon joined by metallic thuds that seemed to be hammers striking spikes and a "sense" that all around the ranger workers were moving swiftly about, in a rush to finish laying the track. Suddenly, the ranger noticed hundreds of tiny sparks all along the railbed, precisely what one would see when sledgehammers drove home the iron spikes.

When the ranger related the events of the night before to his friends the next morning, he found that his experience was not unique. Some said they had experienced the same, eerie events while camping near other abandoned rail lines.

His later inquiries uncovered the information that stories had been told for decades about phantom trains being seen and heard along what is now the county road on the old Central Pacific line near Sinks of Dove Creek. Many locals refused to use the road for fear they would inadvertently encounter an iron horse out of time. Others who had dared walk that path told the ranger they too had heard the faint voices of Chinese laborers. But these were events only whispered in that isolated region. No one dared say aloud that they were frightened of spectral Chinese and translucent locomotives!

Even when the Central Pacific still ran trains past Sinks of Dove Creek, engineers reported seeing lights in the distance that signaled an oncoming train, though they knew that to be impossible. The engineers threw on the emergency brakes, but the approaching train lights grew in intensity until the phantom locomotive thundered *through* the authentic train. All the engineers ever saw was the dazzling headlamp, and all they ever heard was the puffing engine.

The young park ranger never forgot his experience on that August night in 1979. He discovered the truth of Shakespeare's maxim that there is more to heaven and earth than is dreamt of by philosophers. There are those souls condemned to repeat over and over and over again their mortal labors, and who will never know the everlasting sleep which is their due.

Mister Lazarus

The stranger came at dawn.

In his plain, long robes and matted beard and hair, the tall, slim man looked like he had stepped from the pages of the Old Testament. With long, deliberate steps he walked down Alta's empty main street. His gaze took in the hastily built storefronts, miners' tents, and whiskey palaces. Through narrowed eyes that seemed to bore right through the town's facades, he raised his head to look off in the direction of Rustler Mountain. At its foot lay Alta Cemetery. With an almost imperceptible nod, and just the barest hint of a smile, he abruptly stopped in the middle of the dusty avenue. And waited.

Though it was early morning, it didn't take long for people to gather around the stranger. They asked him questions, tried to get him to reveal his purpose in being there. He said nothing until a sizable crowd had gathered.

When he spoke it was to make an offer.

An offer to raise the dead.

Today, Alta, Utah, is known worldwide as one of America's premiere ski resorts, less than an hour's drive from Salt Lake City in the majestic Wasatch Mountains. There are few vestiges of the silver mining boomtown that one hundred years ago boasted five breweries and twenty-six saloons. Its population of five thousand souls embraced a sizable number of brutal gunslingers, brassy dance hall queens, crooked gamblers, and fervid miners.

When the stranger came to Alta, he could not have found a better place to make his bizarre proposal. Over one hundred men had been killed in Alta's saloons alone, while untold numbers of others had been killed in street shootouts and mining accidents, or had died of one of the many diseases rampant in frontier settlements. Alta's boot hill was filled with plenty of "customers" for the outsider's unholy proposition.

As the crowd listened intently, the stranger spun his tale. He had the power to raise the dead, he promised. To bring back to life all those loved ones who had too soon been committed to the hereafter.

Murmurs of delight swept through the audience. If there were any cynics that morning, anyone who doubted this strange man's ability to perform Lazarus-like miracles, they didn't voice their skepticism at such a seemingly impossible assignment.

The thoughts of most must have been on the son or daughter, the father or mother, the friend or lover, who now lay beneath the earth near Rustler Mountain.

There was no hastiness in the stranger's demeanor. He said he was quite content to wait until evening to perform his marvelous deed. At nightfall he would meet the good citizens of Alta at the graveyard—where they could welcome their dearly departed back into the bosom of the community.

Or should they?

Slowly at first, but with an increasing sense of urgency, townsfolk began speaking of the, shall we say awkwardness, of dead friends and kinfolk turning up on one's doorstep. How might we explain to Dad that his old home was sold and is now a bawdy house? That we're now enjoying with unabashed ardor the loving attentions of a new, and much younger, wife? Or that the rich estate left by Uncle Felix has been spread among a dozen relatives who are now quite reluctant to return their inheritances?

It soon became apparent to nearly one and all that this was just about the worst idea anyone had ever heard. The complications for the living presented by the dead arising from their graves would be insufferable.

A committee met the mysterious stranger at the Alta cemetery that night. They asked, begged actually, that he stop his planned "exhumation" and leave town forthwith. It was nice of him to make the offer and all, but the citizens said there just wasn't enough room for the living and formerly living. He shook his head and said it was too late to turn back. He headed into the cemetery.

The leader of the citizens' committee held a hurried conference with his cohorts. They dug into their pockets and came up with $2,500 in gold and silver coins.

Would the mysterious stranger go away if he was given the money?

He looked around at the taut, anxious faces of the men huddled before him. Nodding, he stuffed the money in his pack, turned on his heel and strode away.

The dead were left in peace.

This Utah yarn—for that is what it certainly is—has a curious footnote.

One of Rod Serling's "Twilight Zone" episodes was based on Alta's enigmatic visitor. Entitled "Mr. Garrity and the Graves," the show was broadcast on May 8, 1964, from an unpublished story by Mike Korologos, according to the authoritative *Twilight Zone Companion* by Marc Scott Zicree.

Although the story's location was changed to "Happiness, Arizona," there is little doubt that it was derived from the Alta legend—but with some other interesting differences.

In the TV program, Mr. Garrity (John Dehner) brings a dog back to life after it is hit by a wagon. He then promises to revive the 128 dead people in the cemetery. The town grows apprehensive when it realizes the unfortunate consequences of such an act. Garrity says he will leave . . . for a price. He is paid off and leaves Happiness a wealthier man. With him are the dog he resurrected and the man who supposedly ran it over. Accomplices all.

The Serling twist, as usual, comes in the last scene. As Garrity and his coconspirators pass the cemetery, the dead *are rising out of their graves*. Serling intones, "Exit Mr. Garrity, a would-be charlatan, a make-believe con man and a sad misjudger of his own talents. Respectfully submitted from an empty cemetery on a dark hillside that is one of the slopes leading to the Twilight Zone."

Or to Alta, Utah.

The Seers of Chittenden

Horatio and William Eddy sat in the back row of the little one-room schoolhouse in Chittenden, Vermont. They would have preferred not being there at all because book learning was not their strong suit. But by scrunching down at their desks they made themselves as invisible as possible.

One day while the teacher, Ethel Hale, was writing on the blackboard, a book sailed over her head and crashed against the wall with such force that the spine was broken. Miss Hale wheeled around.

"Who threw that?" she demanded, her face turning as red as the book cover.

No one looked up; all heads were bent over arithmetic papers.

"Who threw that book!" she commanded again, her voice rising. She suspected the Eddy brothers, but of course she had no proof.

"All right," said Miss Hale, "you will all stay after school for one hour."

The next day was even worse for the young country schoolmarm. The heavy dictionary lifted off its wooden stand and soared through the air as lightly as a feather borne by a breeze. Lumps of coal leaped from the scuttle by the stove and erasers arose from chalk trays and fell to the floor.

Miss Hale declared recess. She fled even before the children could get out the door. On the playground she heard loud, penetrating noises following the Eddy brothers. No one was near them. The distraught teacher ran directly to the principal, who promptly expelled both boys. They would never return to school.

Had Miss Hale not been a newcomer to the community she would have known that the Eddy family was "peculiar," that their home had been the center of mysterious events for years. Two daughters and two sons were born to the Eddys. Each time a new baby was in its cradle, unseen hands lifted it out and placed it on the floor or on a bed in another room. Voices whispered in empty rooms and pictures fell from the walls.

Zephaniah Eddy, an evil-tempered and uneducated dirt farmer, blamed his wife, Julie Ann, and her family for these "horrors," as he called them. Mary Bradbury, the great-great-grandmother of Julie Ann MacCoombs Eddy, had been tried and sentenced to death at the Salem witchcraft trials of 1692. But with the help of friends the condemned woman escaped and sailed home to Scotland. She may never have possessed any psychic abilities, but her great-great-granddaughter apparently did.

When Julie Ann was growing up she began to see visions and to speak with the dead. It seemed natural. Couldn't everybody do it? she asked those around her. Upon her marriage to Zephaniah, the couple farmed in Weston and, in 1846, moved to Chittenden.

There, Julie Ann told fortunes and began to predict events with such remarkable accuracy that frightened neighbors shunned the family. The devil's curse was upon her, they said. Zephaniah believed every word of it. He was bitter that his wife had passed this dreadful affliction to their children.

One day Zephaniah watched his boys playing in the yard. Suddenly, he saw two children he did not recognize. When he rushed outdoors the "visitors" vanished before his eyes. He took Horatio and William into the barn and beat them with a rawhide whip. The "spirit" children returned again and again, and each time they came Zephaniah beat his sons until they came to fear and loathe him.

When William fell into a trance at home one day his father poured boiling water over him and placed a red-hot coal on his head. William carried the hideous scars of his father's undeserved punishment for the rest of his life.

After being expelled from school, William and Horatio did not know what would become of them.

Their father did. Incredibly, he decided he would exploit his cursed children, who, he thought, had the power of witchcraft. Ignoring his wife's pleadings, he hired an agent to take William, Horatio, and their sister, Mary, around the country to display their diabolical "gifts." The boys, especially, were said to be able to "materialize" deceased persons. Indians, pirates, soldiers, a girl ghost who skipped rope would cavort on the stage while the children stared blankly at their audiences. Religious zealots and skeptics bent on exposing trickery abused the children unmercifully, pinching and squeezing their little bodies into wooden contraptions so they couldn't escape and pouring hot wax into their mouths so they couldn't talk.

Writer John Mason reported, "They were mobbed in Lynn, Massachusetts and stoned at South Danvers. On a second trip to Danvers they were shot at. William Eddy carried the marks of the bullets that grazed his legs for the rest of his life. William was ridden on a rail out of Cleveland and barely escaped a coat of tar and feathers." South Danvers no longer exists.

But as long as the money poured in, Zephaniah Eddy didn't care how brutally his children were treated.

After the boys had reached young manhood, Zephaniah had another idea. With spiritualism fast replacing the fire-and-brimstone preaching of the fundamentalist faiths, why should he pay an agent to take his children all over the country? And why should he and his wife transport them as they sometimes did? It would be easier and less costly for the people to come to Chittenden.

And come they did, by carriage, by wagon, by horseback. Some even came on foot. From the West Coast, the Midwest, the South, and all parts of New England, the new pilgrims arrived. Some had spent their life savings to get to Chittenden. All sought affirmation of life after death as evidenced by the remarkable talents of the Eddys, and they thrilled to the prospect of seeing loved ones return in the flesh; few would be disappointed.

Most visitors, however, were appalled by the dinginess of the hamlet to which they'd come and repelled by the uncongenial Eddy family, who made them feel ill at ease.

Groups of ten were boarded at the Eddy farmhouse, all crammed into one room on an upper floor that was cold in winter and hot in summer. Plaster was falling off the walls and the floor sagged, yet for only ten dollars a week one had his board and room and the opportunity to rummage through the house looking for any sort of device that might indicate fraud at the séances.

Horatio and William were the catalysts for the phenomena and they held séances every evening except Sunday in a second-floor room that came to be known as the "circle room." Here William sat beside a "spirit cabinet" on a small raised platform. The audience sat on wooden chairs in a semicircle, the room eerily lighted by a kerosene lantern burning in a far corner.

After William slipped into a trance, the curtains of the cabinet would flutter and the first figure emerge. It might be a beautiful Indian maiden with shining black braids and beaded moccasins. It might be an elegantly dressed gentleman in spats and formal evening attire with a bowler on his head. Sometimes a lovely child with golden hair emerged to dance on the stage and sing sweet songs to the amazed spectators. Each figure walked, spoke, and reached out to the audience before fading away. One woman reported touching the cold, clammy hand of a spirit mother with her baby in her arms. As many as forty different spirits might materialize in one evening.

The séances began in August 1874, and one regular spectator was Col. Henry S. Olcott, a correspondent for the *New York Daily Graphic* who was assigned by his editors to investigate the Eddy brothers. Olcott stayed for ten weeks and claimed to have seen no less than four hundred apparitions emerge from the cabinet. He recognized two of them.

Olcott filed fifteen reports, all of which enthralled his readers. In one of his first articles he wrote that the Eddys seemed to represent about every phase of mediumship and seership: prophecy, the speaking of strange tongues, the healing gift, levitations, automatic writing, and, most miraculous of all, the production of materialized phantom forms that became visible, tangible, and often audible to all persons present.

The most astonishing materializations occurred during the visit of one Madame Blavatsky, a Russian woman living in New York. An ardent spiritualist, she had searched for the Christ child in India and would, in later years, establish the Theosophical Society. She and the Eddys became close friends.

One night as she played the organ in the "circle room," a whole series of Russian figures appeared and conversed with the Madame in their native language. Strangest of all was the Kurd soldier in pointed hat, embroidered coat, and purple velvet trousers tucked into his high black boots. In his hand he carried a ten-foot spear. After parading back and forth for a while, he dissolved in a cloud of mist.

One of the audience's favorite figures was a tiny Indian woman named Honto who once exposed her breast and asked a lady present to feel the beating of her heart. The woman claimed she detected a faint heartbeat. Honto, a chain-smoker, returned nightly. Newspaper reporter Olcott measured her on a painted scale beside the cabinet door. She was five feet three. The height of the medium was five feet nine!

Then he produced scales and weighed Honto. He got four readings: 88, 58, 58, and 65 pounds, seeming to indicate that her "body" was a simulacrum that varied in density from one moment to the next. William Eddy weighed 179 pounds.

Another regular "visitor" was a tall Indian named Santum, a taciturn warrior standing six feet three. Curiously, he always wore a powder horn that supposedly

had been given to him by a man in the audience. The powder horn was kept
hanging in the cabinet and donned by Santum whenever he materialized.

During one séance, Colonel Olcott produced two spring balances he had prepared to test the "grip of spirit hands." When a sailor materialized, a member of
the audience held one of the spirit's hands, and Olcott the other. One hand pulled
with a force of forty pounds, and the other with a force of fifty pounds. The first
hand was missing one finger. When Olcott remarked on it the sailor said he had
lost it during a naval engagement.

While William Eddy's mediumship took the form of materializations, Horatio's
talents were strikingly different. He sat in front of a screen with a member of the
audience holding his hands. Suddenly, musical instruments, hidden behind the
screen, began playing wild, discordant music and phantom hands waved on either
side of the screen. When a light was turned on the instruments would be found
smashed and lying all over the floor.

During the oppressive heat of summer evenings, the Eddy brothers held their
séances on a hill behind the house in a wooded area between two boulders. They
called it Honto's Cave. Here, by the flickering lights of the spectators' lanterns,
William materialized Honto, Santum, and sometimes an entire Indian tribe that
danced on the tops of the giant stones, their tomahawks shining eerily in the
moonlight.

But gradually the world shifted its attention to other interests, and the Eddy
brothers' séances became sparsely attended. In 1876 Gen. George A. Custer and
his 264 soldiers of the Seventh Cavalry were annihilated in the Battle of the Little
Big Horn. In that same year, a wonderful book, *Tom Sawyer*, was published by
Mark Twain, a newly discovered writer from Missouri.

When strangers no longer came to Chittenden, the Eddy family withdrew into
a world of their own. They rarely ventured beyond their own farmhouse. Julie Ann
and Zephaniah are buried in the Eddy family plot in Baird Cemetery. William
and Horatio, evidently seeking permanent escape from their tyrannical father, are
buried farther up the road in Horton Cemetery.

The truth behind the Chittenden phenomena is elusive.

Was it all a fraud perpetrated by a greedy father and his subservient children?

Sophisticated magic tricks foisted on a public all too ready to believe in communication with the dead?

The events seem almost too incredible to believe, and yet to this day no one
has fully explained the bizarre and baffling phenomena that occurred in this tiny
Vermont hamlet, once "The Spirit Capital of the Universe."

Bad Manors

When Evelyn Byrd leaves the southeast bedroom of Westover Plantation and brushes past guests and servants on the staircase, she speaks to no one. And no one speaks to her. That's because the beautiful and gentle Evelyn died of a broken heart more than 250 years ago. Still dressed in a shimmering white ball gown, she awaits the lover who never comes.

Evelyn's father was William Byrd II, one of the most prominent and wealthy statesmen of his time. For years he served as secretary of the Virginia colony and later founded the city of Richmond. But he regarded the building of Westover Plantation in 1726, on Route 5 near Charles City, as his most satisfying achievement. It is one of America's outstanding examples of Georgian architecture. A steeply sloping roof accommodates narrow dormer windows, while tall chimneys rise from both ends of the house. The front lawn, shaded by 150-year-old tulip poplars, slopes down to the roiling James River. During the eighteenth century, Westover was the scene of lavish entertainment; an invitation to one of William Byrd's soirees was highly sought.

If there was merriment in the manor house, there was also sadness. When little Evelyn was just ten years old, in about 1718, her father took her to England to receive an "accomplished" education that included lessons in Greek, Latin, and French. While abroad, Evelyn matured into a beautiful young woman with porcelain-white skin, long chestnut-brown hair, and deep blue-green eyes. When her schooling was finished several years later, she visited London, where she met and promptly fell in love with Charles Morduant, the grandson of Lord Peterborough.

The romance was doomed. Morduant was a Catholic, the Byrds were Protestant. Evelyn's father threatened to disown her should she marry the young man. A chastened Evelyn Byrd returned to Westover, there to become a recluse for the rest of her life. Although many eligible suitors from neighboring plantations sought her hand, Evelyn spurned them all. She had but one friend—Anne Carter Harrison. The two young women met daily in a dark grove of trees bordering Westover land near the James.

One autumn day, however, Evelyn felt her life ebbing away. She begged her friend to continue keeping their rendezvous by the river.

"After my death I shall come to meet you there as always," she vowed to Miss Harrison.

In November 1737 Evelyn Byrd died, a sad, dispirited woman who had only reached her twenty-ninth birthday.

Anne kept her promise. Did Evelyn keep hers? Maybe. One night on a visit to Evelyn's tomb, Anne said she saw her friend, dazzling in a white dress.

Succeeding generations of Westover owners and guests claim to have seen the ghost of Evelyn Byrd, drifting ethereally through the house and about the garden and grounds.

In the 1920s when Richard H. Cranes owned Westover, a workman arrived one day to do some repair work in the southeast bedroom. As he entered the room, he found a young woman combing her hair in front of a mirror. He ran downstairs and said to the homeowner, "You didn't tell me someone was in the room." They both went back upstairs but found only an empty room.

Later, the Craneses' daughter invited a school friend to spend the night. Both girls slept together in a large bed. Suddenly, the visiting child awoke to find a woman in white peering at her. She sensed more than saw that the woman was not a real person. In the morning, one of the servants found the woman in white loitering on the steps leading from the kitchen to the pantry.

In December 1929, a house guest of the Cranes was assigned a first-floor room overlooking the garden. She awoke in the middle of the night and gazed idly out the window. On the moonlit lawn stood Evelyn Byrd. The guest later would describe the apparition in these words: "the filmy, nebulous and cloudy figure of a woman, so transparent no features could be distinguished, only the gauzy texture of a woman's form. It seemed to be floating a little above the lawn, almost on a level with the window itself."

The apparition raised its head toward the woman. With a wave of its arm, the ghost seemed to warn her away from the window. She promptly closed the drapes.

Before they bought Westover, the Craneses had feared that they could never find servants. After all, everyone in Charles City County knew that their manor was haunted. But the family, along with subsequent owners, never had problems hiring help. One person, long associated with Westover, thinks that people aren't frightened because the ghost of Evelyn Bird usually appears in three-dimensional form. They think she is a real person and they're only mystified when the lady vanishes.

Not long ago, a visitor leaving Westover turned to see someone following behind her on the walk.

"She had a glow all about her," the woman recalled. "She was wearing a white dress and had black hair. She was very pretty. Then she stopped and just seemed to sink into the ground."

The ghost of Evelyn Byrd is not the only one that haunts Westover.

Evelyn's sister-in-law, Elizabeth Hill Carter Byrd, died in a tragic accident in the house, and her sad spirit too remains.

Elizabeth married Evelyn's brother, Col. William Byrd III, when she was sixteen years old and he twenty. The couple was never happy. Elizabeth, or "Betty" as she was called by the family, bore five children in her short married life of eleven years. Her two small sons were sent away to school in England (she never saw them again) and her mother-in-law, Moriah Taylor Byrd, treated her with disdain. Moriah had never favored the marriage.

One day Moriah said to Betty, "My son never loved you. If you don't believe me, you'll find evidence in the chest upstairs."

Betty was sick. It was true that her husband had two weaknesses: gambling and women, and not necessarily in that order. Although she'd heard rumors of his illicit affairs, Betty dismissed them from her mind. Now she had to learn the truth. Of course, the "evidence" would be in the form of love letters, she thought, letters well concealed in their own bedroom.

Betty knew the chest her mother-in-law referred to. A large chest-on-chest stood against one wall. She pulled out two of the lower drawers and, using them as steps, climbed up to reach the top drawer. The massive chest shuddered, then toppled onto her. She was crushed to death.

Since that day, Westover servants have heard piercing screams coming from Betty's old room.

Some believe she is calling for help; others say the voice is that of Moriah warning Betty away from the chest. It's been said that as long as Moriah lived she never forgave herself for inciting her daughter-in-law to take the action that caused her death. Sometimes it's best to leave secrets alone.

Six months after Betty's death, William Byrd III married Mary Willing of Philadelphia. This marriage was a happy one until William gambled away the family's fortune. Distraught at the thought of losing Westover, he committed suicide in the house.

A century and a half later, a house guest asked to sleep in the room in which William killed himself. At midnight he heard the door opening slowly. A historian wrote of the incident, "... a shadowy, icy presence seemed to glide past the great bedstead and then to the chintz-covered chair. Its vapory unreality filled not only the chair, but the room, and turned the atmosphere into the chill of death."

The guest leaped into bed and pulled the covers over his quaking body. He never slept. He knew for a certainty that he was sharing the room with what was left of William Byrd III.

The Portrait

Martha Hill, known to her family as Aunt Pratt, was, to put it charitably, a problem relative. Most families have one. A vain woman of unremarkable looks, Aunt Pratt sat for her portrait, then insisted that it hang in her brother Edward's plantation home, Shirley, for all to see. In time, Aunt Pratt married an Englishman and moved to Britain. She died there in 1752.

Aunt Pratt, haughty woman that she was, never let her relatives forget her. Her ghost has bedeviled nine generations of the Hill and Carter families.

Long before the hauntings began, Shirley Plantation had become one of the landmarks in colonial America. During the Revolutionary War, it was a supply center for the Continental Army; later, during the Civil War the home survived the struggle for nearby Richmond, capital of the Confederacy. Anne Hill Carter, mother of Confederate general Robert E. Lee, was born here. Her wedding to "Light-Horse" Harry Lee took place in the manor house's parlor.

The plantation, believed to be the oldest in Virginia, was established in 1613 on the banks of the James River. It was granted to Edward Hill in 1660.

In 1723, the third Edward Hill, a member of the House of Burgesses in the Virginia colony, built the present Queen Anne–style mansion as a wedding gift to his daughter, Elizabeth. Her marriage to John Carter, scion of "the first family of Virginia planters" as the son of Robert "King" Carter, united two of Virginia's wealthiest families.

The young couple filled their spacious home with elegantly carved furniture, crested silver, and family portraits. But, for some reason, the picture of Aunt Pratt didn't look right on the sitting room wall. They moved it to a bedroom.

Shortly afterward, a distant relative came to visit and slept in the bed beneath Aunt Pratt's picture. After a few sleepless nights, the woman complained that Aunt Pratt's gaze kept following her around the room. One night, unable to stand the stress any longer, she turned the portrait to the wall. Instantly, something moaned and an armchair rocked backward.

Lavinia Deas, a guest at the plantation during the Civil War, had a similar experience in that bedroom. On a stormy, rain-filled night, the portrait of Aunt Pratt started jiggling around. Lavinia turned its face against the wall. When she suffered a serious accident later, she claimed that Aunt Pratt had something to do with it.

Several decades had passed when a Mrs. Bransford found herself spending the night at Shirley Plantation. Her attempts to settle in for the night were disrupted by the rhythmic creaking of a rocking chair overhead. It was the spirit of Martha Hill, she was told, displeased because her picture had been banished to the attic. Martha could indeed create a mighty disturbance.

Succeeding generations of nervous Hill and Carter children, hearing a commotion in the attic, were calmed to sleepiness after their parents reassured them, "That's just old Aunty Pratt carrying on up there."

In the early 1970s, the picture was loaned to the Virginia Division of Tourism, to be hung in its New York office. There it reportedly continued its gyrations, swinging back and forth on the wall.

An office employee found the portrait standing upright and leaning against a door at the far end of the room. Workers joked that "Martha was trying to get home."

On one occasion, when the tourism office was closed for the weekend, Martha's portrait was locked up in a windowless storage area. When the office manager returned on Monday morning, she faced three anxious workmen. They said they'd heard a commotion in that room and feared someone had been left inside and was hurt. The manager unlocked the door. The room was empty. And Martha's picture again leaned against the wall.

After Aunt Pratt's portrait was returned to Shirley Plantation, art experts, called in to examine its condition, discovered another face beneath Martha's. Itinerant artists often painted one face over another to conserve canvas. Colonial "recycling," one might say.

A psychic identified the buried image as a woman named Cynthia. Oddly, C. Hill Carter, then owner of the plantation, says he did discover a Cynthia in the family tree.

Carter also agreed to allow two ghost hunters to "sweep" the house, searching for errant spirits. Jo O'Shields and her thirty-one-year-old daughter, Karen Benson, arrived late one afternoon in 1986, accompanied by writer David Brill. The women hoped to make contact with Martha's spirit and urge it on to the next world, a world, they said, filled with light and happiness.

Starting on the third floor of the brick mansion, the trio walked from room to room with their arms extended and palms up. Benson explained that her hands were sensitive to electricity given off by earthbound spirits.

The women felt nothing on the third floor. They moved to the second floor. Still nothing.

Meanwhile, Brill had entered the dining room where Aunt Pratt's picture hung above the mantel; ". . . the lights in the chandelier flickered off," Brill wrote of the incident. "I felt my way toward the door and opened it. The lights flashed back on. I quickstepped back into the main entryway, found the others, and breathlessly explained what had just happened."

The psychics moved into the dining room, their palms sweeping the air. They said they felt nothing.

"If you'll communicate with us," O'Shields began, "we'll send you on to a place where you'll be happy."

A moment later, the bulbs in the chandelier went out.

Then they came back on.

O'Shields tried again. "Spirit, if you are here, make the lights go off again at the count of three. One . . . two . . . three."

In a few seconds the lights went out.

The women were perplexed. They felt no presence. Something was wrong.

Brill had left the room in search of Carter. When he told his host what was happening in the dining room, Carter laughed heartily. "That light is hooked to a sound and motion detector. It goes off in seven seconds if there's no sound or motion in the room. When someone enters the room, it comes back on."

As the trio left the plantation, Benson said that she *had* felt the strong presence of a woman in the dining room, "but for some reason she didn't want to communicate with us, and she left."

And what does Carter think? "I haven't seen anything I can attribute to ghosts," he said.

Virginia just might contain more haunted houses, highways, and byways than any other state. Certainly, the ghosts of the Old Dominion are among the most colorful to be found anywhere. Whether this has to do with the state's long history or the fact that Virginians are excellent storytellers is uncertain. But if one wants to find a multitude of creepy ghost stories, Virginia can provide all manner of haunts.

A few other ghosts are well worth mentioning:

Scotchtown

Patrick Henry's old house was haunted when he bought it centuries ago. A blood stain remains on the hall floor, left over when the owner before Henry killed a man who was paying too much attention to his Missus. When the moon is in its quarter, the murdered man revisits his death site.

A woman with a shawl drawn tightly about her head sometimes wanders from the cellar to the kitchen door, and thence to the loft. An odd place, the loft. It's actually the house's second story, but it has no windows. The British taxed colonists for each window they installed, so the wise builders of Scotchtown simply made the second floor a storage room.

Alexandria

A small black dog haunts Robert E. Lee's childhood home. And at Ramsay House, a chair was once seen levitating, and a disinherited son, long dead, occasionally shows himself to startled tourists.

Martha Washington Inn

In the southwest Virginia city of Abingdon, this nineteenth-century inn counts a despondent young girl ghost as a resident. She died of a broken heart. The young Yankee soldier she was nursing back to health, and whom she loved deeply, died of his grave wounds.

Virginia Beach

The infamous Grace Sherwood, the seventeenth-century woman who was the only female "ducked" for witchcraft in Virginia, has given the circumstances of her infamy to Witch Duck Point on the Lynnhaven River.

Trapezium House

Charles O'Hara was afraid of ghosts. A West Indian slave persuaded O'Hara that only right angles germinated ghosts and gremlins—so he built Trapezium House, Petersburg, in 1816 without any right angles. Ghosts have apparently stayed away.

In the 1890s, Centre Hill Mansion, also in Petersburg, was the site of a very strange haunting. It may have grown out of the military siege of the city, which turned out to be the longest in United States history. An entire regiment of soldiers moved about the mansion, according to witnesses. One account states, "Neighbors for many years gathered annually to witness this haunting."

Bacon's Castle

A mysterious ball of fire zips out of Old Lawne Creek Church graveyard, near the castle, and maneuvers between the castle and the cemetery. It always disappears in the ruins of the old church.

Augustine Moore House

Did Augie do it? That's what cast and crew members of the television series "George Washington" were wondering in 1984 when part of the show was filmed at this 1709 Yorktown house. Augustine Moore Jr. was not included in his father's will, perhaps indicating that he died at an early age. Does he haunt the house? A National Park Service ranger told reporters, "There have been situations where people have been uncomfortable in the house." The film's director, Buzz Kulik, declared that the crew heard sounds of plumbing, when there is none in the house. Oddly, none of the noises turned up on audiotape, even when they were clearly audible to the crew members.

Haw Branch Plantation

Established in 1745, this historic plantation in Amelia County has a ghostly tradition going back at least four generations, although recent events may mean the spirits are now at peace.

Soon after Mr. and Mrs. William Cary McConnaughey bought Haw Branch in 1965, a woman's horrified scream shattered the early morning hours on four separate occasions. The cries seemed to come from the attic. When lights were turned on, footsteps on the stairs which had been heard only moments before suddenly quieted. A scent of attar of roses in one bedroom and the aroma of freshly peeled oranges in the library were two other odd events during the McConnaughey family's early tenancy at the plantation.

At least four generations of residents and visitors, including the McConnaugheys, have seen the plantation's mysterious "lady in white."

Another puzzle surrounded a pastel portrait that hung in the house. Originally thought to be a charcoal interpretation, the portrait gradually regained its color over a period of a year and a half without any assistance. The girl in the portrait appears to blush when one looks at her.

But the final chapter in the haunting of Haw Branch may have been written, although it is as strange as the ghost stories themselves.

Mrs. Cary McConnaughey noted the 1988 events: "Oddly enough, since we have gotten back a portrait of my great-great-grandmother, Marianna Elizabeth Tabb Barksdale (Mrs. William Jones Barksdale), everything of an unusual 'ghostly' nature has gone away completely. A long series of coincidences led us to an auction of this portrait a week before it was to go on the block. This house was a wedding gift to her and her husband in 1815. The portrait was presumed burned in a house fire."

Perhaps Marianna was the mysterious "lady in white" and the attic screamer. And all she wanted was her portrait back.

Haw Branch is no longer open—to the *visible* public.

The Conservatory

Footsteps in an empty building. An organ playing by itself. A mysterious growling in the basement. This is how it was in the music conservatory at Spokane's Gonzaga University during the 1974–75 school year.

But even before these reports circulated throughout the campus, some students said that the school's Monaghan Hall was haunted. One had only to look at it—a formidable three-story mansion with a turret and a wide wrap-around porch that darkened the first-floor windows on the brightest days. It could have been part of a horror movie set, but it wasn't. The mansion was built in 1898 by pioneer James Monaghan, and bought by Gonzaga University in 1942.

In the fall of 1974 so many students complained of being afraid to enter Monaghan Hall because of "the footsteps" that Father Walter F. Leedale, an associate professor of music at the Jesuit school, decided to calm their fears by sleeping in his office in the building. He had a rollaway couch. All went well. For a while.

One evening Father Leedale was walking down a corridor with a key in his hand to open a classroom door. Before he could insert the key in the lock, however, the handle turned and the door swung open. The confounded professor carefully stepped into the room and looked around. No one was inside.

On a November evening the Monaghan Hall housekeeper, who worked days in the building, returned to pick up some things she'd forgotten. She later told a reporter that the front door was unlocked and that when she got inside she heard soft organ music, the same steady phrase played over and over. At first she thought someone was practicing, but the door to the organ room was locked and no light showed from beneath it. The woman got a key to the room, opened the door and snapped on the light. The organ continued to play; the keys were being struck in time to the music. The housekeeper had enough presence to note that the window appeared to be shut and locked from the inside before she fled the room and the building.

The unseen musician may have stayed on, though he switched instruments. Two months later, at about 10:30 on a frigid January night, Father Leedale heard a flute playing quite distinctly outside his studio door. As soon as he peered out into the hallway, the music stopped.

One morning two weeks later, still puzzled by the source of the flute music,

Father Leedale sat down at his piano and idly played the refrain he had heard. No sooner had he finished than someone knocked at his door. He opened it to find an ashen-faced housekeeper. Was something wrong? he inquired. Yes, she told him, he was playing the musical fragment she'd heard on the organ the previous November night!

Father Leedale didn't know what to make of it. Something not of this world appeared to be occupying the building, and he was determined to find out what it was.

On the night of February 24, 1975, Father Leedale joined two security guards in a routine check of the building. Daniel Josef Brenner, music department chairman, decided to go along too, as did Steve Armstrong, a student who'd been hired as a live-in guard. The men checked the rooms on each floor and found that all was in order. Father Leedale went back to his studio and the others left. But once outside, one of the guards shouted that he'd seen something moving through a third-floor window. The group hurried back inside and conducted another search of the building. Father Leedale joined them.

It happened on the third floor and, to this day, none of the five men knows what "it" was.

A narrow hallway connected a large practice room and an outside door leading to a fire escape. Once in the hallway the men were seized by something they could only describe later as a "force." One guard reported being "strangled." The other guard said his skin "tingled," while Father Leedale said his skin "reacted to something that was present." Daniel Brenner had difficulty moving and Steve Armstrong felt overcome by what he called an "oppressive presence." None elaborated on his experience, but one, supposedly a guard, spoke anonymously to the press. "I know what I saw," he said. "I know what I heard. And you couldn't pay me to go back in there again."

Father Leedale well understood the fear behind those words. The previous week he and a student had made a complete inspection of Monaghan Hall. Down in the basement, the pair had heard growling coming from the other side of a locked door. The student grabbed the priest's arm. "What's that, Father?" the boy stammered. Father Leedale mumbled something about the wind and the two left. Later, the priest returned alone to the basement and unlocked the door. Only an old bass viola with broken strings was propped in a corner. Could the instrument somehow have produced the strange noise? Neither man could imagine how that would have happened, especially since there was no air movement in the closed room.

But that experience in the third-floor hallway on February 24 convinced Father Leedale beyond a doubt that whatever was in the building was not going to leave . . . voluntarily.

On February 25, Father Leedale began the first in a series of six prayers to expel the tenant of Monaghan Hall.

The priest assembled a small group to participate in the ritual, including Prof. Daniel Brenner, who held the holy water. Shortly after the prayers began, the witnesses gazed in astonishment as a heavy cross around Father Leedale's neck began to flop from side to side. Father Leedale moved it back to its proper position, but it continued to bang back and forth against his chest. He seized it firmly in one hand and grasped a prayer book in the other.

Father Leedale recited the prayers over a period of four days. On one more occasion the cross around his neck moved, but by February 28, 1975, he had successfully finished his attempt to exorcise the "presence" in Monaghan Hall. The entity never again plagued Gonzaga University.

Father Leedale was obviously relieved when he was later interviewed by a reporter. "I have not had any experience of the slightest phenomenon since then [in the music building]. Whatever it was I just don't know, but it's gone. In all my investigations, I cannot come to a conclusion . . . it doesn't fit anything I've read about."

WEST VIRGINIA
A Child of Tragedy

Areas with a long history of violence harbor ghosts aplenty. If that is true, Harpers Ferry is one of the most haunted locales in North America. This village, tucked into the northeast corner of West Virginia and bordering both Maryland and Virginia, has been wracked by years of bloodshed—a "child of tragedy," as one writer aptly described it.

In 1859, John Brown, the fiery abolitionist, left Kansas with eighteen raiders to initiate a slave revolt in Harpers Ferry. Its location in the Blue Ridge Mountains offered excellent hideouts, and a federal arsenal, in full operation, could provide the weapons Brown needed to defeat the slaveholders and establish a free black stronghold.

That was the plan.

But one prominent black leader warned Brown that he was walking into a steel trap and would never get out alive. The prophecy came true. The attack by John Brown's forces was successful—at first. They captured the armory, but state militia and federal forces under the command of Robert E. Lee arrived to wrest control from the Connecticut-born firebrand and his followers. Brown's ragtag army was routed, and this leader who envisioned a stronghold for runaway slaves in Virginia was himself captured, tried for treason, and convicted. Although his righteous indignation at the hideous institution of slavery drew praise from Northern sympathizers, Brown was hanged in a field just outside Charles Town, seven miles from Harpers Ferry.

Two years later, in 1861, the War Between the States broke out, and again blood ran in the streets of Harpers Ferry. Untold numbers of gruesome deaths occurred in the small town, often to women and children caught in the relentless crossfire of battle. Many who survived the skirmishes would succumb later in cholera epidemics.

Natural disasters, too, occurred with some regularity. Harpers Ferry is built at the confluence of the Potomac and Shenandoah rivers, and periodic flooding washed away homes and businesses and exacted a heavy toll of human lives.

Harpers Ferry is now a National Historic Park where, during the summer and on spring and autumn weekends, park employees appear in period costumes to lead visitors around the town, exploring the physical vestiges of one of America's most famous locales. And some folks say that a vast array of ghosts from the town's blood-soaked past also walk the city streets and wander in and out of the old, historic homes.

The Guest House

Marguerite Thayer was staying temporarily in the National Park Service's guest house, the building that is now the library. A government employee from Georgetown, she'd been assigned to a project in Harpers Ferry.

One day she returned to the house at noon to take a short nap. As she walked down the long hallway toward her room, she noticed a man standing at the head of the servants' stairway—a handsome man wearing a beautiful brocade vest and top hat, and holding a cane in one hand. She'd never seen him in the house before and thought perhaps he was a newly arrived roomer, albeit one of formal dress.

"Hello," she said pleasantly. "Can I help you?"

The man glared at Marguerite.

"Who are you?" she snapped.

A dark, menacing look shadowed the stranger's face.

Marguerite reached for her bedroom door, but as her hand closed around the doorknob she realized she'd be trapped if she went in the room. Instead, she lunged toward the door that opened onto a high, outside balcony. Just as she started to step out, a hand pushed her. She stumbled but didn't fall. Marguerite swung around to confront her assailant. He was gone.

Although Marguerite would soon encounter other entities in the house, none was as frightening as the man in the brocade vest.

One day as Marguerite started down the stairway she met a woman in a long, gray, hooded dress, the type of apparel worn in the eighteenth century. The woman held a child by the hand. Neither seemed to pay any attention to Marguerite and as she passed them they suddenly vanished. Marguerite never saw them again.

She didn't mention these two incidents to anyone; a family with small children was also living in the guest house and she didn't want to frighten them.

Marguerite returned to Georgetown and, by doing some judicious questioning, learned that others had had frightening experiences in the same guest house.

In the early 1970s, a year before Marguerite's visit to Harpers Ferry, Horace Fuller arrived to do research on Revolutionary War–era cannon. He was offered the private and spacious house as his temporary home.

One afternoon Fuller was lying on the front room couch when he felt uneasy, as if someone were watching him. Suddenly, Fuller saw a man pass by the couch. He appeared to be a working man, perhaps of the last century, dressed in odd-looking baggy pants with a cap set askew on his head. Even more bizarre was that slung over his shoulder was another man who appeared to be dead. Fuller watched, with horror, until the figures disappeared into the hallway. Then he leaped up and dashed after them. Fuller searched the house and found no one, nor any sign of forced entry.

Fuller told the story all over town. Many people wondered how a responsible researcher could be seeing ghosts. Although discomfited by the ridicule, Fuller stuck to his story. He completed his research and left Harpers Ferry.

* * *

The year after Marguerite Thayer's visit to Harpers Ferry a group of planners from Denver arrived to develop a comprehensive plan for the park. They also stayed in the guest house, two men to a room.

Late one night Jack Peterson was awakened by rhythmic grunts followed by heavy sighs. He had never heard anything quite like it. He sat up in bed. By the light of a full moon shining through the uncurtained window, Peterson witnessed the most peculiar sight of his life. His roommate, Dave Williams, was standing two feet from a wall and pushing against it with all his strength. Peterson imagined, rather than saw, the sweat pouring down his roommate's face.

"For God's sake!" he shouted. "What are you doing?"

Williams never turned from the wall. "Have to . . . have to . . . keep the ghosts out!"

Peterson grew alarmed. Williams was a sober and industrious colleague not given to flights of fancy or belief in the supernatural. What had come over him? Was he acting out a nightmare?

Peterson jumped out of bed and seized his friend by the arm, but Williams broke loose and ran out into the hallway that runs the full length of the rear of the building. Peterson did not give chase.

In the morning Peterson questioned his colleague and Williams told the following story:

"I really don't know what came over me last night, Jack. I don't remember anything about the wall, but as soon as I stepped into the hallway I saw a woman standing by the front stairway. She was dressed in a long, gray traveling outfit of some kind of heavy cloth, and she held a child by her hand. I'd guess the little girl was maybe eight years old. I couldn't imagine who they were, or why the woman was dressed in old-fashioned clothes as if she were going for a ride in a stagecoach. At first I thought they'd come from a costume party and got into the wrong house."

Williams lowered his voice and looked his friend in the eye. "But Jack, they were *not real*! As I watched, the two figures faded from sight. I peered over the banister and saw no one."

Peterson made no comment.

Several nights later Williams awoke again in the middle of the night and padded out to the hallway. He turned to go back to his room and suddenly froze. At the far end of the hall, at the top of the servants' stairway, Williams saw a man—an extremely good-looking man dressed in a brocade vest and top hat and carrying a cane. The man glared at Williams and vanished.

These entities, seen by so many responsible persons, seem to wander the premises at will, their identities and missions unknown.

Of this house Stephen D. Brown, resident writer of the town, said, ". . . [this is] the most documented haunted building in Harpers Ferry."

The Cries in the Night

Jim Cramer and his children lived on the top floor of a historic house in the center of Harpers Ferry. Late one fall night, Cramer was awakened by a sound that he couldn't identify. He sat up in bed and turned on the bedside table lamp. The bright light hurt his eyes as he squinted around the room. Everything seemed in order, but Cramer felt uneasy. Climbing out of bed, he went to the open window and peered out. He saw no signs of life anywhere on the street below, and wondered if he had been dreaming.

He hadn't. No sooner had he returned to bed than he heard a baby crying. Yet no baby lived in the building. Cramer got up quickly and rushed into his children's bedroom. Both were sleeping soundly; they were not in the habit of awakening in the middle of the night.

Back in his own bed once more, Cramer slept fitfully.

Several nights later, he was awakened again by the pitiful cries of a little child. Listening intently, he decided that the sounds were coming from *within* his room. He got up, padded over to the corner closet and put his ear to the door. The cries came from inside the closet; he was certain of that. With trembling hands, Cramer yanked open the closet door. The crying stopped.

For months, off and on, Cramer heard the cries. He never mentioned them to anyone, nor were his children ever awakened by them.

One night Cramer took the children to a nearby drive-in movie. He was glad to be out of the house for a few hours, and the youngsters always looked forward to the treat.

The family did not return until one A.M., and after the children were in bed their father stayed up to wash the supper dishes. Suddenly, the awful crying began. Cramer, tired and impatient, hollered, "Shut up!" But the sounds continued. Finally, he turned and glanced through the open doorway of his bedroom, which adjoined the kitchen. A white object, the size and shape of a football, floated out of his bedroom closet and crossed the room toward his bed.

Wiping the soapsuds from his hands, Cramer dashed into the bedroom, looked under the bed, yanked up the carpet, but found nothing. Still shaken, he returned to his dishwashing. As he picked up the next plate a tremendous crash shook the house. Cramer feared an explosion, yet the sound seemed to have come from his bedroom. Again he rushed into the room, but found nothing to explain the racket. He grew sick with fear that he was losing his mind.

In the morning the couple who occupied the apartment below Cramer's remarked that they'd been awakened by a loud crash. Had Cramer been doing some work in the middle of the night? they wondered. Now he knew that he wasn't crazy. Someone else had heard the same noise.

Was there any explanation for the incidents?

There may be. According to a recently discovered diary kept by a woman who lived in Harpers Ferry during the Civil War, a baby, in its mother's arms, had been crushed to death when the chimney of a building fell during a night of severe fighting.

Could the baby have been killed in the building in which Cramer lived a century later? Some say it's possible the ghost of the tiny one haunts the place of its tragic and untimely death.

John B.

The bearded old man shuffled along the streets of Harpers Ferry on that summer afternoon of 1974 when the town was filled with tourists. Although shabbily dressed, his tattered clothes were clean. He was a pleasant-looking man who bothered no one and occasionally nodded to a passerby. Because of his resemblance to John Brown, this silent wanderer was named "John B." by the Park Service personnel.

A family from Alabama was visiting the park at that time and wanted their pictures taken with a park employee. Suddenly, they spotted the old man and, noting his resemblance to the abolitionist, insisted that he pose with them too. It would be fun to show friends and relatives back home that John Brown himself had given them a guided tour of Harpers Ferry!

Numerous pictures were taken of the group at different angles and by different photographers. The results were perfect—well, almost. In every picture an empty space appeared where the man called John B. had stood!

Unbeknownst to this family, others have experienced the presence of John Brown, and not in altogether pleasant ways. At the Kennedy Farmhouse, five miles from town, the abolitionist's ghost paces the top two floors. The building, actually a restored two-hundred-year-old log cabin, was Brown's headquarters during the three months he planned his strategy for freeing Harpers Ferry's slaves. He and his twenty-one men slept in the small attic on burlap bags filled with corn husks.

Some visitors are uneasy in the place and few want to go upstairs. Sprigg Lynn, who lived in the farmhouse while attending nearby Shepherd College, told a reporter, ". . . it sounds like people are walking up the stairs. You hear snoring, talking and breathing hard. It makes your hair stand on end."

Psychics have declared the presence of an "aura" in the attic, and one woman claimed to have communicated with the dead abolitionist. He said he was "pleased" with the restoration of his old headquarters.

(Authors' Note: The names used in this account have been changed. All other events have been reported as fact.)

The Phantom Army

When Catherine Fenston heard the sound of boots marching down the street at two o'clock in the morning, she became understandably alarmed. Rolling over in bed, she woke her husband, Aaron.

"Catherine, you're dreaming," he mumbled. "Go back to sleep."

Catherine never dreamed. She said so. She got out of bed and tiptoed to the window that overlooks High Street. Only a solitary cat padded over the moonlit paving. But then Catherine heard the high trills of the fife and the roll of drums. The steady beat of boots on the pavement grew louder and Catherine heard men's voices, muffled, in the distance. She never took her eyes from the street below, but saw nothing. When the sounds ceased, she went back to bed.

Over on Ridge Street, Clarence Tuttle was reading. His brother, Lou, had gone to bed earlier and was now up to take his medication. With spoon in hand, Lou suddenly turned to Clarence.

"What's that noise?" Lou asked.

Clarence put aside his book to listen. "It's people marching."

Lou went to the window and glanced up and down the deserted street. "Yeah," he said. "Like an army, but nobody's out there."

However, in 1799, an army did march through the village streets. In that year, war with France was anticipated and federal troops were sent to Harpers Ferry to guard the arsenal. Diplomatic negotiations were lengthy and the soldiers, having little else to do, filled their time by marching through town to the accompaniment of a fife-and-drum corps.

After the threat of war had passed, many of the troops settled in the town. And for 180 years they have marched by day and night—a ghostly army defending Harpers Ferry from a nonexistent foe.

Shirley Dougherty, who gives tours of the haunted sites on Friday, Saturday, and Sunday evenings, told a reporter, "Just about everybody in town has heard the phantom army—the fife and drums—at one time or another. One night, I had just finished the story and it happened and everybody on the tour heard it."

And the legends, too, of other ghosts in old Harpers Ferry continue on: a little drummer boy, tossed out a window by a Union soldier during the war, cries for his mother; a young girl who burned to death in the 1830s still screams for help; and at the door of St. Peter's Church on the hill, the ghost of Father Costello prays for his flock. There is no repose for the restless spirits of Harpers Ferry.

The Drunken Man

Doug O'Brien, his wife Annette, and their two children—one-year-old Nathan and eight-year-old Valerie—moved into the 140-year-old house on November 1, 1985. Annette was pregnant with their next child.

The white frame structure on a quiet street in a small western Wisconsin city had undergone three additions and a number of remodelings through the years. It featured a front porch, a large entryway that served as a play room, a living room, kitchen, four bedrooms, a bath, and a basement under a portion of the original structure. It also had an attic. The yard was spacious.

The O'Briens thought they'd be comfortable there. But by August 1986 they started having doubts. Some things eerie and unusual came with their old home.

One hot night during that month of August, Doug had gone to bed early, leaving Annette and daughter Valerie downstairs. He'd had a long, hard day at work and was unusually tired. Adjoining the master bedroom was a room in which his infant son, Trevor, four months old, slept peacefully. Doug was almost asleep when the baby started crying. Doug was somewhat reluctant to leave the comfort of his bed. He rubbed his eyes and glanced toward the open door of his room. A woman in a long, light-colored dress walked past, toward little Trevor's room.

The baby quieted down immediately. Though Doug didn't quite believe it, he thought the woman *must* have been Annette. He got up and went downstairs. Mother and daughter were still there. Neither one had been upstairs and neither had seen anything of another woman in the house.

"I was shaking when they told me that," Doug confessed. "It was just unbelievable."

Annette O'Brien is a calm, easygoing woman. She wasn't alarmed by her husband's story. He'd been dreaming, she reasoned. Yet what if he hadn't been? A strange woman prowling around her house was not something that made her comfortable. Particularly a lady who seemed to vanish suddenly.

A short time later, Doug encountered a second "visitor."

He was sitting alone on the living room couch watching television. A connecting door opens into a downstairs bedroom. Doug said he saw "a little blond-headed boy standing in the doorway." The child wore pants similar to old-fashioned knickers and a blue shirt. His outfit was clean and neat, definitely not play clothes, Doug observed.

"He just came into the room," Doug went on. "I asked him who he was and what he wanted, but he didn't answer."

The child vanished as quickly as he had appeared.

In the morning, Doug told Annette about the little boy. She said she almost wished she'd seen him, too. Annette's love of children is evidenced by the day care business she operated from her home.

The little boy ghost may also be mischievous. Once Doug was relaxing on the couch when a small, bright-red ball came bouncing out of the back bedroom. And disappeared. "It was a little four-inch ball," Doug remembered. Although he searched for several minutes he found neither the ball nor the person who had tossed it.

That bedroom was one of the centers of what the O'Briens, by this time, were satisfied was ghostly activity in their house. Doug reached that definitive conclusion late one afternoon when he went into that room to take a nap and closed the door to the living room.

"Just as I was dozing off there was that lady again," Doug said. "She was standing beside the bed wearing a red jacket. I just looked at her. I didn't speak. I didn't see her face or arms, but I knew it was that lady I'd seen upstairs. I covered my head with the bedclothes for about ten seconds and then I just laid there calm until she went away."

Amazingly, the red jacket modeled by the spectral lady belonged to Annette!

"It *was* my jacket," she recalled. "I remembered leaving it there on the bed in the back bedroom."

Later in that fall of 1986, a stranger appeared at the O'Briens' front door. She was an elderly woman who said her name was Ethel and that she lived in Texas. Her grandparents had once owned the O'Brien house.

Annette and Doug invited her in. Ethel immediately said, "There's a closet in that back bedroom off the living room."

Annette nodded. Her son Trevor was napping in the bedroom at the time.

"My grandmother used to lock me in that closet and make me pray," Ethel divulged.

Doug was curious. He wondered if his ghostly visitor might have been Ethel's late grandmother.

Then there is the smoke detector. It's installed at the top of the basement stairs. The door into the kitchen is always kept closed. Annette and her sister, Sue, were chatting in the kitchen one afternoon when the detector went off.

"I went running," Annette recalls, "and smelled for smoke by the door. I didn't smell anything and I didn't feel any heat either. I carefully opened the door. The smoke alarm was set on TEST."

No one had been near the smoke detector.

"It's like someone is trying to tell us something," Annette summed up.

Doug worked ten-hour shifts at a company in Bloomington, Minnesota, an hour's drive from his home. When he started working nights, leaving the house at two P.M. and getting back home well after midnight, Annette, for the first time, became frightened in the house. What she feared did not come from anything mortal.

"I had all the lights on when I went to bed. I was really terrified. But once I was in bed and my eyes were closed, I was fine," she said.

Annette often waited up for Doug because, as she said, "just as long as somebody was downstairs before I went to bed I was all right."

One of the couple's greatest fears was that the children would be frightened or harmed. For some time they were not. Only Valerie, the eight-year-old, had a curious experience. She and a friend were playing in her upstairs bedroom one afternoon when the door closed.

"Suddenly, the door handle turned," the little girl began, "so I just thought somebody was outside the door. I opened it and nobody was there. We have corners that people could hide in, so I went and looked in every corner. There wasn't anybody."

After searching for a few minutes, Valerie shrugged her shoulders and returned to her room. Her friend, Abby, was not so composed. She thought she heard something at the door before Valerie opened it, a sound that made her feel "real weird," the girl said.

Both of the girls abandoned their toys and flew down the stairs, Annette adds.

A short time after that, the O'Brien children started having bad dreams—not really nightmares, but scary dreams they could not remember in the morning. Their parents knew then that they all needed help. Something was definitely wrong with their house.

Annette's sister suggested they bring in a psychic to rid the house of its ghostly residue.

In May 1988, Jacki, a Minneapolis psychic who said she sometimes worked with police departments, made her first and only visit to the O'Brien house. She asked that her last name not be used. Jacki had never been to the O'Briens' city and knew nothing of the history of the house. In fact, she came to the house the day after the O'Briens called her.

As long as they live, Doug and Annette O'Brien will never forget the psychic's visit.

"Jacki walked through our entryway into the kitchen," Annette began. "She said we had three spirits—a woman, a young boy, and an old man. Doug and I would never see the man, but one of our boys would. She explained that the ghost child had shown himself to her [Jacki] right away. At first she thought he was one of our boys, but then he vanished. The ghost woman was a nanny who will never leave as long as there are children here. The old man was an alcoholic who had died of starvation in the house."

Jacki went room to room in search of the spirits. With her were Annette, Doug, and Annette's sister, Sue, the one who had suggested seeking a psychic's help. The children had been sent to a neighbor's house for the afternoon.

Annette continued: "In the living room, she said there was a crib with a bird above it and a changing table against one wall. I got really spooked. When we looked at this house a girl with a baby was renting it. The crib was in the living room along with the changing table—exactly where Jacki said they were. And there was a bird mobile hanging over the crib!"

A woman was lying in a coffin against the north wall of the room, Jacki pointed out. Unbeknownst to the psychic, the O'Briens had been told earlier that two people had been laid out for funerals at different times in the room. The room had once been called the parlor, and it wasn't unusual decades ago for a funeral to be held in the deceased's home.

The quartet headed for the back bedroom, where Doug had seen the old woman.

"The psychic said that a little girl was locked in the closet at one time and was down on her knees reading a Bible," Annette said. That was nearly an identical description of what their visitor from Texas had told them.

Upstairs, Jacki became a historian.

"She told us the different dates when our house was added on to," Annette said. "When we got to our bedroom, she said that was where an old man had died and where he was now. That really scared me!"

The O'Briens' bedroom is at the front of the house, above a porch. Jacki said there used to be a door leading out to a balcony and a stairway to the ground. The couple knew about the door as they had replaced it with a window and put a roof over the porch.

"Jacki said the old guy used to escape that way at night to go drinking. So his wife wouldn't know," Annette said.

Then Jacki seemed to solve another of the hauntings. "Our bedroom had been Valerie's room when she and Abby saw the door handle turn. I guess the old man was going in to shoo the kids out," she speculated.

The psychic also told them the little boy she saw sometimes played in the attic. Each time he went up there he carved his initials on a cross-beam. However, the O'Briens have never seen evidence of that.

In a later interview, Jacki provided a more detailed account of the spirits in the O'Brien house:

"The little girl in the closet was requesting help for her stepbrother, who had died of child abuse. But the whole thing was kept very quiet. Even the girl didn't know what he died of. The poor little fellow had been starved. He was about six or seven years old, but was no bigger than a three-year-old. His shoes were made of hard leather and they were too small. They pinched his feet. I saw the little boy outside the closet door. The girl was inside.

"The ghost boy led me upstairs to where the old man was. You see when the child was healthier he spent some time up there. Then, I told him it was time to leave, that it was better on the other side and that there were places for him to play. He asked, 'What's play?' He had never known what it's like to play outside.

"The old man was not of the child's generation. He came later. He had a terrible drinking problem, always boisterous and as loud sober as he was when he was drinking. He was not a nice man. I started talking to him and he told me he didn't like the children in there. The way they made noise. I explained to him that these children lived in the house now and they were allowed to make noise. I also told him that he was not to frighten them."

Jacki had a clear understanding that the man was as mean *after* death as he had been in life.

"He was a large man fighting back at the world [when he was alive]. He was not eating to spite people who were trying to make him eat. He starved himself to death. He was sneaking alcohol because he'd been told he couldn't have it. That it would kill him. Late at night he would go out the door of his bedroom and down the outside stairs. That was his way to go to the bar. His wife . . . had some kind of nursing degree and was trying to save him. He eventually died in the house."

And remained there, it could be added.

Jacki could not recall specific information about the nanny other than that she seemed a benevolent spirit. After Jacki "clears" a house she loses much of the information about the spirits. Sometimes she can bring back strong memories of forceful, persuasive spirits, but the gentler ones, such as the nanny, usually elude her. It is possible that the ghost Doug saw tucking in little Trevor was the nanny.

Before Jacki left the house, the O'Brien children returned home. She told them that an old man had been giving them the bad dreams, but they didn't have to worry anymore. She had put a circle of protection around each of them.

"It's called a red aura," Jacki explained, "and protects each individual in the family and the house itself. Only spirits who are there with love in their hearts can stay. Any living thing in the house has got superiority over anything that has passed on."

If one of the O'Briens should tell a spirit to leave, it has to leave. The spirits don't have any control over the living. Once people realize that, she said, trouble with spirits usually goes away.

Unlike some psychics, Jacki said she doesn't drive spirits out of a house. "I tell earthbound spirits that they have passed into the next world. They don't have to hang around anymore. Usually they go."

The O'Briens *think* the ghosts are gone—yet, in the spirit world, as in life itself, there are no guarantees.

The Housekeeper

In June 1981, Gloria Bruch and her three school-aged children moved into their new home—an elegant Queen Anne–style house on Lake Street in Waupaca. Although the house had not been lived in for fourteen years, it showed evidence of having been well cared for.

Built in 1893 by Calib Shearer, a Waupaca attorney and lumberman, the mansion is graced by two round turrets, fishscale and shingle ornamentation, and inside, stained and beveled glass, burled wood in several rooms, and intricately carved stairways and mantels at the three fireplaces. It is known locally as the Cristy House after the family who owned it from 1907 until 1981. Joseph T. Cristy, the patriarch of the family, operated a dry goods establishment in Waupaca. He bought the house for $7,000. The Cristys made it a happy place, filled with children and laughter.

Gloria Bruch was thrilled with her purchase of such a beautiful and spacious house, but less thrilled to discover that another family, an incorporeal one, appeared to be already living there.

On her first night in the house, Gloria slept in the former maid's room in a rear corner of the second floor. At shortly after three in the morning, she was awakened by the whinnying of horses. There was no mistaking their gentle neighs. Gloria got up, peered out the window into the backyard. Pale moonlight washed over the grass and dappled the leaves of the trees. She saw nothing but felt distinctly uneasy. Back in bed, she lay awake for a long time. Much later, while researching the history of the house, Gloria learned that ponies had once been kept in the old carriage house.

The next morning Gloria wondered if perhaps she had imagined the night's disturbance. The move had been difficult and she had become overly tired. Now, as she unpacked boxes and arranged furniture, she tried to put the phantom horses out of her mind.

She worked through the morning, her mind occupied with the reality of making this big old house a comfortable home for her family. Entering one room, Gloria pulled gently on an old roller shade at the window to raise it to let the sun shine in. The shade fell on her head. A man's sharp laughter came from behind her. She wheeled around. As she suspected, no one else was about.

At noon that day, two of Gloria's children, eleven-year-old Barbara and twelve-year-old Mike, had an eerie experience in the musty basement. They both wanted to take showers, but the shower was in the basement. Being a bit apprehensive about basements anyway, they decided to go down together. While Mike took his shower, his sister stood by the washer in the adjacent laundry room.

Suddenly, Barbara screamed, "Something hit me!"

Gloria takes up the account from that point: "When my daughter screamed, it was very loud, frightening. . . . The next thing I knew both of those kids were running up the basement stairs into the kitchen. Barbara said that something had hit her in the face and one lens of her glasses was shattered. My son said he stuck his head out of the shower just in time to see the glasses shatter, but he didn't see anything else. I just assumed it was a bat, but Barb said it was definitely *not* a bat."

Gloria thought steam from the shower might have caused the lens to break, but an optometrist who later examined the glasses said the lens had definitely been struck by something.

Gloria had not shared either of her previous experiences with her children. She didn't want to upset them.

Soon, the night walker started on his rounds. Night after night someone climbed the wide central staircase from the grand entrance hall to the second floor, walked the length of the corridor, then went back downstairs. The first time, Gloria assumed that it was one of her children, but when she got up to check their bedrooms she found them all asleep.

Going back to her own room, Gloria felt a cold draft envelop her at the top of the staircase.

"And that's when I screamed," she said, although she didn't actually see anything. "It was so frightening. It was really cold right in the middle of nowhere." The presence of a ghost is often characterized by sudden cold.

Gloria's screams brought her children running, but she sent them back to bed. She had just "tripped over a rug," she told them. She especially did not want Mike and Barbara to be more frightened than they already were. Their older brother, Jeff, had not been in the house during the incident in the shower room.

The walker finally went too far. As Gloria lay in bed late one night, she heard pacing in the attic directly above her head. Originally designed as a ballroom by the mansion's wealthy builder, it was never finished and had always been used for storage. Now, Gloria heard something being pulled across the attic floor.

"It was as if a heavy box or heavy chains were being dragged back and forth," she remembers. And there were muffled voices, too indistinct to understand what was being said but most assuredly the sounds of human activity. "I was very frightened and I absolutely refused to go up there."

The attic noises gradually dissipated over the next several hours, much to Gloria's relief.

Other oddities did occur in the house, but Gloria didn't find them frightening anymore. "That was the part that was really strange. It was as if whatever was in the house accepted us," she said, and the Bruch family accepted "them."

The kitchen door would open and close by itself, and the swinging door that led from the kitchen to the front hallway would do the same. The family learned to ignore the phenomenon.

The restless one never ceased his nocturnal wanderings. Gloria even heard foot-steps upstairs during the daytime when all the children were in school.

One night, fifteen-year-old Jeff decided to play ghost hunter. He set up a tape recorder in the parlor and let it run while the family slept. Perhaps, he explained, the tape would pick up some of the sounds they'd been hearing.

In the morning, everyone crowded around while the tape was played back. For long minutes there was little noise of any kind on the tape, save an occasional truck going past the house. But then came a series of "loud, rhythmic noises," Gloria said. No one in the family could identify the source, but Jeff is certain they originated from somewhere inside the house.

Gloria said she detected the squeak of her rocking chair on the tape as if someone were sitting in it, and occasional rappings "like somebody was holding a pipe and tapping it on a table." The only readily identifiable sound on the tape was the grandfather clock at the foot of the staircase chiming every fifteen minutes.

The Legend of Wild Rose

Near the headwaters of the Wisconsin River is a lake called Naghibic. Generations of Ojibwa and Menominee also knew its shore as the location of a glen in which good spirits would gather. They were healers, these good spirits, and to the glen would travel warriors suffering from illness or battle wounds.

A spring bubbled near the center of the glen. The waters seemed to have magical powers. Once the feverish or hurt warrior drank its soothing waters, his ears would catch the soft song of a young Indian girl, coming from everywhere, yet nowhere.

The story of the glen and its mystical spring is that of a Ojibwa girl, Wild Rose, and the Menominee warrior captured by her father in battle.

Wild Rose pleaded for the youth's life. She had fallen in love, but her begging was ignored. The day of the boy's death arrived. Wild Rose awoke before dawn and stole quietly past the guards to where her lover was being held. She cut the ropes binding his wrists and ankles and led him to Lake Naghibic. There was a canoe waiting with which he could make his escape across the waters.

He implored her to escape with him. Leave your family, he said, and join my people. You will know no more war or cruelty, he promised.

Wild Rose confessed her love, but refused his entreaties. She had given her heart to him, but her life belonged with her father and her people. He paddled away, his eyes never leaving his savior until the morning mists shrouded his canoe in darkness.

Wild Rose sat on the beach, watching her heart leave with the brave young Menominee. A low, mournful chant came from her lips as she rocked to and fro.

That's where her father and the rest of the tribe found her. They had awakened to find that the brave had escaped. When Wild Rose's father discovered that his daughter was responsible, he beat her unmercifully. She accepted the punishment without complaint.

Others in the tribe suggested that she be punished further by being forced to marry a man for whom she had shown particular disdain. In this she refused adamantly. They could beat her, even put her to death, but never would she marry another.

And so they left her alone. Wild Rose was as before, but more silent. Each evening she would walk to the lake shore and, sitting beneath a giant oak, sing the mournful song begun on that earlier morning. On occasion, she would stop and stare intently across the lake. But what she was listening for, watching for, never came.

Month after month Wild Rose continued her vigil. The song became more sad with each passing moon, her voice hoarse and sorrowful.

In time, Wild Rose passed on and was buried beneath that oak. But the song didn't stop. It is said the old tree learned the sad chant, and at night the soft voice of Wild Rose swept from its branches. The fir and pine joined in the song, its eerie melody echoed by the spirits of Lake Naghibic.

The song continued for many years, until the great oak tree was no more. It was in that glen, near the grave of Wild Rose, that the gurgling spring appeared, the waters giving new life to those who drank of it.

The Lady in Green

The opening of the West is a saga of hardship and heartache, of families in wagon trains gambling their lives to reach the rugged, unsettled territories of Oregon and northern California. But the prairie is unforgiving; its frigid winter winds and sudden blizzards claimed untold numbers of men, women, and children. And some who might have made it were cut down by sickness or Indian attack, their makeshift graves marked, if fleetingly, by a cairn or perhaps a single prairie flower.

The lifeline of these vast migrations was the army post, where the wagons were supplied and weary travelers found safe shelter.

Fort Laramie, situated as it is along the North Platte River, in southeastern Wyoming, served as the supply hub for many of these wagon trains. From the fort's beginnings, tales have been spun of visitors who apparently never left . . . even after they died.

The best-known ghost story of Fort Laramie, and possibly of the entire state of Wyoming, is about a lady in green—a lovely equestrienne who, sometime around 1850, rode out over the hills and vanished. Her ghost appears every seven years, watching over her beloved Wyoming range.

This is her story:

In 1871, Lt. James Nicholas Allison arrived at Fort Laramie to command a cavalry unit. Allison was a new graduate of West Point Military Academy, where he'd been an honor student. Proving himself a capable and likable officer, he was soon included in all the social affairs of the post. In fact, he often wrote to relatives remarking on the fine assignment he'd been given.

A few weeks after Lieutenant Allison's arrival at Fort Laramie, a group of junior officers invited him to join them in a wolf hunt along the hills east of the fort. Lieutenant Allison had brought with him from the East his horse, and also a handsome hunting dog that was part borzoi, or Russian wolfhound. Although he had never hunted wolves with the dog, he was eager to get started. Smaller dogs would run down the wolf, then the borzoi would seize the animal just behind the ears and hold it fast until the hunters could dispatch it. The afternoon promised to be full of challenge and camaraderie and certainly a welcome respite from the daily routine of the fort.

The group set out over the wide, rolling plains beyond Laramie. Lieutenant Allison, a superb rider, soon outdistanced the others. Within a short time, he saw no one in sight. His "halloos" were lost on the wind. Disappointed that the others couldn't keep up with him, he headed back to the fort, but suddenly his horse went lame. He stopped and removed a stone from one of her shoes.

Then he saw her—a lone figure galloping eastward along a trail that intersected the one he'd been following.

The woman wore a long, green riding dress and a veiled hat with her dark hair evidently tucked up under the brim. She rode a coal-black stallion and, as she dashed past Lieutenant Allison, she whipped the horse's flanks with a jeweled quirt that glittered in the sunlight.

Lieutenant Allison galloped after her. A woman riding alone in this rugged land faced peril from man and beast. But the chase was futile. He mounted a small rise and looked in all directions. He saw no one, nor, to his astonishment, were any tracks visible. With a chill, he realized that he'd didn't remember hearing any hoofbeats either as the woman's horse pounded past him. Now, looking down, he saw his dog, with hackles raised, cowering and pawing the dry dust. The lieutenant reined his horse in the direction of the fort, with the hound slinking behind.

That night, at dinner, Lieutenant Allison was unusually silent and when someone asked if he was ill he said no. He studied the women at the table and decided that none of them matched the description of the mysterious rider. In fact, he could scarcely picture some of them astride a horse. The thought made him smile. The galloping vision he'd seen had been an expert rider moving as one with her beast. Where had she come from? Where was she going? More important, who *was* she?

The questions nagged at the lieutenant until he finally decided to confide in his commanding officer.

The commander listened attentively to the young officer's story and nodded. "Yes, Lieutenant," he began, "you have seen our lady in green. She appears near the fort about every seven years, and she means no harm."

Comfortably situated in the corner of a near-empty lounge, the commander told Lieutenant Allison all about her:

"Years ago, when Fort Laramie was a trading post of the American Fur Company, the agent in charge brought his beautiful daughter out here with him. She had been educated in private schools in the East and was an accomplished horsewoman. Although her father was uneasy about her safety on the frontier, she begged to stay with him. He made her promise never to leave the compound without an escort, and he warned his assistants to keep a guarded eye on her.

"One day, however, the agent was called away from the post, and his daughter slipped away, saddled her favorite horse, a beautiful black, and rode off. Two post workers, alerted to her absence, charged after her, but could not catch up with her, nor did she heed their calls. As if on wings, horse and rider vanished on the Oregon Trail. Now, she may have lost her way and starved to death or drowned in the river. No one really knows. At any rate, neither she nor her horse were ever seen again—alive."

The commander sighed and lit his pipe.

"Her father, of course, was distraught. He spent months, maybe even years, searching for the girl, but, from what I hear, he never bore ill will toward those to whom he had entrusted her care. He seemed to understand that his daughter's obstinacy and foolhardiness could not be contained.

"Years later, a legend grew among the Indians and traders of the valley that every seven years the ghost of the agent's daughter would ride along the old trail east of Fort Laramie."

Lieutenant Allison leaned back in his chair, entranced by the story. He thanked the commander and returned to his quarters. But he could not sleep. He was determined to learn more about this mysterious lady in green.

The next morning, Lieutenant Allison was directed to an elderly Indian woman who had lived near the post when the agent's daughter made her fatal ride. How had she been dressed, he wanted to know. The old woman squinted up at him, her face a wreath of wrinkles in the morning sunlight.

"Always the same. A green dress," she said, nodding. "And the hat with cloth covered her face. The whip had many jewels in it." She shielded her eyes with a hand and scanned the horizon. "A sad thing, so sad."

The young lieutenant paled. He knew now, beyond a doubt, that he'd met the ghost of the lady in green.

Many years later Lieutenant Allison was riding in a train across Wyoming. When it stopped to take on water, he heard cowboys on the depot platform talking about a rancher who had just seen the ghost of the lady in green. He wanted to question them, but his train pulled out of the station before he had the chance.

If the lovely lady ghost appears every seven years, as the legend goes, she should be seen next in 1997, her horse a Pegasus riding the Wyoming winds.

CANADA

Beware Amiable Spirits

The ghosts of British Columbia are sociable beings—they seem to congregate in the southwest corner of the province. From Kelowna, midway between the Pacific Ocean and Alberta, to the small coastal communities of Courtenay and Nanaimo, and on to the cosmopolitan cities of Vancouver and Victoria, the haunted places in this province provide gentle chills for its three million living souls. As far as can be determined, tales of screaming banshees and reanimated corpses can only be found in Vancouver's many bookstores, filed under horror fiction. But encountering a real ghost, even one of a most temperate disposition, can be quite disconcerting if one is unprepared to make such an acquaintance.

The Haunted Gallery

Halloween, 1986. Several employees of the Burnaby Art Gallery, housed in an old mansion known as Fairacres, decide to investigate the unused, abandoned third floor of the building. They find dust covering the floor and cobwebs in dark corners. Poking around, the group finds boxes of decades-old debris, an ancient wringer washer. A sink roosts incongruously in the middle of the floor.

They didn't uncover what they were really looking for—some evidence of ghosts. Nor were there signs of recent human habitation. The strangest discovery was the life-size face of a woman, apparently clipped from a magazine and taped to a window. The eyes had been cut out, as if it had once been used as a mask.

The desolation encountered on the third floor was all the more disconcerting because at least one member of the small band had once heard strange noises coming from there, noises that made her think someone lived up there.

"I would hear 'them' opening the window and closing the window," the young woman told a reporter. "And I would hear them walking and banging things."

The experience was so "real," the woman said, that when coworkers told her the third floor had been abandoned years before, she was very surprised.

Had the young art gallery worker known something of the history of Fairacres, she would have understood that eerie sounds ought to be the least of her concerns.

For years, various employees have told stories of wispy figures floating down hallways, footsteps in abandoned rooms, and odd sensations of being watched by unseen eyes.

Vancouver businessman Henry Ceperley and his second wife Gracie built Fairacres as their retirement home in 1909. Situated on a rise with a commanding view of Deer Lake Park, the mansion is known for its unique architectural design, stained glass windows which allow sunlight to cast dazzling rainbows on the oaken staircase, and black enamel columns.

Gracie Ceperley died ten years after the home was completed. For possible legal reasons, the house and grounds were in her name. Her will required that the property remain with Henry until he died or sold it. Any money realized from a sale was earmarked for a children's playground at Stanley Park.

For reasons unknown, Henry Ceperley disregarded his wife's will. First Henry Buscombe leased, then purchased the three-story Edwardian-style mansion from Ceperley. After Buscombe sold the house, and over the ensuing thirty-five years, Fairacres was an extension to Vancouver General Hospital, a private home, and then, from 1939 to 1954, a monastery for the Order of St. Benedict; the monks left when the new Westminster Abbey in Mission was finished.

Fairacres next entered its darkest period, one that some believe may be responsible, in part, for the supernatural events reported there.

For several years in the late 1950s and early 1960s, a charlatan who called himself Archbishop John I, leader of the Society of the Foundation for a More Abundant Life, held sway over untold numbers of Vancouverites. In reality, the so-called archbishop was one William Frank Wolsey, known to law enforcement authorities in the United States and Canada as a convicted bigamist who was also wanted on charges ranging from embezzlement and strong-arm collection tactics to wife beating.

Born in Estevan, Saskatchewan, in 1904, Wolsey was a compelling personality with piercing blue-gray eyes above an iron-gray beard. He bought Fairacres and turned it into his church and school.

The lessons he taught were dreadful.

Children were told they would die unless they believed what was taught to them. One boy with a communications disorder was mocked during a sermon and became so traumatized that he reverted to baby talk. A young mother kept her infant son in a darkened closet for several months on instructions from Wolsey. The regular curriculum was called "bio-psychology"; Wolsey personally taught a class in sex and hygiene.

The Vancouver *Sun* published an exposé of Wolsey in 1959 and his purported miracles, but his "religious" empire didn't collapse until the mid-1960s, when members started leaving and the courts froze the church's assets of $2 million. Wolsey fled Canada and disappeared.

The Burnaby council purchased the property in 1966 as a centennial project and converted it into an art gallery, which it remains to this day.

A wife whose final wishes were ignored by her husband and a fraudulent religious sect whose traumatized members may never have recovered from their experiences: either event may of itself be enough for all manner of paranormal activity, but taken together there seems to be evidence that Fairacres' history provides some explanation for the experiences various persons have said they had there over the years.

A former gallery director told a reporter about the ghost of a woman in a dark blue gown:

"People have seen and heard a presence in the building. A woman in an evening dress . . . She was seen once upstairs and once downstairs. People are uncomfortable in the building. No one likes to stay late by themselves. [But] there's been no murders or no deaths that we know of—no real stories to explain it."

The problem of staff not wanting to work after hours was so serious that this former director included a lengthy reference to it in his final report to the gallery board, five months after his resignation.

"Staff members have first-hand experience of the presence of 'spirits' and usually decline to work in the evening (even early evening) alone," he wrote. "While this situation may be taken lightly by the Board, it IS a matter of concern when staff are not willing to work in the evening."

But a gallery director in the late 1980s said that he'd had no experience at all with ghosts at Fairacres, even on those late evenings when he was responsible for locking up.

Several news articles from the mid-1960s discuss the appearance to some staff members of the "wispy shape" of a woman. A caretaker said he saw a woman in "a long, transparent, flowing gown" walking down the corridor of the abandoned third floor. That's where "Archbishop John I" housed the children of his followers.

A gallery worker in the mid-1980s found that whatever might haunt Burnaby Gallery is something of a prankster. Working over a basement workbench, he had been removing prints from their frames using a hammer and screwdriver. He was distracted for a moment, and when he turned back his tools had been placed neatly on a wall rack—six feet away from where he'd been working!

Later, he took some empty picture frames to an old wine cellar used for storage. As he approached, the padlock on the cellar door was swaying back and forth, though he hadn't touched it. He watched the movement for some time before it stopped.

Another employee learned that not only have people seen the ghost of a woman on the uppermost floor, but that she may also traipse down the stairs to the second floor. He was preparing walls on the main floor for an upcoming exhibit and a colleague was working in the basement (the same man whose tools moved of their own accord). He told a reporter what happened next:

"I heard someone walk from the outside deck [at one time a bedroom balcony] from one corner of the second floor across to the other diagonally. This is a very old building and when someone walks across the deck it sounds throughout the building. The floors weren't carpeted then—it wasn't shoes, you could hear the pressure on the wood like slippers or stocking feet."

He called his friend up from the basement and together they scoured the building.

"There's no way they could have got past us, not with two people. If they went out the french doors the alarm would have gone off. There were no open windows, and even if there were, it's a long two-story drop, twenty-five feet or more."

Sometimes the sense of a presence is so strong that one has to leave a room or a building to keep one's balance. This was the case with a gallery officer in 1984. She was at the front desk waiting for several others to arrive for an evening meeting when she heard the rustle of satin or taffeta coming from behind her.

"I was very intent on preparing my notes and I heard this noise," she said. "I wasn't frightened, I looked over and there was nothing there. About four minutes later the sound grew louder. My intuition warned me that something was trying to communicate. I knew there was something there that was not of this world. . . . I certainly didn't want to see it."

She walked outside and waited in her car until her colleagues arrived for the meeting. That's where they found her, in the parking lot with her car doors locked.

If there are entities at Fairacres trying to communicate with the living, psychic Joan Fontaine identified at least a few of them for a CBC special in 1987.

She found two areas of the mansion to be especially heavily "populated"—both locations are in the basement, including the wine cellar with the oscillating lock.

Fontaine also heard children crying. "This is a very unhappy place," she concluded.

In an upstairs room once used as a maid's bedroom, Fontaine felt someone invisible brush past her, a man who gave her his name as Joseph.

In the television program, Fontaine said an exorcism wouldn't work. Fairacres would simply attract more ghosts.

The current management of Burnaby Art Gallery will not discuss the ghostly legacy of Fairacres.

The Rider

Lest one mistakenly believe that the only phantoms in Vancouver reside in old mansions, this spectacular city on the Strait of Georgia has provided refuge for all manner of forms from another world.

The tragic death of a young woman, a student at the University of British Columbia, is the impetus for another Vancouver ghost tale. She has become a hitchhiking ghost, a Canadian version of Chicago's famous Resurrection Mary.

It is said the woman was a passenger in the speeding car of another student when it crashed on University Boulevard, killing her. She lingers there, waiting for a ride to her parents' home. She vanishes when a car stops, one version of the story goes, but in another climbs in and gives her parents' address. When the driver arrives there, she has disappeared.

Ethereal young women waiting alongside highways appear in ghost tales known in virtually every state and province of North America. The Vancouver variant differs only in localizing it to a UBC student.

Uh-huh

In June 1993, employees of Mushroom Studios on West Sixth Street in Vancouver told reporter Peter Clough about a mysterious "back-up" singer whose voice was heard singing "Uh-huh" on an album recorded by folksingers Bourne and MacLeod. There is no apparent connection between the ghostly voice and a well-known Ray Charles soft drink commercial.

The manager of the studio said the voice may belong to the same ghost who has haunted the building since the late 1970s.

"No one knows for sure who the ghost is, but we discovered that a long, long time ago, this was an Indian ceremonial grounds," the manager said.

She said the spirit is attracted to the music, especially when it includes drums or vocals. Two engineers briefly glimpsed what they thought was the ghost, but could not provide any description.

Death Bed

Will remodeling a house remove an "uncomfortable" feeling that may presage a haunting? Can a single, spectacular apparition exhaust a ghost's energy?

Those are the interesting questions posed by a turn-of-the-century story from Vancouver's West End.

A middle-aged couple built their new house there but lived in it for only six months before the wife died. Her husband sold the place and moved from the city.

From the very beginning, the new owners were decidedly uncomfortable on the home's main floor, especially in the master bedroom. They decided that remodeling might help alleviate their anxiety. A small drawing room adjacent to the former master bedroom was enlarged to include the old bedroom, walls were moved, new rugs and furniture were purchased for every room, and the walls were refurbished.

It didn't work.

The couple held a party to celebrate the home's new look. Two women told newspaper columnist Harold Weir about the festivities—sixty years after the event. They had remained silent all those decades, and refused to give Weir even the names of the family involved. All the revelers had been pledged to secrecy.

"At precisely eleven o'clock when all was going merrily," Weir wrote of the women's account, "the guests suddenly became conscious of something strange going on at the end of the drawing room where the bedroom had been. It was like a whirlwind of nothingness, sensed rather than seen.

"The room grew unaccountably cold and tongues were not so unaccountably silenced."

A four-poster rosewood bed emerged from the "whirlwind."

"A woman was lying [on the bed] clearly at the point of departure from this life," the women told Weir.

What truly frightened the assembled guests was that the woman was staring in wide-eyed horror at the indistinct figure of a man sitting in a Victorian chair near the bed. The astounding scene remained visible for some time and then faded away.

Everyone except the owners left, but not before they swore never to reveal what they had seen. Within a very short time the couple who had taken so much time and energy to "remodel the ghosts away" had themselves sold the house and put all the furniture up for auction.

Weir said one of the women who had told him the story saved the strangest part for last. She told him she had later attended the auction of the owners' furniture.

Weir wrote:

"The new drawing room rug, where the phantom four-poster had rested, was marked by four well-worn indentations, exactly as though some heavy piece of furniture had rested there for a matter of months." Nothing was sitting in that position on the rug after the remodeling.

The house was eventually torn down, replaced by an anonymous, and presumably unhaunted, apartment building.

Disturbing the Dead

His name was Johnny.

For a period of time in the 1970s, he was the best friend of a little boy who lived in a Premier Street condominium with his single mother.

Johnny was every lonely boy's dream pal. Tall and rugged looking, he made the child laugh out loud as he talked about all kinds of good stuff for hours on end, even if those chats did take place after midnight, which his mother did not especially appreciate.

Unfortunately, Johnny presented a problem for the little boy's mother. He was a ghost with whom only her son could communicate. And she most certainly did not appreciate his presence.

"It started when [my son] was four months old. I found him one night sitting up in bed roaring with laughter—he was completely exhausted," the woman told reporters at the time. "As he grew older, the number of experiences grew. When he was two, I went into his bedroom one night and found it in chaos. Bedding had been ripped, toys smashed and the legs of his bed had been torn off. I had heard no noises prior to entering his room."

She disciplined the boy, but regretted it later when she realized a two-year-old could not have caused such damage.

Further compounding her anxiety was the speculation by the Burrad Indian Band that Johnny was one of their ancestors—the condominium in which mother and son lived had allegedly been built on the site of the band's ancient burial ground. An officer of the Vancouver Psychic Society and a Burrad chief tied the haunting to the burial grounds.

Not until the summer of 1976, when the boy was about three, did his mother seriously ponder the reasons for her son's strange behavior. That summer was a time of bizarre events: a lampshade spun around, cupboard drawers and doors flew open, a food mixer leaped from a wall, and an ornamental bottle took flight and struck a large sofa.

She started reading about psychic phenomena and even experimented with a Ouija board. Until the night the planchette moved of its own accord. A Catholic priest told her to burn it.

Her doctor thought she was having a nervous breakdown until her friends confirmed her stories.

One neighbor said she watched as the mother emptied dirty water from a vase of flowers. After she returned to the kitchen table where the neighbor was sitting, they both noticed water was mysteriously back in the vase.

The same neighbor had seen a swag lamp swinging, while her daughter reported hearing growling voices in the house, had seen pictures move, and saw the lampshade spinning.

Why didn't the mother act earlier? She told a reporter that it wasn't that easy to face what was happening in her home: ". . . for the past couple of years Jason has woken regularly at midnight and talked to Johnny until 4 A.M.—I've heard a grown man's voice talking to [my son]. I just hide under my bedcovers . . . it's really scary."

She said her son first called the invisible visitor Johnny and provided the description of a tall man with fair hair. The boy said he looked like "Daniel Boone in buckskins."

While the local psychic and members of the Burrad Indian Band claimed Johnny was from the disturbed burial grounds, others were not so certain.

A Vancouver psychologist who investigated the case said the events might have been caused by psychokinesis, the ability of some individuals to possess enough "mind energy" to move objects, and that "Johnny" was merely the boy's way of explaining the events.

The psychologist noted, for example, that the child described Johnny as tall and blond, the same as his father, who was no longer living with the family. "It could be that the child has anthropomorphized the psychic energy," the doctor said.

The boy's mother said the child "suffered a traumatic experience when his father left home. He's extremely lonely, and every child has an imaginary playmate."

For her part, the mother was much more comfortable thinking the cause of the problem was psychokinesis, and not a ghost aggravated that his grave had been disturbed.

The Raven, Nevermore

Men and women of the sea know better than to ignore maritime superstitions. No other group may have as many omens, premonitions, or warnings of impending doom as do those who make their living upon the world's oceans.

A penknife that mysteriously changes its shape into a coffin has predicted a death; a captain whose wife is thousands of miles away sees her suddenly materialize in a corner of his cabin, pointing to a faintly seen bed upon which his daughter lies dying; and glowing phantoms have foretold shipwrecks in some parts of the world.

There are two other superstitions that should not be disregarded if one is to travel safely across the seas, for to do so is to risk facing the same fate as the *Raven*, a yacht manned by Canadian sailors that was wrecked on a Caribbean reef a quarter-century ago.

The ketch was under two oppressive shrouds—its name had been changed, from the original *Danebrog* at its launch to the *Raven*, and worse still the name was now that of a bird. Wise sailors avoid those taboos.

But there was more to the *Raven*'s problems than her transgression of seafaring superstitions. The ghost of her original builder prowled the decks.

The 110-foot ship, then called the *Danebrog*, was under construction in Denmark in 1921 when the builder fell to his death from the dock. It is not clear if there was an investigation, and neither is it certain whether the death was simply an accident.

From 1921 to 1972, when the ship was wrecked on a Caribbean reef, the record of the *Danebrog* is unknown. But in the early 1970s, Jan deGroot, head of the Vancouver Sailing Academy, set out to bring the Danish ship to British Columbia. He offered Vancouver sailing students the opportunity to serve as crew for $1,000, including airfare to Nassau. They would assist deGroot in the long voyage to British Columbia.

But when the sailing students, deGroot, his wife, and twenty-four-year-old Joan Whiteley arrived in Nassau, the group found a serious problem on board the now-renamed *Raven*.

The American crewmen who had steered the ship from Denmark to the Bahamas said the ship was cursed. Accidents plagued the yacht during its transatlantic voyage, footsteps clattered across the decks when no one should have been there, and, worst of all, the ship had almost sunk in the Bay of Biscay.

Some crew members whispered that they had even seen the ghost of the dead builder. Not one of them volunteered to stay aboard to Vancouver.

So deGroot and his twenty-two-member crew left Nassau under Dutch captain Bert Mooy. The plan was to briefly dock in Haiti and contravene the superstition about the boat's name by changing it back to the *Danebrog*. But since the captain was Dutch, the change had to be made in a Netherlands-governed port. DeGroot decided to leave Haiti for Jamaica and then sail on to the port of Curaçao in the Netherlands Antilles.

Shortly after leaving Port-au-Prince, however, the curse of the *Raven* became visible.

Joan Whiteley was sleeping belowdecks shortly before her four A.M. watch began when something awakened her.

"I was in my cabin trying to get some sleep. . . . Suddenly I felt a creepy feeling and when I looked up there was a man in blue standing there," she later reported. "He appeared to be ordering a crew about and waving his arms in the air."

The ghost was middle aged, dressed in clothing of the 1920s. Whiteley thought it was the ghost of the ship's builder.

Four hours later the *Raven* struck a reef near Haiti. Whiteley then had her second brush with the supernatural as she sat in the wheelhouse with deGroot's wife, Elsie.

"We were firmly stuck on the reef and in no danger of sinking. I felt this clammy and creepy feeling again. Tears started to come from my eyes and I felt the ghost leave the ship."

Joan Whiteley believed there was nothing that could have been done to save the ship. The *Raven* was jinxed from the moment the builder was killed. It was just a matter of time. . . .

Close Encounters

It sounded like a voice. A wail. Someone in deepest agony. Yet it wasn't quite human. Not like any human they'd ever heard. The family thought it might be their little dog, whining in a most singular way. That is until the night when they heard the yowl and at the same time saw the dog cowering at the foot of a bed.

Then they knew something else was in their house. And they didn't want any part of it.

The nine children lived with their fisherman father in a house they'd occupied for twenty-four years. The mother had recently passed away. It was summer 1978.

An official of a Vancouver psychic society, Linda Klor, learned about the story. She said the family first heard the alarming noise in the middle of the night, but it seemed "more like a voice than a noise."

On the second occasion, the family mistakenly thought their dog was the source of the problem. They also heard the "voice" utter a word that sounded like "die" or "why."

When it happened on a third night, father and children decided to spend the next night elsewhere. A tape recorder was left on, however, to pick up any sounds in the ostensibly empty house. Their dog also remained behind.

Linda Klor told reporters that the recorder taped the dog's barks—but also what "sounded like someone in deep agony. And whatever the entity was, it was using the energy of that dog's bark."

The distressed voice on the tape was not the only noise recorded. Heavy footsteps pounded across the floor, rattling glasses on a nearby table.

Klor and another medium visited the house. They sensed a man present, "a very confused entity," but one whom they could not otherwise identify.

The house seemed to quiet down after that. There was a final wailing sound, but then silence. Klor reported that an electronic analysis of the tape found the voice was not human. She said there did not seem to be an explanation for the events.

The shadowy figure stood at the window staring out to the darkness below. It was definitely male, but dressed in an odd sort of hat and long coat from another, vanished era.

The man in the bed saw him out of the corner of his eye. Something had awakened him seconds earlier, perhaps a slight rustling from this stranger across the room.

As the man turned his head to see who had so stealthily entered his bedroom, the figure faded away. The family with whom the man was staying had a dog. She had been sleeping in the room.

Now she was hiding under the bed. Did she, too, see the vanishing intruder?

The thirteen-room, turn-of-the-century Victorian mansion certainly *looked* like a haunted house. From its fishscale wooden shingles and meandering porch to the picket fence with old, wrought-iron hinges and heavy latches, the New Westminster home seemed pulled from a Charles Addams cartoon. Its situation on a dark, tree-shrouded avenue added to its gloomy bearing.

Looks are deceiving in this case. When the couple with their three teenagers bought the place in 1967, they knew that an extensive renovation was needed. A series of owners had left it in serious disrepair. The father was a carpenter and so he undertook a room-by-room facelift, taking down walls and doors and building new rooms.

It wasn't until two years after the family moved in that their friend staying in a guest room saw the mysterious figure at the window. And even after he learned what happened, it was especially hard for the father to believe his "project" might be haunted. He was a person who believed there was an explanation for everything. His wife was more open-minded about the possibility of ghosts.

Later, other mysteries were added, including the sight of a female specter gliding down the staircase. "The shadow of a woman," the mother told a reporter. "It was the only thing it could have been. She was wearing a long dress."

There were the times when one had the sense of someone being at one's side. Sometimes it happened on the couch while a family member watched television, a sensation that an invisible figure had sat down close by.

Late at night a kind of cold "whirlwind" enveloped the mother and followed her as she did housework.

Despite his avowal that events should be explainable, the father had his own shocks. The first occurred one night as he headed off to bed. He'd flipped off the downstairs lights and started up the stairs when "someone or something grabbed my hand." He said it was as if there was a person next to him holding his hand as he climbed the steps. He finally jerked his hand away, not quite knowing what to think.

There was a bathroom light that took a solid pull on the switch to turn it on. Family members downstairs would hear it click on and off—when no one was upstairs.

Was there an explanation for the haunting?

A Vancouver psychic who visited the mansion "saw" an older man in an upstairs room standing over a washtub scrubbing clothes.

Shortly after the house was built, a family lived there who used to employ a Chinese man to wash clothes. Could that be who the psychic saw? Perhaps, he said, although the particular ghost he had seen might have been just "passing through" and not the resident haunt.

The psychic said there might be another candidate. He surprised the mother by detailing her family history, even stating accurately that her father's sister had died young. And, he added, her spirit now frequently visited the niece she never met in her mansion at New Westminster.

Every region has its tantalizing fragments of ghostlore. A headless phantom here, a haunted road there, but never quite enough to call the ghost truly celebrated. But given time, and enough witnesses, even the most transitory specters may find themselves in the haunted annals. Here are a few interesting candidates from British Columbia:

Disturbing the dead can produce unforeseen consequences, as a young single mother discovered in Coquitlam.

One night in 1986, she reportedly saw the figure of a monk as she came out of the bathroom. She and her four children were out of the rented fourplex forthwith.

Tenants in the other units said unusual things happened to them, too—television channels switched unexpectedly and beds changed position.

It turns out the paving stones making up the fourplex's front walk were taken from 130 graves at the Woodlands Hospital cemetery. Children's graves.

When the owner of the fourplex returned the stones, all was quiet once again.

The Guisachan House in Kelowna was the retreat for the Earl of Aberdeen, Canada's governor-general in the 1890s. Guisachan is Gaelic for "the place of the fir." The earl's wife gave it that name and planted firs along the driveway.

Guisachan House may also be the place of ghosts. Sleigh bells and horses' hooves have been heard coming up the driveway—in winter, of course—beneath the soft canopy of ancient firs.

*　*　*

There was the comedy club in Gastown with a haunted basement. At one time the place was a slaughterhouse and, according to legend, ten workers died in a fire there during that time. Later, the location housed a bar where a prostitute was murdered by her pimp.

Old Hub Clark the railroad ghost may have moved on.

He was a brakeman who fell off a moving boxcar and was decapitated by the wheels of a passing train. The 1928 accident gave rise to many reports of Hub's ghost wandering the tracks at the north foot of Granville Street in Vancouver, below today's Granville Square. Hub's headless torso staggering out of the tunnel now used by SkyTrain scared the wits out of many a trainman.

But SkyTrain also doomed Hub. He hasn't been seen since it started running.

BRITISH COLUMBIA

Victoria's Secrets

Victoria, the enchanting capital of British Columbia, is known for its many green spaces, including Beacon Hill Park on Finlayson Point, its pleasantly mild temperatures and its breathtaking scenery. Founded over a century and a half ago as a Hudson's Bay Company post called Fort Camosun, the city of over seventy thousand residents on Vancouver Island boasts a diversified economy of tourism, wood processing, fishing, and grain shipping.

The typical visitor has a variety of options during his stay in this English-like city. One may enquire about visiting the Dominion Astrophysical Observatory or perhaps tour the University of Victoria or Camosun College. One might observe the fishing fleet, visit the nearby Canadian naval base, or stroll through the buildings of parliament. A Victoria Harbor boat tour is available.

But in this bustling city only a few miles across Juan de Fuca Strait from Port Angeles, Washington, there are other sights a bold tourist might investigate.

The Woman In Chains

Take the oldest house in Victoria, for instance. The Tod house on Heron Street in Oak Bay could justifiably have been called Victoria's most haunted dwelling.

Built in 1848 by Scotsman John Tod, the chief trader for the Hudson's Bay Company for over forty years, the sprawling white mansion was originally located on a four hundred-acre tract of land. The enormously wealthy and influential Tod was a member of the first legislative council of Vancouver and, some have written, one of Victoria's first idle rich.

At his death in 1882 at the age of ninety-one, the tall, gaunt Tod was the oldest living resident of British Columbia. One of his pallbearers was the notorious "hanging judge," Matthew Bailey Begbie.

Interestingly, a picture of John Tod that once hung in the house shows an uncanny resemblance to former Canadian prime minister Pierre Elliott Trudeau.

The Tod house is a wooden structure with giant timbers as its foundation. An owner some years ago, Waveney Massie, and her husband took great pride in restoring the house to its earlier glory. They filled the house with early Canadian antiques and period furnishings. One observer said the Massies were so effective in their restoration that one could easily believe "John Tod is still master of this house, and can be expected momentarily." The table was always set, as though the Massies were expecting Tod and his dinner guests.

The haunting of Tod house is attributed to Tod's last wife—he married seven times and fathered ten children—a Native American woman who may have gone crazy and been kept in chains in a small room.

Two guests in the house many years ago were awakened in the night by the moaning of a female specter, her wrists and ankles fettered. "They say she was reaching out, as if to implore them to remove her chains," Waveney Massie told a reporter.

Mrs. Massie was always willing to detail the history of the house and its ghostly legacy. She even had her own odd experiences to add.

"This door leading down to the basement and the secret tunnel . . . used to swing open all by itself. And in the sitting room—the rocking chair—it just rocked and rocked. And this old cookie jar, hanging on a hook by the fire, it rocked, too. And one Christmas, the tenants found all their Christmas decorations lying in the middle of the living room floor, and no one knew how they got there," she said.

The entrance to the old tunnel to which Mrs. Massie referred was boarded up, but it supposedly led to a beach below the house.

Mrs. Massie said the Tod house ghost became more restrained after a disquieting incident in the garden. "One of the earlier owners of the house was digging in the garden to install a new oil tank, when he dug up human bones, which crumbled to the touch. No one knows to whom they belonged, but from that time there were no more ghostly experiences."

The experiences of two *Vancouver Sun* reporters who spent a night in the Tod house back in 1950, years before the Massies bought it, lend credence to the Massies' story.

Reporter Chris Crombie and photographer George Vipond didn't actually *see* any ghosts, but there were plenty of other incidents the men were "at a loss to explain."

Crombie wrote:

"In the night we heard the squeak of the white picket fence gate outside as it turned on its hinges, followed by the crunch of footsteps on the path; but nobody came to the door and when we looked there was only the black path and the white fence, brilliant in the moonlight."

The reporter noted that it was three years earlier when the events to which Mrs. Massie referred had taken place. Not only had the owners seen the cookie jar swinging about, but hats were thrown from a rack, a door opened by itself, and "indistinct" voices and footsteps were heard.

At the time Crombie and Vipond visited, the Tod house was owned by Col. T. C. Evans, who had bought it in 1944. The journalists came away "half skeptical, half convinced."

"Shortly after midnight we sat huddled in the guest room where no visitor has ever spent a complete night in slumber and where few have been willing to return for a second night," Crombie wrote. "We heard four muffled but distinct thumps and thought of John Tod's last wife who went insane and was chained in a small lean-to, which is now gone, but once opened into the guest room. We thought of the crazed woman's vain attempts to escape by throwing her body against the walls of her small, stifling prison.

"The light, soft tread of bare feet sent us into the long, high ceilinged hall, but there was nothing, only a splotch of moonlight on the grey-carpeted floor."

And the remembrance of things past.

A Beach Ghost

The Tod house was (is?) not the only haunted place in the Victoria neighborhood of Oak Bay. A casual stroll along a beach near the Victoria Golf Club can bring chills to visitors, but it's not because of the cold breeze off Haro Strait. The ghost of a murdered woman sometimes intrudes upon one's anticipated solitude.

The woman was killed by her husband on that beach early in 1936. He buried her body in a sand trap on the eighth hole and then committed suicide by flinging himself into the sea. His body was found entangled in a kelp bed.

A 1964 account of the ghost sighting is quite detailed. It was provided by a high school student who was described by his principal as a "good student and not overly imaginative." The boy and a friend were walking on the golf course at twilight when they noticed the woman.

"She was about 1,000 yards away," he said, "and appeared to be running over the stones on the beach without touching them. I assumed it was the ghost of a woman because it appeared to have a dress on. She was luminous gray with an aura about her. When she reached the furthermost point of land she stopped and looked out into the sea as if she were expecting someone. . . . We must have watched her for five minutes and my friend assured me I wasn't seeing things."

The figure seemed almost to float across the rocks, the boy said, with an ease that was not human. Her arms moved gracefully, but the rest of her body was indistinct.

There were no land formations that might have been mistaken for a person, he said. "I am certain of what I saw."

He didn't want to go back to the beach, however. It was an "unnerving" experience.

The beach ghost is usually seen in March, about the time the sixty-year-old murder took place. Keep your eyes open for her, but give her plenty of room as you play through on that eighth hole. Ghosts simply loathe interference from the living.

Pest House

The shortest history of any haunted house in North America may very well have been that of Beckley Farm, built in the late 1860s or very early 1870s (the records are unclear) between Dallas Road, along Victoria's waterfront, and the shore. Within just a few years it had been demolished, but not before it brought death and misfortune to many who lived there—and the belief among Victorians that its unhappy dead wandered the premises.

George E. Nias erected the house, a horse stable and other outbuildings that he called Beckley Farm. Nias never lived there. For some reason he moved to Australia, and Beckley Farm was abandoned.

The real story of Beckley Farm begins in 1871, when a smallpox epidemic aboard the ship *Prince Alfred* brought renewed attention to it. The vessel traveled among San Francisco, Victoria, and Nanaimo. During a stop in Victoria, seven passengers were found to have the dreaded disease. A decision was quickly made that the infected people would be sent there to live in isolation. Beckley Farm was hurriedly repaired, and a yellow flag was put up to give notice that the farm was now a "pest house."

The *Prince Alfred* continued on its route to Nanaimo, further up Vancouver Island on the Strait of Georgia, and then back down to Victoria. A crewman was diagnosed with smallpox at the second Victoria stop, and he too was sent to Beckley Farm.

One of the original seven passengers, a teenager named Bertha Whitney, died on June 23, 1872. The sailor from the *Prince Alfred* also succumbed to the disease. Both were buried on the grounds of Beckley Farm.

The two deaths were responsible for the first rumors that Beckley Farm was unlucky, even though the six other passengers from the ship fully recovered. Once they got well and left, the farm was again abandoned.

A few months later, a stranger who gave his name as P. Lackle of San Francisco checked into Victoria's old Angel Hotel. He stayed to himself for several weeks, but then revealed to the hotel manager that his wife would soon be arriving from England and they would need some place to live.

The manager suggested he look into the old pest house, Beckley Farm.

That he did. For several days, he was seen wandering around the property, taking notes on what presumably would be the repairs needed to make the house habitable.

Then one morning quite a strange incident was reported. A tenant at the Angel Hotel happened to be walking near Beckley Farm. As he neared the house, he noticed the man known as Lackle and a woman engaged in a heated argument. The woman suddenly struck Lackle and fled. Nobody reported seeing her again.

The man who called himself P. Lackle was found dead of a self-inflicted bullet wound on February 17, 1873, in a Beckley Farm stable. His last name was actually Stocker and he was from Scotland. No one could find out what his real business in Victoria had been, nor why he had assumed a false identity.

Since the woman who struck him had vanished, the speculation was that he had murdered her and then killed himself. Four deaths were now tied to Beckley Farm. Victorians started reporting weird things at the place—lights glimpsed in some of the old buildings, and a woman's dreadful screams.

The haunting did not last long. The buildings mysteriously burned down in late 1873. A cause was not found, although it was presumed the lights people saw were somehow responsible.

There is a final, tragic footnote to the saga of Beckley Farm.

A woman who had been one of the original passengers quarantined at Beckley Farm, and who survived the ordeal, had settled in New Westminster. Once as she was sorting through her clothing, she came upon a dress she had owned for many years. She sent it to a dressmaker for alterations. Within days, the dressmaker and several assistants became virulently ill and died. A doctor diagnosed the deaths as smallpox, and speculated that the pox virus had been transmitted in the dress.

Any physical evidence that Beckley Farm ever existed has long since vanished and been forgotten. There is no sentimentality for such a cursed existence.

Emily Carr

The old St. Ann's Academy was a girls' school and convent at one time. It was also the spectral home of eccentric Victoria artist Emily Carr . . . and maybe a few of her friends.

In 1991, retired businessman Arthur Knight told reporters he saw "twin ghosts" while he was out walking. "I was startled out of my wits . . . shaking like a leaf."

He described the figures as two women in hooded cloaks, one shiny white and the other gray, standing upon the front steps of St. Ann's. One woman was taller than the other. They disappeared at his approach.

He took several photos, one of which shows an indistinct shape in a window of the building. Another photo of the path and steps shows no footprints in the freshly fallen snow.

"Now, I'm not a religious person and I'm not a superstitious person, but I do believe in this phenomenon. I was really shaken," Knight told a reporter. He added that he didn't tell many people about his experiences. "I didn't do anything else because it sort of makes you seem silly."

At the time Knight saw the ghostly duo, a group called the Concerned Citizens Association was opposing a plan to turn St. Ann's into a tourist attraction. A spokesman for the group said many people had seen the ghost of artist Emily Carr there, but nothing else.

A local cable television producer wanted to interview Carr's ghost, especially after he too saw it.

"It was early evening," the man said, "and we were walking past St. Ann's. We looked up and saw a figure in one of the top windows. . . . If she's trying to communicate, TV is a good medium."

There were no reports that Emily took him up on the offer.

The Haunted Hill

About midway up Vancouver Island, some 140 miles northwest of Victoria, are the communities of Courtenay and Comox. Courtenay is inland, but Comox lies right on the Strait of Georgia, directly across from Powell River, B.C., which can be reached by ferry from the island.

Today the two communities are placid island settlements with a combined population of about sixteen thousand. However, many years ago the area was visited by a female apparition that became the talk of the towns.

The ghost was described as a lanky woman, garbed in a brown cloak, with no arms or legs visible, only an indistinct blur. Her face was especially hideous— "nothing like a human face," one man who had seen her said—and marked by two deep black holes where the eyes should have been.

Siwash Hill, on the Comox–Courtenay Highway, was the place where local residents and even some tourists said they had seen her. The hill is some six hundred feet from the sea. The speculation was that the ghost was somehow connected with an ancient battle that had taken place some five hundred yards from the top of the hill between the Comox Indians and their enemies, the Haida Band, from the Queen Charlotte Islands. The Comox burial ground was at the bottom of the hill. It was from that direction that the ghost most often appeared.

The first verified sighting of the apparition came in mid-December 1940, when farmer William Day had an unnerving experience as he walked past the old Indian graveyard. He was carrying a few groceries home when the bouncing shafts of light from his oil lantern fell upon a figure standing alongside the road about twenty feet in front of him. It quickly vanished and Day continued up the hill.

A few feet farther on, however, the figure reappeared almost directly in front of Day. It was a woman who appeared to be staring out toward the sea.

The woman slowly turned toward farmer Day, and that's when he noticed her eyes. "They were piercing holes that seemed to look through me," he said. She had long, luxuriant hair that moved gently in the soft sea breezes.

Day thought someone was playing a trick on him. He disabused himself of that notion very quickly. "I have always laughed at ghosts and things of that kind, but I was in my sober senses, and I have told you exactly what happened," Day said.

A sailor returning to his ship one night saw *and* heard the ghost of Siwash Hill. "I saw a thing about halfway up the hill," he told reporters. He was so frightened that he ran all the way back to the harbor—and right off the end of Comox Wharf.

Construction projects seemed to disturb the ghost. Whenever repairs or work projects were undertaken, drivers on the Comox–Courtenay Highway said they would see a woman standing in the roadway, directly in front of their cars. Unable to stop from hitting her in time, the drivers were astonished to see the figure vanish just before impact.

One of her last reported appearances came after a highway crew putting in a new water main alongside Siwash Hill stumbled upon a human skeleton. The next night the specter was glimpsed hovering above the disturbed grave.

Possessions

Sometimes people are haunted through no fault of their own. They stumble upon an event out of time and suddenly their lives spin out of control, guided, it seems, by a force far beyond their ken.

The Bed

The idea that a piece of furniture can harbor ill will for the living seems a preposterous idea. Surely nails and glue and wood cannot combine to create an entity capable of producing emotional responses, or cause afflictions for its owner.

Yet there is the story of the young mother of two teenage daughters from Scarborough, Ontario, who endured a nightmare of bad luck—because of an old bed. She said it was cursed, and the curse touched all who came in contact with it.

She told her story to reporter Tony Carr:

The woman, whom we shall call Sarah, ran a successful business in the Toronto suburbs in the late 1970s, lived with her two daughters in a nice apartment complex, and, in general, had no reason to doubt that her life would continue on a steady course.

Until the night she found the bed.

"Walking from my car to the elevator, something made me glance at the far corner of the underground parking lot. That's when I first saw the bed. It was beautiful and appeared to have been abandoned," she recalled.

She hauled it up to her apartment, put it together and wondered why anyone would throw away such a splendid piece of furniture.

"I was studying the bed when this weird, very chilling sensation came over me. Blaming it on fatigue, I got ready for my bath and decided the next morning I would buy a mattress and make this lovely old bed my own."

On the night the new mattress was delivered, Sarah was asleep in the bed, which she shared with one of her daughters.

"Something caused me to sit bolt upright," she said. "There at the foot of the bed stood my best girlfriend. Her lips were moving but there was no sound." Sarah's friend lived two floors above her in the same building.

"I remember glancing at the clock. It was 2:03 A.M., and I said, 'Marian, what on earth are you doing here at this hour?'"

Her friend didn't answer, but Sarah's question awoke her daughter.

"Who are you talking to, Mother?" the girl asked. "Mother! What's that blue light by the end of the bed?"

Marian's apparition, appearing only as a blue light to the girl, faded.

Mother and daughter were too upset to go back to sleep. As they sat at the kitchen table, someone knocked at the door. Sarah cautiously opened it a crack.

Two policemen stood at the threshold. After confirming her identity, one of the men asked:

"Do you know a Marian Ducot?"

"Yes, I do," Sarah replied.

"Well, I'm sorry to have to tell you this," one of the officers said, "but she's just been murdered."

The story they told was that Marian had been walking to the elevator in the parking garage when she was jumped by a man wielding a heavy wrench. She was beaten to death. Her killer lived in the apartment directly above Sarah ... and just below Marian Ducot. The killing had taken place in the parking garage below Sarah's apartment and in almost the same place where she had found the abandoned bed.

The killer could offer no rational explanation for his actions. "I don't know what came over me, it's as though I was possessed," he said later.

Sarah claimed that after the murder of her friend, the bed seemed to become a living thing. She felt the bed "trembling" as she tried to go to sleep later on the night of the killing.

"There was something strange about that bed. Who had thrown it out in the first place? And why? Although I hadn't mentioned the trembling in the bed to my daughters, neither of them would sleep in it. My youngest, who wanted to sleep in it, ran from the room screaming: 'Someone's laughing at me from under the bed.'"

Even more bad fortune descended on the young woman. Her business failed, she said, because of a fire and "unscrupulous wholesalers"; her car was demolished in an accident after the brakes failed "for no apparent reason."

It was the bed, she reasoned. Her problems started when she hauled the bed up to her apartment. Perhaps if she got rid of it, her troubles would cease.

"I tried to sell, but as soon as people saw it, they became frightened. I tried giving it away.... A junk dealer took it. The next morning my bed was lying against the side of the apartment building."

Finally a friend offered to take it off her hands. He thought the trouble was with Sarah and not with the bed.

But as they reconstructed the bed in his home, Sarah was so overcome with anger she started pounding the bed with a hammer. She really blamed it for her troubles. Her friend chuckled and asked if she thought the bed might start weeping if she hurt it enough. She stopped and agreed that what she was doing seemed pretty silly.

"We were still laughing when I glanced at the bed, and saw something that stopped me cold. Trickling from the hammer marks were little streams of water, as though the bed was crying!"

Her friend attributed the water to condensation dripping from some overhead water pipes. Sarah said they weren't close enough to have that kind of effect.

Unfortunately the bed continued its menacing ways. Seven days later, Sarah had the bed back. It seems her friend's marina business had suddenly folded after a series of freak accidents. He said all the problems had begun the day the bed came into his possession.

There was more, her friend said:

"I wasn't in it [the bed] for an hour when it started vibrating . . . trembling— or something. I didn't believe I'd ever hear myself say this, but the thing seemed to be laughing at me!"

After a visit to a Toronto psychic who claimed a man had died in agony in the bed after being poisoned and then urged her to burn it if necessary, Sarah's fortune seemed to change.

An antiques buff who specialized in fine, old furniture had heard about the bed and offered to buy it. "It's gorgeous," he said after viewing it. "I must have it."

Sarah was honest in telling him about her painful history with the bed, but he would not be dissuaded. He offered her cash and took it the same day.

"My nightmare had ended. I felt as though a great burden had been lifted from my shoulders," she recalled.

The man who bought Sarah's bed added an ironic footnote to the story. It seemed that since he bought the bed, nothing but *good* luck had come his way. His business more than doubled and he gave up the idea of closing it down, which he had been contemplating before he bought the bed. "It's right out of the blue," he said of his successes.

He hadn't slept in it, he said. "But I will, sure. Bad luck won't happen to me."

Sarah hoped her life would return to normal. But she wasn't entirely certain. "Maybe, just maybe, my life and that terrible bed will be intertwined once again. . . ."

Hexed Houses

Sudden and unexpected changes in what one expects to find in a home one has lived in for some time can lead to the assumption that strange forces may be at work.

A family in Keswick, Ontario, had that discomforting thought in their fifty-year-old frame house. They called it an "evil spirit" and claimed it manifested itself in weird stains and peculiar bumps and rattles.

Keswick is about fifty miles north of Toronto on the southern end of Lake Simcoe. The family name was Matthews.

As reported in 1963, Mrs. Matthews said the "spirit" first appeared as a brown stain that looked like a skull and crossbones embedded in the kitchen floor. Another stain on a kitchen cabinet was the image of a woman in a hoop skirt.

Later, the cabinet doors swung open of their own accord, and dishes could be heard rattling day and night, almost as if a vibration undetected by the family rumbled through the house.

An occasional tapping at the front door was equally puzzling.

The family's attempt to get rid of the kitchen floor stain by holding a Bible over it just made the stain appear even brighter the next day.

In the end, Mrs. Matthews said, she just hoped the "spirit" would go away. It apparently did.

* * *

Another Toronto family, this one in the community of East York, had somewhat similar problems.

The Edward Jowett family had their nerves nearly shattered by mysterious knockings around their house. First they'd come from the front door and then seem to move to other rooms, even coming from under the dining room floor once.

The nuisance always began at midnight and kept the family awake until the wee hours of the morning, listening, wondering, and fearful.

Two police constables summoned one night when the Jowetts could no longer tolerate the disturbance hid behind the front door. Precisely at midnight there came a knocking at the door. The constables threw it open ... to find no one outside.

Gracie the Ghost presented quite a different sort of dilemma at the old William McKay homestead in Havelock, Ontario, northeast of Peterborough.

Gracie was the wife of a former owner. She died in about 1917, but not before threatening to return to haunt the house. She did, some claim, five years later, and set fire to the place, burning it to the ground. The ghostly arsonist was quiet for the next quarter century.

But in 1946, Lorne McKay, a descendant of William McKay, rebuilt the house on the charred foundation of the original.

That's when he said Gracie returned.

"Gracie is back in that new house and she's got my poor dog, Major, nearly in a state of hysterics. She either walks, steady-like, thumps, or whistles around the house."

McKay did say the whistles were "pretty."

Sometimes it's best not to fool with a force that may be stronger than you are.

Like a curse.

That's what may have happened in Hamilton, Ontario, a number of years ago when there was a proposal to change the name of the century-and-a-half-old Honest Lawyer Hotel, reportedly the oldest inn in Hamilton.

Barristers in that city were upset with the name and lobbied the hotel's owners to change it. They didn't like the implication that they frequented taverns, or that honorable advocates were hard to find.

Interestingly enough, that's precisely why the hotel had that name. The original owner, one Henry Upton, paid homage to an attorney friend who kept a fortune for him while he, Upton, fought in the American Revolution.

A sign above the front entrance warned that a curse would fall upon the hand that would "change in any way this old memorial sign."

And so it stayed.

The Mill

Anna Crosby Currier could not have been happier.

She had just returned to Manotick, Ontario, from a honeymoon in New York with her wealthy new husband, Joseph Merrill Currier. On this night in 1861 she held tight to her husband's arm as the couple proudly showed guests around the five-story mill Joseph and his partner, shipping magnate Moss Kent Dickinson, had built on the Rideau River, south of Ottawa, the primary shipping lane between Ottawa and Kingston, Ontario.

Dickinson and Currier had spent lavishly to equip the mill, originally built in 1860 to grind flour but then expanded to house woolen and sawmills. Hand-carved woodwork could be found throughout the mill, the walls were plastered, and imported Buhrstone quartz from France was used for the millstones.

Currier had thrown himself into his new venture in part to help recover from the loss of three of his four children to scarlet fever and the subsequent death of his first wife, Christina.

Joseph Currier had asked Anna Crosby to marry him about a year after the mill opened. So it was that after the wedding and honeymoon, the couple had invited friends to join them at the mill for a reception and tour of what was then one of the most important businesses in northeastern Ontario.

Exquisite in a floor-length gown, Anna strolled through the mill at her husband's side, smiling delightedly as he pointed out the mill's costly details.

It was on the second floor that the unimaginable took place.

Large grain bins spread over the floor had forced the Curriers and their guests to split into several smaller parties. Somehow Anna got separated from the rest. Suddenly her long skirt became ensnared in one of the gears and she was yanked toward a large, spinning shaft. Her screams were drowned out by the pounding din of the grinders and the thundering water turbines. The shaft spun her about and heaved her against a wood beam, crushing her skull. That's where the revelers found her minutes later.

Moss Dickinson bought out the distraught Joseph Currier's shares and owned the mill for a number of years. Several owners ran the operation until 1972, when the Rideau Valley Conservation Authority bought what was by then called Watson's Mill. After fully restoring it, the Authority opened it for public tours in 1975.

Anna Crosby Currier became a highlight on some of the tours. Her *ghost*, that is.

There was that second-story window from which a pale young woman sometimes stared. She would quickly duck away whenever someone gazed too long or too hard at her. Then she would resume her forlorn pacing on that floor, the same one on which she had been killed.

An official with the Authority said people usually saw Anna "on summer nights when the shadows are tall."

Baldoonigans

Old John McDonald had a farm. A haunted farm, and a most famous one in Canadian ghostlore. The sleepy hamlet of Baldoon, in southern Ontario, rarely saw activity of any sort in 1829. But when farmer McDonald came into town to report what was happening at his place, the rest of frontier Canada soon took notice. McDonald said supernatural forces had nearly succeeded in destroying his family. What he had was the work of a poltergeist.

Large chunks of timber were flying around his barn. Soon, pots and pans and other household objects were being hurled through the air without any sign of human assistance.

Small projectiles—which Mrs. McDonald called "witch balls"—pounded against the outside walls.

The poltergeist fired objects inside and outside the house on an almost daily basis. The intensity of the peltings varied, but rarely let up entirely. Sightseers flocked to the farm to see for themselves the strange phenomena. A few said they heard "strange moans" that seemed to come from everywhere, yet nowhere.

For a long three years the poltergeist kept up its antics. The McDonalds grew increasingly despondent. They tried all sorts of methods to rid their farm of the haunting—even calling in a "witch hunter"—but to no avail.

The phenomena stopped without explanation in 1831. Nothing more was seen, felt, or heard of the Baldoon poltergeist. The McDonalds resumed their quiet, rural life. It remains one of Canada's enduring supernatural mysteries.

A Poetic Death

"The Good Gray Poet" is the lamentable nickname by which American poet Walt Whitman came to be called, erroneously suggesting a harmless, kindly old man when actually he was considered daring and even "immoral," particularly after the publication of the first edition of his famous *Leaves of Grass* in 1855.

Although it was not well received by critics upon publication, the initial collection of twelve untitled poems and his subsequent work catapulted Whitman into the front ranks of literary geniuses. Whitman, also an essayist and journalist, grew in popularity and stature so that upon his death in 1892, the man who had only a few years of schooling and had once toiled as a carpenter and contractor was known as the "bard of democracy." His verse commemorating the assassination of Abraham Lincoln, "O Captain! My Captain!", was memorized by generations of schoolchildren.

There is quite another reason Whitman occupies a niche in the annals of Canadian hauntings, however, one that has less connection to his poems and more to do with his personal character.

The poet's biographers have written extensively of his devotion to the wounded during the Civil War. When his brother came home a casualty in 1862, Whitman went to Washington to nurse him. He stayed on as a volunteer in army hospitals. Never one to let his experiences lie fallow, he wrote his impressions of the war and published these poems as *Drum-Taps* in 1865.

That theme of selflessness, of his devotion to comrades, was one of Whitman's primary traits. Is it any wonder then that Whitman's devotion to his close friends might transcend death?

That is exactly what several people say happened in the summer of 1919, nearly thirty years after the poet's passing at his home on Mickle Street in Camden, New Jersey.

The event that summer was peculiar in itself. It was the dedication of a peculiar crag on a bluff known as Bon Echo Rock, near the village of Bon Echo, Ontario, to the memory of Walt Whitman. The Rock itself is nearly two miles long and four hundred feet high. Ancient Native American paintings have been found on it, and a local legend holds that a treasure hides in a lost cave somewhere in the cliff.

The reason for its dedication to Whitman was that from certain directions and in certain lighting conditions, the crag was said to look like the head of an old man with whiskers. It was given the nickname "Old Walt," because some thought it resembled the poet; more pragmatic observers said it more closely paralleled the Egyptian Sphinx, if it looked like anything other than stone at all.

Several notables connected with Whitman came to Bon Echo for the ceremonies, including Horace Traubel. He was one of the "band of disciples" who gathered at Whitman's New Jersey home during the final years of the poet's life. Traubel, whom some called Whitman's Boswell because he wrote several books about Whitman's life which he called the *Diary*, was one of the literary executors of his estate.

Traubel was very ill when he arrived in Bon Echo. A heart ailment had become acute; it was apparent that his last days might be spent in that Ontario hamlet.

Traubel's host in Bon Echo was Mrs. Flora MacDonald Denison, one of the leaders in the effort to dedicate the Bon Echo Rock crag in Whitman's honor. During Traubel's stay in her home, Mrs. Denison claimed that the spirit of Walt Whitman was at the dying man's side. Several other witnesses backed up her claim. The story was published in the local newspaper several years later, and signed affidavits were obtained from Mrs. Denison and others at the behest of the Society for Psychical Research.

At the end of August 1919, Traubel was so ill that he was confined to Mrs. Denison's home, moving only from his bedroom to the veranda, from which he had a picturesque view of "Old Walt." Traubel's wife, Anne, stayed at his side, relieved only occasionally by Mrs. Denison.

Traubel had been utterly depressed by his deteriorating health, but that changed on the evening of August 28. He had been sitting on the porch watching as twilight descended across the crag. As he was being assisted inside, he suddenly brightened and pointed into the distance.

"Look Flora! Quick, quick, he's going!"

Mrs. Denison turned but couldn't see anything. "What? Where, Horace?" she asked.

"Just over the rock. Walt was there, head and shoulders and with his hat on, brilliant and splendid. He beckoned to me, and spoke to me. I heard his voice, but I didn't understand all he said, only 'Come on!' "

Traubel's mood changed dramatically. He was cheerful, grateful for even the smallest of kindnesses from his many visitors, and confident in what he, alone, had seen. Mrs. Denison hadn't shared the vision, but she was able to see his disposition change. Sadly, his physical health continued to decline.

Over the next few days, he told Mrs. Denison that he heard Whitman's voice again urging him to "come on," and said that he saw visions of several of their mutual friends, including the politician and orator Robert Ingersoll. He smiled when he thought of Ingersoll in particular. It was he who had written to Whitman shortly before the latter's death: "May the Lord love you, but not too soon."

The visions of a dying man would have been dismissed as typical deathbed hallucinations were it not for the fact that the most dramatic incident—the actual appearance of the ghost of Walt Whitman—was witnessed by Traubel *and* Canadian army colonel L. Moore Cosgrove. Colonel Cosgrove wrote a detailed report for the American Society for Psychical Research the following year:

"During the months of August and September, 1919, I was in close touch with Mr. Horace Traubel, whom I had known through his numerous writings. I had not previously known him personally, nor had I a deep knowledge of the works and ideals of Walt Whitman. This I state to show that my mind, conscious or subconscious, was not subject to illusions concerning them."

Colonel Cosgrove noted that he had served in France during World War I and thus was familiar with death and the "atmosphere surrounding the dying." He was not particularly emotional during Traubel's final days, and he described the dying man as having thoughts that were "very clear," and said he was "without pain and seemed perfectly conscious."

The army colonel was with Traubel quite late one night a few days after he said Whitman had spoken to him:

"[Traubel's] eyes were closed and after some time he stirred restlessly, his eyes opened and he started as if to change to the other side of the bed. His lips moved as if he were trying to speak. I put back his head, thinking he needed more air, but he moved again and his eyes remained riveted on a spot some three feet above the bed. At last my own eyes were irresistibly drawn to the same point in the darkness—there was but a small, shaded light behind the curtain on the farther side of the room.

"Slowly, the point at which we were both looking grew gradually brighter, and then a light haze appeared. It spread until it assumed bodily form, and it had the likeness to Walt Whitman, standing beside the bed, a rough tweed jacket on, an old felt hat on his head and his right hand in his pocket. He was gazing down at Traubel, a kindly, reassuring smile on his face. He nodded twice as though reassuringly.

"Whitman . . . moved closer to Horace from the farther side of the bed. The strength of the dying man was ebbing and he was forced to allow his head to roll back.

"Suddenly [Horace] said, 'There is Walt!'

"As he said this the ghost passed, apparently through the bed and toward me, and appeared to touch my hand as though in farewell. I distinctly felt it as though I had an electric charge. The figure gradually faded from sight."

Colonel Cosgrove said Traubel's features softened, almost as if the strain of dying had been lifted by the poet's startling deathbed appearance.

"I did not regard the event as extraordinary at the time," Colonel Cosgrove said. "I had experienced similar phenomena at crucial moments during heavy casualties in France."

Horace Traubel died two hours later.

Enigmas of the Unknown

Is it their geographic isolation that causes Canada's Atlantic Provinces—New Brunswick, Newfoundland, Nova Scotia, and Prince Edward Island—to have such a wealth of ghost stories? Perhaps on those long, fogbound nights when the weather is foul and travel perilous, the entertainment that seems most fitting concerns phantom schooners, portents of death, ghost lights, and inescapable curses.

Possibly, too, it is the matter of living on the edge, of having to carve an existence from the sea or the forests on land that is fundamentally inhospitable. The people who reside there may understand more than others that life is tenuous at best, and that death is a loyal mate.

The Widow

The strangest house in the old city of St. John's, Newfoundland, was situated in the East End, before the calamitous fire of 1892 destroyed that neighborhood. Well into the mid-twentieth century, however, many people were still alive who remembered the dreary house and the widow and her son who lived there. It was impossible to forget such a drab dwelling, and the chilling curse placed on its future tenants by the old woman.

A written description of the dwelling is all we have left as no photographs of it are known to exist. It was a house in perpetual darkness, with a narrow cornice and clapboard siding long unpainted; roofboards showed through where the shingles had rotted away. Yellowed shades covered dusty, perpetually unwashed windows that were never opened, though the shades were usually drawn up halfway each morning. The front door was flush with the street, but swung on rusty hinges each time it was opened.

The woman who lived in the house married late in life, had a baby boy and then watched as her husband died when the child was but an infant. She reared him as best she could, taking on menial housekeeping jobs or the washing and ironing for neighbors. As the boy grew he too took on his share of work, delivering newspapers or performing odd jobs around St. John's. Though his mother was illiterate, the boy finished enough school to read and do his figures.

St. John's in that era had a unique housing covenant. The custom of the period was to build houses on ground "leased" from landlords so that even though one owned the dwelling, rent had to be paid for the land upon which it had been built. This was the case with the widow and her son. Each year mother and son gathered enough money to pay their ground rent for the following year. In turn, the landlord gave them a receipt which the widow knew, even though she could neither read nor write, entitled them to continue living in the home in which she was raising her son. She carefully placed each year's receipt in a bureau drawer lest anyone challenge their occupancy.

In time the widow's son became a man. He decided that his mother had worked long enough and hard enough to support their meager existence and now he would become the head of the house. He had no training for anything but humble labor, but that was plentiful in St. John's and provided enough income to put food on the table and simple clothes on their backs and pay the yearly ground rent. He followed his mother's custom in the latter task, delivering the rent to the landlord and requesting the receipt which he dutifully turned over to his mother.

The son fell in love. The young woman who became his bride agreed that she would move into the old house with her new husband and mother-in-law in order to save money. She was an expert decorator and soon the dreary house sparkled with new lace curtains and shades, freshly scrubbed floors and walls, and windows extricated from the accumulation of years of dust and grime. Even the hinges on the front door were oiled. A coat of "Dr. Bunting Green" paint was applied to the exterior. Never before had residents in St. John's East End seen such a glorious transformation.

But life for the widow, her son and his wife would not mirror the heartening changes in their home.

A baby was born to the son's wife. Now there were four mouths to feed, four persons to clothe, four persons who relied upon the son's slight income for all their worldly needs. And the baby, most especially, required a level of care that made the son's weekly pay sadly inadequate.

He thought long about the problem. At night he walked down to the harbor where he would sit on the pier and think through his alternatives. There were few.

He concluded that he had but one choice. He would put off paying the yearly ground rent for a few weeks, maybe a month or two at the most. That savings would give his baby extra food, perhaps his wife and his mother an item of clothing apiece, and the rest he would set aside to pay the landlord. It wouldn't take many weeks to make good on the rent, he reasoned, only long enough to get ahead a little bit. After all, what was more important, the landlord who had plenty of money or his own family with their meager existence?

There was the problem of the receipt. His mother would expect the slip of paper after the yearly payment; he had carried on the custom over the years he had supported the household and had made sure his mother always got the receipt so she could put it away. He felt guilty about deceiving her, but what choice did he have? She would only see marks on the paper and assume they were in the landlord's handwriting. It was a small deception, he decided, although the guilt he felt over misleading her was great.

He found a sheet of white paper similar to the previous years' receipts and proudly gave it to her the year he decided to "delay" the ground rent. She smiled at her thoughtful son and placed it carefully in the bureau.

A few weeks passed and the son found that he still didn't have enough saved for the landlord, who didn't complain for he knew the family was honest. After six months, though, the son grew worried. His modest savings weren't nearly enough for the payment. He called upon the landlord with a story of an ill mother, a sickly child, and unexpected expenses, none of which was true but which trickery the son excused as necessary.

"During all the years since your father took out the lease," the understanding landlord said, "every payment but this one has been met on time, and I can understand how it is with you. If everybody paid up as well as your father, your mother, and yourself have done, there would be small cause to worry over bad bills."

Even a deception based upon the best motives can lead to tragic consequences. So it was with this family. Several years passed and each year the son put off his ground rent, being always careful to forge a receipt for his mother. The landlord, who was at first caring and understanding, grew impatient. He demanded payment in full. When the son confessed that he could not oblige, the landlord foreclosed on the house.

The widow wept on the day she was forced from the home in which she had lived most of her life. Her son was to blame, in her heart she knew that, but as with many mothers she refused to think ill of her child. Instead, she cursed the landlord for the indignity of being tossed out of their home.

The family had no choice but to move into a tenement apartment which, it so happened, was just around the block from their home. Even the backyards adjoined and a window in the apartment looked out at their old house.

Since he didn't want the house to sit empty for too long, the landlord placed it on the market. It was all too much for the widow, who sat each day at the dingy tenement's back window, crying over the loss and screaming at anyone who seemed to be looking over the property.

Nearly everyone in the neighborhood learned of the widow's plight, and watched as she kept vigil at the window. Potential buyers of her home were scared off by her angry imprecations that should they buy the house a curse would fall upon them and their families.

A prominent St. John's business owner scorned the idea of an old woman's curse. He was without superstition, the house was in adequate condition, and thus he could find no logical reason not to buy it.

On an evening after he'd made arrangements with the landlord to buy the new property, the businessman was sitting at his home when a knock came at the door. He opened it to find the old widow kneeling at the threshold, her hands clasped beseechingly before him.

"Please, sir, I beg of you not to buy the only home my son has ever known and the one in which I have lived my life," she wailed. "I know that you are a kind man at heart and would not trample upon an old woman's last wishes. I will pray for you every day and ask God to bring you and your family good fortune if you would only do as I ask."

In her delusional mind, the widow thought that if the house remained vacant the landlord would relent and allow her family to move back in. *He* was to blame! *He* was the one who had tossed them out on the street! She still believed her son deserved no culpability in the matter.

"I am sorry, my dear woman," the businessman replied. "It is unfortunate that you lost your home, but that is none of my concern. I paid a fair price for the property and intend to move in with my own family as soon as needed repairs can be made. I'm sure you will understand that it's just business. Nothing personal."

With that he closed the door. The old woman's tears stained her shawl as she pulled herself to her feet and turned to leave. Through narrow, reddened eyes, she glanced back at the door. He had not heard the last from her, she promised.

The businessman hired carpenters to repair his new house's roof and siding, painters to give it a fresh coat of paint, and handymen to replace the old windows with modern sashes. Light, diaphanous curtains allowed sunlight to penetrate the dark rooms for the first time in many years.

All the while, the old widow sat at the window of her tiny apartment watching the activity at "her" house. Though her health was rapidly failing, she was vitriolic in her denunciation of this man who "has taken the roof from above my head."

Soon the house was in readiness. The businessman, his wife, and two bright, vivacious teenage daughters—ages seventeen and fifteen—were thrilled with the remodeling and thought this would be just the place to spend the rest of their lives.

The yard had not been kept up for a very long time and after the remodeling was completed had become the family's main chore. Planting flower beds, a vegetable garden, and new grass took up most of their free time.

Shortly after his family moved in, the father was clearing an area in the backyard quite close to the picket fence that divided the property from the tenement in which the widow and her family lived. He often saw her sitting at the window, muttering to herself and cursing her ill fortune, but did his best to ignore her.

On this day she was again at the window. He wasn't looking her way when he heard her voice rising to a pitch he had never heard before. When he looked up he saw that she had thrown open the window and was leaning out in his direction, shaking her wrinkled fist at him.

"My curse upon you, you robber of the widow's mite," she screamed. "May your life be blasted and may the brightest flower of your family soon fade and perish."

With that she fell back from the window. The businessman was afraid she had collapsed and ran to a neighbor's door. He explained what he had seen (but kept to himself what she had said) and asked the neighbor to check on the old woman. He explained that it was probably best for him not to go himself to her apartment.

The widow had collapsed unconscious on the floor. She was taken to her bed, and there she remained for the final days of her life.

"I'll haunt him! I'll haunt him! My curse upon him!" she muttered over and over again as she lay in bed.

Her priest, neighbors, and even her son and daughter-in-law tried to persuade her not to depart with a curse against the businessman and his family upon her lips. She ignored them.

Then one night she clasped a neighbor woman's hand and said, "I'm nearing the end. I can feel myself slipping away."

"God is good and we must always hope for the best," the woman friend whispered, leaning close. "If you should die tonight, you would not want to enter the world beyond the grave with a curse upon your conscience."

The old woman nodded.

"And so you won't haunt him?" the friend asked.

"I will! I will haunt him for all eternity!" the old widow screeched, and fell back against her pillows. She died without saying another word.

A few days later the businessman was asleep in his bed when he suddenly sat bolt upright. Still groggy from sleep, he was vaguely aware of a distant, tolling bell— one . . . two . . . three times it chimed. He was frightened. Something within him said these were familiar sounds, yet he could not focus his consciousness on their source. His brain was still too clouded from sleep, but he had to know—where had he heard them before?

He lifted himself slowly to a sitting position at the edge of the bed and felt the soft, cool evening breeze drift in through the open window. Of course, the bells were from the old town clock! It could not possibly be as late as three o'clock in the morning; surely he must have slept through the first nine chimes and only become conscious of the final three strokes.

He got to his feet and tiptoed to the window, which looked out over the back-yard. The moist air felt good upon his face as he leaned out and gazed into the night..

And then he felt his legs go weak and his heart started pounding so that he thought his chest would explode. He gripped the window ledge and stared trans-fixed across the yard at the widow's apartment . . . and into the dead woman's face! She was at the window where she had sat vigil for so many months, shaking a bony finger at him. A pale light seemed to surround her.

He leaped back into his own bed and pulled the covers over his head, shaking and moaning so that his wife was roused from her sleep.

"Wake up, Jim! You're having a nightmare," she scolded.

He did not respond, but continued to burrow into the bedclothes as if he could escape the horrible sight so easily.

"Jim! Jim! Wake up, poor man," his wife cried.

He grew quiet and finally sat up.

"I must have been dreaming," he said, not daring to speak to his wife of what he had seen for fear she would think him crazy.

"What time is it?" he asked.

"It must be after midnight," his wife assured him. "You're all nerved up. You must have had a very upsetting dream. Lie down and think of pleasant things before you go back to sleep."

"But I don't think I was dreaming . . . all of it," he insisted. "I'm sure I was awake and heard the town clock striking. I must see what time it is."

He struck a match, and in its flickering glow saw that the small clock on the bedstand showed one minute past midnight.

Nothing more was said of the incident. Whether it had all been a dream or whether he had seen the ghost of the dead woman gnawed at his brain, but he could neither resolve the dilemma nor escape the fear its continual presence in his thoughts brought to even the most mundane of daily tasks.

All was quiet for some time until an evening several weeks later. The wife was alone. Her husband was away on a business trip and their daughters were visiting schoolmates.

She was sitting in the kitchen with a collection of mending on her lap. The evening was rapidly shifting from daylight to darkness, and in the twilight she had lighted an oil lamp to help her see her sewing needles and thread.

A gust of wind abruptly swept through the room, extinguishing the lamp. A chill went down the wife's spine at the suddenness with which heavy dusk settled in the room. She had not entirely believed her husband's explanation on that earlier night that he had simply had a nightmare. And, too, she had learned about the old woman's supposed curse.

As she reached for a match with which to relight the lamp wick, the deep silence was broken by three sharp, distinct raps that resounded throughout the house, yet seemed to emanate from no one place in particular. She jumped at the unexpected sound. Carefully setting the sewing on the kitchen table, she got up to see if someone had come in through the front door.

She froze as she peered through the kitchen doorway. Standing inside the front entrance was a small, old woman with a shawl covering her shoulders and drawn up to obstruct most of her face. With an outstretched hand, the hag started shuffling down the hallway toward the doorway in which the terrified homemaker stood.

With a scream, the wife fell back into the kitchen and collapsed.

The next thing she knew, soft voices were urging her to awaken. She opened her eyes to see her daughters and a neighbor leaning over her. She was in her own bed, warm blankets pulled up to her chin.

"Wasn't it all dark?" she asked.

"Yes, that it was," said the neighbor. "I heard you scream and came rushing over. I found you there on the floor of the kitchen and not a lamp lit in the entire house. And the front door was wide open. Seems to me the wind blew out the kitchen lamp. The chimney was still hot."

"Did . . . did . . . you see anyone?" the wife stammered, still very agitated from the events.

"Nobody," the neighbor said. "Well, nobody but an old beggar woman limping down the street." The girls added that they too had seen a stranger some distance from the house.

"Oh, I was terribly scared," the mother said. "The draft must have blown out the light—and then the beggar woman suddenly coming into the hall . . . at least I think it was a—." She broke off her final words, not daring to think about who else it might have been.

All of these elements must have combined at the right moment to produce this weird effect, the mother reasoned. The wind gust must have blown open the front door and then put out the lamp at the same moment the beggar woman rapped. Yet that wind was so cold as it came down the hallway ahead of the stranger . . . so cold that it seemed to penetrate to her very bones.

There was nothing conclusive in these two incidents to suggest that the widow's curse had taken hold of the businessman's family. Each might have been attributed to simple coincidence were it not for what happened on an exquisite late Newfoundland spring night several months later.

A thin strand of daylight remained on the western horizon as the deep blue sky darkened on its journey toward night. A sprinkling of stars twinkled their greetings to the shadows that fell softly over St. John's. Boats in the harbor swayed gently at their moorings. The world seemed a warm and generous place.

On that street and in that house where the widow once lived, the dinner hour had passed as pleasantly as usual. Father and mother had retired to the parlor, he to finish some paperwork and she to resume some intricate crocheting. The younger daughter was in her upstairs bedroom overlooking the street. The older daughter, the blooming rose of her father's eye, sat by the window in her room using the fading daylight to finish a piece of embroidery.

The soft air coming through the open window nudged the lace curtains aside and blew softly across the girl's face. She let the embroidery drop to her lap as she leaned back in the soft chair cushions. Her eyes closed. She let her mind wander among the million thoughts that young girls everywhere have at that age.

Minutes drifted by. The room settled into darkness. Suddenly the girl who had been wandering among the stars felt a slight chill. She opened her eyes. From where she sat there was a clear view across the backyards. At first there was only darkness at the dead widow's apartment, but gradually a pinpoint of light appeared in the one window where the woman had sat screeching her disgust to the girl's family. The light grew in intensity and in its glow the girl saw the old widow sitting in her chair at the window, but this time she was a corpse in a torn dress and ragged shawl. She raised her arm and pointed a bony finger toward the young girl.

The light growing in intensity about the specter became like a shaft of rays spilling out across the yards, up the side of the girl's home and finally through her window and into her room, where she felt ensnared by its intensity.

As the beacon stretched between the two windows, the widow's ghost glided out her window, along the path of light, and hovered outside the girl's window. She rested her rotting arms on the sill and raised her grisly face. Shreds of flesh hung like streamers from her skull; where the eyes and nose should have been there were only dank holes. She stared through the window, her mouth pulled back in a hideous, toothless grin. She reached toward the girl.

The scream brought the girl's parents rushing into the bedroom. They found their daughter writhing on the floor, hysterical, crying and speaking gibberish about lights and faces and old women, but completely unable to make any sense to her tormented parents.

A doctor came the next day and diagnosed the condition as "paralytic epilepsy" brought on by some sort of shock. He gave her medicine, and even brought in several colleagues to help in the diagnosis, but it was all to no avail.

The girl grew weaker with each passing day, unable to eat or to communicate with those around her. The doctor surmised that her brain had suffered such trauma from whatever event transpired that night that she was lost forever.

And in that condition this girl, this burnished flower in her parents' garden, passed from the earth. The widow's curse had triumphed.

The Presbytery

Father Cody built the presbytery on the hill in Tors Cove, Newfoundland, a hundred years and more ago. Locals called it "the palace," because the good minister used only the finest materials to build the house—ornate outside moldings, hand-carved woodwork, an angled staircase.

With so much attention to detail, is it extraordinary to learn that Father Cody never let go and continued to preside over his quarters?

The mystery of the presbytery begins when Cody still lived there. He was gone one weekend and his housekeeper invited a friend to stay over. The friend awoke at 3:45 the next morning after a dream in which her seafarer son had spoken to her, had in fact bid his mother good-bye. Father Cody's housekeeper learned a few days later that her friend received word that her son had drowned—at precisely the same time his mother had reportedly seen him in her dream.

More recently, a Newfoundland artist rented the "palace." He didn't know of its haunted history, but soon discovered for himself its peculiar qualities.

A kitchen door leading to a "mudroom" that separated the kitchen from the back door kept opening. Going out that way was also the quickest way to the church. Since he lived there alone, the artist blamed it on "the wind." One night while he was working at the kitchen table, however, the artist heard a noise behind him and turned to see the door opening as if to allow someone to enter.

He nailed the door shut. That worked for several months until he went away for a few days and returned to discover the nail on the floor and the door wide open.

Many people in Tors Cove wouldn't go near the presbytery, even during the day. Tradesmen were reluctant to provide repairs. A carpenter told the artist that he had been laying a new floor in the house when Father Cody "spoke" to him. He also saw someone going up the staircase, even though he was alone.

A plumber refused to shut off the water when the artist eventually moved out. The reputation of the presbytery on the hill was enough to keep him away.

Holyrood

This small community of two thousand people on the south end of Conception Bay has an ancient connection to the sea and seafaring ways.

Back in the 1860s, John Mackay and his stepfather, John Cunningham, had a big fishing business in the village, in what is called the North Arm of Holyrood. Mackay's schooner was the seventy-ton *Isle of Skye*, a fore-and-after.

In early October 1865, Mackay, Cunningham, and their crew had a full catch from the Labrador banks and made for home. They were last seen on the night of October 10 crossing Notre Dame Bay, northwest of Fogo. There was a frightful nor'easter early the next day and the *Isle of Skye* was lost.

A curious incident on the night of October 11, however, led some Holyrood residents to think Mackay and Cunningham had weathered the storm. At about ten o'clock that night, people living along the seashore on the South Side, west of Runaway Rock, heard loud cries and shouts of "Hello! Breakers ahead!" coming from across the water. Men jumped into their boats and rowed out into the bay to help what they thought was a ship in distress. Bonfires were lit onshore to guide the stricken craft.

Though the search went on for hours, no sign of a ship was ever found. The shouts had died away; the rescuers went home puzzled. And afraid.

Shortly after retiring for that same night, Denis Penney, who lived along the coast near North Arm, heard the splash and dropping chain of an anchor. His son had been aboard the *Isle of Skye*. Penney was certain the schooner had returned. He got up to light the fire, fully expecting his boy to walk through the door soon.

It didn't happen.

Sometime later, wreckage of the *Isle of Skye* was found at Moulton's Harbor Head, near Twillingate on the northeast coast, several hundred miles from Holyrood.

Many believed Mackay and Cunningham attempted to make it home in spirit, if not in the flesh.

*   *   *

Jim Curran's ghost proved the adage that one had better follow a dying man's wishes, or face the consequences.

Curran told his son-in-law, James Butler, that he wanted to be buried in the new cemetery on Holyrood's South Side, even though it wasn't technically "open" as of yet.

"If you don't," Curran said, "I will return and give you not a moment's peace."

Curran died just before Christmas. Butler passed along his father-in-law's request for burial in the new cemetery to Father Walsh.

"Impossible," the pastor pronounced. "I won't hear of such a thing. The cemetery is not consecrated. We'll bury Mr. Curran on the North Side and if he's set to come and haunt anyone, let it be me."

Butler said that would be fine, as long as the ghost didn't come to visit him.

Jim Curran was laid to rest on a snowy afternoon shortly after Christmas. Father Walsh and his driver made for home, which was at Harbor Main. The snowstorm got worse and the men found the road blocked. They took a path across a pond but wandered for three hours before they found their way back. Father Walsh's driver, a superstitious fellow named Harry, was badly rattled.

"It's Jim Curran's ghost what led us wrong," he swore.

Father Walsh heard grumblings among his congregation that maybe the old man should have been buried in the new cemetery. In church the next Sunday, the priest explained his reasons for not allowing anyone to be buried in the South Side graveyard until it was blessed. He would take more convincing, it seemed.

Later that night, Walsh heard a knock at his front door. He opened it to find no one there, but did hear distinct footsteps cross the threshold, walk across the floor and thence up the staircase to a bedroom.

Another priest in the region, Father O'Donnell, came to visit the next day. He inquired about the visitor Father Walsh had received the previous night. Walsh denied anyone had been there, but Father O'Donnell said he knew better.

That was enough for Father Walsh. He ordered the cemetery opened immediately. The first order of business was the exhumation of Jim Curran's body from his North Side grave and reburial in the new cemetery.

The old man who was disobeyed has rested serenely ever since.

Smoker

Irving Penny was a trapper. On this afternoon he thought he was going to die. He drove his ten-dog team of huskies onward through the wet, pelting snow. All he could see from his sledge was the whiteness of the bleak Partridge Hills of Labrador. The squalling sou'easter tore at his fur parka, sending occasional clumps of snow through its flaps so that they fell cold and wet against his skin.

Penny thought he was hallucinating when he heard a faint sound in the near distance. But there it was again, a musher's cry. Out of the swirling snow a team of fourteen pure white dogs appeared pulling a sled loaded down with mounds of furs. On it was a large man, dressed all in white furs, and pushing his team into the face of the storm.

Penny called out, but the stranger said not a word as he sped by. Trusting some unknowable instinct, Penny followed.

Not thirty minutes later, he saw looming before him the winter shanties of the fishermen at Frenchman's Island. The mysterious musher pushed ahead past the settlement, but Penny stopped at the first hut and pounded on the door. The fisherman welcomed him and helped put the team down for the night. Then Penny collapsed by the fire.

When he had thawed a bit, he asked the question that had been gnawing at him: "Who was the fella in white who came in, in front of me?"

"I didn't see anyone else, not a soul," the fisherman said, squinting past the fire and into the face of his unexpected guest.

When the trapper related his experience, the fisherman nodded his head.

"You saw 'Smoker,' " he said. "He brought you here. Whenever there's a blizzard, he always turns up. He has to, to save his soul from eternal damnation."

The apparition Penny encountered was known as the "ghostly trapper of Labrador," one Esau Gillingham, a Newfoundlander who, in 1910, migrated to Labrador to trap. Not much is known about his life before he crossed the Strait of Belle Isle to Battle Harbour and began setting his trap lines up and down the Atlantic coast.

The life of any trapper in those years before World War I, particularly in the harsh terrain of Labrador, was one of bare subsistence. And daily survival in isolated settlements like Red Bay, Goose Bay, Holton, and Hopedale depended on a man's ability to hunt, fish, and trap. Without those skills, there was no food on the table. Any cash money came from selling what you fished from the icy waters or trapped in the wilds.

Gillingham was not an incapable trapper. He ran lines clear up the coast to Nain; some claimed he even went as far north as Hebron in the Torngat Mountains and Cape Chidley on the Labrador Sea. He discovered, however, that the harsh living conditions made it possible to earn a living, a handsome living, giving the isolated settlers what they desired most but had no access to: liquor. And rum, in particular. Gillingham concocted a mixture of spruce cones, sugar, and yeast to form a devilish drink he brewed at a secret still in the impenetrable black spruce forest.

In the summer, Gillingham sold the firewater among the isolated coastal settlements, traveling stealthily by boat so as not to alert the Mounties. Even when he ran his trap lines in the winter, Gillingham kept a keg aboard his sledge, hidden beneath the furs he brought in. The name for his virulent moonshine was "smoke." Thus Gillingham's nickname, the "Smoker."

The rum did its work, but in a way Gillingham didn't anticipate or, it's more likely, didn't pay much attention to. It was such noxious stuff that many who drank too much went mad, others beat their wives and children; there were cases where men who got drunk from it thought they were invincible and ran coatless into blinding blizzards, ending up frozen to death in snowbanks.

The Mounties finally caught up with Gillingham, smashed his kegs and sent him to jail in St. John's for six months. If they thought that would mend the bootlegger's ways they were mistaken.

"They'll never see me inside that jail again!" Gillingham swore upon his release.

He quickly disappeared into the Labrador wilderness. Soon stories started to spread about him, how he was buying every white dog he could find, or stealing those whose owners refused to sell; how he was trapping only white fox or ermine; how he had made a new sledge and painted it pure white.

Smoker's plan was simple. He had no intention of stopping sales of his moonshine, but in order to accomplish his deed he needed a means of escape. Dressed in white furs, atop a sledge pulled by a team of pure white dogs, he could move virtually undetected against the deep winter snows of Labrador. In the summer he could hide his boat in the many coves impossible to reach by land.

He nearly succeeded. For years, Smoker moved among the settlements selling his poison. Madness and death followed in his wake, yet the authorities were never able to catch him. Finally, a snitch revealed his hiding place. The Mounties caught him and took him to the black spruce forest where his still lay hidden.

"We know your still is in there," a Mountie declared. "Now lead us to it. We'll throw you in jail for the rest of your life if you don't."

Smoker knew they were bluffing because without any evidence of his illicit trade they could not file charges.

He leaned back and smiled. "My still's in there, that's right. Go right ahead, Sergeant. Find it if you can . . . but you ought to know there's fifty bear traps all around that still. Mind where you take a step."

One Mountie who had started for the wood stopped in his tracks. He knew a bear trap could snap a man's leg in two as easily as if it were a matchstick.

Smoker went free. He continued his ways, but became even more deranged when he took to drinking his own moonshine. He kidnapped a woman and held her in his log hut for weeks until he released her. She was raving mad and couldn't testify against her captor. White dogs disappeared from the settlements.

Mothers who feared for the lives of their sons and daughters warned, "Smoker'll get you if you don't watch out!"

The end of Esau "Smoker" Gillingham came in 1940, after he moved back to Newfoundland. He fell off a cod-drying platform, called a "flake," near the Gander River and broke his back. He was in agony until he died several days later.

Some say he was a changed man after his return to Newfoundland, an old sinner who had found religion in his twilight years. That may be so if what are reported to be his last words are accurate.

"Lordy, Lordy, God!" Smoker supposedly cried with his last breath. "I don't want to go to Hell. Let me drive my dogs along the coast to the end of Time. I'll make up for all the bad I've done."

If we are to believe the stories of the madness, death, and terror Smoker brought to so many innocent people in Labrador, it may take *longer* than to the end of Time for him to make penance. Even a half-century later, Smoker must still be showing lost trappers the way home.

"The Spookiest Place I Know"

With those words Jack Conrod, a longtime caretaker on Devil's Island, a twenty-five-acre chunk of sand and bushes near the harbor entrance to Halifax, Nova Scotia, described the place he knew well. Although it's only a half-mile from Eastern Passage, Conrod said, "it might as well be in the middle of the Atlantic. You can get stranded. . . ."

But it's not getting stranded that's worried people, it's wondering if all the hair-raising tales about the island are even remotely true.

Although it was settled in the early eighteenth century, the small, windswept island gained its reputation only in the past century. The reasons are probably twofold: when the sun rose and set, it shone through the lighthouse windows so that it seemed the building was on fire; and many people have died in the rough waters of the reef-rimmed island. Families only occasionally lived there, making a living from fishing, but most of them left decades ago.

In 1977, a man from Whitehorse, Yukon, took up an offer by the island's owner, Bill Mont, to live there rent-free. He is said to have lasted one week before taking off for parts unknown.

Clarence Henneberry spent the first sixty years of his life on Devil's Island, until he and other residents were forced to leave in 1945 because of wartime military restrictions. Government officials thought they could see too much of the naval activity in and around Halifax Harbor.

Henneberry did not believe in ghosts, but he had enough strange experiences on the island not to fool around with the supernatural.

Across the island from where he grew up there was a house that was thought to harbor evil spirits.

"There was something wrong with the house," Henneberry said. "I've seen the roof of that house ablaze a half dozen times. Once I went up to it and put my hand on it. It was as cold as that kitchen table."

Then there was the "walking light."

The unheld lantern "used to go from the house to the bush, then walked back . . . I wanted to go see it but my father wouldn't let me. I wasn't scared," Henneberry insisted.

In Nova Scotia, as in many other regions of the world, there has been a belief in "forerunners," sometimes called "tokens." These are appearances by dead relatives, or omens of a tragedy to come.

Clarence Henneberry witnessed a forerunner. His brother Charlie appeared to him late one night.

"I woke and he was in my room with wet clothes on. I asked him what he was doing home and he didn't answer me. He was there only a minute."

Henneberry didn't think any more about the incident until the next day. His family received word that Charlie had drowned the night he appeared to Clarence.

Phantom of the Strait

The ancient three-masted schooner was on the move once again, her spare masts spurting fire and her decks ablaze from stem to stern. Slowly she made her way down Northumberland Strait as she has done for several centuries.

Mrs. Aldon Langille saw her. From the window of her cottage in the village of Cape John, Nova Scotia, she gazed out over the wind-chopped sea. The schooner came into view, gliding up the strait, fire spurting from her sails and hull. She and her neighbors watched the ship for nearly an hour.

A few days later after supper, nearly everyone in Cape John watched again as the mystery ship plied its way down the Strait.

"It has to be seen to be believed," one resident said.

Just when the phantom ship of Northumberland Strait first appeared is lost to history. To make matters even more confusing, there may be more than one candidate for the phantom. But it is entirely accurate to say that over the years literally hundreds of people—young and old, men and women, believers and nonbelievers—have sworn upon all that is holy to have witnessed this blazing ghost of the sea.

Northumberland Strait lies in a generally southeast to northwest direction, separating the mainland of Nova Scotia and New Brunswick from Prince Edward Island. It varies in width from 8 miles between Cape Tormentine, New Brunswick, and Borden, P.E.I., to over 30 miles at Hillsborough Bay, P.E.I. The Strait is about 180 miles long, roughly from Pictou, Nova Scotia, to Richibucto, New Brunswick.

A turbulent body of water, Northumberland Strait acts as a kind of funnel for the surrounding Gulf of St. Lawrence. The name itself may come from the ship *Northumberland*, which was supposedly lost in the Strait in about 1747. The explorer Jacques Cartier named part of it "St. Luniare," and its southern end was once called the "Red Sea."

Some reports to the contrary, the phantom ship, or fire-ship as it is sometimes called, appears at any time of the year and at the most unexpected places. Those who witness it are sometimes reluctant to speak of their experiences. Nonbelievers scoff at such nonsense, but those who know better say the event is unique.

Each village along the Strait has its own version of the phantom ship.

One region holds that it is the revenant of a Scottish immigrant ship bound for Quebec. Every person on board perished when the ship was struck by lightning and burned to the water.

Another version of the ship's identity is that it is the phantasm of a pleasure craft. It seems that during a drunken brawl at the captain's table, an oil lamp was overturned and exploded. All hands died in the ensuing conflagration. She still looks for the way out of Northumberland Strait.

If the tale is told in Pictou, N.S., the fire-ship becomes a different Scottish immigrant ship, this one bound for Nova Scotia, that never made land after it left Scotland. The origins of this version supposedly came from the 1773 arrival of the *Hector*, carrying Scottish settlers from Loch Broom.

Farther northwest along the New Brunswick coast, the phantom is "the *John Craig* light," after a ship by that name that was wrecked many years ago off Shippegan Island, between Chaleur Bay and the Gulf of St. Lawrence.

Sea-borne apparitions are common all over the world, even those which seem ablaze from their crow's nests to their waterlines. Whatever sails through Northumberland Strait is unique only in the variations of what event is responsible for the haunting.

Or is it an event at all in this case? The more sensible folks familiar with the legend of this phantom ship insist the unearthly glow is caused by gaseous vapors from undersea coal beds breaking through the water's surface.

But try telling *that* to Mrs. Langille and her neighbors.

Across Nova Scotia at Mahone Bay, southwest of Halifax, a spectral fire-ship that is said to be the *Teazer* from the War of 1812 appears as a bright glow offshore, usually in foggy conditions.

There were two American privateers named *Teazer* during the war. The old *Teazer* was under the command of a Captain Johnson. He and his ship were captured by the British. He was paroled with the understanding that he would not fight against the British until a prisoner was exchanged for him. If they caught him before the agreement was carried out, he would be hanged.

Captain Johnson ignored the stipulation and signed aboard the young *Teazer* when it sailed for Nova Scotia under the command of a Captain Warren. They plundered several Nova Scotian coastal villages, but the cruise was generally uneventful. One community they had raided was Chester at the north end of Mahone Bay. They hadn't gotten much the first time through, so Captain Warren decided to try again several weeks later. That was a mistake. A British man-of-war trapped the young *Teazer* in Mahone Bay.

Captain Johnson knew what would happen if he was captured by the British. As Captain Warren was discussing with his crew a way around the blockade, Johnson slipped belowdecks and blew the ship apart, killing all but six men.

As late as 1948, Mahone Bay fishermen sometimes pulled up pieces of the ship, which they promptly sold to tourists.

The young *Teazer* appears as a specter, usually in heavy fog and usually as a precursor to bad weather. One witness said, "I happened to be in Mahone Bay and saw a glow in the fog and was told it was the *Teazer*, and was advised that a gale was imminent. It arrived the next day."

Only visitors seem to be awed by the sight. Locals are so accustomed to the young *Teazer* rising from her watery grave that they only nod and say, "Aye, it's the *Teazer* burning again," and go back to their work.

Even ghost ships can get tiresome if they appear too often.

Bibliography

UNITED STATES

Alabama

PERIODICALS

Campbell, Dwayne, and Tim Willoughby. "There ain't no such thang as 'haints' . . ." *The Cullman Tribune,* June 23, 1977.

Dunnavant, Bob. "Yankee soldier is still lurking at old depot." *Birmingham Post-Herald,* July 26, 1979.

Hogan, Ann. "Rocky Hill Remembered for Its Grandeur." *Moulton Advertiser,* July 26, 1973 (reprinted from the *Huntsville Times,* March 12, 1967).

"The McEntire House." The Decatur Chamber of Commerce, Decatur, Alabama, March 14, 1957.

McGuire, Buster. "The Ghost House of Camden." MA, November 14, 1976.

Nagel, George. "Interesting Tale Told of Old McEntire House in Decatur." *Birmingham News,* July 7, 1940.

———— "Mrs. Charles Walker Actually Has Seen a Real Apparition." *Birmingham News,* September 29, 1940.

Rawls, Phillip, and Ginger Grantham. "South Alabama Abounds with Eerie Ghost Stories." *The Montgomery Advertiser Alabama Journal,* December 31, 1976.

Salter, Charles. "A Ghostly Tale from Stover Creek." *The Atlanta Journal and Constitution,* May 28, 1978.

————. "Ghosts? No, But Footsteps Are There." *The Atlanta Journal and Constitution,* September 10, 1978.

Sentell, Lee. "The Ghosts of McEntire." *Decatur Daily,* June 20, 1971.

"Spirit 78." *Powergram,* October 1974.

Spotswood, Frances. "Fall cleanup seems assured at Homewood haunted house." *Birmingham News,* October 27, 1966.

Truchon, Frank. "Ghostly goings-on in Alabama related by Mrs. Windham." *Birmingham News,* November 21, 1977.

Windham, Kathryn T. "The ghosts of Alabama." *The Sun,* July 15, 1971.

UNPUBLISHED WORKS

Eskridge, Dena Fay. Letter from Courtland Public Library, Courtland, Alabama, September 4, 1984.

Alaska

BOOKS

Johnson, John F. C., ed. *Chugach Legends: Stories and Photographs of the Chugach Region.* Anchorage: Chugach Alaska Corp., 1984.

Keithahn, Edward L. *Alaskan Igloo Tales*. Anchorage: Alaska Northwest Publishing Co., n.d.
Smith, Warren. *Strange Hexes*. New York: Popular Library, 1970.

PERIODICALS

"Iliamna's Monster: Fact or Legend." *Anchorage Times*, c. February 1968.
"Legend of Sleeping Lady." *Alaska Legends*, vol. 2, no. 8 (n.d.)
"Mystery Fish: Fresh Water Giants Reported from Lake Iliamna to Arctic." n.p., n.d.
Sherwonit, Bill. "Mystery of 'Iliamna Monster' has logged many miles." *Anchorage Times*, April 28, 1985.

UNPUBLISHED WORKS

Correspondence from Bruce Merrell, Alaska Collection Librarian, March 24, 1986.

Arizona

BOOKS

Peterson, Thomas H., Jr. *Fort Lowell, A. T. Army Post During the Apache Campaigns*. Published by the Tucson Corral of the Westerners (Fall 1963, Revised 1976, No. 8).
Smith, Susy. *The Power of the Mind*. Radnor, PA: Chilton Book Co., 1975.

PERIODICALS

Biere, Francine. "Ghosts of the Old West." *Accent*, October 1983.
Bowden, Charles. "When things go bump in the night." *Tucson Citizen*, October 29, 1982.
Collins, Christina. "Ghosts." *Tucson Citizen*, October 29, 1977.
Fowler, Larry. "Ghost in Catalina High Halls?" *Tucson Citizen*, October 31, 1980.
Huff, Dan. " 'Ghost's' house is sold, but memories linger on." *Tucson Citizen*, n.d.
Hunt, Nancy Lee. "Old-time ghost in modern building." *Arizona Daily Wildcat*, October 31, 1989.
Knight, Susan M. "Reporter's past puts her in ghostly spirit." *Arizona Daily Star*, October 30, 1980.
———. "Spooky goings-on send family fleeing to new home." *Arizona Daily Star*, October 30, 1980.
Porter, Claire. "Tucson 'haunts': spirits, places of local legend." *The Territorial*, October 25, 1984.
Rosenblum, Keith. "Ghosts—Hunt for spirits' haunts fruitless task in Tucson." *Arizona Daily Star*, October 28, 1979.
Schellie, Don. "Phantom hitchhiker time once again." *Tucson Citizen*, May 25, 1979.
———. "Where are the Tucson ghosts?" *Tucson Citizen*, June 28, 1979.
Sinclair, Murray. "One of Tucson's Variety of Ghosts Doesn't Like Children or Dobermans." *Arizona Daily Star*, n.d.
Sorenson, Dan. "Guess who might be coming to dinner?" *Tucson Citizen*, December 5, 1983.
"The youthful ghost of Suarez house." *Tucson Citizen*, May 17, 1980.

Arkansas

BOOKS

Allsop, Fred W. *Allsop's Folklore of Romantic Arkansas*. Volume II. New York: The Grolier Society, USA, 1931.
Randolph, Vance. *Ozark Magic and Folklore*. New York: Dover Publications, Inc., 1964.

PERIODICALS

Dickinson, Sam. "Tales of Ghosts." *Arkansas Democrat*, May 27, 1962.

Hicks, John C. "The Legend of Skeleton Hollow." *Arkansas Democrat*, September 10, 1961.

Johnson, William. "Ghosts and 'Hants' Play Their Part in Folklore of Arkansas." *Arkansas Democrat*, August 9, 1931.

Shell, Lilith. "The Strains of a Violin." *Arcadian Magazine*, November 1931.

California

BOOKS

Albion, Robert G. *Five Centuries of Famous Ships*. New York: McGraw-Hill Book Company, 1978.

May, Antoinette. *Haunted Houses and Wandering Ghosts of California*. San Francisco: The San Francisco Examiner Division of The Hearst Corporation, 1977.

Smith, Susy. *Prominent American Ghosts*. Cleveland and New York: World Publishing Company, 1967.

Taylor, L. B. *Haunted Houses*. New York: Wanderer Books, 1983.

PERIODICALS

Arnold, Thomas K. "Investigative Team Stalks the Supernatural in San Diego Houses." *Los Angeles Times*, October 25, 1982.

———. "The Spirits of San Diego," *San Diego*, October 1985.

Bardacke, Frances. "The Swinging World of 'Yankee Jim.' " *San Diego and Point*, January 1966.

Burgess, Michele. "The Winchester House: A Marvelous Mystery." *Sky* (Delta Airlines Inflight Magazine), April 1982.

Randall, Gale. "Spirited Mansion." *Sonoma Press Democrat*, April 23, 1987.

Rose, Frank. "Where the Mystical Meets the Bizarre." *The New York Times*, July 12, 1987.

Shoup, Mike. "Winchester House Was Built to Ward Off Evil Spirits." *Omaha World Herald*, July 10, 1986.

Sullivan, Gail Bernice. "How About a Ghost Story?" *San Francisco Sunday Examiner*, January 9, 1972.

Sweeney, Thomas W. "A Royal Dilemma." *Historic Preservation News*, June 1992.

Weisang, Myriam. "Hearts for Art's Sake (A profile of the San Francisco Art Institute and its second annual Artists Valentines Exhibition/Auction)." *The San Francisco Bay Guardian*, February 6, 1985.

UNPUBLISHED WORKS

Interview with Mrs. June Reading, San Diego, July 7, 1988.

Material from San Francisco Archives, Public Library, Civic Center, San Francisco, California 94102.

Mulford, Harry. *Legends of a Ghost*, July 20, 1976.

San Francisco Art Institute Séance Press Release, October 26, 1976.

Colorado

BOOKS

Brandon, Jim. *Weird America*. New York: E. P. Dutton, 1978.

Gaddis, Vincent H. *Mysterious Fires and Lights*. New York: Dell, 1967.

Martin, MaryJoy. *Ghosts Ghouls & Goblins: Twilight Dwellers of Colorado*. Boulder, Colo: Pruett Publishing Company, 1985.

Smyth, Frank. *Ghosts and Poltergeists.* Garden City, N.Y.: Doubleday and Company, Inc., 1976.

PERIODICALS

Fry, Eleanor. "Townsite of Rosita officially abandoned." *Pueblo Star-Journal,* August 21, 1978.
Kelly, Bernard. "So you don't believe in GHOSTS!" *Contemporary Magazine of The Denver Post,* October 28, 1962.
Linehan, Edward J. "The Rockies' Pot of Gold Colorado." *National Geographic,* volume 136, no. 2 (August 1969).
Little, W. T. "County seat battle raged for years." *Canon City Daily Record,* October 6, 1980.
————. "Dancing Ghosts Carry Own Lights." *Rocky Mountain News,* April 19, 1956.
————. "Hunting Ghosts in a Ghost Town Out West." *The New York Times,* August 20, 1967, XX, 19:1.
"Old, new melds in Silver Cliff." *Pueblo Star-Journal and Sunday Chieftain.* March 18, 1979.
Parker, Dorothy. "Leadership encompasses 30 years." *Canon City Daily Record,* May 7, 1980.
"Three Brigands of Rosita." *The Denver Tribune,* August 28, 1881.
Wilkinson, Bruce M. "Silver Cliff Respects Heritage." *Pueblo Star-Journal and Sunday Chieftain,* October 24, 1965.

UNPUBLISHED WORKS

Francis, Irene. Tape recording entitled "The Lights in the Silver Cliff Cemetery," Westcliffe, Colorado, November 1987.
Local History Center of the Public Library, Canon City, Colorado.

Connecticut

BOOKS

Blackington, Alton H. *Yankee Yarns.* New York: Doubleday & Company, 1954.
Bolte, Mary. *Haunted New England.* Riverside, Conn.: The Chatham Press, Inc., 1972.
Cahill, Robert Ellis. *New England's Ghostly Haunts.* Peabody, Mass.: Chandler-Smith Publishing House, 1983.
Federal Writers Project. *American Guide Series for Connecticut.* Boston: Houghton Mifflin Co., 1938.
Stevens, Austin N. *Mysterious New England.* Dublin, N.H.: Yankee, Inc., 1971.
Wilcoxson, William Howard. *History of Stratford, Connecticut.* n.p., n.d.

PERIODICALS

"Death of Phelps Mansion." *The Stratford Bard,* February 17, 1972.
Decerbo, Esther. "Historical, Haunted Mansion Finally Ends Its Stormy Life." *Bridgeport Sunday Post,* March 5, 1972.
Jarman, Rufus. "Mystery House on Elm Street." *Yankee,* October 1971.

UNPUBLISHED WORKS

Information from Franklin, Connecticut, Town Hall.

Delaware

BOOKS

Cullen, Virginia. *History of Lewes, Delaware*. Revised printing. Lewes, Del.: Col. David Hall Chapter, NSDAR, 1956.

Delaware: A Guide to the First State (American Guide Series). Compiled and Written by the Federal Writers' Project of the Works Progress Administration for the State of Delaware. New York: Viking Press, 1938.

Frank, Commander. *Stories and Legends of the Delaware Capes*. Published by Miles Frederick, n.d.

Reynolds, James. *Ghosts in American Houses*. New York: Bonanza, 1955.

Smith, Susy. *Ghosts Around the House*. Cleveland and New York: World Publishing Co., 1988.

————. *Haunted Houses for the Millions*. New York: Dell Publishing Co., 1967.

PERIODICALS

Dover Evening Journal, March 24, 1972.
Dover Post, June 30, 1976.

District of Columbia

BOOKS

Alexander, John. *Ghosts: Washington's Most Famous Ghost Stories*. Washington, D.C.: Washingtonian Books, 1975.

Brandon, Jim. *Weird America*. New York: E. P. Dutton, 1978.

Datsun Student Travel Guide, 1978.

Greenhouse, Herbert B. *In Defense of Ghosts*. New York: Simon and Schuster, Inc., Essandess Special Editions, 1970.

Jeffrey, A. K. *Across the Land from Ghost to Ghost*. Lahaska, Pa.: New Hope Publishing Company, 1975.

Smith, Susy. *Haunted Houses for the Millions*. New York: Dell Publishing Company, Inc., 1967.

Steiger, Brad. *Real Ghosts, Restless Spirits and Haunted Minds*. New York: Award Books, Universal-Award House, Inc., 1968.

Walker, Danton. *I Believe in Ghosts*. New York: Taplinger Publishing Company, 1969 (a reedited version of *Spooks Deluxe*, published in 1956).

PERIODICALS

"5 'authentic' ghosts in Capitol." *The Montgomery Advertiser, Alabama Journal*, October 30, 1977.

"Ghosts may haunt corridors of Capitol." *The Tuscaloosa* (Ala.) *News*, October 30, 1977.

"Who's whooo: Unexplained tales lure many tourists." *Cleveland Press*, October 31, 1978.

Florida

BOOKS

Kettelkamp, Larry. *Haunted Houses*. New York: William Morrow and Company, 1969.

Roll, William G. *The Poltergeist*. Metuchen, N.J.: Scarecrow Press, Inc., 1976.

Steiger, Brad. *Real Ghosts, Restless Spirits and Haunted Minds*. New York: Award Books, Universal-Award House, Inc., 1968.

————. *True Ghost Stories*. Rockport, Mass.: Para Research, 1982.

PERIODICALS

Achenbach, Joel. "For sale: Home with ghost." *The Miami Herald*, May 1, 1985.
———. "Ghosts here? It's their night." *The Miami Herald*, October 31, 1985.
Browning, Michael. "A Chance of a Ghost." *Miami Herald Tropic Magazine*, October 31, 1982.
Epstein, Warren. "Haunting grounds." *Tampa Tribune*, October 19, 1984.
Glass, Ian. "A cloud of smoke grabbed me . . . this is it." *Miami News*, May 30, 1974.
———. "Ghost house for sale—only $110,000." *Miami News*, March 22, 1976.
———. "Knock, knock, who's there at Villa Paula's?" *Miami News*, March 22, 1976.
———. "A pall of confusion called by séance and may be Paula." *Miami News*, April 5, 1976.
Grimes, Sandra. "A Ghost Story." *Tampa Tribune*, February 19, 1982.
Nordheimer, Jon. "Even Police Can't Locate 'Spook in the Stockroom.'" *The Miami Herald*, January 18, 1967.
Roberts, Jack. "I Paid a Visit to Our City's Spook House." *Miami News*, January 18, 1967.
———. "There Was a Boy, a Very Strange . . ." *Miami News*, March 2, 1967.
Werne, Jo. "I'm Not the Shelf Spook, 19-Year-Old Clerk Says." *The Miami Herald*, February 3, 1967.

Georgia

BOOKS

Miller, Harriet Parks. *The Bell Witch of Middle Tennessee*. Clarksville, Tenn.: Leaf-Chronicle Publishing Company, 1930.
Perkerson, Medora Field. *White Columns in Georgia*. New York: Rinehart, n.d.
Roberts, Nancy, and Bruce Roberts. *This Haunted Land: Where Ghosts Still Roam*. Charlotte, N.C.: McNally and Loftin, Publishers, 1970.
Taylor, L. B. *Haunted Houses*. New York: Wanderer Books, 1983.
Windham, Kathryn Tucker. *Thirteen Georgia Ghosts and Jeffrey*. Huntsville, Ala.: The Strode Publishers, n.d.

PERIODICALS

Broussard, Richard. "The Ghost of Orna Villa." *Atlanta Magazine*, October 1984.
Denholtz, David. "Old Faculty Members Never Die . . . ?" *The Spokesman* (Oxford College Student Newspaper), May 30, 1980.
Jordan, Vera. "The Alexander Means Home: Haunted House of Oxford." *The Spokesman* (Oxford College Student Newspaper), March 1972.
St. John, Wylly Folk. "Ghost That Eats Biscuits?" *The Atlanta Journal Magazine*, October 13, 1946.

UNPUBLISHED WORKS

Davis, M. L. "The Surrency Ghost," Special Collections Division, The University of Georgia Libraries, Athens, Georgia.
Interview with James Watterson, May 1987.

Hawaii

BOOKS

Brandon, Jim. *Weird America*. New York: E. P. Dutton, 1978.
Coffin, Tristram Potter, and Hennig Cohen. *The Parade of Heroes*. Garden City, N.Y.: Anchor Press/Doubleday, 1978.
Westervelt, W. D. *Hawaiian Legends of Volcanoes*. Boston: Ellis Press, 1916.

PERIODICALS

"Al Pelayo 'Legendary' Host at Volcano House." *Hawaiian Times*, vol. II, no. 1.

Apple, Russ, and Peg Apple. "Pele's Signal to a Mother." *Honolulu Star Bulletin*, May 12, 1973.

Bruggencate, Jan Ten. "Pele is an old acquaintance for Sadie Brown." *Honolulu Advertiser*, December 6, 1986.

Gilmore, Alice. "The Lady in Red." *OAHU*, vol. 4, no. 3 (April 1980).

Hardy, Barlow. "Mme. Pele Re-appears." *Paradise of the Pacific*, February 1946.

Howard, Vol. A. "Fire Goddess Pele, Real or Imaginary?" *Paradise of the Pacific*, March 1944.

Maguire, Eliza D. "Madame Pele's Last Legend." *Paradise of the Pacific*, December 1926.

Martin, Marlene. "Pele's Fury." *Los Angeles Times*, October 18, 1987.

Tabrah, Ruth. "How Madame Pele Got 'The Word.' " *Honolulu Magazine*, n.d.

Idaho

BOOKS

d'Easum, Dick. *Sawtooth Tales*. Caldwell, Idaho: The Caxton Printers, Ltd., 1977.

PERIODICALS

d'Easum, Dick. "Footsteps of Idaho Ghosts." *The Idaho Statesman*, November 3, 1963.

"A Haunted House." *Idaho Daily Statesman*, November 15, 1892.

"Haunted House Changes Owner," *Idaho Statesman*, June 5, 1927.

Rushforth, Desirai. "Do You Believe in Ghosts? They Do." *Idaho State Journal* (Pocatello), October 31, 1986.

UNPUBLISHED WORKS

Correspondence from Elizabeth P. Jacox, librarian, Idaho State Historical Society, Boise, November 24, 1986.

Illinois

PERIODICALS

Hughes, T. Lee. "Peoria Library on 'Cursed' Site." *Peoria Journal Star*, October 31, 1974.

Michael, William M. "I ain't afraid of no ghosts!" *Herald & Review* (Decatur), n.d.

Norman, Frances. "Old Curse Dooms Library Site as Eternal Source of Ill Fortune to Owner." *Peoria Journal Star*, January 30, 1944. Reprinted in *Peoria Journal Star*, February 10, 1957.

" 'Old Book' . . . The Tragic Story of a Demented Soul and 'The Graveyard Elm.' " *Peoria Journal Star*, October 31, 1980.

"True Tale of Peoria." *Peoria Herald*, September 15, 1895.

UNPUBLISHED WORKS

Bryan, William W. "Historical Sketch of the Peoria Public Library." Compiled 1980.

Indiana

BOOKS

Baker, Ronald L. *Hoosier Folk Legends*. Bloomington: Indiana University Press, 1982.

Ellis, Edward S., A.M. *The History of Our Country, Volume III*. Cincinnati: The Jones Brothers Publishing Company, 1918.

Panati, Charles. *Supersenses*. New York: Quadrangle/The New York Times Book Company, 1974.
Rogo, D. Scott. *Parapsychology: A Century of Inquiry*. New York: Taplinger Publishing Company, 1975.
Roll, William G. *The Poltergeist*. Metuchen, N.J.: The Scarecrow Press, Inc., 1976.

PERIODICALS

Bell, Steve. "Scary Places." *Indianapolis Monthly*, October 1984.
McLayea, Eunice. "This old house still has 'ghosts.' " *Indianapolis Star*, March 22, 1981.
Ward, Joe. "Ghost stories." *Louisville* (Ky.) *Courier-Journal*, October 29, 1974.
Whyde, Kathy. "Cities have their own folklore." *Indianapolis Star*, April 4, 1982.

Iowa

PERIODICALS

Annals of Iowa, Spring 1965.
Bluhm, Donald A. "The Duke of Winterset." *The Milwaukee Journal*, August 12, 1984.
The Festival Flyer, Supplement to the *Winterset Madisonian*, vol. 6, October 11 and 12, 1975.
Hopkins, Julie. "Tales to make your blood run cold." *The Des Moines Register*, October 31, 1976.
Today's Dubuque, 1987.

UNPUBLISHED WORKS

Smeator, Mrs. Guy. Federal Writers' Project, Folklore Series ms. ca. 1940, 240 Folklore., Iowa State Historical Society, Iowa City.

Kansas

BOOKS

Ghost Stories of Fort Leavenworth. Compiled by The Musettes, 1984.

PERIODICALS

Conley, Manuel A., Maj. USA. "Haunted Fort Leavenworth." *The Retired Officer*, October 1979.
Lazzarino, Evie. "Ghostly tale still haunts Sigma Nu house." *Lawrence Journal World*, October 31, 1982.
Mouze, Victoria, SSgt. "Getting into the Spirit." *Soldiers*, October 1982.
Seifert, Allen. "They're around, all right—in spirit." *St. Joseph News-Press/Gazette*, October 26, 1986.
"Wichita psychic probes legend of Theorosa's Bridge." *Valley News*, May 26, 1976.

UNPUBLISHED WORKS

Heffley, Deborah Anne. "Haunting Tales of Emporia, Kansas," written for Studies in American Folklore EN 740 C, Emporia State University, July 15, 1983.
Koch, William E. The William E. Koch Folklore Collection, Kansas State University, Manhattan.

Kentucky

BOOKS

Winer, Richard, and Nancy Osborn Ishmael. *More Haunted Houses*. New York: Bantam Books, 1981.

PERIODICALS

Kopach, Kathy. "Ghost Story: The Lady in Gray Walks at Carneal House." *Cincinnati Enquirer*, n.d.

"Let the Spirit Move You." *Automobile Bulletin*, September/October 1970.

"Liberty Hall at Frankfort Is to Be Presented to Colonial Dames." *Louisville Times*, November 11, 1922.

Niemtus, Laurice. "The Schoolgirl, the Friendly Spook of New Albany, the Grey Lady and Other Haunting Tales." *Louisville Times*, July 24, 1982.

Page, Lane. "Old Kentucky Haunts." *Springfield* (Ohio) *Sun*, December 2, 1965.

Ramsey, Sy. "Kentucky Ghosts Haunt Old House." *Springfield* (Ohio) *Sun*, December 2, 1965.

"Relics and Ghost Fill Old House." *Louisville Times*, November 13, 1922.

Stacy, Helen Price. "A Ball of Hair and a Pinch of Salt." Commonwealth of Kentucky, Department of Public Information, October 23, 1970.

———. "It's Time to Make Friends with Goblins." Commonwealth of Kentucky, Department of Public Information, October 20, 1972.

———. "Shades of Ghosts Provide Stories for October Reading." Commonwealth of Kentucky, Department of Public Information, January 12, 1973.

Teagarden, Oressa. "Do Ghosts Keep Vigil Forever." *Louisville Courier-Journal*, December 8, 1940.

Thierman, Sue McClelland. "Haunted by History." Courtesy Kentucky Historical Society, n.d.

Warren, Jim. "Trio Take in Ghostly Air of White Hall." *Lexington Herald-Leader*, October 30, 1984.

Louisiana

BOOKS

Botkin, B. A. *A Treasury of Southern Folklore*. New York: Crown Publishers, 1949.

Cohen, Daniel. *The World's Most Famous Ghosts*. New York: Pocket Books, 1978.

Hurwood, Bernhardt J. *Monsters and Nightmares*. New York: Belmont Productions, Inc., 1967.

Saxon, Lyle, et al. *Gumbo Ya-Ya*. New York: Bonanza Books, 1945.

Smith, Susy. *Prominent American Ghosts*. Cleveland and New York: World Publishing Company, 1967.

PERIODICALS

Alexander, Bill. "The Myrtles' Friendly Ghosts Provide Extra Entertainment for Some Overnight Guests." *The Old News Is Good News Antiques Gazette*, July 1990.

Burrough, Bryan. "As Spooky Places Go, an Inn in the Bayous Goes a Bit Too Far." *The Wall Street Journal*, October 31, 1984.

Foster, Mary. "Big easy ghosts find many places to hang around." *New Orleans Times-Picayune*, October 28, 1989.

Lewis, Joy Schaleben. "This Bed and Breakfast Is a Scream." *Los Angeles Times*, September 27, 1987.

Munson, Richard. "At the Zumo Home, Ghosts Just Move in with the Furniture." *Sunday Advocate*, March 5, 1978.

Rivers, Bill. "Louisiana's Gentle Ghosts." *Morning Advocate*, September 28, 1952.
Veach, Damon. "Ghost Tales of Baton Rouge." *Baton Rouge Enterprise*, October 29, 1981.
Wonk, Dalt. "The Fall of the House of Orchard." *New Orleans*, June 1975.

Maine

BOOKS

Beck, Horace P. *The Folklore of Maine*. Philadelphia: J. B. Lippincott Co., 1957.
Botkin, B. A., ed. *A Treasury of New England Folklore*. New York: Crown Publishers, 1947.
Noyes, Sybil, Charles T. Libby, and Walter G. Davis. *Genealogical Dictionary of Maine and New Hampshire*. Baltimore: Genealogical Publishing Co., 1976.
Simpson, Dorothy. *The Maine Islands in Story and Legend*. Philadelphia: J. B. Lippincott Co., 1960.
Skinner, Charles M. *Myths and Legends of Our Own Land*. Philadelphia: J. B. Lippincott Co., 1896.
Sylvester, Herbert M. *Maine Pioneer Settlements: Old York*. Boston: W. B. Clarke Co., 1909.
———. *The Romance of Old York*. Boston: Stanhope Press, 1906.

PERIODICALS

"Catalogue of the Relics and Curiosities in Ye Olde Gaol, York, Maine." 1980 reprint of 1900 catalogue, n.p.
"The Jonesport Raffle." n.p., n.d.
Paper, Hank. "Portland's Famous Ghost Stories." *Portland*, Fall 1985.

Maryland

BOOKS

Anderson, Elizabeth B., with Michael P. Parker. *Annapolis: A Walk Through History*. Centerville, Md.: Tidewater Publishers, n.d.
Ellis, Edward S. *The History of Our Country*. Cincinnati: The Jones Brothers Publishing Company, 1918.
Hammond, John Martin. *Colonial Mansions of Maryland and Delaware*. Philadelphia and London: J. B. Lippincott Company, 1914.
Merriam, Anne Van Ness, comp. *The Ghosts of Hampton*, n.d.
Skinner, Charles M. *Myths and Legends of Our Own Land*. Philadelphia: J. B. Lippincott Company, 1896.
Stevens, William O. *Unbidden Guests*. New York: Dodd, Mead, 1946.
Taylor, L. B. *Haunted Houses*. New York: Wanderer Books, 1983.

PERIODICALS

AAA World, September/October 1986.
Burdett, Hal. "Brice House ghost stories." *Evening Capital*, n.d.
Challmes, Joseph J, and Tom Horton, comps. "Marylanders compile rich legacy of ghostly tales and legendary lore." *News American*, August 11, 1976.
Jackson, Elmer, Sr. "Jennings House." *Anne Arundel Times*, January 15, 1970.
Randolph, Evan. "The Spirit of Commodore Truxton." *Yankee*, June 1977.

UNPUBLISHED WORKS

Communication from Ellen Berkov, Anne Arundel County Public Library, Annapolis, Maryland, May 15, 1992.

Massachusetts

BOOKS

Botkin, B. A., ed. A *Treasury of American Folklore*. New York: Bantam Books, 1948.

———. A *Treasury of New England Folklore*. New York: Crown Publishers, 1947.

Brimblecom, Deborah. *The Screeching Lady of Marblehead*. Beverly, Mass.: Wilkscraft Inc., 1976.

Chamberlain, Samuel. *New England Legends and Folklore* (adapted with additions from A *Book of New England Legends and Folklore* by Samuel Adams Drake, 1884.) New York: Hastings House, 1967.

Drake, Samuel Adams. A *Book of New England Legends and Folk Lore in Prose and Poetry*. Boston: Little, Brown and Company, 1910. Rpt. Detroit: Singing Tree Press, Book Tower, 1969.

Miles, Dorothy. *The Wizard of Orne Hill and Other Tales of Old Marblehead*. Privately published, 1985.

Snow, Edward Rowe. *Fantastic Folklore and Fact*. New York: Dodd, Mead, 1968.

PERIODICALS

Allmaker, Ali Martin. "Local Haunts." *The Berkshire Eagle*, July 6–12, 1984.

Coppage, Noel, and Walter D. Mosher. "A Mighty Hole in the Ground." *Yankee*, November 1973.

"Even John Barnard Believed the Story of the Screeching Woman." *Marblehead Messenger*, January 26, 1938.

"Historic Marblehead." *Lynn* (Mass.) *Item*, July 22, 1952.

Kuperschmid, Eileen. Untitled article. *The Berkshire Sampler*, October 30, 1977.

Schacht, Susan. "Miles' book chronicles local lore." *Marblehead Reporter*, September 26, 1985.

"The Screeching Woman." *The Boston Globe*, August 28, 1929.

Taft, Lewis A. "The Legend of Peter Rugg." *Yankee*, October 1960.

Michigan

BOOKS

Eberle, Gary. *Haunted Houses of Grand Rapids, Volume Two*. Ada, Mich.: Ivystone Publications, 1982.

Farrant, Don. *Haunted Houses of Grand Rapids*. Ada, Mich.: Ivystone Publications, 1979.

Hurwood, Bernhardt J. *Monsters and Nightmares*. New York: Belmont Productions, Inc., 1967.

PERIODICALS

Covert, Colin. "Bumps in the night." *Detroit Free Press*, October 26, 1980.

Franklin, Wade. "America's Haunted Houses: You Can Walk in the Footsteps of Ghosts," *Detroit Free Press*, May 22, 1977.

"Ghost sightings are dead serious matter for many." *Eau Claire* (Wisc.) *Leader Telegram*, October 10, 1992.

McPherson, Mark. "Who Ya Gonna Call?" *Detroit Free Press*, October 25, 1987.

"Mysterious Incident Recalled." *Sault Ste. Marie Evening News*, August 1952.

Minnesota

BOOKS

Blegen, Theodore C. *Minnesota: A History of the State*. Minneapolis: University of Minnesota Press, 1963.
Collections of the Minnesota Historical Society, Vol. V. St. Paul: Published by the Society, 1902.
Minnesota: A State Guide (American Guide Series). New York: The Viking Press, 1938.

PERIODICALS

"Coroner to Probe House of Mystery." *The St. Paul Pioneer Press*, February 20, 1911.
El-Hai, Jack. "Nights of the Living Dead." *Minneapolis St. Paul Magazine*, October 1987.
" 'Ghost' Excites a St. Paul Family." *The St. Paul Pioneer Press*, February 18, 1911.
"Rosaries Increase Mystery of Ghost." *The St. Paul Pioneer Press*, February 19, 1911.
"When 'things go bump in night,' Mack listens." *Plainview News*, October 30, 1984.

UNPUBLISHED WORKS

Interview with Tim Mack, August 14, 1990.

Mississippi

BOOKS

Botkin, B. A., ed. *A Treasury of Southern Folklore*. New York: Bonanza Books, n.d.
Colorful Moments from Mississippi's History. Meridian, Miss.: Junior Food Stores, Inc., n.d.
Crocker, Mary Wallace. *Historic Architecture in Mississippi*. Jackson: University Press of Mississippi, 1973.
Datsun Student Travel Guide, 1978.
Newton, Carolyn, and Patricia H. Coggin. *Meet Mississippi*. Huntsville, Ala.: Strode Publishers, Inc., 1976.
Roberts, Nancy, and Bruce Roberts. *This Haunted Land*. Charlotte, N.C.: Heritage Printers, Inc., 1984.
Windham, Katherine Tucker. *13 Mississippi Ghosts and Jeffrey*. Huntsville, Ala.: Strode Publishers, Inc., 1974.

PERIODICALS

Aden, Marky. "House is history plus mystery." *Delta Democrat-Times* (Greenville), n.d.
Bergeron, Kat. "Gulf Coast spooks, old ones and new, still can produce a nightmare or two." *The Sun/The Daily Herald, Mississippi Gulf Coast*, n.d.
Brigham, Allegra. "Potpourri . . ." *Columbus Dispatch*, February 12, 1978.
Burdsal, Bill. "Ghost Stories." *Mississippi*, September/October 1985.
Campbell, Nanci. "Suspicion of Arson in Cahill Fire." *The Daily Herald* (Biloxi-Gulfport), July 19, 1970.
Chidsey, Judge Charles E. "The Mysterious Music of Pascagoula." *Four Centuries on the Pascagoula* (article is an abridgment of author's article in *Popular Science Monthly*, 1890).
Culbertson, Jean. "State Folklore Abounds in Ghosts." *The Clarion-Ledger*, October 31, 1967.
Ehrbright, Nan Patton. "Gentle Coast ghosts have haunted houses for years." *Mississippi Gulf Coast*, n.d.
Ewing, Jim. " 'Witch's Grave' still chief haunting site in spooky Yazoo City." *Jackson Daily News*, October 27, 1983.
Flynn, Pat. "Who's buried in the witch's grave?" *The Yazoo Daily Herald*, July 2, 1978.

Fox, Marion Laffey. "The Natchez Way." *Adventure Road*, Spring 1983.
Gerrard, Ben. "Did the Witch Cause the 1904 Fire?" *Bookends 1983*, Yazoo City High School yearbook.
"Ghost Tales Include That of 'Miss Nellie.'" *Columbus Dispatch*, December 25, 1974.
Gorringe, Maybelle. "'Spirits' Visit Haunted House." *Jackson Daily News*, December 19, 1969.
Harrison, Martha. "Madison Chapel Hallows Ground Where Pioneers Sleep." *Jackson Daily News*, February 20, 1938.
Mangum, David. "Graveyard—Where Ghosts Appear—At Chapel of Cross." *The Clarion-Ledger*, October 28, 1973.
Ryan, Pam. "Legend of Spirits Ends with Fire." *The Daily Herald* (Biloxi-Gulfport), July 19, 1970.
Simmons, Rebecca. "Ghost's Hostess Won't Tempt Fate." *Columbus Dispatch*, November 26, 1978.
———. "Ghosts Find Conditions Favorable in Columbus." *Columbus Dispatch*, October 28, 1979.
Skipper, Deborah. "Boo or balderdash? We'll let you decide." *The Clarion-Ledger, Jackson Daily News*, October 30, 1983.
"Two ghosts at old King's Tavern blamed for erratic clock, eerie sounds, lights." *Press Register* (Mobile), July 3, 1977.
"Where a Ghost Walks." *The Delta Democrat-Times*, December 31, 1943.
Wright, Carol von Pressentin. "Plantation Mansions on the Mississippi," *The New York Times*, February 10, 1991.

Missouri

BOOKS

Collins, Earl A. *Legends and Lore of Missouri*. San Antonio: The Naylor Co., 1951.
Missouri, a Guide to the "Show Me" State (American Guide Series). New York: Duell, Sloan & Pearce, 1941.
Moore, Tom. *Mysterious Tales and Legends of the Ozarks*. Philadelphia: Dorrance & Co., 1938.
Randolph, Vance. *Ozark Magic and Folklore*. New York: Dover Publications, Inc., 1964.
Rayburn, Otto Vance. *Ozark Country*. New York: Duell, Sloan & Pearce, 1941, from the American Folkways series edited by Erskine Caldwell.
Steiger, Brad. *True Ghost Stories*. Rockport, Mass.: Para Research, 1982.

PERIODICALS

Bergmann, Joe. "Spirits in the House." *Columbia* (Mo.) *Daily Tribune*, October 25, 1987.
Clayton, Joe. "Legend Season." *Springfield News & Leader*, October 27, 1957.
Shroyer, Jo Ann. "Spirits of St. Louis." *St. Paul Pioneer Press*, October 31, 1993.

Montana

BOOKS

Murray, Earl. *Ghosts of the Old West*. Chicago: Contemporary Books, Inc., 1988.

PERIODICALS

Liberty, Margot. "Ghost Herder's Battlefield." *Hardin Tribune-Herald*, June 22, 1961.
Palmer, Tom. "Helena's Haunted House." *The Independent Record*, October 29, 1984.

UNPUBLISHED WORKS

Interview with Dorothy Card, May 14, 1987.

Nebraska

BOOKS

Vaughan, Alan. *Incredible Coincidence—The Baffling World of Synchronicity.* New York: J. B. Lippincott, 1979.

PERIODICALS

Chadron Citizen, February 9, 1893.
Lincoln Evening News, November 22, 1892.
Madison County Reporter, March 8, 1900.
The Bridgeport News-Blade, October 10, 1913.
The Enterprise (Pawnee), July 7, 1880.
The Hastings Tribune, October 29, 1985.

UNPUBLISHED WORKS

Files of Federal Writers' Project of the Works Progress Administration in Collections of Nebraska State Historical Society.

Nevada

BOOKS

Guiley, Rosemary. *Encyclopedia of Ghosts and Spirits.* New York: Facts on File, 1992.
McDonald, Douglas. *Camels in Nevada.* Las Vegas: n.p., 1983.
O'Brien, Dolores K. *Meet Virginia City's Ghosts.* Virginia City: n.p., 1969.
Roberts, Bruce, and Nancy Roberts. *America's Most Haunted Places.* Garden City, N. Y. Doubleday & Co., 1976.
Young, Richard, and Judy Dockery. *Ghost Stories from the American Southwest.* Little Rock: August House, 1991.

PERIODICALS

Earl, Philip I. "Lee Singleton: A man haunted by a ghostly past." *Nevada State Journal,* October 25, 1981.
————. "Nevada has its ghostly past." *Nevada State Journal,* October 31, 1982.
————. "Six-Mile's haunted treasure." *Sparks Tribune,* July 28, 1982.

UNPUBLISHED WORKS

Correspondence from Phil Earl, Nevada Historical Society, August 1986.
Correspondence from Susan Jarvis, librarian, University of Nevada, Las Vegas, 1986.
Correspondence from Jeff Marcinik, assistant director, Humboldt County Library, July 1986.

New Hampshire

BOOKS

Back, Horace. *Folklore and the Sea.* Brattleboro, V.: The Stephen Greene Press, 1983.
Botkin, B. A. ed. *A Treasury of New England Folklore.* New York: Crown Publishers, 1947.
Cahill, Robert Ellis. *New England's Ghostly Haunts.* Peabody, Mass.: Chandler-Smith, n.d.
Carmer, Carl. *The Hurricane's Children.* New York & Toronto: Farrar & Rinehart, Inc., 1937.

Drake, Samuel Adams. *New England Legends and Folk Lore in Prose and Poetry*. Boston: Roberts Brothers, 1884.

————. *Nooks and Corners of the New England Coast*. New York: Harper & Brothers, 1875. Rpt. Detroit: Singing Tree Press, Book Tower, 1969.

Rutledge, Lyman V. *Ten Miles Out: Guidebook to the Isles of Shoals*, 4th ed. Boston: Isles of Shoals Unitarian Association, 1964.

Simpson, Dorothy. *The Maine Islands in Story and Legend*. Philadelphia and New York: J.B. Lippincott Company, 1960.

Smith, Susy. *Prominent American Ghosts*. Cleveland and New York: World Publishing Company, 1967.

————. *Worlds of the Strange*. New York: Pyramid Publications, 1963.

Steiger, Brad. *Real Ghosts, Restless Spirits and Haunted Minds*. New York: Universal-Award House, Inc., 1968.

Taylor, L.B. *Haunted Houses*. New York: Wanderer Books, 1983.

PERIODICALS

AAA World, September/October 1986.

Napolitan, Joseph. "Season is open for New England Ghosts." *The New York Times*, July 28, 1957.

Roberts, D.W. "Star Island." *New Hampshire Profiles*, April 1986.

"Shoals Marine Laboratory." *Yankee*, February 1987.

"To Be a Legend in Your Own Time." *Yankee*, July 1972.

New Jersey

BOOKS

Cohen, David Steven. *The Folklore and Folklife of New Jersey*. New Brunswick: Rutgers University Press, 1983.

Fort, Charles. *The Complete Books of Charles Fort*. New York: Dover Publications, Inc., 1974.

McMahon, William. *South Jersey Towns: History and Legend*. New Brunswick: Rutgers University Press, 1973.

New Jersey: A Guide to Its Present and Past. Compiled and Written by the Federal Writers' Project of the Works Progress Administration for the State of New Jersey (American Guide Series). New York: Hastings House, 1939.

Skinner, Charles M. *American Myths and Legends, Volume 1*. Philadelphia and London: J.B. Lippincott Company, 1903.

PERIODICALS

Axelrod, Robin Hope. "Don't wait for the spirit to move you." *The Spectator* (Somerset, N. J.), n.d.

Lewis, Peggy. "The Graisberry's Ghost." *Interact*, October 1976.

Marks, Peter. "Chronicles of Jersey's 'ghosties.'" *Sunday Star-Ledger*, October 28, 1979.

Szathmary, Richard. "Ghost of a Chance." *New Jersey Monthly*, October 1983.

Waldron, Martin. "The State's 'Bicentennial Ghost' Fades from Sight Again." *The New York Times*, November 21, 1976.

"The World Turned Upside Down." *Psychic: The Magazine of New Realities*, vol. VII, no.5.

UNPUBLISHED WORKS

Correspondence with David C. Munn, Cherry Hill, New Jersey, March 19, 1986; February 15, 1989.

New Mexico

PERIODICALS

Brewer, Steve. "Hotel Ghosts Return to Old Haunt." *Albuquerque Journal*, December 6, 1987.

Drabanski, Emily. "Haunted Casas: The Spirits of Santa Fe." *Santa Fe New Mexican*, October 31, 1982.

Kahn, Russell. "The Ultimate Fear." *Santa Fe Reporter*, October 31, 1982.

Klaus, Rob. "The Ghost of La Posada." *Impact Magazine of the Albuquerque Journal*, October 26, 1982.

Peipert, James R. "Cimarron's St. James Hotel plays host to ghost." *Minneapolis Star Tribune*, October 31, 1993.

Reed, Rita. "A Night in the Old West." *Minneapolis Star Tribune*, December 11, 1994.

Thompson, Fritz. "Ghosts, Ghosts, Ghosts." *Impact Magazine of the Albuquerque Journal*, October 30, 1979.

UNPUBLISHED WORKS

Correspondence and interview with Greg Champion, Cimarron, New Mexico, January 12, 1995.

The National Historic St. James Hotel brochure, n.p., n.d.

New York

BOOKS

Blundell, Nigel, and Roger Boar. *The World's Greatest Ghosts*. New York: Berkley Books, 1984.

Botkin, B. A. *New York City Folklore*. New York: Random House, 1956.

Brandon, Jim. *Weird America*. New York: E. P. Dutton, 1978.

Canning, John, ed. *50 Great Ghost Stories*. New York: Dell Publishing Co., 1971.

Huggett, Richard. *Supernatural on Stage*. New York: Taplinger Publishing Co., 1975.

Jones, Louis. *Things That Go Bump in the Night*. New York: Hill and Wang, 1959.

Kettelkamp, Larry. *Haunted Houses*. New York: William Morrow and Co., 1969.

Smith, Susy. *Prominent American Ghosts*. Cleveland and New York: World Publishing Co., 1967.

Walker, Danton. *I Believe in Ghosts*. New York: Taplinger Publishing Co., 1969 (a revised version of *Spooks Deluxe*, published in 1956).

PERIODICALS

"Ghost Story," The Talk of the Town, *The New Yorker*, May 15, 1995.

Klinglesmith, Dan. "Backstage Passes Unveil Shows' Secrets." *St. Paul Pioneer Press*, August 22, 1993.

"Lost: One Poltergeist," *The New York Times*, n.d.

Miller, Joy. "If Your House Has to Be Haunted, Pick an Entertaining Poltergeist." *Mobile Press Register*, February 7, 1960.

Quindlen, Anna. "About New York: Belief in Ghost Haunts a Historic Mansion." *The New York Times*, October 31, 1981.

North Carolina

BOOKS

Brandon, Jim. *Weird America.* New York: E. P. Dutton, 1978.
Gaddis, Vincent H. *Mysterious Fires and Lights.* New York: Dell Publishing Company, Inc., 1968.
Harden, John. *The Devil's Tramping Ground and Other North Carolina Mystery Stories.* Chapel Hill: The University of North Carolina Press, 1949.
———. *Tar Heel Ghosts.* Chapel Hill: The University of North Carolina Press, 1954.
Rankin, Hugh F. *The Pirates of Colonial North Carolina.* Raleigh, N.C.: Department of Cultural Resources Division of Archives and History, 1977.
Roberts, Nancy. *Ghosts of the Carolinas.* Charlotte McNally and Loftin, Publishers, 1962.
Whedbee, Charles Harry. *Legends of the Outer Banks and Tar Heel Tidewater.* Winston-Salem, N.C.: John F. Blair, 1966.

PERIODICALS

"At Night Do Spirits Stalk?" *Milwaukee Journal,* April 19, 1985.
Mintz, Frances. (Untitled). *Fayetteville* (N.C.) *Observer,* October 25, 1959.
Pressley, Sue Anne. "Things Go Bump in the Night at North Carolina Capitol." *Charlotte Observer,* July 20, 1979.
"The Queer Lights on Brown Mountain." *Literary Digest,* November 7, 1925.
Schlosser, Jim. "State to celebrate its Capitol as wise 150-year investment." *Greensboro News & Record,* June 30, 1990.

North Dakota

BOOKS

Devils Lake Illustrated. W. L. Fudley, Publisher, Press of *Grand Forks Herald,* 1898.
Gaddis, Vincent H. *Mysterious Fires and Lights.* New York: Dell Publishing Company, Inc., 1968.
North Dakota: A Guide to the Northern Prairie State (American Guide Series). Written by Workers of the Federal Writers' Project of the Works Progress Administration for the State of North Dakota. Fargo: Knight Printing Company, 1938.
Skinner, Charles M. *Myths and Legends of Our Own Land,* Vol. II. Philadelphia: J. B. Lippincott Company, 1896.

PERIODICALS

Hope Pioneer, Steele County, July 28, 1893.
North Dakota Historical Quarterly, Collections of the State Historical Society of North Dakota, vol. 1 (October 1926–July 1927).
North Dakota History, vol. 13, no. 4 (October 1946).

UNPUBLISHED WORKS

Federal Writers' Projects, Folklore Series, Folder 38; Series 550, Box 88, North Dakota State Historical Society, Bismarck.
Fannie Dunn Quain Papers, State Historical Society of North Dakota manuscript collection.

Ohio

BOOKS

Bromfield, Louis. *Pleasant Valley*. New York: Harper & Brothers, 1943.
Woodyard, Chris. *Haunted Ohio*. Beavercreek, Ohio: Kestrel Publications, 1991.
———. *Haunted Ohio II*. Beavercreek, Ohio: Kestrel Publications, 1992.

PERIODICALS

" 'Ghost' Sightings Reported in Ohio State Parks." *Akron Star-Beacon*, October 25, 1978.
Malabar Farm State Park brochure (n.d.), Route 1, Box 469, Lucas, Ohio 44843.
Richland Shield and Banner, July 25, 1896, October 17, 1896, and October 24, 1896. (Microfilmed edition of 1979, Ohio Historical Society, roll dated January 5, 1889, through December 5, 1896).

Oklahoma

PERIODICALS

Downes, Brian. "Second Wild West billing." *Chicago Tribune*, December 11, 1994.
"Ghost Routs Family." *Tulsa Tribune*, November 13, 1968.
Ruth, Kent. "Heard any ghost stories lately?" *Daily Oklahoman*, October 24, 1976.
———. "Oklahoma has ghost of its own." *Daily Oklahoman*, October 4, 1981.
Sarchet, Mark. "Eerie Sounds by Moonlight." *Daily Oklahoman*, April 14, 1957.
Wooley, John, Jeanne Forbis, and Tom Ewing. "Oklahoma Haunts: The Hills Are Alive." *Oklahoma*, October 31, 1982.

Oregon

BOOKS

Finucane, Stephanie. *Heceta House: A History and Architectural Survey*. Printed jointly by Lane Community College and USFS for the Heceta House Development Fund. Revised February 6, 1980.
Helm, Mike. *Oregon's Ghosts and Monsters*. Eugene: Rainy Day Press, 1983.

PERIODICALS

Bauguess, John. "Lighthouse Tract Suits Pair." *Oregon Journal*, May 14, 1975.
Eals, Clay. "Spirits roam real haunted house." *The Oregonian*, October 31, 1977.
Hesseldahl, Norman. "Heceta Head: A Picturesque Postcard with An Interesting Past," *Oregon Coast*, April/May 1987.
Miller, Mark. "Oregon's Lovely, Lonely Coast." *National Geographic*, December 1979.
"Mystery lures Duffy home," *Minneapolis Tribune*, December 5, 1982.
"Oregon Beacons—one hit by a ship, one haunted," *Sunset*, February 1986.
Ward, Darrell E. "Lighthouse gets painstaking restoration." *The Oregonian*, November 8, 1983.

UNPUBLISHED WORKS

Interview with Loyd Collette, July 6, 1988.

Pennsylvania

PERIODICALS

Bull, John V. R. "General Wayne Inn maintains a tradition of fine food." *The Philadelphia Inquirer*, April 27, 1986.

Carynnyk, Carol R. "A colonial inn with a penchant for surviving." *The Philadelphia Inquirer*, September 16, 1984.

Ciccarelli, Maura C. "A ghostly tour along Main Line." *Main Line Times* (Ardmore, Pa.), October 30, 1986.

McManus, Betty. "The General Wayne Inn." *Main Line Times* (Ardmore, Pa.), January 22, 1987.

Mendte, J. Robert. "General Wayne Inn." Anthony Wayne Historical Association, Merion, Pa. (Originally printed in the *Main Line Chronicle* from a paper read before the Anthony Wayne Historical Society, n.d.)

Patterson, Doris. "Are Hessian Soldiers' Ghosts Floating Around Main Line?" *Main Line Times* (Ardmore, Pa.), October 30, 1986.

Thompson, R. E. S. "Scribe Disappointed (?) in Search for Ghost." *Pittsburgh Post-Gazette*, March 21, 1938.

UNPUBLISHED WORKS

Interview with Barton Johnson, June 1986.

Rhode Island

BOOKS

Brandon, Jim. *Weird America*. New York: E. P. Dutton, 1978.

Chamberlain, Samuel. *New England Legends and Folklore* (adapted with additions from A Book of New England Legends and Folklore by Samuel Adams Drake, 1884). New York: Hastings House, 1967.

Reynolds, James. *Ghosts in American Houses*. New York: Bonanza Books, a division of Crown Publishers, by arrangement with the original publisher, Farrar, Straus and Cudahy, 1955.

Smyth, Frank. *Ghosts and Poltergeists*. Garden City, N.Y.: Doubleday and Company, Inc., 1976.

PERIODICALS

Powell, Noel. "Block Island's Fiery Ghost." *Yankee*, July 1956.

Rhode Island Collection, Providence Public Library, Providence, Rhode Island.

South Carolina

BOOKS

Fireside Tales: Stories of the Old Dutch Fork. Dutch Fork Press, 1984.

Graydon, Nell S. *South Carolina Ghost Tales*. Beaufort, S.C.: Beaufort Book Shop, Inc., 1969.

Greenhouse, Herbert B. *In Defense of Ghosts*. New York: Simon and Schuster, Inc., Essandess Special Editions, 1970.

Kellogg, Day Otis, ed. *The Encyclopedia Britannica*, vol. V. New York and Chicago: The Werner Company, 1900.

Rhyne, Nancy. *Coastal Ghosts*. Charlotte: The East Woods Press, 1985.

Roberts, Nancy. *Ghosts of the Carolinas*. Charlotte: McNally and Loftin, Publishers, 1962.
Willcox, Clarke A. *Musings of a Hermit*. Charleston, S.C.: Walker, Evans & Cogswell Company, 1966 (privately printed).

PERIODICALS

Chadwick, Bruce. "The Charms of Charleston." *American Way*, March 18, 1986.
Leland, Jack. "Ghosts Part of Lowcountry Lore." *The News and Courier* (Charleston), October 28, 1985.
Ralston, Edwina. "Nineteenth Century Lady in White Is Resident of Twentieth Century." *Knoxville* (Tenn.) *News Sentinel*, April 9, 1989.
Sparks, Andrew. "I Spent the Night in a Haunted House." *The Atlanta Journal and Constitution Magazine*, October 29, 1961.
Yancey, Kitty Bean. "The Laid-Back Life on Pawleys Island." *USA Today*, December 6, 1985.

UNPUBLISHED WORKS

Letter from Robert J. Thomas, November 9, 1989.
Letter from Clarke A. Willcox, October 18, 1988.

South Dakota

BOOKS

Karolevitz, Robert F. *Paper Mountain*, n.p., n.d.

PERIODICALS

Lollar, Kevin. "Halloween spirit lurks in theater." *Sioux Falls Argus Leader*, October 31, 1985.

UNPUBLISHED WORKS

Interview with Ray Loftesness, May 1987.
Interview with Jack Mortenson, May 1987.

Tennessee

BOOKS

Bell, Charles Bailey, with Harriet Parks Miller. *The Bell Witch of Tennessee*. Originally published 1934; facsimile reproduction. Nashville: Charles Elder, 1972.
Botkin, B. A. *A Treasury of Southern Folklore*. New York: Crown, 1949.
Ingram, M. V. *Authenticated History of the Bell Witch and Other Stories of the World's Greatest Unexplained Phenomenon*. Originally published 1894. Nashville: Rare Books Reprints, 1961.
Jarvis, Sharon, ed. *True Tales of the Unknown*. New York: Bantam, 1985.
Miller, Beaupre Olive. *Heroes, Outlaws and Funny Fellows of American Popular Tales*. New York: Cooper Square Publishers, 1973.
Smith, Susy. *Prominent American Ghosts*. Cleveland: World Publishing Corp., 1967.
Smith, Warren. *Strange Hexes*. New York: Popular Library, 1970.

PAMPHLETS AND PERIODICALS

Barr, Gladys. "Witchcraft in Tennessee." *Tennessee Valley Historical Review*, Fall 1973.
Beatty, Floy. "Bell Witch Broke Her Date!" *Nashville Tennessean*, n.d.

Bell, Richard Williams. "The Bell Witch, or Our Family Trouble." Reprint of pamphlet. Nashville: Mini-Histories, 1985.

"The Bell Witch." *Tri-County* (Tenn.) *News*, September 2, 1966.

"Bell Witch Returns, but This Time in a Play." *Knoxville* (Tenn.) *News-Sentinel*, October 31, 1976.

"Bell Witch of Robertson County, Tennessee's Most Famous Ghost." *Whitehaven* (Tenn.) *Press*, July 21, 1966.

Brehm, H. C. "Echoes of the Bell Witch in the Twentieth Century." (pamphlet). Nashville: H. C. Brehm, 1979.

"Bryan's Cantata 'Bell Witch' Presented in Carnegie Hall." *Knoxville* (Tenn.) *Journal*, April 15, 1947.

Burnette, Martha. "Beware Tennessee's Bell Witch." *Nashville Tennessean*, March 19, 26, 1933.

———. "Tennessee's Bell Witch." *Chattanooga Times*, March 26, 1933.

Burt, Jesse C. "General Jackson Meets the Bell Witch." *Nashville Tennessean*, n.d.

Cobb, Irvin S. "A Witch Was a Witch." *McClure's Magazine*, March 1923.

Day, Annie Mae. "Bell Family Stages Reunion, but Will the Witch Attend?" *Robertson County Times*, August 15, 1937.

"Does the Bell Witch Still Haunt Adams?" *Brownsville* (Tenn.) *States-Graphic*, December 23, 1977.

Dromgoole, Will Allen. "The Bell Witch of Middle Tennessee." *Nashville Banner*, February 22, 1931.

"Famous Witch Due to Return in 1935, Says Dr. C. B. Bell in New Volume." *Nashville Banner*, November 4, 1934.

Hill, Marion. "Bell Witch Story Stirs Great Interest Locally." *Whitehaven Press*, August 23, 1966.

Hinton, Elmer. "The Bell Witch Still Around?" *Nashville Tennessean*, October 28, 1964.

Hockenheimer, J. M., and J. H. Howell, with G. W. Boswell. "The Secrets of the Bell Witch." Pamphlet, n.p., 1971.

Holder, Bill. "The Rowdy Witch." *Nashville Tennessean*, March 21, 1948.

Lucas, Urith. "Stories of Illinois' 'Angelic Spirit' Revives Memories of Robertson County's Mysterious Bell Witch Activities." *Nashville Banner*, October 1, 1949.

Morton, M. B. "Authentic Bell Witch Story." *Nashville Banner*, February 19, 1937.

Mynders, Alfred. "Next to the News." *Nashville Tennessean*, October 25, 1957.

Preston, Bill, Jr. "Does Witch Still Spook Bell Farm?" *Nashville Tennessean*, October 30, 1971.

———. "Has the Bell Witch Returned Home?" *Nashville Tennessean*, November 28, 1965.

Rogers, Joseph W. "Ghosts: Can the Dead Come Back?" n.p., n.d.

———. "Ghosts: What Was the Bell Witch?" Nashville: n.p., n.d.

Russell, Katie Ruth Jackson. "Scenes of the Bell Witch Legend." n.p., 1972.

Spivey, Louis E. "Halloween Brings Up Tale of Bell Witch." *Springfield* (Tenn.) *Times*, October 22, 1964.

Sprivey, Louise E. "Bell Witch Called Phenomenon of All Time." *Clarksville* (Tenn.) *Leaf-Chronicle*, November 7, 1964.

Talley, Robert. "Will America's No. 1 Ghost Return to Tennessee Tonight?" *Memphis Commercial Appeal*, October 31, 1937.

"Tennessee Ghost Stories." n.p., October 31, 1984.

Vincent, Bert. "Strolling." *Knoxville News-Sentinel*, July 7, 1968.

Walker, Hugh. "Here Comes Kate!" N.p, April 2, 1972.

Wick, Don. "The Strange, True Story of the Bell Witch of Tennessee." Tennessee Department of Tourist Development, n.d.

UNPUBLISHED WORKS

Author interview with Carney Bell, April 1987.

Author interview with H. C. Brehm, April 1987.

Correspondence, Kelly Barnett, August 15, 1987.

Correspondence, H. C. Brehm, March 23, 1987.
Correspondence, Audrey Campbell and Hope Barton, November 1975–June 1976.
Correspondence, Hugh B. Johnston to H. C. Brehm, April 4, 1987.
Huntwell, Jeffrey. "The Secrets of the Bell Witch." Unpublished manuscript, 1971.
Interview with Carney Bell by H. C. Brehm, March 5, 1979.
Interview with Lynda Fay Butler by H. C. Brehm, October 23, 1977.
McFadden, Sharon. Untitled manuscript, 1983.
McRaven, Henry. "Tennessee Prodigies." Unpublished manuscript, December 14, 1966.
Mears, Mary. "The Bell Witch of Adams, Tennessee." Unpublished manuscript, Federal Writers' Project, April 27, 1937.

Texas

BOOKS

Brandon, Jim. *Weird America.* New York: E. P. Dutton, 1978.
Gaddis, Vincent H. *Mysterious Fires and Lights.* New York: Dell Publishing Company, Inc., 1968.
Greenway, John, ed. *Folklore of the Great West.* Palo Alto, Calif.: American West Publishing Company, 1969.
Roberts, Nancy. *Ghosts of the Wild West.* New York: Doubleday, 1976.
Syers, Ed. *Ghost Stories of Texas.* Waco: Texian Press, 1981.

Utah

BOOKS

Brunvand, Jan Harold. *Studies in Western Folklore and Fiction.* Prepared by the Printing Service, University of Utah, for sale through the University Bookstore to students in the Folklore of the West course, Salt Lake City, 1972.
Carter, Kate. *Heart Throbs of the West.* Salt Lake City: Daughters of Utah Pioneers, 1945.
Coffin, Tristram Potter, and Henning Cohen, eds. *The Parade of Heroes.* Garden City, N.Y.: Anchor Press/Doubleday, 1978.
Coleman, Loren. *Mysterious America.* London and Boston: Faber and Faber, 1983.
Dorson, Richard M. *Buying the Wind: Regional Folklore in the United States.* Chicago: University of Chicago Press, 1964.
Greenway, John, ed. *Folklore of the Great West.* Palo Alto, Calif.: American West Publishing Co., 1969.
Murray, Earl. *Ghosts of the Old West.* Chicago: Contemporary Books, 1988.
Zicree, Marc Scott. *The Twilight Zone Companion.* New York: Bantam, 1982.

PERIODICALS

Kapaloski, Gayle. "Ghost Stories." *Utah Holiday,* October 1984.
Valentine, Dan. "Spirit of the West." *American Essays,* 1969.

UNPUBLISHED WORKS

Correspondence with K. Haybron Adams, Reference Librarian, Brigham Young University, May 1987.
Correspondence with Carol Edison, Folk Arts Coordinator, Utah Arts Council, July 1987.

Vermont

BOOKS

Doyle, Arthur Conan. *The History of Spiritualism, Volumes I and II*. New York: Arno Press, 1975. A facsimile of the 1924 edition.
Stevens, Austin N., ed. *Mysterious New England*. Dublin, N.H.: Yankee Publishing, Inc., 1971.

PERIODICALS

Fagan, Tom. "State Sprinkled with Evil Curses, Spooky Goings-On" (Eddys of Chittenden Were Focus of Occult), *The Sunday Rutland Herald* and the *Sunday Times Argus*, October 29, 1978.
Green Mountain Whittlin's, published by Green Mountain Folklore Society, vol. XXXIV, 1982–83.
Rubin, Cynthia. "State Sprinkled with Evil Curses, Spooky Goings-On" (Emily's Bridge Haunted by Several Odd Legends), *The Sunday Rutland Herald* and the *Sunday Times Argus*, October 29, 1978.

UNPUBLISHED WORKS

Low, Gilman. "Superstition and the Supernatural as They Pertain to Folk Cultures in Vermont," 1977. Ms. Courtesy of the University of Vermont Special Collections.
Correspondence with Richard Sweterlitsch, Assistant Professor of Folklore, University of Vermont, Burlington, May 1987.

Virginia

BOOKS

Greenhouse, Herbert B. *In Defense of Ghosts*. New York: Simon and Schuster, Inc., Essandess Special Editions, 1970.
Lee, Marguerite DuPont. *Virginia Ghosts*. Berryville: Virginia Book Company, 1966.
Olmert, Michael. *Official Guide to Colonial Williamsburg*. Williamsburg: The Colonial Williamsburg Foundation, 1985.
Taylor, L. B. *The Ghosts of Williamsburg . . . and Nearby Environs*. Williamsburg: Progress Printing Company, Inc., 1983.
———. *Haunted Houses*. New York: Wanderer Books, 1983.

PERIODICALS

Bonko, Larry. "M'lady is invisible." *Norfolk Ledger Star*, April 17, 1978.
Briel, David. "Ghost Hunt." *America*, Spring 1987.
Carpenter, Bill. "Are Spirits of Historic Persons Walking Williamsburg's Streets?" *Richmond Daily Press*, October 31, 1965.
Dietz, F. Meredith. "Ghost of 'Antique Virgin' Said to Haunt Westover." *Richmond Times-Dispatch*, September 17, 1950.
Farkas, Harold M. "The V.I.P. Ghosts in Virginia: A Spectral Who's Who." *The New York Times*, January 24, 1971.
"Happy Halloween." *College of William and Mary News*, October 30, 1979.
Howard, Tom. "State Ghosts Are Legendary." *Richmond Times-Dispatch*, n.d.
Mahoney, Mary Reeves. "Virginia's Haunted House Highway." *Ford Times*, October 1979.
McLaughlin, Bill. "Who frequents rooms and stairwells within CW's long-empty buildings?" *Richmond Times-Herald*, October 30, 1981.
Spano, Susan. "Their Old Virginia Homes." *The New York Times*, March 22, 1992.

Virginia Travel News. Department of Economic Development, Fall 1984.
"Who's whoo: Unexplained tales lure many tourists." *Cleveland Press,* October 31, 1978.
Worldwide Travel Planner, March 1990.

Washington

PERIODICALS

Andrews, Page. "Ghost Stories." *The Seattle Times/Post-Intelligencer,* October 30, 1983.
Morris, Dan. "Jesuit Challenges 'Force' Haunting Old Mansion." *The National Observer,*
    May 3, 1975.
Robinson, Kathryn. "Haunted Seattle." *The Weekly,* October 28–November 3, 1983.

UNPUBLISHED WORKS

Interview with Nan Cauthorn Cooper, December 1987.

West Virginia

BOOKS

Brown, Stephen D. *Complete Guide to the Olde Town, Harpers Ferry.* Harpers Ferry: The
    Little Brown House Publishing Co., 1975.
———. *Ghosts of Harpers Ferry.* Harpers Ferry: The Little Brown House Publishing Co.,
    1981.
———. *Haunted Houses of Harpers Ferry.* Harpers Ferry: The Little Brown House Publish-
    ing Co., 1976.
Musick, Ruth. *The Telltale Lilac Bush.* Lexington: University of Kentucky Press, 1965.

PERIODICALS

Dykeman, Wilma. "John Brown's Landscape." *The New York Times,* November 1, 1987.
Repanshek, Kurt J. "Restless Spirits, Ghosts at Home in Harpers Ferry." Associated Press
    dispatch, April 22, 1984.
Thomas, Dana. "On a Tour of Harpers Ferry's Favorite Haunts." *The Washington Post,*
    October 31, 1989.

Wisconsin

BOOKS

Skinner, Charles M. *Myths and Legends of Our Native Land.* Philadelphia: J. B. Lippincott,
    1896.

PERIODICALS

Bruch, Gloria. "Spooky roommates." *Stevens Point Journal,* October 26, 1988.
Coon, Laura Sumner. "Haunting melody." *The Milwaukee Journal,* October 26, 1984.
Erickson, Lisa. "This house really is haunted." *Antigo Daily Journal,* October 31, 1984.

UNPUBLISHED WORKS

Interview with Jeff Bils, May 3, 1990.
Interview with Gloria Bruch, March 31, 1990.
Interview with Jacki, a psychic, September 30, 1990.
Interview with Douglas O'Brien family, June 12, 1989.

Wyoming

BOOKS

Munn, Debra D. *Ghosts on the Range: Eerie True Tales of Wyoming.* Boulder, Colo.: Pruett Publishing Co., 1989.
Murray, Earl. *Ghosts of the Old West.* Chicago: Contemporary Books, 1988.

PERIODICALS

Hamilton, Brad. "Story of St. Mark's Ghost Tower Re-told." *Wyoming State Tribune,* October 21, 1979.

UNPUBLISHED WORKS

Fifield, Dorothy H. "The Ghost Rides Again." Wyoming State Archives, Museums and Historical Dept., Cheyenne, Wyoming.

CANADA

BOOKS

Beck, Horace. *Folklore and the Sea.* New York: Stephen Greene Press, 1973.
Blundell, Nigel, and Roger Boar. *The World's Greatest Ghosts.* New York: Berkeley, 1988.
Clarke, Ida Clyde. *Men Who Wouldn't Stay Dead.* n.p., n.d.
Creighton, Helen. *Bluenose Ghosts.* Toronto: McGraw-Hill Ryerson Limited, 1957.
Fink-Cline, Beverly, and Leigh Cline. *The Terrific Toronto Trivia Book.* Toronto: Personal Library Publishers, 1979.
Guiley, Rosemary. *Encyclopedia of Ghosts and Spirits.* New York: Facts on File, 1992.
Haining, Peter. *A Dictionary of Ghosts.* New York: Dorset Press, 1993.
Henningar, Ted R. *Scotian Spooks: Mystery and Violence.* Hantsport, N.S.: Lancelot Press, 1978.
Kevan, Martin. *The Best of Montreal and Quebec City.* New York: Crown, 1992.
Mosher, Edith. *Haunted: Tales of the Unexplained.* Hantsport, N.S.: Lancelot Press, 1982.
———. *The Sea and the Supernatural.* Hantsport, N.S.: Lancelot Press, 1974.
Sherwood, Roland H. *Maritime Mysteries.* Windsor, N.S.: Lancelot Press, 1976.
———. *The Phantom Ship.* Hantsport, N.S.: Lancelot Press, 1975.
Singer, Kurt, ed. *The Unearthly.* New York: Belmont Books, 1965.
Smith, Susy. *Haunted Houses for the Millions.* New York: Dell, 1967.
Sonin, Eileen. *ESP-ecially Ghosts.* Toronto: Clarke, Irwin and Company, 1970.
Watson, Julie. *Ghost Stories and Legends of Prince Edward Island.* Willowdale, Ont.: Hounslow Press, 1988.

PERIODICALS

Armstrong, John. "The Gallery of Ghosts: The eerie and unexplained in old Burnaby mansion," *Vancouver Sun,* October 31, 1987.
———. "Ghost eludes our intrepid reporter." *Vancouver Sun,* October 31, 1987.
Bolan, Kim. "The haunted gallery." *Vancouver Sun,* October 31, 1986.
Bon Echo (Ont.) *Sunset,* May 17, 1928.
Carr, Tony. "Goodnight, Ghost." *Vancouver Sun,* December 9, 1977.
Clark, Victor. "Metro's Ghostliest Places." *The Subway Link,* vol. 1, no. 2 (October 31–November 20, 1986).

Clough, Peter. "Daily Planet." *Vancouver Province*, June 11, 1992.

Cobb, Michael. "She's Hostess With Ghostess." *Vancouver Sun*, May 30, 1966.

"Courtenay Man Insists Ghost Woman Danced Right at Him." *Canadian Press*, ca. 1940.

Curtin, Fred. "Ghosts back at old haunts." *Vancouver Province*, April 9, 1964.

"Emily Carr Haunts Halls," *Vancouver Province*, May 12, 1991.

"Escape in a haunted house." n.p., n.s. June 17, 1966.

"Evil Spirit Hits House in Ontario." *Canadian Press*, June 12, 1963.

Fitzhenry, Jack. "The Widow's Curse." *The Newfoundland Quarterly*, December 1945.

Fralic, Shelley. "A ghost that stayed away." *Vancouver Sun*, November 1, 1982.

"Ghost Fee Ruled Out." *Vancouver Sun*, July 21, 1966.

"Ghostly Guests at Beckley Farm." n.s., May 8, 1955.

"Ghostly Presences Aid Atmosphere." *Vancouver Province*, n.d.

"Ghosts host haunted." *Vancouver Province*, June 24, 1966.

"Gracie the Ghost Back After 22-Year Holiday." *Canadian Press*, January 23, 1947.

"Haunted house sold." *Vancouver Sun*, April 2, 1973.

Herman, Wendy. "Ghost town Toronto." *Toronto Star*, April 27, 1980.

Jamieson, Charles. "Are There Such Things as 'Tokens'?" *The Newfoundland Quarterly*, December 1928.

———. "The Ghostly Light Off Come-By-Chance Point." *The Newfoundland Quarterly*, October 1928.

"Jim Curran's Ghost." *Commercial Annual Christmas Number*, 1921, n.p.

Johnson, Eve. "So you don't believe in ghosts? Prepare yourselves for a shock." *Vancouver Sun*, October 30, 1981.

Marshall, Roger. "Dead builder 'walked' doomed *Raven's* decks." *Vancouver Province*, February 10, 1972.

Mills, Philip. "Mother, son share house with ghost." *Vancouver Province*, December 22, 1976.

"Motorists Report Strange Happenings on Highway." n.s., April 12, 1960.

"Mystery Knocks Alarm Home." *Canadian Press*, October 13, 1933.

"Night in a Haunted Home Long." *Vancouver Province*, May 15, 1950.

"Not a Chance," *Vancouver Province*, July 20, 1966.

Oberlyn, Ros. "Spook-hunters seem to be having a wail of a time." *Vancouver Sun*, October 24, 1978.

Odam, Jess. "Hetty's Haunted by Ghost Fans." *Vancouver Sun*, June 8, 1966.

———. "*Sun* Team Sees No Ghost—But What Was That in Hall?" *Vancouver Sun*, June 2, 1966.

"OOOOOOOOOHH, Ghostly Tales." *Vancouver Province*, May 12, 1991.

Rimes, Les. "Sun Man Sleeps on as 'Ghost' Gives Fiddle Solo." *The Island*, September 24, 1959.

"Scare Still On." *Vancouver Sun*, June 1, 1966.

Schaefer, Glen. "Our Scariest Haunts." *Vancouver Province*, October 28, 1990.

"The Schooner 'Isle of Skye.'" *Commercial Annual Christmas Number*, 1921, n.p.

Senn, Roma. "Things that go bump in the night." *Atlantic Insight*, October 1983.

Shortis, H. F. "Ghost Stories." *The Evening Telegram* (St. John's, Newfoundland), December 15, 1928.

"Spooky Trouble at mill." *Canadian Press*, March 9, 1985.

Stockand, Dave. "B.C. has its fair share of spooks." *Vancouver Sun*, October 29, 1977.

Stroud, Carstens. "The Case of the Missing Snipe," *Toronto Star*, December 9, 1979.

"Sunday Séance Seeks Shy Spook." *Vancouver Sun*, June 3, 1966.

Sutter, Trevor. "Ghost in Nightclub." *Regina Leader-Post*, April 27, 1992.

"Two visits by 'phantom' tied to wall's tombstone." *Vancouver Sun*, October 26, 1982.

Volgenau, Gerald. "Ghostbusters: Pair Claims to Banish Spirit From Home." *Montreal Free Press*, n.d.

Weir, Harold. "Ghostly Secret." *Vancouver Sun*, November 2, 1961.

White, Scott. "Legislature's Past Spooky." *Vancouver Sun*, July 5, 1984.

"Who Wants Haunted House?" *Vancouver Province*, March 31, 1973.

UNPUBLISHED WORKS

Correspondence from Judy Curry, Metropolitan Toronto Library Board, November 1986.

Correspondence from Mrs. E. M. Darke, curatorial assistant for historic houses, Toronto Historical Board, January 1987.

Correspondence from Marie V. Gibbs, Moose Jaw, Saskatchewan, October 1993.

Correspondence from Jennifer Harrand, secretary, Burnaby Art Gallery, November 1994.

Correspondence from Laura Jantek, coordinator of reference services, Halifax City Regional Library, n.d.

Correspondence from Jean Moore, Regina, Saskatchewan, n.d.

Correspondence from M. R. Mulvale, Greenwood, Nova Scotia, December 1993.

Correspondence from Miriam Siwak, Sydney, Nova Scotia, October 1993.

Authors' Note

If you would like to share an experience you've had with a haunting, or know
of a ghost story from your community or region, please send the information to:

Michael Norman
c/o Tom Doherty Associates
175 Fifth Avenue
New York, New York 10010